Harper's Encyclopedia for Horsemen

Harper's Encyclopedia for Horsemen

The Complete Book of the Horse

Louis Taylor

Illustrations by Rosemary Taylor
and others

Harper & Row, Publishers

New York, Evanston, San Francisco,

London

Excerpt on pages 495–496 by H. Tom Fulton
from "The Tennessee Walking Horse—
His Origin and Development."
Reprinted by permission of the Tennessee Walking
Horse Breeders' Association of America.

FIRST EDITION

STANDARD BOOK NUMBER: 06-014226-X

LIBRARY OF CONGRESS CATALOG CARD NUMBER: 72-79697

Designed by Dorothy Schmiderer

This book is respectfully dedicated to the
Master Horseman, Antonio Aguilar, whose
facility in establishing rapport with horses
is an inspiration to every serious student
of horsemanship who witnesses it.

Contents

Preface

Serious study of horsemanship in America is not very old (though until the turn of this century the horse was as vital a part of our culture as the automobile is today). Toward the end of the first quarter of this century the first course in equitation was offered at Ohio State University (certainly a large and representative educational institution now offering excellent facilities for education in this field—with fine horses owned by the school). It was purely a lecture course with a grand finale at Frank Mitchell's stable, which then supplied the mounts for Troop B National Guard Cavalry. At this final session the class was actually mounted, and for one hour put into practice some of the principles learned during the lecture course.

Later the author of this book succeeded his friend and lifelong counselor, Frank Talmadge, as instructor in equitation at O.S.U. Fortunately, with the help of Mr. Talmadge, the powers that be increased the budget for the course sufficiently to permit the use of the instructor's horses, and Dr. Carl Gay, chairman of the Animal Husbandry Department, allowed use of the Judging Pavilion for the classes. Horsemanship had arrived at Ohio State. More than that, the seed of the present book was firmly implanted in the author's mind, for even with the kind and efficient cooperation of the University library staff, he could find no suitable text and no reference work.

Riding and Driving for Women, by Belle Beach, and *Patroclus and Penelope*, by Theodore A. Dodge, were finally selected as required reading. If I were teaching a course today, I would require all of the latter and much of the former, for while terminology of gaits has been changed and standardized and wonderful discoveries have been made in the field of jumping since this Civil War amputee served as model for the photography in his book, it is doubtful that Caprilli (discoverer of the forward seat) or Tom Bass (one of greatest among gaited-horse riders) could have done better at the things Dodge did. Certainly neither of them could perform in (or had any knowledge of) the other's field, while Dodge was master of all fields of horsemanship known in his day.

Subsequent teaching of riding at Denison and Ohio Wesleyan universities produced continuing frustration in a search for a text and adequate reference books. One other authority did prove useful, De Sousa; but apparently he, like all the others who excelled in any field, seemed oblivious of the fact that there were things many people wanted horses to do and be that he had never thought of.

Of course this narrowness of field is partly a matter of snobbery, as I came to realize. My greatest love at this early time of life was hunting. I hunted with the Rocky Fork Hounds as often as I could steal the time. I also played a little polo. Ohio State had an artillery unit, attached to which was a Captain Hill. He somehow managed to get a few fair polo mounts issued to the outfit and, by procuring some University backing, got a polo team going. It was helpful to have faculty come out and play at practice, so I enjoyed polo whenever I could get an hour off. Thus I knew excellent horsemen on the polo field and riding after hounds and many of them had a supercilious attitude toward fields of horsemanship outside their own.

Following the depression and the advent of the New Deal of the Roosevelt era, interest in horses mushroomed. Books about horses crowded booksellers' display windows. Horse interests broadened as the national population trend headed westward. I too went west, where I bred a few horses of the kind later to be called Quarter Horses (the American Quarter Horse Registry was not established until 1940) and found a type of horsemanship startlingly different from any I had ever before encountered, the kind depicted in my *Out of the West* and much more beautifully in Tom Lea's *The Hands of Cantu*. It was older and even prouder than the horsemanship that calls itself the only educated horsemanship (dressage). I searched for a book by a practicing horseman in this field and found one: *El Charro Mexicano*, by Don Carlos Rincon Gallardo, Duke de Regla, Marques de Guadalupe. But while Don Carlos gives a good picture of his kind of horsemanship, he is just as rigid and oblivious to all others as is any devotee of the Spanish Riding School or military regiment.

Among the plethora of books relating to horses, I kept looking for one that would be more than a eulogy of one or more breeds, one that would not shush away the faults and abuses in the horse world that inquiring minds, especially young ones, want explained.

Much of the beautiful Big Horn country around Sheridan, Wyoming, was originally settled by titled Englishmen. While judging a show in Sheridan in the late forties, it was my good fortune to become acquainted with a descendant of one of those intrepid aristocrats. He was interested in my quest for a reference book and felt sure that it would come from England; a few years later he sent me one written by an Englishman, a book he thought a possible answer to my problem. It was an excellent work, probably one of the two best in English in its decade, but the author's grasp of things American is typified by his entry *Trapaderos* (tapaderos), which explains them as mere decoration. However, we do not have to go to England to find confusion about Western lore. The best and most popular American reference in the field spells *serape* with an *x* and says it is a saddle blanket, and makes some other errors.

Since I cannot find a book to my liking, I must try to make one.

I am sure that even after my lifetime of observation and note taking, and these last four years of intensive writing, many errors have crept in and persisted. For them I offer humble apology. Most of what is good in the book horses have taught me; for the rest I sincerely thank many good and kind horsemen.

Harper's
Encyclopedia
for Horsemen

Accidents

That the untrustworthy nature of the horse is the chief cause of accidents is a popular misconception firmly fixed in the public mind. Careful consideration of that misconception sheds light on the real causes of accidents and gives a hint about prevention.

The horseman who says, "Never trust a horse," is honest and wise. *He* can never trust a horse. Though he may have cut his teeth on a saddle horn and inhaled corral dust every day of his life, his ability to communicate with a horse is very limited. The feel of his horse under him; the sight and sound of the horse he is leading; the stance or subtle move of ear, eye, or muscle of a loose horse—these things he misses or misinterprets. Moreover, he often fails to make or time his own movements so the horse can understand them. The horse can't trust *him,* either. The horse has been hurt by whip, spur, bit, club, boot toe, or what not unexpectedly and surprisingly. To such a horse, man is a source of pain against which an animal must always be on his guard.

Much time and some natural endowment is needed to learn to communicate sufficiently with the horse in order to avoid accidents with any but the most lethargic. Excepting only those few horses taught voice signals by rather eccentric trainers, communication with horses must be kinetic—that is, by movement of some part of the horseman's body, whether in contact with the horse or standing near him in the corral or stable. Attempts at verbal communication with a strange horse may cause accidents. Many a horse, galloping good-naturedly, has been terrified into a hysterical runaway by frantic screams of "Whoa! Whoa!"

Learning the use of aids (*see* AIDS) helps prevent accidents but goes about as far toward learning to communicate with horses as a semester of French in high school goes toward learning to communicate with Frenchmen.

Until a horseman learns to communicate with (*to understand and be understood by*) horses well enough to anticipate them and have them anticipate and understand him, he can avoid accidents by entrusting himself only to wise, mature horses and never allowing his mount to attain a speed that is uncomfortable. This means weeks or months at the walk before jogging, weeks at the walk and jog before trotting, etc. Even a wise, mature horse can be startled by idiots rushing up behind him at a mad gallop on the bridle path or trail. So the amateur should avoid trails frequented by idiots. If some do appear, he should turn his horse around, face them, and ride back trail until his horse is composed.

Action

The word *action* means very different things to different horsemen. An owner of a Saddlebred horse who says his animal has "good action" means that he picks his forefeet and hind feet up higher than do most horses, that hind action is as high as front action, and that the movement of each foot (when viewed from the side) is circular—each foot moves as if it were attached to the rim of a wheel. There is no hesitating, pointing, or "dwelling" of the foot when it reaches the most forward part of its circular orbit. Viewed from front or rear, the movement of each foot is in a plane parallel to the horse's line of progress—no foot swings outward or inward as it moves forward or rearward. The good action the Saddle Horse owner talks about, because of its circularity, has the appearance of being very "snappy," especially when the horse develops a little speed; however, it must not become "trappy": that is, the height of the action must not exceed the length so that the foot describes an upright oval rather than a circle. The fine-harness horse enthusiast and the Hackney owner mean the same thing by "good action," although the latter wants such extreme performance that the knee rises above the level of the elbow and the hind pastern sometimes brushes the stifle.

If a knowledgeable Western horseman comments on the good action of an animal who has just won a reining class in a horse show or a cutting horse contest, he means that the horse's balance is exceptionally good. The horse's legwork is quick and fast, with a hind foot always right under the center of balance when it is needed. If the term *good action* is applied to a rope horse, it means much the same thing. If the roping is being done in actual range work, there always comes the time of a freak accident (especially in brush country) when the miraculously quick movement of the horse is all that can save the rider's life, and his own, too, probably. Any one of a thousand things can (and does) happen—a rope snarls around a bit of brush; a critter darts back in a rough spot and drags the rope around the horse's hocks; or a rock slides and the horse and rider drop a few feet down a mountainside. The good action of the rope horse has cheated the undertaker in many such situations.

The careful observer of a good horse working a difficult range can see many of the movements of Olympic dressage, sometimes done with a precision and quickness that might put a school horse to shame. Such action in a stock horse is called good action.

To the fancier of the Arab, *good action* refers to the way a horse moves his feet backward and forward (just as the Saddle Horse enthusiast thinks of it, although the Arab moves the feet differently). The Arab owner wants action confined to the same plane in its back-and-forth motion as does the Saddle Horse owner; he wants no paddling (swinging outward) or dishing (swinging inward). However, the Arab owner wants action that is quite different from that of the Saddle Horse when viewed from the side. When the action is good, the Arabian points or "dwells" with each foot for an instant when it reaches the limit of its forward movement. The movement of the Arabian has been said to make the horse appear as if he were suspended from a wire and were floating forward, not striking the ground at all.

In recent years the Arabian horse has been competing so successfully for popularity that he is entering fields dominated by breeds in which extreme action has been induced by abnormal foot growth, weighted shoes, etc. This has caused some change in the action of Arabs destined to compete in, for example, park horse classes. In Arab shows there are also classes comparable to the fine-harness classes for other horses. They are called formal driving classes. There is a trend toward higher action in both park horse and formal driving classes for the Arabs. In the former is to be seen much higher action than Arabs have displayed in other classes; however, the reach-and-point is still an obvious characteristic.

Fashion in action changes—not so rapidly or radically as in other matters, but just as surely. In 1915 Astral King successfully fought two hours and five minutes against Cascade, Richelieu King, Easter Cloud, and four other great stars for the Champion Five-Gaited Stake at Louisville. Rarely in those days did the battle for the title "World's Greatest Saddle Horse," held annually at Louisville, last less than an hour. The length of such contests and the pictures of the winners clearly show that the feet of show horses of the time were about half as long as they are today. (No modern show horse wearing the long feet of our day could perform for such a long time.) Of course, without the long feet the action cannot be as high as it is today.

The fashion in Saddle Horse circles today demands action so high that it can be attained only by the use of extreme length of foot, special shoeing, and expert handling by rider-trainers. No rules for getting action are very useful, for each horse responds a little differently (or very differently) to shoeing and to handling. However, generally speaking, height of action is aided by length of foot (both toe and heel) and by weight of shoe. Horses that will not grow enough heel to keep up with the growth of toe can be helped with pads. By the use of rubber "driving pads" frog pressure can be maintained and foot health preserved on a moderately long foot. When the first pair of pads is due for a reset job, often that first pair can be turned upside down and a new pair of pads put on between the old pads and the shoes so frog pressure can be maintained even when walls have grown to considerable length. Wedge-shaped pads made of plastic are also used to help heels keep up with toes, though wedge pads do not help frog pressure. No matter what precautions are taken, it is doubtful that a horse can long remain sound and carry the feet that produce winning action today.

It is relatively easy to get high action in front by proper shoeing and collection; however, the higher a horse is made to go in front by artificial means, the lower his hind action is likely to be. It is also appropriate here to mention that if a horse has a tendency to paddle, the more he is collected or worked "on the bit," the worse he will paddle, in spite of any corrective shoeing. Hind action can be helped sometimes by keeping the angle of the feet very steep, or by the use of Memphis bar shoes with blocked heels and squared toes.

The Walking Horse people go to such extremes in getting action that the shoes cannot be held on the feet by nails alone and have to be secured by bands over the foot. There is a general notion that the deliberate crippling of Walkers, as so well pictured and explained in *Life,* October 3, 1969, is done for the purpose of attaining high action. It is true that in some instances the "soring" or crippling does increase action. However, it has the more important function of making the gait done in the show-ring resemble the original running walk, a gait "done at the speed of from six to eight miles an hour with economy of effort of both horse and rider" (words of Burt Hunter, one of the most influential originators of the breed registry). In the modern show-ring, Walkers perform at up to 18 miles an hour. To make the gait look like the original running walk (hind feet scooting far forward under forefeet and head nodding at each step) the trainers "sore" the horses. A few trainers are adept at producing ringbone, which is not as obvious to audiences as the results of "soring."

To get the long, low action of the Arab, procedures for getting high action have almost to be reversed. However, individual differences are even greater when the problem is to get "daisy clipping and dwelling action." Usually light shoes are a necessity. Slight toe weights sometimes help. As a rule the feet must be kept almost short enough to satisfy a cowboy. Any handling that tends to get the horse "behind the bit" (oversensitive to the bit) defeats the purpose of the trainer. The Arab with good action usually goes mostly on the snaffle bit and is ridden with a very loose curb chain or strap. The difference (except for speed) between what he does when asked for a collected trot and what he does when asked for an extended trot is so slight that only the trained eye of the Arab enthusiast can detect it. The horse that has been taught noticeable collection is likely to lose some of the quality of action desired in an Arab.

What the Western horseman means by good action is a long story. In some details, it is as gruesome as that of the Walker. The feet must be kept short and the toes light, so the story is painless in that area. However, the Western horse of good action works on an extremely light rein. To a German dressage expert he would be said to work behind the bit—extremely behind the bit. This, of course, means that he is capable of extreme and instant collection. Some 10 or 15 years ago cutting horses made their debut in the polite society of the horse show. Their popularity was almost instantaneous. The first ones shown were natural-born cutting horses. They worked without cues. Reins were of large, braided cotton rope enabling the audience to see that they did not signal the animal as they flapped loosely. Such horses, of course, work with their heads low, for the bovine is of shorter stature than the equine, and the horse kept his head pretty close to the animal he worked, though when ridden outside a corral, most good cutting horses had as nice a head carriage as anybody's mount. This rise to glory of the cutting horse brought to life many trainers and owners of horses destined to be cutting horses. About as many natural-born cutting horses are foaled each year as there are great prize fighters or opera singers. Thus the demand for cutting horses far exceeded the natural supply, so most trainers armed themselves with equipment to turn ordinary horses into cutting horses. The most common piece of equipment was a piece of iron pipe with one end wrapped with tape for a handle. This little gadget "learned him to keep his head down."

As the cutting horse's popularity grew, cutting horse action was imitated by others of Western persuasion. For about a decade, good action in any Western horse meant, among other things, the ability to collect with head low and nose out—a neat trick, frequently learned with the aid of a piece of pipe.

Today, praise be to Allah, most show judges are asking Western horses in performing classes (not cutting contests) to have flexion of the neck behind the head and to carry the head in a natural position. A lot of iron pipes will go to the junk heap.

Whatever fashion decrees as good action, trainers will teach horses to have. Unfortunately there is always a tendency to value most highly a kind of action which is unnatural for the horse and almost impossible for him to perform. Such is the nature of what Mark Twain called "the damned human race."

Age

Age and Value

Comparison of the age of any mature horse to that of a human being is obtained by multiplying the horse's age by three. Thus a seven-year-old horse's age is comparable to that of a 21-year-old man.

Until he is five or six, some parts of a horse's skeleton are soft or cartilaginous. Therefore, the horse less than four years old that is raced or shown, especially in classes that demand speed and action, is usually permanently damaged. Such a horse is likely to be unsound by the time he is six or seven, if not sooner. This fact, plus the practice of bad shoeing and careless use that makes many Western ranch horses unfit for hard work after 12 or 14 years of age, has created the too-popular notion that a horse in his teens has seen his best days. The performance of 17- and 18-year-old horses in Olympic teams, the unequaled record of Goldsut Maid on the trotting track when she was 18, and countless similar feats on record disprove this idea that a horse's best years are his early ones.

Two old sayings are far more pertinent today than ever before, according to Dr. J. P. Ellsworth of Prescott, Arizona, and many of his fellow veterinarians. The first is, "A horse is as old as his feet and legs"; the second is, "Many a good tune has been played on an old fiddle." Dr. Ellsworth and his colleagues say that until modern veterinary science and modern methods of horse care came into being, most horses in populous areas of the country endured worms (*see* PARASITES) all their lives. Few horses had proper dental care. Most, especially those in parts of the country where feed grows under irrigation, suffered dietary deficiency (including lack of certain trace elements and vitamins). Horses suffered more infectious diseases than they do now, when inoculations against many of them are available. A modern horse 20 years of age, if he has not been raced or otherwise strained in infancy or youth, may be in better physical condition than was a 12-year-old in horse-and-buggy days.

An important afterthought with implicit warning is that modern horses are not forced to endure as many quack "cures" and drenchings as did their great-grandsires and granddams.

The owner who sells or gives away (usually to be abused by a thoughtless child) the old horse is a disgrace to the human race. If he cannot afford to care for the old one, he should sacrifice the few dollars selling him would bring and call a veterinarian to put him to sleep painlessly and without fright.

Determining Age

The time-honored way of telling a horse's age is to look at his teeth, or to "mouth him." Though this is the most accurate method known, it is not infallible. Horses differ in what they eat and in the hardness of the teeth they inherit. At one time during World War I, light artillery horses were in such demand that the army accepted mares. One receiving depot was at the fair grounds in Columbus, Ohio. Each animal was examined by a team of officers before he was accepted. Two mares, well known by the writer, were presented to the examining officers, competent men. The first mare was rejected as overaged. The second mare, her dam, was accepted.

By and large, of course, the officers screened animals by age correctly, and they were probably well aware that their guesses would not be 100 percent correct.

For description of dental features that indicate age, *see* TEETH.

Like people, horses show age in face, hair color, joints, and other anatomical changes. The very old horse usually has deep cavities above the eyes. If he is gray when young, he turns white or white with flecks (called *flea-bitten*); if he is a darker color, he usually turns gray around the eyes or over his entire head. His joints lose their flexion. He often tends to be buck-kneed (knee joints farther forward than pasterns), and sometimes his hind pastern joints cannot straighten completely. His withers become sharp and high. Sometimes he sags in the back. His molars wear down or drop out, so he has to have special feed.

Aged

The term *aged* appears on some show catalogues and sale listings. It designates that a horse is nine years old or over. The common term is *smooth-mouthed*, because, after his eighth year, a horse normally has no cups in his lower front teeth by which his age can be estimated (*see* TEETH).

There is an old saying that "In the trader's stable there is no horse over nine."

Agoraphobia

Agoraphobia is a term rarely if ever used by American horsemen, but it designates a condition to be avoided, one that every prospective buyer should know about if he thinks of buying from a show or training stable.

Some horses kept continuously in a stable and never ridden outside a ring are terrified at the great outdoors. They will shy at everything and anything. The term for this state is *agoraphobia.*

Patience and care will sometimes cure the condition, but not always. Prevention of it is the wisest course. From colthood, the animal should be allowed to run either on the range or in open pasture. If neither is possible, he should be led into the open frequently. If the mature horse is seldom ridden, he should have at least a small enclosure to move in, from which he can "see the world."

Aids

Unless he is young, extremely well-coordinated, and athletic, the good horseman can move the body and legs of his horse more precisely and easily than he can move his own. Whether he ever heard the word *aids* or not, he uses the aids in directing his mount. Broadly and loosely employed, the term covers the rider's use of hands, legs, body, and voice. In the machinelike, highly stylized performance of dressage (*see* DRESSAGE) the aids can be readily categorized. Each move of the rider is in accordance with convention; each calls for a specific movement from the horse. With the somewhat less machinelike performance of the reining horse (show horse) of the West, movements merge into one another almost imperceptibly. When the reining horse is taken out of the show-ring and puts his skill to actual use on the range, the variety and gradations in use of the aids are almost infinite. The shifting of his center of balance may for many minutes at a time be continuous. The sidewise movements of either his whole body or just the forehand or quarters may be continuous but never twice the same. His rider's use of the aids would be difficult to categorize, but it must be perfect. One false use of an aid may throw the horse as well as the rider in fast rein work.

All riding is a matter of balance between impulsion and restraint. The aids that provide impulsion are the pressure of legs, heels, or spurs. Restraint is provided by the use of reins. If the horse has been taught to understand, pressure of one leg or heel behind girth or cinch will move the quarters away from the leg or heel or will stop progress toward it. If the horse has been taught to understand it, a slight pressure of rein on the neck accompanied by a raising of the hand will prevent forward motion and cause the horse to put his weight on his haunches and turn his forehand away from that subtle pressure on the neck. If his quarters are held in position by leg aid, he will execute a quarter-turn on the haunches, or a complete spin if the use of rein aids continues.

If leg aids are properly used to keep the hindquarters moving sidewise at proper speed (one leg used to keep quarters moving fast enough and the other to keep them from moving too fast) and reins are used to prevent forward motion and induce sidewise motion, he will do a perfect sidepass (*see* SIDEPASS). All use of aids must, of course, be adapted to the understanding of the mount. The green, untrained horse will usually move toward, instead of away from, the pressure of a leg or heel. Instead of tucking in his chin, flexing at the poll, and bringing his hocks forward when pressure is applied to the reins, he will thrust his head forward against the bit and then toss it skyward, and so on. A horse has to be taught to respond to aids. The well-trained Eastern horse comprehends the aids only if contact is maintained on the reins at all times; that is, some pressure must be kept on reins at all times. The Western horse is trained to work on a slack rein, and so it goes. No two horses are taught exactly alike. If the rider of a strange horse is skillful and the horse has been taught by a sensible trainer, the rider will soon learn the language of the aids the horse understands; if not, chaos will prevail.

The novice "rides one end of his horse only." The expert uses the aids so that every part of his horse responds. The relation between a good horseman and his mount is similar to that between a pair of ballroom dancers. The move of each is anticipated by and responded to by the other. Each meaningful movement of the horseman is an aid.

Albino

Until 1918 when Caleb R. and Hudson B. Thompson purchased a white stallion known as Old King, who served as foundation for the breed they have so faithfully and successfully labored to establish, the word *albino* signified an animal completely lacking pigmentation in skin, hair, and eyes. The albino horse's pink skin was thought to be objectionable in certain climates, and albino eyes were said to be associated with defective vision. The American Albino Association, Inc., explains in its literature how it has developed a breed of white, pink-skinned horses that are uniformly free from the so-called faults or weaknesses formerly attributed to the albino. It should be borne in mind that white coat, mane, and tail are not confined to albino horses. Most white horses have a dark skin and were gray or some other color when young. (*See* AMERICAN ALBINO ASSOCIATION, INC.)

Alter

Alter is a euphemism for *castrate* or *geld* (*see* GELD).

R. R. Snow King, National Grand Champion American White Horse Stallion, Davenport, Iowa, 1970.

White Wings II, first permanently registered stallion of American Albino foundation with a complete four-generation pedigree of snow white ancestry. Bred on the White Horse Ranch in Nebraska, owned by Ingabord Swenson of Aurora, Ohio.

Amateur

An amateur is one who rides or drives for some reason other than to make money. The term is also loosely used to designate one who is not an expert or accomplished horseman. The American Horse Shows Association, whose rules govern all shows it recognizes, has very specific requirements for the classification of "amateur." Only persons fulfilling those requirements may enter amateur classes in shows. Horsemen who have received money for riding, driving, teaching, or use of their names or pictures in advertising cannot be classified as amateurs.

Amble

The amble is one of the slow gaits permitted in a five-gaited horse. It may be considered midway between a very slow pace and a running walk. In the pace, the two feet on the same side strike the ground simultaneously. It is a "two-beat" gait. The sound of it suggests two-four time in music. In the running walk, the feet strike the ground individually at equidistant intervals. It is a "four-beat" gait that suggests four-four time in music. In the amble, when a hind foot strikes the ground, its impact is followed immediately by the forefoot on the same side, those two impacts being almost but not quite simultaneous. Of course, the feet on the opposite side follow the same sequence. The amble rhythm is that of syncopated music. It is done at a speed just a trifle faster than a walk, is easy on the rider, and requires a minimum of effort from the horse. (*See* GAITS.)

American Albino Association, Inc.

The American Albino Association, Inc. (Box 79, Crabtree, Oregon 97335), is concerned with the registration of what it terms the American White Horse and with the promotion and improvement of the breed. A geneticist, a physiologist, or a biologist uses the word *albino* to indicate one of those rare animals of any species that is devoid of pigmentation in hair, eyes, and skin; however, the American Albino Association applies the term *albino* to horses that do not lack pigmentation in their eyes and states that "their eyes are just like any other equine's and they handle sunlight and glare consistent with other breeds. Their stamina is proven over and over again in the grueling route of the circus and show troupes where they excel."

American Andalusian Horse Association. *See also* ANDALUSIAN

The American Andalusian Horse Association (P.O. Box 1290, Silver City, New Mexico 88061) is one of the newest of horse organizations in the country. The annual meeting on February 6, 1971, of the association held in Juárez, Mexico, was called to order with ten members and their families present. A few others, delayed by hazards of the road, appeared before the meeting was over. At the time of the meeting there were 135 Andalusian horses in the United States. They are, of course, registered with the association.

American Association of Owners and Breeders of Peruvian Paso Horses. *See also* AMERICAN PASO FINO PLEASURE HORSE ASSOCIATION, INC., and PASO FINO

The address of the American Association of Owners and Breeders of Peruvian Paso Horses is P.O. Box 371, Calabasas, California 91302.

The president in 1972 is Doug Hart. The most active breeder, past president, and member of the board of directors of the association is F. V. Bud Brown, B-Bar-B Ranches, 12001 N. Ranch Lane, Scottsdale, Arizona 85254.

One of the most effective proofs of the excellence of the Paso Fino as a saddle horse is the history of Mr. Brown's adoption of the Paso Fino as a breed to produce on his B-Bar-B Ranch and use in his Friendly Pines Camp in Prescott, Arizona, a summer camp for youngsters. Mr. Brown and his wife Isabel, affectionately known by hundreds of youngsters and adult admirers as "Brownie," for many years spent part of each year traveling about the world, always with one eye out for a breed of horse in which they could find the perfect saddle animal for Brownie, who, because of an old back injury, needed an animal with an easy gait. In the Icelandic and Norwegian ponies the Browns found some admirable qualities—sturdiness, docility, and natural saddle gaits. However, not until they spent some time in Peru did they come across an animal that seemed to fill the bill entirely. Since the cost of bringing home one or two animals would be prohibitive, Bud decided to collect a sufficiently large shipment so that the importation could be put on a business basis and the cost per animal reduced. Now, several years and two generations of Pasos later, Bud feels that he made a wise choice in Peru.

American Buckskin Registry Association

Among the 25 equines brought to the New World by Columbus on his second voyage and the thirteen horses described in the log of Cortez in 1518 were horses of the colors we now call buckskin, grulla, and dun. Not all horses of such colors are descendants of the Spanish stock selected for import by Columbus or the mounts of the conquistadores, but certainly the majority of horses of these colors in the Southwest carry some of the original Spanish blood. In 1965 the American Buckskin Registry Association, Inc. (P.O. Box 1125, Anderson, California 96007), was incorporated with the purpose of collecting, recording, and preserving the pedigrees of buckskin, grulla, and dun horses and ponies of all breeds as well as those of unknown ancestry.

The association states that it never registers a horse on his color alone.

However, it is very rigid in its rules about acceptable colors. For example, a buckskin must be of what the association considers the true color denoting descent from original Spanish stock—buckskin with dorsal stripe, shoulder stripe, or patch or barring on the legs. The association has made remarkable progress since its incorporation and gives firm promise of establishing a place in the equine sun for horses of its chosen colors.

American Hackney Horse Society

The American Hackney Horse Society (*see* HACKNEY) is located at 527 Madison Avenue, New York, New York 10022. The registration of both the Hackney horse and Hackney pony is vested in the American Hackney Horse Society. In its brochure, "The Hackney," the society gives information about the Hackney pony, which is probably much more familiar to Americans today than is the Hackney horse. The first pony imported into the United States was Stella 239 in 1878. Probably the most important Hackney pony imported into this country was Southworth Swell, imported by Mr. J. Macy Willets of Casillis Farm in 1925. His blood is carried by all of the outstanding Hackney ponies today.

American Horse Protection Association, Inc.

Address: 629 River Bend Road, Great Falls, Virginia 22066.

The uncompromising kindness, intelligence, political know-how, and just plain guts of the people who comprise the membership of the American Horse Protection Association almost surpass belief. Their aid in exposing the cruelty of methods used to capture wild horses (*see* WILD HORSES) has done much to correct this abuse. The association has been successful in promoting legislation to protect the vanishing wild horses. It is absolutely fearless in its attack on the cruelties of Walking Horse trainers. Directly or indirectly credit is due the association for the article "The Agony of the Walking Horse" (*Life,* October 3, 1969), and for passage of the precedent-establishing and enforceable bill to protect the Walking Horse which became effective in Virginia on July 1, 1970. It is certainly to be hoped that the association will turn its attention to the agonies of the three- and five-gaited American Saddle Horse, which equal in intensity those of the Walking Horse, though they are less obvious to the layman.

The cost of membership in the association is nominal. Interested horsemen will find the group hospitable and grateful for interest shown in its endeavors.

American Horse Shows Association

The American Horse Shows Association (527 Madison Avenue, New York, New York 10022) publishes a *Rule Book* and accredits and classifies all shows that apply for such service and conform to the *Rule Book*. Thus the association facilitates avoidance of duplication of dates, so exhibitors do not have to miss a show because it is held on the same day as another of equal or more importance. The *Rule Book* helps to standardize requirements for show classes in order that horsemen will know what to prepare their horses for. It also gives a basis for settling disputes. The association has a system of classifying judges and a prescribed procedure of apprenticeship and other qualifying activities for horsemen (and others) who aspire to become judges. The association is gracious about answering letters regarding its activities.

American Indian Horse Registry, Inc.

The American Indian Horse Registry, Inc. (P.O. Box 9192, Phoenix, Arizona 85020), is dedicated to the preservation and upgrading of the Indian Horse. Though the registry is relatively new, it has already organized some shows for Indian Horses in which classes for an interesting variety of uses were set up.

The secretary, Barbara Huff (1501 E. Aire Libre, Phoenix, Arizona), welcomes questions about the registry.

American Mustang Registry, Inc.

Address: P.O. Box 9243, Phoenix, Arizona 85020. (*See* MUSTANG.)

American Paint Horse Association

The American Paint Horse Association (P.O. Box 12487, Fort Worth, Texas 76116) gives the following information:

The words *paint* and *pinto* are synonymous; both refer to spotted or two-toned horses with body markings of white and another color. However, when used to refer to the two registry organizations—the American Paint Horse Association and the Pinto Horse Association of America—the two words take on vastly different meanings. The Pinto Association registers all breeds and types of horses including ponies, Saddlebreds, parade, and fine-harness horses. The APHA is devoted strictly to the stock- and quarter-type horse and bases its registry on the blood of registered Paints, Quarter Horses (AQHA) and Thoroughbreds (Jockey Club of New York). The APHA was founded on the proposition that color alone is not a basis for a breed, and that the indiscriminate use of all breeds results only in a color registry rather than a breed registry. The American Paint Horse Association is a registry based upon a combination of breeding, conformation, and color.

The words *tobiano* and *overo* refer to the two Paint Horse color patterns. These patterns can be distinguished by the location of the white on the horse. While there are certainly exceptions to practically every **rule** for

(Left) A tobiano Pinto. The tobiano pattern has white as the basic color with markings of any other color in the form of large, distinct spots. The white appears to work from the top down.

(Right) Excellent example of overo Pinto. The overo pattern is basically a dark or roan horse with white markings which extend from the belly upward.

identifying these patterns, the following are the best guidelines to use:

Overo
1. White will not cross the back between the withers and the tail.
2. At least one leg, and often all four legs, will be the dark color.
3. Head markings are often bald, apron, or even bonnet-faced.
4. There are irregular, rather scattered, and/or splashy white markings on body, often referred to as calico patterns.
5. Tail is usually one color.
6. Horse may be either predominantly black or white.

Tobiano
1. Head is marked like that of a solid-color horse—either solid or with blaze, strip, star, or snip.
2. All four legs will be white, at least below the hocks and knees.
3. Spots are usually regular and distinct, often coming in oval or round patterns that extend down over the neck and chest, giving the appearance of a shield.
4. Horse will usually have the dark color on one or both flanks.
5. Horse may be either predominantly dark or white.

Although much formal research remains to be done on the genetics of

Paint Horses, we already know that the tobiano and overo have some basic differences in their genetic implications. The tobiano gene is considered to be of dominant nature, while the overo gene possesses recessive tendencies. Breeders of Paint Horses have, however, continued to have outstanding success in breeding either tobiano or overo to solid-color horses and still maintaining the paint color in the offspring.

APHA registration rules state that for a horse to be entered in the Regular or Appendix Registry he must be a recognizable Paint Horse. All questionable cases are referred to the APHA Registration Committee for a final decision.

The following traits are among Paint Horse characteristics: blue or glass eye(s); white markings above the hocks and knees; multicolored tail and/or mane; apron face, which is white extending beyond the eyes laterally and under the chin; pink skin under white hair; a blue zone between dark skin and white skin.

White markings on a horse's belly which cannot be seen from a standing position are not considered paint markings that will qualify a horse for the Regular or Appendix Registry. Horses who show some paint characteristics but not sufficient to enter the Regular or Appendix Registry are entered in the Breeding Stock Registry; these horses are not eligible to compete in approved Paint Horse shows, races, or contests.

Each year the American Paint Horse Association conducts a National Championship Show in which it awards the titles of "National Show Champion" and "Reserve National Show Champion" to two horses in each halter and working division. This show is a three go-round event, and the final winners are determined by total points won in the three go-rounds. All horses registered in the APHA are eligible to compete in the National Show.

American Paso Fino Pleasure Horse Association, Inc. *See also* AMERICAN ASSOCIATION OF OWNERS AND BREEDERS OF PERUVIAN PASO HORSES, PASO FINO, and CRIOLLO

The American Paso Fino Pleasure Horse Association, Inc., is located in Lorton, Virginia. Its vice-president and registrar is Rosalie MacWilliam (8828 Ox Road, Lorton, Virginia 22079). The writer is indebted to her for the following list of horse shows that regularly feature Paso Fino classes: Atlanta Charity Horse Show, Georgia; Winter Haven Charity, Florida; and Tri-County Horsemen's Association Shows, Pompano Beach, West Palm Beach, and Hialeah, Florida. She also gives a list of all the current outstanding horse-show contenders of the breed: Mar de Plata LaCE, Malsama, El Capricho, Casa Blanca, Sortibras LaCE, Dominico LaCE, Faetón, La Noche, Doña Ines, Sureña, El Pirata, Bolero LaCE, and El Pastor.

The 1971 Show Rules of the association clearly indicate that it relentlessly pursues a course of making the Paso Fino in America an animal of excellent conformation (e.g., "long backs should be penalized in halter classes"). There is also a determination to eliminate the cruelty in training methods used on the Paso in his native land (one example is the extremely tight noseband used just above the nostril which obtains sedation by limiting oxygen supply and by use of pain similar to that caused by a nose twitch). Rule 4 states: "Any sign of new scars from a training device on the nose or any part of the horse will disqualify the horse. Many imported horses show old scars, but these scars are not permitted on horses trained in the United States. Members of the American Paso Fino Horse Association must not allow their horses to be trained by cruel methods. Sharp unwrapped nose devices are cruel."

The association bids fair to achieve the goal of producing a horse of beauty, versatility, and delightful, natural gaits requiring no special gimmicks of shoeing, bitting, or trick training devices such as tie-downs, tight nosebands, or tail sets. While the group hews to the line of a horse that will perform exclusively the gait characteristic of the breed, it promotes a versatility in that gait achieved by variation of collection and difference in speed. The pamphlet published by the association, "The Paso Fino Horse: The New Horse That Is 400 Years Old," categorizes the performance of the gait under four headings: *paso fino, paso corto, paso largo, sobre paso,* and adds *andadura,* which the animals of the breed use for extreme speed in place of the gallop—it is a straight pace and lays no claim to comfort. All performance of the paso gait is what we would call a rack (*see* GAITS). The *paso fino* is slow, highly collected, and done with extremely high action of front feet and paddling (*see* ACTION); the *paso corto* is similar in speed but less extreme in collection and action; the *paso largo* is a rack of moderate speed and extension; the *sobre paso* is done on a slack rein with complete extension and relaxation at about the speed of what we would call a slow-gait.

American Quarter Horse Association

The American Quarter Horse Association (P.O. Box 200, Amarillo, Texas 79105) is the world's largest and fastest-growing equine registry. In addition to registering Quarter Horses, it performs many functions for Quarter Horses' owners, including recording transfers of ownership, establishing and enforcing rules and regulations of approved shows and contests, maintaining and publishing records of recognized Quarter Horse race meets, sponsoring free clinics throughout the nation (usually at state universities), maintaining a free motion-picture film library for nationwide use, and working closely with state and regional Quarter Horse associations which share in the increasing growth of the breed and of the industry.

The association publishes the *Quarter Horse Journal,* an illustrated monthly magazine which carries current news about Quarter Horses and the people who use and enjoy them, together with helpful information about breeding, care, feeding, racing, auctions, and regional and state shows.

The association now has registered over 800,000 horses throughout the country, by far the largest number of any one breed in the country.

American Saddle Horse

Members of the National Saddle Horse Breeders' Association, started in 1891 by producers of the long-established and then most valued breed of multiple-use horse in Kentucky and surrounding areas, wanted a name to distinguish their horse from the Thoroughbred (race horse). By 1899 they arrived at the name *American Saddle Horse* and changed the association name to American Saddle Horse Breeders' Association. However, the long name took over a quarter of a century to be accepted and used by horsemen in general. Many fine stallions of the breed went to the range country of the West to improve native stock and were called Kentucky Thoroughbreds, or simply Thoroughbreds. In the Midwest, Kentucky Saddler was the popular name for the breed.

In 1908 the ASHBA proclaimed Denmark, a four-mile race horse, a Thoroughbred, foundation sire of their breed. However, credit due him for

Three-year-old, 16.1 hands, American Saddle Horse filly—natural tail and feet—ideal type.

transmission of desirable characteristics of the Saddler results almost entirely from the influence of one, and only one, of his get, Gaines Denmark, a son of a Cockspur mare. The Cockspurs were of the old, easy-gaited Colonial stock which preceded the advent of the Thoroughbred on this continent. Infusion of Thoroughbred, Arab, Morgan, and other blood probably benefited the American Saddle Horse, but its most distinctive characteristics can be traced to its foundation, the old English saddle horse of easy gaits and good temperament.

The Saddler started out as a multiple-purpose breed, tiller of the soil, mount for easy and rapid transportation, family buggy horse, fancy carriage horse in cities, and attraction at county fairs. He was usually little more than 15 hands high. He had a finely chiseled nose, eyes large and wide apart, a high forehead, ears close together, neck long and flexible, shoulders long and sloping, a short back, ample heart girth, ribs well sprung, forelegs well forked (joining body in a Gothic arch), arms strong and gaskins flat, cannon bone short and of ample size, croup long and level, and tail carried naturally high.

This horse survived the coming of the automobile as a spectacular attraction at shows, where until the advent of Western classes he was the featured part of every horse show in the Midwest and an important part of some Eastern shows.

His change in role from utility item to showpiece caused change in conformation and performance. The original gaits (*see* GAITS) permitted the breed by the ASHBA in 1902 were the walk (flat-footed), trot, canter, rack, and slow-gait (which could be the amble, slow pace, running walk, or fox-trot). In three-gaited classes and in three-gaited combination classes (those in which the horse was shown both in harness and under saddle), only the walk, trot, and canter were displayed. The average height of the breed at this time was 15.2 hands. As the Saddler changed his role to showpiece, he gained in height, because 16- or 17-hand horses make a more impressive spectacle than smaller ones. Refinement of head lost importance. Gaudy browbands and cavessons (tabooed in an earlier day) covered the formerly high forehead and delicate nose. The very slow trot or jog replaced the less showy flat-footed walk, and the slow rack became popular as a slow-gait; so the five-gaited show horse today usually displays only three gaits—trot, rack, and canter—unless, as sometimes occurs, he shows a slow pace as a slow-gait. In three-gaited classes he ordinarily shows only the trot and canter (for a walk, he usually does a very slow or broken trot).

An effort is now being made by the American Saddlebred Pleasure Horse Association (Irene Zane, secretary-treasurer, 801 South Court Street, Scott City, Kansas 67871) to expand the role of the Saddle Horse. As a result of its efforts, many recognized shows are including Saddlebred pleasure classes. So far, the standards for judging them for performance and conformation seem to be identical with those of other three- and five-gaited classes, with the possible exception of less emphasis on height of action.

High prices for show specimens of the breed have caused increasing occurrence of animals with deficient heart girth, narrow chests (both forelegs "coming out of the same hole"), and heads with "blobby" noses and eyes set high. However, such animals are not typical. The breed in general is still one of good fork, good bone and middle, fine head, and extreme versatility. Individuals here and there excel in the fields of jumping, polo, range work, and genuine pleasure riding.

American Saddle Horse Breeders' Association

Headquarters: 929 South Fourth Street, Louisville, Kentucky 40201. (*See* AMERICAN SADDLE HORSE.)

American Shetland Pony Club

Address: P.O. Box 2339, Route 52 North, West Lafayette, Indiana 47906. (*See also* SHETLAND PONY.)

American Shire Horse Association

Address: 300 East Grover Street, Lynden, Washington 98264. (*See* SHIRE.)

American Suffolk Horse Association

Address: 300 East Grover Street, Lynden, Washington 98264. (*See* SUFFOLK.)

Andalusian. *See also* AMERICAN ANDALUSIAN HORSE ASSOCIATION

When the Moors brought Barb horses into Spain they formed the foundation of two types of horses in Andalusia by crossing the North African blood onto native Spanish stock. One type was the jennet or genet (*see* JENNET), and the other was of somewhat heavier bone and stockier build, a type of horse to be seen in some of the paintings of Velásquez. This stockier Andalusian was called "Villanos" and was a favorite of the nobility in Castile.

Anthrax

Anthrax is an acute infectious disease which occurs in practically all mammals. The horse is less susceptible than cattle and sheep but more easily infected than man. The pathogenic organism in the disease is *Bacillus anthracis*, which forms spores that may retain their vitality for more than 25 years. Obviously, animals housed where infected animals have previously lived are in great danger of infection unless the place has been thoroughly disinfected.

There are three forms of the disease, but the symptoms of any of them are easily confused by the layman with those of other serious illnesses. A sensible horseman will employ the services of a veterinarian if his animal or animals become seriously ill, regardless of the specific variety of the ailment. A veterinarian, with the aid of modern clinical facilities, can readily diagnose positively a case of anthrax. All such cases must be immediately reported to the proper state authorities.

Until recently anthrax was generally considered an incurable disease, but today it is sometimes possible for a veterinarian to treat an animal successfully. Obviously, afflicted animals should be quarantined.

While vaccination properly done constitutes a safe and effective prophylaxis in most cases according to *Equine Medicine and Surgery,* any vaccination procedure should be done under supervision of state and federal veterinarians.

Antitoxin

Antitoxins, "toxoids," and serums for treatment and/or prevention of diseases of horses should be used only by or under the close supervision of licensed veterinarians. Every horse owner should consult his veterinarian concerning the need for preventive vaccination.

Annual vaccination for sleeping sickness and for tetanus is imperative in all localities.

Major pharmaceutical firms utilize horses in the preparation of anti-toxins for human use. Such animals are, of course, well cared for and humanely treated. It is sometimes possible to persuade such a firm to take a horse that is to be pensioned.

Appaloosa

Of all strikingly colored horses, the Appaloosa seems to be gaining popular favor most rapidly. He comes in at least four different color patterns (frost, leopard, snowflakes, and spotted blanket), but to the casual eye he is most commonly recognized as the horse that looks as if a giant-sized wet paintbrush had been shaken at his rump.

Horses of the color and type we now call Appaloosa were probably domesticated somewhere on the steppes of Russia two or three thousand years B.C. Pictorial evidence indicates they were in China by 500 B.C. and in Spain by A.D. 700. They are commonly depicted in Persian art of the fourteenth century.

In the seventeenth century, horses of Appaloosa color and type were brought to America by the Spaniards. By the latter part of the eighteenth century, these horses became the first equines to be systematically and carefully bred in the West. The Nez Percé Indians, the only tribe to indulge in systematic horse breeding, inhabited parts of what are now Washington, Oregon, and Idaho. They prized above all other horseflesh the type we call Appaloosa. Their best horse-raising country was drained by the Palouse River.

The coming of the white man destroyed the Nez Percé horse breeding. However, the Indians had so well established their type of horse that late in the nineteenth century, when circuses and Wild West shows began to look for striking-looking horses, enough of the Nez Percé influence was still alive to produce Palouse horses (as they were then called). These sold to circuses for as much as $3,000 a pair (purchase price paid by dealers in the Palouse area was about $100 a head).

Appaloosa horses registered today by the Appaloosa Horse Club (Box 403, Moscow, Idaho 83843) trace their ancestry to a horse won in a poker game in Fossil, Oregon, about 1900. He was known as Painter and, later, as Old Painter. His prepotency so stamped his progeny in both type and color that he became famous. Bred to a black mare from a rodeo string, he sired a good Appaloosa colt named Young Painter. A daughter of Young Painter was bred to an Arab stallion, Farras, and foaled an Appaloosa colt named Flash. Flash was bred to a daughter of Young Painter, called Marvel's Angel #4. The result of that mating was a colt named El Zorro, now known as one of the most illustrious progenitors of the modern Appaloosa. Fixation of type and color by this judicious (or lucky) inbreeding has created such a uniformity of color and type in the modern Appaloosa breed that it is to be hoped that present and future breeders will not change it by outcrossing to Quarter Horse, Thoroughbred, or other blood.

The Appaloosa is a rugged horse of excellent heavy bone, good feet, ample heart girth, well-sprung ribs, short back, and powerful quarters. The medium-length neck is set on shoulders sloping enough to give the Appaloosa a head carriage a little higher than that of the Quarter Horse. Though not extremely refined, the head is well proportioned and supplied with wide, strong jaws. The eye is set fairly low and surmounted by a forehead indicating ample brain room.

Though courageous and supplied with all the "heart" a horseman desires, the Appaloosa is amenable to instruction and does not become flighty when he warms to his work.

Color requirements for registration were originally stated by the Appaloosa Horse Club as follows: "A horse must have white rump starred with round or oblong spots and also flesh-colored spots around the eyes, nose, and genital organs. The stallions must be dominating leopard-spotted with white rump covered with dark spots. Any base color, such as bay, gray, chestnut, cream, white, roan, etc., is acceptable."

As to size, registration requirements demand that an animal be between 14½ and 16 hands in height and weigh between 900 and 1,100 pounds.

Other distinctive characteristics of the breed are the dark stripes that run from coronet to shoe on the tough hoofs, the wispy manes and sparse tails, the mottled skin coloration, and the white sclera around the eyes.

The Appaloosa is finding favor in all fields where Western horses are useful, such as roping, cutting, and trail riding. Appaloosas are also distinguishing themselves as jumpers. Some of the leading racetracks are featuring Appaloosa racing with pari-mutuel wagering.

Appaloosa Horse Club, Inc.

Beginning in 1938, the Appaloosa Horse Club (Box 403, Moscow, Idaho 83843) advertised in leading horse magazines and livestock journals to promote the Appaloosa breed. It published the first *Appaloosa Stud Book* in 1947, the second volume in 1950, the third in 1957, the fourth in 1961, the fifth in 1965, the sixth in 1966, the seventh in 1967, the eighth and ninth in 1968. In 1950 the club hailed *The Appaloosa Horse*, by Francis Haines, Robert L. Peckinpah, and George B. Hatley, as the first complete authentic text on the Appaloosa and so advertised and promoted it.

By operation of the registry, breeding and pedigrees of Appaloosas are being preserved, and their increase is being encouraged. Registration has grown from 266 in 1954 to 14,911 in 1967. More than 100,000 Appaloosas have been registered since the registry was established. The club has made available for loan 20 sets of 48 colored 35-mm. slides with written commentary. These slides and commentary trace the history of the Appaloosa and show his present uses. They are lent without charge to service clubs, 4-H clubs, FFA chapters, riding clubs, etc.

To help educate and qualify Appaloosa judges, the club sponsors an Appaloosa Judging School. The official judge covers all the points of judging, places some classes, and gives reasons. The participants then judge several classes, fill out judging cards, and write reasons. Those who prove their ability are accepted as Appaloosa judges.

The club has been successful in having the American Horse Shows Association accept the breed and include a section on Appaloosas in its *Rule Book*. Such acceptance helps standardize judging and rules that apply to classes of the breed in open shows.

For the benefit of trail riders and owners who enjoy the historical aspects of the Appaloosa, the club sponsors the Chief Joseph Trail Ride. Each year this ride covers 100 miles of Chief Joseph's War Trail. The trail starts at Wallowa, Oregon, in the Blue Mountains. It then crosses the Snake River, goes over Clear Water, then over Lolo Pass into Montana, then south into Big Hole, then into Camas Meadows, then east through Yellowstone Park, then north across the Missouri River, ending forty miles from the Canadian border in the Bear Paw Mountains—a total of 1,500 miles. The Chief Joseph Trail Ride covers a 100-mile segment of this War Trail each year.

Appetite

A good appetite is an asset in any kind of livestock. It is one indication that the animal is in good health and congenitally rugged. In his so-called natural state a horse is an eater of grass and browse. He does not eat large quantities of feed at a time as he does when domesticated and fed only two or three times a day. Rather, he nibbles throughout the day and often throughout the night, depending upon the lushness of grass and browse. More or less continual nibbling of food in small quantities is quite appropriate for an animal with a small stomach like the horse. It is also appropriate for him to have a good and continuous appetite.

A good rule of thumb in feeding a horse is to follow feeding practices that keep the horse slightly hungry. If convenience dictates that he is to eat only twice a day, he should be fed enough so that starvation does not make him gorge on his feed, and he should receive quantities small enough so that his appetite is never completely satisfied. The horse owner who is concerned with getting the most out of the feed he buys and keeping his horse in the best condition will feed frequently and in small quantities. The amount he provides in a 24-hour period will not exceed the total supplied by the man who feeds his horse only twice a day.

When a horse of normally good appetite leaves feed in his manger, the uneaten feed should be removed and the manger cleaned. The horse's rations should be cut at least in half until he cleans up what he is fed. Then the rations should be increased very gradually until back to normal. It is possible that the so-called normal ration was too big for the horse and he was being overfed. Evidence that this is the case will be more feed left in the bottom of the manger after the horse is back on full rations. Another cause of lack of appetite, of course, is illness of some sort. If the horse treated as indicated above does not regain his appetite, you should call a veterinarian. If the veterinarian is fearless and competent, he may tell you that the horse has lost his appetite because of bad handling, that is, the bad riding or driving by the owner. Many well-bred, sensitive horses become so nervous when mishandled that their digestive systems cannot function properly.

There is an old saying, possibly Biblical in origin, that "the eye of the master fatteneth his cattle." No more important truth can be stated about a horse's appetite than this. The appetite is a good indicator of the horse's general health and well-being, and the intelligent owner will keep a constant watch over it.

A final and valuable word on the consideration of appetite is that the feeding of red bran is extremely important, especially for horses who have access to nothing but dry feed. The writer never feeds a horse without giving it a two-pound coffee-canful of red bran. This is good insurance against colic caused by impaction. It is also a help in preventing laminitis in overfed horses, and for horses on dry feed it is the best preserver this writer knows of.

Apples

An apple or two cut into pieces small enough to prevent choking is good feed for a horse. Its effect on his general condition may not be noticeable, but it can strongly influence his opinion of his owner. Too many apples at one time and any amount of green apples will cause colic. At the first sign of colic (a horse looking at his sides repeatedly, lying down and getting up repeatedly, kicking his belly, etc.), you should call a veterinarian. While you wait for the veterinarian, it is important to stay with the horse and keep him from lying down and thrashing about on the ground. Many a horse whose life could easily have been saved has tied his intestines in knots and sealed his own death warrant by rolling and thrashing on the ground from pain. When a horse is in extreme pain from colic, it is sometimes very difficult to keep him from going down. Lead him at a walk and keep him moving, even if somebody has to follow him with a switch. This writer has witnessed at least one case of colic from eating green apples in an area too remote from a veterinarian for professional help. The owner kept the horse walking. He enlisted the aid of two or three helpers whom he ordered to cut a sapling some 8 or 10 feet long. This was placed under the horse's belly, and a helper walked at either end of the sapling, raising it against the horse's belly to give a little pressure. It was then rolled back and forth under the horse's belly as the horse walked along, massaging it gently. An enema of soapy water, warmed of course, is sometimes helpful if it can be administered without allowing the horse to go down. The one old-time home remedy to be avoided is the drench, that is, medicine administered by mouth. Use of a drench is dangerous because it frequently results in getting liquid into the horse's lungs and he dies of foreign-body pneumonia.

The wise horseman avoids colic from apples by using them only as a treat and avoiding those that are not ripe.

Appointments

In practically all classes of all major horse shows, appointments are as important as the horse. Until the formation of the American Horse Shows Association there was much greater confusion in the matter of appointments than exists today. That association now publishes a *Rule Book* which covers appointments in all kinds of major horse shows. There is, for instance, a very definite rule about the number of buttons on the tails of a coachman's coat in certain classes for harness horses, classes seen only in the East. There is a rule about how the poncho or raincoat is to be rolled and tied on the rear of the saddle in a Western pleasure class. There are rules about the length of a horse's mane, rules about whether the mane should be braided or unbraided, rules about the way tails should be trimmed or not trimmed, and so on. Any adequate treatment of appointments would require a book the size of the present one or larger. The newcomer wishing information on appointments will find that the *Rule Book* of the American Horse Shows Association is his best source. If this is not available to him, the previous year's catalogues of major shows will

Acceptable curb chains for Western classes.

	Coat	Vest	Buttons	Breeches or Leg Garments
Master	Square cornered single-breasted frock. Melton or heavy twill. Scarlet or hunt livery color. Two flap pockets, one on either side, and whistle pocket permitted. Collar of colors adopted by hunt.	Preferably of plain white buff or yellow cloth.	Must conform to hunt livery; brass on coat and vest engraved with emblem of hunt.	White (buff or brown, according to livery of individual hunt), of leather, cord, twill, or any other suitable material. Should show 3 small buttons close together at knee. Lightweight breeches of silk or cotton not permissible.
Honorary Huntsman, Professional Huntsman	Same as Master.	Same as Master.	Same as Master.	Same as Master.
Honorary Whipper-in, Professional Whipper-In	Same as Master, with large hare pocket on inside of skirt.	Same as Master.	Same as Master.	Same as Master.
Gentleman Member	Scarlet, hunt livery color or black; of melton or heavy twill. Accepted formal Cuts: A. Frock with rounded skirts B. Swallow tail (shad belly) C. Cutaway (weasel belly) D. Dublington (weasel belly)	Same as Master.	Must conform to hunt livery. Brass or bone on vest. Black bone on black coat.	White breeches must be worn with scarlet, hunt livery color, or black coat of A, B, C, or D. Black derby and buff or brown breeches may be worn with black coat of accepted formal cut. Hunt silk hat and white breeches preferable.
Lady Member *(Astride)*	Regulation Hunting Coat of: B. Swallow tail (shad belly) C. Cutaway (weasel belly) D. Dublington (weasel belly) of melton or dark material	Same as Master.	Same as Gentleman Member.	Buff or brown (not white) cord, twill or leather.
Junior Member	Same as Lady or Gentleman Rider in classes not restricted to Junior Exhibitors. In those classes restricted to Junior Exhibitors same as Lady or Gentleman Rider except hunt caps are permitted.			
Hunter Division, Appointment Classes	Non-members of recognized hunt (amateurs or professionals) are permitted to ride in appointment and hunt team classes. Appointments same as those for Huntsman, Whipper-in or Member, except collar must be the same material and color as coat. Buttons must be plain.			
Equitation, Hunter Division	Any tweed or melton suitable for hunting. Conservative wash jacket in season.	Optional.	Optional.	Breeches or jodhpurs.
Saddle Seat, 3-and 5-Gaited Informal	Conservative solid colors are required. These include black, blue, gray, green, beige or brown jacket with matching jodhpurs, white jacket in season, and derby or soft hat. Spurs of the unrowelled type, whips or crops optional.			
3-and 5-Gaited Formal	Even more conservative solid colors required for evening wear, including dark gray, dark brown, dark blue or black, tuxedo type jacket with collar and lapel of the same color. Top hat, jodhpurs to match, and gloves, or dark-colored riding habit and accessories. Spurs of the unrowelled type, whips or crops optional.			

Neck-wear	Hat	Gloves	Footwear	Boot Garters	Spurs
Plain white hunting stock with plain gold safety pin worn horizontally.	Black velvet hunt cap. Ribbon worn up for unpaid wearer. Ribbon worn down for paid wearer.	Heavy wash leather or brown leather. Rain gloves, white or colored, carried under girth, each glove on proper side of saddle, thumb against palm of glove and against saddle, fingers toward front of saddle.	Boots of black calf (not patent leather) with brown or colored tops sewn on boot. Tabs sewn on but not sewn down to tops.	White (buff or brown) to match breeches. Worn between 2 lowest buttons. Buckle against buttons on the outside.	Of heavy pattern with moderately short neck. Preferably without rowels worn high on heel.
Same as Master.	Same as Master.	Same as Master.	Same as Master.	Same as Master.	Same as Master.
Same as Master.	Same as Master.	Same as Master.	Same as Master.	Same as Master.	Same as Master.
Same as Master.	Silk hat with hat guard worn with Coats A, B, C or D. Derby worn with black coat of any accepted formal cut. Hat guard required.	Same as Master.	Same as Master except black boots without tops must be worn with bowler hat. Patent tops not permitted.	Black if boots are without tops. Must Must conform to color of breeches if top boots are worn.	Same as Master.
Same as Master.	Black hunt derby. Silk hat required with B, C or D coats. Hat guard required.	Same as Master.	Hunting boots of plain black calf with or without tabs. Patent leather tops with tabs, which must be sewn on boots, are permissible. Tabs should be sewn on but not sewn down.	Plain black or patent leather if worn with patent leather tops.	Regular hunting spurs preferably without rowels.

Same as Lady or Gentleman Rider in classes not restricted to Junior Exhibitors. In those classes restricted to Junior Exhibitors same as Lady or Gentleman Rider except hunt caps are permitted.

Nonmembers of recognized hunt (amateurs or professionals) are permitted to ride in appointment and hunt team classes. Appointments same as those for Huntsman, Whipper-in or Member, except collar must be the same material and color as coat. Buttons must be plain.

| Optional. | Dark blue or black hunt cap, black or brown derby. | Optional. | Optional. | Optional. | Optional, unrowelled. |

Conservative solid colors are required. These include black, blue, gray, green, beige or brown jacket with matching jodhpurs, white jacket in season, and derby or soft hat. Spurs of the unrowelled type, whips or crops options.

Even more conservative solid colors required for evening wear, including dark gray, dark brown, bark blue or black, tuxedo type jacket with collar and lapel of the same color. Top hat, jodhpurs to match, and gloves, or dark-colored riding habit and accessories Spurs of the unrowelled type, whips or crops optional.

contain much information about appointments, as will the catalogues of the leading horse equipment supply houses. For example, the Miller Harness Company, Inc., 123 East 24th Street, New York, New York 10010, includes in its catalogue a chart showing correct hunting appointments so far as dress is concerned for the master of foxhounds, for the gentleman member, for the lady member, and for the junior member. The Miller catalogue also contains a chart covering the appointments for correct clothes for riding three- and five-gaited horses in the show-ring and also for riding in equitation classes. It describes the proper clothing for formal five-gaited evening classes, for informal morning and afternoon classes, and for formal and informal three-gaited classes, as well as for hack horse classes. See pages 26–27.

Since matters of appointment change sometimes from year to year, especially appointment in equitation classes, and even more drastically appointment in Western classes, it is advisable to get information from the most recent catalogues or other sources before one goes into the show-ring to compete for prizes.

The following are requirements of the American Horse Shows Association for appointments in hunter seat equitation: Snaffle bits shall be used with or without nosebands. Pelhams are permissible, as are full bridles. Martingales are optional in classes of jumping and hacking. However, martingales are not permitted in classes in which there is no jumping.

Stock Seat Equitation—Appointments

Here are the appointment requirements of the American Horse Shows Association for Stock Seat Equitation classes: Western hat and cowboy boots must be worn. The local management of the show may designate whether chaps are to be used. Spurs are optional.

Appointments of tack are as follows: The saddle, which should fit the rider, may have slick or swelled fork. The cantle may be high or low but must be appropriate for the size of the rider. For all classes except medal classes, any standard Western bit is acceptable; but local show management may designate any type of Western bit if such is needed for local conditions. Curb chains may be used if they are one-half inch wide and lie flat against the jaw. No trick device may be used in connection with a leather chin strap. Hackamores, tie-downs (running martingales), and draw reins are not allowed. If the rider chooses to use closed reins he must carry hobbles. These may be tied below the cantle or on the near side of the saddle. If he chooses split reins and the horse can demonstrate his ability to be ground-tied, the rider may dispense with the hobbles. Bosal or cavesson-type noseband is allowed. A lariat must be carried. It may be of either fiber or rawhide. Silver equipment is permissible but it must not be given preference by the judge. Any nonstandard type of horseshoes may be penalized at the discretion of the judge.

Appointments required by the American Horse Shows Association for

Gymkhana classes are as follows: A Western hat is to be worn by Western riders. They must also wear a shirt but with a collar. Its sleeves should be long and its tail tucked in. Cowboy boots are required. Chaps and spurs are optional. If spurs are worn, they must not have sharp points and the rowels must not be wired or taped. Western saddles in Gymkhana classes may have either a slick or a swelled fork. The height of the cantle is optional. No lariat may be carried. The rider may have his choice of hackamore or type of bit, but the judge may eliminate a rider who he thinks is using a bit or any other equipment that is too severe. The only type of martingale permitted is the running martingale.

English riders in Gymkhana classes may use snaffle bits with or without dropped nosebands, Pelhams, or full bridles. Again, the only martingale allowed is the running martingale. The English rider should wear tweeds or a dark-colored coat, though plain-colored light jackets are permitted in season. Either breeches or jodhpurs are permitted, and either boots or jodhpur boots may be worn. The English rider may wear a hunting cap of dark blue, black, or brown or he may wear a black or brown derby. Spurs are optional but must be devoid of rowels.

Heavy-Harness Classes—Appointments

For many years one of the most colorful features of any major horse show was the heavy-harness classes, so called to distinguish them from classes for horses wearing light or fine harness. The heavy-harness class is now almost obsolete in our horse shows. However, the appointments are still of interest, many of them carrying over into our classes for Hackney ponies or other harness pony classes. The following sections include the most important appointments for heavy-harness classes.

Four-in-Hand

Four-in-hand means a team of four horses, matched in color and driven in park harness to a park drag of solid color in which ride two servants in livery. In addition to the two servants, the park drag must be equipped with an extra collar, traces, reins, brakeshoe, quarter blankets and cooler, lap robes, water pail, and tool kit.

Lady's Phaeton

A variety of rigs of the phaeton class was permitted, but the rest of the appointments included no options. They were as follows: umbrella and cover for the servant's hat, a wheel wrench, two raincoats, collar, lap robe, a card case, a lash whip, and wet-weather gloves. The horse's mane was not to be braided. He had to wear a standing martingale, a buxton bit, breeching, and bearing rein.

Gig Class

Gigs are two-wheeled vehicles, very sturdy, with seats rather higher than the horse's back. Any one of several types of gig was permitted; however, one called the Tillbury was considered appropriate only for a horse from

15.3 to 16 hands in height and an animal of great presence and lofty action. Again, the mane was not to be braided. The standing martingale was a must, the bit was a gig bit, and the horse's head was held up with a bearing rein attached to a bridoon or snaffle bit. A buxton bit and full bearing rein were permissible but not preferred. One appointment for this class seems rather odd to modern show-horse exhibitors. It was a kicking strap. Presumably, this appointment was included because the seat of the gig was in such a position that the reinsman was in a particularly vulnerable position if his horse decided to kick.

In addition to the foregoing list of appointments, there were the appointments for the servants and coachman. If the servant was a footman, he had to wear a single-breasted coat with six buttons in front and six buttons on the tails. He also had to wear a full striped waistcoat, silk hat, and hand driving gloves. His boots were tan or pink with tops of mahogany, and he wore a white ascot tie. His coat was either black or the color of the upholstery of the gig. His breeches and coat had to be excellently tailored, and his boots fitted perfectly with tops that hugged the leg snugly.

If the servant was a coachman, he had to wear what was called a coachman's coat, which had six buttons in front and four on the coattails.

Appuyer

Appuyer is a French word similar in meaning to the old cavalry term *two-track*. (*See* TWO-TRACK.)

Arabian Horse

The songs and stories in which the Arabian horse has been extolled have some basis in fact. Any excellence of form or temperament in any present-day breed of horse owes a debt to Arabian and Barb (North African) horses, with probably the major share of the debt due the Arab.

History reveals the quarrelsome, violent nature of the peoples of the part of the globe in which the Arabian horse developed (any perspective on current world events adds to the same picture). Another trait of these peoples of the Near East is their fondness for beauty, as evinced in their rugs and other artifacts that have acquired considerable monetary value in the Western world. The Arabian horse's outstanding qualities are attributable to these two dominant traits, the warlike and the aesthetic, of the people who created him. They made him their best tool of war and a thing of beauty.

The history of the breeding of this horse stretches back into legend. The five original families, according to most sacred traditions, sprang from the daughters of five mares of a band of horses withheld from water and then turned loose; as the band rushed toward a nearby pool, Allah gave the command to stop. Only the five mares obeyed. From this legendary source, reckoning lineage by maternal lines, the Bedouin developed the most agile, intelligent, and enduring of war horses, as the Crusaders learned to their sorrow. These horses were part of the Arab's family, the foals playing in and outside the tents with the children, sharing their milk in dire times and enjoying plenty when it came. The horses at times would subsist, barely, on a little camel's milk and a handful of dates, but regardless of condition, they would perform unbelievable feats in battle, and on occasion (though the camel was the more usual means of transportation) they would cover distances in flight or pursuit that would make a modern endurance ride look very tame.

Though for many centuries the horse was at the center of Bedouin life, changes in weapons and methods of warfare changed his role. After some two years of study of the Arabian horse in his native habitat, Lord Byron's granddaughter, Lady Anne Blunt, and her husband, the Victorian poet Wilfrid Scawen Blunt, wrote in the 1870s that there were few more than 200 *Asil* horses (an untranslatable term signifying of royal blood, or of the true, pure, "noble" strain) left in Arabia. Bringing home with them some Asil Arabians, the Blunts founded the most famous of English Arabian horse breeding establishments at Crabbet Park, which was made even more famous by their descendant, Lady Wentworth.

It was probably the love of beauty that preserved the Asil Arabian in his native habitat after his role as war-horse was ended. Great potentates kept stables of the wonderful little animals, though they knew of nothing to do with them but run races or sit and contemplate their beauty (which, true enough, some did by the hour!).

Long before the establishment of Crabbet Park, and before the Arabian in his native land had changed his role from war-horse and intimate companion of humans to that of race horse kept in elaborate quarters by hirelings, Charles II and his equerry, the Duke of Newcastle, had developed a breed of horse in England that no purebred Arabian could match in speed. However, when Oriental blood was infused into the English horse, largely through four sires—the Godolphin Barb, the Darley Arabian, the Byerly Turk, and the Alcock Arabian—a strain resulted that had speed far beyond any previously demonstrated by any horses in the world. This strain, of course, became the Thoroughbred, the modern race horse.

Bloodlines

The powerful influence a small amount of Arabian blood can have when infused into any other breed is due in no small measure to the passionate devotion to purity of strain of Arabian camel and horse breeders (the source of the greatest horses because in drought and famine camels' milk was all that kept horses alive; camels could eat tiny herbs unavailable to horses as food, and their ability to survive drought exceeded that of the horse). Carl Raswan, a devoted lifelong student of the breed, translated some of the notes of Prince Amir Faysul Sha'lan (born about 1800) now in the archives of the Royal Agricultural Society of Egypt. Prince Faysul's notes were always written in the presence of and subscribed to by a council of breeders who came to his tent from all parts of the desert. Enemies with their slaves were guaranteed inviolability on their journey to and from the council. At such meetings, horses were brought before the council and discussed. A stolen mare, if she was pure in one family and without taint of outside blood, would be agreed upon as to future breeding so her blood would be kept pure. The two enemies (thief and former owner) would be "partners" in ownership of the expected foals.

To the prince and his peers, purity of family was of far greater importance than any consideration of "improvement of strain," and what Raswan called "incest breeding" was frequently practiced to keep families pure from the taint of outside blood.

Families or substrains as known over the past century or two can be classified under three main bloodlines, each with its substrains. These main strains are the Seqlawi (Seglawi or other spellings), the Kuhaylan (also alternate spellings), and the Muniqi (spelling apparently dependent upon the mood of the scribe). If for brevity's sake we typify each major strain by its outstanding characteristic, we might call the Seqlawi the horse of utmost refinement. (A fact beyond the comprehension of Occidental nervous systems is that a Bedouin or a group of Bedouins can stand and contemplate the beauty of a Seqlawi much as some Orientals are said to be able to sit and contemplate a beautiful flower.) The Kuhaylan is the horse of strength; the Muniqi, the horse of speed.

The Seqlawi and the Kuhaylan are closely related. They are the "classic" or "antique" strains. The Muniqi is a few centuries younger than the other two. The Darley Arabian was of Muniqi strain. He was imported into England in 1703, when it was still almost impossible to get mares of pure strain out of Arabia (because of their religious significance and involvement). The Darley Arabian was the ancestor of the great Eclipse, one of the most famous race horses of all time.

Some of the substrains of the Seqlawi are as follows: Abayyan, Dahman, Rishan (very small), Tuwasan (very small and superrefined), Milwah, and Mu'waj (last two not found in America). There are also numerous substrains among the Muniqi and among the Kuhaylan. The Seqlawi have constituted almost all the early importations into America; however, there is no evidence of any interest in keeping families pure in this country. Very generally speaking, our practice is to breed winner to winner without respect to pedigree. Of course, there are breeders who have great prejudice in favor of horses from a certain country. One such recently told me he would never have a drop of blood on his ranch that wasn't Polish (Arabian, of course). A neighbor of his is equally adamant about blood from Egypt. Yet both of them revere the blood of a horse that brought $150,000 at public auction in his twentieth year and is now standing at $10,000. That horse, Naborr, foaled in Russia, was purchased in Poland by an American dowager and now is standing at stud on a ranch in the wilds of Arizona. It

Nineteen-year-old Naborr, Arabian stallion imported from Poland by Mrs. Anne McCormick. Picture taken October 12, 1969, three days before he was sold at public auction for the highest price ever paid at auction for an Arabian horse, $150,000.

might help clear the air (and even improve breeding practices) if we would concentrate more on bloodlines than exclusively on geography in conversation about Arabian breeding.

Specifications

The characteristics of the Arabian horse as specified by the Arabian Horse Club Registry of America are in part as follows:

Skeleton: The skull is relatively short; the lower jaw is slender, although wide at the throttle. His brain case is large. He has fewer vertebrae in his back and tail than do other breeds. The pelvic bone is more horizontal than it is in most breeds. The usual callosities of the hind legs are very small or absent and are of small size on the forelegs. The ergots on the fetlocks are small and often indistinguishable.

Head: The upper part of the head is larger in proportion to the whole size of the horse than is seen elsewhere, especially in depth across the jowls. It has a triangular shape, diminishing rapidly to a small and fine muzzle, giving the impression of a gazelle or deer. The muzzle is small, and may be enclosed in the palm of the hand. The lips are thin and fine. The nostrils are long, thin, and delicately curled, running upward and projecting outward. When the animal is excited or in action, the nostrils are capable of great dilation and, seen in profile, project beyond the outline of the muzzle, giving a bold, square, sharp, and vigorous expression. The face is slightly dished below the eyes. The cheekbones are sharply cut. The eyes, set far apart, somewhat on the side of the head, are large and lustrous. They are set more nearly in the middle of the head than in other breeds, with plenty of brain capacity above them. The distance from the top of the head to the top of the eyes is often within one inch of the distance from the lower eyelid to the top of the nostril. Added brain capacity is frequently given by a slight protrusion over the forehead and extending to just below the eyes, called the "Jibbah" by the Arabs and greatly prized. A ratio of two-and-one-half to one between the circumference of the head around the jowls and that directly above the nostrils is not uncommon. The cheekbones spread wide apart at the throat, often between five and six inches, enabling the muzzle to be drawn in without compressing the windpipe and the animal to breathe without distress when running. The ears, smaller in stallions and of good size in mares, are pointed, set evenly together in an upright position and of great flexibility. In general, the head should be lean and full of fine drawing.

Neck: The neck of the Arabian, according to the Arabian Horse Club, is long, arched, light, set on high, and run well back into the withers. (A parenthetical statement is needed here to explain that the term *long neck* is relative. While the Arabian usually carries his head high and is capable of great flexion of neck, the neck itself leaves something to be desired in the matter of length in the eyes of devotees of some other breeds.) The throat is particularly large and well developed, loose and pliant when at rest. The head is set onto the neck at a slightly more oblique angle than it is in other breeds. The direct way in which the neck leaves the head for a slight distance before curving is called the "Mitbah" by the Arabians and is greatly prized.

A. and E. Exaggerated drawings showing outline of Muniqi contrasted with ancient strains.
B. Photograph of Muniqi mare.
C. The Darley Arabian, from the life-size contemporary painting in Aldby Hall.
D. Typical head of a Muniqi horse bred pure-in-the-strain. Note the unmistakable resemblance to the Darley Arabian painting.
F. Classic (antique) Kuhaylan-Seqlawi mare.
G. Classic (antique) Kuhaylan stallion.
H. Head detail of classic Kuhaylan stallion.

Straight, angular lines: Muniqi and related strains.

Rounded lines: Kuhaylan, Seqlawi, and related strains.

Height: Measurement from the withers is from 14.2 to 15.2 hands with occasional individuals above or below this height.

Forequarters: The withers are high and set well back and heavily muscled on both sides beyond the usual European standard. The shoulders are long, deep, broad at the base, and powerful but light at the points. The arm is long, oblique, and muscular. The knees are large, square, and deep. The cannon bone is short, flat and clean, and of good size and shows remarkably strong, heavy tendons. The fetlock joint is exceptionally large. The pasterns are long, sloping, very elastic, and strong. The hoof is large, hard, round, wide, and low at the heel. The legs should be set parallel in front and straight from the side and toe squarely ahead.

Middle: Looking from the front or rear, the ribs will be seen to bow out and protrude beyond the quarters. The ribs run to a notable depth beneath the chest and give room for great heart and lung capacity. The ribs hold their size and are close coupled to the point of hipbone. The back is unusually short because of the absence of one lumbar vertebra and the oblique angle of the shoulder. The body is long below with a low belly capable of holding feed. The transverse measurement of the thorax is equal to or a little greater than the vertical measurement.

Hindquarters: The croup is even with the withers in height; the loins are broad; the haunch is long in proportion and quite horizontal. The tail is set on high; it is arched and carried in the air at the first motion of the animal. The quarters are long, well muscled, and somewhat narrow with a fine line denoting speed. The hams are well filled out. The hocks are clean, well let down, of almost abnormal size and strength, giving great leverage to the tendons at the gaskins. The shank bone is flat, clean, short with large tendons. The pasterns are sloping, long, and muscular. The fetlock joint is of exceptional size. The hoof is hard, large, round, wide, and low at the heel. The hind legs are placed in a vertical position squarely under the hindquarters and parallel to the body.

Coat: The mane and tail are long and very fine in texture. The coat is thick, close, fine, soft, and silky.

Color: In Arabia 50 percent are bays, 30 percent grays, and the rest various shades of chestnut and brown and, rarely, a pure white or black. Stars, strips, or blaze faces occur, as do snip noses and a white foot or more with one or more white stockings. Solid white, while much prized, is comparatively rare. Duns, piebalds, and yellows are not seen. Specking, however, is fairly common, often a red variety on the rump. Parti-colored horses are crossbreds.

Weight: The Arab weighs from 800 to 1,000 pounds according to size, with occasional individuals exceeding this weight.

Gaits: The natural gaits of the Arabian are the gallop and a fast walk. In the latter, the hind foot often oversteps the forefoot from one to three feet. While the trot is not his natural gait, he can develop a good trot with cultivation. (Parenthetically, the horse with no intermediate gait between the walk and the gallop is of very limited use under saddle.) Certainly, the intermediate gait of the Arab is the trot, for the lateral gait is rarely seen among Arabians. Being trained to cover long distances, the Arab's natural action is long and low, sufficient to maintain good footing and stride without undue height of action of knees and hocks.

Recent Trends

Very recently the Arabian horse has enjoyed a tremendous increase in popularity in America, with accompanying rise in price. His role here ranges from that of riding horse on trail and bridle path to article of "conspicuous consumption" (status symbol) and show horse in a multitude of categories. This shift of role from war-horse (his original reason for being) to plaything triggers some radical changes in this oldest of all breeds. The first and most obvious change is in size. The big prices go for animals much larger than those the Bedouins knew. The general conformation of the Asil Arabians, the Seqlawi and the Kuhaylans, was, as Carl Raswan so frequently emphasized, typified by a roundness and a strength in all parts. The haunches of those great little equines were especially powerful, rounded and well muscled, with tail set high. Today's American show standards still require the high-set tail but instead of the rounded, muscular haunch, they demand a long, straight, level topline of croup, a feature so well attained by one other show-ring breed that it often results, in some strains, in a lowering of the back at a very early age.

The cow-hocks (see COW-HOCKED) which once enabled the Arabian to shoot his stifles forward to attain a stride almost unbelievable in an animal of his size and to keep his hind feet under him in the rapid footwork of battle are frowned upon as a deviation from the conformation of other show breeds and they are disappearing. The great width of jowl and roomy throttle, which facilitated respiration in the Arabian's former strenuous feats in battle, pursuit, and flight, and probably were a factor in his freedom from respiratory ailments, made his profile so different from that of other show breeds that not only do breeders select for finer throttles but they pose their animals with outthrust noses and, when the horses are stabled, keep their throttles tightly wrapped in fleece-lined leather "sweaters" to reduce size (and possibly to accentuate the "mitbah").

The dish, "jibbah," great broad forehead, and delicate nose of the head of the "antique" strains are not common in American Arabian shows, possibly because concentration on other "improvements" is not compatible with maintaining them or possibly because they are not spectacular enough to be assets in the show-ring.

In performance, show-ring emphasis is on the pointing and dwelling at the trot. The Arabian organizations, acting through the American Horse Shows Association, have wisely limited the length of toe and weight of shoe that can be worn in the show-ring, so any considerable increase in peculiarity or uniqueness of action must be achieved largely by breeding and selection.

The one kind of modern American use with any remote resemblance to that for which the breed was created is the cutting contest. In this stylized version of cutting cattle, horses must keep their heads down at all times. Almost any Arabian is smart enough to keep his nose down and close to a cow if he can be interested in working one (if he can't, he, or a horse of any other breed, will make a sorry fake of a cutting horse), but he objects to hanging his head all the time he is in the ring. To obviate this "contrariness" various expedients are resorted to by trainers, some of them extremely painful. The effect of the desire for a low-headed Arabian is hardly perceptible on breeding farms as yet, but it may ultimately strengthen.

At the present time, the qualities most prized in American shows, as outlined above (with the exception of the low head for cutting horses), are found most frequently not in pure strains from the Sheriff or Wentworth stock but in horses from Poland, where at the dawn of the sixteenth century the aristocracy became interested in founding Arabian breeding establishments. (One of the most notable was the Sanguszke Stud in 1506.) This was long before it was possible to get mares of pure Asil strain out of Arabia. (Because of their descent from the Five Mares of the Prophet, such animals were not to be touched by infidels. To be a party to the export of an Asil mare was a crime worse than murder, rape, or arson. It is said that the first importation of Asil mares into Europe was accomplished by a Polish horseman who "went native" in Arabia, acquired a band of mares, and then escaped to his homeland.) Possibly some of the characteristics, such as size and long, straight croup, so highly prized in modern American show-rings but atypical of horses of the desert, stem in some small part from the distaff side of early Polish pedigrees.

Of the greatest international fame is the stud of Count Potocki, founded about the middle of the sixteenth century. The Antoniny Stud of Poland was the source of Skowronek, perhaps the most highly respected Arabian stallion of our time in England and America.

The Arabian in Poland is bred and kept for racing. Selection and mating in Poland has been on a very different basis from that of Prince Amir Faysul Sha'lan (mentioned above) and Ali Pasha Sherif, who "bred within the same strain or within related strains of the Kuhaylan and Seqlawi, producing those priceless and perfect animals which artists and breeders from all over Europe came to admire—or if they were fortunate, to acquire" (Carl Raswan).

Though Polish Arabians are still favored among the elite breeders in some parts of America, there is a growing regard for blood from Egypt, which could mean a return to favor of some of the pure, Asil blood of "antique" type.

The outstanding shows in which Arabians compete on this continent are the U.S. National Championship Show, until recently, held Labor Day weekend in Oklahoma City, Oklahoma; the Scottsdale All-Arabian Show held mid-February at Scottsdale, Arizona; the Canadian National Show held in August of each year. In addition to these, most of the 108 member clubs put on one show annually, and most states have at least one major Arabian show.

Arabian Horse Club of America, Inc. *See also* ARABIAN HORSE and
INTERNATIONAL ARABIAN HORSE ASSOCIATION

The Arabian Horse Club of America, Inc. (1 Executive Park, 7801 East
Belleview Avenue, Englewood, Colorado 80110), conducts the registration
of Arabian horses in this country. It and the International Arabian Horse
Association are in no small part, through their excellent management,
courteous treatment of the public and promotional programs of various
sorts, responsible for the phenomenal growth in popularity of the Arabian
horse during the last two decades.

One of the most helpful achievements of these associations is the insurance program through which any member can insure his Arabian stock in
one of the old-line insurance companies at rates that are below those available to other horse owners.

Arms (of a horse)

The arm of the horse is the portion of his anatomy between his elbow and
the most forward point of his shoulder (see diagram p. 130). Less fuss is
made in literature and in talk about this part of the horse than about his
shoulder, or about conformation and its relation to performance. However,
the arm is no less important to proper action, whether that of a hunter or
of a harness horse, than is the shoulder—the more nearly horizontal the
arm, the less reach and freedom of forward and upward motion of the
foreleg; the more nearly perpendicular, the greater the freedom of forward
and upward motion of the foreleg.

Arroyo

The term *arroyo* is borrowed from the Spanish. It indicates a deep channel
that has been eroded by water. The sides of the arroyo are perpendicular. It
may reach depths of over 100 feet. In some arroyos water runs the year
round. In others water runs only during the rainy season. Arroyos are
common in certain parts of New Mexico and surrounding states.

Arthritis

Arthritis in horses is quite similar to arthritis in human beings. Among
horses as among people, it is unfortunately not uncommon in older individuals. Successful treatment is unusual.

Asthma

Fortunately, asthma is rare in horses. However, the uninformed sometimes
confuse another ailment of horses with asthma, an ailment which is all too
common. The layman's term for this ailment is *heaves*. The correct term is
pulmonary alveolar emphysema. (*See* HEAVES.)

Australian Horses

The early stock of Australia had a history similar to that of the early horses of our West. Like the latter, the Australian horses had Barb and Arabian blood in their veins. But because of lack of careful breeding, there was considerable degeneration of type. However, at the beginning of the nineteenth century, good stock was imported from Arabia and England, chiefly by what was called the Australian Agricultural Company. Since most of the horse breeding was carried on in New South Wales, Australian horses came to be called "Walers." Walers were characterized by stamina, good bone, and size. In the late 1800s the British government purchased many of them and sent them to India for military purposes.

Azoturia

Before tractors and trucks became common, azoturia was one of the most common and serious diseases of the working horse. It is known all over the world and still occurs frequently, though not as often or seriously as in the days before the truck and the tractor.

Azoturia usually takes the following course: A horse that is worked daily and kept on a high-grain ration of feed is rested up for a day or two without any reduction of the grain feed. Returned to work after the day or so of rest, he begins to be a little sluggish in his action behind. If the rider or driver is aware of this trouble immediately and stops the horse, covers him up, keeps him warm, and calls a veterinarian, the chances are that no permanent injury will occur. However, in the days of delivery horses, many a good animal met a painful death at the hands of a driver who took to the whip as soon as the horse began to slow down.

Today we have few delivery horses who are worked daily, so the classic pattern of the disease does not appear as frequently as it once did. Azoturia may occur in horses of any age and under a variety of conditions. It is usually associated with a high-grain ration in the feed. The first symptom is always a slowing down of action in the hindquarters. Occasionally a horseman who is unacquainted with azoturia thinks that the horse will "warm out of it" if he is moved; so the horseman insists on keeping the horse going until he is completely paralyzed and goes down. There are instances of recovery by horses who have gone down with azoturia, but they are rare.

Formerly a common and dangerous disease and in modern times still a menace, azoturia baffles veterinary science. "Tying up," a muscle spasm similar to a crick in the back in man, is considered by many veterinarians to be merely a mild form of azoturia; others believe that "tying up" is a separate entity. To the horseman, however, it seems to be the same thing, for the symptoms are identical at the beginning—the horse slows down in his action behind.

The number of treatments of azoturia that veterinary science has found helpful is legion and will disconcert the layman—partly because of lack of basic knowledge. However, if the disease is recognized and a veterinarian promptly called, any horse stricken with azoturia will make a complete recovery. Although there is still much to be learned about azoturia, veterinary science has learned a great deal and is able to handle it if it is recognized early and the horse is stopped and kept warm until the veterinarian arrives.

If the horse survives the initial attack, care must be taken to prevent recurrence. This includes limiting or eliminating grain from the diet for a while, getting the horse accustomed very gradually to work, and, in some cases, having a veterinarian inject a compound containing selenium and tocopherol.

Back

In any consideration of conformation, the back of the horse is very important. The horseman uses the term *back* to designate that part of the animal which is between the rear of the withers and the croup. The word *croup* designates the highest point of the horse's hindquarters. When a horse is very thin, the croup frequently appears to be farther back than when a horse is carrying a lot of flesh, for on a thin horse the croup is merely a point of bone with little flesh on it. Conversely, when a horse carries considerable flesh, the croup seems to be farther forward and therefore the back seems shorter. Desirable conformation calls for a relatively short back—short, that is, in comparison with the length of the belly of the horse from elbows to stifles. This proportion is due partly to the fact that a horse of good conformation has very sloping shoulders. The back of the horse should not sway downward between withers and croup. Neither should it bow up just in front of the hindquarters in a manner that is called "roach back" or "hogback." As a horse grows old, the back tends to become a little lower immediately behind the withers. For politeness' sake, we sometimes say that the old horse's withers have risen.

Backing

The proper time to teach an equine to move backward is shortly after he places his feet for the first time on earth. If the little fellow is handled gently from the time he is a few hours old, he can be pushed a few feet backward or forward or to the side. The owner who is careful and kindly will find that it is possible to pick the little colt up without frightening him. An equine who is handled in this way makes a much more delightful personal mount than one who is not handled until he is old enough to be ridden. At whatever age a horse receives his first lesson in backing, he should not be required to take more than one or two steps at the first lesson. One excellent way to start the mature horse to learn to back is to ride him directly up to a gate and then have a helper open the gate toward him so that it forces him backward. The best way to create trouble when first asking a horse to back is to sit on his back pulling violently on the reins and yelling, "Back." Slight repeated pulls on the reins when the horse is standing still should be the signal for him to back.

When the horse has learned the meaning of the signal on the reins to back, and when he has learned the meaning of the aids (*see* AIDS), he should be collected as he is asked to back. When he is backing, the direction he takes is controlled by the use of leg pressure and of the indirect rein (*see* INDIRECT REIN). No horse can be considered well trained unless he is as responsive to his rider while he is backing as he is while he is going forward. And any well-trained horse can be made to take a step very,

Seven-year-old son of Antonio Aguilar enchanting a capacity audience in the Phoenix, Arizona, Coliseum with a song of his homeland as he moves his mount like a dancer on a stage, including backing it half the length of the large arena (note extreme collection on light rein and correct head position of horse).

very slowly in a backward direction or to back at a fair rate of speed. Most trail horse classes include a maze through which the horse must back. The maze is constructed of rails laid on the ground, and the horse must back through the maze without disturbing any of the rails.

Backing Race

A backing race can be an interesting event in a gymkhana. In an informal backing race for beginners, the horses may simply line up on the starting line with their tails toward the finish line, which is some 50 or 60 feet away. They must move toward the finish line with their heads approximately in the proper direction and must cross the finish line hind feet first. A more sophisticated backing race for more advanced riders can be a little longer. A course for each contestant can be laid out with rails on the ground far enough apart so that a horse can back between them easily without kicking them over. If a very advanced group is competing, a turn or two can be made in the course.

Balance

A wise cavalry officer who had been sent abroad to study the cavalries of foreign nations for two years told the writer when he returned, "All riding is a matter of balance." Asked whether he meant balance of horse or rider he said, "Balance of both." As far as the horse is concerned, he "is balanced between impulsion and restraint."

This is perhaps an oversimplification of horsemanship, but it certainly covers most of the things done on a horse's back. The center of a horse's balance when he is walking in a leisurely fashion in pasture is not far behind his forelegs, somewhere in the region of his withers. The center of balance is about that same place when he is running fast. When a horse is performing some of the more intricate movements of the dressage, the center of balance may be in the region of his loins. The balance of a horse is controlled by collection (*see* COLLECTION)—by opposing the signal for impulsion, given by the legs, body, or what not, with pressure on the reins. The highly trained Western horse needs no pressure on the reins; taking some of the slack out of the reins serves the same purpose as pressure on the reins with the Eastern horse. Impulsion of the Western-trained horse is given by subtle movements of the rider's legs. The center of balance of the rider should be over the center of balance of the horse. Each seat of the rider (*see* SEAT) is designed for a kind of riding in which the center of balance of the horse is, most of the time, in one certain place. Thus, the monkey seat of the jockey places his center of balance over the horse's withers because the running horse's center of balance is far forward. The balanced seat, explained below, is one in which the rider is able to shift balance as the horse shifts his center of balance for various gaits and movements. The show seat of the rider of the gaited horse is well back on the horse, partly to show off the horse's forehand but also because the gaited horse, putting up his spectacular performance in the show-ring, has his center of balance well back. If the rider's center of balance is behind that of the horse, he adds to the horse's problems considerably, as evidenced in Western riding by the ignorant rider's leaning back when he asks his horse to do a sliding stop. This leaning back puts the rider's center of balance far behind the center of balance of the horse, and the poor animal will skin his pasterns unless he has sliding boots (*see* SLIDING STOP) on his hind legs.

Balanced Seat

A balanced seat is one that keeps the body in constant alignment with the horse's line of thrust. For example, if a horse is running at top speed, which means that he is certainly not collected at all, his line of thrust is more nearly horizontal than perpendicular, for he is pushing hard with his hind feet when they are extended far behind him. When a horse is cantering at a good, extremely collected canter with his hocks under him, the line of thrust may be very nearly perpendicular. The torso of the rider using a balanced seat leans far forward on the fast-running horse and is nearly upright on the horse doing the collected canter. In using the balanced seat, the rider sits in the middle of the seat of his saddle. His weight is carried on his inner thighs and his pelvis, not on the fleshy part of his buttocks. The back of his heels should be directly under the pelvis at all times, and his weight is extremely flexible, so that he can keep his body constantly aligned with the line of thrust of his horse. The legs from knees to ankles are in the "saddle groove" of the horse, that is, the smallest part of the horse's barrel, which lies just behind its shoulders. The insides of the calves (not the backs of the calves) and knees are against the horse. The heels are kept down. If his legs from knee to ankle are in proper position, the rider does not need to worry about the angles of his feet, because the toes must be turned just slightly out (as in walking) if the leg position is correct. On turns, especially fast ones, he does not lean too far to the inside. It is better to be on the too upright than too leaning side. Many a horse has been pulled off his lead behind by the heavy rider who leans too much, especially if he rides a trifle behind the center of balance. In stopping a fast working horse, the rider must lift him just enough to bring his hocks under him as he stops, and his quarters must be held steady with the heels of the rider. If the horse is lifted and squeezed too much, the forequarters will come up in the air too high and bounce. "What goes up must come down" is painfully true of the front end of a fast-stopping horse. On the fast stop, the rider using the balanced seat *keeps his body aligned with the horse's forefeet,* not his hind ones. If the rider aligns his body with the hind feet, as some riders do, he will be leaning back in an almost horizontal position with his weight punishing his horse's loins and interfering mightily with the horse's use of his haunches. When a horse stops quickly, his hind legs are not thrusting back; they are sliding.

Balking (then and now)

The vice (*see* VICES) of balking, common in horse-and-buggy days, is rather rare today. We have something very close to it now and then in horses whose mouths have been punished severely to make them collect or to give them extremely high action. This vice is called "getting behind the bit"; and if the horse gets behind the bit sufficiently, he will rear or run backward or do anything else to keep the rider from putting pressure on the bit. The true balker simply stands still and refuses to move. The best pulling horses in draft-horse days were sometimes made into balkers by being whipped when they were pulling their hardest. The causes of balking are too numerous to mention, and some of them elude observation.

In the days when balky horses were common, recommended cures were numerous. The only trouble with them was that most of them didn't do much good. They varied from picking up the horse's foot and pounding on the shoe, in order to distract his attention and get his mind off his troubles, to pouring sand in his ear, which made him shake his head and, again, was supposed to have him shake the idea of balking out of his head. One of the legendary cures was to build a fire under the horse, and it always suggests the old story of the balking team hitched to a load of hay. The owner built the fire under the team; the team started up and moved forward just enough to let the fire burn up the hay. There is one element of truth in most of the theories behind the old-fashioned cures: The horse refuses to move in spite of beatings or punishment because he has a fixation or "mental block" that makes him oblivious of anything except his determination to stand still. Anything that will relax the horse and get his attention on something other than his determination to balk will serve as a cure. Many a balker has been induced to move by a horseman whose patience rivaled that of Job. No horse will stand still forever. Sometimes a horse will be intrigued by the horseman's getting out of the buggy and picking blades of grass at the side of the road. In such an instance, an assistant should be left in the buggy to handle the reins if the horse does decide to move. On rare occasions, balkers have been induced to move by some startling noise or something that diverts the attention quickly. In this case the horse may start with such a violent lunge that he does damage to the vehicle or harness or the occupants of the vehicle. The best remedy for balking is prevention—the avoidance of extremely high checkreins, severe bits, and senseless use of the whip.

Ballasting

A few horsemen use the term *ballasting the horse*. Though the term is not common, the performance it refers to is important: shifting of the weight of the rider to signal the horse and to help him perform as the rider wants him to perform. An obvious illustration is the extreme forward seat, which helps the horse get his balance forward and also signals him to extend. Another instance of ballasting not so well known in this country is one being emphasized by Monte Foreman and some other horsemen. It is the use of the body in helping the horse take the proper lead on the canter or gallop. This use of ballasting consists simply in getting the weight *off* the shoulder the rider wants the horse to lead with. That is, if the left lead is required, the rider leans slightly to the *right* and, in extreme cases, he may lean slightly back. Such action is quite the reverse of what is usually seen in gaited-horse classes in the show-ring. However, German and Swiss authorities and now some Americans have proved that it works. The main thing to keep in mind about ballasting is that, except for a few brief special purposes, the rider should keep his center of balance over the center of balance of the horse. Many riders, if not most riders, forget this important principle at times, as is especially evident in a group of riders going downhill—someone will always get his balance way behind the horse's balance. If the hill is steep, it is better, if one is not with the horse, to have one's balance slightly ahead of the horse's balance than behind it.

Bandages

Bandages can do harm to a horse's leg as easily as they can do good. The beginner is likely to overuse bandages. The horse's leg is very complicated, with its intricate circulatory system and its lubrication of tendon sheaths. The pressure of a bandage or a change of temperature caused by wetting the sheet cotton under a bandage certainly interferes with the natural circulation in the leg. Beginning horsemen, seeing expensive race horses or show horses being led out or even worked with bandages on their legs, often assume that this is the way fine horses should be treated. So the tyro immediately goes to the harness store and buys a set of bandages. He forgets that a high percentage of horses running on the racetrack and a certain percentage of show horses are unsound, and bandages are used as therapy. The best thing to do with a sound leg is to leave it alone. Much that is diagnosed as lameness of the leg is actually lameness of the foot, and veterinarians frequently say that the most good done by firing (*see* FIRING) the leg in many cases is the rest it makes the owner give the horse. Wise horsemen use bandages according to competent veterinary advice. There are instances in which a bandage, not too tight, put on over plenty of sheet cotton may protect a horse from injury. For example, when the horse is being shipped by trailer, car, or boat, such a bandage may prevent bruising. Another legitimate use of the bandage on a healthy horse is to wrap the tail when a horse is being hauled in a trailer, or to wrap the mare's tail when she is being bred. The best bandages for such a general purpose are what used to be called Derby bandages. They now are usually known as track bandages. One variety that is very good goes under the name of Grey River Track Bandage. These bandages are made of closely knitted material, largely wool, which is elastic. When used on a tail, such a bandage does not require sheet cotton. The first wraps on the tail should be as close to the body as possible and fairly tight. (A tightly bandaged tail will slough hair and hide if left on for many hours.) As the wraps continue down the tail for several inches, the bandage can be given half a turn to compensate for the decreasing diameter of the tail. Since a good track bandage is at least three yards long, the wraps can be continued down the tail about half the length of the tail bone and then worked back up the tail toward the top. All tail wrapping should be finished at the top of the tail near the body so that the strings which are at the end of every good track bandage can be tied close to the top of the tail.

When used on the leg, bandages should be put on over sheet cotton. Sheet cotton can be bought in rolls. There is also a variety on the market now which is quilted and can be washed; it is easier to use and will wrinkle or bunch up less than ordinary sheet cotton. If the sheet cotton is put on wet, or if the bandage is wet after it is put on, it should be kept wet because wool shrinks when it dries after wetting, and the resultant extra pressure on the leg may do some harm to the circulation.

When track bandages are used for *any* purpose, each bandage should be rolled starting with the end that has strings attached to it. With the strings thus rolled inside, obviously they will be in proper place for tying when the leg or tail is bandaged. To bandage a leg properly, take a couple of rolls at the top of the cannon bone just under the knee and then progress down to the pastern joint; then come back up to the knee again, finishing there so that the bandage may be tied at the top.

There are many varieties on the market for use on horses' legs. Each variety attempts to compete with the old Derby or track bandage. The new "Equihose" looks like a bandage when it is on a horse's leg but it is made all in one piece and slips on over the hoof like a stocking. Rubberized bandages are good for some therapeutic purposes, but the old track bandage is probably useful for more purposes than any other type.

The beginning horseman should be told that most liniments, even though they do not blister when applied without a bandage, will put a severe blister on a horse when used under a bandage. The beginner should also be warned repeatedly that bandages are to be employed only when needed. The wise horseman uses them according to a veterinarian's advice.

Barb

The word *Barb* applies to horses indigenous to the part of North Africa that lies west of Egypt. According to at least one reliable authority, the Barb breed is considerably older than the Arab. Barbs were taken by the Moors into Spain and were probably the foundation of the Andalusians and other Spanish types. Thus there is Barb blood in horses brought to our continent by the Spanish. The Criollo of South America shows Barb influence, as does the Mustang of North America. If a vestige of the hardy little cow pony of the Southwest is still left in the Quarter Horse, then some Barb blood can be said to run in its veins. The most talked-about ancestors of the Thoroughbred are the Godolphin Barb, the Byerly Turk, and the Darley Arabian. For some years there were those who argued that the Godolphin horse was an Arabian. Earl Farshler in his good book *The American Saddle Horse* gives conclusive proof that the Godolphin horse was a Barb and includes an authoritative picture of the Godolphin Barb. This picture illustrates to an extreme degree the characteristics that typify the Barb.

The Barb today is being carefully bred in Algeria and in Morocco. The modern Barb is slightly larger than the Arab. His head and back are longer. His hips are sloping with the tail set low. He is a very hardy horse and is said to have an excellent disposition and the ability to live on poor fare.

Bar Bits. *See* BITS

Bardot

Bardot is a borrowed French term to designate a hinny (*see* HINNY). (If the French film star realizes the superiority of the hinny to other related creatures, she will appreciate the compliment.)

Bareback Riding

Bareback riding properly done can be an excellent aid in developing balance. It can even be a help in developing good hands, for the person who has learned to ride bareback without reins, his arms folded, will not be so likely to use his reins to help his own balance as the rider who has not had such an experience. Needless to say, bareback riding improperly done can be harmful by setting up bad habits that are extremely hard to break. The child who has started riding by using his reins to help him stay on top of his horse will find it very difficult to develop good hands or to do anything else properly after he starts using a saddle.

There is, or was, at least one competent instructor in a Texas school who used a rather severe method of teaching. She would put a class of riders up bareback without reins, arms folded. She would then stand in the middle of the arena with a long coaching whip. Any rider who "tight-legged" a horse would receive a crack with the coaching whip. By "tight-legging" she meant gripping the horse with the back of the calves of the legs.

It is important in bareback riding to avoid the overuse of grip, even proper grip. Proper grip when riding bareback is the same as proper grip when riding the balanced seat (*see* BALANCED SEAT). The insides of the knees and the insides of the upper part of the calves of the legs are used for the grip. The inside of the upper thigh comes in close contact with the horse.

Xenophon's cavalry knew nothing of stirrups or saddles. Those expert horsemen used the perfect bareback seat, as can be seen in any picture of the frieze of the Parthenon. The bareback pad is extremely popular today, and many youngsters begin their riding experience bareback, but unless they are made to practice regularly riding without reins, a generation of bad hands may result.

A warning is in order here: The addition of stirrups to the so-called bareback pad is a rather dangerous practice, for it is very difficult to keep the bareback pad from turning, and it is apparently impossible to supply it with stirrups with open bars which will allow the stirrups to come off if the rider is thrown from the horse and his foot hangs in the stirrup. (*See* SADDLES for method of decreasing the danger of the pad.)

Barn Rat

A horse who refuses to leave the stable unless in the company of other horses and sometimes not even then is called a barn rat. He is also said to be barn sour or stablebound. The stablebound, barn-sour horse is a tragic and dangerous case. It is not safe for any but an expert to attempt to break the horse of this habit. Severe measures have to be taken. The remedies are numerous, ranging all the way from throwing the horse to extreme use of whip and spur. Sometimes the explosion of a blank shotgun shell is used, but this has side effects on other animals in the area. The nonprofessional who has acquired this pitiable beast, if he cannot afford to employ a professional horseman to rid the animal of the vice, had best lead the horse some distance from the stable before mounting him, and he should ride him only in company for many, many rides. There is always the possibility that if the new owner treats his horse well and follows this procedure, the horse will gradually get over his vice. Such recovery, however, is exceptional. The barn rat is made, not foaled. His vice is the result of much bad handling. If the animal is extremely valuable, he can be given enough training of the dressage variety to make him quickly responsive to all the aids. Then when he is mounted and starts his resistance to leaving the barn, he can be controlled in hindquarters and forequarters and kept facing in the desired direction until he is willing to proceed. The horse who has had proper dressage work can be controlled in any situation. If the horse is so well trained, the rider will have to be trained well enough to communicate with him. Such training of horse and of rider requires time and money, but if the barn-sour horse is valuable, this method is by far the best.

It is unfortunate that a vice very similar to if not identical with being barn sour sometimes afflicts valuable hunters. One reason is that some trainers of hunters are so preoccupied with jumping that they do not give enough work in responding to the aids. The hunter who had not been taught to yield properly to the leg aids or to an indirect rein (*see* REINS) may well become what in the West is called "herdbound." That is, he may refuse to leave a group of horses, or to leave any spot in which he has been standing, unless accompanied by another horse. Such an animal will use the same defenses as will a stable-bound horse. He will rear or whirl or fly backward or do anything else he can to avoid properly obeying his rider. The hunter taught to yield properly to the bit and to respond properly to the leg aids will not fall victim to this vice unless ridden by an extremely ingenuous and bad rider over a considerable period of time. The herdbound horse is extremely dangerous not only to his own rider but also to others in any group in which he is ridden.

Barrel (of the horse)

The barrel of the horse is his body, the portion of his anatomy that lies between the shoulders and the hips.

Barrel (for racing)

In barrel racing, the objects used to form the pattern of the course of the race are called barrels. Since barrel racing had its origin in Texas, the home of many oil wells, these objects are usually 50-gallon oil drums made of metal. (*See* BARREL RACING.)

Barrel Racing

Barrel racing is a relatively new sport, scarcely more than two decades old. It started in Texas, which abounds in good horses, pretty girls who can ride them, and 50-gallon oil drums (the barrels). It was probably inevitable that these items should organize. The pattern of the barrels has varied considerably and may change in the future. The number of barrels has ranged from two to four. They have been arranged in a straight line, a square, and a triangle of varying proportions. Today the number of barrels is three, and the pattern is that of an almost equilateral triangle. The size of the triangle varies somewhat with the size of the arena, but the GRA (Girls Rodeo Association) recommends that the two barrels equidistant from the starting line (20 yards) be 30 yards apart and the third barrel be 35 yards from each of the others. The contestant may choose to go either direction of the pattern, but most seem to prefer starting with the right barrel. It must be circled to the right, and the other two to the left. A flagman signals the finish of each contestant. Knocking over a barrel (even if it flips completely over and rights itself bottom side up) disqualifies a contestant, as does failure to follow the pattern completely.

Basic Seat

The good horseman can ride reasonably well on any kind of horse that is fit for any use. We might except the bucking horse of the rodeo and the top race horse, though a good American rider should be able to weather the storm of a few modest bucks now and then, and he could ride the monkey seat of the race rider, even if he could not boot home a winner.

Balance should be appropriate to the kind of riding done, but we might regard all balance in riding as a departure from a basic or "normal" seat. The more specialized the purpose, the farther we get away from the basic or "normal" seat and balance. Man o' War was ridden to glory with a monkey seat (rider over the withers, center of balance over the forelegs).

Hell-to-Sit, one of the greatest bucking horses of all time, was ridden a very few times and then only after he was 15 or 16 years old (he was still throwing riders in Madison Square Garden when past 20). The few men who rode him used a seat we might call exactly the opposite of the monkey seat, the rider keeping his body well behind the middle of the saddle and the center of balance over the loins.

All kinds of expert riding, from the monkey seat to the forked-radish seat of the charro in a Western parade, have some of the common elements of the basic seat. Each special seat is a modification of the basic seat, the seat which most comfortably joins man and horse and enables them to move more nearly like one living body. The basic seat can be seen in much Greek sculpture. The frieze from the Parthenon shows it. Watch a polo player jogging or cantering onto the field and you will see it. The old fox hunter jogging to or from the hunt uses it, as does the cowboy on the trail.

In the basic seat the body is erect; that is, the shoulders are directly above the hips. The back is straight or slightly convex (contrary to what is prescribed for the riding-school seat or "equitation seat"). The weight of the body is carried farther back in the saddle than in any other seat except that used in showing gaited horses. The upper parts of the thighs carry some of the body weight, especially at movements faster than a slow, uncollected walk.

From hip to knee, the leg inclines forward, approximately at a 45-degree angle with the body. The position of the upper portion of the leg depends on the size of the rider and the size of the horse. A tall long-legged rider on a small horse will ride with his thigh more nearly horizontal than perpendicular because the curve on the inside of the rider's leg just below the knee should contact the horse just ahead of the girth, the part just behind the shoulder (the part of the horse that Monte Foreman calls the saddle groove). A short-legged rider on a good-sized horse will carry his upper leg more perpendicular. A very short-legged rider on a very large horse will find this seat impossible (which does not mean that a short-legged rider cannot ride well on a large horse, though he may have to use excellence of balance to make up for slight difficulties in seat). Many authorities state that it is the inside of the thigh that should contact the saddle in any seat. Taken literally this advice is impossible to follow if the rider sits down in his saddle. However, the contact, especially with the lower thigh, is made more nearly with the inside of the thigh than with the back of the thigh. If the back of the thigh makes the contact, the calf of the leg just below the knee will not touch the saddle at all; and the back of the calf, not the inside of it, will be the only part of the lower leg in contact with the horse. This position will make the toes stick straight out away from the horse. With proper position of legs, the rider does not "grip the horse with his knees," as some fictional writers claim. He does not grip the horse at all when riding along casually. His muscles, all of them, are almost imperceptibly and unconsciously keeping in rhythm with one another. If the horse makes a sudden unexpected move, the legs grip the horse. Or if the rider wishes the horse to make a sudden move, he grips with his legs and seems to lift the horse with them in the desired direction.

The grip of the basic seat is not a knee grip. It is a grip with all the inner part of the leg from midcalf to upper thigh. As the knee is just above the thickest part of the horse, a grip with the knees alone would tend to force the rider up and off the horse. The good rider of the basic seat rides with his legs relaxed but in the right position for gripping, and his stirrups are directly below his kneecaps.

If a proper contact is made with the horse from hips to midcalf, the feet of the rider will satisfy any critic except the poor soul born to self-torture who insists on riding, sometimes for hours, with his feet parallel to his horse's sides and his heels far below the balls of his feet. Though there are some purposes for which the heels should be well below the balls of the feet, in the seat we are now talking about, the soles of the feet should be parallel with the ground. With the leg position as we have described it, the feet will be at about a 45-degree angle with the horse's sides. The beginner should have the balls of his feet on the stirrups with any seat; the experienced rider using this seat *may* ride with his feet home (stirrups under the arch of the foot).

We have talked about this seat at length and in detail because it is the basic seat from which others are deviations. As we have said, most old, experienced riders use it in relaxed moments, and it is to be seen in the old Greek art as well as the Roman and early Italian art. A word of caution is needed by people who would study this seat in early Greek art. Some of the most expert horsemen the world has known (Xenophon, for instance) rode before saddles or even horseshoes were invented. The bareback seat they used varies from the basic seat with saddle and stirrups in but two details. The feet were carried with the toes down and much farther forward than we carry them when using stirrups. Stirrups change the position of the lower leg completely.

Except with the very large rider on the very small horse, the basic seat puts the center of balance of the rider directly over the center of balance of the horse when the horse is moving at an easy rate and not extremely collected. It is the seat for the beginner to use while he is learning the rhythm of the horse.

Basketball (on horseback)

Basketball on horseback is said to have originated with the Cossacks. They used a sheepskin instead of a ball and showed great skill throwing the sheepskin far ahead of a rider and catching it on a fast gallop. In the days when horses were used by the United States Cavalry, basketball was played by cavalrymen. They used a regular basketball, and the game was a pretty rough business, but it was considered a very good exercise for cavalrymen.

Baubling

Baubling is a term used to refer to a horse who makes a mistake or objects to performing a required act of any kind.

Bay

The term *bay* is used for quite a range of color shades in the horse, reddish brown through deep cherry color to a rather pale, almost clay color. The bay horse can be distinguished from a chestnut or sorrel by his black mane and tail. The bay usually has some black around the lower part of his legs. Most bays are called red by the uninformed.

Beach, Belle

Probably no greater horsewoman has ever lived than Belle Beach. Her book *Riding and Driving for Women,* published in 1912, contains much information that is of great value for horsemen today. Belle Beach's death in 1933 drew comment from leading newspapers. More than one of them mentioned that on occasion Belle Beach's reins in the hunting field were No. 50 cotton thread.

Bean

A "bean" is an accumulation of smegma in the head of the horse's penis. This may increase in size until it interferes with urination and causes serious or even fatal illness. Geldings and stallions should be watched for any difficulty in urination and should periodically be examined by a careful, experienced and cleanly horseman or a veterinarian to see if cleaning is needed. (*See* STOCK.)

Belgian Draft Horse Corporation of America

Blanche A. Schmalzried is the secretary-treasurer of the Belgian Draft Horse Corporation of America. Her address is P.O. Box 335, Wabash, Indiana 46992. The corporation keeps the registry of the Belgian horse in America.

Belgian Horse

The Belgian horse was one of the three or four most popular breeds of draft horses produced in this country. He is a descendant of the Great Horse of Flanders, the grandparent of the horses used by the knights in armor and of other draft breeds. In the early part of this century, careful

Rube and Champ, Belgians, winning Heavyweight Class, were subsequently sold to Larry Lansburg. Champ stars in the film *Chester, Yesterday's Horse*. Gilbert Owsley, driver.

breeders greatly improved the Belgian horse, particularly in the quality of feet and bone. During the second decade of this century, draft horse breeders put up an extremely hard fight to keep a place in the sun in spite of the rise in popularity of the tractor on the farm. They bred horses of great size so that one man could control a great amount of power. The Belgian was bred up to a size that ran well over a ton. His great intelligence and quiet temperament also found favor in the race against the tractor. In 1913 the Belgian horse Farceur brought the record price for a draft horse, $47,000. Though tractors finally took the place of horses on most American farms, Belgians are still being bred and classes for them are held in state fairs in the Middle West. There are still jobs that a Belgian horse can do better than any machine, according to James Potter, of the Arizona Pulp and Paper Company, Inc., which conducts one of the largest logging operations in northern Arizona. Recently one item on the large bill for new equipment for the company was a package deal with C. G. Goode and Son, breeders of Belgian horses. It included four mares and a young stallion, all descendants of the original Farceur. According to Potter, more and more logging outfits, especially in eastern Canada and the northern New England states, are going back to using horses. He says he likes the Belgians best of all because of their great intelligence, docility, and strength.

Bending Race

For a bending race, a row of jump standards or other similar objects should be set up about ten or twelve feet apart. Each contestant leaves the starting line, weaves in and out among the stakes, and returns to the starting line, racing against time. Touching a standard disqualifies a contestant. Obviously, a horse who changes leads handily has a great advantage in this race over one who does not.

Bight (of the reins)

The portion of the bridle reins extending from the hand to the end of the reins not attached to the horse's bit is called the bight. In equitation classes the bight should fall on the off side of the horse, according to the current *Rule Book* of the American Horse Shows Association.

Bike

The vehicle used on harness racetracks in races between trotters or pacers is known as a "bike." The modern racing sulky is extremely light and rides very close to the horse. The wheels, of course, are the bicycle type.

Billet

A billet is the end of a strap that goes through a buckle.

Birthday

Most breed organizations have a ruling that makes January 1 the official birthday of every animal registered by the breed association. Therefore, if a foal draws its first breath on December 31, the next day it will technically be one year old.

Bits

Until very recent times, horsemanship was largely considered a matter of finding out how to hurt a horse and where to hurt him to make him react in a desired fashion. In my book *Bits, Their History, Use and Misuse* there are illustrations and descriptions of bits that display the enormous ingenuity of man and his ability to devise contraptions that will cause excruciating pain. The late Henry Wynmalen, M.F.H., is probably the first authority who wrote fully and clearly about the necessity of teaching the horse what pressure on the bit means before pressure is used to direct the horse into the movements which we finally want him to execute.

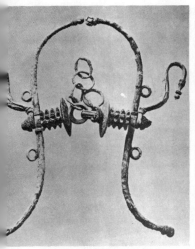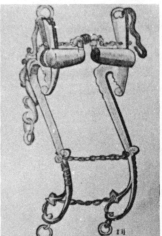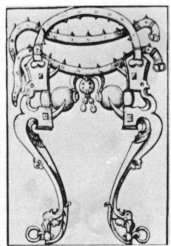

(Left) Fourth-century Greek bit with disks and echini, discussed by Xenophon. The side-pieces are turned in the picture to show their S shape. When worn they lie flat against the outsides of the horse's mouth.

(Center and right) In the seventeenth century curb bits of the European riding schools became so complicated that sometimes some teeth had to be removed from the horse's mouth to accommodate the bit.

Since communication with the horse is largely kinetic—that is, largely a matter of movement and pressures rather than of words or other signals—the bit is the most useful instrument. What the horse does with any part of his body usually depends upon what he is doing with his head and neck, for they are the most important controllers of his balance; so what the bit tells him will control his entire body.

Early bits were constructed to cause pain in various parts of the horse's mouth and head. The very earliest ones hurt the outside of the jaws; later on, about 400 B.C., the part of the bit that went inside the mouth was intricately designed to inflict pain of different kinds. The practical Greeks devised bits that would cause pain on the outside of the mouth by pinching movements, from which our snaffle bits are descended, and on the inside of the mouth as well. Today most of our top horsemen feel that the curb and snaffle, the double bridle of English variety, will serve any ordinary purpose of training or of riding. The curb with its lever action tells the horse (after he has been properly taught) to bring his chin in and hocks under him—in other words, to collect himself. The snaffle (*see* SNAFFLE) encourages the horse to put his center of balance forward, to get his nose to the front. There are excellent horsemen who use the old California method of the spade bit and hackamore, but such riders never use a spade bit to cause pain. It is, they say, the most versatile bit ever designed, and with it they, those rare excellent horsemen with light, deft hands, can get any exact balance or movement they desire.

Varieties of Modern Bits

For horses in harness, bits can be classified easily into three types. (1) The most common bit, the jointed snaffle, has no leverage action. (2) The bar bit resembles the snaffle except that the mouthpiece is not jointed. (3) The leverage bit is used on some horses in harness, Hackney ponies for instance, the Budweiser team, and what used to be called heavy-harness horses (see discussion of curb bit below). Driving bits with leverage action are descended from those of the coaching days and they are of several kinds. The bar bits and the snaffles come in various forms. Some are rubber covered; some are made of hard rubber; some are leather covered.

Varieties of modern bits. A. Mexican half-breed bit; B. Santa Barbara spade; C. Mexican ring bit; D. Western Pelham; E. original Walking Horse bit; F. U.S. Cavalry bit of frontier days.

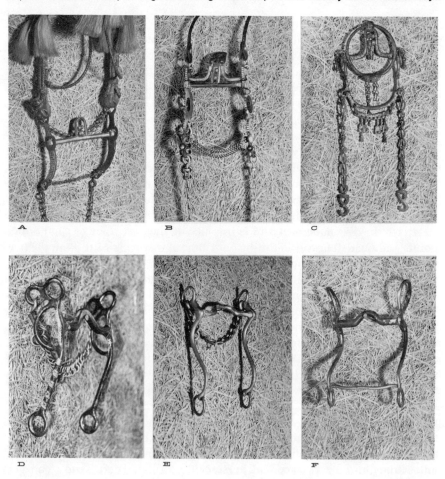

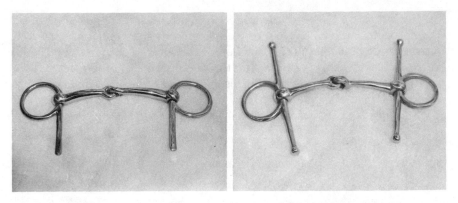

(Left) Half-cheek snaffle (sometimes called driving bit). (Right) Full-cheek snaffle.

Most driving bits today that are not of a leverage variety are what we call half-cheek bits—that is, at each end of the mouthpiece there is a ring and also a short bar that extends downward. A full-cheek bit is one in which the bar extends both up and down on the outside of the mouth and the end of the mouthpiece. Though the full-cheek snaffles are not seen in driving harness, they are still used when the horse is under saddle.

Riding bits today include the leverage bit, the snaffle, and the bar bit. The leverage bit, commonly called the curb, comes in a number of forms. The mouthpiece occurs with or without a port, and ports come in various sizes. The sidepiece or the shank of the curb determines its severity. In English curb bits the commonest length of shank is seven inches, but some English bits seen on gaited horses have shanks as long as ten inches.

In addition to curb bits, the general class of leverage bits includes the spade bit. In the spade bit there is in place of the port a long spoon which presses against the roof of the horse's mouth when pressure is applied to the reins. Chains are sometimes used on spade bits, but proper adjustment of chain length is a very intricate and delicate matter and has a great deal to do with the exact balance the rider will achieve.

Perhaps least common in this country among leverage bits is the ring bit. Its origin is attributed differently by various authorities. It is sometimes called the Moorish ring bit, sometimes the Turkish ring bit. In our country it is seen commonly only in localities where there are Basque stockmen. As its name implies, it is equipped with a ring which entirely encircles the horse's jaw and goes through an opening in the top of the very high port of the bit. When the reins are pulled, the port goes upward pulling the ring up against the bottom of the horse's jaw. Obviously no chain is needed, since the ring applies the pressure usually supplied by the chain. As a rule the shank of the ring bit is somewhat shorter than that of an ordinary curb.

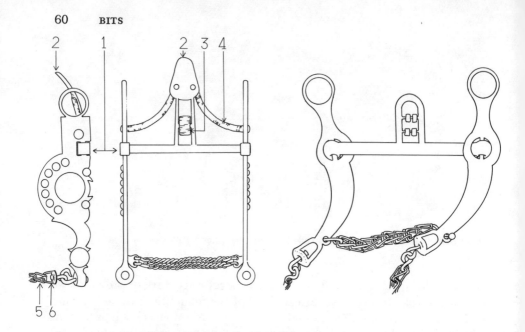

(Left) Spanish spade bit. 1. Swivel clasp; 2. spade; 3. copper; 4. copper-covered brace; 5. chains; 6. swivel. (Right) Half-breed bit; this may also have single roller instead of four small rollers.

All English curb bits are supplied with little loops for a lip strap. The loop is on each shank midway between the mouthpiece and the ring to which the rein is attached. The lip strap is attached to the loop on one side; it then goes through a ring in the center of the curb strap and thence down to the lip strap loop on the other side of the bit. A shoestring or piece of cord will do in place of a lip strap, but the wise horseman always uses a lip strap on an English curb, for most horses will lip the bit—that is, take the shank of the bit into their mouths—if it is not supplied with a lip strap. Western bits do not have lip strap loops, but the shanks are usually S-shaped or made in some other design that will discourage the horse from taking the shank into his mouth.

Choosing a Bit

The choice of a bit should depend more upon the hand of the rider than upon the mouth of the horse. However, some horses, especially some spoiled horses, can be used with only one kind of bit. And some horses have been so cruelly hurt with a leverage bit that they can never be ridden satisfactorily with anything but a snaffle or hackamore. Similarly, there are riders whose hands are so bad that they should never be allowed to ride a horse with anything but a cotton rope halter. The best bit for any horse ridden by a particular rider is the bit with which that horse and that rider can best communicate with each other.

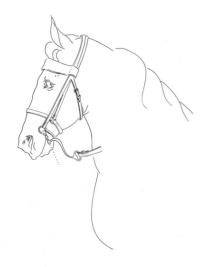

Angle of bit. Proper adjustment of curb strap to prevent pinching corner of mouth (strap or chain must be short enough to prevent bit shank from coming back farther than a 45-degree angle with mouth).

Fitting the Bit

When a single bit is used, it should fit snugly into the corner of the horse's mouth but not pull the corners up and make a wrinkle just above the mouth. When a double bridle, or a full bridle—that is, a curb and snaffle—is used, the curb bit should be fitted not too snugly into the corner of the horse's mouth and the snaffle should be fitted quite snugly. A very slight wrinkle caused by the snaffle bit is not bad for most horses. One of the most important matters in fitting a bit to a horse is that of adjusting the curb chain or curb strap properly. The chain or strap should be of such length that the shank of the bit when pulled will be at a 45-degree angle with the mouth and can be pulled to no great angle. If a Western bit is used, the shank below the mouthpiece may be so curved or constructed in such a fancy design that the 45-degree angle rule will be difficult to determine. But even in Western bits a part of the shank from the mouthpiece to the bridle is usually straight; and if one can imagine this part of the shank extended downward, he can so adjust the chain or strap that the angle of the imagined shank will be 45 degrees and no pull on the reins can make it greater. If the curb chain or strap is any longer than has just been indicated, the corners of the horse's mouth will be pinched between the chain and the mouthpiece of the bit. This is a very common occurrence, and on many old rental horses and ranch horses one can see calluses at the corners of the mouth that have been made by this pinching of a too long strap or chain. If the chain is too short, a pull on the curb bit will simply pull the bit upward toward the horse's ears and will not create any leverage action at all.

Adjustment of the Bit. See BITS, Fitting the Bit

Bitting

The term *bitting* when used by an intelligent horseman means the process of teaching the horse what the teacher means when he uses the bit. There are almost as many ways of doing this as there are horsemen. However, in general, the Eastern method consists in using a snaffle bit and some kind of bitting rig (*see* BITTING RIG), working a horse on a lunge line with this bitting rig on it, and then working the horse carefully after he is first mounted, with a snaffle bit or a full bridle (*see* BITS), using only the snaffle reins. Western horsemen do not use the term *bitting* as frequently as do Eastern or English horsemen, but they are just as careful about the process. Western trainers usually start a green horse out with a bosal, which is a kind of braided noseband (*see* BOSAL). Reins are, of course, attached to the bosal, but frequently the Western trainer will hang a bit in the green horse's mouth without any reins attached the first few times the horse is ridden. Later on, two sets of reins will be used, one on the bosal and one on the bit, so that the transition from bosal to bit can be made gradually. The bit used is ordinarily a snaffle; however, at least one excellent trainer in California still uses the spade bit. The spade bit should not be used by anyone who is not expert at handling it, for the inept can do much harm with it (*see* SPADE).

Bitting Rig

The simplest form of bitting rig is a surcingle or roller (a web or fiber band 2½ or more inches wide, padded on either side of the backbone to keep pressure off the top of the spine). It is provided with rings at the top, sides, and bottom for reins, overcheck, and tie-down and attached to a crupper by a backstrap. Refinements and elaborations of the bitting rig are many. It may be provided with a backstrap and pad like a harness; it may be provided with terrets and a hook for attaching overcheck or sidecheck. When the bitting rig has arms going well above the horse's back so that reins may be attached to them at about the height they would be held by a rider's hands, the contraption is called a dumb jockey.

The ways of attaching the bit or bits to the bitting rig or dumb jockey are as varied as are the types of dumb jockeys. Practically all users of bitting rigs or dumb jockeys employ side reins that attach each bit ring to a ring on the side of the bitting rig. Frequently these side straps either are made of elastic or have a strip of elastic in them. The horse's head is held up by a checkrein or an overcheck attached either to the main bit or to a special overcheck bit. In most instances there is a tie-down going from a noseband to a ring on the center of the belly of the bitting rig. Some trainers put a horse in the bitting rig when he is being worked on a lunge line. Others, including those who work on the lunge line, will turn the horse loose in paddock, corral, or stall with the bitting rig on him.

The theory behind the use of the bitting rig is that it teaches the horse the meaning of the bit and also trains him in how to hold his head. Some expert trainers have achieved good results with the bitting rig, but many a good animal has been ruined or had his mouth spoiled or his neck made rigid by its use. Keeping a horse in the bitting rig too long the first few times it is used on him, or having the straps too tight, will certainly do more harm than good. The most important reason for using the bitting rig is that a busy and harassed trainer can be working several horses at one time by putting bitting rigs on some of them and turning them loose in paddock or corral.

Black Hawk Family

The Black Hawks are a famous strain of Morgan horses stemming from one son of the great Justin Morgan (*see* MORGAN HORSE).

Black Points

The term *black points* refers to dark coloration of manes, tails, and lower legs as seen on all bay horses and some duns and buckskins.

Blankets

The size of horse blankets is reckoned in inches measured from the center of the breast, where the blanket fastens, to the rear end of the blanket. As a general rule, cheap blankets are more expensive in the long run than higher-priced ones. A long-time favorite is the old Baker blanket, but its initial cost is rather high. If the health of the horse is the prime consideration of his owner, the horse will not wear a blanket winter or summer except in very unusual climates. If the horse has proper food and shelter and a little place to exercise (by that is meant a corral at least 50 feet square), or even if he is enclosed in a box stall, he will be much better off as to health without a blanket than he will be blanketed. In extremely cold climates or in places like Arizona and New Mexico, where diurnal variation is extreme, blankets are sometimes used to advantage if put on during the night and taken off during the day. However, if the blanket happens to become wet from rain or other cause, it should be taken off. There are occasions, usually emergencies, when the use of a blanket is imperative. For example, if after a hard ride a horseman has no opportunity to cool his horse out properly before loading him in a trailer, the horse must be blanketed (the wise horseman always carries one or more blankets in his horse trailer). But the blanket should be removed from the horse and the animal given a good rubdown as soon as possible. A blanket wet with sweat will cause illness just as readily as will a blanket wet by rain.

Bleeder

The word *bleeder* is applied to horses used by laboratories for producing serum.

Blemishes

Blemish indicates a scar or lump or other unsightly result of an accident which does not interfere with the horse's usefulness—that is, does not interfere with his way of going, his wind, or his vision. Blemishes do not greatly affect the price of some kinds of horses, for instance, rope horses or cutting horses. However, the horseman can sometimes pick up an animal directly suited to his needs at a bargain price because the animal has a blemish. The horse (and any other animal, for that matter) should be examined by a veterinarian of the buyer's choice before any money changes hands. Many an unwary buyer has been told by a former owner that a lump or scar is merely a blemish and in no way affects a horse's usefulness when that lump or scar actually makes the animal unfit for service.

Blind Staggers. *See also* STAGGERS

Blind staggers is an old-fashioned term which means nothing more than fainting or falling down. The horse may go down from any one of a number of causes. In horse-and-buggy days a horse would get "blind staggers" from too tight a throatlatch or too tight a collar. If a horse has been starved for salt, a very rare occurrence in this day of commercial feeds, and is suddenly given access to an unlimited supply of loose salt, he may have a fainting spell and go down. An even more old-fashioned word for the same sort of phenomenon as "blind staggers" is *megrims*. Obviously, if a horse staggers or falls down, a veterinarian should be summoned. If the veterinarian is not immediately available, the horse should be kept quiet and some sort of shade constructed that will keep direct rays of the sun off his head. Cool compresses quietly and carefully applied to the horse's head are sometimes good first-aid treatment until the veterinarian arrives.

Blistering

For many generations, blisters have been induced on horses by the use of salves, liniments, and ointments (most of them having as a base red iodide of mercury) in hope of curing everything from ringbone to poll evil. The amount of useless agony caused horses by this practice is appalling. There are cases in which a blister is useful, but one of the most important factors, if not the most important, in any ailment or illness is correct diagnosis, and the wise horseman will rely on his veterinarian for diagnosis and prescription of treatment.

Whether or not the increased circulation of the injured part caused by a blister benefits a sprain depends upon the individual case. However, when an uninformed horseman blisters a sprained leg, the blister has one good effect—it makes the horseman rest the horse over a period of time. In the case of a pulled tendon there is one very bad effect of the use of a blister— it gives the horseman the notion that the horse is being helped, and he does not call a veterinarian. With modern veterinary knowledge, a bowed tendon, if not extremely bad, can be cured completely if a veterinarian is called immediately. One important item in the modern technique of handling bowed tendons is a semirigid cast which keeps the upright tendon in place, even though the lateral ligaments are torn (*see* BOWED TENDON).

Blood

The word *blood,* when applied to horses (as distinguished from its application to hounds or huntsmen) means the amount of Thoroughbred blood in a horse's pedigree or the evidence of that blood as shown by the quality, fineness, spirit, and stamina of the animal. There is an old saying, which may or may not have some basis in fact, that "an ounce of blood is worth a pound of bone." This maxim implies that quality of bone is more important than quantity.

Blood Heat

The normal temperature of a horse is approximately 100° F. The age and sex of a horse have some effect on the temperature.

Bloom

The term *bloom* denotes gloss of coat, sparkle of eye, spriteliness of movement, and other evidences of well-being in a horse. Bloom is best attained by confining an animal's contact with people to those whose actions make sense to the horse, and by proper feed, water, and general care (*see* TONICS).

Bog Spavin

A bog spavin is an injury to the vascular system of the hock joint. The soft parts of the joint swell and extend out beyond the bony parts. Sometimes a bog spavin on a young animal if detected soon enough can be successfully treated by a veterinarian. Home remedies usually increase the trouble.

Bolt. *See also* BOLTING

When a horse eats his grain too rapidly, he is said to bolt it. A remedy is to place rocks in the grain manger so that he cannot get his grain as fast as he would like to. There are various patent food mangers that are designed to cure bolting in a horse. Most of them are useful.

Bolting

A horse is said to be bolting when he is running out of control of the rider. The term is used chiefly to denote a horse who does this sort of thing habitually. The vice of bolting, like every other vice a horse may have, is caused by bad handling. A very usual way of causing a horse to bolt is as follows: An inexperienced rider takes a horse out for a ride, possibly with a group of less inexperienced riders. Somebody starts to gallop. The tyro's horse, of course, goes along with the others. His rider becomes frightened, screams, and starts yelling "Whoa!" at the top of his voice, which is enough to make any horse run. The green rider raises his hands in the air because he has been holding the reins so far back that he has no place else to put them if he wants to pull. He puts his heels back in his horse's flank; he leans forward. In fact, he does everything a rider can do to make a horse go faster. If he is fortunate, he will stiffen up and fall off in a place where there is deep sand or grass, and he will not be much the worse for wear. But the horse will not soon recover from his trauma.

There are, of course, other ways of causing a horse to become a bolter. The cure will depend a great deal upon the anatomy of the horse, his temperament, and the way in which he was caused to become a bolter. The old remedy of letting a horse bolt and then making him run farther than he wants to run by use of whip and spur may be effective, but it may also damage the horse's heart or wind. If he can be induced to bolt where the terrain is fairly level and the footing safe, his head can be pulled around to the side, even clear around to the rider's knee, and he will stop. Of course, doing this quickly at the wrong time will cause a horse to fall down. This trick can be observed by watching almost any Western movie in which horses are made to fall down. Quick, short, hard pulls on one rein or on both are more effective than a long steady pull, no matter how hard, for a steady pull will only make a horse go faster.

The best thing to do with the horse who has developed the habit of bolting is to turn him over to a competent, reliable trainer, or to sell him or have him put to sleep by a competent veterinarian.

Bone

When a horseman praises or disparages a horse's bone, he is referring to that part of a horse's leg between the knee and the pastern joint. He may also have in mind the part of the leg that lies between the hock and the pastern joint. Whether in a front or hind leg, the bone in the part referred to is called the cannon bone. Actually what the horseman is thinking of is more than just the bone; it is the entire section of the leg between knee and pastern or hock and pastern. The proportions of this part of the horse's leg are a pretty good indication of his entire skeletal structure. They also tell something about his endurance. The part of the leg referred to as bone should be short in comparison with the part of the leg between the knee and the elbow, which is called the forearm. Ideally the cannon bone should resemble an old-fashioned straight razor in shape. When viewed from the front, it should be narrow; when viewed from the side, it should be wide and should be about the same width from just below the knee to just above the pastern. A common fault is for the cannon bone to be "tied in" just below the knee—that is, for the top of the cannon bone when viewed from the side to be much narrower just below the knee than it is just above the pastern joint.

When a horseman boasts about his horse's bone and states the number of inches it comprises, he has in mind the length of a tape measure when placed around a horse's leg just below the knee. There is an ancient saying: "An ounce of blood is worth a pound of bone." It means that refinement, evidence of good breeding, is more important than size of bone. However, the wise horseman is not misled by maxims; he knows that no matter how fine a horse is, if his feet and legs are not sufficiently large and sturdy, he will break down.

Boots

Boots for the Horse

Boots for the horse, very generally speaking, are for either of two purposes. The first is to protect the horse from injury sustained by striking a leg or a heel with a foot, bruising a shin while jumping, or burning the skin off hind pasterns while executing a sliding stop. Some of the many varieties of boots are quarter boots to prevent bruising of a front heel with a hind toe, interfering boots, and shin boots. There are also polo boots to prevent injury by the mallet.

Another purpose of boots is to cover the unsightly scars on the forelegs of Walking Horses made by the cruelties inflicted on them during training (see SORING).

Boots for the Rider

Boots are almost a fetish for both Eastern and Western horsemen. They are useful for many kinds of riding, e.g., protection from heavy brush, horse's sweat, polo mallets, but anyone who thinks they are indispensable for good riding needs to be reminded of the horsemanship of the Nez Percé Indians of the past and of the South American gauchos of the present.

Certainly formal English riding requires one to wear black boots. To avoid suffering, the wearer should be sure that his boots are not too tight. If the tops are too short, the wrinkles at the ankle may allow the tops to slip below the desired height. The person whose instep is so high that putting on boots is a great difficulty had better resort to the use of talcum powder and boot hooks rather than the wearing of field boots, those having laces at the instep, because laced boots are entirely incorrect.

If one rides a gaited horse or a Walking Horse it is quite proper to wear jodhpur boots (ankle length with elastic sides or buckle-over front).

In Western boots, convention allows more latitude than in English boots; but the Western horseman is just as insistent upon wearing boots as is his friend of the "pancake saddle." He will usually avow that a good pair of boots, with steel arches, is the most comfortable footgear made—even though his own gait may be visibly on the "gimpy" side. At least one prominent Westerner wears especially made patent leather boots at formal dances.

Modern Western boots all have sharply pointed toes. Work boots are frequently made with the flesh side of the leather out, called "rough out." For other than workaday use, the sky is the limit in beautification of the tops of Western boots. Exotic leathers such as crocodile or ostrich are fashionable. The softest and most comfortable leather is kangaroo. Ankle-length Western boots are correct but not serviceable in brush country or in any riding that is vigorous enough to cause the rider's pants to creep up. It seems a pity that Western boots are usually worn inside the jeans or pants, for the tops are often very attractive.

The high, undershot heel of the Western boot, once so popular, has given way to lower heels which are fairly straight. Many claims were made for the old high heels. It was said that they kept the feet from going completely through stirrups and that they could be dug into the ground for good footing when the wearer held a critter on foot by a rope. However, bulldoggers and calf ropers, idols of young Western horsemen, found they could make better time with boot heels that were lower and larger, just as they found that lower cantles saved fractions of seconds; so boot heels, like cantles, have changed in accordance with the preference of rodeo stars. If they adopt the custom of some old-time cavalrymen and present-day Argentine gentlemen (the polishing of boot soles, evidently for proof that the wearer rarely walks), we shall doubtless see the arena reflected from boot soles as the bronc rider makes his ascent.

Bosal

The bosal is a noseband of braided rawhide of any one of a variety of diameters—from a half-inch (in rare instances) to as much as three inches where it crosses above the nostrils (in some very extreme gringo bosals as explained below). Properly used, its front rides on a horse's nose just above the soft cartilage. The rear of the bosal terminates in what is called a heel knot, which keeps the reins (usually a hair rope) in place. If the bosal is correctly adjusted, the heel knot rests lightly against the horse's chin when reins are slack. When reins are pulled, the bosal exerts

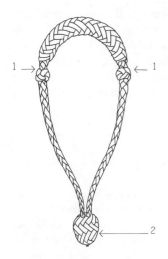

Bosal. 1. Movable buttons; 2. heel knot. Arizona horseman Monk Maxwell using bosal in early education of reining horse. Note extreme collection with light rein pressure.

pressure on the lower jawbones just above the point at which a curb chain would exert pressure. The diameter of the bosal is greater where it rests on the nose than elsewhere. Movable buttons on either side keep the strap which goes over the horse's head far enough forward so that it just misses the horse's eye.

The bosal is an important part of the horsemanship brought to this country by the conquistadores. It is charmingly described in *The Hands of Cantu* by Tom Lea and less charmingly but more specifically explained in my book *Ride Western*.

Contemporary gringo trainers often use bosals of huge diameter, some of them made of plastic. Many modern trainers so adjust the bosal that its pressure is chiefly on the nose. This produces a very different kind of balance and response from those produced by the original users of the bosal, who adjusted it so that its authority was exercised on the lower jawbones.

Bottom

When a horseman claims that his animal has lots of bottom, he means that he has great endurance.

Bowed Tendon

A horse is said to have bowed a tendon when he tears the lateral ligaments that hold in place the big tendon behind the cannon bone. This tendon is perpendicular and straight in a healthy horse. If the injury to the lateral ligaments is not attended to immediately by a competent veterinarian, the big tendon at the back of the horse's leg will bow outward and the horse will never be as serviceable as he was before. However, modern veterinary science has developed techniques of handling such an injury, including the use of a semirigid cast, and if a veterinarian takes care of a bowed tendon at once, the chances are that the horse will be as serviceable as ever in the future.

Bowing

The easiest way to teach a horse to bow or kneel is to use a Rarey strap (*see* RAREY STRAP). After a horse has worn such a strap for a few minutes and is not excited about it, it is usually possible to induce him to move his hind feet backward a step or two. Then the trainer standing behind the leg that is held up by the Rarey strap grasps the reins just above the horse's withers. He uses the indirect pull or neck rein lightly to pull the horse toward himself. This will force the horse's nose slightly away from the trainer. If the pull is continued in a backward direction still applying some neck rein, the horse is very likely to come down on the knee of the leg that is held in the Rarey strap. If he does not do so at once, he will hop about some and the trainer should start the process all over again. In due time the horse will become somewhat weary, and if the trainer does not get excited or in too much of a hurry, he can induce the horse to touch the ground with the knee that is held in place by the Rarey strap. When the horse does touch the ground, he should be immediately rewarded with a bit of carrot or something else which he enjoys. One touching of the ground at the first lesson is sufficient. At subsequent lessons the horse can be asked to bow more than once, but patience and intelligence in getting the horse to understand what is wanted will pay off in the end, and both horse and rider will enjoy having learned a new trick.

Box

In rodeo parlance a box is a pen beside the chute (a pen confining calf or steer to be released for roping). The roper or ropers must remain in the box until the instant specified for release by the rules governing the event in which they are competing (*see* SCORE).

Box Stall

The usual size for a box stall is 12 feet by 12 feet. The sides of the stall should be of two-inch planking; above that there should be iron grating to the ceiling. Flooring is always an important matter in any horse stall (*see Floors* under STABLES). No matter what kind of flooring is used, drainage must be supplied. *See Model Small Stable* under STABLES for discussion of drainage. Each stall must also be supplied with mangers, as explained under STABLES.

Provisions should be made for fastening the door of a box stall open, especially if it is a Dutch door. Many a horse has had to be destroyed because the wind blew a door shut as he was entering his stall. In this event a horse will lunge forward invariably, and damage is bound to be done.

There should be no light sockets within the reach of a horse in a box stall. Incredible as it may seem, more than one valuable animal has met his death by sticking his nose or tongue in a light socket. A horse can take much less electric current than a man.

In the matter of windows and lighting, there is great disagreement among horsemen. Some horsemen purposely keep horses in totally dark stalls. The idea seems to be that if the horse is kept in the dark, when he comes out in the open, he will look lively and spirited. The humane horse- man and the one who keeps his horse because he enjoys the friendship of an animal will see that there is light in the box stall. It may be wise to have the windows high enough so that the horse cannot touch them with his nose; but if the windows are lower, they can be protected from the horse by a grating (*see* WINDOWS).

Bran

The feeding of bran, that is, wheat bran or so-called red bran, has long been known as a very good thing for horses. Old books recommend the feeding of hot bran mashes (*see* COLDS) for certain purposes. However, not until fairly recent times has the importance of bran been emphasized properly by veterinarians (some of whom prophesy formula feeding in all good stables in the near future). Today more than ever, bran is a necessary part of every horse's daily ration, for horses are owned by Sunday riders all over the country, most of whom do not have grooms or children to keep the horse properly exercised during the week. Furthermore, appreciation of older horses is increasing, and the life expectancy of a good horse is greater now than formerly because a good deal more is known about proper shoeing and taking care of him after he matures. The older a horse is, the more important it is for him to have bran in his daily ration so that there will be no "tie-up" in his intestinal tract.

Methods of feeding bran vary. Some good horsemen feel that the daily feeding of bran is not as good as a weekly or biweekly feeding. However, most of the veterinarians consulted by the writer of this book recommend daily feeding of bran. The writer himself feeds a two-pound coffee can of red bran to each of his horses twice a day.

Breaking

Much that used to be done under the heading *breaking* is now obsolete. The kind of performance in horses people are willing to pay money for today cannot be obtained by the old method of breaking the horse—that is, taking the young, frightened horse who has no idea what is wanted of him, mounting him, and then by main strength and ability to stay on his back teaching him that he cannot throw his rider. The word *break* implies a breaking of the spirit of the horse. Modern methods are discussed under TRAINING, COLTS, and other headings (CAVALLETTI, ROPING, HUNTER, etc.) in this book.

Breaking Cart or Break-in Cart

The conventional training cart has always been and still is a very useful piece of equipment in any stable in which horses are taught to work in harness. Even horses who are to be used entirely under saddle can profit by a little training in harness. The conventional training cart has fairly high wheels, long, heavy hickory shafts, a single platformlike seat, and a platform behind the seat on which an assistant can stand. The long, heavy shafts put the green horse far enough away from the driver and the bulk of the vehicle so that if the kicking strap should break, the colt's hind feet could do little damage. The heaviness of the shafts prevents breakage and injury to the horse should the animal throw itself while in the shafts.

Breaking carts of the conventional variety are still being manufactured and can be purchased. However, some modern authorities advocate an "improvement" on the old breaking cart. The improved model is equipped with automobile wheels and brakes that can be operated separately on each wheel. The use of such brakes could be helpful in teaching a young horse to stop and in teaching him to turn. But the old breaking cart is still extremely useful, and any horseman having a number of horses to train should look carefully into its merits.

Break in Two

Break in two is a slang phrase for bucking.

Breastplate

A breastplate encircles a horse's neck at the shoulders. It may be attached to the saddle by short straps just below the withers. It is attached to the girth or cinch by a strap that runs from the lowest point of the breastplate to the girth or cinch. It keeps a saddle from sliding back when a horse is used for jumping or in mountainous terrain. In the West, breast collars are more popular for this purpose than breastplates. The breast collar or breast strap is made exactly like the breast collar in a driving harness; that is, a strap goes around the front of the horse just below the juncture of neck and body. This strap is attached to the saddle on either side. Then there is a strap that goes over the horse's withers to keep the strap going around his front from getting too low. Usually another strap goes from the center of the breast strap between the legs and attaches to the center of the cinch.

In using either a breastplate or a breast strap, one must avoid having the strap attached to the girth so short that the girth or cinch will not come forward or be pulled forward until it causes injury right behind the forelegs.

Breastplates or breast collars are very necessary on horses whose ribs are not well sprung and on horses used in mountainous country where the horse is going up steep inclines frequently. By using breast strap or breastplate, the horseman can avoid the necessity of "pulling the horse in two" with the girth or cinch. Obviously the saddle will stay in place with a looser cinch if breast strap or breastplate is used in mountainous country.

Breeching

The breeching is a part of a harness that goes around the horse's rear just above his stifles and enables him to hold back on the vehicle to which he is attached. Breechings are not used in racing harness.

Breeding. *See also* ESTRUS and BROOD MARES

The man who owns one or two good mares is often tempted to breed his animals. The question always arises: Is this venture profitable? The best answer is "No"; for the cost of raising one or two colts is usually greater than the cost of a green three- or four-year-old animal of good quality. However, the fun of raising a colt may offset the cost, and there are a few things the beginning breeder should be told.

First let us say that only a good mare is worthy of raising a colt, and she should be bred to the best stallion available. If she is a good representative of her type, she should be bred to a stallion of that type. The crossing of types or breeds is always a precarious matter and usually leads to disappointment.

An old story told about Bernard Shaw and Eleanora Duse has it that Duse wrote Shaw saying, "It is well known that I am the most beautiful woman alive and it is reported that you are the most intelligent man. It seems a shame that we should let this combination of qualities vanish from the earth without being perpetuated in a new generation." Shaw is reported to have replied, "It is true that I am the most intelligent man alive, and I have heard great praise of your beauty; however, did it ever dawn on you that the offspring might have your brains and my beauty?"

The point of this story is that offspring may have the faults of either or both parents as well as their virtues.

In the breeding of horses, the probability that the colt will resemble one parent more than the other will depend on the amount of inbreeding in each parent. If on the mother's pedigree no one name occurs more than once, and on the father's pedigree there is a name that appears over and over again, the chances are pretty good that the colt will resemble the father more than the mother.

The wise owner of a good mare will send her only to the court of a stallion owned by careful horsemen. There is one excellent stallion in the Southwest whose owner turns him loose at the time of service with the mare in a corral. Most mares have survived this practice without injury, but not all. The careful stallion owner keeps his stallion well in hand at time of service. His stallion is trained to mount the mare carefully. Each mare at the time of service wears breeding hobbles (*see* BREEDING HOB-BLES). These not only protect the stallion from being kicked but also protect the mare; for if a mare starts to kick at a stallion, no matter how well-mannered he is, he may want to kick back. Breeding hobbles are so made that a mare can walk freely without being hampered by the hobbles, but they completely prevent her from kicking. A mare's tail should always be wrapped before service, and the bandage should be removed from her tail as soon as the service is finished.

Breeding Classes

Horse-show classes in which animals (colts, adults, male or female) are exhibited wearing only halter or bridle are sometimes called breeding classes. In some such classes the animals are said to be shown "in hand." Breeding classes are frequently referred to as halter classes. Presumably the word *breeding* implies that such classes are for the purpose of improv-ing the breed or of displaying the evidence of good breeding in the classes shown. Some breeding classes are open to stallions and their get (sons and daughters). Others are for mares and their get.

Breeding Hobbles

Breeding hobbles are designed to allow a mare to walk freely and to prevent her kicking. They consist of a heavy strap that goes around the neck at the juncture of neck and shoulder. From this collar strap another strap extends down between the mare's front legs to a point a few inches behind her front legs, where it is attached to a pulley. Through this pulley is a rope or another strap terminating in a snap at either end. Each snap is attached to a strap that goes around the mare's hocks in a sort of figure-eight fashion so that it will not slip up or down. It can easily be seen that a mare can move either leg forward in walking without interference, but if she strikes out with a leg, the hobbles will check her.

Breeds

A breed of animals is a group of individuals fairly uniform in type that are sufficiently prepotent to produce offspring of similarly uniform type. It is true that if one looks long enough within any of the breeds, even the old and well-established ones, he can find a horse of almost any type. How-ever, each breed has characteristics that are more frequently found within that breed than elsewhere.

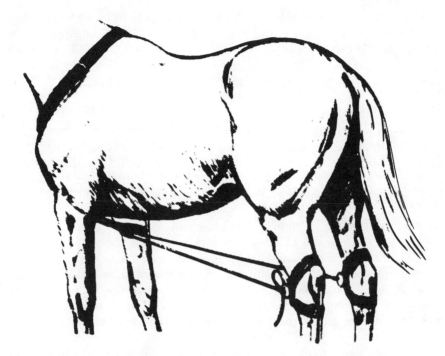

Breeding hobbles.

The old question of which breed has the most desirable characteristics is, of course, unanswerable. There is no such thing as the best breed.

Breeds vary in age and in uniformity. The oldest breed of horse that has any popularity in this country is the Arab. The next oldest breed is the Thoroughbred, although the American Saddle Horse Registry is said to be two or three years older than the American Registry for Thoroughbreds. The American Thoroughbred, of course, has his foundations in the English Thoroughbred who dates back to the time of Charles II.

A discussion of each American breed and the address of the association or associations that register it and promote it are given alphabetically in this book.

Breeze

To breeze a horse is to give him a short gallop for exercise or to stimulate his circulation. When a horse is breezed, he is never allowed to attain full speed. Sometimes the breezing is done while the horse is wearing a hood or even a blanket.

Brida, à la

Riding with long stirrups, the "forked-radish" seat, the conquistadores called *à la brida*. The conquistadores and other sixteenth-century caballeros prided themselves on being able to ride "in both seats." That is, they could use the extremely old-fashioned "forked-radish" seat, which was appropriate for parade and some other purposes, and also the seat with very short stirrups, a Moorish invention considered especially useful for fighting, which was called riding *à la gineta*. (*See also* GINETA, À LA.)

Bridles

See BITS for proper adjustments of bridle.

The main purpose or function of a bridle is to hold the bit or bits in the desired position in a horse's mouth. The bridle should do this without chafing the horse's head or being uncomfortable in any other fashion. A bridle should be adjustable so that it can be worn by different horses and so that the position of the bit in a given horse's mouth can be changed if the horseman wishes to change it. A bridle must be easy to care for, that is, easy to keep clean and to keep soft and pliable. It should be made of material that is durable and can be repaired easily. A bridle must be so constructed that the part of it that goes over the head behind the horse's ears will not slip back on his neck and thereby cause the bit to be pulled upward in his mouth. Furthermore, the bridle must be so constructed that the horse cannot shake the part that goes behind his ears off his head easily.

One bridle that fulfills all these requirements fairly well is the English bridle, the so-called Weymouth bridle. This is a full bridle or double bridle made of flat English leather. It has a browband which keeps the part of the bridle that goes over the horse's head behind the ears from slipping backward on the horse's neck. It has a throatlatch (sometimes incorrectly called a throatlash) which prevents the horse's shaking the bridle over his ears and off his head. The flat English leather is easy to clean and easy to keep soft and pliable by the use of soap and neat's-foot oil. It is also relatively easy to repair, especially in comparison with a stitched bridle or bridle consisting of round leather. Most modern Weymouth bridles are equipped with what are called French hooks for attachment of bits.

The English or Eastern bridle to be used with a Pelham bit or a single curb bit is exactly like the Weymouth except for the omission of the snaffle headstall and rein. Most good English bridles have a cavesson which may or may not serve the purpose of keeping a horse's mouth shut. The English bridle used for a snaffle bit only is sometimes equipped with a so-called dropped noseband or dropped cavesson. This is simply a cavesson that is put on the horse just below the bit. (The conventional cavesson goes around the horse's nose just above the soft part of the nose cartilage.) The purpose of the dropped noseband is to give more control of the horse with the snaffle bit than is gained without such a noseband. It also tends to keep the horse from thrusting his nose out (that is, forward) and making the bit pull toward his ears rather than on the bars of his mouth, as is very frequent with the use of the snaffle bit without a dropped noseband.

Of course there are many, many other kinds of bridles to be seen on horses ridden with flat saddles (English saddles or Eastern saddles). On some of them, the strap holding the bit in place is entirely separate from the strap used for the throatlatch. Those two straps go through the ends of the browband and are separated by a rosette on either side. Such bridles are rather a nuisance, for it is not long until the browband drops down on one side when the bridle is not in use, letting the throatlatch slip out of place, and then the rosette falls off and is lost. Also, whenever a horse rubs his head, he is likely to knock one of the rosettes off.

Another kind of bridle, seen rather frequently as part of both Eastern and Western gear, is one in which the strap holding the bit in the mouth is long, with a single buckle on it. The strap goes through the bit on one side of the horse's mouth, over the head, through the bit on the other side of the horse's mouth, over the head again, and back to the single buckle. The buckle, of course, should be on the left side of the horse. This strap is separate from the throatlatch, and strap and throatlatch both go through the ends of the browband and are separated from each other by a rosette on either side. This bridle is easier to repair, perhaps, than the ones described above, but it puts more leather on a horse's head than is necessary.

As far as appearance is concerned, the kind of bridle a horse wears to best advantage depends somewhat upon the construction of his head. A horse with a beautiful, fine head deserves a bridle that covers as little of the head as possible, one that does not detract from the head's natural beauty. The heavy-headed or coarse-headed horse may look better in a highly decorative bridle. If the horse is used with Western gear and has an exquisite head, the split ear bridle will probably give the best appearance. The split ear bridle consists of a single strap which goes from one side of the bit, over the horse's head, to the other side. The strap is split to admit the right ear to protrude through it. Some split ear bridles have buckles on either side of the cheek for adjustment of length. Others have the bit attached on either side by a Conway buckle, and this permits the length to be adjusted at the point of attachment of the bit. Some split ear bridles are provided with a throatlatch and some with a noseband. However, the horse with the beautiful head deserves a split ear bridle made of a very narrow strap which will not detract from the beauty of the head.

Western bridles range all the way from the very simple split ear bridle to the extremely complicated, heavily silver-mounted parade bridle with chains that cross the horse's face between the browband and the noseband. The type of bridle selected will, of course, depend upon the purpose for which the horse is used and also upon the kind of head the horse has.

Bridling

Bridling a horse is a simple operation for a horseman with any experience, but many an inexperienced horseman has made a horse very foolish by

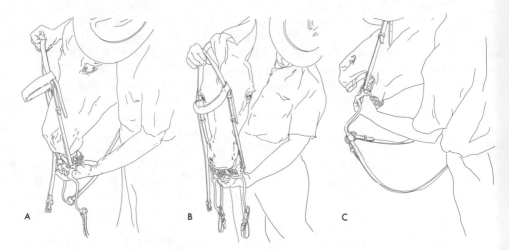

A   B   C

ineptness at bridling time. The horse who has been so spoiled had best be handled by an experienced horseman until he gets over his foolishness; continued attempts on the part of the inexperienced will make the horse worse each time he is bridled.

To bridle a horse properly, hold the bridle by crown and reins in the left hand, which is the only way to pick up or carry a bridle. If the reins are not fastened at the ends, tie a knot in them for the present purpose. Stand at the horse's left, just behind his head and close to him. With your right hand slip the reins over the horse's head, right behind his ears. Remove the halter. If the horse starts to wander, you can control him by grasping the reins under his throttle. That's why you put them behind his ears instead of way back on his neck.

Now take the crown of the bridle in your right hand and bring the palm of your left hand up under the bit, but never use the left hand to raise the bit. With your right hand, raise the bridle and bring it into position so that the horse's nose is between the cheekpieces of the bridle and in the nose-band, if your bridle has one. With your left hand you are now *guiding* the bit so that it comes between the horse's lips and against his teeth, but you are *lifting* the bit with your right hand.

If the horse does not open his mouth, a finger or thumb put between his lips will probably get him to do so. (An all-wise Providence made the horse with a mouth that has no teeth where the bit goes.) If this does not work, the pressure of a thumbnail or a fingernail on the bar of the mouth (the part the bit rests on) will prove effective. As the horse opens the mouth, your *right* hand should raise the bridle so the bit slips into place. Then you slip the crownpiece over the ears and buckle the throatlatch. Buckle it about three holes looser than you think it should be. When a horse tucks his chin in, he needs plenty of room in the throatlatch. Greenhorns buckle

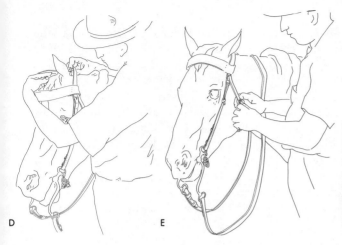

Bridling the horse. A. Bridle crown in right hand, left palm under the bit; B. nose between cheekpieces of bridle; C. right hand lifting bridle; left hand guiding the bit. D. Slip crownpiece over the ears. E. Buckle the throatlatch.

the throatlatch so tight that the horse suffers when collected. They also do dreadful things with a curb chain or strap, as you will find explained under the heading BITS.

Bridoon

Bridoon is a very British term for a snaffle bit. It usually refers to one with large rings and a mouthpiece made of metal of larger diameter than usually used in snaffles.

Such a bit is ideal for use on a horse afflicted with a rider who hangs onto the bit or maintains his own balance by means of the reins. In Ireland in bygone days, according to old Irish grooms, the large-mouthed bridoon was frequently used in the Old Country when the resident magistrate went ahunting.

Brisket

In most parts of the United States the term *brisket* denotes that part of a bovine located between and just in front of the front legs. When the animal is butchered, the brisket makes excellent corned beef. In some parts of the country, especially where there is considerable reverence for British terminology, *brisket* refers to the top of the fork, the juncture of forelegs and body, of a horse.

Broken Amble

The term *broken amble* is used only by people who are uninformed about any horse except those whose gaits are confined to the walk, trot, and gallop (*see* AMBLE).

Broken Knees

Broken knees is a loose and deceptive term. It does not mean that the horse's knees have been broken. Of course, if a horse's knee joints have been broken, the horse is no longer serviceable. In such case the horse is usually destroyed. The term *broken knees* refers to knees that have scars or lumps on them generally due to falls or bruises of some kind. While broken knees may be an indication that a horse stumbles readily, they may simply be the result of a cruel kind of training used in some places to train jumpers. Sometimes it is possible to buy a serviceable horse at a reasonable price if the horse has broken knees that do not hurt him and that are not an indication of stumbling. Certainly, however, anyone who contemplates buying a horse with broken knees should have the animal inspected by a veterinarian to make sure the scars or lumps will not interfere with the horse's usefulness.

Bronc

Bronc is a slang term for *bronco*, a Spanish word meaning wild. The term is applied to a horse who is not yet suitable for an ordinary rider. Horses of the bucking string in a rodeo are usually referred to as broncs.

Brood Mares

The gestation period of mares is 11 to 12 months. There is a current notion that male foals are carried a little longer than female ones. It is true that as a mare reaches an advanced age she is very likely to carry her foal longer than she did when she was younger. Usually a mare's bag will fill with milk several weeks before she foals. When a mare is carrying her first foal, the bag may fill and then be slack and then fill again repeatedly. A day or two before the mare foals, little specks of wax will appear on the ends of her nipples. A healthy mare will not take long for the process of foaling; 15 to 30 minutes is normal. If the mare strains for a longer period with no evidence of the foal's appearing, a veterinarian should be called at once.

Some mares foal while standing, and others lie down for foaling. Usually a mare will give some sign just before she foals that the event is about to take place. She may nip at her flanks or she may appear quite restless. At this time she should be left alone and not be disturbed by humans or other horses. However, she should be watched carefully. The foal should appear forefeet and nose first, the nose between the forefeet, one of which may be slightly behind the other. If the foal does not appear in this fashion—for instance, if the head is bent back or some other part of the foal's anatomy appears first—he must be turned so that he will present himself properly. Almost any person knowledgeable about horses, if his hands and arms are sterile, can push the improperly presented foal back into the mare and turn him so normal foaling will occur. However, if difficulty is encountered, a veterinarian should be summoned immediately.

A valuable mare deserves the attendance of a veterinarian at time of foaling as surely as a human mother deserves the attendance of a physician at time of giving birth. However, thousands of foals come to life every year on the open range or in pastures without the aid of any human being and do so in a perfectly healthy fashion. A clean pasture in which a mare will not be disturbed by other animals at foaling time is an excellent place for her to foal. If a pasture is not available, a clean box stall will do very well. A few minutes after a healthy foal is born, he will struggle to his feet and start nursing. Usually he will break the transparent sack in which he is born, but if not, of course, the sack must be broken so the little animal can breathe. Any mucus should be wiped from his nostrils, and iodine (*see* NAVEL) should be applied to the navel cord, which is ordinarily broken when the colt is foaled but must be cut by an attendant if this is not the case. As a rule, mares "clean themselves," that is, pass the afterbirth, soon after foaling, but this process may be delayed as much as 12 hours even if the mare is quite healthy. If it is delayed longer than this, a veterinarian should be called. Some mares, especially range mares, will eat the afterbirth, but a careful horseman will see signs of this and will assume that the mare has cleaned.

Valuable mares should be fed during pregnancy in accordance with veterinary advice, as they should be fed after foaling. However, a general rule that can well be followed is to give the mare red bran regularly, at least as much as a two-pound coffee-canful once a day. Immediately after the mare foals, she may well be given a bran mash (*see* FEED) if she will take it. Her grain ration should be cut severely immediately after foaling, or the grain should be withheld entirely, and the mare should be returned to full ration very gradually.

Brood mares who are confined, that is, kept in small corrals or stalls, should be given quiet exercise daily. Nothing is much worse for a brood mare than to stand idle day after day. Back in the days when draft horses were used on farms, many an excellent mare was taken out of a plow to foal in the field, where she dropped a perfectly healthy foal and was ready to return to quiet work a few days after foaling. Such mares usually had sturdier, healthier foals and were themselves healthier than the mares who were kept in corrals or stalls during pregnancy. If a mare is habitually used under saddle, she can be ridden quietly right up until the day of foaling. She should not, of course, be asked to run at extreme speed or to jump great heights; but under a careful rider she can do from 10 to 30 miles in a day without harm.

Broom Polo

Broom polo is good fun and practice. The rules for indoor polo may be followed or may be varied to suit the conditions of the group playing.

Brooms are used in place of mallets. The ball may be a softball or a basketball.

Broomtail

Broomtail is a Western term for the wild horses that are fast disappearing from the ranges (*see* WILD HORSES).

Brown

A brown horse is darker in color than a bay but usually has the black points common to the bay horse. The brown horse is frequently a little lighter on his belly and in his flanks than elsewhere.

Brush

In horse-and-buggy days an informal race between rigs on the highway similar to the illegal automobile "drag race" of today was called a "brush."

Brushes (for grooming)

The most useful brush for the body of a well-groomed horse is one with short bristles and a leather back with a wide strap for a handle which goes over the back of your hand. Brushes with wooden or fiber backs and longer bristles (called dandy brushes) are generally used for removing caked mud or sweat. The best ones for use on the hair in mane and tail are similar in appearance to the dandy brush but made of the roots of rice and should be used only when wet; otherwise the bristles break off. For the horse who is kept in healthy condition but not necessarily show shape— that is, the horse that is used until he sweats and his dried sweat is removed by grooming—can be well groomed with an ordinary scrub brush with stiff bristles, a brush that costs less than 50 cents. After the dirt has been brushed from the coat with such a brush, the coat can be smoothed with a rub rag of burlap. (*See also* GROOM.)

Brushing (interfering)

Brushing is a rather old-fashioned term for interfering, that is, the act of striking one ankle or foot with the foot on the opposite side. This fault can be corrected sometimes by proper shoeing. However, if the cause is extremely bad conformation, it is very difficult for a farrier to effect a permanent cure.

Buckaroo

Buckaroo probably had its origin in southern Texas. It is about as near as the gringo could come to pronouncing the Spanish word for cowboy, *vaquero*. The word is still heard on occasion in the cattle country. It is used usually in a friendly or jocose manner.

Bucking

When a horse bucks, he throws his head downward until his nose or more of his head is between his front legs. Simultaneously he lunges high into the air. At the top of the lunge he usually kicks violently. There are many variations of bucking. The horse may throw himself sideways at the top of his lunge or whirl as he goes upward. The rodeo horse, who bucks under the impetus of a flank cinch and the raking spurs of his rider, goes through motions quite similar to those of the voluntary bucker, but he does so with

Rodeo bucker. Note flank cinch and position of rear cinch of saddle.

even more violence than the horse not wearing a flank cinch and being spurred. Many a novice thinks his horse is bucking when he is hopping up and down slightly. However, no novice stays aboard a horse who puts out a real job of bucking.

The horse who bucks can usually be broken of the vice. In fact, one of the big problems of the operator of a rodeo string is that of keeping his horses bucking. Few rodeo horses (and those few are the notable ones) continue to buck after one rodeo season. Many a rodeo bucker has become a good, serviceable, and safe saddle horse. Years ago in Florence, Arizona, where junior rodeos were first invented, an old gray gelding used to come in to the junior rodeo every year ridden by a youngster, sometimes a girl not over six or seven years old. The horse could be seen walking around outside the arena under a child who was watching events until time for the old gelding to do his stuff. Then he would be put in the bucking horse corrals and thence into a chute where he would be fitted with a flank cinch. When he came out of that chute he always did a magnificent job of bucking. As soon as the event was over, he was returned to his juvenile rider, who would again use him as a movable perch from which to observe rodeo events.

Bucking Horse

Rodeo contractors (those who supply stock for rodeos) are willing to pay high prices for horses who will buck violently, with or without the stimuli of bucking straps (*see* BUCKING STRAP), hot shots, etc., for repeated performances. Most horses will stop bucking after the first season or even the first few performances. Almost every horse, even an old docile one, can be made to buck by the use of the bucking strap and hot shot, but few horses will buck hard enough to make a good show, and most will quit bucking and start running if spurred hard.

Bucking Strap

A bucking strap is one that is attached to the rear of a Western saddle on either side and passes under the flanks of a horse. Obviously, such a strap will cause any horse to buck. Bucking straps are seen only in rodeos in saddle bronc events. The amount of tension needed on a bucking strap to make a bucking horse put up a good show in a rodeo depends entirely on the horse. In some instances the bucking strap need not be very tight and a horse will put up an excellent show of bucking. On other horses the bucking strap has to be twisted so that it causes considerable discomfort. The art of managing bucking horses for rodeos is certainly as great as the art of handling any other kind of horse in equine exhibitions or contests. Some people are horrified at the use of a bucking strap to make a horse buck, yet these same people will watch a Walking Horse class in a horse show in which every horse who displays the desired kind of performance is in agony. And his performance in the ring is of much longer duration than the few seconds of bucking put on by a bucking horse in a rodeo (for an explanation of the "Agony of the Walking Horse" see *Life*, October 3, 1969, pp. 77–78). Of course, the discomfort to the bucking horse ends after his very short exhibition of bucking. The Walking Horse or his cousin, the three- or five-gaited horse, who is almost as horribly treated so far as shoeing and tail setting are concerned, performs many times longer in each class than a bucking horse wears a bucking strap, and the discomfort for the gaited horse or the Walking Horse does not end with the class. It continues throughout his show season and sometimes much longer than that, while the pain (if any) from a bucking strap lasts for only the few minutes of performance in the ring.

Buck-kneed, Buckling Over, or Over at the Knees

If, when a horse is standing still, his knees are farther forward than his pastern joints, he is said to be "buck-kneed," "buckling over," or "over at the knees." If the horse is young and the knees are not extremely bucked, the trouble may be the result of overwork and bad shoeing and may possibly be corrected by rest and proper shoeing. However, if the horse has some age and is badly over at the knees, he has, as the saying goes, "had it."

Bulldogging

The term *bulldog* means to throw a steer by leaping from the saddle, grasping the bovine's horns, and twisting its neck. This is a popular rodeo event. The bulldogger is assisted by a hazer. The rules of the event are very exact. The requirements are two excellent horses and two expert performers.

Bullfinch

A bullfinch is a high thorn fence, too high for jumping except through some holes that may be in the fence. Such fences occur with some frequency in England. Here we have only replicas of them at hunter trials in parts of the country in which there is great reverence for things British.

Bun-eating Contest

The requirements for a bun-eating contest are a starting line and, some distance from it, a rope or wire from which are suspended on strings wiener rolls or buns, and a group of enthusiastic riders. If the riders are quite expert, the game may be played by having them stand in the saddle while they eat the buns. If the group is not so experienced, the bun eaters may remain seated. Of course, hands cannot be used on the buns.

Burns

Burns on the horse should be cared for much as they are on human beings. If they are severe, professional help must be called at once. If they are minor, ointments that are procurable at the drugstore may be applied. There is one kind of burn on a horse, however, that the horseman should be especially careful of: the rope burn.

Many horses are caused much suffering by horsemen too ignorant to know how to tie a horse. If a horse is tied so that he can get a foot over the rope by which he is tied, he is very likely to get a rope burn on the back of his pastern. Such a burn is difficult to heal. It must be kept clean, and an ointment must be applied daily.

Busqué

Busqué is an esoteric term meaning Roman nosed.

Busting

Busting is a slang phrase for breaking a horse in the old-fashioned Western manner (*see* BREAKING and STEER BUSTING).

Buying a Horse

Skillful professional horsemen find the horse auction useful, both as a place to sell and as a place to buy, but for the nonprofessional horseman the auction is the most dangerous place to try to buy a horse. The next most dangerous source is the individual owner who advertises a horse in the newspaper. A reputable dealer or breeder is the best source of horses for the nonprofessional. The reputable breeder or dealer is perfectly willing to have the horse tried out. If he can assure himself that the prospective buyer will not ruin the animal immediately, he will let the prospective buyer take the horse home and try him out. Furthermore, the reputable dealer or breeder is perfectly willing to have the prospective buyer select a veterinarian to examine the horse for soundness. This is a must for any nonprofessional horseman, and a good many wise professional horsemen follow the practice of having a horse checked by a veterinarian before purchase, especially if a good deal of money is involved.

Perhaps the most common blunder of the nonprofessional when buying a horse is that of insisting that the horse be young, that is, less than eight years old. The less experienced the buyer, the less wise is it for him to purchase a young horse. "Many an excellent tune has been played on an old fiddle," said Belle Beach, one of the greatest horsewomen who ever lived. The horse who is a dozen years old or more will teach his rider a great deal, and it will be much harder to spoil him than to spoil a younger horse. Moreover, if a horse reaches the age of eight or nine years and is still pronounced sound by a competent veterinarian, the chances are he will remain sound the rest of his life. If he has any conformational faults that tend to make him unsound, the unsoundness will have shown up by the time he is eight or nine years old. The horse that has escaped bad or show-ring shoeing and all other kinds of misuse until he is 20, and so remains entirely sound, has many good years left in him. The prospective buyer may find that the price of such a horse is very reasonable compared to that for one not quite so long in the tooth.

When buying a horse, the nonprofessional horseman should be sure that the horse's temperament is good, that he is old enough to be settled in his habits, and that he is pronounced completely sound by a competent veterinarian. He should try the horse out at the place of his present owner or, if possible, take him home and try him for a few days.

Bye Day

Bye day is a hunting term which designates an unscheduled hunt.

Byerly Turk

The Byerly Turk is one of the three most commonly known foundation sires of the Thoroughbred breed. The other sires are the Godolphin Barb and the Darley Arabian. The most famous son and chief transmitter of the blood of the Byerly Turk was a horse called Herod.

Caballero

Caballero is the Spanish word for horseman. It is equivalent in many respects to the French word *cavalier*. When *caballero* is applied to a horseman in the Southwest, it is usually a term of respect.

Cadence

The word *cadence* is used to indicate the rhythm of the horse's hoofbeats at various gaits. For example, the cadence of the walk is four-beat. It is done in four-four time. On a good, flat-footed walk the same interval follows each hoofbeat. The trot is a two-beat gait, the feet striking the ground in pairs, as do the feet in the pace (*see* GAITS). The gallop is a three-beat gait unless it is done with great speed or collected (*see* COLLECTION) extremely into a good canter, in which case the fourth beat can be heard; but it is very close to one of the others. The rack is also a four-beat cadence, as is the running walk; but those gaits are faster than the walk. The amble, the fox-trot, and the stepping pace produce a cadence that could be called syncopated; that is, you can count the hoofbeats, "one and, two and, one and, two and." A horseman with a good ear can tell a good deal about a horse's soundness by listening to the cadence of his gaits and he can certainly tell a good deal about the way the horse has been trained.

Camp

Camp is an obsolete term now replaced by the word *pose*. Vernacular variants of *pose* are *park* and *stretch*. All three- and five-gaited show horses are made to pose when they stand still in the show-ring. That is, they are made to stand with their forelegs straight up and down and their hind legs pushing forward a trifle. Back in the days of horses and buggies and coaches, coachmen used to teach their horses to pose so that they would stand perfectly still while important personages were getting into or out of the vehicles. (*See* STRETCHING.)

Camuse

Camuse is an esoteric word borrowed from the French to indicate a dish face like that of a classic Arabian (*see* ARABIAN HORSE, *Specifications*).

Canadian Pox

Canadian pox is one of the innumerable skin afflictions of the horse. It is characterized by tiny eruptions, frequently behind the elbows. These scab over, and when the scabs come off, there are little bare spots on the horse. This particular kind of skin eruption can be treated successfully with Lysol solution. However, the wise horseman does not rely on first-aid remedies for skin troubles very long. He calls a competent veterinarian, for there are some skin disorders of a very serious or even fatal nature that have a simple and seemingly innocuous beginning.

Cannon Bone

The cannon bone is the part of a horse's leg that is between his knee or his hock and his pastern joint.

Frequently when a horseman speaks of the cannon bone, especially if he is talking about its length, he is referring to the entire part of the leg between the pastern joint and the next joint above it—including bone and tendons.

Canter

The word *canter* is used differently in different parts of the world, in different parts of this country, and by different kinds of horsemen in each part of the country. However, it always indicates the gait performed by the same sequence of hoof impacts on the ground (*see* CADENCE), that denoted by the words *gallop, canter,* and *run.* This pattern of hoofbeats gives the gait the sound of three-quarter rhythm in music: one, two, three; one, two, three. The sequence is performed on what is called either of two leads. When the horse is performing a gait called canter, gallop, lope, or run on the left lead, let us say, he may start off with the right hind foot. This is followed by a simultaneous impact with the ground of the left hind foot and right forefoot. That is followed by the impact of the left forefoot, which is said to be the leading foot. If the horse is performing the gait on the right lead, he may start off with the left hind foot, which is followed by a simultaneous impact with the ground of the right hind foot and left forefoot. This is followed by the impact of the right forefoot, the leading foot.

In the days when the horse cavalry was an active part of our military services, some military writers on horsemanship made even further divisions of the gait performed with the sequence of hoofbeats just described, some of them giving as many as six or seven different names to different speeds and balance of this gait. Today we frequently add another term, *hand gallop;* and there are those who even talk about a collected and uncollected canter. The latter term seems to the writer to be a contradiction in terms. Lope, hand gallop, gallop, and run are discussed under other headings in this book. It is our purpose here to explain the uses of the word *canter.*

Overly fastidious devotees of the three- and five-gaited show-ring seem to be allergic to the word *gallop* and call any gait performed in the one, two, three rhythm a canter. Though some horses in the show-ring do perform a highly collected, slow gait when asked to canter, one frequently sees the gaited horses performing a rather rapid and not too collected gait in response to the request to canter. While Western riders usually talk about the lope, when they put on Eastern togs and ride their horses with flat saddles, they frequently call any gait done in the rhythm of the gallop and done at a speed of less than 10 miles per hour a canter. In the early days of horse shows in America and up until fairly recently, the word *canter* denoted a gait done with extreme collection and at a speed of not more than eight or nine miles per hour. It is possible to slow an uncollected gallop down to even less than this speed. The appropriate term for such a gait is *lope,* a gait frequently used when the horse under saddle was the only means of transportation in the West. Today many horsemen and would-be horsemen make no distinction between the lope and the canter and use *canter* to indicate either gait.

Cantle

The cantle is the rear of the seat of the saddle. On early Western saddles the cantle was quite high and straight. Modern Western saddles rarely have cantles over four inches high. Many of them, especially the roping saddles, have much lower cantles.

Capped Elbow

A horse confined in a tie stall or very small box stall and given insufficient bedding may bruise his elbow with a shoe when he lies down. If a chronic swelling is thus produced a horse is said to have a capped elbow or shoe boil.

Capped Hock

When the covering of the rear or point of the hock joint is thickened, the horse is said to have a capped hock (*see* HOCK).

Capping Fee

Some hunts require a fee from a nonmember, even though he is invited by a member. It is said that there was an old custom according to which an official of the hunt would pass among the field of riders with his cap held out for donations from nonmembers and that this is the origin of the term.

Carriage (of the head). *See* HEAD SET

Cast Horse

When a prone horse is unable to get to his feet because of his position in relation to stall, fence, objects (tree, rock, or bank) or because of the nature of the terrain, he is said to be cast. Many a horse has lost his life by being cast for some length of time. If a veterinarian is available, he may give the horse a tranquilizer to prevent his injuring himself until the confining object is removed or sufficient help is summoned to get the horse to his feet. If a horse is sensible and not struggling violently, it may be possible to get cotton ropes or straps around the pasterns of the legs *nearest the ground.* By pulling on these straps the horse may be rolled over away from the fence, partition, or other confining object. If it is at all possible, it is usually better to remove the object than to disturb the horse.

Castrate

Castration of a horse should be done only by a competent veterinarian who will practice asepsis and use modern anesthesia. Castration can be done successfully at any age; however, for convenience' sake most colts are castrated early in their second year. A few horsemen advocate castration of the newborn foal as soon as the testicles come down into the scrotum. They claim this causes least shock to the animal. Some horsemen favor letting a horse go until four or five years old before castration if the animal's head and neck are not developed well in colthood.

Catchweights

In a race advertised as "catchweights," no horse is required to carry any specific weight.

Cavalletti

The cavalletti is a set of bars (usually seven or eight) and four jump standards. The most readily available bars in metropolitan areas are four-by-fours. They are usually from eight to ten feet long. Jump standards are posts four and a half or more feet in height. They are fastened to bases consisting of lumber laid flat on the ground, of such weight and area that it will prevent the posts from being knocked over easily. Each post is provided with pins on one of its faces. These are set in at a slope and are just long enough and stout enough to hold rails. The pins are usually spaced about six inches apart so that rails may be placed at any desired height. There are many variations on the type of standard just described.

The cavalletti is generally thought to be an invention of Caprilli, the great Italian horseman, author of forward-seat riding, who died in 1912. Actually Kentucky horsemen, though ignorant of Italian nomenclature, were using split fence rails (milled lumber was not then available) for schooling horses long before Caprilli was born.

The common use of rails (cavalletti) in pioneer Kentucky to promote flexibility, handiness, and surefootedness is indicated by the following story, familiar to all old-time Kentucky horsemen:

Using the cavalletti to teach horse and rider to jump. A. Mounted on a Hungarian Furioso stallion, Linda Tellington demonstrates correct hunt seat. B. Cavalletti set up for beginning work. C. Graduate student of the Pacific Coast Equestrian Research Farm at Badger, California, puts horse over the cavalletti to lengthen stride at a walk. D. Putting horse over the cavalletti to lengthen stride at a trot. E. Starting horse over single jump after cavalletti work. F. Horse starts over low double jump. G. Height of double jump increased. H. Double jump with second rail raised higher than first. I. Taking closely spaced in-and-out jumps with outstretched arms—excellent balance exercise. J. Clearing triple bar jump using light cord, no bridle (rider demonstrating complete rapport with horse).

Tom Hal, one of the most illustrious progenitors of the American Saddle Horse breed (and of the Tennessee Walker if the truth would out), was owned by a physician in Lexington, Kentucky, a Dr. Boswell. In addition to being famous for speed, endurance, and ease, Tom Hal was also known as the most surefooted of stallions. Once, when this quality of Tom's was questioned, Dr. Boswell ordered 10 rails to be placed on the ground. He bet the questioner $10 that Tom could rack at top speed over the rails without touching any of them. The doctor never lost a bet on Tom Hal.

Of course, contemporary American Saddle Horses would fall and break their necks (because of their long feet and show-ring training) if ridden over the cavalletti. Schooling over the cavalletti today is employed exclusively by a few trainers of hunters and jumpers. It is enjoying a deserved increase of popularity. There is no one set program of cavalletti training that is perfect for all horses, as is well pointed out by Captain Vladimir S. Littauer in his *Common Sense Horsemanship*. However, Bulletin No. 5 of the Pacific Coast Equestrian Research Farm of Badger, California, is devoted to a step-by-step program that is certainly generally useful if tempered by the discretion of a skilled horseman.

Initial use of the cavalletti may well be at a quiet, relaxed walk over rails laid parallel from four to six feet apart. The spacing should be that of the normal stride of the particular horse being started. The cavalletti should be part of a figure eight, and the horse should be worked over it the first day until he will walk quietly with loose or extremely light rein over the rails with no tendency to hesitate, rush, or walk out to the side. The number of days or weeks this work should continue depends upon the temperament and intelligence of the horse and the skill of the rider in communicating with him. The horse's work during this period should not be an exclusive diet of cavalletti. He should continue whatever other kind of activity he is used to, which should certainly include some cross-country or trail work.

The second step with the cavalletti may involve placing the standards at either side of one of the end rails. When the horse is used to seeing the standards so placed, the end rail can be raised to not more than 18 inches on the standards. When the horse can quietly traverse the cavalletti so arranged at a walk, he is ready to be trotted over the "course."

By similar slow stages, the horse can learn to gallop over the course. The jump rail can be raised to two feet, and other rails nearest the standard can be removed. Always leaving a few of the rails on the ground is a valuable aid in controlling takeoff. Until the horse is completely relaxed, the rails on the ground should be so placed that they do not interfere with his natural stride as he takes off for his hop over the jump. However, when the proper time comes, a judicious slight change of the rails may correct a fault in takeoff, if correction is necessary. An unwise or too great shift of the rails may cause a justifiable refusal, which, if followed by sufficiently severe punishment, will result in a spoiled horse.

By placing the rail in the standards at 18 inches and setting up the second set of standards 19 or 20 feet beyond it with a rail two feet high, one can introduce the horse to an in-and-out jump. (In horse shows, in-and-out obstacles are usually 24 feet apart.) The first jump should be fairly solid and kept at 18 inches, as its use is merely that of a marker. The horse should first learn to trot into the jump and shift to gallop or canter to jump out.

The foregoing is certainly not a rigid, universal recipe for every young horse destined for the hunting field or show jumping. The possible arrangements of rails and jumps and progressive uses of them are infinite. The rails can be used to lengthen or shorten stride. They can be used in connection with the standards to control habits of takeoff. The cavalletti is also an aid in correcting faults in spoiled, mature hunters and jumpers— rushing, running out, refusing, etc. Of course, no device of training is better than the skill of the trainer allows. A horse will "tell" a knowledgeable trainer (one who has learned that communication with horses is a two-way activity) when he is making a mistake, usually that of attempting to progress too rapidly.

Cavesson

To William Cavendish, Duke of Newcastle (1592–1676), favorite member of Charles II's Privy Council, we owe the widespread use of the cavesson. Prior to the time of the Duke of Newcastle, the training of horses in the elaborate riding halls frequented by the great lords and ladies was a cruel affair. Horses were tied securely between two great pillars and whipped to get desired results. When they were ridden, they were ridden with bits having shanks several times longer than any seen today and mouthpieces consisting of disks and spikes and other torturing devices. In modernizing the methods of training horses, the Duke reduced the number of posts to one (the Spanish Riding School of today still uses two) and replaced the extremely severe bits by the cavesson for many parts of training. The cavesson Newcastle used slightly resembled the cavesson designed by the late United States Cavalry for the purpose of lunging young horses. Such a cavesson is a noseband about two inches wide made of several thicknesses of leather stitched together and supplied with rings at the sides, at front, and at back. The cavesson is held in place by a strap which passes over the horse's head behind his ears.

Today most full bridles or double bridles are equipped with a cavesson that is considerably simpler and lighter than Newcastle's. The modern cavesson seen on the full bridle is a noseband an inch or so in width, held in place by a narrow strap that goes over the horse's head. This narrow strap passes through the ends of the browband. It rides under the strap or straps that hold the bit or bits in place. In modern show-rings, for five-gaited and Walking Horse classes, horses wear nosebands that are broad across the nose and of bright color or colors. On many show horses the

Cavalry-style lunging cavesson.

cavesson serves another purpose in addition to that of decoration. It is worn very tight so that it will keep the horse's mouth shut. This practice is quite necessary with horses whose mouths have been spoiled in training and with other horses who have different faults caused by mishandling.

Cavvy

Cavvy designates the herd or band of horses in use on a working cow outfit. It is the Northwestern equivalent of *remuda* (*see* REMUDA).

Cayuse

Cayuse is a term indicating a horse of the variety now native to certain parts of the Southwest, a Mustang. The Cayuse is said to be descended very largely from the Spanish horses brought to this continent by the conquistadores (*see* MUSTANG).

Originally the word meant a horse or pony owned by or bought or stolen from the Cayuse Indians.

Centaur

The centaur was a mythical creature made like a horse from the shoulders back. From the shoulders forward, it had a man's figure from hips upward. This figment of the imagination symbolizes the ideal of all good horsemen, that is, the complete fusion of man and horse.

Center Fire Rig. *See also* SADDLES

Western saddles are held on the horse by straps called *rigging* that go over the saddletree at either end of the saddle and terminate in rings. To these rings the latigo straps are attached. The latigo straps fasten the cinches to the rigging rings. When a so-called full rigging is used, there are two cinches kept a few inches apart under the horse's belly by a "spacer strap." The front cinch, of course, is attached to the front rigging rings and the hind cinch, usually a wide flat strap, to the hind rigging rings.

The so-called center fire rig, at one time the favorite in California, employs a single cinch. Straps from the front rigging ring and rear rigging ring to cinch ring were of equal length.

The center fire rig has the advantage of keeping a cinch well behind a horse's elbows, but it has the disadvantage of allowing the saddle to slide forward and, if a horse's conformation is faulty, to pinch the shoulder blades or bruise the withers. In heavy roping it has a further disadvantage in allowing the back of the saddle to tip upward when a rope exerts a strong forward pull on the horn.

Certification

In horse shows there are some hunter classes that require each horse to be certified; that is, the rider must have a statement signed by the master of a recognized hunt that the horse has hunted for a season with a registered pack. Such a horse is called a qualified hunter.

Challenge Trophy

A challenge trophy is a cup, plate, plaque, or similar article donated with certain rules under which it is to be won. Frequently, the rules specify that the first animal to win the trophy for three years is allowed to keep it. Sometimes the trophy is to be perpetually the property of a given show or organization while the winner each year is given a duplicate of the original trophy. In such a case each winner's name and the date of his winning is inscribed upon the original trophy.

Champing the Bit

In speaking of teaching the horse to learn the "language" of the bit, Henry Wynmalen says that the horse knows the language of the bit only when he will flex with a smile and champ the bit. To champ the bit means to play with it with mouth and tongue. When a horse does this, some saliva will make foam which forms on the bit, and the horse who will not so champ the bit is called a "dry mouth." Crickets (little rollers in the port of a bit) and sliding shanks are used in the hope of making a horse stop being a dry mouth. However, champing the bit with a smile and flexing at the pole is the sign of a well-trained horse for whom the bit is a meaningful and comfortable thing; no gimmicks will quite produce the same effect as careful training.

Championship, Grand

In the hunter-jumper division of shows, Grand Champion awards are given on the final afternoon or evening of a show on the basis of points horses have won throughout the entire show. As in the matter of championship classes, a letter to the American Horse Shows Association or consultation of its *Rule Book* is the safest way to be sure one's information is correct.

Championship Classes

Championship classes are competitions between individuals who have won in limited classes in a given division of a horse show. As rules are likely to change slightly from year to year, the person needing information about championship classes should consult the current *Rule Book* of the American Horse Shows Association (address given in this book). The association is prompt in answering correspondence and has been willing to give answers to specific questions.

Change of Lead

When a horse gallops or canters (or "lopes"), two diagonal feet strike the ground at the same or almost the same time (*see* CANTER). Each of the other two diagonal feet strikes the ground individually. The horse is said to be on the right lead if the sequence of the hoof impacts on the ground is as follows: left hind, right hind and left fore, right fore. The horse is said to be on the left lead if the sequence is: right hind, left hind and right fore, left fore.

The number of methods employed to teach a horse to take the desired lead or to change leads is legion. The best method to use depends upon the particular horse being trained and the ability of the particular rider. However, the method most often useful on the totally green horse is to trot him into the desired lead—best done in an arena or ring. Keeping close to the railing, the rider posts to the trot, *rising with the horse's outside foreleg*. As he approaches a turn, he keeps the head turned slightly toward the rail; leaning slightly *toward* the rail with his own body, he urges the horse into a gallop. If the horse fails to take the lead with the foot nearest the center of the ring, the rider stops the horse and tries again, this time leaning farther toward the *outside* of the ring and back over the horse's *outside* loin. This leaning out and back is especially useful if the horse tends to take the proper lead with the forefoot but not behind, a performance called "disunited canter" or "cross-firing," and done more frequently by a sluggish horse than by others. Sometimes this mistake can be corrected by use of

whip or bat to urge the horse into a gallop more suddenly. (*See also* FLY-
ING CHANGE.)

Chaparreras or Chaps

Chaparreras or chaps are leather or fur coverings for the legs. They have
no seat but extend to the waistline in front and are held up by a heavy belt.
In actual work on the range, the chaps worn are made of fairly heavy
leather or fur. If of leather and oiled to be made waterproof, they become
quite stiff and heavy. In some parts of the Northwest, cowboys prefer fur
chaps. The legs of some chaps are held together at the side by snaps and
rings, which are covered by a flap that extends the entire length of the
chaps. Such chaps are known as batwings. Another type, called shotgun
chaps, has legs closed like those of a pair of pants. Shotgun chaps have to
be pulled on. Some horse-show classes for Western pleasure horses require
that the rider wear chaps. Chaps for this purpose may be quite light and
decorative. There are also highly decorative chaps for use in parades.
Rodeo bronc riders wear batwing chaps that will flap and give more style to
their riding.

A very complete discussion of chaps is to be found in Chapter 25 of a
useful book by Fay Ward, *The Cowboy at Work.*

Chaparajos is a word sometimes used improperly for chaparreras or
chaps by Easterners.

Charger

In the days when the cavalry used horses, horse shows frequently included
classes for officers' chargers. They were very colorful classes. The officer's
charger was a fairly large horse capable of carrying weight, but he had to
be extremely handy and capable of some speed. He had to be able to
change leads on a full gallop at every second stride so that as the officer
swung his saber from side to side the horse could change leads in order to
support the officer as the saber swung.

Charging

Charging is a word used principally only by those who are proud of their
knowledge of esoteric horsey terminology. If, when he is loose in corral or
pasture, the horse rushes with teeth bared and ears back at anyone who
enters the enclosure, he is said to be charging. If the terrain of corral or
pasture is such that the horse will not break his knees when thrown, the
vice can quickly be broken by a competent roper who can forefoot the
horse when he makes his charge. Another method is to stand one's ground
and strike the horse across the nose with a stout bat or stick as he approaches. This requires care to avoid putting out an eye when striking the
horse.

The great majority of horses having this vice (fortunately they are not many) will usually forget it if handled by a competent horseman who will go into the corral, stand his ground, and quietly halter the animal. Few horses will actually injure the person who enters the corral. Of course, the horse who has been tortured by human beings sometimes develops adequate defense.

Some years ago at one of Kentucky's largest Saddle Horse establishments, Land O'Goshen, there lived a venerable mare habitually ridden by a diminutive 10-year-old girl. This mare would charge a stable hand in paddock or box stall, so she was never disturbed by having anyone enter her stall to feed her. The feed was poked through an opening made in the grill in the upper part of her stall. At stall-cleaning time, the help carefully passed a rope around the old mare's neck as she thrust her head over the lower half of the Dutch door, then put a halter on her and tied her up until the stall was clean.

The little 10-year-old who rode the mare would put a bridle over her arm and open the stall door. When the mare rushed toward her, the little miss stood still. As the mare came up within arm's length, the youngster would slap her on the neck, saying, "Oh Adele!" quietly slip reins over the flattened ears, and then bridle the mare. However, not a stableboy on the place would enter the box stall until Adele was securely tied or removed.

Charro

A charro is one who practices the traditional art of horsemanship in Mexico. This is one of the oldest and most exciting kinds of horsemanship in the world. It was brought to Mexico by the conquistadores, and much of it had been taken from the Moors. The horses of the charros execute all the movements of the Spanish Riding School horses with the exception of those movements taught by tying a horse between pillars and whipping him (the "above-ground movements"). The charros' horses do not have the mechanical appearance of the performing Lippizaners. Their movements suggest the dancer on the stage rather than the performing member of an acrobatic drill team.

The training methods of the charro differ from those of all other horsemen by the use of the bosal. They achieve a quickness and subtlety of response seldom seen in any other horses.

Unfortunately, the best book on the charro and his methods has not been translated from the Spanish. It was written by one of the outstanding practicing charros, Don Carlos Rincon Gallardo, Duke de Regla, Marques de Guadalupe. The title of the Duke's book is *El Charro Mexicano*. Translation of the portion of the book describing the bosal is given in my *Out of the West*.

Charro or Western parade seat.

Checkreins

Checkreins are of two general types. One consists of a strap that is divided on the bridge of a horse's nose, from which it goes on either side to the bit. Upward, it goes between the eyes and through little loops on the crownpiece of the bridle that lie each side of the poll and close enough together so that the straps will not rub the horse's ears. From these loops, the strap passes back to a hook or other similar fastening on the harness of the horse. This type of checkrein is called an overcheck.

The other type, called a side rein or bearing rein, goes from the bit on either side through loops which are attached to the bridle at the juncture of browband and crownpiece. From there the checkrein goes back to the hook on the backband on the horse.

Checkreins serve many useful purposes, but they can also be a means of torturing a horse and giving him bad habits. A checkrein is generally used on a bitting rig. When a horse is being driven, a checkrein is necessary so that the moment he stops, he will not put his head down to eat the grass or examine the terrain with his nose. A pony or horse ridden by a child who is just beginning to learn to ride may wear a checkrein to keep him from putting his head down to eat grass every time he stops. Checkreins that are so short that they keep a horse's head in an unnaturally high position and are used for any length of time will not only cause the horse misery but usually engender some bad habits in him.

Cheek Strap or Cheekpiece

A cheek strap or cheekpiece is the part of a bridle that lies against a horse's cheek. At one end it fastens to the bit; at the other end it fastens into the crownpiece. (See illustration of bridle.)

Chestnut Color (Chestnut Sorrel). *See* SORREL

Chestnuts (Callosities). *See* MALLENDERS

Chickasaw Horse. *See* NATIONAL CHICKASAW HORSE ASSOCIATION

Chicken Coop

A chicken coop is a kind of jump used in horse shows. It is a replica of a panel which covers a wire fence in hunting country so that the fence may be jumped with safety. Good wire fences on farms are four feet high, so the chicken coop covering them is usually a little over four feet.

Chief (family)

The Chief family was founded by a horse (Harrison Chief) who was admitted to registration by the American Saddle Horse Breeders' Association because of his own winnings and the winnings of his get. Prior to the advent of Harrison Chief in the show-ring (he was foaled in 1872) American Saddle Horses were uniformly fine and fine headed and not large—most of them were around 15 to 15.2 hands high (*see* HAND); occasionally, one might reach the height of 15.3. Harrison Chief was a horse of Standardbred ancestry. He was by Clark Chief, who was by Mambrino Chief, who was by Mambrino Paymaster, who was by Mambrino, who was by Imported Messenger. His dam was called Lute Boyd, a Standardbred mare by Joe Downing, who was a great Standardbred sire. One of Joe Downing's sons, Abe Downing, had set a record of 2:20 3/4, and another son, Dick Jamison, a record of 2:26. Lute Boyd was a very beautiful mare, much finer than most of the Standardbred horses of that day. Her son, Harrison Chief, though not so fine as the Saddlebreds of his time, was not nearly so coarse as many of the Standardbreds. He was a big horse—16 hands high—and his performance in harness pointed him toward the show-ring in harness. Of course, at that time a horse of his size would have looked almost freakish under the saddle in gaited classes had he ever been gaited. For eight years he was shown in harness and was defeated only four times, once by his own daughter. This means, of course, that he defeated many Saddlebred horses, for the Saddle Horse was the one usually shown in harness classes then. Not only did he defeat Saddlebred horses in harness classes, but his progeny also soon began to defeat them in classes under saddle as well as in harness. He had three sons who gained fame during his lifetime and afterward. They were King, Bourbon Chief, and Bracken Chief. (King is not to be confused with Bourbon King. This early King was sometimes known as Wilson's King.)

When Bourbon Chief was bred to a granddaughter of Harrison Chief, the result was Bourbon King, one of the most illustrious Saddle Horses that ever lived. For years the most important five-gaited stakes for Saddle Horses were won exclusively by animals sired by Bourbon King and out of dams of Denmark or Highlander breeding. This Chief-Denmark cross, as it became known, was considered the ultimate in breeding for several years.

While Harrison Chief's progeny through Bourbon Chief was attracting so much favorable attention, other progeny of his through Bracken Chief was causing considerable hostility toward Chief blood on the part of Saddlebred breeders. Some of Bracken Chief's get were 17 hands and weighed over 1,300 pounds and were very coarse. The only virtue they had was speed (perhaps we should also include size in view of what is favored today, though at that time size was not considered as desirable as it is today).

The pros and cons among Saddle Horse breeders as the result of the winnings of the progeny of Bourbon Chief and the coarseness that seemed to come through Bracken Chief and King intensified. The pros were insistent that Harrison Chief be included in the American Saddlebred Registry. The cons objected violently, contending that the quality of the Saddle Horse would be greatly impaired by the inclusion of such blood. However, the pros finally won, and Harrison Chief was admitted into registry by the American Saddle Horse Breeders' Association. As time went on, the crossing of the Chief family with the Denmark became almost meaningless because the practice of breeding winner to winner without respect to family so diluted each family that families became indistinguishable. Today it is practically impossible to find an American Saddle Horse who can with any justice be called a Chief or a Denmark, or a Highlander. We do, of course, have animals that show almost exclusively the characteristics of one of these families, but such animals are rare.

A note of caution should be added to any explanation of the Chief family. Some people confuse the blood of Indian Chief with that of the Chief family. While the progeny of Indian Chief crossed with the members of the Chief family often resulted in excellent animals, Indian Chief himself, a horse foaled in 1857, did not have a drop of the blood that we include under the term *the Chief family*. Even today there is considerable doubt as to his breeding. The American Saddle Horse Breeders' Association included him in the registry and finally agreed on a pedigree for him stating that he was sired by Blood's Blackhawk and out of a mare named Lou Berry. Blood's Blackhawk was a Morgan horse and Lou Berry was also a Morgan but had a trace of the blood of the Kentucky Whip family, a very old family of Thoroughbreds that was responsible for much of the quality in early American Saddle Horses. Whatever his breeding may be, there is evidence in descriptions of him and his progeny that he, Indian Chief, was very largely Morgan, though many animals three or four generations removed from him had a length of neck that greatly exceeds that of typical Morgans, and some of them lacked the smoothness of the hips of the early Morgans. Their croups were level, but the points of their hips were quite prominent. Most of them were beautifully gaited animals and had delightful action.

Chinese Tag

In Chinese tag, the one who is tagged must keep his hand on the place where he has been tagged until he can tag someone else. For example, if a rider is tagged on the shoulder, he must keep one hand on his shoulder until he tags someone. This, obviously, means he must use his bridle hand to tag with, a difficult and not too safe stunt for beginners unless mounted on very sluggish mounts.

Chin Strap

A chin strap passes through the rings at the top of the sidepieces on either side of a curb bit, then under the horse's jawbone just above the chin. The strap should be buckled just behind where it goes through the top of the left curb shank or sidepiece.

There is a current notion among amateur horsemen that a curb strap is kinder to a horse than a curb chain. However, under certain conditions the curb strap may cause a horse considerably more pain than a curb chain properly adjusted. A strap will stretch; if the curb strap stretches and the owner does not shorten it to compensate for the stretch, the strap may pinch the corners of the horse's mouth against the mouthpiece of the bit. Furthermore, if the curb strap is not kept clean and pliable, it may irritate the horse's skin. Again, the keeper on the curb strap may be allowed to slip downward and press against the horse's jaw, causing a sore. If the buckle is not kept in the proper place, the rivet or stitching which holds the buckle may press against the horse's jaw and cause a sore.

Chuck Wagon

In the days of the large cattle herds, the chuck wagon, a specially built wagon drawn by two or more teams, was used at roundup time to carry everything from food to such spare gear as was absolutely necessary. Today the chuck wagon has given place to the pickup truck.

Chute

Chutes for livestock are of two general classes. One is used for branding, de-horning, doctoring, etc. It is just wide enough to allow an animal to enter and is so constructed that it can be closed at either end.

The other kind of chute is considerably larger. Chutes are usually located under the grandstand in the rodeo ground. Immediately behind them is a corral for holding animals that are to be used in bucking contests. Animals are forced into the chutes from the corrals and held for saddling and mounting. The latter operation is performed by the rider dropping down on the animal's back from the top of the fence. When all is ready, a chute gate leading into the arena is opened, and an animal comes out of the chute, usually with the rider on his back.

Circus Horse

The term *circus horse* covers a wide range of animals. A circus horse may be an excellently trained hunter who gives an exhibition performance in a circus. Or he may be a horse trained to do tricks on his hind legs with no one on his back.

The circus horses used by the people who do stunts on them, standing or jumping through hoops and lighting on the horse's back, are draft animals usually weighing around 1,500 or 1,600 pounds. Percheron blood is evident in most of them because of the predominance of grays among Percherons—grays which turn to white with age. The white color has an advantage because these horses all have to have resin on their backs to help keep the barefoot performers from slipping, and resin is not as obvious on the back of a white horse as it is on the back of a horse of darker color. This use of resin has led to the term *resinback* for circus horses who serve the purpose just discussed. A resinback, of course, must be a horse of pleasing appearance, as most draft horses containing Percheron, Belgian, Shire, or Clydesdale blood are. He must also be of good temperament and have sufficient impulsion so that he can easily be taught to continue doing a canter or hand gallop as long as his trainer desires.

Claiming Race

In a claiming race, the value of entries is stated before the race is run. After the race, any horse may be "claimed" or bought for the stated value.

Classes. *See also* HORSE SHOWS

A mere listing of the classes that may be seen in horse shows across this country from east to west would fill a book the size of this one. Fortunately, the American Horse Shows Association has done much to standardize the kinds of classes seen in important shows. Until some 30 years ago, horse-show classes were fairly limited. They consisted of classes for hunters and jumpers, for horses shown in harness (either in heavy harness to gigs, broughams, or other carriages of some weight, or in fine harness driven to lighter vehicles). Then there were classes for the gaited horses and the so-called breeding classes, in which the horses were shown "in hand"—that is, wearing only a halter or a bridle with the attendant on foot beside them.

Later, plantation classes were added (these were the forerunners of the Tennessee Walking Horse classes). A horse wearing a Western saddle would have been as out of place in those shows as levis would be at a formal dance.

With the coming into our shows of Western horses (in the second quarter of this century), the number of kinds of classes endlessly increased. We now have classes for reining horses, for cutting horses, for stock horses, for Western pleasure horses, etc., all shown in Western gear. Any individual or group contemplating putting on a horse show will do well to consult the *Rule Book* of the American Horse Shows Association, explained elsewhere in this book.

Cleaning. *See* GROOM

Clean Legs

The term *clean legs* is used to designate legs that are free from blemishes of any kind, such as scars, spavins, and ringbones (each discussed under appropriate headings in this book).

Cleveland Bay. *See also* CLEVELAND BAY SOCIETY OF AMERICA

The breed Cleveland Bay was established in Cleveland, England, and was designed for general utility. It is actually a draft breed with a good deal of Thoroughbred blood in it, lighter than the Shire, Belgian, Percheron, etc. It found some favor in this country as a carriage horse before the advent of the automobile.

The Cleveland Bay is not a tall horse, usually about 15½ hands high, but weighs up to 1,400 pounds or a little better. A horse of uniformly good disposition and square gaits, he is, however, not possessed of great speed or high action. That is probably because no one thought to grow his feet to crippling length for high action, or to do anything else to make him have spectacular performance suitable for the show-ring. He is thus a horse almost unknown in this country though he is still used in some places for crossbreeding to produce hunters. There certainly is a possibility that he could be made into a showpiece. The very fact that all Cleveland Bays are of the same color (bay with black points) may attract some breeders.

Cleveland Bay Society of America

The Cleveland Bay Society, White Post, Virginia 22663 (A. Mackay-Smith, secretary), maintains a registry. While its promotional activities are marked by modesty and restraint, the society seems to be pointed toward importation of Cleveland Bay stallions during the next few years to breed to Thoroughbred mares to produce weight-carrying hunters. The feasibility of this intention is proved by the present use of two stallions, one in Virginia and the other in California, and by the fact that some of the best

One of the two Cleveland Bay stallions (November 1970) standing in America.

jumpers on the Canadian and British teams at the present time carry Cleveland Bay blood.

Cleverness

In some localities in North America the word *clever* is used by horsemen for a very special purpose. It is applied to a horse who has a good disposition, is trustworthy, and is free of all vices. In other places the word *clever* applied to a horse means that the horse is nimble and can do whatever he is supposed to be good at with great agility and promptness. It is equivalent to another, more colorful term used in many parts of the West. The Westerner says that the horse "has a handle on him," by which he means that the horse responds quickly to the aids, will shift balance readily, and will do exactly what a good Western horse is supposed to do.

Clipping

Clipping the horse is often an expedient for eliminating the labor of careful grooming. Sometimes a horse comes in off pasture or range with a coat so long that it will not dry out readily after the horse sweats. At such times clipping may be advisable. But if a horse is clipped and the weather turns chilly, he must be blanketed to prevent illness. The horse who will not readily shed his long winter coat is more in need of a veterinarian than of clipping.

A wise practice is followed in some stables of hunters where horses are clipped. The hair is left unclipped under the saddle and even sometimes on the legs. There is no better pad than horsehair, whether it is the horse's own hair or that of some other horse made into a blanket. And the hair on a horse's legs sometimes cushions the blow of sticks and brush which the horse gallops through.

Close-Order Drill

Any kind of drill is excellent practice in learning to control a horse. There are few riders who are able to keep their stirrups in close proximity to those of another rider. Occasionally in horse shows one sees in pair classes riders who keep their stirrups clicking with those of their partner while performing all the required gaits.

Eight Clydesdales, each a show-ring champion in his own right. Average height 18 hands.

Close-order drill as specified in the old Fort Riley cavalry manual or elsewhere is of use to every riding instructor. Valuable as formation riding is, riding instructors cannot indulge in too much of it because their pupils will find it boring and their custom will drop off. However, anyone who wishes to improve his ability to control his horse should now and then, for a brief time, attempt to keep his horse exactly beside that of another rider while the other rider varies his speed.

Clover Hay

In parts of the country where clover hay is available, the horseman can feed it advantageously if he can procure clover hay that is made properly. Either alsike or red clover should show some of the color of the blossom. The rest of the hay should have a greenish cast. If the hay is black or shows any mold, it should certainly not be used. Old-time horsemen of the trotting horse circuit used to say that the best hay in the world was about one-third clover and two-thirds timothy.

Clucking

Clucking is a noise made by the rider with tongue and teeth. This ubiquitous and iniquitous practice has caused many accidents on the trail and lost tempers in the show-ring. The rider who insists on clucking had best ride alone so he will not inadvertently excite the horses of other riders.

Clydesdale. *See also* CLYDESDALE BREEDERS ASSOCIATION

The Clydesdale horse is from 16 to 17 hands high and weighs close to a ton or more. Ninety percent of the Clydesdales are either bay or brown. Many have white markings on face or legs. The legs are provided with long silky hair below knees and hocks. Since the undiscriminating person sometimes has difficulty distinguishing between the Clydesdale and the Shire, it may be useful to quote from the late Henry Vaughan, an eminent authority on livestock breeds. Dr. Vaughan said that Clydesdale breeders emphasize quality, set of legs, size and shape of feet, slope of pasterns, and superb action, whereas Shire breeders select for size, bone, and extreme draftiness and ruggedness.

The known history of the Clydesdale horse dates back to the middle of the sixteenth century, when the Duke of Hamilton is said to have imported six fine black stallions from Flanders. These undoubtedly were the Great Horse of Flanders, the breed used by the knights in armor. There is no written record of the duke's importations. However, there is written record of an importation by a John Paterson, a Lanarkshire farmer who imported a black Flemish stallion about 1720, which he crossed on native mares with good results.

The Clydesdale, like the other great draft breeds, reached the peak of his popularity during the last years of the nineteenth century and the early years of the twentieth. Baron's Pride, foaled in 1890, is said to have earned upward of $150,000 in prize money and stud fees. Today the Clydesdale is still the popular horse for exhibition purposes of multiple-hitch teams, for example, the Budweiser team. Six- and eight-horse teams of Clydesdales continue to be popular exhibits at some horse shows. (See page 109.)

Clydesdale Breeders Association of the United States

The secretary of the association is Frank Martin, Route 1, Plymouth, Indiana 46563. (*See* CLYDESDALE.)

Coat

The quality of a horse's coat of hair is the result of many factors. It tells the careful horseman much about the internal condition of a horse, his breeding, and about the way he is being used. Because of his inheritance, a horse may have a short, tight, glossy coat, or a long, somewhat coarse coat. These natural qualities of the individual can be altered considerably by other factors. For instance, parasites can cause a coat to lose its brightness. Feed that is not properly balanced, or lack of feed, may cause a coat to become dull and long. Careful grooming will improve the looks of any horse's coat and will improve his general health, but the coat of a healthy, vigorous horse will have a sheen or luster that will show through dust and dirt.

Cob

The word *cob* does not indicate a breed of horse but a type. This is a small compact animal with good bone, one that is suitable for a variety of purposes, from light draft work to hunting (when ridden by not too heavy a rider). The original so-called bulldog type of Quarter Horse and the original Morgans were of the cob type.

Coffin Bone

The coffin bone is a little bone located in a horse's heel. Race horses not infrequently fracture this bone. In horses whose heels are contracted over a long period of time, this bone may become irritated so that the periosteum (covering of the bone) becomes enlarged and makes movement of the horse's foot painful. Any injury to a horse's coffin bone (also called pedal bone) is a great disaster.

Cold-Blooded Horse

A cold-blooded horse is one who shows little or no evidence of having Thoroughbred or Arabian ancestry—in other words, a coarse animal. The opposite term is, of course, *hot-blooded*. It is used to indicate any animal showing evidence of having much Thoroughbred or Arabian blood in his veins, that is, a horse showing extreme quality, sensitivity, and spirit.

Colds

Since a horse's respiratory tract is highly developed and large in proportion to his size, any infection of it may be a very serious matter. Any symptom of a cold in a horse is a signal to call a veterinarian, not to reach for a home remedy. Good first aid calls for keeping the horse warm and dry in a well-ventilated but not drafty place and giving him a bran mash. (*See* FEED.) The first time a horse is offered a bran mash he may refuse to have anything to do with it, so it is a good idea to introduce him to it by hand. Put a little of the mash in your hand and sprinkle over it some sweet feed, sugar, or anything else that you are sure the horse likes. After he has eaten two or three handfuls of bran, the entire mash may be presented to him. It is important to see that the mash is cool enough before being given to a horse.

Colic

Pain in a horse's belly (abdomen) is called colic. It is not hard to diagnose. If a horse has pain in his abdomen while he is being ridden, he may slow down or, if ridden by a sympathetic rider, he may stop. If there is perfect rapport between rider and horse, he may then look around at his side or kick his belly with his hind foot. The horse ridden by a martinet who prides himself that his horse "minds perfectly" will give no evidence of his pain; if the illness is severe enough, the horse will go until he drops.

If a horse is loose in paddock, corral, or box stall, he will give evidence of belly pains in the manner described above for the horse ridden by a sympathetic and intelligent rider. A horse showing such signs should be haltered immediately so that he can be kept from lying down and rolling. This maneuver may be rather difficult if the pain is severe, and requires one man at the halter and another behind the horse with a switch or length of rope. Of course, a veterinarian should be called immediately. Many a horse has died from foreign-body pneumonia caused by medicine given orally by his owner when the horse has colic (see DRENCHING).

In severe cases of colic a horse will lie down and get up repeatedly, then finally roll violently. This rolling sometimes produces a tie-up in the intestines worse than the original ailment. Where a veterinarian is not available, the best home remedies are to keep the horse warm and on his feet and give him enemas and light massage. Of course, it is possible that the abdominal pain is caused by an illness that will not yield to any home corrective, but the remedies just mentioned can do no harm.

Although the causes of colic are too numerous to mention in a book of this size, two of them are so important that they cannot be left out. The first is improper feeding, including too rapid change of diet. The second is internal parasites (worms and bots) (see PARASITES).

Collected Gaits. *See also* GAITS

At every gait except the true or natural running walk and the canter, a horse may perform in either a collected or an extended manner (see COLLECTION). When he is collected, he arches his neck, bringing his head back to a point almost directly over the front of his shoulders, and brings his hocks well under him. This moves his center of balance farther to the rear than it usually is. When a horse is collected, his action is usually higher than at other times, and he travels with more ease to his rider. In a few kinds of horse-show classes, notably performance classes for horses of specific breeds, the horses are required to show a collected trot and an extended trot. In many of these classes it is interesting to watch what the riders do for a collected trot. Some of them merely slow the horse down and bring his chin in slightly. Of course, for the extended trot they let him get his nose out and exhibit whatever speed he is capable of.

The true canter is a gait performed only with a large degree of collection. The canter might be described as a highly collected gallop. With the exception of the gait displayed by five-gaited horses in the show-ring as a slow-gait, the canter is the single gait that is done only in a collected manner. What the Tennessee Walking Horse now does in the show-ring for a running walk has some appearance of being a collected gait. However, it is a gait done with extreme action and considerable speed but in a manner made to resemble as closely as possible the original or old-fashioned running walk, which was a very uncollected, loose sort of gait. The modern show-ring running walk can hardly be classified either as collected or as extended. It is produced, as *Life,* October 3, 1969, so well pictures and explains, by soring the horse in front with chains or caustic medicines (*see* SORING) and by use of great growth of hoof and weight of shoe. The soring makes the horse put his hind feet far forward to get his weight off his hurting forefeet, and the long toes and heavy shoes make him pick his front feet up very high. The gait that he does could well be called a deformed rack, slightly collected.

Collection

What we may call the language of the bit (*see* REINS, *Use of*) is transmitted from the hands of the rider by the reins. The well-trained horse knows this language perfectly and responds to it happily and instantly. The bit, of course, is not the only means of communication between horse and rider. Every movement of leg and body of the rider has meaning for the well-trained horse (*see* AIDS). The relation between horse and rider resembles that between ballroom dancers. The good dancer does not poke his thumb in the ribs of his partner to make her move her right foot forward or backward; the communication of dancers is far more subtle. Each move has meaning and is responded to by the partner. So it is with the good horse and rider. However, we may generalize and say that the well-trained horse is constantly balanced between impulsion and restraint. This does not mean that he is being jabbed in the ribs by the spurs to give him impulsion and simultaneously punished on the mouth by a bit to give him restraint. The reins of the well-trained Western horse are rarely taut, and the spurs of his rider touch his sides very lightly, if ever at all.

On the well-trained horse, the impulsion and restraint given by the rider determine where the center of balance of the horse will be. When the unmounted horse is walking freely in the pasture, his center of balance is just behind his withers. He walks with his neck fairly straight and thrust forward from his withers. His hind legs swing well out behind. If this same horse is well trained and mounted by a good horseman, the rider can flex the horse's neck—that is, raise the horse's head and put an arch in the horse's neck just behind the head. The rider can also, as we say, "pull the hocks under the horse." Of course, the very act of pulling the head up and back into an arch moves the center of balance of the horse to the rear. This shifting of the center of balance by raising his head, flexing his neck, and pulling his hocks under him is called *collection*. It shortens the horse's stride and increases the height of his action.

It is not unusual to see an unskilled rider on a well-trained horse over-collect the animal and cause him to rear. Rearing in such a situation certainly should not be punished, for the horse is doing exactly what he is told to do. The head of the horse has followed the hand of the rider, which was too high. And the hind legs of the horse have followed the signal of the legs of the rider and provided too much impulsion. In other words, the rider shifted the horse's balance entirely onto its hind legs and raised the forelegs off the ground. This, of course, in actuality, is what is done when a good reining horse makes a quarter- or even a half-turn on his haunches. The horse is simply collected until all of his weight is carried on his hind legs, and then he is turned to one side.

There are as many methods of teaching a horse to collect as there are kinds of horsemanship and then some. However, the best results are usually obtained by slowly and carefully teaching the young horse to respond to the bit, that is, to know what pressure on the bit means. When the horse is first ridden, any pressure on the reins will be responded to by resistance of some sort. (A child's natural reaction if someone grabs his arm is usually to pull away.) So the rider must proceed carefully to let the colt know what is wanted when the rein is pulled. After the colt has learned how to be started, stopped, and turned by the reins, a little pressure can be applied to the reins and at the same time the colt can be urged to keep on walking. This pressure and urging should be only momentary. The first time or two it is tried, the result will very possibly be just a tossing of the head and a pulling against the bit. But as the colt becomes more familiar with the bit as a signal for turning and for stopping, there will come a time when for a moment he will flex his neck slightly and mouth the bit when pressure is applied and he is asked to keep on going forward. When he does this even for a moment, he should be stroked on the neck or given some other sign of approval which he might recognize. Teaching a horse to have a good mouth and to collect properly are practically one process, a process that can be carried on successfully only by an experienced horseman.

Color of the Horse

The colors common to those breeds of horses for which there have been registries for many years in this country are brown, black, bay, chestnut, roan, and gray. Until fairly recently there was another classification of colors, sorrel. However, there were many arguments about the listing of sorrel horses in show catalogues. Any owner of a sorrel horse that was fairly dark wanted to list it as chestnut because the old-fashioned chestnut, which was the color of raw liver, was a favorite color. To squash such arguments, all horses who were sorrel or chestnut were permitted to be registered as chestnut, and the term *sorrel* was kept out of show catalogues. Horses who are brown, bay, or what was formerly called sorrel are of a reddish cast. The browns and bays all have black manes and tails and usually black hairs on the lower parts of the legs. The brown horses are of such a dark shade that they are frequently mistaken for black, but there is lighter coloring shading almost to tan around muzzle, eyes, belly, and the inside of the legs. The body color of bay horses occurs in shades all the way from the darkness of mahogany, in which instance the horse is called a mahogany bay, to a very light sandy shade sometimes, though rarely, referred to as sandy bay. A bay of deep-cherry-red body color is called a blood bay. The horse whose color is called roan has a coat composed of white hairs interspersed with hairs of a darker shade. Sometimes the darker shade is such that the coat has a bluish cast, in which case the horse is called a blue roan; if it has a reddish cast, the horse is called a strawberry roan.

Roan coats do not show dirt as readily as do some other colors; on the other hand, they rarely have the sheen seen in some bay, black, brown, or chestnut horses. Gray horses usually turn white with age or white with little flecks of chestnut, a color which is called flea-bitten. There is one shade that might with a little imagination be classified as gray, a color seen more frequently in Western horses with some Spanish blood in them than in others. It is sometimes referred to as mouse color. The term used for it in the Southwest is *grulla* (pronounced *grewyer*). Oddly enough, it is rare to see a grulla horse who does not have excellent bone and good hard feet and many other desirable characteristics.

A buckskin horse is colored, as the name implies, like buckskin. The term *dun* includes buckskin and shades considerably lighter than buckskin. Dun horses and buckskin horses frequently have a black stripe down the back and some stripes on the upper parts of the legs. Such horses are sometimes called zebra duns or zebra buckskins. *Claybank* is the name for a shade of dun that verges on the sorrel. The Palomino's body color matches a newly minted gold or copper coin. His mane and tail must be pure white. The color of a Palomino has found favor among horsemen only within the past 30 or 40 years.

The history of the organization of Palomino breeders is a rather stormy one, and there are still at least three organizations registering Palomino horses. Bones of contention have centered around color, among other things—color of coat, color of skin, and color of eyes. One organization has always contended that the only true Palomino is the horse with a black skin and hazel eyes. White on face and lower legs occurs occasionally in Palominos and seems to be permissible in all camps. But there is still prejudice in some quarters against what is called a pumpkin skin (that is, a skin with a pinkish shade) and against freckles on the nose and around the eyes.

Parti-colored or spotted horses include the Appaloosa, the pinto, and the paint. Their color patterns are explained under the heading COLOR PATTERNS.

The most thorough study of color and color inheritance was done by Dr. Fred Gremmel at the Texas Experiment Station. It includes a table of probability percentages of color from matings of animals of various color combinations. Dr. Gremmel, lecturing while a member of the faculty of the University of Arizona, explained one of the conclusions of this exhaustive study which was quite surprising to older horsemen. It was to the effect that all coat colors of horses derive from a single pigment. The amount of the pigment, the way it is clustered and arranged in the hair shafts, and the distribution of the clusters determine the color of the coat. The color of the pigment itself has been called Isabella. It is observable most readily in the flecks on the coat of a flea-bitten gray.

Color Patterns

See COLOR OF THE HORSE for color patterns of bays, browns, and Palominos.

One color that has had a phenomenal rise in popularity in this country over the last quarter-century is the color of the Appaloosa. The color pattern of the Appaloosa as specified by the Appaloosa Horse Club is as follows:

A horse must have a white rump starred with round or oblong spots and also flesh-colored spots around the eyes, nose, and genital organs. The stallions must be dominately leopard spotted with white rump covered with dark spots. Any base color, such as bay, gray, chestnut, cream, white, roan, etc., is acceptable.

Spotted horses other than Appaloosas are called paints or pintos. The English classify paint horses as piebald, which means white and black, and as skewbald, which means white and any color other than black. The Pinto Horse Association of America classifies pintos as follows:

Pinto markings are divided into two patterns, Tobiano and Overo. These patterns are described: *Tobiano*—clearly marked pattern. White as a base with black, brown, sorrel, or dun as the other color. Markings distinct and the colors usually divided half and half. Mane and tail the color of the region from which they stem. Legs white. Head dark or combined with star, strip, snip or blaze. *Overo*— a colored horse, roan, dun, sorrel, bay, brown or black, with white extending upward and irregular in pattern. Mane and tail dark or mixed, head usually white or bald. Legs give a combination of both colors.

Most white horses have black skins and dark eyes and came into this world a dark color. However, there are albino horses, for which there is a registry. These horses lack pigmentation in skin and eyes as well as hair, so that they have pink skin and pink eyes, which are a decided disadvantage in some climates. An effort is being made by the White Horse Ranch in Nebraska to breed a white horse that has a black skin and brown eyes and good conformation. The ranch started with a Saddlebred stallion named Silver Mac and is said to be making laudable progress.

Colt (as a term)

The word *colt* is often used very loosely, except by the precious (or the tyro hoping to impress his fellows by his "correctness" in equine matters), to indicate any equine less than three or four years old. Strictly speaking, *colt* is the designation for a male equine from the time he is weaned until he reaches the age of four years. The female is called a filly. While the little ones are still nursing, both sexes are called foals. The term *weanling* is used sometimes to designate young animals of either sex from the weanling stage to the age of one year. The term *yearling* also applies to both sexes, as do *two-year-old, three-year-old,* and *four-year-old.*

Colts

If foaling is normal it takes a colt only a few minutes to be born. From 5 to 20 minutes after he is foaled, he struggles to get to his feet. It usually takes him a couple of attempts before he can get up, get his balance, and get a few swallows of milk. This first milk, the colostrum, has a very special composition, which the little newcomer needs to stimulate all the functions of his body. As a rule, after his first nip of colostrum he will take a little nap and then have another nip of the life-giving fluid. No matter how many foals one watches coming into this world, it is always astounding how short a time is required for a little one to gallop about after his mother as he becomes steadier and the spills become fewer.

If the baby does not have a pair of upper and a pair of lower teeth when he comes into this world, he gets them within a week or so. His fuzzy thick coat protects him from the rain, but his excuse for a tail has little function, and he soon learns to stand where Mother's tail will keep the flies off. Some of the skeleton of a horse is cartilage until he is five years old. Some horses continue growing until the age of seven, though few horses ever gain much in height after their second or third year.

Although strenuous work is injurious to any horse before he is five years old (as can be seen by observing the great majority of race horses who are lame before they have matured), the kind of disposition a horse has, the kind of attitude he has toward human beings, is best cultivated by handling from the time he is born. When the West was young, rarely did a horse feel the touch of a human hand except for branding and castration until he was at least four or five years old. However, the first American voice of authority to advocate handling the young colt gently came from the West. It was that of Charles Marvin, who handled what was once the greatest home of trotting horses in the country: Leland Stanford's Palo Alto Farm, Menlo Park, California. At least one excellent trainer favors haltering a foal before its legs become entirely steady (*see* HALTER BREAKING). A suckling carefully handled from this stage on has no fear of people and no resentment against them. He can be gently pushed around and taught to lead and back (*see* BACKING) with very little effort. On many good breeding and training farms, yearlings are worked on the longe line, are driven in longlines (*see Longlines*, below), and sometimes in breaking carts. Two-year-olds can be ridden for short periods of time by light riders without any injury to the colt. At three, some serious training for the career for which the animal is destined may be given. But the owner who wants the animal to have many years of sound usefulness will not put him to any strenuous work until he is five or six years old.

Early Care

Because of his need for the stimulation of colostrum, the newborn foal must nurse as soon as possible. On rare occasions it is necessary for someone to help him nurse the mare the first time. In other rare instances it is necessary for the mare to be restrained, for now and then a young mare has so much milk that her udder becomes tender and she will kick or bite when it is touched. Sometimes it is necessary to tie up a mare's front leg and twitch her (*see* TWITCH) and let the foal approach from the side on which the front leg is tied up.

A foal soon learns to eat grain with his mother. As soon as he is eating grain readily, a creep may be constructed which will enable a foal to get to a supply of grain that the mare cannot reach. Mares, like other equines, do best when fed frequently in small amounts. It is wise to feed a mare grain three times a day at least. If she is moved from paddock or corral to stall that many times a day for feeding, so much the better, because the foal will get used to being handled. Clean water must be available at all times. A tiny foal will suffer and die from dehydration in some climates (as in parts of Arizona, New Mexico, and California) if he is not protected from the sun during the heat of the day. Fortunate indeed is the foal with access to good pasture. In lieu of this, or even to supplement it, chopped carrots are good. In the area of the greatest concentration of Arabian breeding farms, on one of which is located the price-record-breaking $150,000 Naborr, there is considerable feeding of sprouted grain raised hydroponically in rather expensive machines. The practice is so new that there is little scientific information on it, but it is certainly finding favor among the Arabian breeders of the Scottsdale, Arizona, area.

Weaning

There is considerable disagreement among horsemen about the proper age to wean a foal. If nature is allowed to take charge of the matter, a mare usually weans a colt when he is about a year old or less. However, if the mare is pregnant, suckling a foal for more than six months is likely to have an undesirable effect upon the next foal. Weaning at less than five months usually has an undesirable effect upon the suckling. Six months has long been a standard for the age of weaning a foal in most areas of this country.

Before being weaned, the suckling should have become used to eating grain. If he has been wisely and gradually worked up to the point where he can be given all the whole crimped oats he will consume, he may at weaning time have free access to crimped oats. He also should have free access to good, green, leafy hay and, of course, to clean water at all times. The mare at weaning time must have her feed cut back. The bran part of her grain rations should be continued, but all other grain should be omitted. When she has completely dried up and is returned to grain feeding, the grain feeding should be resumed very gradually. Inexperienced horsemen are always tempted to milk the mare when her bag becomes distended at weaning time, but milking increases her troubles. A mare's bag should not be touched, as any massaging stimulates the production of milk. If she seems to be in pain, a veterinarian should be consulted. It is best to separate the mare and foal as far as possible at weaning time, on separate ranches if convenient, and they should not be allowed to run together again until the mare has entirely dried up and the foal has ceased giving any signs of wanting his mother.

Longlines, Hackamore, and Longe Line

After the youngster has been taught to lead and to stand tied, as explained under the main heading HALTER BREAKING, it is appropriate to introduce him to the longe line (also called lunge line), the longlines, and, possibly, the hackamore.

Longlines may well be the first of these new pieces of equipment. They may be of rope, leather webbing, or nylon. They reach from the animal's mouth to the hands of the trainer, who should walk far enough behind the animal so that no playful kick will make contact with him. At the horse's head the lines may be fastened to a snaffle bit, a bar bit (*see* BITS), a halter, a hackamore, or what not, anything the ingenuity of the handler dreams up as long as it does not cause pain to the horse (of course, no bit that utilizes leverage, such as a curb bit, should ever be used). With longlines properly used as is described below, a hackamore exerts pressure only on the nose; there is, therefore, little point in using a hackamore when a halter will serve exactly the same purpose. Many a tiny colt has learned a good deal with longlines attached to a halter. While being worked in the longlines, horses wear a variety of things depending upon the ideas of the handler. Some handlers use a bitting rig; others, a driving harness; some, a surcingle provided with a ring at each side through which the longlines will run freely. Still others use a saddle with stirrups tied on either side to a rope or strap passing under the horse's belly, in which instance the longlines go through the stirrups. A driving harness with

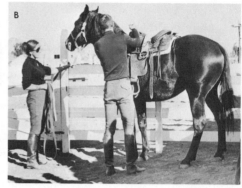

The following series of pictures were taken at a horse training clinic in Phoenix, Arizona, under the auspices of the Arizona State Horsemen's Association, November 1970.

A. Linda Tellington, Pacific Coast Equestrian Research Farm, using unbroken four-year-old stallion fresh from Montana range, demonstrates introducing horse to tack.

B. First saddling; saddle is very gently placed on horse's back.

C. Using care (one handler on each side) in fastening cinch.

D. Close-up of longlines in correct position on back legs of horse.

E. Starting horse on longlines using assistant at halter.

F. More work with longlines.

G. Giving horse approval and confidence and dismissing helper.

H. Resuming longlines without help.

I. Light pressure is put on stirrup for the first time. After this successful step horse was unsaddled and put back in his stall.

breeching is perhaps the most satisfactory because the longlines can be passed through the shaft lugs (the loops at either side of the horse through which the shafts pass when he is hitched to a buggy) if they are properly held down by a bellyband. The longlines can also be run through rings tied at the juncture of hip strap and breeching, or they can be passed through the hip strap's lower end where it divides (if it does divide) for attachment to the breeching. When a driving harness is used for longline training, the horse should wear a breast collar, and the tugs should be tied into the breeching rings so that the breeching is held comfortably snug where it passes behind the horse's stifles. It should not be tight enough to interfere at all with his movement but must be tight enough so that it cannot be pulled upward to the root of his tail.

The point in using surcingle, saddle, harness, or other similar device is that the longlines must be kept from getting under the horse's feet, and they must also be kept from sliding up over his rump if he turns suddenly. Because the use of the driving harness keeps the lines where they belong at the quarters, it is undoubtedly the best thing to use in conjunction with the longlines.

An assistant is a great advantage on the first day of using longlines with any young animal. The colt does not have any idea of what is wanted of him. To convey to him that his handler wants him to move forward, it is far better to have someone at his head leading him (of course he has long ago been taught to lead) than for the handler to startle him by slapping him on the rump with a line or throwing a pebble at him. As soon as the youngster learns to walk in a reasonably straight line without yawing his head about or tossing it up and down, he can be taught to turn to left and right and to start and to stop on verbal command. There is a great variety of things a young animal can be taught to do while on the longlines. A row of barrels can be useful, as can some low objects to step over. Longlines are not an imperative necessity in the training of every equine, but they are extremely helpful for the city or suburban dweller raising a horse without much room for exercise. Unless the handler is quite skillful at using the longe line (see LONGE), longlines are much better than the longe line for teaching the colt to keep his head in front of him when he travels. They also obviate the possibility of the youngster's whirling on his forehand and bowing a tendon, which is sometimes done on a longe line if the handler is not experienced. Of course, the longlines and the longe line can be used at alternate lessons for variety's sake, and each device can obtain some results impossible with the other. The two are supplementary.

Though a hackamore (see also HACKAMORE) has no advantage over a halter when the colt is being used in longlines, it has some advantage over a halter if the colt is on the longe line. However, when so used, the hackamore must be loose and held up at its rear by a fiador (see FIADOR). A flip of the longe line will produce a quick movement of the hackamore which has more authority because of its weight and stiffness than would a movement of the halter. This is beneficial in teaching the young animal to stop on verbal command or to reverse direction or to come to center. With a raising of the hand on high or a simple word spoken distinctly, but always the same, he can be taught to stop at the command "Whoa" by a simple flip of the longe line, which at all other times has been held slack but high enough to clear the ground and to be safe from a playful foot getting over it.

Of course, foals vary greatly, and a very light flip of the rope, which is always the first thing to try, may not stop the little fellow. Then a slightly more definite flip should be given. As soon as the foal stops, the handler should walk up to him and let him know that he has done well.

For full explanation of longe (or lunge) *see* LONGE.

Bitting Rig

The bitting rig (*see also* BITTING RIG) is useful chiefly to save time and effort of the trainer. Although a poor substitute for the good hand of a skillful horseman, it is relatively harmless if used intelligently. If none of the straps restricting the horse's head movement (overchecks, bearing reins, side reins, standing martingale, etc.) are so tight that the horse cannot stand in a comfortable relaxed position, his mouth will receive little damage from the bitting rig unless it is left on too long. Theoretically, one important purpose of the use of the bitting rig is to give the colt the proper "head set." Another purpose for which it is thought useful is to teach the horse to give to the bit. Every wise old trainer knows that no care need be given to head set if a horse is trained to accept the bit properly and to balance himself properly. When a horse does these two things, he will automatically have the best head set that his conformation will permit. However, the trainer whose living depends on pleasing owners will do well to use a bitting rig on a colt owned by someone who wants to see results quickly. If the straps going from either side are of such length that the horse has to bend at the poll very slightly, and the overcheck or bearing rein is of such length that his head must be held a little above the level of his back, he will soon learn to assume the desired posture of the head and neck. If the bitting rig is not left on more than a few minutes the first few times, the length of time can be gradually increased until a weanling, let us say, can wear it for 15 or 20 minutes. Some trainers achieve good results by using rubber inserts in the reins that hold the chin in. The overcheck or side rein can be fastened to the terrets with rubber to avoid bruising from the bit if the head moves up and down slightly. Terrets are the two rings attached to the pad or backband through which lines can be run. The use of a bitting rig for such long periods that the animal becomes tired will do nothing but harm.

Use of Breaking Cart (*see also* HARNESS, *First lessons in*)

If a colt has been worked carefully in longlines and handled a great deal otherwise, he will have little fear when being hitched in a vehicle the first time. However, the breaking cart (*see* BREAKING CART) is the ideal vehicle to use for the first lessons between shafts. A bare substitute for a breaking cart for the first few lessons between the shafts can be made of a pair of long saplings. An assistant can walk behind the colt carrying the butt ends of the saplings, or they can be lashed into a travois to drag on the ground. If the latter is employed, the saplings must be quite long; if they are short, they will be very low to the ground close to the horse's heels, and he may get a hind leg over them when he turns.

When a colt is perfectly relaxed and all bystanders have been shooed out of the area, a breaking cart may be quietly pulled up and the shafts put through the shaft lugs. Of course, the important thing for the trainer to see to is that the bellyband is stout and in good order and that the kicking strap (*see* KICKING STRAP), no matter how gentle the colt may be, is a good one and is properly adjusted for this first lesson.

No sensible horseman jumps in the cart and starts clucking and flapping the reins to make a colt move forward when he is first hitched to any vehicle. It is a good idea to let the colt stand as long as he wants to and allow him to make the first move forward. Ten or fifteen minutes spent in this fashion are well spent. More than one colt has been ruined by being startled at this juncture. The colt should be allowed to move forward for some distance without being asked to turn. When he is asked to turn, the turn should be very gradual. Sometimes an assistant at his head is quite an aid in getting the colt to understand that he is being asked to turn. A safety device used frequently in horse-and-buggy days, a trip rope, may be advisable with highly nervous colts. It should be used first with longlines. It is simply a long cotton rope fastened to a front ankle, run through a ring in the center of the bellyband and then to the hands of the driver. When the command to stop is given orally and on the reins, the forefoot is pulled off the ground and held there until the colt stands quietly. He may hop around a little at first but not for long. Properly used, the trip rope has a quieting effect upon a nervous animal.

Mounting the Colt

Before he is mounted, the colt should be so familiar with a saddle that he pays no more attention to being saddled than to having a blanket put on. First saddling must be done very gently. It can be done when the animal is a tiny foal as well as immediately prior to lessons in mounting. Whenever it is done, a light saddle (of racing or English type, if possible) should be used. Stirrups should be removed or tied securely across the seat so they will not flop. All saddle strings should be tied up. If the youngster is especially nervous, it may be best to remove girth or cinch and gently lay the saddle on his back for a moment, the first time he is introduced to it. When girth or cinch is applied, it should not be pulled tight. After the colt has become well enough acquainted with the saddle to walk in a relaxed manner around his stall with it on his back, the girth or cinch may be gradually tightened. (No sensible horseman ever "pulls a horse in two" with cinch or girth unless he is showing off on a bucking horse.) When the young horse is completely relaxed under a saddle and not before, he is ready for first mounting.

The first mounting should be done in a stall unless the roof is too low, in which case the mounting may have to be done in a corral. Place the colt where he can be held or tied facing a fence. Of course, the colt will previously have become acquainted with the saddle so that he can move about with stirrups flapping without the slightest fear. An assistant might well hold the colt's head toward a fence so that he will not be tempted to move forward. Then his trainer can step quietly onto his back, sit for a moment or two, and possibly stroke the colt's neck gently before dismounting. It is wise to repeat this lesson from either side until the colt is not at all nervous when he is mounted. Then he can be mounted and the assistant can convey to him the fact that his rider wants him to move. If the assistant is not at hand, the rider can quietly reach down and pull the colt's head to one side much as he would do if he were standing by the colt's side and wanted him to move to the side. If by some misfortune the colt is startled and starts to move rapidly, it is wise to slow him down by pulling his head around to the side as far toward his tail as possible. By going in ever smaller circles the youngster will soon slow down. A colt quickly becomes hysterical with speed at this stage. For the vast majority of horsemen, the big-ringed bridoon or other snaffle that is so designed that it will not pull through the colt's mouth is by far the best bit. For the first riding of the colt, the plow rein, euphemistically called the direct rein, is more useful than the neck rein. At first, the colt's only reaction to a pull on the bit may be to resist it. How does he know that a pull on the right rein means "turn right" or that a pull on both reins means "stop"? Of course, if he has been worked in longlines, this will be old stuff to him. However, any turning, starting, or stopping should be done very slowly for the first few rides with the colt. Hands on the reins should communicate to the colt with short meaningful pulls. The hands should not maintain a constant dead pull on the reins. A green colt who keeps throwing his head up and down or yawing it sideways is giving a pretty good sign that his rider is hanging on to the bit. If the rider continues to do this, he will have a horse with a very bad mouth and one that always tosses its head.

(For further lessons for the colt see TRAINING.)

Combination Horses

Combination horses are those shown both in harness and under saddle. The horse is brought into the ring in harness and shown as directed; then he is unhitched in the ring and put under saddle to be shown again as

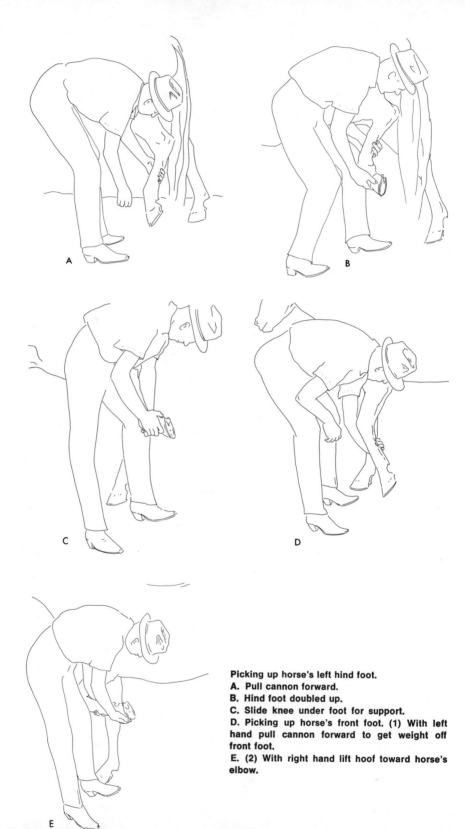

Picking up horse's left hind foot.
A. Pull cannon forward.
B. Hind foot doubled up.
C. Slide knee under foot for support.
D. Picking up horse's front foot. (1) With left hand pull cannon forward to get weight off front foot.
E. (2) With right hand lift hoof toward horse's elbow.

directed. Three-gaited combinations are usual events in horse shows all over the United States. Five-gaited combination classes are now a rarity. Winning animals are usually American Saddle Horses, though no horse-show classes, except a few breeding classes, are confined to American Saddle Horses.

Competitive Rides

Competitive trail riding and endurance riding are rapidly becoming two of the nation's most popular horse activities. While in both of these activities horses are ridden over distances, the two sports are quite different and should not be confused. The modern endurance ride is actually a controlled race against time over a given distance, usually 50 or 100 miles. The competitive ride is a much more sophisticated thing than the endurance ride. The distance of a competitive ride is usually between 25 and 40 miles, depending on the terrain (to be covered between 6½ and 7 hours' riding time). The novice division covers a shortened course of around 20 miles. The rides are judged by a team of at least two judges, one of whom must be a practicing veterinarian. The open division, for horses over five years of age, is divided into: junior division (riders age 10 to 17), light-weight division (rider and tack weighing between 155 and 190 pounds), and heavyweight division (rider and tack weighing over 190 pounds). A fourth division, always very popular, is the novice division. Over a shortened course, this is primarily for young horses (three to five years old) and for newcomers to the sport. It is often large enough to warrant dividing it into junior and senior classes.

The judging is based on each horse's starting the ride with a score of 100, evaluated as follows: soundness, 40%; condition, 40%; manners, 15%; way of going, 5%. While all of the judging is on the horse, the riders also compete for horsemanship awards and are judged on the care and handling of their mounts throughout the entire weekend.

The parent of modern competitive trail rides is the Vermont 100-Mile Ride. It is an annual affair at Woodstock, Vermont, with permanent head-quarters there and a permanent trail, which is covered in three days of 40 miles the first day, 40 the second, and 20 the third. The rules are virtually those of the North American Trail Ride Conference, a sample of which is given in the preceding paragraph.

Florida, Maryland, New Jersey, and Oklahoma now have 100-mile rides patterned after the Vermont affair. The North American Trail Ride Conference was incorporated in 1961. The organization has now spread over five states—Colorado, California, Arizona, Washington, and Utah—and will soon cover more. Rides are scheduled throughout the year. They may be either three-day or one-day rides, and awards consist of a schedule of points. Individual riders go from ride to ride, and at the end of the year national awards are given. Mounts are classified into two divisions: open and novice. The open division is subdivided into lightweight, heavyweight, and junior. The novice division is limited to riders 10 years of age or older who have never won a national championship or placed third or higher in the annual high scores in any division in any previous year. This division will ride over a shortened course and may be divided into junior and senior sections.

Horses over five years of age may compete in the novice division until they have accumulated 32 points. Thereafter they must enter other divisions. The 32-point limit does not apply to horses under five years of age. Horses less than five years old must compete in this division regardless of the previous experience of the rider. Horses under 36 months may not compete in any division.

The scoring of competitors is a complex matter. There are checkpoints along each ride at which horses are all examined and penalties are imposed according to the rules of the North American Trail Ride Conference. Complete information can be obtained from the North American Trail Ride Conference, Inc., 1955 Day Road, Gilroy, California 95020. The annual award ceremony is held at a convention of the group each November.

It is interesting to note that competitive riding does not center on any breed or breeds. Horses of any breed (or no breed) are welcome to compete in any of the rides of the North American Trail Ride Conference. So far, the winners of the annual award have been confined largely to a few breeds. Winners have been: in 1961 Little Joe, a grade Morgan; in 1962 Suds, a Morab (Morgan-Arabian cross); in 1963 Shamas, a registered Arabian; in 1964 a registered Missouri Fox Trotter by the name of Warrior's Merry Lady; in 1965 a registered Quarter Horse, Posse, and the same horse in 1966; in 1967 a registered Arabian, Rafftez; in 1968 a registered Quarter Horse, Dandy Bar V; in 1969 a registered Arabian, Shafarr; in 1970 a grade Morgan by the name of Dusty Thursday; a grade gelding, Casey, won in 1971.

Conditioning

"Conditioning," said a wise old horseman, "is just as important as the quality of the animal you start out with if you want to win a championship or a race." That remark should be memorized by all beginning horsemen. It should be taken to heart by anyone who thinks that the big stables are given an unfair advantage by most horse-show judges. Close and constant observation is necessary for successful conditioning. No two horses will do well on exactly the same amount or kind of feed. The rule of thumb may say 12 pounds of grain and 20 pounds of roughage daily, but some horses may develop laminitis (founder) on such a ration and for others it may not contain sufficient grain. The condition of the manure, the brightness of the eye, the luster of the coat, and the evidence of good spirits are the more obvious signs of the result of a good conditioning program. (*See* FEED and TONICS.)

Conestoga Horses

In 1629 a Dutchman by the name of Pieter Evertsen Hueft, a resident of New York, imported some horses from his native land. Like most of the horses of Holland at that time, they carried the blood of the Great Horse of Flanders, progenitor of the horses used by the knights in armor and of all important draft breeds. The progeny of the Hueft importations found favor among the farmers of Pennsylvania and were used in the teams that pulled the Conestoga wagons, vehicles used in transporting freight before railroads were invented.

Conformation

The term *conformation* denotes the shape and relative size of the various parts of a horse and the way these parts are put together. Each breed has its own idea of the way a horse should be shaped. Specific breeds may lay emphasis on the shape of one or more particular parts of the horse. One, for instance, may emphasize the need for a sloping shoulder and great heart girth; another, length of neck and carriage of tail (even if resulting from use of knife, tail set, ginger, etc.). However, most horsemen, regardless of the breed they espouse, will agree to the following generalities regarding conformation: round feet of ample size with convex soles and heels well off the ground; flat legs with good bone below the knee; flat, clean joints; short cannon bone; long, well-muscled forearms; clean hocks and well-muscled stifles; long sloping shoulders; short strong backs with powerful loins and long hips; great heart girth; well-set necks; clean throttles; smart ears, well set; big, intelligent eyes set wide apart midway between top of nostril and base of ear; finely chiseled heads with neat muzzles possessing nostrils that can expand prodigiously when need be.

Congestion of the Lungs

There is probably no animal whose lungs have greater demand placed on them than the horse. Only by tremendous development of the lungs has the species survived. However, this has its disadvantage, for the horse's great lungs are susceptible to many afflictions, most of which would come under the general heading *congestion* (inflammation, expansion of the capillaries, filling with fluid, etc.). Before the discovery of modern antibiotics, death from the various forms of influenza, distemper, strangles, etc., was frequent in sale barns, usually by way of pneumonia. The wise horseman

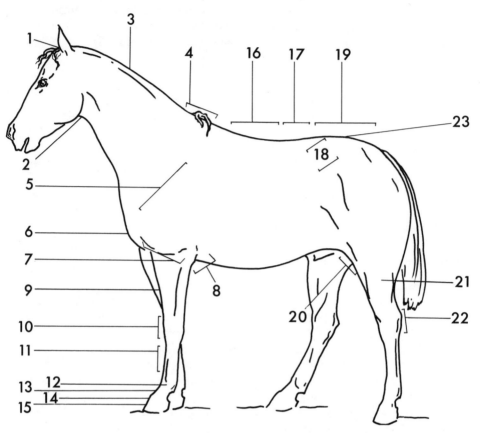

Anatomy of the horse. 1. Poll; 2. throat; 3. crest; 4. withers; 5. shoulders; 6. chest; 7. arm; 8. elbow; 9. forearm; 10. knee; 11. cannon; 12. fetlock joint; 13. pastern; 14. coronet; 15. hoof; 16. back; 17. loin; 18. point of hip; 19. hips; 20. stifle; 21. gaskin; 22. hock; 23. croup.

today will elicit the aid of a veterinarian the moment any symptom of a respiratory ailment occurs in his horse.

Constipation

"The eye of the master fatteneth his cattle." Not the least important function of that eye is to keep constant tab on the horse's droppings. Death in old horses frequently occurs from intestinal obstruction. When the manure of any horse, especially an old one, is dropped in the form of hard tight balls which cannot be easily disintegrated by pressure from a boot toe, his daily ration of red bran should be increased and perhaps his grain should be decreased. Following the advice of leading veterinarians, the writer has for years been scrupulously careful to see that every horse in his stable or corral gets a two-pound coffee-canful of red bran twice a day. There are horsemen who prefer to use a bran mash (*see* COLDS) once or twice a week rather than the dry bran fed daily. The writer has found that with some horses the regularity of his method serves to prevent colic and periodic diarrhea.

Of course, if a horse fails to drop manure between feedings, a veterinarian should be called.

Contracted Heels

Contracted heels are the curse of horses kept shod in hot, dry climates. As the heels grow closer together, the bars of the hoof, instead of sloping outward toward the ground, tend to be straight up and down. The frog atrophies, sometimes to one-fourth its normal width at the heel. Contracted heels cause a horse as much pain as ingrown toenails and excruciatingly tight shoes cause a human. There are various remedies, most of which entail weakening the wall of the heel and putting pressure on whatever frog the horse may have left, well known to all good farriers. One remedy is to use a stout spring which tends to press the walls of the heels outward. This spring has been known to work, but frequently it does more harm than good. Whatever the method of cure, the first thing to do with contracted heels is to increase their moisture content. Clean mud or water in which the horse stands while eating and/or drinking may help some.

Prevention of contracted heels should be a very important part of management in any stable, especially those in hot, dry climates. Proper shoeing is essential, with shoes which are wide enough at the heel and are perfectly flat or sloped ever so slightly at their hind extremities so that the wall of the foot at the heel will not be forced inward at each impact with the ground. Any paring away of the frog by the horseshoer invites contraction of the heels, as does shoeing a horse continually with long heels which prevent frog pressure. To preserve the natural moisture content of the hoof, daily painting of the entire foot, sole, frog, heels, wall, and coronet, with the following mixture, well shaken or stirred before each application, is helpful: six parts of fish oil (cod-liver or similar oil available in quantity at poultry supply stores), one part of Creoline, one part of pine tar, and two parts of glycerin.

The experienced horseman never buys a horse with badly contracted heels, hoping that he can cure the malady and have a sound horse. Heels that are badly contracted over any period of time cause permanent damage to the interior bony structure of the feet. (*See* COFFIN BONE.)

Controlling the Horse. *See also* TRAINING and VICES

The prerequisite for any control of a horse not involving constant violence (and often final failure) is communication with the horse, which means the rider's understanding and anticipating the horse's actions and his ability to let the horse understand what he, the rider, wants. With horses who have been mishandled, the development of such communication may be very time-consuming.

If the problem of control is largely that of making the horse reduce speed, any one of the multitude of pain-producing bits, hackamores, figure eights, draw reins, or gags may be employed. In some instances on the polo field one can see such devices used with some effectiveness. However, they sometimes merely add fuel to flame.

The best way to cure a horse of refusing to stop is to lighten his mouth by the use of good hands and in most instances by bits that have been made milder by having the mouthpiece covered with leather or rubber and the curb strap or chain padded. In some instances bad adjustment of the bit (*see* BITS) may be the initial cause, easily corrected by proper adjustment.

The beginning rider on the knowledgeable old-school horse usually has control problems because he has not learned to anticipate the horse or to communicate with him, and because the old fellow is wise in methods of minimizing effort. Practice in riding in formation and in making his horse leave a group or go past it and return to it continuing rearward beyond it without stopping may help the tyro cure himself of making every one of his movements, using each aid, just a split second too late.

Coolers and Cooling

A light woolen blanket made of New Zealand or Australian or other long-staple wool, large enough to reach from a horse's ears to his tail and to come nearly to the ground on either side when the horse is covered, is known as a *cooler*. The nature of the wool is such that the fibers of the blanket act like tiny wicks and pull the sweat from the horse's coat to deposit it on the outside of the blanket in a form that resembles dew. It is wise to put a cooler on a horse the moment he is dismounted after having done work strenuous enough to make him sweat profusely. Tack can be removed from under the cooler, and the horse can be kept moving slowly until his circulation begins to come back to normal.

When an extremely hot horse comes out of the ri..g or off the track, not more than a few seconds should be spent in scraping the excess sweat from his body with scrapers. A cooler should then be thrown over him, and he should be walked slowly. If help is plentiful, he can be rubbed with linen rub rags over loins and shoulders, the groom reaching up under the cooler. As soon as his respiration and heartbeat approach normal, he may be cross-tied and rubbed with more dry linen or Turkish towels. He may be allowed a few swallows of water, and his nose and head may be sponged with clear warm water. After the vigorous rubbing and sponging of nostrils and head, he may be walked by rider, groom, or mechanical walker until respiration and pulse are completely normal. A little water should be given him at intervals until his thirst is entirely quenched.

There are horsemen who advocate bathing the feet and legs of a hot horse with cold water, but most veterinarians can relate instances in which founder has been caused by such sudden change of temperature of the feet. Any water applied to feet and lower legs during cooling out should be tepid. Failure to cool a horse out properly may result in laminitis (founder), a condition in which inflammation of the feet (expansion and gorging of the capillaries) results in separation of the layers of horn of the feet and in the dropping of the sole (see LAMENESS). There are remedies, but a foundered horse seldom becomes completely useful after foundering.

Coon-Footed

The term *coon-footed* signifies that a horse has hind legs that suggest those of a raccoon. His pasterns are long and very sloping. Sometimes the pastern joint is as close to the ground as the coronet (top of the hoof). This is generally considered a great weakness in a horse. However, many a horse slightly coon-footed has lived a long and serviceable life.

Copperbottom

1. The Copperbottoms were a strain of horse highly esteemed in the Southwest before the American Quarter Horse Registry was established. They were usually sorrel and had many of the characteristics now highly prized by Quarter Horse breeders.

2. Copperbottom is the name of one or more of the early or foundation sires in at least two American breeds of horses, the American Saddle Horse and the Quarter Horse. Because of the custom in an early day of giving the colt the name of an illustrious sire, authenticating the original bearer of a popular name of a horse is difficult. It is possible to document the statement that a horse known as Copperbottom was imported into Kentucky

from Canada about 1812. He had all the qualities of gait, conformation, and temperament then prized in Kentucky horses, and he is considered one of the founding sires of the American Saddle Horse.

Corinthian

A Corinthian class in a horse show is one in which riders and horses are wearing proper hunting appointments (*see* APPOINTMENTS).

Corn

Corn is an excellent feed for horses if used judiciously. There is an old notion that corn is "more heating" than oats. This idea has been exploded by experimentation with draft animals on university farms in the heat of summer. Corn is not quite as foolproof a feed as whole oats; since the latter feed has considerable bulk in the hull, a horse can eat a great deal more of it by bulk than he can of corn without suffering from laminitis (also called founder), which is an almost certain result of overfeeding on grain (overfeeding in one large amount or in smaller amounts over time). For use of corn in a horse's ration, *see* FEED.

Coronet

The coronet is the top of a horse's hoof, the part just below the hairline. It is the growing part of the hoof and corresponds to the light-colored crescent on a human fingernail. Unless he has great good luck and the immediate attention of a very competent veterinarian, any horse sustaining an injury to his coronet will have a permanently injured hoof.

Coughs

A horse, like a person, may cough from any one of an almost infinite number of causes. However, because of the great development of a horse's respiratory tract, a wise horseman always pricks up his ears when he hears a horse cough. If the horse is eating dusty hay at the time, the wise horseman will sprinkle the hay lightly. If the horse coughs when the wind rises and the horse is in a dusty corral, the wise horseman will sprinkle the corral. Persistent coughing is a cause for calling a veterinarian, and if the coughing is accompanied by a nasal discharge and a temperature above 102 degrees, the call should be a hurry-up one.

Courtesy

Courtesy on horseback does not differ greatly from courtesy anyplace else. Like sanitation, courtesy is an attitude of mind. Probably the golden rule will cover normal aspects of courtesy on horseback. Here are some rules that might well be borne in mind when riding on a trail:

1. Don't allow your horse to do anything that will disturb or interfere with others.

2. When you are on a tricky part of the trail, don't stop and make others stand in a difficult position; if you want to hesitate, drop out to one side and let others pass.

3. Keep at least one horse's length between you and the horse ahead. If the man behind you rides too close, don't criticize him; just drop out and choose another part of the line to ride in.

4. If you are the last man through a gate, be sure it is left the way the first rider found it, either open or closed.

5. Never tie your horse where there is any chance that the horse nearest him may reach him with its heels.

6. Never hold on to a branch you pass under; it may swing back and hit the next rider.

7. Never play with your rope or indulge in horseplay on the trail.

8. Never be among the idiots who gallop or trot the last quarter-mile or so into camp—there is at least one on every trail ride.

One rather controversial matter of courtesy has to do with whether a group riding across field or desert or on the bridle path or trail should accommodate itself to the slowest rider in the group. Of course, no reasonably civilized riders will go dashing off on a mad gallop and leave behind one or two more sensible riders. However, the controversy arises in relation to the walk. Many horses in rental strings and many horses owned by amateurs cannot walk more than two miles an hour. If such horses are ridden in a group with riders who have well-trained animals able to do that best of all gaits, a good brisk walk close to or more than four miles an hour, one of two things will have to happen. Either the two-mile-an-hour walkers will have to jog, or the riders of horses with good walks will have to hold their horses back to the speed of the slow walkers. It seems a pity to ruin the walk of a good horse in order to keep pace with that of a poor one. Perhaps courtesy should be exercised by the rider of the two-mile walker and he should allow his horse to jog and keep up with the good walkers.

Few things in this world are more tiresome than riding a two-mile-an-hour walk for any length of time. There is no follow-through in the movement of a two-mile-an-hour walker. Each foot seems to hit the ground with a thud. Before long, the knees of the rider begin to ache. On the other hand, a horse with a good, brisk flat-footed walk will carry his rider for hours on end without tiring either the rider or the horse. If the owner of a horse with a good walk wants to ride with the person whose horse cannot walk, and courtesy, he feels, demands that he slow his horse down to the walk of the poorer horse, he will be wise to leave his own horse in the stable and rent a horse who will walk with his friend's mount.

A real working cowboy outfit. Seasoned, experienced cowhands on a roundup at the 88 Ranch in the Superstition Mountains, Arizona. The white mule is representing the Craig Ranch, which used mules on its extremely rough terrain.

Covert (cover)

A covert is a bit of brush or woods in which hounds search for fox or scent of fox.

Cowboy

Strictly speaking, a cowboy is a hired hand on a cattle ranch. Today the term is very loosely used, and often it is used facetiously to designate anybody who dons Western gear and mounts a horse. Sometimes he doesn't even have to mount a horse. The work of the cowboy before the advent of barbed wire, pickup trucks, and squeeze chutes is well explained in *The Cowboy at Work,* by Fay E. Ward.

Cow-Hocked

When a horse habitually stands or travels with his hocks closer together than his stifles and his pasterns, he is said to be *cow-hocked.*

Cow Pony

Cow pony is a term no longer often heard in the West, but it was once used to denote any horse suitable for working cattle on a ranch.

Cremellos (also Creamalos)

Cremellos were white horses with a faint yellow tinge to their coats, white manes and tails, and, frequently, light-colored eyes. There were two or three serious breeders of these animals before the day of the Palomino.

Crest

The crest is the top of a horse's neck.

Cribbing

Cribbing or wind sucking greatly diminishes the monetary value of a horse. A cribber or wind sucker is considered unsound. Such a horse hooks his front upper teeth over any available object, frequently a post or stump (hence, the name stump sucker in some regions), pulls backward, distending the tissues of his throttle, makes a grunting noise, and sucks air into his stomach. Horses that develop this vice lose weight, becoming thinner and thinner, no matter how well they are fed.

It is possible to control the vice by the use of a cribbing strap. The simplest form of cribbing strap is a piece of leather about two inches wide that goes around the horse's neck just behind his head. There are many "improvements" on this. Some have pads where the strap touches the windpipe; others are wider at that point than elsewhere; still others, made of two layers of stitched leather, have a sort of groove, fitting around the windpipe. Any of these will work fairly well, and they do not seem to interfere with the horse's drinking or eating; they merely prevent the distention of his throttle. The horse who needs to wear a cribbing strap is not worth as much money as he would be if he were free of the vice. (*See also* VICES.)

Cribbing straps.

Cricket

A cricket is a copper roller, rollers, or other loose piece of copper in the port of a curb or spade bit.

Criollo

The word is *Criollo* in the Spanish-speaking countries of this hemisphere, and *Crioulo* in those countries of this hemisphere in which Portuguese is spoken.

While in the northern part of our hemisphere the blood of the horses brought to this continent by the conquistadores was considerably diluted by that of European horses brought west by pioneers—some searching for gold, some for wealth in cattle breeding—in the southern half of our hemisphere the blood of the Spanish horses was not so diluted. Change also came about through careless breeding or through natural selection, but except in the few breeding establishments owned by members of the tiny wealthy minority who love horse racing and polo, the horses of Central and South America still carry almost purely the bloood of the Spanish horses of the Conquest.

The term *Criollo* (or *Crioulo*) is generally used to include all South American strains carrying the original Spanish blood. Selection and careful breeding practices in some parts of the continent, however, have caused considerable differentiation of types. For example, the Costeño and the Paso Fino of Peru are Criollos, but their easy gaits (done naturally from the time of foaling), modest coloring, and smooth conformation are in sharp contrast to the Criollos of Argentina. The Argentine horses are of many and bizarre colors. They are somewhat heavier of bone than the Andalusian and Barbs from which their blood is said to stem. Their Roman noses and small eyes (a very frequent feature) do not appeal to North American taste, but they are extremely sturdy, useful animals. Not until 1920 was any attempt made to breed these horses in anything that might be called a scientific manner. In that year a college professor in Buenos Aires selected and bred the foundation stock of modern Criollos in his country. He collected 2,000 of the most typical Criollos he could find and from them selected 15 mares and a few stallions to serve as the foundation stock for breeding.

In 1925 a Swiss friend of the professor selected two Criollos, 18 and 19 years old, to use as mount and packhorse to ride from Buenos Aires to Washington, D.C. That ride was one of the toughest ever made. It was 13,350 miles long and led over some of the highest mountains and broadest rivers in the world. It went through swamps at sea level and below. Some of it was across deserts without water. When these horses arrived in Washington, they aroused some attention for the trip made by their rider, Mr. A. F. Tschiffely. Several horsemen evinced interest in the breed from which Gato and Mancho, Mr. Tschiffely's horses, came. However, the breed failed to catch on in this country because it was so different from anything we had learned to revere as fine horseflesh. Mancho and Gato, the valiant Criollos that made the trip from Buenos Aires to Washington, were returned to their native land by ship, and they lived at ease on the professor's ranch until they were both more than 30 years old.

Critter

Critter, a corruption of *creature,* is sometimes heard in rural Western conversation. It denotes a member of the equine or bovine species.

Crop

A crop is a stick of wood, hawthorn, leather-covered rawhide, or what not, having a prong of a deer's antler attached at one end, ostensibly for use in pulling a gate open or shut, and a flat loop of leather at the other to which a long lash may be fastened.

Crop-eared

A bovine or equine that has had the tips of the ears or the tip of one ear cut off is called "crop-eared." Sometimes this is part of the marking for ownership in the range country. It is said that farther east the ears of horses are sometimes trimmed if they appear too large, and hence, a horse with small ears is sometimes referred to as crop-eared.

Croup

The croup is the highest point of the hindquarters of a horse.

Crownpiece

The crownpiece of a bridle is the part that goes over the head just behind the ears.

Crupper

A crupper is a padded loop at the rear end of the back strap of a harness, through which the horse's tail passes.

Cryptorchid

A cryptorchid is a male equine whose testicles have failed to descend into the scrotum. (If only one testicle is involved, he is called a monorchid.) The testicles may be retained in the inguinal canal or in the abdomen. Such retention keeps the temperature of the testicles too high for the formation of spermatozoa. Therefore, the cryptorchid cannot reproduce, though the monorchid can. Monorchids should not be bred, however, because the condition is thought to be hereditary. Cryptorchids are usually nervous and irritable and possessed of an abnormal libido.

Testosterone has been successfully used by veterinarians for correction of some cases of retained testes. More frequently, the best solution to the problem is surgical removal of the testes.

The term *ridgling* (corrupted occasionally into *original*) is sometimes used for *cryptorchid*.

Cubbing

Several weeks before regular hunting season opens, hounds are taken out so that young ones may learn what to do, and so that young foxes may learn to run rather than to hide and be routed out. These "hunts" do not usually start before daylight as is the custom with other hunts, and the apparel of the riders is very informal. Young riders and horses are ordinarily welcome at cubbing time if they do not interfere with the serious business of educating hounds and foxes.

Cuff

Cuff is the slang word for *curry* or *groom*.

Curb

A curb is an enlargement at the back of a horse's hock. It usually makes him lame and always reduces his value to whatever is the going rate at the canneries.

Curb Bit

Any bit that employs the mechanical principle of the lever and fulcrum is called a curb bit.

Curb Chain. *See* BITS, *Fitting the Bit*

Curby Hocks

A curby hock is a hock on which a curb exists (*see* CURB).

Currycomb

Currycombs are tools for grooming horses. The very old-fashioned currycombs were made of metal and had wooden handles. The metal part had teeth. These tools were useful principally in removing mud and sweat from long-haired draft horses. The first improvement, since the old-time currycombs were pretty rough on a horse with a thin coat, was to make them ovoid and put a canvas or leather strap on them to go over the back of the

Original rubber currycomb.   **Modern "rubber" currycomb (peg tooth).**

hand. The new currycombs had no teeth but were composed of little corrugated metal ovals which scraped off sweat and mud. The great improvement came when rubber replicas of those currycombs were manufactured. Today an up-to-date currycomb has little pegs for teeth; it is made of plastic; and the strap that goes over the back of the hand is adjustable.

Cutting. *See also* NATIONAL CUTTING HORSE ASSOCIATION

Cutting is the name for the performance of a cutting horse. A cutting horse has to do three things: (1) separate an animal from a herd, (2) take it to a designated place, and (3) keep it from going back where it came from.

No use of horses for pleasure is increasing faster than is the sport of cutting cattle. Part-time ranchers, professional men (and women), young and old, are active in the sport. While everyone likes to be a winner, the desperate struggle to be a show-ring champion that infects so many areas of horse activity has not yet deadened the fun of the amateurs in the cutting arena. Of course, second-rate trainers abound to cater to owners who bring in a horse with the hope that in a few months (or even weeks!) the trainer will transform him into a champion cutting horse.

With short iron pipes for beating heads into low carriage, sawed-off ice picks for gouging shoulders, tacks in boot toes for pricking elbows, and other gimmicks, the struggling trainer will produce in a short time an animal who will appear to the inexperienced and undiscerning eye to be performing like a cutting horse. The experienced eye immediately sees the signs of such training. The horse who has been punished on the bit will not drive freely after a cow. If he has been jabbed and gouged for fancy side movements, he will be choppy and afraid to turn and move out when he should. Such a horse may display a lot of agile footwork that will enthrall some spectators, but the knowing will detect his hesitation, his choppy movement, and his failure to get away from a cow and work her when the moment calls for such action.

Cutting horses, like opera stars and prizefighters, must be born for their jobs; the great ones are not born often. If a young horse has that rare natural bent for cutting, a good trainer can help him a great deal.

Cutting Horse. *See* CUTTING

Daisy Cutter (Daisy Clipper)

Daisy cutter is a disparaging term for a horse displaying a kind of action commonly seen at the trot among Thoroughbreds and Arabians. It is long and low in comparison with the trotting action of other breeds.

Dally

To dally means to take a turn around the saddle horn with a lariat to hold a roped animal. Some ropers tie the rope "hard and fast" to the saddle horn; others carry the rope in their hand until an animal is roped, then take up the slack and "take a dally round the horn."

The word comes from the Spanish *dar la vuelta,* meaning to give a twist. It was corrupted into *dally welty* and *dolly welty,* then shortened to *dally.*

Dam

A dam is a mother of a horse. The term *second dam* is frequently used to designate the maternal grandmother.

Dandy Brush. *See* BRUSHES

Darley Arabian

The Darley Arabian is one of the three most famous progenitors of the Thoroughbred horse. The other two are the Byerly Turk and the Godolphin Barb (*see* THOROUGHBRED).

Dead Heat

A dead heat occurs when two or more race horses cross the finishing line at exactly the same time. Modern photography has greatly diminished the number of dead heats proclaimed from the judges' box.

Dealers

Horse dealers, like merchants in any other field, vary. Some are men of impeccable honor and honesty who zealously guard a reputation beyond reproach. Others, unfortunately, are superb masters of chicanery and devious conduct. If the new horseman can find a dealer of the former variety, he will do well to place himself in that dealer's hands, telling him exactly how much money he can afford to pay for a horse and just what he wants to use the horse for. He may get some valuable advice from the dealer. Frequently, the beginning horseman insists that he wants a young horse of such and such description. The wise dealer will diplomatically steer him onto a wiser and older horse and may also see that the kind of horse the inexperienced horseman describes will not do what the horseman wants to do with it.

Denmark

Denmark F.S. is designated as the foundation sire of the American Saddle Horse. There is probably not an American Saddle Horse alive today who does not trace his ancestry many times to Denmark F.S. Denmark was a Thoroughbred four-mile race horse who lived in the middle of the nineteenth century. He probably receives more credit for the breed he is said to have founded than he deserves, for every great horse who comes from him traces its ancestry through one son, Gaines Denmark, who was out of an easy-gaited mare of a strain already well developed in this country before the first Thoroughbred was imported. To that mare the breed owes as much as or more than it does to Denmark F.S.

Derby

The Derby was established at Epsom Downs in England by the Earl of Derby in 1780. It was so famous that later the word *derby* came to be used to indicate any important race. The most important one in this country is the Kentucky Derby, which is run annually at Churchill Downs just outside Louisville. Englishmen pronounce the word as if it were spelled d-a-r-b-y. Americans say it the way the spelling indicates.

Diagonals

When a rider posts to a trot, he rises as one diagonal pair of a horse's feet strikes the ground and sits down in the saddle as the other diagonal pair hits the ground. If he rises as the left fore and right hind hit the ground he is said to be posting on the right diagonal, for he is rising as the right forefoot comes up. If he rises as the right fore and left hind hit the ground, he is said to be posting on the left diagonal, for he is rising as the left forefoot rises. When showing in the ring, rise with the outside forefoot. I.e., going counterclockwise, post on right diagonal; clockwise of the ring, use left diagonal.

Direction (changes of)

The horse worked exclusively or almost exclusively in a ring or arena should have the direction of his travels around the ring or arena changed rather frequently so that he will go one way as well as the other and will take one lead as readily as the other. When a horse is shown, directional changes are called for by the judge. If the class is an equitation class (one in which the rider only is judged), the rider may demonstrate his ability to reverse by turning the horse toward the rail as well as toward the center. In other classes it is customary to make the change of direction by turning the horse toward the center of the ring. (*See also* LEADING.)

Direct Rein. *See* REINS, *Use of*

Dishing

When a horse travels, each foot should move forward and backward in one perpendicular plane, moving neither outward nor inward from that plane as the foot passes forward and back. Any deviation from this so-called straight action is indicated by any one of three terms: *dishing, paddling,* and *winging.* There is not complete uniformity in the way these terms are used. *Dishing,* according to one authority, applies only to the action of the hind feet—when the hocks are thrown in and the hind feet thrown out. An equally respectable authority applies it to action in which any foot or feet are thrown outward as the horse travels. Other authorities use the term *dishing* to indicate that a horse turns his foot *inward,* even so much as to hit the other foot or leg as it passes forward and back. There is confusion over the other two terms also, though *paddling* almost always denotes throwing the feet outward, a fault which is considered a virtue by Paso (*see* PASO FINO) breeders because, they claim, it aids quick turning on the forehand, so imperative in bullfighting, for which Pasos are used in some places.

Dismounting

There are several respectable ways to dismount from a horse. Here is the currently fashionable one: The rider puts the reins in his left hand, which also grasps the mane, or the front of the saddle if the horse has no mane; he places his right hand palm downward on the pommel or horn of the saddle; and he leans forward putting his weight almost entirely on his hands. He then swings the right leg across the horse's rump just high enough to miss the croup. When he has turned so he is facing the horse's croup, he removes his left foot from the stirrup (of course, putting all his weight on his hands at this moment) and descends to terra firma. There has always been considerable argument about which way the rider should be facing when he finally lands with both feet on the ground. There are those who claim he should be facing the same direction as the horse, because if the horse moves, the rider should be in a position to go with him (*see* illustration on page 146 and RIDING).

Distance

One use of the word *distance* is to designate the length of the space on the trail between one horse's nose and the tail of the horse immediately ahead

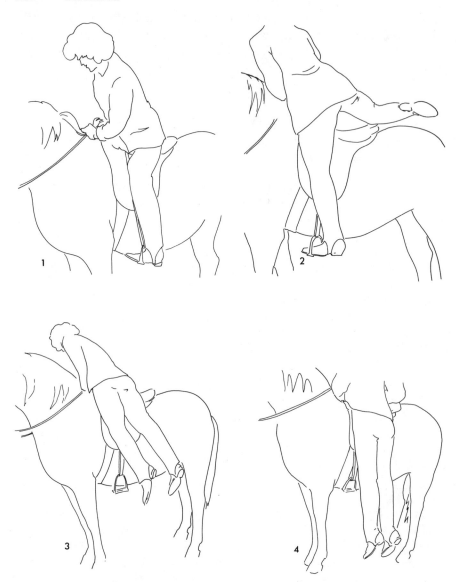

Prepare to dismount.
1. With reins in left hand, which also grasps mane (or front of saddle if horse has no mane), and palm of right hand downward on pommel or horn of saddle, put weight on hands and left stirrup.
2. Swing right leg across rear of horse; rider may either step down with right leg or slide down, depending upon his size.
3. To slide down, put weight on both hands and take left foot out of stirrup.
4. Both feet reach ground at same time.

of him. Traditionally, that distance was supposed to be the length of a horse, and any less distance than that was considered unsafe. Today, however, in much formation riding, four feet is considered a safe distance. Common sense dictates that in the hunting field or on a trail with steep ascents and descents a much greater distance must be kept, for in the event that a horse refuses a jump or falls at a jump when riders are galloping fairly fast, obviously the riders must be farther than a horse's length apart if an accident is to be prevented. In rough, mountainous country, horses must keep well apart because a horse descending a steep grade may fall, or he may run into an obstacle that causes him to stop abruptly, or he may pick up a cholla which will cause him to buck, rear, or whirl, creating great confusion in a line of riders if ample distance is not kept.

Distemper. *See also* STRANGLES

Distemper (strangles) is endemic in many sale barns and in some show stables. It is epidemic in cold weather more frequently than in summer, though a horse may run into it on the show circuit at any season of the year.

Disunited

Disunited is a term used to indicate a gallop or canter in which a pair of feet on the same side, instead of the diagonal pair, strike the ground simultaneously. Such horrible performance is sometimes called galloping with one lead in front and another behind (*see* RIDING).

Dock

The bone in a horse's tail, which is made up of the end vertebrae of the spine, is called the dock.

Docking

Docking is the cutting of a horse's dock (*see* DOCK) some distance from the end. The practice of docking is becoming quite rare in this country.

Dog

Dog is a slang term for a sluggish, rather worthless horse, a "plug."

Dog Carts. *See* BREAKING CART

Door in a Stable

A stable door should be wide enough to allow a horse to pass through easily with no danger of bumping his hips. It is also very important that each door be equipped with some device by which it can be fastened open. Many a fine horse has had to be destroyed because he knocked a hip down as a result of wind blowing a door top against him as he was entering his stall. If a horse is entering his stall and the door bangs against him, he will lunge forward violently. Every horse should be trained to enter and leave a stall quietly while his handler precedes him or while his handler stands to one side and gives the animal enough slack to enter or to leave the stall. Training for this latter method is helpful when the time comes to teach the horse to enter a trailer.

Doping

The term *doping* is used for the practice of giving a horse medicine either orally or by injection, or any other means for that matter, to produce a certain kind of performance. Race horses have been doped almost as often to make them lose races as to make them win them. However, doping has been pretty well eliminated from the racetrack through the use of the saliva test. (A sample of a horse's saliva is tested in a laboratory to ascertain whether he has been given any kind of medication prior to a race. If he has been so medicated, his owner, stable, and trainer are punished by the racing authorities.) There is today some doping of show horses. Tranquilizers are given some show horses to calm them down, especially in equitation classes. But tranquilizers for this purpose have their limitation because a tranquilizer in any considerable dosage causes the penis of a gelding or a stallion to drop down and be quite obvious.

Double Back

The term *double back* is used sometimes in the eastern United States to indicate a horse whose loin muscles rise above his backbone.

Double Oxer

Double oxer is a hunting term for all jumps that are over obstacles having a railing or fence on either side. For instance, a hedge protected on either side by a rail could be called a double oxer. In England some very impressive jumps come under this heading. A hedge having a ditch and a low rail on either side is called a double oxer. If the hedge is so high that the horse cannot see the ditch on the far side, this is indeed a formidable obstacle.

The term *oxer* comes from *ox fence,* which meant a hedge about three feet high protected on one side by a fence.

Drag

1. *Drag* is a slang term for a coach kept for private use as distinct from a stagecoach.

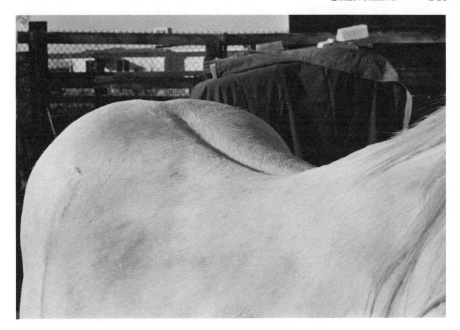

Loin muscle development sometimes called double back.

2. In hunting parlance, *drag* or *drag hunt* indicates a hunt in which the hounds follow a scent made by some artificial means.

Drain

Any culvert or pipe large enough to be refuge for a fox is called a *drain* by hunting folk, especially if they are British.

Draw Rein. *See also* MARTINGALE, *German*

A draw rein is a rein fastened to the saddle rigging, running freely through a snaffle bit ring and back to the rider's hand.

Drenching

Back in the days of the old "hoss doctor," before the advent of our great schools of veterinary medicine, drenching a horse was a common practice; nobody knows how many poor animals died of foreign-body pneumonia because of this. Of course, some skilled people could drench a horse without killing him. Luck was now and then on the side of others. The writer of these lines, by the grace of God and great good fortune, drenched horses with no fatality. But he is a timid soul and probably always erred on the side of losing the medicine rather than using too much force to get it down the horse.

While wine bottles were the commonest utensils for drenching, special drenching bottles were at one time manufactured. They were shaped like wine bottles and were covered with leather so that they would not easily slip out of one's hand. One inserted the drenching bottle's long neck into the horse's mouth just ahead of his molars, pointed it toward the rear of his mouth, raised his head, and hoped that he swallowed the medicine. If any of it passed into his lungs, he was sure to develop a case of foreign-body pneumonia.

An eminent veterinarian remarked recently, "I hate like blazes to be called to the racetrack for a case of colic, for usually if I ask, 'Has the animal been given any medicine?' someone says, 'Well, we drenched him with such and such.' Then when I put my stethoscope to the animal I hear the expected rattle indicating pneumonia."

Racetracks seem to harbor addicts of the drenching bottle more than training stables; however, the wise horseman will make sure that no trainer to whom he entrusts his horse will ever use a drenching bottle on it.

Dress. *See also* APPOINTMENTS

In addition to the familiar meaning, the word *dress* had for many years a special meaning for horsemen; and it is employed in this meaning in all early writing on horsemanship. The meaning is simply "to train." From that use of the word comes *dressage,* which in strictest usage means "training" (*see* DRESSAGE).

Dressage. *See also* REINS, *Use of;* SCHOOLING; TWO-TRACK; SHOULDER-IN; PIVOT, etc.; and COLTS

Dressage is included in a group of phrases glibly used but having virtually no meaning because they are used in such a loose fashion. Foremost among these perhaps, besides *dressage,* are the terms *pleasure riding, equitation,* and *schooling.*

There is precious little riding done today for any reason other than that it gives pleasure to the rider. Perhaps we might except those who ride to keep up with the Joneses. There certainly is no practical use for the hunter today. We have no area so badly infested with foxes that men have to get on horses and run them down. Even the cutting horse has lost his use. What with chutes and other modern conveniences, any good cow pony can do whatever cutting is necessary on a ranch these days. The best practical cutting job this writer ever saw was done by a pony bought from the Pima Indians for $7. The modern cutting horse, expensive as he is, is certainly ridden for pleasure. However, as that dean of American horsemanship Captain Vladimir S. Littauer so aptly puts it, the phrase "riding for pleasure" is usually a genteel substitute for the admission "I am not interested in riding well." The term *equitation,* which according to most

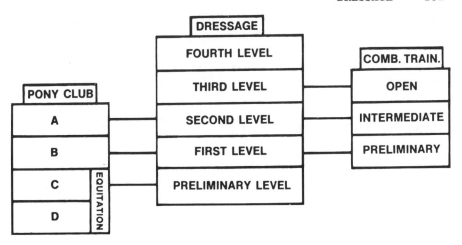

Levels of tests below the Fédération Équestre International Prix St. Georges established by the American Horse Shows Association, the United States Combined Training Association, and the United States Pony Club. Horses may not be entered in classes differing by more than one level at any one show (i.e., horses may enter levels 1 and 2, 2 and 3, 3 and 4, Prix St. Georges and F.E.I. Intermediate, Intermediate and Grand Prix, but may not enter levels 1 through 3, etc.).

dictionaries covers all kinds of horsemanship, is usually used in this country to indicate intermediate or elementary horsemanship. The term *schooling* is used to indicate everything from the training of jumpers or five-gaited horses to what is done in many Western training establishments, including the beating of a horse over the head with an iron pipe to "teach" him to keep his head low.

The term *dressage* is as carelessly and confusingly used as those just mentioned. It comes from a French verb meaning "to train," and when a Frenchman uses it to tell you what he has been doing with his hunter, he means that he has been schooling it over obstacles. The first time I put a horse in a crosstie and place my hand on his hip to make him move his quarters to one side, I can use the word *dressage* perfectly correctly to indicate what I am doing. However, in this country we have at the moment what might be called a dressage explosion. There is such a rapid increase of interest in what Captain Littauer calls "a game people play with horses and call dressage" that the word is beginning to take on a rather new and fairly definite meaning. We now talk about levels of dressage. At the lowest level, a rider simply comes into a ring from one end and halts at the center area of the arena. That is, he makes his horse stand perfectly still without bobbing his head for several seconds. On this same level of dressage there are various other movements a rider must execute; for instance, he must demonstrate his ability to change his line of progress from, let us say, east to south by traversing a 30-foot arc, keeping front and hind feet on the same line of progress. This means that he rides "both ends of his horse" and cannot allow his horse to swing his quarters away from the line of progress or to yaw his head from one side to the other. If the emphasis upon this kind of "dressage" continues to grow, we will have a much better quality of riding and certainly our horses will suffer much less than they do now.

The current "game of dressage" includes levels up to what is called the Grand Prix and Olympic Dressage. These highest levels smack of the methods of the Spanish Riding School of Vienna and the French system of Saumur. There are almost as many and as violently conflicting "schools" of dressage as there are of psychology today. One school with a rather Teutonic scent hangs on to the horse's mouth and insists on complete rigidity of the rider's anatomy from a point between the shoulder blades to the horse's mouth. Then there is the Tellington School in California which rides with light hands and flexible wrists. Fortunately no proponent of dressage in this country shows any interest in tying a horse between pillars and whipping him to get desired performance (a custom of the old riding schools). Practice in any of the forms of dressage (except those advocating stiff wrists and heavy hands) will improve the skill of any horseman. It will certainly teach him to ride the entire horse, not just the front end.

Of course, the dressage horse is highly specialized and quite limited in ability, though he may be able to jump, in addition to his dressage performance. A horse trained by an advocate of dressage, if ridden in any area where the Saddle Horse is popular, will cause amusement, for the natives will say, "He cain't saddle none," meaning that the horse is incapable of doing a gait deemed suitable for a riding horse. However, it seems reasonable to assume that the practices of many leading Saddle Horse and Walking Horse stables are causing some horsemen to change their allegiance to the dressage horse (see *Life*, October 3, 1969).

Detailed information about dressage is available in two books very understandably and charmingly written: *Dressage*, by Henry Wynmalen, and *Common Sense Horsemanship*, by Captain Vladimir S. Littauer. Another more recent and highly technical and comprehensive book is *Effective Horsemanship*, by Noel Jackson. Some devotees of dressage insist that the finest work on the subject done to date is *The Complete Training of Horse and Rider*, by Podhajsky.

Driving

After the automobile assumed its important place in American life, the use of a horse in harness declined until by the 1930s practically no use was made of a horse in harness except in the show-ring. During the past two decades, however, driving has become more and more popular. In California there are groups of people, some of them organized, who are enthusiastic about driving. Many of them are enthusiastic about horse-drawn vehicles of long ago, and they either search out those that are left over from a bygone age or make replicas of them. The activities of these groups have been written about in *Western Horsemen* and *Horse Lover* in recent years.

Arabian breeders are also promoting the use of the horse in harness. At Arabian shows, classes called informal driving are becoming more and more popular, and in Arizona and California some use is made of the Arabian in harness for what might be termed pleasure purposes, though it is doubtful that many young men wash their buggies and curry up their horses on Saturday night in anticipation of Sunday sparking as was the custom long ago. The Morgan horse, once so widely esteemed in this country as a driving animal, is being used more and more in harness; in his native state of Vermont he is seen with increasing frequency as a harness horse on country roads.

Proper use in harness never injured any horse, and many trainers drive horses at some stage in the training. The use of longlines (*see* LONGLINE) is common with trainers all over the country. Rope horsemen, especially those who use their animals for team roping, drive them (*see* LOG). For the suburban dweller who raises a horse or two, the use of harness is almost indispensable, for the suburbanite rarely has access to good pasture with safe fences in which the colt can exercise, and he can drive his colt much earlier than he can ride him.

Skill in driving depends upon the skill of one's hands even more than does skill in riding. In driving, impulsion must be supplied by the voice, the sound of a whip, or at times, if one is sufficiently intelligent to use it properly, the touch of a whip. The use of longlines is as good a method for the horseman to use in learning to drive as it is for the trainer to use in teaching a young horse to be driven. By walking behind a colt with long-lines attached as indicated under the heading LONGLINE, the beginning horseman can learn much about how to get a horse to respond to pressure on lines while the animal is in harness. The best way to begin is to put longlines on a mature animal who is familiar with harness. After the beginning horseman has learned how to start, stop, turn, and control the speed of a horse by using the longlines, he can then hitch the animal to a two-wheeled cart. The two-wheeled cart is much safer than a four-wheeled vehicle for the beginning horseman to use, just as it is a safer vehicle in which to start driving a very young animal. Carts can be procured from manufacturers who advertise in any of the leading horse magazines, and it is not difficult to build one if the horseman is handy with tools.

When driving, it is quite important to see that the horse is so hitched that he is comfortable. The quarter straps (the ones that attach the breech-ing to the shaft) should be just tight enough to keep the vehicle from running up on the horse and not so tight that they interfere with his movement. The shafts should be long enough so that their front ends are well ahead of the horse's shoulder and do not poke him in the shoulder or side when he is asked to turn. If the horse is hitched without breeching it is the bellyband which keeps the vehicle from running up on the horse, sometimes called an extra bellyband. This band wraps around the shafts on either side, and there must be some sort of knob on the shaft to keep that extra bellyband from slipping back on the shaft. Furthermore, it must be just tight enough to do its job but not so tight that it will chafe or cause pain to the horse. The beginning horseman will always do well to use a blind bridle and a running martingale, though the martingale must not be so adjusted that it pulls the horse's head downward. An overcheck or side rein is also a must for the beginning driver, but whichever type is used, it must be just short enough to keep the horse from putting his head down below normal carriage and not so short that it causes him discomfort. The wise horseman makes sure that he and the horse have come to a complete mutual understanding with longlines before he uses a vehicle. When the vehicle is first used, an assistant is necessary. The horseman with whom the horse is familiar holds the horse while the assistant quietly pulls the vehicle up on the horse. All this should be done without spectators and in a place where, should the horse get loose, he will not tangle himself up in wire or otherwise hurt himself.

Driving with Long Reins. *See* LONGLINE

Drop Jump

A drop jump is one having the landing side lower than the takeoff side, a very dangerous jump for an inexperienced horse.

Dropped Noseband

A dropped noseband is a cavesson (noseband and strap going through ends of browband and over the head) which encircles the nose just below the bit. It is used with snaffle only. Such a noseband increases the control of a snaffle. It also is sometimes effective in stopping tongue lolling (keeping tongue out of mouth) and continual opening of the mouth.

When a standing martingale is needed too, both a conventional cavesson and a dropped noseband may be used by stitching the dropped noseband to the center of the cavesson (on top of the nose) and not attaching it to the strap going over the top of the head.

Dry Mouth

The term *dry mouth* designates a horse who keeps his mouth closed on a bit constantly and apparently does not move his tongue. Such a horse rarely gives to the bit and does not have a light mouth. One method of attempting to cure such a horse is to put a bit with a cricket in his mouth (*see* CRICKET).

Dude

In the Southwest the term *dude* was once a slang expression for a winter visitor in the range country; in the Northwest it was applied to a summer visitor. It is rarely used today.

Dude Ranch

Dude ranch was once a popular term for a ranch whose income was mainly or completely from extending hospitality to winter or summer visitors. The term *guest ranch* is now more prevalent. However, Wickenburg, Arizona, still claims to be the "dude capital of the world" because many large and charming guest ranches operate in the vicinity.

Dumb Jockey. *See* BITTING RIG

A dumb jockey is a harness consisting of surcingle, back strap, crupper, side reins, overcheck or sidecheck, standing martingale, and some sort of projection rising above the top of the surcingle to which reins may be attached.

Ears

Any generalizing about a horse's ears is dangerous. It is usually said that well-bred horses, that is, horses having a lot of Thoroughbred blood, have fine ears held alert and close together at the tips. In the main, this is the case, but the writer hunted for years with fine Thoroughbreds from a family in which the name Adair occurred very frequently. These excellent hunters, all straight Thoroughbreds, invariably had the lop ears that we associate with very cold-blooded horses.

A horse expresses himself with his ears much as people express themselves with their hands, and horses vary as greatly in the amount of use they make of their ears in expressing themselves as people do in the amount of use they make of their hands in expressing themselves. Unfortunately, few horsemen are adept in interpreting a horse's ear movements. It is generally thought that any time a horse moves his ears back he is angry or wants to fight, but a horse has as many ways of putting his ears back as a human has of raising his hands. Only careful observation of a particular horse will lead to proper understanding of the language of his ears.

Easy Rider Gaited Horse Association of America, Inc.

Before the sixteenth century, a time when Italy became the teacher of all Europe in matters of artistic refinement, a horse who trotted was considered fit only for servants to ride or for packing freight. Until the development of roads and the universal use of wheeled vehicles, horse-drawn of course, preference for an easy-gaited horse continued. However, the fancy or cultivated riding of nobility and royalty, which had its origin in sixteenth-century Italy, became so popular among the aristocrats of Europe that practically all the writing on horsemanship had to do with horses that performed only three gaits, the walk, the trot, and the gallop. Nevertheless, horses who were used for transportation (and the horse was the only means of transportation for centuries) were, by and large, easy-gaited animals. No man who could afford an easy riding horse would keep in his stable for his transportation about town or in the countryside a horse who was not possessed of easy-riding gaits.

The cultivated riding of the European aristocrats culminated in the Spanish Riding School of Vienna and it was looked upon then as the only "educated" type of riding. And, in fact, it is so looked upon today by many horsemen. However, with riding becoming more and more popular than it ever has been in America, there seem to be more and more people who appreciate the comfort of an easy-riding horse. For that reason the Easy Rider Gaited Horse Association of America, Inc., Box 365, Herrin, Illinois

62948, was recently organized and incorporated. The rules for registration of horses in the registry kept by the association designate no particular breed. Eligibility depends, first of all, upon size. A horse must be at least 13 hands high. The rules state that all under 13 hands will be registered as ponies. And the horse must be inspected and certified to be truly an easy rider with a four-beat gait. "A horse must be natural gaited with an ambling movement, using no artificial techniques." The rules of this association provide for registration of the progeny of a mare and stud if both are registered in the ERGHA registry.

Since we already have several organizations, each promoting a breed that is naturally easy gaited, to wit, the Tennessee Walking Horse, the Missouri Fox Trotter, and the Paso, the ERGHA may seem superfluous. However, this new organization places all emphasis upon the easy-riding quality of horses, and, as yet, puts no premium upon showing, action, speed, or any other performance that is almost beyond the natural endowment of a horse. In the association's literature there is an implication that the object is to produce a horse who will be good for trail riding and other practical uses rather than for spectacular performance under a professional rider in a show-ring.

What will happen in the matter of conformation remains to be seen. But the aptitude for performing easy gaits, whether a running walk, a fox trot, a rack (or paso as it is sometimes called), can be traced to the North African Barb, even more specifically to the genet (*see* JENNET). The modern Andalusian, the modern version of the genet, frequently shows a natural tendency to do a four-beat gait, so there may be some correlation between the propensity to do an easy gait and the type of conformation to be seen in the Andalusian. On the other hand, in the case of the Walker, by deliberate effort of breeders the original conformation of the horse who does the running walk naturally has been greatly changed, and his size has been tremendously increased. The little Paso's conformation frequently shows resemblance to that of his North African ancestry. It may be that, as the Easy Rider Gaited Horse Association matures, it will set up a goal for similar conformation. Certainly, those who are familiar with horses of naturally easy gaits will be sympathetic toward the activity of this organization.

Egg and Spoon Race

An egg and spoon race can be adapted for use with riders of any degree of proficiency. The boiled egg is carried in a spoon and cannot be touched by the fingers. Beginning riders can be told to walk for the entire race; other riders can be told to walk until the command is given to trot, and so on. Even a jump can be negotiated by advanced riders without dropping the egg from the spoon.

Egg butt snaffle.

Egg Butt

An egg butt is a kind of snaffle bit in which the juncture of mouthpiece and sidepiece has some resemblance to the shape of an egg for observers with a vivid imagination. The egg butt tends to prevent the ring of a snaffle bit from passing into a horse's mouth when the opposite ring is pulled by a rein. This bit has its popularity from time to time; fashion changes.

Elbow. *See* CAPPED ELBOW

End Gate

End gate is a slang term for the cantle of a saddle, especially for the cantle of an old-fashioned Western saddle, which used to be quite high and perpendicular.

Endurance. *See also* ENDURANCE RIDES

Unfortunately for the horse, his endurance has been a matter of controversy for several centuries. Debates over the relative endurance of various breeds have generated more heat than light. During the last years the United States Cavalry used horses, it held endurance rides theoretically open to horses of all breeds. Those rides, over terrain of all kinds, lasted for several days. Each day the horse had to complete 60 miles in 10 hours. If he completed the distance in less than 10 hours, he had to keep moving for the allotted time. In those days the cavalry was promoting the breeding of Thoroughbreds through its Remount program, which also used a few Arabians and still fewer Morgans. According to cavalry records, Thoroughbreds showed up best in the endurance rides, Arabians next, and Morgans next above all other breeds. However, it is important to bear in mind that breeders of Hackneys, Standardbreds, Saddlebreds, Cleveland Bays, and others of the time (the Tennessee Walking Horse, as we know him today, had not yet been invented) were certainly not interested in sending their best horses to compete in endurance rides; such representatives of those breeds that did compete (with two notable exceptions) were probably inferior animals.

The notable exceptions were the animals of a Pittsburgh attorney by the name of McCready. He was rather incensed at the idea that the breed he considered most highly developed for carrying a man with ease to both horse and rider had not been given what he thought was a fair chance in the endurance rides. The story of his remarkable performance is told in my book *The Horse America Made*.

As a result of tests and long experience, authorities in the cavalry generally concluded that 25 miles a day over long periods of time carrying a full load was about what the average horse could endure and stay in good condition, provided he was well fed and cared for. However, the limits of the endurance of horses go far beyond this, as illustrated by Morgan's march, which was a matter of several weeks. The march started in August with a 90-mile ride accomplished in 25 hours as a prelude to a surprise attack. Later, Morgan's men fought their way over 300 miles in two weeks. This feat was followed by what was approximately a 90-mile march in 35 hours.

The endurance of any individual animal depends on the way he is bred, the way he is built, the way he is cared for, the way he has been exercised, and what he has been and is being fed. Therefore, there can be no hard-and-fast rule of a horse's endurance. In addition to the stamina of the horse, what an individual horse can do in a given amount of time is almost as dependent upon the horseman who rides or drives him. When Linda Tellington rode an Arabian mare over the grueling 100 miles of the Tevis Cup race in 16 hours, bringing the mare in in such good condition that she won another endurance ride a few days later, many horsemen thought she had made a record that could not be broken. Yet broken it was by several hours within the next year or two by an Indian, who brought his mount in in just as good condition as Linda's. To state with any degree of assurance what any individual horse can endure, one must first know who is going to ride or drive him while he is enduring.

Endurance Rides

The first endurance rides in the Western world were conducted by nobility and royalty. They were rather simple affairs; the horses were assembled and raced until each horse except one dropped dead. The horse remaining alive the longest was the winner. If he died the next day, that was immaterial. Endurance rides in America today, fortunately, are of an entirely different type. They are controlled, and no record exists of a horse's having been ridden to death on any endurance ride of note. There is not an organization of endurance rides as there is of competitive rides. Individual endurance rides are held all over the United States. One of the best known is the Tevis Cup Ride, held at Auburn, California, each August. It is over extremely rough terrain, and the time limit is 24 hours. There are two kinds of competition at the Tevis Cup. One is simply a race over the 100-mile course; the other is for the best-conditioned horse that completes the ride in 24-hours' time limit. There are three mandatory one-hour rest stops on the ride. In 1970 over 200 competitors started on the Tevis Cup Ride and 160 finished. The winning horse made the ride in approximately 11 hours.

Another well-known endurance ride is the Jim Shoulders Ride in Oklahoma. Like the Tevis Cup Ride, it is 100 miles long and it is run with similar rules. Properly conditioned horses, sensibly ridden, can make either of these rides without suffering any ill effects.

England (development of the horse in)

When the Romans landed in England, they found two distinct types of horse. One was a small easy-gaited horse, highly regarded as a saddle mount in England until the seventeenth century—typified by the Hobbies and the Galloways (*see* HOBBIES and GALLOWAY). These showed the conquering Romans the joy of a gaited horse; and the amble very early became a popular gait for a riding animal in Rome. The other horse developed in England, says Sir Walter Gilbey, Bart., in *The Great Horse,* was the Great Horse (*see* GREAT HORSE). Until the seventeenth century, it was the little easy-gaited horse that supplied the transportation needs of England. A horse that trotted was called a "bone shaker" or a "bone breaker" and considered fit only for servants to ride or to pack freight. In addition to this horse of everyday utility, other breeds arose in England.

When knighthood was in flower, the Great Horse was the favorite mount of the knights who wore armor. Following the days of heavy armor on horseback, it became fashionable for nobility to ride in great riding halls. The ultimate development of what their horses were and did is seen in the Spanish Riding School horses today. Horses with some Oriental blood were bred for the riding halls.

During the days of heavy armor, English nobility learned about the virtues of the little horses of the Mediterranean area the hard way. The Great Horses of the Crusaders were no match on the field of battle for the little horses of the infidels.

With the passing of heavy armor and the rise of the great riding halls, the blood of the horses of the nobility was infused more and more with Mediterranean blood. The Andalusian horse of Spain became a popular source of blood. Because of the kind of training horses were receiving at the time of the great riding halls, too much Mediterranean blood, hot blood, increased mortality during the training period, so considerable cold blood was kept in the mounts used in the riding halls.

When Charles II returned from exile in France and brought along his good friend the Duke of Newcastle, he laid the foundation for the hot-blooded horse in England and America. Doing something very surprising in a country which always had and still does put so much emphasis on the sire in a horse's pedigree, he ordered the duke to assemble a band of twenty mares to be used as the start of a breed. Perhaps Charles or Newcastle had learned some of the wisdom of the Orient, where the breeding of a horse is reckoned by the mares from which the horse is descended. Whatever the reason for the selection of that band of mares, they were assembled in the king's stable and called the Royal Mares. From then on, the horses descended from them and the stallions in the king's stable were called "Thoroughbred." Argument still goes on about the breeding of those mares. While some horsemen claim they were all of Oriental (Arabian, Barb, and Turkish) blood, the most reliable records show that a considerable number had the blood of the little native English horses in their veins.

Great though the influence of those mares was on the development of English horses, credit is given today to four stallions for being the foundation of the English Thoroughbred. Certainly, to the blood of those four stallions and the Royal Mares the Thoroughbred owes the beauty and the elegance he had before he began to be selected and bred for speed without regard for any other quality. Even today we occasionally see a Thoroughbred with the big, low-set eyes, delicate little nose, beautiful neck, and elegant carriage so admired by early breeders of Thoroughbreds. Such animals show the influence of Oriental blood most strikingly.

However, the great speed of the Thoroughbred could not have been achieved without the homely little horse native to England. When the first Oriental horses were brought to England, they were raced against the native English horses. The owners of the imported horses were always put to shame. But when the blood of the native English horses was crossed with the blood of the Oriental imports, faster horses than had ever before been seen were the result. Such is the mystery and fascination of horse breeding.

The four great Oriental stallions (three widely known and a fourth less widely known) now considered the founders of the English Thoroughbred were all imported into England in the first half of the eighteenth century. Within a few years after their being established as sires in England, only horses who descended from them through their fathers (that is, whose fathers or grandfathers were sons of one or more of the four foundation stallions) could be called Thoroughbreds. Even today, every Thoroughbred in England and America traces his ancestry through his male line to those four stallions. They were the Byerly Turk, the Darley Arabian, the Godolphin Barb, and the Alcock Arabian.

English Hunting Seat

Certainly today the English are as well aware of the value of getting the weight forward on a horse when he jumps as are Americans. However, the traditional English hunting seat was one in which the rider sat well down in his saddle and carried his feet forward. When the rider did not lean back on the reins, this position had advantage, considerable advantage over some kinds of obstacles—for instance, the double oxer (*see* DOUBLE OXER).

English Saddle

Both the pommel and the cantle of an English saddle are low. The stirrups are put on well forward. Stirrup leathers are held to the tree of the saddle by devices that turn the leather loose if the rider is thrown from the horse and his foot hangs up in the stirrup. The seat of the English saddle is padded, as are the bars or panels where they rest on the horse's back. The English saddle is also called the flat saddle.

Entering a Stall

To sudden fright, that is, to being startled, a horse's automatic reaction is flight or kicking. If he is in a stall, flight is impossible. Almost any horse is startled by sudden entrance into his stall. Common sense dictates that before entering a horse's stall, whether it is a tie stall (in some localities called a straight stall) or a box stall, one should speak to the horse so that he is aware of the person's presence.

Equestrian

The term *equestrian* is used to denote one who rides. However, in a small Western cow town, when the roundup is over and the boys have drawn their pay, it might not be conducive to health and well-being to call a mounted hand an equestrian.

Equipment. *See* APPOINTMENTS

Equitation Classes

Equitation is the art of riding. An equitation class is one in which the rider only is judged. The American Horse Shows Association specifies many equitation classes. They are categorized according to age, experience, previous show-ring winnings, and type of riding to be done. (English classes include Hunt Seat and Saddle Seat; Western ones to date have unofficially been divided into Cutting Seat, Roping Seat, Parade Seat, Pleasure Seat, and Balanced Seat.)

Ergot

The ergot is a small, round, horny growth at the back of a horse's fetlock joint.

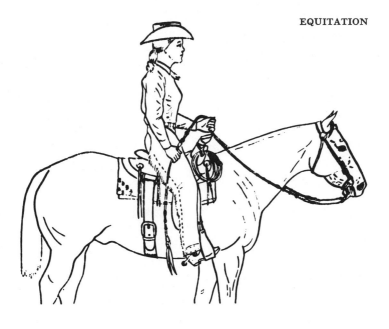

Stock seat equitation. Rider should sit in saddle with legs hanging straight and slightly forward to stirrups as in figure at top or with knees slightly bent and weight directly over balls of feet, as above. In either position stirrup should be just short enough to allow heels to be lower than toes. Feet should be placed in stirrups with weight on ball of the foot. In wide stirrups the foot may have appearance of being "home" when in reality weight is on ball of foot. Rider should sit jog. At lope should be close to saddle. All movements of horse should be governed by imperceptible aids.

Saddle seat equitation. "To obtain proper position, rider should place himself comfortably in saddle and find his center of gravity by sitting with a slight bend at knees, but without use of irons. While in this position, adjust leathers to fit. Irons should be placed under ball of foot (not toe, nor 'home'), with even pressure on entire width of sole and center of iron. Foot position should be natural (neither in nor out). Height of hands above horse's withers depends on how and where horse carries head. Method of holding reins is optional, except that both hands shall be used and all reins must be picked up at the same time. Bight of reins should be on the off side."

Hunt seat equitation lessons. 1. Linda Tellington indicating correct points of pressure of inside of leg against horse on hunt seat. 2. Linda describes how to hold reins in demonstration of hunt seat riding. Elbow, wrist, and hand form straight line; wrists and fingers are flexible, not rigid; thumb is flat with gentle firmness on reins, neither rigid nor too loose.

Hunt seat equitation. "Rider should have a workmanlike appearance, seat and hands light and supple, conveying the impression of complete control should any emergency arise. Hands should be over and in front of horse's withers, knuckles thirty degrees inside the vertical, hands slightly apart and making a straight line from horse's mouth to rider's elbow. Method of holding reins is optional. However, all reins must be picked up at the same time. Rider's eyes should be up and shoulders back. Toes should be out at an angle best suited to rider's conformation; ankles flexed in, heels down, calf of leg in contact with horse and slightly behind girth. Iron may be either on toe, ball of foot, or 'home.' " *1970 Rule Book.*

3. Linda demonstrates one faulty manner of handling reins—fingers clenched tightly, wrist rigid, and hand turned out at wrist with thumb held incorrectly. 4. Student practicing hunt seat at recent clinic at Horse Lovers' Club, Phoenix, Arizona. 5. Student practicing posting trot with hunt seat.

Estrus

Estrus is the word for the period during which a mare will accept a stallion. She is said at that time to be "in heat." Normally, mares average from five to seven days in heat. However, mares vary greatly, and there are annual seasonal factors, never explained, which seem to cause mares in a given area during a given season to be extremely irregular in their estrus cycles. For example, in the Paradise Valley area of Arizona, early in 1971, breeding farms and veterinarians reported unheard-of irregularities in mares. Estrus periods of more than 18 days were frequently noted.

Mares are seasonal breeders and most readily conceive when the days of the year are longest. This characteristic is attributed by some authorities to a susceptibility of a mare's pituitary glands to the effect of sunlight. Certainly, the fact that mares on pasture get a goodly supply of vitamins from fresh spring grass suggests other factors.

The time from one estrus to the next is called the estrus cycle. It ranges from 18 to more than 30 days, averaging about 21 days. Many horsemen maintain that the longer the heat period, the longer the estrus cycle. Heat periods in underfed or very old mares are likely to be longer than average.

A mare will conceive only if sperm comes in contact with an egg. Generally, an egg will be discharged from a follicle on an ovary about 24 to 48 hours before a mare goes out of heat, so it is wise to breed her about the middle of her estrus and every other day thereafter until she goes out of heat. More frequent breeding is unnecessary because the sperm cells live from 24 to 72 hours. The life of an egg is shorter, about 12 hours, and it takes sperm 6 to 12 hours to travel up the fallopian tube, the place where fertilization takes place.

Mares vary greatly in behavior during estrus. Some mares show obvious signs such as frequent urination, "winking" of the vulva, raising of the tail, and even a slight discharge in rare instances; other mares show very slight or no visible signs unless brought close to a stallion. The wise breeder keeps a record of the estrus cycle of each mare and in difficult cases employs a veterinarian to examine the mares. (*See also* BROOD MARES.)

Ewe-Neck

Old horsemen used to say that a horse's neck was put on upside down if he had a ewe-neck. The term applies to a neck that sinks instead of rises between the horse's head and his shoulders.

Exercise (for a horse)

If properly fed and watered, a horse can do with very little exercise. In the days of horses and buggies, before the automobile was invented, some city horses would stand for weeks in the stalls without exercise and without apparent harm. However, if a horse is kept without exercise, he must be started very gradually when exercise begins. He is much like a man who has spent days in a hospital bed. He cannot get up and immediately play a game of baseball. Probably the most unfortunate horse today, so far as exercise is concerned, is the horse owned by the Sunday rider. He stands in a box stall or a small urban or suburban paddock or corral all through the week. Then on Sunday his rider, who often is not particularly versed in things pertaining to horses, gets on him and, if he is the kind of person who thinks he is riding only when he is going at full gallop, gives his horse more exercise than he is able to take.

The horse who is exercised daily and kept on good feed, then rested for a few days without having his ration cut, is likely to develop azoturia if after this period of rest he is put to sudden and strenuous work. (*See* AZOTURIA.)

Exmoor Pony

While he has never reached this country in great numbers, in the early part of this century the Exmoor pony was highly prized here as a mount for children and small adults. He runs wild on Exmoor, in the southwestern part of England, as do the Mustangs in certain parts of our own West.

In size the Exmoor is similar to or even a little smaller than the Mustang. However, at least until very recent years, he has been harvested more economically than our own Mustang. Up to a few years ago, there were annual roundups of Exmoor ponies, and they were brought into the towns and sold at auction. Some of them went to the mines as draft animals, but this market is, of course, disappearing with the increased use of mechanical power.

Eyes

The eyes of most horses are brown with a black pupil. There is also the so-called glass eye. The pigment of this eye is light blue instead of brown, and the eyeball is perfectly clear. White edging is rare in the eyes of horses, and when it does appear, it is sometimes thought to indicate meanness. This supposition is without foundation. Any milkiness or bluish tinge in a horse's eye (except the blue of the glass-eyed horse) is an indication of defective vision.

There is one disease of the eye of which the uninformed horseman should be very wary. It is periodic ophthalmia, often called moon blindness, because it recurs about as often as the moon changes. A horse suffering from this disease will have defective vision for a few days, and then his eyes will clear up and be apparently normal, although a discerning person can see a little lacy curtain on the iris. This faulty vision and the clearing up will occur several times before the horse goes perma-

By voluntary effort comparable to holding one's breath, the horse can momentarily suspend his normal binocular 360-degree vision and focus monocular gaze on an object (usually distant). When he does this he usually assumes the pose pictured here.

nently blind. During those intervals when the eye is normal the horse may be sold at auction "as is," and the unwary buyer may assume he is buying a sound horse.

Because of the location of his eyes, a horse's field of vision is almost 360 degrees. There is just a little spot some 10 to 15 feet directly behind him which a horse cannot see without turning his head. Since the only protection against most predators of the horse when he is in his wild state is flight, this kind of vision is necessary for survival. Some authorities claim that a horse is completely color blind—that he can see no difference in colors. However, there is considerable evidence to support the notion that while a horse may not have the same experience when looking at red or blue or yellow, say, as we do, he certainly can distinguish difference in colors.

A horse has what in professional jargon is called "binocular vision." That is, because of the location of his eyes and their structure, his brain receives two images simultaneously, just as we sometimes receive two images at the same time from our television tube. This is the usual way a horse receives his view of the world. But by an act of will as voluntary as yours is when you hold your breath, he can focus his eyes so that he has temporarily "monocular vision"; that is, one image only is conveyed to his brain, giving him vision like ours. A striking and picturesque example is probably what the leader of a wild herd is doing when he repeatedly appears atop a ridge, just a valley beyond his pursuers, strikes a pose with head high and neck arched, while he looks intently at his hunters for several minutes before he disappears, to repeat the performance at the next ridge.

Domestic horses rarely display this activity because few horsemen allow their mounts to stop at will and fix a monocular gaze upon anything. However, the writer, whose sanity has been questioned by more reasonable horsemen, gets much of his enjoyment in riding from sharing experiences with a favorite mount. So little does he inhibit the natural inclinations of that horse that the horse will stop and strike the pose mentioned above, especially in nearby hill country when snow has driven deer out of the higher mountains so that they can be sighted frequently.

The binocular vision keeps the horse apprised of his total environment—almost all 360 degrees of it. His monocular vision gives him excellent, detailed information of a particular part of it.

F

False Starts

If a rider asks a horse for a certain gait (by whatever cue may be appropriate and by use of aids) and the horse takes a different gait, the animal should be brought to a walk immediately. Then he should be asked again, much more definitely, for the desired gait. If a horse is asked for a canter, let us say, and starts to trot, the first step at the trot may be the horse's mistake. The second step, if he takes it, at the trot is the mistake of horse and rider. The third step, if taken, is entirely the fault of the rider, for the rider should have brought the horse to a walk immediately.

In all horse-show classes in which horses are asked to display different gaits, it is always proper to bring a horse to a walk before starting him on a new gait. Almost without exception, a judge will ask a class to walk before he asks for a change of gait. However, if a judge should fail to do so, each rider should bring his horse to a walk before starting on the new gait. The one exception to this is the five-gaited class. When, in a five-gaited class, horses are performing a slow gait, they are sometimes told to "rack on." If this request comes, they move from the slow gait directly into a fast rack.

Farcy

Farcy is a disease of the horse quite similar to the dreaded, and fortunately rare, disease of glanders. The symptoms are abscesses of the mucous membranes, usually easily observed in the nostrils. A horseman of at least moderate intelligence will immediately telephone his veterinarian if he observes such symptoms—or any other unusual symptoms, for that matter.

Faults

In Parade Classes

Faults in parade classes cannot be scored as definitely as they can in hunter and jumper classes. However, the American Horse Shows Association states that they shall be penalized. The faults are excessive speed, bad manners, switching tail, exaggerated opening of mouth, hard mouth, lugging on bridle and fighting bit, halting or hesitating, zigzagging or sidewise movement, carrying sour ears.

The following faults disqualify the entry from competing in a class: executing other than specified gaits (slow-gait, dressage steps, canter, pace, running walk, etc.); use of tie-downs, martingales, draw reins, boots, and other appliances; any artificial change of color or markings other than in mane or tail; extreme or vertical position of tail. The tails must be carried naturally and not gingered or put in a tail set prior to showing. That a horse's tail has been set does not exclude him from the class (*see* SET TAIL).

In Hunter Classes

Faults in hunters are of four general kinds: touches, knock-downs, disobediences, and falls. Light touches are not to be considered but may be scored according to the following scale when elimination of horses is difficult:

1. With any part of a horse's body behind the stifle	½ fault
2. With any part of a horse's body in front of the stifle	1 fault
3. Touching standard or wing, in jumping obstacle, with any part of horse, rider, or equipment	1 fault

Knock-downs are considered major faults. An obstacle is considered knocked down when its height is lowered by a horse or rider. Knock-downs are scored as follows:

1. With any part of horse's body behind the stifle	4 faults
2. With any part of the horse's body in front of the stifle	8 faults
3. Knock-down of standard or wing in jumping obstacle with any part of horse, rider, or equipment	8 faults
4. Knock-down of obstacle by touching a wing or post shall count as a knock-down of obstacle with above penalties.	
5. Placing any foot in liverpool, ditch, or water	8 faults
6. Hind knock-downs, not the fault of bad jumping, shall not necessarily eliminate a horse from an award but shall be scored against in a comparative manner.	
7. When a horse touches an obstacle, causing a rail of an adjoining panel or wing to fall, it shall not be considered a knock-down.	

Disobediences, major faults

Circling once upon entering the ring and once upon leaving is permissible. Faults of disobedience are scored as follows:

1. First refusal, runout, bolting on course, extra circle	8 faults
2. Second refusal, runout, bolting on course, extra circle	8 faults
3. Third refusal, runout, bolting on course, extra circle	elimination
4. Jumping an obstacle before it is reset	elimination
5. Bolting from ring	elimination
6. Failure to keep proper course	elimination
7. Jumping an obstacle not included in course	elimination

A horse and rider falling in competition means elimination. A horse is considered to have fallen when shoulder and haunch on the same side touch the ground or the obstacle on the ground.

In Jumper Classes

A jumper who touches an obstacle with any portion of his body behind the stifle is scored for half a fault. Each of the following scores as one fault:

1. Touch of an obstacle with any part of a horse's body in front of the stifle or any part of rider or equipment
2. Touch of standard with any part of horse, rider, or equipment
3. Touch of flag, number, or marker at obstacles included in the course, or of flag, or automatic starter, or equipment other than designated markers on starting or finishing line with any part of horse, rider, or equipment during the round

Any disobedience counts as three faults. Each of the following will be scored as four faults:

1. Knock-down of obstacle, standard, or wing with any portion of the horse, rider, or equipment
2. Knock-down of flag, number, or marker at obstacle included in course, or of flag, automatic starter, equipment, or other designated markers on starting or finishing line with any part of the horse, rider, or equipment during the round
3. Placing any foot in the liverpool, ditch, or water, or knock-down of any obstacle placed before, in, or beyond water or ditch

A second disobedience of the horse will be counted as six faults. A horse will be eliminated from the class for any of the following faults:

1. Third disobedience
2. Fall of horse and/or rider (except in fault-and-out classes) (see TOUCH-AND-OUT)
3. Jumping obstacle before it is reset or without waiting for signal to proceed
4. Starting before judges signal to proceed; jumping obstacle before start whether part of course or not; jumping obstacle out of order; off course
5. Failure to enter ring within one minute of being called
6. Failure to cross the starting line within one minute after judge's audible signal to proceed
7. Jumping any obstacle before crossing starting line unless the obstacle is designated as a practice jump
8. Failure to jump in designated order

In Stock Horse Classes

Faults of stock horses cannot be scored as exactly as can those of hunters and jumpers, but the following faults are to be considered in making awards: switching tail, exaggerated opening of mouth, hard or heavy mouth, nervous throwing of head, lugging on bridle, halting or hesitating while being shown (particularly when being run out), indicating anticipation of being set up (which is characteristic of an overtrained horse).

Fear (in horses)

No factor is more important in the survival of the horse as a species than fear. In his natural state the horse has practically no defense against his enemies; he is more defenseless than any other animal in his wild state. He has no fangs, no horns. Fear and subsequent flight are his lifesavers. His fear is aroused by anything unusual in his surroundings, no matter how tiny or how large (*see* EYES). The rustle of something almost too small to see in the grass at his feet may cause alarm as quickly as something three times his own size. With this natural propensity in his makeup, it is little short of miraculous that the horse can be domesticated and turned into such a creature as the fearless hunter we all admire or the dependable children's mount that is safer than a good many baby-sitters. Adequate treatment of the subject of overcoming fear in horses would require a volume larger than this one. However, the general principle is to introduce anything new to the horse very gradually and to give him plenty of time to determine its harmlessness. At the turn of the century John S. Rarey, possibly the greatest horseman who ever lived in this country, trained and rode a little bunch of wild Western horses without having any of them ever show signs of panic or fear after he started to work with them. Rarey's method, of course, would take too much time to be useful on the kind of animals he was training, for they were not worth very much money. But he did prove that it is possible to overcome the fear in the wild horse and teach it to be a serviceable animal without any of the violence usually associated with the breaking of Western horses at that time.

The horse who shies at every little thing on the side of the trail is usually more afraid of the whip and spur of his rider than of the object at which he is shying. It is the part of wisdom to ride an overly timid young animal in the company of a quiet old horse until the youngster gains confidence on the trail. While many a spoiled animal comes out of the backyard of a city dweller, colts raised in urban or suburban surroundings have at least one great advantage. From the time they are foaled they are used to seeing and hearing and smelling everything they are likely to encounter when they grow up and are being ridden or driven.

A wise old horseman once said, "You have to be half as smart as the horse in order to get along with him. And your biggest job is having sense enough to let the horse know what it is you want of him." Certainly, in helping a horse overcome fear, considerable ingenuity is often required in devising some way to let the horse discover the harmlessness of a new object or a new movement. Constantly forcing a horse to do what he is afraid to do is like adding fuel to flame. Likewise, the horseman who always allows a horse to refuse to do whatever he is afraid of will soon have a worthless animal. With the green horse, discretion is always the better part of valor. But when one finds himself in a situation in which a horse refuses to obey because of fear, it is wise to take plenty of time to let the horse see the harmlessness of what he is afraid of (often by the rider's dismounting and touching the object) and then proceed casually and firmly.

Feather (also Feathers)

Feather is the term used in some places for the fetlock, that is, the long hairs that grow at the back of the pastern and extend sometimes upward toward the knee. In some breeds great pride is taken in the length and silkiness of the feather.

David Fyffe, who for many years had charge of all the livestock at Ohio State University and was one of the most highly respected judges of livestock in this country, was very fond of the Clydesdale breed, which of course originated in his native Scotland. When talking about Clydesdales, he often repeated the following saying: "Plenty of bone and lots of feather; top may come, but bottom never." In other words, you can improve the body by putting on more flesh, but legs and feet can't be so improved.

Feed

No amount or variety of feed will keep a horse in good condition unless he is properly watered. A horse's stomach is relatively small. If he is given grain when he is a bit thirsty, and then watered, the grain will wash out of his stomach, do him little good, and possibly produce colic (*see* COLIC).

While the old method of watering a horse from a pail two or three times daily in summer and once daily in winter has kept many a horse fat, there is no more important rule to lay down in horse care than that clean water should be available for the horse 24 hours a day. Better for a horse to have to break the ice on his water in winter than to have to lick his thirsty chops and wait for his master to bring him a drink of warmed water. Of course, salt should be always available for a horse, preferably the iodized variety in most areas.

A horse will recover from emaciation resulting from underfeeding, but few if any horses recover completely from laminitis resulting from overfeeding. Why laminitis or founder is the price paid for such a great variety of mistakes made by horse owners, no one has ever discovered. Gorging on feed when he gets into the feed bin, overheating on the track or in the show-ring or in the hands of ignorant riders, improper cooling out after a workout, excessive fever during illness, extreme concussion on hard roads, and other causes compete with bad feeding practices in bringing on founder or laminitis. Laminitis resulting from bad feeding practice is probably the most insidious form of the disease, for it comes on so gradually that the horseman is scarcely aware that his horse is ruined until he is past saving.

Dr. Elmer Powell, old and highly respected veterinarian of the Scottsdale, Arizona, area, says, "That line between top condition of a horse and over conditioning which causes founder is extremely narrow and often hard to discern." Of all modern horsemen, probably the Sunday rider is the one most likely to err in his feeding practices, for he may not adjust the amount of feed accurately to the amount of exercise his horse gets. If he feeds a pelleted feed which contains both roughage and grain, it is impossible for him to vary the amount of grain properly in case the exercise of a horse varies considerably.

Although the horse can be ruined by overfeeding and other bad feeding practices, he is probably, of all domestic animals except his cousin the ass, best endowed with the ability to survive under very diverse conditions of feeding and shelter or lack of shelter. The amount and nature of feed required to keep him in good flesh can be varied widely to suit local needs and pocketbooks. Corn can be the grain fed, but the most foolproof and satisfactory grain is whole oats. Whole grains, as modern dietitians have discovered, are generally preferable to milled or otherwise mutilated grains, though many horsemen prefer "rolled" oats to feeding whole oats. However, the writer is now living in Arizona, where barley is the most readily available grain; and since whole barley must be soaked or rolled to be thoroughly usable in a horse's digestive apparatus, he sometimes uses the steam-rolled barley with excellent results.

Some horse owners are so situated that an abundance of good clean roughage, like corn or hegari fodder, is cheap, and grain is perhaps relatively high. In such a case, the horse will do well if given plenty of roughage and a quart or so of oats three times a day. No scales are needed to determine how much roughage a horse may safely and economically be given. He may be fed all he will clean up, though he must be accustomed to alfalfa very gradually. On the other hand, if transportation of feed is an item, making hay expensive, the horse can be given, let us say, oats in the amount of a gallon and a half three times a day, and his roughage may be cut to eight or ten pounds daily (provided the grain is whole oats). Often when fed oat hay, containing the grain, a horse doing only light pleasure work exists with no additional grain.

A handful of whole flaxseed soaked overnight in water may be fed once or twice a week if extra gloss of coat is desired. Bran is beneficial and a must for all modern horse owners. A two-pound coffee-canful of so-called red bran (wheat bran) must be fed once or twice a day if the modern horse owner wants to avoid colic and keep his horse in good condition. The old practice of giving a bran mash once a week seems satisfactory enough (a bran mash is made by filling a 2- or 2½-gallon bucket half full of bran and then pouring enough boiling water on it to make it a bit sticky to the hand, after which the bucket is covered with a blanket and allowed to sit until it is cool enough to eat). However, the present writer has found that the feeding of dry bran daily is much more satisfactory and is not extremely laxative.

In spite of the fact that the horse is so versatile and adaptable in the matter of using whatever feeds are available, so long as they are clean and unspoiled, a study of the nutritive value of various feeds is a profitable expenditure of time for the horseman and will occasionally save money.

For little or no charge, any horseman can get bulletins from the agricultural department of his state university. The Department of Agriculture at Washington also has information available in bulletins. Any county agent will be glad to direct a horseman in the matter of obtaining bulletins on horse feeding.

The horse, like his master, needs green vegetables in his diet. Even a handful of grass now and then is helpful, and little else than grass is necessary to fill his need for the "green" part of his diet. Carrots and other root plants as well as apples and other fruit are appreciated by the horse but are not absolutely necessary.

As we have said, the amount and to some extent the nature of the feed given a horse should depend on the work he is asked to do and on the conditions under which he lives.

Feeding and Watering Dos and Don'ts

1. Be sure that water has been available to the horse before feeding.

2. When possible, feed in small quantities, and feed often. On the same total daily amount of feed a horse will put on a good deal more weight if fed four times a day than if fed twice a day.

3. Feed hay before grain, if possible. It is usually satisfactory to feed grain first in the morning, since the horse probably has been nibbling at his hay through the night.

4. Heavy hay feeding, where practiced, should be done at night.

5. Rope nets for hay are very helpful if mangers are not available.

6. Feed grain in clean boxes or nose bags. A satisfactory nose bag can be made out of a gunnysack (*see* MORRAL).

7. Feeding of grain is most economical if done at least three times a day.

8. If the horse's manure becomes hard and dry, increase the amount of bran or give a bran mash or green grass. Make some effort to see that the horse gets green grass whenever it is available (but *never* grass cuttings unless fresh and cool). Oleander leaves in grass cuttings will kill a horse.

9. If the horse slobbers, holds his head to one side, or evinces other difficulty in eating, have a veterinarian look at his teeth. If a horse does not respond properly to good feeding and care, he may be wormy. Call a veterinarian. *Worms and bad teeth account for a vast majority of the cases in which horses are getting enough feed and still are thin. Both should be checked twice a year.*

10. Have clean water and salt available to the horse constantly when in stall or paddock.

11. Do not feed grain to a horse when he is hot. Hay will not hurt him.

12. Do not work a horse hard right after feeding. If you must work him immediately afterward, cut his feed in half.

13. Do not give a tired horse a full feed of grain.

14. Do not let the horse bolt his grain. If he does, put some rocks in his manger.

15. Never feed the horse moldy or dirty feed. Watch hay carefully for mold or spoilage.

16. If it takes a horse longer than 25 minutes to clean up his grain, feed him less and examine his teeth.

17. *Don't* be alarmed by or follow the advice of a quack's "diagnosis": "Your horse has lampas [usually pronounced lampers]. Gimme your knife and I'll cut them for you." *See* LAMPAS for full explanation.

18. *Never* allow anyone to scarify or burn lampas.

19. *Don't* take the advice of any layman or rely too much on your own judgment in the matter of ailments of your horse, minor or major. If the horse is worth feeding, he is worth a veterinarian.

20. *Don't* experiment with home remedies for colic. A physic is fatal to some kinds of colic. Again, call a veterinarian.

21. *Don't* allow your horse to eat clover when it is frosted. It is usually fatal. Pasture containing some clover is usually kept sufficiently short to make the clover harmless; but on many farms second growth in meadows usually looks about right to turn a horse on when time for frost arrives. It is danger from this that we warn against.

22. *Don't* turn a horse on Johnson grass or any other of the sorghums fed in subtropical regions unless you are sure that they have not suffered from the peculiar stunting caused by faulty irrigation, which renders them capable of producing hydrocyanic acid poisoning. If they have been correctly grown, Johnson grass and other sorghums are good feeds whether green or properly cured.

23. *Don't* ask the horse to eat chewed-over hay or grain. If the hay manger is full of trash or unpalatable stocks, throw them out. If the horse leaves good edible food, cut down his ration.

24. *Don't* water a hot horse. As he begins to cool off, let him have a half-dozen swallows every few minutes until he is satisfied. In feeding newly cut alfalfa, there is danger that some of it may not be completely dry (it will feel tough rather than brittle when twisted in the hand). Feeding such hay will cause colic. The remedy is to open each bale, spread it out to air, and allow it to dry thoroughly before feeding any of it.

25. Become familiar with the book *Feeds and Feeding* by William Morrison, published in 1957 by the Morrison Publishing Company of Ithaca, New York.

Feed Bag. *See* MORRAL

Feeding (principles of). *See* FEED

Feed Manger. *See Mangers* under STABLES

Feet (of horse)

A horse's feet should be large enough to carry him. Unfortunately, it is not uncommon to hear horsemen who ride only in the show-ring boast, "What tiny feet my horse has!" The writer has even heard working cowhands, who should know better, boast about the fact that a certain 1,200-pound horse took a number zero shoe.

It would be hard to think of any living tissue that takes a more severe pounding and strain than does a horse's foot. The bigger it is, the better, provided (and this is an important provision) it is of the right shape. It should be larger at the shoe than at the coronet (top of hoof), concave in the sole, open at the heel, and supplied with a good, big, flexible frog. When properly trimmed by a competent farrier the hoof should have an angle with the ground of around 50 degrees, depending upon the slope of the pastern; and the heel should be well off the ground.

The perfect conditions for foot health are those obtained when a horse is running barefooted on good sod. Most of the ills of a horse's feet are caused by some sort of departure from this ideal—something the amateur horseman should bear in mind so that when he is forced to keep his horse in some extremely unnatural situation or to use him in extremely unnatural work he will attempt to compensate for the lack of normal conditions. By way of illustration, the United States Army kept large numbers of horses at a post in Texas where the footing is very dry and hard and the weather often very hot. These horses were tied in clean mud for certain periods daily. Police horses and delivery horses, it has long been known, go better with rubber pads on their feet to lessen the concussion of their work, which is entirely on paved city streets. The space between the rubber pad and the sole of the horse's foot is packed with pine tar and oakum, which keeps the foot soft and the frog pliable.

The horse whose leg and foot circulation has been tampered with by overzealous and self-confident grooms will be more likely to succumb to adverse conditions than will more fortunate horses. The chief way in which leg and foot circulation is ruined by the ignorant is with bandages.

Of course, many horses have their feet ruined by improper shoeing. In the matter of shoeing, it is well to remember that the long toes of the show horse should be reserved for the show-ring. The pleasure horse or the working horse should never be allowed to carry a hoof that has grown beyond the live sole. If the horse is used on rocky ground, as in the mountain area of the Southwest, a fairly wide-webbed shoe must be worn for protection; but in all cases the lighter the shoe the better, so long as it affords ample protection for the work done and does not wear out so fast that the nails of the new shoe have to occupy the old nail holes. No good blacksmith needs to be told to shoe the foot full and not to draw the shoe in at the heel. Likewise no competent blacksmith needs to be told to keep his knife away from the frog and bars of the horse's foot. If a good blacksmith is not available, it is a wise plan to allow the horse to go barefooted for a fortnight or so every two or three months. This will irritate the blacksmith, but it will give Mother Nature a chance to overcome the ills to which faulty shoeing will lead if continued over any considerable time. No shoe should be left on until the wall of the hoof grows far down below the living sole. To see whether the wall is grown below the real sole, an old screwdriver or other blunt instrument can be used to brush away the part of the sole normally shed while the horse is barefooted. Force should not be used in this process, as it is merely to remove sloughed tissue.

A good blacksmith will keep the foot at an angle that is merely a continuation of the angle of the pastern. It is obvious that if either heel or toe is too long or too short, the angle of the foot when the horse is at rest will be different from the angle of the pastern. Of course, viewed from front or rear, the hoof should be level. A line drawn through the center of the frog and on to the toe of the hoof should bisect the bottom of the hoof. If it does not, the fault should be gradually corrected over a period of four or five shoeings, unless the horse is aged and has a fixed structural peculiarity. In the case of a badly misshapen foot, it is always safest to call in a good veterinarian.

Sometimes, to correct or change a horse's stride, a farrier will change the angle of his foot. Unless the farrier is expert and has been well trained, this is a dangerous practice, for a sudden change of angle of a horse's foot can lead to any one of several kinds of joint lesions such as sidebones, ringbones, or bone spavins. Any corrective shoeing should be done either by a highly specialized and trained farrier or under the supervision of a veterinarian who is knowledgeable about feet and leg ailments.

A wise horseman will watch his horse when the horse is running barefooted on pasture for any considerable period of time, to see that his feet do not become too long or misshapen. It is especially important to watch the feet of growing colts. A lowering of one side of the colt's foot, as from chipping off a bit of the hoof by stepping on a sharp rock or other foreign body, will cause a slight change in the colt's way of going, that is, in his trueness of stride (see ACTION and DISHING). If the foot is not properly leveled at once, the shift in stride may tend to increase the wearing of the foot at the wrong level until a misshapen or even faulty bone structure of the foot results, or the joints of the leg grow to accommodate the peculiarity of stride induced by faulty level of hoof. Many a colt of naturally good action has been ruined because his owner never dreamed that little colts need to have their feet watched. The paring or leveling required by a colt's feet is usually very slight but it is nevertheless extremely important.

Feet (position of rider's feet)

The correct position for a rider's feet in relation to his body can easily be determined if the horseman will stand on a floor with his feet fairly close together and place his weight on the part of the foot that will be pressing down on the stirrup when he is mounted. Thus if he is going to ride with the ball of his foot on the stirrup, he will stand with his weight on the ball of his feet; if he is going to ride with his feet home, that is, with the instep of his foot pressing on the stirrup, he will stand with his weight evenly distributed on ball and heel of foot. Standing on the floor with his weight properly placed as indicated above, the rider will bend at his knees and hips to the angle they will assume when he is mounted. Obviously, if he intends to ride a jockey seat, he will have to be almost squatting on the floor; if he intends to ride a forward seat, his knees and hips will not be as extremely bent as if he is intending to ride the jockey seat. If he intends to ride the parade seat or the so-called gaited horse saddle seat, he will be standing with his knees and hips almost straight. If the horseman performs this exercise correctly, it will be observed that a plumb line dropped from the top of his pelvic bone will intersect that part of his foot which is carrying his weight. Incidentally, this exercise is also useful in determining the angle of the torso, for it is impossible to maintain one's balance in the position just described unless the torso is at the proper angle. When imitating the jockey seat, one will have to bend the torso far forward to maintain balance. At the other extreme, for the parade seat, the torso is almost erect.

The exercise described above will show that when the rider is mounted, the stirrup should be directly under the top of his pelvis. The level of the foot is important. The heel should always be slightly lower than the stirrup. While many riding instructors keep repeating the command "Keep your toes in," the correct position as far as the angle of the foot is concerned is not keeping the toes in. It is not even keeping the feet parallel but keeping the feet at about a 45-degree angle with the horse. That is, the toes are turned slightly out. Keeping the toes in or even keeping the feet parallel with the horse will result in cramped ankles or knees. If the toes turn out too much, there will be daylight between the rider's knees and his saddle. When the feet are carried properly, the inside of the rider's knee and the inside of his leg just below the knee will be in contact with the horse. This is almost putting the case backward, for if the rider's leg at the knee and just below the knee is at proper position, the angle of the feet is necessarily correct.

Feet on the Dashboard

Feet on the dashboard is an expression used to indicate riding with the feet placed too far forward and the heels too far down, pushing the rider back in his saddle.

Fencing

The varieties of fence behind which horses may be kept is seemingly infinite. Wood probably makes a fence of the most pleasing appearance.

The kind of wood depends upon the locality. In a region where lumber is fairly cheap, a wood fence is most economical if one can devise a way to keep horses from chewing it. The writer has seen a horse chew entirely through a two-by-six in a single night. Nobody has solved the mystery of why horses chew wood or how they chew it. Sometimes in certain localities horses can be kept behind a wood fence for years without damaging it with their teeth. In other localities it is impossible to keep a horse behind a wooden fence for 24 hours without having it damaged considerably unless it is painted with creosote or protected by an electric wire.

Any fence for horses should be at least four feet high—higher than that if the horse has a tendency to jump. If there are horses on both sides of the fence, the wise horseman will string an electrified wire (here may we warn that no device should be used to electrify a fence except one sold by a reputable dealer and underwritten for safety) six inches above the top of the fence. Stallions must be separated from other horses by a solid board fence five or six feet high, depending on the temperament of the stallion.

In pastures of 10 acres or more, it is possible to keep horses behind ordinary woven wire fence without great risk unless there are horses on the other side of the fence who tend to want to fight over the fence. However, when horses are kept in fairly close quarters, the danger of putting a foot through an ordinary woven wire fence is too great. In this case wire fencing should be one of three kinds—either the so-called V-mesh which is too small for a horse to get his foot through, or the two-by-four "horse mesh," or the chain link fence. Any one of these varieties must be made of material heavy enough so that a horse will not break it if he paws it. The writer has observed wire fences in suburban areas behind which horses are kept, many of them put up with iron posts and iron posts for braces, but he has never seen one so constructed that it has stood straight for more than a few months. Horses will rub their tails; some of them will rub their manes. When they rub against a fence supported only by iron posts, the fence will give.

If the corner posts of a corral are well braced, sunk four feet in the ground, and of a size similar to that of a railroad tie, the fence may remain reasonably upright if the intermediate posts are all metal. However, the writer has found that an electrified wire placed three feet inside a metal fence is a very economical kind of construction. All gates for a horse corral, pen, or paddock should be at least three feet wide, and there should be provision for hooking them open. A horse may have his hip knocked down and have to be destroyed because a gate blew against him while he was entering or leaving a corral. Each corral should have one removable panel or a gate wide enough to admit a truck for purposes of hauling out manure or hauling in dirt to fill holes. In suburban areas it is always necessary to fence horses away from an oleander hedge. While a horse who is not starved rarely eats oleander, accidents will happen; the writer has known at least two fat and well-fed horses who died from nibbling oleander leaves. One of them, it is true, ate the leaves when they were cut up in grass cuttings from a lawn.

It is always wise to separate horses who are kept in close quarters. In the old days when horses were used hard every day all day, it was possible to let them stay together in a corral overnight without danger of great damage. But modern use of horses is such that horses will rarely stay together in a corral without scarring each other up, to say nothing of breaking each other's bones. It is easy to separate horses in a corral by running an electrified wire between them. Electrified wire alone is not extremely satisfactory as an outside fence in suburban areas. Horses are continually getting loose in suburbia, and an excited runaway horse who is not used to an electric fence will run right through one, doing damage to himself or to the horses who are kept behind the electric fence. Outside fences should be made of wood, wire, or cement. If necessary, electric wire can be put two feet inside the outside fence and six inches on top of it. However and whenever an electric fence is used, a horse should be educated about it. The easiest way is to hold the horse by the halter shank fairly close to the electric fence and allow him to move about at the end of the halter shank so that he will come in contact with the fence. If he does not care to move, a helper may shake some feed on the far side of the fence to get him to move toward it. Touching the fence once or twice is all the education most horses need to stay away from an electric fence. Such an education will make them stay away from the fence for several hours after it is turned off. With some horses the current may be turned off forever, after they have been educated. Others are fairly smart and in an hour or so will examine the fence with their whiskers or nose; if the owner is careless about leaving the fence off, a smart horse will always determine whether the wire is on or off and act accordingly. The writer has had two such irritating animals.

No matter what material a fence is made of, it should be strong enough to withstand any punishment a horse will give it. A fence that is falling down is one of the greatest dangers a horse encounters. If the fence falls down far enough for him to get a front foot over it, he will almost invariably pull back and cut his pastern, usually down through the coronary band. If he gets over it with his forefeet and hangs a hind foot up in it, he will usually tear his hock on the fence. Proper use of electric wire has saved many horses from painful injury.

Fender

A fender is a piece of leather attached to a stirrup leather to protect a rider's leg from contact with a sweaty horse. Fenders are not commonly used on English saddles. However, no law says that one who rides an English saddle is forbidden to avail himself of the convenience of a fender.

Any saddlemaker can cut out a piece of leather and put some slots in it through which the stirrup leather can run to keep it in proper position and protect the rider's legs from the sweat of the horse.

Fever

A horse's normal temperature is approximately 100° F. A horse's temperature is taken with a clinical thermometer placed in its rectum. If the temperature runs much above 100, it is time to call the veterinarian.

Fiador

The fiador is a browband and throatlatch, the latter constructed of cleverly knotted doubled rope of small diameter, used with a bosal to prevent the latter from dropping or being pulled from beneath a horse's chin.

Field Master

The term *field master* indicates a certain official on a fox hunt. In the layman's terms, every rider on a hunt who is not an official constitutes a part of the field. In other words, the field is all the riders who are not officials of the hunt. The field master is in charge of this field. In the past, hunts in certain parts of the country were rather informal, and non-members were always welcome. In such a situation the field master is a very important person, for a member of the field who is discourteous, ignorant, or a show-off can ruin a hunt, interfere with the hounds, or cause trouble in other ways. Just keeping the field quiet while hounds are drawing cover is sometimes a pretty big job for a field master.

Fighting

Fighting in the corral when horses are turned together can often result in broken bones, which necessitate destroying a horse. Horses may run in a small corral or paddock together for years without trouble; then, usually at night, something may start a fight, and in the morning the owner will find one horse injured so severely that he has to be destroyed. The suburban dweller who keeps two or three horses can easily separate them with one wire of an electric fence run between them. Today, electric fencing units are very reasonable and simple to install; there is no need for allowing horses kept in small quarters to run together.

The horse who tends to fight other horses while ridden in company by either biting or kicking is usually one who has run in a group of horses where he was kicked and bitten. If a colt runs with older horses who fight him away from feed, he will quickly learn to be on the defensive, to "put up his dukes," so to speak, in the presence of any other horse.

Unfortunately, the horse who has thus learned to be on the defensive can be cured of the habit only by being severely punished whenever he shows any tendency to fight another horse. This punishment should be administered by an experienced horseman, for timing is important and punishment administered improperly will do much more harm than good. If the horse tends to use his heels whenever another horse approaches, the rider should be on the alert to pull his mount's head toward the approaching horse; obviously his mount cannot kick until his rear end is toward the approaching horse.

Of course, the properly schooled horse, responsive to leg aids and with a good mouth, will never give trouble as far as fighting is concerned, for he is attuned to his rider just as a ballroom dancer is attuned to his partner; he has no more time or attention to devote to kicking or biting another horse than does the ballroom dancer have to devote to kicking the shins of a passing couple. However, it is a sad fact that many of the horses encountered on trials and in group riding in general are badly schooled. The partially schooled horse should be kept off bridle paths and trails until he is thoroughly broken of the habit of fighting.

Fighting the Bit

The term *fighting the bit* is a rather loose one used to indicate a great number of things a horse can do to avoid responding to signals on the bit. One of the commonest among short-necked horses, especially those with heavy shoulders and low withers, is called "boring." In this particular vice the horse arches his neck, lowers his head until his chin comes in against the chest (overflexing), and then seems utterly insensitive to pulls on the rein. Any fighting of the bit is an indication of previous bad handling and, possibly, present misery from maladjustment or bad choice of a bit. The commonest cause of discomfort of a horse ridden with a curb bit is maladjustment of length of chin chain or strap (*see* BITS). Perhaps the main cause of head fighting is bad hands on the part of the rider. The use of a hackamore or hackamore bit may help stop the trouble if it is entirely with the horse. If the cause of the trouble is the bad hands of the rider, the only sure remedy is a funeral (*see* HANDS).

Filly

The term *filly*, like the term *colt*, is fairly broad. Those most exact and careful in its use and most critical of anyone who is not careful are the people whose knowledge of horses is largely academic or gained through conversation at a cocktail party. *Filly* may be applied to any female equine under the age of four. However, the term *foal* is usually used until the animal is weaned. People who are extremely fastidious in word usage about horses reserve the term *colt* for male equines under the age of four.

Fine-Harness Horse

According to the *Rule Book* of the American Horse Shows Association, a fine-harness horse is one who is shown with a full mane and undocked tail hitched to an appropriate vehicle, preferably a small buggy with four wire wheels but no top. A light harness with a snaffle bit and overcheck is required. The fine-harness horse is required to show a walk and a park trot (high stepping, stylish, moderate speed). He is not required to back. In open classes, sometimes the command "Show your horse" is given. This signifies that each contestant may do with his horse whatever he thinks shows it off to the best advantage, which is usually a park trot. A fine-harness horse must be able to stand quietly unchecked; however, during a workout the horses not involved may be checked. Good manners count heavily in fine-harness class, and speed; excessive speed is penalized. An attendant may "stand the horse on its feet," which means make it pose, but he must stand at least two paces from its head at all other times. The fine-harness class in a horse show belongs in the Saddle Horse division, and most of the entries are American Saddle Horses.

Fiord Pony

The Fiord Pony is the most popular of three breeds in Norway. It is also called the Norwegian or Westland Pony. It is undoubtedly related to the Iceland Pony, for both have the extremely stocky build and dun color. The dun may be any one of several shades, but the ponies always have a dorsal stripe and a black upright mane, which is usually kept clipped to preserve its uprightness. These dun ponies of the northern countries have unusually good dispositions, extremely hard bone, and considerable resistance to all equine ailments. The ones that appear in Iceland are naturally very easy-gaited. They, like the Paso of South America and the Tennessee Walking Horse of North America, naturally have a four-beat gait. They do this gait from the time they are foaled, and rarely is one of them ever seen to trot.

Firing

Firing is an operation performed by a veterinarian ostensibly to cure some kinds of lameness, unfortunately sometimes reluctantly, at the insistence of owners. It is done by using a highly heated iron or "needle" on or in the affected part of the animal. Usually a horse who has been fired will have little flecks of white hair on his legs, sometimes in regular patterns like domino spots. There is some prejudice against a horse who has been fired because of fear that the old injury may have resulted in a permanent weakness and may return even if the firing has produced a "cure."

According to *Equine Medicine and Surgery*, one of the most recent and respected of reference works in the field of veterinary medicine, "The value of firing for the treatment of injuries to tendons and ligaments is open to considerable debate." Pin firing, the text goes on to say, especially in heavily muscled areas, though questionable, may be beneficial because of the enforced rest required for the fired area to heal.

Fistula

The layman's term *fistula* is usually used to indicate an abscess that forms in the vicinity of a horse's withers. The abscess may break out toward the top of the withers or lower down. The first sign is a swelling of the tissues around the withers. The cause is sometimes a blow or a bite; in any case, the injury is extremely serious and should be treated by a veterinarian. If it is not attended to early, it is more economical to destroy the horse than to go through the long process of curing it, unless the horse is particularly valuable for breeding.

Fistula is also used sometimes in the phrase *fistula of the poll*, which is also called "poll evil." These terms apply to an abscess just behind the horse's poll, which is the highest point of the horse's head. In the days before electric power in coal mines, coal was moved in the mines by horse, and almost invariably a horse so used had poll evil. This was the result of bumping his head while he was moving forward against the top of the tunnel. The coal miners would say the horse was "topped." In many mines where the tunnel was not high, Shetland ponies were used. They, too, were almost invariably "topped." Before the time of modern antibiotics, fistula of the poll was generally considered incurable and fistula of the withers nearly so, although every livery stable "hoss doctor" had a remedy, sometimes an extremely severe and gruesome one. With the great advances in veterinary science and modern antibiotics, there is today much hope for a horse with fistula if his ailment is diagnosed early. Radical surgery is usually necessary unless the fistula is treated very early.

Five-Gaited Horse. *See also* GAITS

The five-gaited horse is one that walks (flat-footed), trots, canters, racks, and does one of the accepted slow-gaits (amble or stepping pace, running walk, or fox-trot).

In modern show-rings, because spectacular performance is all-important, a slow, broken trot is often substituted for a walk, and a slow rack is substituted for a slow-gait.

Flat Racing

The term *flat racing* simply means racing without any obstacles for the horse to jump. The existence of this term tells us something about the history of the development of racing. Earlier racing was usually over country in which there were natural obstacles to be jumped.

Flat Ribs

A horse is said to have flat ribs when his ribs are not rounded out well, when they come down straight on the sides. This kind of a build is also called "slab-sides." The horse whose ribs are well rounded is said to have ribs that are "well sprung."

Flexing

A few horsemen in certain localities talk about flexing the jaw of a horse. More commonly horsemen talk about flexing at the poll. This is almost a misnomer because the poll of a horse is the highest part of his head and the flexing spoken of is done just behind the head. These phrases are used to indicate the same sort of thing as *setting the head*. They are all concerned with getting the horse to understand and respond to the bit. It is possible to make a horse bend his neck at the desired spot by using a bitting rig. However, a horse so trained is rarely the delightfully responsive animal who is obtained by the trainer with good hands willing to use a lot of time in training his horse. When the horse has finally found out what the bit is for, what the rider intends by the bit, there is no need to worry about his head set because he will respond. The exceptions are usually horses with very short thick necks or with extremely straight shoulders or some other unusual conformational defect. When a careful trainer with good hands has finally "developed the horse's mouth," that is, enabled the horse to understand what pressure on the bit means, nobody needs to worry about the horse's head set; it will *be* set.

Float (teeth)

The process of floating is merely that of filing off the rough edges of a horse's teeth which would cut the tongue or the cheek. Not all horses wear their teeth unevenly and develop such sharp edges, but a good many do. Today a veterinarian should be employed to perform this operation.

In the days before modern veterinary science, itinerant teeth floaters used to come around annually or semiannually to every stable to float the teeth of all the horses. Undoubtedly, in many instances their services were superfluous, and if the floater was honest, he would so indicate and would go to the next animal.

Flying Change

A horse is said to execute a flying change when he changes leads at a gallop without slackening speed. A properly trained horse will do a flying change if he is given the proper aids, that is, a slight increase of pressure on the rein on the side with which the horse is leading and a light pressure of the leg on the same side just behind the stirrup leather.

A horse who has not been trained to respond properly to aids (*see* AIDS) may be induced to execute a flying change if the rider follows these directions:

Have your horse at a full gallop along the arena rail or outer boundary of your riding area. Reverse his direction just as he completes the turn at an end of the arena by turning him to the *inside* of the ring and continuing the turn until he is going the reverse of the direction you have been galloping. As you finish the reverse, lean toward the *outside* of the arena and increase speed quickly to change leads. If necessary, hang on to the horn of your saddle. (It took a good many years for Western horsemen to discover that a horn was "good for more things than to tie a rope to.")

Every horseman who has attended one of Monte Foreman's excellent clinics will recall his admonition to riders attempting this maneuver: "The more you get behind the horse and lean to the inside, the harder for the horse to change!"

A horse who is particularly difficult in this maneuver or any other involving change of lead should be taught to perform the "sidepass" (*see* SIDEPASS). When the horse has learned the sidepass, his hindquarters can be controlled. The usual trouble with difficult horses in lead change is their failure to change behind. Hindquarter control is necessary. The older horseman may well remark that all I am saying is that the horse should be taught the leg aids (*see* AIDS) and to flex properly—matters of mere routine in all long-established riding schools. However, Mr. Older Horseman, please remember that a host of today's riders spend neither the time nor the money required for conventional riding-school routine. The new method is an economical way to get the results they want.

When the horse has been taught to sidepass, his quarters can be moved slightly off his line of progress and toward the side of the lead he is asked to take. Obviously, this shift puts him temporarily oblique to his line of progress. Furthermore, it will almost surely make him change leads behind when he changes in front—correcting his error. Such handling of the quarters will obviate the necessity for "being too Western" and dangerous, running the horse at extreme speed.

Foaling. *See* BROOD MARES

Foals. *See* COLT

Food. *See* FEED

Forearm

The forearm is the part of the horse's leg that extends from the elbow to the knee.

Forefooted (horse)

The term *forefooted* signifies being roped by the forefeet. The practice of forefooting is practically obsolete today. But when the West was younger and many more horses were used in the cattle industry than today, they were handled very differently. Most of the horses used on ranches were worth less than $20, so not much time could be spent on their training or handling. When horses were needed for a certain job of work on the ranch, they were herded into a corral called a remuda corral, where each horse was caught, saddled, and bridled for the day's work. A few ranchers would never allow horses to be roped in the remuda corral, for a horse that is accustomed to being roped is difficult to catch in any other way.

Horses used to being roped in a corral would soon learn to stop immediately when a rope touched them in any place, partly because the first time or two they were caught they may have been forefooted. That is, when they were raw, green horses just off the range and were first put into a remuda corral, they tore wildly round and round the corral until a deft roper caught them by the two forefeet, pulled those feet out from under them, and they fell suddenly to the ground. Two or three treatments of this kind usually made a horse extremely respectful of a rope. However, if the roper happened to catch the horse by only one forefoot, the chances of a broken shoulder or even a broken leg were very great, but the loss of an unbroken horse was not financially too important. (For further description of roping horses see Fay Ward's *The Cowboy at Work.*)

Forelock or Foretop

The forelock or foretop is the strand of hair that grows at the top of the horse's head and hangs down between his eyes. If properly cared for, it will usually grow well enough to help protect the horse's eyes from flies in the summertime.

Forging

Forging is hitting the front shoe with the hind foot. This is common among very young horses and very thin and listless ones. The young ones need time to develop muscles and plenty of good feed to overcome the fault. Faulty shoeing may be a cause. No one method of corrective shoeing will work on all individuals. Shortening of the front toes and raising the heels slightly (but never enough to prevent good frog pressure) will help the horse pick his front feet off the ground (turn his front feet over) more quickly and get the front feet out of the way of the hind ones. Lengthening of the hind toes will help slow down the break-over behind. Sometimes the hind toes have to be squared off in front, which procedure, of course, does not slow down their break-over, but it prevents them from reaching quite as far forward as naturally.

Forward seat. Gail Ross, former member of the Canadian Olympic Jumping Team and Grand Prix winner. Note use of forward seat in high jumping (rider's weight over horse's center of balance and body in line with line of thrust).

Fort Riley

Fort Riley (Kansas) was the greatest cavalry school and cavalry post the United States ever had. When it existed, one could drive through it for miles with corrals of horses and mules on either side.

Fort Riley Seat

The term *Fort Riley seat* is not often heard today, but it used to mean the seat adopted by the United States Cavalry at Fort Riley. It is now called the balance (or balanced) seat (*see* SEAT).

Forward Seat

The forward seat was as revolutionary an invention as the pneumatic tire. Shortly after this century began, an Italian cavalry officer by the name of Caprilli made a remarkable discovery and gave important advice to all horsemen competitive and athletic in their tastes. Like other great discoveries, Caprilli's seemed simple and obvious after he made it. The discovery was that a horse's balance, his center of gravity, is in a constant state of flux—a finding very much in line with all thinking about the physical world in this century. Caprilli proposed that the chief aim in riding should be to avoid interfering with the horse's balance. This advice is more important to competitive riders than to a horseman who rides neither to win a trophy nor to keep up with the Joneses. Important to all, however, is his emphasis on the fact that there is no one best seat. It has been amply demonstrated that the horse's center of gravity ranges from over his withers to a point well behind his shoulders and that a rider interferes least with his mount when the rider's weight is directly over the horse's center of gravity. In the hunter and jumper and the dressage horse, this center of gravity is well forward. The cavalry show horse falls in the same category, so it is the forward seat, the seat originally advocated by Caprilli, that with slight alterations is the American forward seat so popular in all athletic riding in America today.

In this seat, the body leans forward until the weight is directly over the stirrups. The shoulders are "open," and the back is straight or slightly concave. The seat in the middle is so far forward that "the crotch of the britches touches the pommel." Relatively little weight is carried on the seat of the saddle, and this is carried by the bones of the pelvis, not by the buttocks. The upper leg's position in relation to the body is the same as that in the basic seat (*see* BASIC SEAT). Because of the position of the body, the knee, then, is farther forward on the saddle and lower than in the basic seat. The stirrup leathers are vertical, as in the basic seat. The foot is carried much farther back than the knee. The heels are pushed as far as possible below the ball of the foot so that all the weight of the rider seems to be "pushed down into the heels." The feet are carried at about a 30-degree angle with the horse's sides. They are placed in the stirrup so that the foot touches the inside bar of the stirrup, and more weight comes on the inside than on the outside of the foot. The feet may be either "home" or with the ball of the foot on the stirrup. (The latter gives more opportunity for use of the ankle in rhythm with the horse, but the former gives more security.)

The position of the feet makes the calves hard—thus most effective for gripping. More weight is carried by the feet in this seat than in most others, but the lower pelvis and upper thighs should be snugly down on the saddle. Lower thighs, inner surfaces of knees, and upper calves are relaxed but in close contact with the horse during slow, quiet riding. During jumping or any other violent movement, these three parts of the leg grip the saddle.

Hands and arms are used uniquely in this seat. The elbows are carried in close to the sides. From the elbow to the horse's mouth, arm, wrist, and reins form a straight line.

This seat gives the fluid balance that goes with every movement of the horse. The hips, knees, and ankles give a springy seat. It is a seat that seems formidable to the Kentuckian, who says, "For unrequited labor, nothing beats using a bucksaw or riding a three-gaited horse." However, the forward seat is extremely uncomfortable only for those who forget that the grip is relaxed in all but very energetic movements of the horse. Certainly, it is not the seat to be used for casual pleasure riding on trail or bridle path. Probably few of the riders who developed and use this seat have ever ridden the uniquely American horse, bred and trained not solely for jumping or for speed over turf, but for ease and delight of the rider for any distance over any terrain (*see* AMERICAN SADDLE HORSE).

Founder. *See* LAMENESS

Fox-trot. *See also* FOX-TROTTER

The fox-trot is one of the gaits permissible for the five-gaited horse (the five gaits are the walk, trot, canter, rack, and slow-gait; the slow-gait may be a slow pace, an amble, a running walk, a stepping pace, or a fox-trot). It is also the most important gait of the Missouri Fox Trotter, who is also permitted a flat-footed walk and canter (*see* FOX-TROTTER). The fox-trot is a diagonal gait, one in which the left hind foot and right forefoot move almost simultaneously, as do the right hind and left fore. However, the forefoot strikes the ground an instant before the hind foot on the opposite side, so the rhythm of the hoofbeats is like that of syncopated music. The speed of the fox-trot is usually about the same as the speed of the original running walk (not to be confused with what one sees in the show-ring now under the name *running walk*), a gait of some seven or eight miles an hour. The fox-trot can be done at a speed much faster than the true running walk. Some of the Missouri Fox Trotters will perform their gait as fast as the Tennessee Walker now performs his gait in the show-ring— some 16 to 18 miles an hour. The Missouri Fox Trotter, incidentally, is incapable of any gait that is not easy for the rider—that is, easy enough for him to carry a glass of water without spilling it. The virtues of the fox-trot are that it is easy on both horse and rider and can at moderate speeds be kept up almost indefinitely. It is rarely seen today in the show-ring in five-gaited classes because it is not as flashy as other slow gaits permitted the five-gaited horse.

Fox-Trotter

The Fox-Trotter (*see* FOX-TROT) is a horse who naturally prefers the fox-trot to other gaits (*see* GAITS). Until recently, there was no recognition of Fox-Trotters as a definite breed, but for many years before the advent of good roads and automobiles, horses appeared in frontier Kentucky, Tennessee, and Missouri who did the fox-trot naturally about as frequently as did those who did the running walk naturally. Indeed, there was little preference and not much distinction made between animals who fox-trotted and those who did the running walk. All of them were said to "saddle." As late as the second decade of this century, the writer overheard conversations in rural Kentucky backwoods general stores in which the question frequently came up when a promising young horse was the topic: "Kin he saddle?" If the answer was affirmative, the horse in question could certainly do a running walk or fox-trot, and it mattered little which. As the saying went, "He could tote the grain to mill"—meaning he could give an easy ride.

If records had been kept, such horses could undoubtedly be traced through the Narragansett Pacers or the Canadian Pacers or the Cockspurs to the Galloways and Hobbies of the British Isles, or to the jennets of Iberia. To the strains represented by these horses that could "saddle" the American Saddle Horse owes the beauty and ease of his movement. Recently, an organization has been formed to select fox-trotters of uniform type capable of passing on their own characteristics, to register them and their progeny, and to promote the sale thereof (see MISSOURI FOX TROT-TING HORSE ASSOCIATION). It chose for the name of its breed the Missouri Fox Trotter. As yet, the American Horse Shows Association has not recognized the breed, but classes for Missouri Fox Trotters are already included in the programs of some shows. So far, specimens exhibited have shown a little more refinement than do the Tennessee Walking Horses. They do not attain the size of the Walkers nor do they give evidence of having been subjected to the artificialities of shoeing, tail setting, etc., used on Tennessee Walking Horses.

In 1964, Warrior's Merry Lady, registered Missouri Fox Trotter, won the Annual Award of the North American Trail Ride Conference.

Fresh Forage

No horseman can escape the advice "Give your horse all the green grass you can." This advice is good if taken properly. Even five minutes of holding on a lawn where he can eat, if the lawn is free from oleander leaves or other noxious matter, will do him some good. The writer grew up near a harness horse track and recalls a daily sight of harness horse owners holding their horses out and allowing them to nibble the bluegrass which was encircled by the track. Some caution is in order. Many a horse kept in urban or suburban areas has died from nibbling oleander leaves. The wind carries these leaves, and lawn mowers cut them up into fine bits, and they mix with lawns. Johnson grass (see FEED) under certain conditions is deadly poison, though under proper conditions it can be used as a feed. Grass cuttings that are free of noxious plants may be fed to a horse in moderate amounts if fed immediately after cutting. However, grass cuttings that have been piled up and allowed to develop some heat will cause serious digestive ailments, which may be fatal even under the best care a veterinarian can give. Short, new growth of any grass is richest in nutrients, vitamins, etc.

Freshness (in horses)

The amateur horseman, especially if he lives in parts of the country where inclement weather is common, often finds "freshness" in his horse quite a problem. If a horse is not used for several days, the grain should be taken away from him not only to prevent freshness but also to prevent founder and azoturia (*see* AZOTURIA). Even with the grain taken away, some horses become very "high" or "fresh" when they stand up in a stall during a spell of bad, snowy weather. If a horse is used to working on a longe line, the line affords the best means of letting him work off excess energy. If the horse is not used to working on a longe line, there is a possibility that he will flop his rear end around the forequarters and bow a tendon his first time out.

Another way to let him work off excess energy is to saddle and bridle him and then be sure to put the reins over the saddle seat and to put the stirrups over the reins so that when he kicks and plays he will not get the reins under his feet. It is even a good idea to tie the stirrups under his belly with a good stout cord so that he will not flop them up in the air and toss them off when he plays. Then turn him in a paddock where he may kick and play with a saddle and bridle on. He may be encouraged to do so by clapping the hands. However, no horseman in his right mind will use a whip or throw a clod at a horse to make him play.

If neither of these methods is possible, perhaps a neighbor with an old, quiet, steady horse will volunteer to accompany the rider whose horse is too high, in which event a good steady trot for some 20 or 30 minutes will get the freshness out of him. In such event this caution is needed: If the horse has been on high-grain feed and worked regularly and then laid up for a day or two without lessening the grain, he will develop azoturia when taken out and worked faster than a walk for the first 20 minutes or half an hour he is out (*see* AZOTURIA).

Front

The word *front* is used by horsemen to denote several rather different things. It may mean a fancy browband and cavesson used on gaited horses in the show-ring. It sometimes designates the chest of the horse. The three-gaited, five-gaited, and fine-harness enthusiasts speak of a horse's having a good front if his shoulders are sloping, his neck is long and well arched behind the head, and the action of his forelegs is bold and high.

Futurity (races and classes)

In futurity races and horse-show classes, competition is between young animals who are usually entered or nominated for entry right after foaling or even before they are foaled.

Gag Bit

A gag bit is a snaffle bit (*see* SNAFFLE) having sidepieces (usually rings or semicircles) so made that round leather cheek straps or ropes (sash cord size) will run through them freely. If rope is used, it serves in lieu of bridle cheek straps and may run through the ends of the browband. With the gag bit, neither the reins nor bridle cheeks are buckled into the bit. The reins are attached to the ends of the cheek straps or rope, which run freely through the sidepieces of the bit.

Gag bit.

The action of this bit is identical with the action of a gag rein (*see* GAG REIN). When a gag bit is used in place of an ordinary snaffle or bridoon, in a double bridle (full bridle), it is called a Shrewsbury or a Duncan, depending upon the design.

Gag Rein

A gag rein is one fastened at the top of a horse's bridle and run freely through snaffle bit rings and thence to the rider's hand. Obviously the gag rein makes the bit pressure operate upward on the corners of a horse's mouth rather than downward on his bars. It is used on the racetrack perhaps more than anyplace else, although trainers of barrel horses are now recommending the use of the gag rein in training. Although it has other uses in the hands of professional trainers, the novice will do well to avoid it except under the guidance of an expert.

Gaited Horse

The term *gaited horse* refers to the five-gaited horse. This animal is usually an American Saddle Horse, which breed is also frequently developed as a three-gaited horse. Oddly enough, the three-gaiter is not referred to as a gaited horse. Perhaps the reason is that his gaits (the walk, trot, and canter) are more nearly those of the natural gaited horse (usually walk, trot, and gallop), though the trot of the three-gaited show horse is certainly very different from the natural trot of a horse, and his so-called walk is far from the flat-footed gait a horse does naturally. The five gaits are the walk, trot, canter, rack, and slow-gait. The slow-gait may be any one of several gaits which are just faster than a walk: the amble, the stepping pace, the running walk, the fox-trot, and the slow pace. In the show-ring, however, the horse usually shows as a slow-gait either a very slow rack or an amble because these are much flashier than the other slow-gaits. (The crippled gait of the Tennessee Walker in the show-ring is not to be confused with what was originally called the running walk and included as one of the slow-gaits.) For further treatment of each of the five gaits, see their respective headings in the book.

Gaits. *See also* COLLECTED GAITS

In the days when the cavalry was equipped with horses, many profound articles came out of Fort Riley describing the gaits of the horse and classifying them on the basis of the patterns hoofprints make on the ground. German and French authorities have used other classifications. However, all such classifications have concerned themselves with performance that is most easily considered under—and is limited to—three headings: walk, trot, and gallop.

In 1902 the American Saddle Horse Breeders' Association (*q.v.*) cleared the air considerably by designating the terminology it would use and the gaits it would approve. Up until that time (and for some time thereafter by many careless people) the term *pace* was used for any gait other than a trot if it was slower than a gallop and faster than a walk. The terms *single-foot* and *rack* had been used interchangeably. Following the work of the ASHBA concerning gaits, the clearest method of classifying them is by the sequence of impacts of hooves on the ground.

The first three of the gaits recognized by the ASHBA are the most common among riding horses: the walk, trot, and canter. When a horse walks, he strikes the ground with one foot at a time. When he walks on dry ground, the sound makes us think of four-four time in music. We can count the steps: one, two, three, four. The sequence is as follows: left hind foot, left front, right hind, right front, left hind, left front, etc.

When a horse trots, his feet strike the ground in pairs. The left front foot and right hind foot strike at the same time. So do the right front foot and left hind foot. The trot is like two-four time in music: one, two; one, two.

The gallop or canter (they differ only in collection—see COLLECTION—and speed) is more complicated. If a horse starts to gallop or canter with his left hind foot, it strikes the ground and is followed by a diagonal pair, the right hind and left front feet, which hit the ground almost simultaneously. Then the right front foot strikes the ground. All this makes the gallop sound like three-four time in music: one, two, three; one, two, three. (If the left forefoot is striking the ground alone, not paired with the diagonal hind foot, we say the horse has the left lead. If the right fore is striking alone, the horse is on the right lead. See CHANGE OF LEAD.)

In addition to the walk, trot, and canter, the ASHBA recognized and specified the rack and the slow-gait. The latter could be any one of four gaits performed just a trifle faster than a walk; they were the slow pace, the stepping pace (sometimes called the amble), the fox-trot, and the running walk.

The rack has the same sequence as the walk, but the horse leaps, so there is an interval following each impact when no foot is in contact with the ground. This interval must be of exactly the same length after each impact. The rhythm must be true four-four time. Any tendency toward syncopation is unpardonable. If anyone wonders why, he need only sit on a horse whose rack is not true. (The true rack is delightfully smooth; the untrue, unbearably rough.)

The slow pace, like the pace done at speeds exceeding 30 miles per hour on the track, is one in which the two feet on each side work in unison, the left hind and left fore striking the ground simultaneously and the right hind and right fore doing likewise. The slow pace of the five-gaited horse is done just a little faster than a walk.

In the stepping pace, the hind foot on each side strikes the ground just a trifle ahead of the forefoot, creating a syncopated rhythm. This gait, like the slow pace, is done at a rate just faster than a walk. The fox-trot, done at speed similar to the other slow-gaits, is a diagonal gait like the trot, but the forefoot of the diagonal pair strikes just a trifle ahead of the hind foot, thus creating a syncopated rhythm with sound similar to that of the stepping pace. The running walk as designated by the ASHBA and by the late Burt Hunter, who might well be called the godfather of the Tennessee Walking Horse (q.v.) is a four-beat gait like the walk and the rack. It is executed, according to both above-mentioned authorities, at a speed of from six to eight miles an hour with "economy of effort to both horse and rider" (Hunter's wording). Like the flat-footed walk, it is done with a foot in contact with the ground at all times (not leaped as on the rack), but the stride is much longer than that of the flat-footed walk. To get that stride, each hind foot must hit the ground many inches ahead of the track left by the corresponding forefoot. The head swings to help lengthen the stride. The entire body is, relatively speaking, loose and relaxed to aid the swinging motion. Sometimes the teeth are heard to click as the head swings up and down with the rhythm of the gait.

Obviously, a true running walk has a fairly low limit of possible speed. When a horse doing a four-beat gait exceeds nine, or at most rare possibility, ten miles an hour, he must leap. That is, there must be an interval when no feet are in contact with the ground, in which instance he is said to *rack*. Because of its lack of speed and because of its "economy of effort to horse and rider," the running walk as originally designated was not a very showy gait. The five-gaited show people abandoned it years ago as a show-ring gait. However, after the death of Burt Hunter, who kept the Tennessee Walker true to type, the Walking Horse enthusiasts made their play to capture show-ring prominence by pushing their horses' speed beyond 15 or 16 miles an hour and raising the action as high as that of any five-gaited horse. To keep the gait from being classified as a rack—that is, to retain the resemblance to the original running walk—they made the horse sore in the front feet and legs by chains, blisters, and what not, so he scooted his hind feet far under him to keep the weight off his sore front ones. The soreness sometimes helped increase height of action, too. This leaped four-beat gait of the Tennessee Walker in the show-ring is called a running walk, but it hardly fits the description given it by the men who set up the registry for the breed or by the ASHBA in its 1902 meeting.

Whatever it may be called, the gait of the show-ring Walker is a brand-new gait, one never done by horses before.

Gallop. *See also* GAITS

The gallop is one of the natural gaits of most horses. The sequence of hoof impacts on the ground is as follows (right lead): left hind, right hind and left fore almost simultaneously, right fore. From the gallop the horse can be taught to run, which is the gait with the extreme speed seen on the racetrack, or to canter, which is the gait with extreme collection as seen in the show-ring, especially in such classes as the three-gaited class. The impact of the feet of the galloping horse produces a three-beat rhythm, but when that same horse is collected into the slow and highly collected canter, the rhythm may be almost four-beat, for the diagonal feet that normally hit the ground nearly simultaneously strike individually; and the same is true of the rhythm of the extremely fast run of the race horse.

Gallop Depart

The term *gallop depart* is a rather sophisticated—we might also almost say precious—one used to indicate the start of the gallop. In gaited classes, the gallop depart must be from the walk. In the old days of the cavalry, the gallop depart was from a trot. In some dressage work, the gallop depart is from a halt. The race horse man does not use the term *depart;* however, if the gallop depart of his horse is good from the starting gait, he says that the horse "breaks well."

Galloway. *See also* HOBBIES

The Galloways of Scotland, like the Hobbies of Ireland, were small, sturdy animals about 14 hands high, developed for their easy riding gaits, their good disposition, and their tremendous endurance; they were the foundation of the most popular horse in England until some years after the Restoration. It is interesting to note that in 1700 no Englishman of any affluence would have in his stable of horses that were kept for transportation purposes a horse who trotted. By 1800 he would not have in his stable a horse who did not trot.

These sturdy, easy-gaited horses—"pacers" they were called—did a four-beat gait. They were the foundation stock of the American Saddle Horse and the Tennessee Walking Horse. Undoubtedly they were related to the Paso Fino of South America. Certainly they were the forebears of the famous Narragansett Pacer, whose extreme ease of riding made him so popular in foreign courts that he entirely disappeared as a distinct breed in this country.

Gaskin

The gaskin is the muscular development of a horse that lies between the hock and the stifle.

Geld

The word *geld* comes straight down from Old English. It means to cut straight. To geld is to castrate.

Gelding

The spinster schoolmarm is quoted as having defined *gelding* as a gentleman horse who has been deprived of his biological influence in the community in which he resides. He is, therefore, a castrated male.

Genet. *See* HINNY and JENNET

Gig

The word *gig* as a noun denoted the heavy two-wheeled vehicle that was once used to show heavy-harness horses with in horse shows. In the West the word also means a punch of the horse's sides with spurs.

Gimpy

A horse is said to be gimpy when he has a slight limp. Sometimes the lameness is so slight, or the horse has been so treated, that there is little evidence of it in his gait. However, the experienced horseman may detect it and say the horse is "gimpy."

Gineta, à la

Riding *à la gineta* means riding with extremely short stirrups in the old Moorish style. It is the extreme opposite of the style of riding used by the Crusaders. Horsemen of Mexico and the southwestern United States in the sixteenth and seventeenth centuries prided themselves on being able to ride "in both saddles," meaning that they could ride both *à la gineta* and *à la brida,* the latter being the seat with very long stirrups, the seat of the Crusaders.

Girth

When horsemen possessing a well-made horse speak with justifiable pride of their horse's large girth, they are referring to the circumference of the horse's body just behind his withers.

When a horseman goes into a saddle shop to purchase a girth, he is looking for a wide strap, piece of webbing, or several strands of mohair fastened together to make a flat straplike contraption. Any of these girths will have from one to three buckles on either end, and they are used to keep the saddle on a horse's back. The girth passes underneath the horse a few inches behind his forelegs. Any girth should be at least as wide as the palm of a man's hand, wider if possible, and should be as strong as cowhide. Any girth should be kept clean and pliable. Many horses, especially if they are not used regularly, develop girth sores just behind their elbows if girths are not properly cared for. The so-called Fitzwilliam girth comes in two pieces. One is a wide girth with two buckles on either end, and the other piece is a narrower one with a buckle on either end. The narrow one passes under a couple of narrow straps attached to the outside of the wide girth. All buckles attach to billets on the saddle on either side.

Probably the most popular girth in good stables is the folded-leather girth. It is quite satisfactory if kept clean and pliable. Canvas girths, especially of white canvas, are frequently used in show-ring classes. Probably the best girth of all for practical purposes is of mohair, commoner in the West than in the East. It is made of strands of mohair fastened together so they form a wide surface about the width of the folded-leather girth and having two buckles on either end. These buckles are metal that will not rust, and the whole girth can be washed in the washing machine—preferably in cold water. Canvas girths must be watched very carefully, for they deteriorate easily when used on sweaty horses and will break or become stiff and harsh.

Girths are used on English or flat saddles. Western saddles are held on the horse by cinches (from the Spanish *cincha*). A cinch is considerably shorter than a girth because of the rigging of the Western saddle (*see* WESTERN SADDLE).

Adjustment of Girth

Proper adjustment of a girth is an "iffy" matter. If the horse has good, high withers, and the saddle fits him well, the girth need not be exceedingly tight. If the horse has mutton withers, as the saying goes—that is, low withers—the girth will have to be tighter; and if he has broad, flat withers, as do some Quarter Horses, the saddle will have to be almost uncomfortably tight to keep from turning. In such a situation a breast strap, or a breastplate fastened to the top of the saddle on either side, having a strap that goes between the horse's legs and fastens to his girth, will help considerably. With a horse that is used regularly, a man must be extremely stout and somewhat violent to pull a girth tight enough to harm him. However, if the animal is young and has not been ridden for quite a while, he should not be "pulled in two with the girth." One old-time test for tightness is to run three fingers under the girth just below the side of the saddle and then push them down until they come to the place where the girth passes under the horse. It should be possible to insert the fingers easily at the side of the girth, but the girth should be tight enough so that three fingers cannot pass under the horse. Of course, the Fitzwilliam girth is the one that can easily be pulled the tightest, and care must be taken to see that it is not pulled too tight. There are on the market some girths made of leather of single thickness. These are very likely to cause a sore behind a horse's elbow. If such a girth is extremely desirable, it can be used without harm by putting foam rubber under it, so that the foam rubber extends out beyond the edges of the girth.

Glanders

Glanders is one of the few diseases, if not the only one, that infect both horse and man. It was a great curse in Europe for years because it was endemic throughout that part of the world. There have been only a few outbreaks in this country, and our relative freedom from it is due, according to many people who should know, largely to the efforts of one man, a Dr. Detmars, for many years dean of the College of Veterinary Medicine at Ohio State University. Having grown up in Germany and seen the havoc wrought by glanders, he was prompt to take drastic action whenever he knew of a case. Early in this century, a few cases occurred in Dayton, Ohio. Dr. Detmars immediately went to Washington and with fiery zeal got action enough to have all horses who had been exposed to glanders destroyed and properly disposed of. His fervor in this matter aroused a good deal of hatred, but he stuck to his policy; wherever glanders occurred, he took immediate measures.

So far as the layman is able to observe, the symptoms of the disease are eruptions in the mucous membrane. These can be seen in the nostrils. Any case of glanders, of course, has to be reported to the proper authorities at once. Some states still require a test for glanders on any horse that is to enter the state from outside.

Gloves

For English and Eastern riding, string gloves are as proper and sometimes more practical than leather ones. Gloves made of material other than leather or string are not generally practical. String gloves are useful in rainy climates because they do not slip on reins. In Western riding, especially in brush country, horsehide gloves are quite useful. Gauntlets are a nuisance, but in extremely brushy country they save the sleeves of shirt jackets, to say nothing of the skin on wrists.

Godolphin Barb

The Godolphin Barb is one of the three best-known progenitors of the Thoroughbred. (The other two are the Darley Arabian and the Byerly Turk.) The original name of the Godolphin Barb was Scham. That name means Damascus, and hence it is assumed that that was his place of origin, which includes the Syrian Desert. Records have been found that indicate that this horse was of the Muniqi strain of Arabian (*see* ARABIAN HORSE) the largest and fastest of the three main strains of Arabians being bred in this country today. There is now documented proof that the Godolphin strain name *Jilfan* is directly related to that particular Muniqi family from which came the Darley Arabian.

Gone Away

Gone away is the cry that all riders to hounds love to hear. It is given when the fox has started to run, and the hounds are in pursuit.

Good Hands

Theoretically, good hands are those that get immediately any desired response from a horse. There are good hands classes in many horse shows. In such classes the rider must keep constant pressure on the reins at all times. The amount of pressure depends upon the kind of horsemanship the judge is addicted to. If he happens to be of the German horsemanship persuasion, the rider should hang on to the reins fairly strongly all the time. If the judge is one who emphasizes "lightness" of hands, the pressure must be slight; however, it must be constant if the rider expects to win a prize. The position of the hands, too, is important. They must not be thrust out far in front of the body, the knuckles should be toward the horse's ears, and the hands should not be too high above the saddle. In starting, stopping, turning or changing the gaits of the horse, hand movements should be very slight, hardly perceptible by the audience. Of course, the horse must respond readily and without tossing his head, opening his mouth, or showing other signs of distress or defense.

The kind of "good hands" just described cannot be maintained on many well-trained Western horses. The requirement of good hands of this sort rules out many excellent Western riders because they ride well-trained Western horses who perform with what is called a "slack" rein. With such riders and horses there is constant communication through the reins, but the good Western horse and the good Western hands do not require bit pressure for this communication. The slightest shift of the hand on the so-called slack rein is recognized by the horse and responded to. This slack rein is not one that flops down below the line between bit and hand, but it is a rein that is not held taut by the hand. It gives the horse some chance to move it by his manipulation of the bit even if he does not change the position of his head. Anyone interested in the superior subtlety of the Western hand will find it interestingly depicted in a book by Tom Lea called *The Hands of Cantu.*

The expert horseman learns with each horse the kind of hand movements that will carry the message. Though certain generalities can be made, such as "Raising the hand tends to lighten the forehand" (which communicates the direction "Get your hocks under you!"), each horse is unique. The horseman is supposed to be more intelligent than the horse and therefore should go more than halfway in finding the perfect kinesthetic communication for the particular horse he is handling. When the communication has been established, it is maintained by movement and by "passive resistance," *never by constant pulling at the reins.* Examples of the uselessness of pulling on the reins of a runaway (a horse that has been startled into a hysteria of running) are endless.

Some months ago, a highly bred young horse I was riding was thrown into a panic. The situation was such that I could not turn him (circling will sometimes stop the panic). I found, however, that he would respond to a lift of the forehand. The first movement of my hand got very slight response. I had sense enough not to intensify the movement and try by force to get the response. As I lifted him repeatedly in rhythm to his mad gallop, he began to respond and was soon coming up high enough in front to check his speed. Also, I got his attention. That squashed the hysteria.

I relate this incident not as a panacea for bolting horses (many of them have been mishandled so repeatedly that there is no cure that is not more costly than the price of a replacement for the horse) but to illustrate that good hands do not use the reins as a means of force—a forceful pull on the runaway is met by a forceful pull by the horse and more speed, if any is left in the animal. Kinesthetic communication, like verbal communication, is not made more understandable by increasing its volume. If a "word" is not understood, repeat it more distinctly (perhaps you were mumbling!). Sometimes it has to be repeated in rapid succession several times, as was my "word" to the hysterical youngster who was running so fast.

Good Hands Classes. *See* GOOD HANDS and HORSEMANSHIP CLASSES

Good Hands Horse

A good hands horse is one on which a rider can win in good hands classes in horse shows. This means, first of all, that he is a horse who will give the rider no problems. His performance must be practically automatic, with no initiative on his part. A good hands horse can be a show horse who has passed his prime, if one can find such a horse whose feet have not been crippled by shoeing for the show. He will not be excited by the audience, music, or anything else connected with a horse show; and he will be sufficiently good-looking to enhance the appearance of his rider. Sometimes it is possible to find an American Saddle Horse who has not quite enough animation for winning ribbons in open classes, or one whose tail has been ruined during the process of setting (of course, if the tail is too unsightly, the horse will not serve). If this kind of horse has had some training in three gaits, he can usually be taught to respond to the aids easily and can have his mouth developed into a good light mouth that will make him suitable for showing in a good hands class. It should be pointed out, however, that if the horse has been taught to do any gait other than the walk, trot, and canter, he is entirely unsuitable for use in a good hands class; only a very experienced rider can keep a gaited horse from showing signs of a lateral gait. Horses in good hands classes are asked for only three gaits.

Goose-Rumped

A horse is said to be "goose-rumped" when his croup (from highest point of hips to root of tail) is extremely steep.

Governess Cart

A governess cart is a low, two-wheeled vehicle with a door in the center of the back and two seats that face each other. It is most frequently used with ponies in this country.

Grass

Most owners of horses are eager to see that their animals have access to green grass. Certainly fresh, new growth of grass in a clean pasture is excellent food for any horse. It is often the best medicine for an ailing animal. On the other hand, grass by itself will not keep a horse in condition to do hard work and must be supplemented by other feeds. Certainly, a horse who has any use at all should have some dry hay and grain in addition to pasture, no matter how good the pasture. If the pasture has been used for many years, it is very likely to be infested with worms or worm eggs, and a horse who uses it should be wormed at 21-day intervals. In urban areas one frequently sees little plots of so-called pasture in which there are great spaces where the grass has been gnawed down to the roots, and smaller spaces filled with grass that has grown to maturity and dried. Such pastures are worse than useless. If the urban horse owner has only an acre of ground, he will do well to divide it into two or three parts, allow the horse to graze it down fairly short in one part, then turn the horse on another part while the first part grows a little. This will ensure a constant supply of new growth of grass, which is the kind most useful to the horse. Such a dividing of a pasture will be a great help if the horseman lives in an area where irrigation is the method used to raise grass. Any horseman will do well to consult his county agricultural agent about the best kind of grass for his purpose. An attempt is frequently made in the arid regions of the Southwest to grow alfalfa for horse pasture. Alfalfa will not stand the trampling of horses. In this area Bermuda is the best grass. There are permanent pasture mixtures which will do well if one has sufficient area, but they will not take the punishment that Bermuda will take. In parts of the country where rainfall is ample, a mixture of grasses will often provide proper pasture for a horse. Bluegrass is excellent, and several of the bent grasses, such as redtop, are useful. Clovers, generally speaking, will not stand much trampling.

As a final note, it may be suggested that the electric fence (*see* FENC-ING) is a great help to the horseman in dividing a small pasture.

Gravel

Occasionally (fortunately not often) a small piece of sand or gravel will work its way up between the wall of a horse's foot and the tender part of the foot. In this event, the foreign particle keeps working its way upward and will finally form an abscess at the coronary band. When the abscess breaks or is opened by a competent veterinarian, it can be treated like any other open wound. Usually, when properly treated, a horse that has been graveled recovers completely; if, however, during the process of working its way upward in the foot the foreign particle has caused enough inflammation to do structural damage to the foot, permanent lameness may result.

Any horse of value showing lameness should be examined by a competent veterinarian. If he is worth keeping, he is worth such care. The diagnosis of lameness is often a difficult matter. Many would-be authorities will look at a horse and prescribe a medicine for blister or even recommend that the horse be fired (*see* FIRING). As a rule, the only virtue of the remedy prescribed is that it makes the owner rest the horse. Sometimes, prompt attention to lameness by a veterinarian means the difference between permanent damage and complete cure. For example, a horse with a bowed tendon, if attended to immediately by a competent veterinarian, will, unless the damage is extreme, completely recover, thanks to modern treatment; but if the bowed tendon is not taken care of promptly, the bow will be permanent.

Gray. *See* COLOR OF THE HORSE

Grazing Bit

A grazing bit is a curb bit with a low port and short, curved shanks. Its construction makes it possible for a horse to eat grass with the bit in his mouth without putting pressure on the shanks of the bit.

Great Horse

The earliest horses in England of which written account is available were of two distinctly different types. One was the small, easy-gaited horse, typified by the Hobbies and the Galloways (treated under their respective headings in this book), probably of origin similar to that of the Iceland Pony (*see* ICELAND PONY), whose easy gait is attributed by some writers to genets brought back to the land of the Vikings by Varangians returning from Constantinople in the eleventh century.

The other type was a gigantic animal of uniformly white color, according to Sir Walter Gilbey, Bart., in his book *The Great Horse*. In partial support of his theory, Sir Walter offers the following translation from Caesar's account of his experiences in England:

Most of them [the natives of England] use huge chariots in battle. They first scour up and down on every side, throwing their darts; creating disorder among the ranks by the terror of their horses and noise of their chariot wheels. When they get among troops of [their enemies'] horse they leap out of the chariots and fight on foot. Meanwhile, the charioteers retire to a little distance from the field. . . . They become so expert, by constant practice, that in rough hills and precipices they can stop their horses at full speed; and, on a sudden, check and turn them. They run around the pole stand on the yoke, and then, as quickly, into their chariots again. They frequently retreat on purpose, and after they have drawn men from the main body, leap from the pole and wage unequal war on foot.

Another bit of evidence of the Great Horse in England during the first century is the British coin bearing the likeness of a horse which was clearly an animal of draft type.

Sir Walter tells us that the Shire horse gets his excellent temperament, intelligence, and hardiness, as well as his size, from the Great Horse that was used to manipulate so cleverly the big clumsy chariots of the first century B.C. in England. According to Sir Walter, the Great Horse was the progenitor of the Suffolk, the Clydesdale, and the Shire. The Percheron descended from the massive equines of Flanders. It has been well established that the Great Horse of Flanders existed at a very early date, long before the Christian era, not only in western Europe but also in the fen lands of Lincolnshire and adjoining territory on the eastern coast of England. In this lush grassland developed the largest breed of horse the world has known.

Green Horse

The term *green horse* is a loose one and may be applied to any horse who has had very little handling. In the East, it is sometimes used by dealers to indicate a horse who has been shipped in from the area in which he was raised and has not been handled much.

Green Hunter

The American Horse Shows Association *Rule Book* states that "a green hunter is a horse of any age that is in his first or second year of showing in any classes at Regular Member Shows of this Association, or the Canadian Horse Shows Association, requiring horses to jump, except horses which have jumped over an obstacle lower than three feet, only to demonstrate obedience, i.e., trail horses."

Green Hunter Classes

A green hunter class is one in which only green hunters are shown. The height of jump for first-year horses is three feet and six inches. The height for second-year horses is three feet and nine inches. (These are minimums established by the American Horse Shows Association.)

Gretna Green Race

Gretna Green in England was the well-known marrying place for runaway couples. In the Gretna Green Race, a book, supposedly representing a register, is placed at one end of the arena or riding ring opposite the starting place. Couples holding hands race from the starting place to the book. One member dismounts and signs both names. He then remounts and they race back to the starting place. The couples must hold hands continually. If the hand hold is broken, the pair must start over again.

Griffin

A Griffin is the name given to one of the numerous breeds of ponies directly descended from *Equus przewalskii* (see PRZHEVALSKI). Being so closely related to this horse of the Pleistocene age, this tough, ugly little pony is particularly quick and has tremendous endurance. He is used in China for polo. Probably his quickness and his ability to stand up under the cussedness of the human race have contributed a great deal to the development of this oldest of games on horseback.

Gringo

Gringo is a slang border term for a non-Mexican originally signifying extreme contempt. It is still usually pejorative but is sometimes used today in a semihumorous way as a term of affection. It is said that during the war by which we relieved Mexico of the burden of Texas a song that was very popular with and sung frequently by the United States soldiers was "Green Grow the Violets." Hearing this sung so often, the Mexicans started calling the American soldiers "Gringos," which is about as close as they could come to "Green Grow." After all, that's about as close as the Texans came with their *buckaroo* to the Mexican *vaquero*.

Groom

Every well-kept horse is groomed once a day, whether he is worked or not. If he is worked until sweaty, he is groomed after he has dried out from his workout. The usual method of grooming is to use a rubber currycomb first. Starting at the hocks (only brushes and rub rags should be used below hocks and knees), one should curry every hair on a horse's body, with a circular motion, ending at his ears. Next, a dandy brush should be used in the same way, and vigorously. Then a rub rag, preferably one made from a linen salt sack (if the linen is not available, a good turkish towel will do) should be used vigorously both ways of the hair, again starting with the hocks and ending with the ears. The good horseman is careful to see that not a hair on a horse is missed, especially hairs between his forelegs and under his belly, inside the hind legs, etc. The rub rag can be used to wipe the dock and the underside of the tail, as well as to wipe the ears and the head and around eyes and nose and the legs below knees and hocks. The final use of the rub rag should be *with* the hair of the horse.

There is quite a trick to using a rub rag properly. It should not be held wadded up in a ball. The center of the rag, when the main part of the coat of the horse is being rubbed, should be grasped firmly and the ends allowed to flop back and forth. They will help get the dust out of the coat—especially important when cooling out a hot horse, for the ends of the rag help in the cooling process.

The final work should be done with a body brush, that is, a brush with fairly short bristles and a leather back. This should be used *with* the hair. Brushes should be kept clean and should be cleaned frequently during the process of grooming by being rubbed on a currycomb. All rub rags should be washed often.

Gymkhana pole bending. "Two entirely separate and distinct competitions are available, known as Table 1 and Table 2. Any show may offer sections in either or both tables. In both tables the rider shall have his choice of the side on which to pass the first pole. If more than one lane of competition is used, management should allow ample room between all running lanes and between the lanes and walls or fences." Table 1:

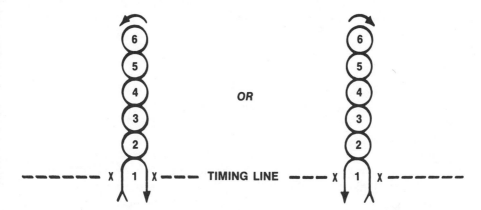

"Six poles shall be placed 20′ apart (18′ if competition is restricted to ponies) in a straight line down the approximate center of ring. The timing line shall be formed by two markers, one placed 15′ on each side of pole 1, so that pole 1 and the two markers forming the timing line be in a straight line perpendicular to the straight line formed by poles 1 through 6. The entry shall cross the timing line, bend between the poles, circle pole 6 (farthest pole), return through the course by bending between the poles, and cross the timing line."

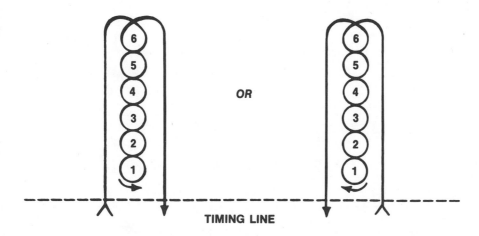

Gymkhana pole bending. Table 2: "Six poles shall be placed 21′ apart (18′ if competition is restricted to ponies) in a straight line down the approximate center of the ring, the first pole being 21′ from the timing line. The entry shall cross the timing line, move in an approximately straight line to pole 6 (farthest pole) make a 180° turn around pole 6, and cross the timing line, by moving along the poles on the side opposite that on which it first approached pole 6."

If the horse has sensitive skin, the part of his foot just above the heel, the part below the pastern, should be cleaned with the fingers only, for it is frequently very tender; any roughness or chapping here should receive immediate attention. Zinc oxide is usually effective in clearing up what are called scratches, a chapping of the little hollow just above the horse's heel. Feet should be cleaned with a hoof-pick. Often a nail or a rock can be detected entering the horse's foot before it does any damage (*see* GRAVEL).

Gymkhana

The gymkhana originated in India, and its original purpose was to relieve the boredom of life in a British military post. Since horses of show caliber were, of course, scarce, events for mounted contests had to center on the playing of games.

There is much to be said for the gymkhana, for it does not seem to engender as many petty jealousies as does the small horse show. The most successful gymkhanas are the product of ingenuity in devising events of a wide variety. Water races, egg and spoon contests, bun-eating races, ring-spearing contests, walking races, bedroll races (bedroll must be rolled, tied to saddle, taken to appointed area, unrolled, lain upon by horseman, re-rolled, tied to saddle, and returned to starting line), boot races, etc., can be indulged in by relatively inexperienced horsemen and gymkhanists. For more experienced horsemen the gymkhana may include various kinds of gymnastics on horseback similar to the monkey drill of cavalry days or stunts of the Cossack riders in circuses.

Habit

See APPOINTMENTS for information on apparel. *See* VICES for information on bad habits of a horse.

Hack (noun)

The term *hack* is used in the eastern part of the United States to designate any horse used for purposes other than racing, hunting, or showing. In some areas it means exclusively a horse that is kept for hire (a rent horse).

Hack (verb)

In the East, a person who rides for any purpose other than to show his horse or to hunt is said to *hack*. When a hunt moves from one covert to another, each of the mounted personnel is *hacking*. Their proper gait is the slow jog trot.

Hack, Hunter Hack

According to the American Horse Shows Association *Rule Book,* the hunter hack is to be shown at a walk, trot, and canter both ways of the ring, to jump two fences three feet six inches high, and to gallop one way of the ring. In Green and Young Hunter classes, hunter hacks are not to gallop.

Hackamore

Hackamore is a corruption of the Spanish *jáquima.* But *jáquima* denoted a specific piece of headgear as used in old Baja California, while *hackamore* is used very loosely. It denotes a bosal used with or without a fiador (*see* BOSAL and FIADOR), or any one of a great number of mechanical devices more specifically called hackamore bits (*see* HACKAMORE BIT) though with one exception they do not include a mouthpiece, and any homemade gear to put on a horse's head.

The jaquima, progenitor of all hackamores, is still used by the charros of Mexico. It is described by Don Carlos Rincon Gallardo, Duke de Regla, Marques de Guadalupe, celebrated charro, as follows:

Jáquima: es otra cabezada con ahogador, frontal, cabezal, trocillos, fiador y bozal, que tiene en su parte posterior una gaza con rozadero para que de ella se amarre el cabestro. Las hay para amansar y son de cerda, y otras de uso comun para apersogar animals. Estas se hacen de ixtle. Las primeras, claro esta, son mas fuertas que las segundas . . .

Very liberally translated and interpreted, the Don's description is of a rawhide bosal, a rather elaborate headstall that keeps the bosal in exactly

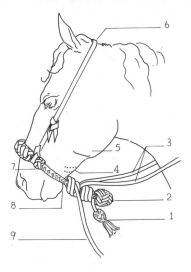

Simple hackamore. 1. Rope tassel; 2. heel knot; 3. reins; 4. point of pressure when reins are pulled; 5. cheek; 6. whang leather; 7. button; 8. chin; 9. lead rope.

Rope hackamore. 1. Rope tassel; 2. strings; 3. reins; 4. lead rope.

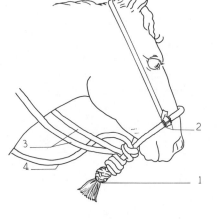

Hackamore with fiador (or theodore). 1. Reins fasten here.

the proper place, and a fiador that keeps the bosal from slipping below the chin but allows instant release of pressure on the jaw when the reins are released. The description includes reins (of hair) and lead rope. The *rozadero* (rough material) of the bosal where it contacts the bottom of the jaw indicates that the jaquima's authority worked on the jaw, not on the nose as do some of the gringo bosals. Northern cowboys, using larger and colder-blooded horses than do the charros, habitually use strong-armed methods including bosals of great diameter, their authority operating on the nose of the horse rather than on his jaw. Though they sometimes create excellent reining horses, it is doubtful that they ever attain the subtlety and immediacy of response attained by the charros of lower California and other parts of Mexico.

Hackamore Bit. *See also* HACKAMORE

Few humans live today whose hands are subtle enough to use successfully the jaquima (corrupted to *hackamore* by gringos) of the old Baja California horsemen. Some get along fairly well by using a bosal that depends largely upon nose pressure for authority rather than on jaw pressure as did the original jaquima. However, the best device for modern hands that would use a hackamore is one called a hackamore bit. The term is slightly misleading as it suggests something that is inside the horse's mouth. This is not true of most hackamore bits, though some are equipped with a removable mouthpiece, which it is claimed is helpful in the transition from hackamore to bit. The original hackamore bit, which was said to be originated by border Mexicans, consisted of two T-shaped metal sidepieces, a chain or rawhide nosepiece, and a chain under the jaw. The top of the T and the bottom of the T and both extremities of the crosspiece of the T terminated in holes large enough to admit the fastening of rawhide or

(Left) Hackamore bit, leather-covered flat metal nosepiece. 1. Hinge. (Center) Hackamore bit with padded nosepiece and removable bar. 1. Removable bar; 2. hinge. (*See* HACKAMORE BIT.) (Right) T-shaped hackamore bit. 1. Reins fasten here; 2. bridle fastens here; 3. flat metal band. (*See* HACKAMORE BIT.)

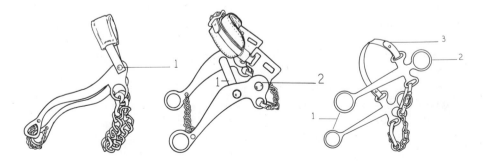

chain. The top of the T was attached to the cheekpiece of the bridle on each side. To the forward extremity of the crosspiece on each side was attached the nosepiece. To the rearward extremity of the crosspiece the jaw chain was attached. The reins were attached to the bottoms of the sidepieces. When the reins were pulled, the rawhide or chain over the nose was tightened, as was the chain under the jaw. Many variations of this original hackamore bit have been devised, some of them very fancy, but they all involve the principle of the old T-shaped hackamore bit.

Hackney

On the distaff side, the Hackney springs from the Norfolk Trotter. This was a breed that supposedly sprang originally from Norwegian horses brought to England by Norse invaders. We do know for certain that from the beginning to the middle of the eighteenth century there were heavy, round-boned, and more or less cart-horse-shaped trotters in Norfolk. They were of varied sizes and types but were referred to as Norfolk Trotters. In 1760 a horse called the Shales horse was foaled. He, like Justin Morgan, Gaines Denmark, and Allen F. One, was extremely prepotent, so prepotent that he fixed the type of his breed.

Shales was sired by a Thoroughbred called Blaze. Blaze was by Flying Childers, who in turn was sired by the Darley Arabian, one of the foundation sires of the modern Thoroughbred (*see* THOROUGHBRED). The breeding of the Shales horse to Norfolk mares produced horses of extremely fine action and refined the conformation of those old trotters. Like Justin Morgan, Shales's prepotency was so great that not only were his immediate get of uniform type but for two and three generations the conformity continued.

Before the railroads came to England, the Hackney's position was very similar to that of the progenitors of the American Saddle Horse. That is, he was a road horse but was used under saddle to carry the farmer to market and occasionally the farmer's wife as well, riding behind her spouse on a pillion. On other days the Hackney was used for jobs about the farm. In some instances, the trips to market were long ones, and the Hackney was highly valued for his ability to trot fast over an extended time. It is not well known that the Hackney was the first horse in the world to trot fast. He was also a long-distance trotter. There are records of seventeen miles an hour over ordinary roads. In 1794 a mare known only as Ogden's Mare trotted 4 miles in 12 minutes and 14 seconds. Subsequently she trotted 30 miles in 2 hours carrying 252 pounds in the saddle. Another Hackney named Phenomena trotted 17 miles in 56 minutes and the same distance another time in 53 minutes. At 23 years of age this mare trotted 9 miles in 28 minutes and 30 seconds. In 1815 Fenton's Mare trotted a mile on the road in 2 minutes and 58 seconds. Then she covered a mile on Sudbury

Common in 2 minutes and 53 seconds. In 1832 a mare named Nonpareil trotted 100 miles in 9 hours 56 minutes and 57 seconds.

The establishment of railroads and the improvement of highways almost caused the extinction of the Hackney. He was not heavy enough to be kept purely as a draft animal on farms, and the lighter driving horse replaced him on the highway. During the latter part of the nineteenth century much of the breeding stock was sold. But a few of the old faithful breeders kept at the improvement of the breed, and they so improved its action and its style that the Hackney became the most prized carriage horse, or heavy-harness horse as it is called, in the show-ring in the world. In the 1880s Danegelt sold for $25,000. From the turn of the century until about 1925 the popularity of the Hackney increased, and the Hackney was the personification of style and excellence in the show-ring.

Of course, the automobile greatly reduced the demand for heavy-harness horses of all breeds in America, including the Hackney. There are a few studs of Hackneys in Eastern states, and a few importations are still being made. However, the present demand for Hackneys is limited entirely to the show-ring, and the breeding of these horses is certainly on a limited scale, more limited, in the writer's view, than they deserve, for it has been proved time and again that a Hackney cross produces an excellent hunter and jumper. Some of the greatest records (high jumping records) have been made by horses with some Hackney blood. Why the Hackney was never used in the West, where a compact, handy, hardy horse is highly prized, is a mystery, for this is a horse of great intelligence and stamina and can easily be taught the things that Western horses are asked to do.

The Modern Hackney and Pony

In 1931 Henry Vaughan stated that among 1,000 Hackneys taken at random from the *American Hackney Stud Book* there were 545 chestnuts, 255 bays, 137 browns, 29 roans, 28 blacks, and 6 grays. Dark chestnuts, bays, and browns are preferred. At the time he was writing, over half the breed were chestnuts and 93 percent were chestnut, bay, or brown. The Hackney frequently has flashy white markings such as a star or strip and one or more white ankles or stockings. His height varies from 14 hands to 16.3, but he is usually 15 or 16 hands. He weighs well for his height. He possesses true heavy-harness type, including compactness and fullness of form, roundness of middle, great smoothness and finish, length and arch of neck, a smartly carried tail, medium length of leg. He is upheaded, clean-cut, alert, and stylish to a degree. He is muscular throughout and has substance in bone and quality as well. The modern Hackney is a more refined horse and has more finish than the Hackney of yesterday. The head of the Hackney is rather square in outline yet clean-cut and with a good eye and ear. The neck is middling long and well crested but frequently a bit heavy and full at the throttle. The shoulders are sloping and smooth, the back strong, the rib round, and the coupling good. The croup is long, level, and well muscled, and the thighs and quarters are also muscular. The joints are large and strong, yet clean, and the bone is plentiful and of excellent quality. Pasterns are of good length and slope. The Hackney has a good foot, and the breed has a reputation for soundness.

The Hackney has a remarkably high and flashy "all-around" way of going which is often accentuated by his white ankles or stockings. He is an active, snappy, true, rapid walker but excels particularly at the trot. His stride is very high and fairly long, and is elastic and easy; he usually displays excellent manners in harness. He has the spirit, mettle, boldness, poise, and a natural action which enable him to put up a big show.

Perhaps the fame of the Hackney is more widely spread by the Hackney pony than by the full-sized horse. Obviously, it is easy to select for the smaller size, and the Hackney ponies have all the qualities of the full-sized horse. There are many kinds of classes for Hackney ponies—roadster classes, harness classes (similar to what used to be called heavy-harness classes), and sometimes classes called cob-tailed pony classes. The flashy action and brilliance of these ponies always appeals to the spectators, and the proud little fellows in harness seem to be fond of the applause they get. Both the Hackney horses and the Hackney ponies are registered under the authority of the American Hackney Horse Society, 527 Madison Avenue, New York, New York 10022. Other Hackney horse organizations are the following: Canadian Hackney Horse Society (Mrs. W. A. Burke, Port Stanley, Ontario, Canada); England Hackney Horse Society (16 Bedford Square, London, W.C. 1, England); Midwest Hackney Association (Mrs. Paul Hanks, Pittsfield, Illinois 62363); South Central Hackney Association (Mr. E. P. Woods, Maple Avenue, Danville, Kentucky 40422); New England Hackney Association (Mrs. Barbara Doane, 49 Pinhill Road, Swampscott, Massachusetts 01907); Ohio Hackney Association (Mrs. James W. Watkins, 136 High Street, Canfield, Ohio 44406); Southeastern Hackney Association (Mrs. Sylvia Gettys, Westland Drive, Concord, Tennessee 37720).

Hackney Pony. *See* HACKNEY and AMERICAN HACKNEY HORSE SOCIETY

Half-Arab and Anglo-Arab Registries

The Half-Arab and Anglo-Arab records are kept by the Half-Arab and Anglo-Arab Registries, 224 East Olive Avenue, Burbank, California 91503. As the name implies, a foal by a registered Arabian can be registered in the Half-Arab Registry, and a foal from an Arabian and a Thoroughbred is eligible for registration in the Anglo-Arab Registry.

Half Halt

The term *half halt* is used more by people who display their horsemanship verbally at cocktail parties than by those who spend their lives with horses.

It designates that very momentary hesitation which some horses require for change of leads when executing the figure eight. The change of leads comes in the middle of the figure, when the horse is starting to change directions in the ring—in other words, where the lines of the figure eight cross. The horse is not brought to a complete halt. He is collected on his canter slightly and slowed down almost to a halt; then, usually while he has his weight on one hind foot, he shifts his balance and changes his lead. Overcollection or complete stopping at the point of change in the figure eight will defeat the rider's purpose entirely.

Half halt is also used as a balancing and suppling exercise in dressage (*see* DRESSAGE).

Half-Turn

The command *half-turn* is used by some instructors in equitation. When a group of riders is going in single file next to the fence or wall of the arena or riding hall and the command "Half-turn" is given, each rider individually turns toward the center of the ring. He then proceeds to the opposite side of the ring and thence goes in the direction the reverse of that from which he started. The half-turn may be done at any gait, but whatever gait the horse is on when the command is given is the one he should maintain throughout the maneuver. To the Western rider, this maneuver suggests a rather watered-down version of the rollback (*see* ROLLBACK). It is done much more slowly; and the original turn is that of a half-circle, some six to eight feet if the horse is at a walk and a larger half-circle if he is at a faster gait. When the horse reaches the opposite side of the arena if he is at a gallop, he should change leads as he takes up the new direction.

In Reverse

Some equitation instructors vary the half-turn as follows: The riders circling the ring next to the fence or wall at the given signal pull away from the fence on a diagonal and then make a half-turn toward it, reversing their direction around the ring. This, too, suggests to the Western rider a rollback, and, of course, if it is done at any speed at all it actually is a rollback (*see* ROLLBACK).

Halt

Most well-bred horses, if they are well cared for and in good health, have to be taught to stand still for any length of time. Just as most children find it difficult to remain still, so do well-bred horses. In the show-ring it is permitted, after horses are lined up, for a horse to move about in a small circle if the lineup has to wait for one or two horses to work out on the rail. For some kinds of show-ring classes horses are taught to stand with their feet in a certain position. Sometimes this position is called camping or stretching or parking. For many years the standard horseman's term for this particular stance was *posing*. The term *stretch* was a bit humorous because the horse who stretches his forefeet forward naturally is a lame horse, horses with sore front feet almost invariably stretch, and so do male equines when they urinate.

Until recently, the proper pose was one in which the horse's forelegs were straight up and down and the hind legs pushed forward slightly. That is, the hind feet were a little farther back than they would be if the horse stood naturally. However, lately the amateurish *stretching* has grown in popularity in show-ring circles, and in respectable horse-show classes one now often sees horses stand with their front and hind feet stretched apart. Horses shown in what are now called halter classes should, when standing still, have their feet squarely under them. That is, they should not have one hind foot or one forefoot stuck out ahead of its mate. To have one *hind* foot *slightly* ahead of the other is not a bad fault when the horse is standing. Special ways of standing are fashionable from time to time in certain specific classes. For instance, in Arabian halter classes now, it is quite the thing to have the horse stretch his nose forward just as a stallion will stretch his head out when sniffing at a lady newcomer. In some American Saddle Horse halter classes, it is the prevailing mode to have the horse pose with his forelegs straight up and down and his hind legs extended a little farther back.

Six-day-old Arabian colt (sired by Naborr) being taught to lead by owner, Marylou Namesnik. (*See* HALTER BREAKING.)

Halter Breaking. *See also* COLTS

The competent horseman who handles horses of some value usually shudders or swears, at least inwardly, at the word *breaking*, whether used alone or in the phrase *halter breaking*, when it is applied to a horse. If an animal is properly handled from foaling time onward, there is no traumatic experience in his education that merits the term *breaking*. The foal who is handled from the time he is dropped will not fight a halter. Many good horsemen have a tiny halter ready to put on the foal as soon as he is dry and finds his sea legs.

When the halter is put on the little fellow, it is a good idea to make a browband out of muslin or some other soft material, for a halter will slide back on its neck, pulling the nosepiece up to an uncomfortable position.

When a tiny foal is haltered and handled gently and quietly, he can be maneuvered around the stall by the handler, who puts his left hand on the halter and his right hand on the baby's rump. Of course, the addition of a short rope to the halter can be made as soon as the baby finds out what is wanted. At this stage, no lesson should be very long, for the infant equine, like the infant human, has a short attention span. If the owner of a colt has failed to acquaint him with a halter until he has reached some months

Rope momentarily too high under tail, causing colt to kick.

or even years of age, the problem of getting him used to a halter is quite a little greater than it would have been had the job been done at the proper time. The first thing to do is to get the halter on the animal without exciting him. This, of course, can best be done in a stall where the animal is fed and used to being comfortable.

The first lesson should consist simply of having the halter worn and handled gently by the trainer without his exercising restraint for the first few days. Then a lead rope or shank can be attached to the halter. It should be long enough so that it cannot easily be jerked out of the trainer's hand. With this shank or rope, the colt can be turned a step or two to either side in the stall. With a few repetitions at each lesson, the colt will soon realize that a pull on the halter means that the trainer wants him to go in a different direction.

A colt's first reaction to a pull on the halter shank is usually the same kind of reaction one would get from a child if one attached a rope to his wrist and pulled on it. The child would pull back. With some colts, a gentle stroking of the animal and a gentle tone of voice can persuade him to do what the trainer is trying to get him to do when he pulls on the rope. With other animals, it may be necessary for the trainer to use enough force to make the animal move one foot in the desired direction. As soon as he does so, he should be given to understand that he has done what is wanted.

Pulling *forward* on a halter is always an error. The first pulling on a halter may be done to the side. If the colt can get the idea that what is wanted is for him to step to one side when the halter is pulled to the side, the most difficult lesson will have been learned. This lesson is best learned in a stall or some enclosure.

To teach the colt to move out, the best help is a rope long enough to be doubled around the animal's rump. It may then be run through the halter, in which case both ends of the rope have to be run through the halter and should be kept even. It is a good idea to have a lead shank (*see* HALTER SHANK) as well as the doubled rope in the trainer's hand when he is attempting this maneuver. The rope around the rump obviates the necessity for any strong pull forward on the halter. When it is desired to have the colt move forward, a *slight* pull, just enough to be a signal, on the halter may be given; then the rump rope is used to provide impulsion forward. Frequently, when the colt does respond, he may kick, play, and buck a little. At this point the lead shank comes in handy to keep his head going in the desired direction.

Of course, every horse should learn to stand tied. No attempt should be made to teach the colt to stand tied until he is taught what the halter is for and until he leads readily, easily, and obediently. Then he can be led up to the place where he will be tied, where he should be held for a few minutes by hand. The same thing should be done repeatedly until he gets the idea that when he comes to this spot, he is supposed to stand. To tie the colt solid for the first time, the best place is a good, stout wall, in which a ring has been securely fastened at about the height at which the colt holds his head when he is walking or trotting. If the wall is not available, whatever the colt is tied to should be strong enough so there is no danger of breakage, and there should be some provision (possibly a swivel) to prevent the colt from winding the rope around the post or tree. Furthermore, if he is tied to a fence, the fence must be of such construction that there is no danger of his putting a forefoot through it and injuring himself. The violence of a colt's struggle when first tied up can be minimized and the speed of his education accelerated by using a stout piece of rubber, such as a small inner tube. The rubber must be very securely wired or tied to the ring in the post or wall. Then the stout halter rope must be securely tied to the rubber. The entire distance from halter ring to ring in post or wall should be not much greater than the distance from the post or wall ring to the ground; otherwise the colt may continually get his forefoot over the halter rope.

The colt should be left tied until he is completely convinced of the futility of pulling against the halter rope. He should not be frightened or yelled at during this lesson. Any and all violence must be on his part only. It is not unusual for this first lesson to require several hours, and the wise trainer will very quietly offer the colt water if the weather is warm. Some trainers like to place a little good, green leafy hay at the base of the post or wall for the colt to nibble while he is standing tied. This will not stay in place long if the colt is nervous. However, it can be replaced often; and a small amount at a time is better than too much.

No colt should be left unattended during this first lesson. Somebody must be within earshot and close enough to be able to see the colt at all times in case he throws himself in a bad position or otherwise needs attention.

Halters

Halters are of as great a variety as bridles. The choice of a halter for the show-ring should be made only after the purchaser has observed the current fashion in halters in his particular show-ring because this changes almost annually. A halter for use around the stable may well be of leather with brass fittings that will not rust. The ordinary halter used around the stable of show horses is fairly heavy so that it will last. However, if a halter is to be left on a horse while he is unattended, it is very wise to have it of extremely light leather so that should it be hung up on anything protruding in the stall it will break easily.

Some leather halters are so constructed that they tighten up under the jaw when the halter shank is pulled. It is difficult to imagine why such halters were invented; for if punishment under the jaw is desired, it can readily and effectively be obtained by using a halter shank (*see* HALTER

SHANK) one end of which is chain. The snap of the halter shank may be run through the D on the near side of the halter. Then the snap with chain attached can be passed under the horse's jaw and snapped into the D on the off side of the halter. Obviously any shaking or jerking on the halter shank will pull this chain sharply against the horse's jaw. Some trainers prefer to pass the chain over the horse's nose rather than under the jaw.

If the kind of halter that tightens around a horse's nose and under his jaw is used, a horse should never be tied up with it. It is possible with halters of this variety to snap the halter shank into the ring through which the strap under the jaw runs and thereby eliminate the tightening-up action.

For many years in the West, the standard halter has been the Johnson rope halter. It comes usually in three sizes, and the middle-sized one can be adjusted so that it will fit almost any horse. This halter used to be made only out of cotton rope, but now nylon is also used. If you buy such a halter you should tighten up the metal fastenings because any severe pull will make them slip on a nylon halter. The tightening up is easy to do. The fastening can be placed on a piece of metal and then hit with a hammer until it squeezes down tightly on the nylon. Nylon web halters of gay colors are now popular. They too are adjustable and come in various sizes. No halter, whether it is nylon, cotton rope, or leather, should be left on an unattended horse unless it is of such light construction that it can easily be broken. The halter should be so adjusted that the nosepiece or the D joining the nosepiece to the cheekpiece does not rub against the cheekbones. With leather halters, there are usually adjustments for the length of the strap over the head and the length of the strap under the jaw. The only caution as far as length of the strap under the jaw is concerned is that the halter be not taken up so tight that it rubs on the horse's jaw when he eats. The part over the head, the strap that runs behind the horse's ears, should be tight enough so that it will not be thrown over the horse's ears when he shakes his head, but it should not be tight enough to come up under his throttle and be uncomfortable if he pulls his chin in and flexes his neck.

Halter Shank

The best halter shank (lead rope or strap) for most purposes is one which is part strap and part chain. Its overall length is usually eight feet and two inches including a two-inch snap. The chain part is either 18 or 24 inches long. The 18-inch length is preferred as a rule. The strap should be of good leather about an inch wide. It should be kept soft and pliable with saddle soap at all times.

Rope shanks (of which no stable seems ever to have enough) should be of cotton and three-quarters of an inch in diameter. The reason for specifying cotton is that nylon is too slippery for the hands, and a grass rope or a nylon rope will burn a horse's leg quickly if he gets his foot over the rope and saws it back and forth. Worse still, if he gets the rope around a hind leg just above the hoof, he will saw on it and produce a very bad burn which is often hard or impossible to heal. Rope halter shanks are usually from seven to nine feet in length. The longer ones are frequently fitted with an adjustable fastening; the rope can be placed around the horse's neck and then snapped into the adjustable fastening. Every wise horseman knows that no horse should be tied only by a rope around the neck, because horses have died from being tied this way. (When a horse puts his head down, the rope usually slips around on his neck so that the pull is between his ears rather than under his throttle. When he raises his head and feels that pull between his ears, he rears back and either chokes himself to death or breaks his neck.) The advantage of snapping the rope around the horse's neck is that the rest of the shank can be passed through the halter ring before it is tied to a post. Then if there is any pull on the shank, the pull is on the rope shank around the horse's neck rather than on the halter, but the shank is kept down where it belongs. Rope shanks are frequently provided with snaps that have no swivels. However, for the slight extra expense, a swivel snap is to be preferred.

Halting (a group of riders)

If the leader of a group of riders halts suddenly without warning, the chances are very good that some damage will be done behind him. A horse will come up on the rear of the horse ahead of him and be kicked. All riders in the group should be informed before starting on a ride what warning signal will be used. The most common one is the raising of the hand of the leader. Then each rider in turn raises his hand so that the one behind him is aware that a stop is impending. The old rule of keeping at least one horse's distance from the horse ahead is often disregarded, frequently to someone's sorrow. However, when a group of riders is stopping, it is quite important that at least four or five feet separate each horse from the horse in front of it. If a horse is restive and will not stand still on the trail, he should, if it is at all possible, be turned at right angles to the trail. If the country is open and flat, he can be ridden out of line and turned in a short circle. However, in much Western trail riding, this maneuver is impossible. On some mountain trails, stops may be necessary where there is no opportunity to turn a horse at all. In such an event, if the horse is restive, the rider should dismount. Of course if the trail is extremely narrow, he cannot do so, and the only alternative is to attempt to calm the horse by stroking his neck and restraining him with light pressure on the reins, with the bridle hand held as low as possible. The rider ahead of the one whose mount is restive should be warned that there is trouble behind him.

No one should lead a group of riders unless his horse is well mannered and "both ends of him can be ridden." That is, the horse should be one who can be moved sideways, backward, forward, or on a diagonal as readily as the rider can move his own feet. He should, of course, be a horse who will swing his hindquarters around the forehand or the forehand around the hindquarters at the will of his rider. Furthermore, he should be a horse who will not kick if touched on the rump by a horse behind him.

Halting (the horse)

Improper stopping of the horse can be one of the many causes of a bad mouth. Proper signals to stop a well-trained horse are increase of rein pressure in rhythm with the horse's head movements accompanied by light collection or increase of collection, not leaning back and yanking on the reins. (*See* SLIDING STOP.)

Any jerking or otherwise maltreating of the horse's mouth will not increase the speed of his stopping. Rather, it will make the horse throw his head in the air and keep on going. Sometimes it is desirable to teach a horse the verbal signal to stop. This can be done by always giving the verbal signal "Whoa" when one uses the reins and the leg aids to stop the horse. Gradually the reins and the leg aids can be diminished and, finally, entirely dispensed with. There is one big disadvantage to this procedure. If the horse has been taught the lesson too well, he may, when performing in the show-ring at a fair rate of speed, stop very suddenly when someone says "Whoa" right beside him. No matter what method is used in halting or stopping a horse, he should come to a stop without any evidence of discomfort—that is, without throwing his head or yawing his mouth open or hopping up and down. This is the case whether the horse stops casually as might be done in a pleasure ride on a nice bridle path or whether he comes to a sliding stop from a full gallop (as is explained under STOPPING). Furthermore, the horse should stop squarely in line with his line of progress; he should not twist his quarters off to one side—or his forehand, either, for that matter. A horse ridden by a rider who knows how to control only one "end of a horse" will rarely stop properly. If the horse is well trained and the rider is knowledgeable, the hindquarters are as responsive to the rider's legs as is the forehand to the rein. His hindquarters can be easily kept in line when he is coming to a stop, whether from a high rate of speed or from a slow walk.

Hambletonian (Society and Race). *See* HAMBLETONIAN TEN

Hambletonian Ten (Rysdyk's Hambletonian)

Hambletonian Ten or Rysdyk's Hambletonian is the most famous and the most influential progenitor of the modern harness race horse. Like Justin Morgan, he had a very modest beginning of his career. He was sold as a foal with his dam for $125 to William Rysdyk of Orange County, New York, in 1849. Mr. Rysdyk was a farmer of limited means, and the horse earned for him $184,725 in stud fees. During the horse's 21 years in stud, he sired 1,321 foals and became so famous by virtue of bare speed that his fee was placed at $500. When we consider the difference in the value of the dollar in 1849 and today, that was quite a fee for a trotting horse. Like all great progenitors of which there is any accurate record of breeding, Hambletonian Ten was inbred. Hambletonian Ten's sire, Abdallah, was a very unpopular horse at the time of his getting Hambletonian Ten. He was said to be ugly and possessed of a bad disposition. However, he was a grandson of Imported Messenger. Hambletonian Ten's dam was known simply as the Kent Mare. She was a cripple and had been purchased out of sentiment; no one seemed to think much of her. However, her dam was the daughter of Bishop's Hambletonian, a son of Imported Messenger; and the Kent Mare's second dam, Silver Tail, was a daughter of Imported Messenger. So the Kent Mare, though a cripple and not well thought of, was a double great-granddaughter of Imported Messenger; and Abdallah, sire of Hambletonian Ten, was a grandson of Imported Messenger.

Hambletonian was a bay horse with black points and two white hind ankles. He was 15.2 hands in height. His neck and throttle were said to suggest those of a Thoroughbred, and his muscular development has been described as tremendous. It is said that his croup was higher than his withers and that his hind legs were placed well behind his croup rather than under him. He sired 150 sons who were sires of speed and 80 daughters who were successful dams of race horses. He died in 1876, and a monument was erected in his memory. His name is kept alive in the minds of the public, however, better by the work done by the Hambletonian Association than by any monument. That association, formed in 1923, established what is known as the "Hambletonian," a race for three-year-olds for a large stake. It was first held in Syracuse, New York, in 1926. Since then, it has taken place at the Good Time Track at Goshen, New York. This race has caused Goshen to become the leading center of trotting races in this country.

Hamstring

The hamstring is the big tendon that runs upward from the point of a horse's hock, often called the tendon of Achilles. It corresponds to the tendon of Achilles in the human leg, which is the big tendon running upward from the back of the heel. The name comes from the myth that that part of the body was the only part of Achilles which was vulnerable to any injury.

Hand

Hand is the term used in stating the horse's height. A hand is four inches. In old horse-trading days, it was not unusual to see a rough approximation of a horse's height obtained by standing the horse on fairly hard level ground and then placing a buggy whip or a pole upright close to him and opposite the highest point of his withers. The point on the pole that was level with the highest point of his withers would be marked. Then a man would take the pole in his hand and measure the number of palm widths from the end of the pole that had been on the ground to the mark that had been made opposite the horse's withers. Measurement was done by grasping the pole hand over hand from the end to the mark. Presumably, the width of a man's hand is about four inches. When horse trading was as common as is automobile dealing today, most men who dealt in horses were well aware of the width of their hands and could come remarkably close to ascertaining a horse's height by the method just described.

Nowadays, in writing a horse's height, we put a period after the hand. The period is followed by a number representing the inches beyond the number of hands of the horse's height. Thus, 15.2 indicates that a horse is 15 hands and 2 inches high at the highest point of his withers.

Handicap Jumping

In small informal shows when there are not sufficient entries to fill a number of jumping classes, horses and riders of various sizes, ages, and abilities can compete in the same class by varying the jump to suit the horse and rider. This places considerable responsibility on the judge, for if a Shetland pony clears an 18-inch jump in excellent form, he should win over a full-sized horse who does not clear a 3½-foot jump in as good form.

Handicaps (in racing)

Prior to the formation of what was called the Kentucky Association in 1826, race horses were handicapped by a series of head starts. But this practice was very unsatisfactory, and the association standardized not only the length of races but also handicaps so that horses of known speed could compete on more or less equal footing with those whose speed had not been established. This handicapping, as we know, is now done by the requirement of weight to be carried by horses of known speed.

Difference in the weight of jockeys is not as important as difference in the amount of dead weight a horse has to carry, for a good jockey with his live weight and the ability to balance himself can compensate for some extra pounds. The addition of dead weight is a true handicap.

Hands (position of). *See also* GOOD HANDS

When one is concerned purely with establishing rapport between horse and rider, position of the hands is determined entirely by what horse and rider are doing. If the position of hands is observed in one of the great equine competitions in this country (say, the $10,000 Five-Gaited Stake at Louisville), a tremendous variety of positions of hands as well as of methods of holding the reins is found. To obtain speed, action, balance on the hind-quarters, or what not, one rider may carry his hands very high. On another horse with equal speed and action, the rider may carry hands relatively low. However, in show classes in which the rider is being judged, there is a "correct" position. If the horse is excellently trained, quite amenable, and not excitable, all will go well when maintaining this "correct" position of hands. The position is as follows:

ENGLISH (according to the American Horse Shows Association *Rule Book*)

Hands should be held in an easy position, neither perpendicular nor horizontal to the saddle, and should show sympathy, adaptability, and control. The height the hands are held above the horse's withers is a matter of how and where the horse carries his head. The method of holding the reins is optional, except that both hands shall be used and all reins must be picked up at one time. Bight of rein should be on the off side.

WESTERN (according to the American Horse Shows Association *Rule Book*)

In repose, arms are in a straight line with body, the one holding reins bent at elbow. Only one hand is to be used for reining and hands shall not be changed. Hand to be around reins. When ends of split reins fall on near side, one finger between reins permitted. When using romal or when ends of split reins are held in hand not used for reining, no finger between reins is allowed. The position of the hand not being used for reining is optional but it should be kept free of the horse and equipment and held in a relaxed manner with the rider's body straight at all times. Rider may hold romal or end of split reins to keep from swinging and to adjust the position of the reins provided it is held at least 16 inches from the reining hand. Hands to be above horn and as near to it as possible. Bracing against horn or coiled reata will be penalized.

Since good horsemanship is a matter of receiving communications through the reins as well as giving directions through the reins, there should be as much flexibility in the wrist, arm, and hands of the rider as possible. The straight line dictated by show-ring standards for English riding militates against this flexibility. So when one is not in show-ring competition, it is advisable to keep the wrist bent so that the palm tends to bend inward. The writer was pleased to learn from one whose equestrian education had been conducted in Australia that Australian riding masters demand a "roundness" at the wrist rather than the straight arm described. (*See* FORWARD SEAT.)

Hand Up

A relatively small assistant can help a fairly large rider mount without great effort on the assistant's part if he uses the following method. The rider stands opposite the horse's shoulder, facing it. The assistant bends his left knee and places his left hand on his leg palm up a few inches above the knee. Then the rider places his left foot in the palm of the assistant's hand. When the assistant gives the signal that he is ready, the rider can spring up and settle himself into the saddle. As the rider puts weight into the assistant's palm, the assistant straightens his left leg. He does not attempt to lift the weight of the rider by pulling upward on his hand. It is quite important that the rider not give his spring until the assistant signals that he is ready.

Handy Hunter

A handy hunter is one suitable for hunting "trappy" country. Trappy country is territory in which the jumps are not necessarily high but diffi-cult by their very nature. That is, there may not be much takeoff, or the jumps may not be on level ground. It is particularly hard for a horse to negotiate a jump if the landing is lower than the takeoff, for instance. An in-and-out jump with the two obstacles 24 to 26 feet apart simulates the kind of jump a horse may have to negotiate in trappy country.

The American Horse Shows Association *Rule Book* states:

In Handy [Hunter] classes, fences shall simulate those found in "trappy" hunt-ing country. The course must have at least two changes of direction and at least one combination; horses are required to trot over one fence toward the end of the course and may be asked to lead over one fence. A pole over brush and jumps such as triple bar and hog's back and any spread over four feet are prohibited. The suggested distance for an in-and-out when used in a ring is 24–26 feet and on an outside course 26–28 feet.

The *Rule Book* further states that handy hunters should be judged from 60 to 75 percent on their performance and from 25 to 40 percent on their conformation.

Harness (care of)

To prevent discomfort causing misbehavior of the horse and subsequent sores, and also to prevent breakage in harness, all harness must be kept clean and pliable with oil and/or saddle soap. Good castile soap is excel-lent for cleaning harness and saddlery of any kind. Pure neat's-foot oil is excellent for preserving and keeping the leather soft. However, since leather oiled with neat's-foot or a similar preparation is likely to stain a white horse or the clothing of a rider, glycerin saddle soap may be used in place of oil. To oil, all buckles need not be undone each time a harness is cleaned. A periodic thorough cleaning in which every buckle is undone and leather cleaned thoroughly where it passes through buckles should be given. If this kind of cleaning is done by the less experienced stable help, each buckle must be undone individually and rebuckled after the leather is cleaned before the next buckle is treated. If all buckles are undone at once by an inexperienced hand, professional help may be required to reassemble the harness. In some climates a well-oiled harness will mildew if stored over long periods of time without cleaning. Therefore, it is wise to give periodic soaping to a harness that is stored and not in use.

Harness (first lessons in). *See also* COLTS, *Use of Breaking Cart*

The first lesson in training in harness may well begin at an early age. The age at which the colt is first harnessed will usually depend upon the size of harness available to a good horseman. If pony harness is at hand, it does no harm to put it on a very small colt. Of course, he should not be asked to respond to much discipline but he can be acquainted with having harness put on him carefully and then removed. A long yearling may well be harnessed and driven on longlines before it is time to put weight on his back. (*See* COLTS.) The bridle should be fitted, as should a bridle for any purpose, so that the bit hangs snugly in the corner of the horse's mouth. The throatlatch should never be so tight that it pulls up on the throttle when the horse brings his chin in. Breast collars, if used, should be so adjusted that they do not pull up on the windpipe or hang down on the shoulders and interfere with the leg movements. Backstraps should be short enough so that the crupper does not hang down away from the dock; bellybands should be snug but not uncomfortably tight. For the first few lessons, the harness should simply be put on, then taken off. Then long-lines may be used, as explained under *Longlines* (main heading COLTS).

Harness Classes

Until the middle of this century, harness classes in shows were of three kinds: heavy-harness, fine-harness, and roadster.

Originally, heavy-harness horses wore curb bits and collars with hames —black collars with brass hames for the more formal classes and brown collars with steel hames for the more informal ones. At the turn of the century, heavy-harness classes were sometimes won by Saddle Horses, Standardbreds, or horses of mixed blood; but the Hackney finally became the undisputed monarch of the heavy-harness field. He was shown to a variety of vehicles—gigs (rather heavy two-wheeled vehicles), heavy phaetons (some drawn by single horses; others, by pairs), park drags (with four-in-hand), and road coaches. Today, shows include classes such as those just described, but they are for ponies and are not called heavy-harness classes but harness pony classes. The few exceptions—the few shows that include harness classes for Hackneys—are so rare that the American Horse Shows Association *Rule Book* states, "Hackney Horse classes and appointments may be had on application to the AHSA office," and otherwise omits them.

The term *fine harness* is still in use. The Fine Harness Horse Section is to be found in the Saddle Horse (American Saddlebred) Division of the AHSA *Rule Book*.

Fine Harness classes are divided into Junior, Horses Shown by Amateurs, Ladies' Fine Harness Horses, etc. The *Rule Book* states:

Horses must be of predominantly Saddlebred type. The gaits are (1) Park trot: an animated park gait, extreme speed to be penalized; and (2) walk: animated and graceful. Fine Harness Horses are to be shown with full mane and undocked tail. The preferred vehicle today (once a light top buggy with top down) is a small, topless buggy with four wire wheels. A light harness with snaffle bit and overcheck is required.

The AHSA *Rule Book* specifies harness classes for Arabians, Appaloosas, Morgans, Pintos, and various pony breeds. Of all these only the Morgan has a specified class that closely resembles the fine-harness class; it is called Park Horse in Harness. The Arabian Formal Driving class suggests the fine-harness class only in appointments. Both the Appaloosas and the Arabians have specified Pleasure Driving classes. The Appaloosa must show a walk, slow trot, and fast trot, but extreme speed is penalized. Unlike the fine-harness horse he is required to back. The specifications for both Morgan and Arabian Pleasure Driving classes omit word about backing or speed.

The term *roadster* survives today. Even the Arabians have Roadster classes. The Standardbred or trotting-bred horse is the outstanding contender for Open Roadster classes (those open to horses of all breeds). Perhaps the most hilariously noisy classes held are the Roadster classes in the little Kentucky shows. For some of them, the show-rings are round with steeply sloping sides. The faster a horse travels, the higher he climbs up the slope of the side. Such classes are indeed horse races, and races run right under the eyes of the ecstatic and noisy spectators. When rain descends upon such a class, horses, drivers, and front-row spectators are covered with mud by the end of the class. Needless to say, accidents in such classes are quite usual.

Whether in the wild setting just described or in more sedate environment, the Roadster class features speed at the trot. In addition to this, the AHSA *Rule Book* stresses the need for "animation, brilliance, and show ring presence." It also states that there are two types of roadsters: those suitable for a bike (*see* HARNESS RACING) and those suitable for a road wagon. The latter, it states, should have more scale and height than the former.

Harness Racing

Religious bigotry, rivalry of millionaires, Yankee inventiveness, and a few other factors, such as the appearance of prepotent sires and the improvement of roads, engendered the sport of harness racing. In 1802, racetracks

Bret Hanover (current champion of pacers), Frank Ervin up.

Nevele Pride (champion of trotters), Stanley Dancer up.

were closed and racing was banned, thanks to the efforts of righteous reformers. However, a horse race was declared to be a contest of horses at their fastest speed. Obviously a horse can run (gallop) faster than he can trot; so trotting contests continued. In these contests the horses, until about 1830, were under saddle, not hitched to vehicles.

By 1840, progress, including urban growth, made the trotting horse in light harness a very important part of life in the populated areas of this country. Better tracks were built, and men learned more about making light vehicles. Trotting races were largely harness races, and distance races became popular in 1829. Tom Thumb went to England and astounded British horsemen by trotting 100 miles in a little over 10 hours.

By the middle of the century, popularity of harness racing had grown sufficiently to arouse again the righteous indignation of the reformers. Decent folk frowned on anything related to the sport. However, the jingle of the guinea rescued harness racing from total dishonor and disgrace. Cornelius Vanderbilt and Robert Bonner (owner of the *New York Ledger* and a strict churchman) were ardent horsemen and rival reinsmen. Third Avenue and Harlem Lane were the scenes of their informal races. The fame of these "brush" races spread across the country. Although brought back to respectability for a while by the Vanderbilt-Bonner enthusiasm, harness racing again fell into disrepute because, it is alleged, of the gambling and corruption attending races. Again it was rescued, this time by the formation in 1870 of the Trotting Association, predecessor of the National Trotting Association, which in more recent times became one of several regional organizations causing confusion that seemed to spell certain disaster for the sport. Fortunately, it was saved by the formation of the

Equipment commonly worn by the pacer.

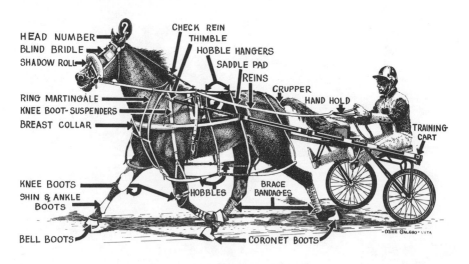

HEAD NUMBER
BLIND BRIDLE
SHADOW ROLL

CHECK REIN
THIMBLE
HOBBLE HANGERS
SADDLE PAD
REINS
CRUPPER
HAND HOLD

RING MARTINGALE
KNEE BOOT-SUSPENDERS
BREAST COLLAR

TRAINING CART

KNEE BOOTS
SHIN & ANKLE BOOTS

HOBBLES

BRACE BANDAGES

BELL BOOTS

CORONET BOOTS

-MIKE GALEGO-USTA

United States Trotting Association. To the formation of the latter is due great credit for giving impetus to the breeding of fast harness horses.

The restoration of order in the sport, accomplished by the Trotting Association, attracted such men as Leland Stanford, whose Palo Alto establishment has been called the greatest breeding laboratory in history (one of its by-products during a photographic analysis of a trotter's leg movements was the invention by Muybridge of the technique of making motion pictures).

While the early breeding of fast harness horses in America was a rather hit-or-miss business marked by a few very prepotent and influential sires (*see* MESSENGER, also JUSTIN MORGAN and HAMBLETONIAN TEN), Stanford established the pattern of subsequent breeding practices based on careful selection, judicious mating of types, and careful use of inbreeding. Earlier breeding methods are not to be belittled, however, for the first recorded mile to be trotted in less than three minutes was registered in 1806 by Yankee, a gelding of unknown breeding. By 1839 the record had been reduced to 2:32 by Dutchman, and in 1845 Lady Suffolk trotted a mile in 2:29½ at Hoboken, New Jersey.

Of course, breeding is not solely responsible for the increase in speed. Improvement in training techniques and in shoeing, and very importantly the invention of the ball-bearing-equipped, pneumatic-tired bike and the hobble, invented in 1885 by John Browning, to say nothing of the improvement in harness, contributed to the increase in speed. The bike was invented in 1892 and was first tried in America on the Detroit, Michigan, track by Ed Geers (the beloved "Pop" Geers of the early years of this century).

Equipment commonly worn by the trotter.

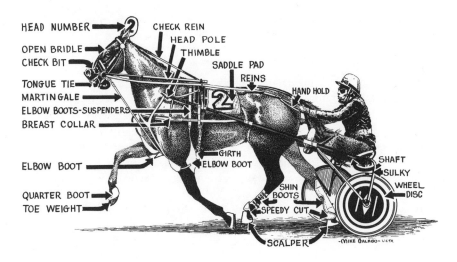

Adios—greatest Standardbred stallion siring primarily pacers.
Measurements (taken in 1960, at age 20): between eyes, 8"; muzzle, 21"; point of nose to between ears, 27"; between ears, 5"; around jaws at eyes, 28"; around neck at poll, 33"; center of eye to back of jaw, 9"; between ears to point of withers when neck is level, 35"; point of withers to tailhead, 52"; girth, 76"; at flank, 74"; elbow to knee joint, 17"; hind cannon, 13¼"; width of hips, 23"; stifle to hock, 22"; front cannon, 11"; around neck to crest, 44"; width of shoulders, 21"; length of fetlock, 5" (both same).

Prior to the invention of the hobble (or hopple), pacers lost so much time breaking that they had not kept their records up with those of the trotters. With the invention of the hobble (which met with considerable resistance from conservative track officials but finally became permissible), pacers, kept in their gait by the new contraption, set new and astounding records. In 1897 Star Pointer paced a mile in 1:59¼. The tracks and equipment of 50 years ago were crude by modern standards; but the immortal Dan Patch paced a mile in 1:55¼, a record that stood until 1938, when Billy Direct paced a mile in 1:55, within one day of the event of Grey Hound's record of 1:55¼ at the trot.

After introduction of the hobble, the relative speeds of trotters and pacers kept very close. The first two-minute trotter was Lou Dillon, trotting a mile in 2:00 in 1903. In 1966, in a time trial at Lexington, Bret Hanover paced a mile in 1:53⅗. In 1969 at Indianapolis, Nevele Pride lowered the trotting record at 1:54⅘.

Trotters and pacers are all of the same breed. Some horses perform creditably at both gaits. The world's champion double-gaited horse is Steamin' Demon, who paced in 1:58⅘ and trotted in 1:59⅕. The world champion double-gaited mare, Calumet Evelyn, paced in 1:59¼ and a week later, without any change in shoes or rigging, trotted in 2:00. She reduced her trotting record to 1:59½ a year later.

However, some families now predominate in pacers with most of the colts going to this gait naturally. Among these are the families of the Abbe, Abbedale, Grattan, and Billy Direct. Many colts from other families are first tried as trotters. If they show no trotting aptitude, or are more inclined to pace, they are put to pacing. Much of the change is accomplished by shoeing, and the hobbles are used to help convert a colt to pacing and to keep him on gait.

A powerful influence in the evolution of the trotter and the steady reduction of the speed limit, aside from the great work of the breeders, has been that of the trainers and drivers, many of whom also have been breeders. The immense improvement in their methods and skill, as compared with those of the formative period, has contributed greatly to progress, the betterment of gait and manners most particularly.

The growth of harness racing in recent years is remarkable. In 1956, 14,622 horses started in races on our tracks, and purses amounted to $21,862,611. In 1969, 33,188 horses started, and purses climbed to $80,683,497. In 1956 there were 4,680 Standardbred horses registered; in 1969, 11,851. This growth of the sport is due in large part to the United States Trotting Association, located at 750 Michigan Avenue, Columbus, Ohio 43215. Publicity Chairman Larry Evans's honest and wise program of education and publicity has made the public aware of the art of training, driving, and breeding harness horses. Some of the literature prepared by the association gives clear and honest information to beginners who may be toying with the idea of owning a horse and wondering about costs, methods of selection, etc. And there are data for the spectator that will greatly increase his enjoyment. Much of this literature is free and sent upon request. Then there is the *Trotting and Pacing Guide, Handbook of Harness Racing,* available from United States Trotting Association, into which is packed more concise and pertinent information on a subject than a dollar will buy anywhere else.

Harrier

The term *harrier* is applied to a hound used in hunting (called coursing by hunting folk) hares (rabbits). The term applies to hunting on horseback, for the shorter-legged beagle is used for hunting rabbits on foot.

Hat Guard

A hat guard is a cord with which a hunting derby or silk hat is kept from flying to the four winds when it is blown or knocked off. It runs from the brim of the hat to a ring in the collar of the coat. A somewhat more serviceable device was used by some cavalry oufits and occasionally is seen even today by nonmilitary folk in the West. It consists of a small strap passing through the brim of the hat just above each temple. From the hole on either side of the brim, the strap passes around the front or back of the hat close to the hatband. Below the brim, the ends of the strap join under the wearer's chin, where they are held together by a sliding braided-leather knot, which can be adjusted to keep the strap tight under the chin or loose, as the wearer desires.

Hat Snatching

In the game called hat snatching, each of a group of riders wears a paper hat or a paper bag turned back at the edges. Each rider tries to snatch another's "hat." When a rider loses his hat, he must leave the scene of combat. The last man on the field wins!

Head (noun)

Few parts of a horse's anatomy are the subject of such a wide divergency of opinion as the head. There are still many horsemen who are firmly of the belief that the shape of a horse's head indicates his disposition and many other qualities. The notion that human head measurements indicate character persisted for years and gave rise to much "scientific" study of what was called the "cephalic index." This sort of thing has long been discredited, but horsemen seem to cling harder to old ideas than even sociologists. Small eyes set close together were said to denote meanness, especially if accompanied by "little pin ears and a long roman nose," as the song goes.

The most beautiful heads in the horse world are those found in two strains of Arabians (each of which is spelled in many ways, even by the same authority in the space of a page!), the Seqlawi and the Kuhaylans. Their heads are not only beautiful but also structurally the most efficiently functional, for the great width between the jowls (unequaled in any other breed), the shortness of the distance from nostril to windpipe, and the delicate, flexible nostril, which can expand unbelievably, all tend to prevent respiratory afflictions and certainly give greater breathing ability than do other types of equine heads.

"Beauty is in the eye of the beholder," but most horsemen concede that the Arab head has it. Any other breed, from Percheron to Saddler, has the Arab influence to thank for whatever beauty the head possesses. Viewed from in front, the beautiful head is shaped like a diamond—delicate nose, width between eyes set midway between nostril and poll, and ears set close together. From the side, the face is straight or slightly dished. Some Arabian families are characterized by a marked dish midway between top of nostrils and eyes, and a fullness, or even a bump, just above the eyes (called a jibbah). Though the jowls are wide and the windpipe is large, the throttle is clean and free of excess flesh. The head is set on a neck flexible and fine.

The early Percherons showed the influence of the beautiful Arabian head, though when the fashion called for horses to weigh over a ton, beauty of head was forgotten in selection and Percheron heads became coarser. The American Saddle Horse until after the first quarter of this century was a thing of beauty testifying to the Arabian blood in his veins, some coming through Thoroughbreds and some coming directly from an Arab named Imported Zilcadi, the progenitor of Benjamin's Whirlwind, one of the great sires in the breed. As the Saddler has become almost exclusively a showpiece, the beauty of his head has diminished as the practice of breeding winner to winner and selecting for size and flash has increased. Today, long noses and narrow foreheads are quite common among winning members of the breed. Even the Thoroughbred, now that the mile dash over the specially prepared track brings the money, shows much less the influence of the Arabian head than he did a half-century ago.

Many Western horsemen consider this departure from the "pretty" head a virtue, maintaining that the best horses often have ugly heads and that a rugged horse rarely has a fine head. Though to this contention the writer does not subscribe, preference in heads is ultimately a personal matter. When buying a horse or deciding upon his value for any other reason, it is wise before making a final choice to become well informed of the standards set up by the authorities of the breed to which a horse belongs.

Head (verb)

1. When handling stock while mounted, a rider may have occasion to stop an animal that is running away from a herd. If he does so by outrunning the escapee, getting in front of it and thereby turning it back toward the path it should follow, he is said to "head it."

2. Another use of the term *head* is to designate the leading of a drive consisting of a number of animals.

3. In roping steers of any considerable size, two riders are usually employed. The one who ropes the head of the animal is said to head it. He is called the "header"; his partner, the "heeler." (*See* ROPING.)

4. In the hunting field perhaps the most offensive display of ignorance (equal to that of undoing the front cinch first on a full-rigged saddle on a green horse) is that of heading the fox, done usually by a witless rider in a manner similar to that of the cowboy heading an escapee from the herd.

Head (to head a fox). *See* HEAD (verb, 4)

Heading (in team roping). *See* HEAD (verb, 3)

Head Set

Horsemen speak of "setting a horse's head" or giving him a "head set." By this they mean teaching him to flex his neck just behind the head and to hold his head high enough to conform to current show standards for his breed or type. A bitting rig (*see* BITTING RIG) is frequently used. When a trainer's living depends upon satisfying owners, he may save time by using a bitting rig, for he can be "working" several horses in bitting rigs at the same time. However, the wise horseman knows that if a horse is to become all that his natural endowments permit, time must be taken to preserve his mouth and disposition. There should be no rush to "set his head." When the horse has learned what movements on the reins mean and responds to them intelligently, he will set his own head, and the "flexion at the poll" will be much more beautiful and responsive than is that of any animal who has had his head "set" for him.

Fashions in head sets change. In certain classes for horses of Western type there was a fashion lasting about a decade for low head carriage. This arose with the advent and rise to popularity in our shows of cutting horses (*see* CUTTING). Cutting horses, like opera stars, are born few and far between. Those so born can be improved by man, but those not so born can become only fakes. Obviously, a good cutting horse keeps his head level with his work, sometimes even using his teeth on a recalcitrant critter. This does not mean that he will always travel with his nose in the dust, however. Trainers, quick to please the fancy of owners, soon learned to use a short iron pipe or heavy dowel to "teach" a horse how hard is the way of a transgressor of the law "Thou shalt keep thy head down at all times." The low-head fashion spread to other Western types and lasted until very recently. The tide seems now to be turning, and many judges declare they want Western horses to flex at the poll and carry a natural head. Anybody in the market for used iron pipe or pieces of doweling?

Heat (in brood mares). *See* ESTRUS

Heat (in stable)

Artificial heat in stables probably does more harm than good. This is not to say that expertly designed and constructed air-conditioned stables are harmful. Many years ago the United States Cavalry was plagued by tuberculosis in horses kept at certain permanent posts. The trouble was eradicated by a rigid rule demanding that horses be tied outside on a picket line for a certain length of time each day, regardless of weather. During an influenza (then called distemper) epidemic in central Ohio in the days before automobiles and tractors, the L. L. Pegg Farm near Columbus was stricken. Fine Percheron brood stock was kept in stables and blanketed against the cold, but such stock suffered more than any other on the farm and some animals died. Young stock and some grade-work stock ran in a large field sheltered only by an open shed. In spite of snows and freezing rain, that stock showed less distress than any other on the farm, and none of these animals died. It might be of interest to note that the unsheltered stock had all the corn fodder it would eat and a little ear corn. Mr. Pegg finally came to the sound conclusion that stock winters best in the open if there is room to exercise and plenty of roughage to eat.

Of course, the owner who uses his horses and wants short coats may have to resort to blankets and warm stables, but he should beware of artificial heat.

At the other extreme, the environment of excessive heat, a horse can maintain good health in areas where the thermometer rises above 120° if he has a spot of shade and water that is not constantly exposed to the sun's rays. The greatest danger to horses in such climates is that of stopping a sweaty horse and letting him stand. In an extremely hot climate, evaporation is so great that a hot horse will chill and founder in a very few minutes, even seconds, if there is much wind. Such a horse should be kept moving until he is dry.

Heats (in racing)

Heats are the individual contests in a harness race. Usually, the race consists of not more than five heats. The horse who first wins three heats is the winner of the race. A heat in a harness race is usually a mile in length. The term obviously comes from the fact that the horse becomes extremely hot as a result of each contest and has to be properly cooled out (see COOLERS AND COOLING) before he is warmed up again for the next race.

Heaves (chronic pulmonary alveolar emphysema)

The horse with heaves or broken wind shows distress in getting his breath when exercised. Following each exhalation he gives an extra effort or "heave" with his diaphragm in a vain attempt to expel air from ruptured lung cells. Exact knowledge of the cause of the disease does not exist. Horses on good, clean pasture never get it. Dust is a contributing factor, as is mold in hay. There is some scientific basis for the belief that allergy plays a part in the disease.

While no horse can be made entirely serviceable after contracting heaves, he can frequently be made comfortable and suitable for light work by feeding hay sparingly and wet (alfalfa must be sprinkled very lightly and only immediately before feeding or it will cause colic) with regular addition of slightly moistened bran (a two-pound coffee-canful twice daily for a 1,000-pound horse—to be reduced if bowels become extremely loose).

Heavy Hands

The term *heavy hands* designates a horseman whose hands are like dead weight on the reins. He does not use short (and, if necessary, repeated) pulls on the reins to signal his horse, and he is utterly oblivious to communication *from* the horse via the reins. Heavy hands are more prevalent among riders who affect the "correct" English riding-school position than among those who ride with wrists slightly bent and flexible, with reins carried nearer the ends of the fingers than toward their base. (The "correct" English position is achieved by maintaining a straight line with arm, hand, and reins from elbow to bit.) (*See also* GOOD HANDS.)

Heavy-Harness Horse

Horses shown in harness other than those in fine harness, roadster, formal driving, and pleasure driving classes are sometimes called heavy-harness horses; at other times, simply harness horses. (*See* HARNESS CLASSES.)

Heel (to heel)

In the days before trailers and occasionally today in some areas, a huntsman (*see* HUNTSMAN) would ride (HACK) to the meet. On such occasions the hounds would travel in a group at the heels of the huntsman's mount. They were kept in place by the men called the whips (the huntsman never disciplines or "rates" his hounds because it is important for them to look to him for protection and affection at all times) riding behind and at either side of the pack. During such a performance, the hounds are said to *heel*.

Heel, Heeling, Heeler (in roping events)

In what is termed *steer roping* or *team tying* one roper, the header, ropes the bovine's head; the other, its heels. The latter is called the "heeler." His performance is called "heeling." He is said to "heel" the critter.

Heels

English riding masters place great emphasis on the position of a rider's heels. They insist that the heels should be lower than the toes. Any rider who wears spurs and rides a horse of any responsiveness maintains this position of heels if he would survive. However, the insistence that beginning riders maintain any position of any part of their body in a perfectly static or rigid way will produce stiff riders and also usually heavy hands.

As the rider learns to be aware of the movements of his horse (to feel his rhythm), he can be coached to ride on the inner part of his thighs rather than his buttocks, to use the inside of his calf rather than the back of it, and to apply his legs when needed to the "saddle groove" (narrowest part of the horse just behind the shoulders) rather than doubling his legs up or thrusting his feet forward. Such coaching will keep the feet where they belong, and a little admonishment to keep heels down may then be beneficial.

Height. *See also* HAND

The height of a horse is taken at the highest point of his withers (the rise in the backbone just ahead of the saddle) and is recorded in hands (units of four inches). Very generally speaking, mature equines under 14.2 (14 hands and 2 inches) are considered to be ponies. However, some of the greatest Arabians of whom there is any record were well under that height, and one of the greatest Olympic contestants ever to defend the honor of the cavalry of the United States (Olympic Don, a Saddlebred gelding) was not much above it. Justin Morgan is said by some to have been exactly 14.2. Nevertheless, all breeds not labeled *pony* show evidence that their proponents are striving for ever-greater height. The American Saddle Horse, before he became almost exclusively a showpiece, was rarely much higher than 15.2. Now he must be at least 16 hands high if he is to bring a price that will pay his board bill. The great Arabian Raffles would indeed look like a pony if he could be brought back to life and led into a modern Arabian horse-show class, as would his sire and grandsire, Skowronek. Horses shown today as hunters are generally over 16 hands high, and Morgans are almost without exception much taller than the great little horse from which they are supposed to be descended.

Probably all this emphasis on height springs from the ever-increasing influence of the show-ring on price. A tall horse always makes a more impressive appearance in the ring than a short one, and the nearer a horse resembles a show-ring winner in appearance, the better price he will bring.

Herdbound. *See also* BARN RAT

A herdbound horse is one who violently resists being ridden away from a group. Usually such a horse will also be "stablebound"; that is, he will rear, whirl, run backward, and use other violent means to avoid being ridden away from the stable.

The habit of riding a horse close to the stable for the first few minutes of exercise when he is mounted often produces such a vice. Horses whose education has been confined to work in a ring or arena often contract it.

Hidalgo

Hidalgo is a Spanish word meaning a person *of high birth.*

Hidebound

Wormy, underfed, or otherwise ill-treated horses may have a coat that "sticks to the ribs," that is, skin that cannot be moved by the fingers. The hair will lack luster and will not lie down properly when groomed. An experienced horseman can usually spot the cause, but the safest remedy is to call a veterinarian if the horse is worth keeping.

High Blowing

High blowing is a noise made by the fluttering of the nostrils. Some horses, especially highbred ones, indulge in it occasionally when galloping. Inexperienced horsemen sometimes mistake the sound for evidence of a respiratory disorder.

Hinny

A mule is the result of breeding a jack (male ass) to a mare. When a stallion is bred to a female ass or "jenny," the result is called a hinny, like all hybrids, incapable of having offspring. It is also sometimes called a genet, a jennet, or a bardot. This is all very confusing because the terms *genet* and *jennet* were used to designate a type of Spanish horse well thought of in the twelfth century, valued for its easy gaits. (*See* JENNET.) The hinny, in parts of the country where travel is done extensively in a saddle, is generally considered an excellent mount. It is usually more pleasing in appearance than the mule and more responsive in temperament.

Hiring a Horse. *See* RENTING A HORSE

Hobbies. *See also* GALLOWAY

The Hobbies and the Galloways were two easy-gaited families of horses, highly prized as utility animals in England up to the seventeenth century. In the late seventeenth or early eighteenth century a priest was given the task of making a survey of the livestock of Ireland. In his report he included the Hobbies. It went in part as follows: ". . . and their gait was that smooth that when mounted one could carry a glass full of liquor and spill ne'er a drop." The Galloways and the Hobbies were almost identical in type and gait. They were small in size, about the size of our Indian ponies. With all their sturdiness and easy-riding qualities they must have had considerable speed, for it was by crossing the Oriental horse and the native horse of England that a racer was produced which no horse of any other breed can equal in speed to this day. We now call that horse the Thoroughbred.

Hobbles (or hopples). *See also* HARNESS RACING

The term *hobbles* (or *hopples*) designates any device used to fasten a horse's legs together (usually the two front legs only). In the early days of "cowboys and Indians," hobbles were usually of rawhide because it was the most readily available material. Later, cotton rope could be purchased at the general store and it made excellent hobbles if unwound and then braided so that it was soft and strong. Such rope makes a good set of hobbles today. The center of the rope is put around the right pastern and secured with a single knot. The two ends are then twisted for about 10 inches. Then another single knot is tied and the remaining ends are put around the left pastern and tied with a square knot. The rope should be just long enough so that not much of it is left to flop around after the square knot is tied. The most popular manufactured hobbles used by pack trains consist of two heavy collars that encircle the front pasterns. Each collar has a ring. The rings of the collars are attached to either end of a short chain in the center of which is a swivel.

Some horse-show classes for Western horses require a set of hobbles to be tied on the rear of the saddle. Such hobbles are usually of fairly light leather. In Western saddlery stores one can usually find quite a variety of hobbles, each designed for a specific purpose.

It is to be hoped that no one who owns a horse needs to be warned that a horse has to be trained to wear hobbles and that putting hobbles on an untrained horse results always in violence and frequently in disaster. The best hobbles for training are those made of soft cotton rope, and the best

Cotton rope hobbles.

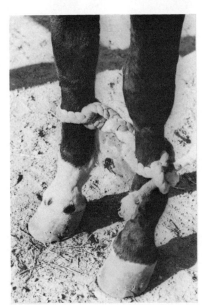

place for training is the center of a smooth field of good sod of an acre in extent. If the training is done in the corral or stall, the floor must be thickly covered with sand or sawdust to prevent broken knees if the horse goes down, as he frequently does when first hobbled. Furthermore, the corral or stall should be carefully inspected for nails, protruding corners of mangers, or anything else that might injure the horse when he struggles. Such objects should be either removed or heavily padded with old pieces of automobile tire or similar material.

Hock

A horse is only as good as his legs and feet. About 75 percent (or more) of lameness occurs in the foot of the horse (though frequently diagnosed otherwise by grooms and wiseacres). A very large proportion of the rest of the lameness occurs in the hock because, next to the forefeet, it is subjected to greater violence than any other part of the horse when he is used. Proper conformation of the hock, like proper slope of the shoulder, is a prerequisite for the kind of performance demanded in the hunting field and the show-ring. The hock that appears extremely thin when viewed from back or front will not hold up. The normal bony parts of the hock should be prominent and free from puffiness.

Bony enlargements which occur low on the inside forward portion of a hock are called bone spavins (*see* SPAVIN) or "jacks." They can be readily detected by a veterinarian or an experienced horseman. They eventually cause lameness. A bowing out of the tendon at the back of the hock is called a curb (*see* CURB). It is frequently the result of too much early work, malnutrition, or both. Puffiness in the joint can frequently be pushed from the inside front of the joint to the outside just in front of the cap. Puffiness may be any one of several kinds of trouble. One is called a bog spavin. Another is called a thoroughpin. It is possible for some of the ailments of a hock to be permanently cured if the animal is young and cared for by an expert veterinarian. Most home remedies merely add fuel to the flame. The purchase of any horse should always be preceded by a veterinary examination, which includes close inspection of the hock joint.

Hogged Mane

A hogged mane is one that is clipped close to the hide.

Hold Hard

Hold hard is a cry given by the huntsman warning the field to slow down and not override his hounds.

Hold on Horse. *See also* GOOD HANDS

The beginner riding outside the riding ring is in danger from two extremes. One is that he will be so fearful of hurting his horse's mouth that he will never exert pressure enough to tell the poor animal anything. On the other hand, some unusual movement of the horse may instill such terror in the rider that his hands will "freeze" on the reins; that is, he will clutch the reins, pull with all his might, and never release that hold. No runaway horse was ever stopped by a steady pull. When a good horseman exerts pressure on the reins to "tell" his horse to collect or to decrease his speed, that pressure is unconsciously rhythmic. The rhythm corresponds to the natural rhythm of the horse's head. Unless riding a spoiled horse, the experienced horseman seldom, if ever, pulls steadily on the reins. It is conceivable that some situation might cause that rider to exert tremendous pressure on the reins, but it will be only momentary. Of course, it may be repeated very quickly and as many times as necessary and as violently as need be (though he must always remember that violence engenders violence). Ordinarily, the pressures exerted on the reins by the good horseman are slight, but their timing must be perfect. In the most important horse-show classes, whether of hunters or gaited horses, the variations of hold on the reins are so subtle that few spectators can observe them.

Holloa

Holloa refers to a cry given when a fox is viewed. This term is equivalent to *tallyho,* which is about the only term of the hunting field known to most laymen.

Honda

A loop at the end of a lariat, just large enough to permit free passage of the rope out of which the lariat is made, is called a honda. Sometimes the loop is lined with metal.

Honda.

Hood

A hood is a covering for the horse's head and neck made of any one of various kinds of material. On rare occasions a hood is used in cooling out a very hot horse. Such a hood should be of the same kind of long-staple wool of which coolers or cooling blankets are made. This material acts like a wick and pulls the sweat from the horse, depositing it like dew on the outside of the hood or cooler. Some hoods are made of waterproof material for protection against rain.

Hoof

The horse's hoof is, for all practical purposes, the most important part of his anatomy. "No foot, no horse" is one of the oldest sayings of horsemen. Probably because of silly notions about dainty feet, voiced at cocktail parties, many well-bred horses have hooves that are too small. This is one of the several reasons why most race horses are cripples before they mature. No horse ever had a hoof too large if it was properly shaped, by which I mean round, open at the heel, concave on the sole, supplied with good strong bars, thick walls, and ample, pliable frog. To keep the hoof healthy when shod, the wall must never be allowed to grow much beyond the living sole. This will mean that the frog is always pressed when the horse has his weight on the hoof. The frog is often called the horse's "second heart," for pressure on the frog pumps some of the blood out of the

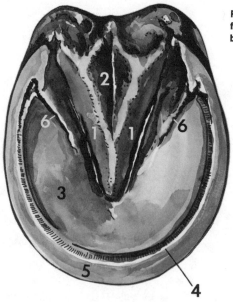

Right front hoof. 1. Frog; 2. furrow of frog; 3. sole; 4. white line; 5. wall; 6. bar.

capillaries of the foot. In hot dry climates there is a danger of dehydration in the hoof (*see* PERIOPLE). Regular soaking of hooves in such climates is beneficial (whether in clean mud or water). However, irregularity, alternating between excessive moisture and excessive dry heat, is worse than no moisture at all. A dressing, excellent if applied daily, is the following: six parts of fish oil (cod-liver or other similar oil procurable at poultry supply stores), one part pine tar, one part Creoline, and two parts glycerin. The mixture must be stirred well before each application. (The old Fort Riley formula called for raw linseed oil instead of fish oil.)

Tennessee Walking Horses fitted for the show-ring usually have mutilated hooves (see *Life,* October 3, 1969, pp. 77 and 78: "Agony of the Walking Horse") and are rarely safe or suitable for use outside the show-ring. American Saddle Horses fitted for the show-ring have carried toes 7 or 7½ inches long (the normal foot of a horse rarely exceeds 4½ inches and is usually much shorter than that) over a period of at least several months. This usually makes them unsafe and unsuitable for use outside the show-ring even after the feet are cut down, because abuse of their hoofs has done structural damage to the foot, circulation, etc.

Farriers (horseshoers) sometimes, in order to make a neat-looking job, rasp off some of the natural enamel (periople) on the outside of a horse's hoof. This of course increases dehydration of the hoof. The rasp should not be used above the clinches of the nails. Another injurious practice of some farriers is paring away the outside of the frog. This "second heart" of the horse should be pared only to permit proper placing of the shoe, if such paring is needed.

Hopple. *See* HARNESS RACING and HOBBLES

Horse

Handling of, in Pasture

A horse turned loose in a pasture with a group of horses that have been running together will be kicked and bitten. Whether or not injury will result depends upon the condition and temperament of the animals in pasture. It is always wise to have animals in pasture unshod, especially behind. If a horse has been kept up and fed well and then turned loose alone in a small pasture, there is a good chance that his first impulse will be to run at top speed. If the pasture is enclosed with wire, there is some chance that he will not stop in time to avoid injury on the wire. Some horsemen think it wise, in such a situation, to lead the horse around the entire perimeter of the pasture before turning him loose.

In some parts of the country in late August pitiable sights can be seen in small suburban pastures. A family of horse lovers, because the summer months are too hot for riding or because they wish to go on a vacation, will put their horse or horses out to pasture, believing or wishing to believe that the horse will enjoy a few weeks of freedom. If the pasture is only average, or less than average, and the horse has been accustomed to good care, his condition will deteriorate at an appalling rate. By the time the family has to return home to get the children into school, the condition of the horse may be pathetic.

Many a horse's disposition has been ruined by owners who did not know how to approach and halter him when he is in pasture. Any horse who has ever been roped cannot be caught single-handed except by roping. Unless one wants to rope him, either help must be called in to corner him or he must be driven into a chute or small pen. The horse who has not been so spoiled can be made equally difficult to catch if his owner walks into the pasture swinging a halter and yelling, "Come here, Joe," or whatever the animal's name is. Keep up your acquaintance with your horse while he is in pasture. Go in to the pasture occasionally when you do not want to take him out and give him a couple of carrots or other tidbits that you know he is fond of. Do this enough so that he will come toward you or at least stand still and wait for you when you go into the pasture. A light catch-rope about four feet long that can be looped over one's belt or thrown over a shoulder is much better than a halter to use when taking a horse from pasture. Such ropes should be tied around the horse's neck with a bowline or square knot, *not with a slipknot.*

In many suburban pastures there is danger of a horse's being panicked by stray dogs. At the time these lines are written, the writer has in his corral a fine Arabian mare who was frightened by a pack of dogs chasing a goat through her small pasture. In her panic, she turned suddenly, slipped, and struck a hind leg against a fence so violently that it has needed weeks of careful nursing. Not only the pasture but also the neighborhood in which it exists should be inspected before a horseman puts a good animal in it.

Handling of, in Stable

Random movements or noises near a horse who is in a stall, whether a box stall or a tie stall, are the mark of gross ignorance. If a horse has his head in the manger and is eating, he may not hear his handler's approach from the rear, so the wise handler always speaks quietly to a horse when he enters a stall. Box stall doors not fastened open have swung shut and broken a hip on more than one horse. When a horse is being led into a stall anything that touches or startles him will cause him to leap forward. If the touch is by a door blown by the wind, he will leap forward violently enough to injure himself.

When a horse is tied in a stall, he should be tied at least as high as the middle of his shoulders and with a shank just long enough to allow him to get his nose to the ground comfortably. If there is any slack in the shank when he puts his head down, he will get a front foot over it.

The horse who is yelled at, slapped, or poked (to make him move to one side) while in his stall will soon become ill-natured. Treat your horse with respect; he may be better bred than you are.

Nature of. *See also* ACCIDENTS and INTELLIGENCE OF HORSES

The fundamental problem of any matter of horsemanship is communication with the horse. By the use of pain or reward a horse can be forced or coaxed to do a variety of things. But that constant rapport between horse and man exhibited by the most intelligent horsemen and best-educated horses can be achieved only with the best possible communication between horse and man. It is almost entirely kinetic and is dependent almost solely upon kinesthesia.

The sensitivity of the horse is such that the relation between horse and horseman can be likened to that between a pair of ballroom dancers. There certainly is no set of signals that a leading partner gives to effect movement of his partner. He does not, let us say, push with his thumb on her lumbar vertebrae to signal her to move her left foot forward. So it is with horse and rider. Movements of each are anticipated by and responded to so rapidly, constantly, and often subtly that a codified set of signals would be a cumbersome nuisance. Nevertheless, since few horses have the good fortune to be ridden by excellent horsemen, a horse must be taught the meaning of a codified set of signals called the *aids* so that the average rider can be told "when you want the horse to do this certain thing, you use this certain aid (or signal)." *See* AIDS.

In the horse's natural state, his most important tools for survival are his eyes (*see* EYES), ears, and nose.

In almost all situations a horse's immediate response to anything unusual in his environment is flight, for neither his heels nor his teeth are entirely adequate defenses against his natural enemies or predators. The writer, in over half a century of close companionship with horses and ponies of all descriptions, has never seen a *naturally* "mean" or vicious equine, though he has personally known some who have killed their handlers and were adept at repeating the performance whenever the opportunity presented itself. The more intelligent the horse, the more mean, vicious, and dangerous he can be made by ignorant handling. The horseman with even a modicum of intelligence refrains from making random movements around a horse, unless that horse and he are on very familiar terms. The same horseman tries to have every movement he makes around a horse be meaningful to the animal. Almost any five- or three-gaited show stable is full of illustrations of horses handled in the opposite manner. Most of the horses in it have been subjected to a variety of pains and punishments that have been without meaning to the horse, and few movements of his handler have signified anything to him except the probability of immediately ensuing pain. Much of the spirit and so-called airiness he displays in the show-ring are the result of his handling in the stable.

Horsemanship

In England and America the only kind of horsemanship that has been conventionalized and organized into a discipline has a long history. It goes back in time and place at least to fifteenth-century Italy. In England, in the time of Henry IV, it was practiced only by royalty and nobility and was typified by violent leaps in air, kicks, rears, and turns, most of which became conventionalized and codified by the Spanish Riding School of Vienna (*see* SPANISH RIDING SCHOOL). Training, survived by only a small percentage of horses, was typified by an official whip bearer (who carried a bundle of fresh whips for riders) and pairs of great pillars between which horses were tied and whipped until they performed or perished. In the reign of Charles II, the Duke of Newcastle brought reforms. His bits were less gruesome. He used only one pillar, and whipping was reduced. However, the 20-foot whip wielded by two hands was still in evidence in a performance of Lippizan horses (Spanish Riding School breed) given by Professor Herman in Tucson, Arizona, in 1969.

This ancient royal type of horsemanship evolved into modern dressage. An offshoot is the horsemanship of the modern hunting man. Forward-seat riding is also a descendant of the baroque riding halls of royalty modified by the wisdom of an Italian, Caprilli. Though dressage and forward seat riding are considered by many the only modern "educated" kind of horsemanship, there are now some very respectable schools of gaited horse riding, Western riding, cutting horse riding, etc., in the United States. Books on these various types of horsemanship are numerous.

In 1885 one of the most sensible books on horsemanship was written by Colonel Theodore A. Dodge, entitled *Patroclus and Penelope*. Even in that early day, Colonel Dodge wrote:

The most common delusion under which the average equestrian is apt to labor in every part of the world is that his own style of riding is the one "par excellence." Whether the steeple chaser on his Thoroughbred, or the Indian on his mustang is the better rider, cannot well be decided. The peculiar horsemanship of every country has manifest advantages, and is the natural outgrowth of, as well as peculiarly adapted to, the climate, roads, and uses to which the horse is put. The cowboy who can defy the bucking bronco will be unseated by a two-year-old which any racing stable boy can stick to, while this same boy would hardly sit the third stiff boost of the ragged, grass-fed pony. The best horseman of the desert would be nowhere in the hunting field. The cavalryman who, with a few of his fellows, can carve his way through a column of infantry, may not be able to compete at polo with a Newport swell. The jockey who will ride over five and half feet of timber or twenty feet of water would make sorry work in pulling down a lassoed steer. Each one in his element is by far the superior of the other, but none of these is just the type of horseman whom the denizen of our busy cities, for his daily enjoyment, cares to make his pattern.

The colonel, if living today, might add something about the unique horsemanship associated with three- and five-gaited show horses. Had he traveled in Tibet, he could have included the words of Rampa (author of *The Third Eye*):

Skill on a horse is essential in a country where there is no wheeled traffic, where all journeys have to be done on foot or on horseback. Tibetan nobles practice horsemanship hour after hour, day after day. They can stand on a narrow wooden saddle of a galloping horse, and shoot first with a rifle at a moving target, then change to bow and arrow. Sometimes skilled riders will gallop across the plains in formation, and change horses by jumping from saddle to saddle.

No list of types of excellence in horsemanship is complete without mention of the hackamore reinsman of Baja California, whose skill can be traced back through the Spanish conquistadores to the Moors and other North African horsemen. This type of horsemanship is charmingly described in *The Hands of Cantu* by Tom Lea.

For information about the kinds of "horsemanship" necessary to win in equitation classes in modern horse shows, the current *Rule Book* of the American Horse Shows Association should always be consulted. Styles in such things as, for instance, the method of holding reins and romal in a Western Pleasure class may change from year to year. It is things like this, or the exact angle of the English rider's toes, that often decide the difference between first and second place in a horsemanship class. Though appearance of the rider is the chief criterion in judging a class in horsemanship, for more "practical" purposes the performance of the horse is the best proof of the ability of the rider.

A goal that might be acceptable to most varieties of horsemen today may be stated as follows:

Complete harmony of horse and rider is the goal. When that is reached, the horse will flex with a smile and champ the bit while the rider holds the reins lightly in sensitive fingers. Through the variation of the slack of the reins, he understands what the horse is communicating by the movement of the bars of his mouth. The horse is interpreting the mind of the rider by the movements of the fingers affecting the slack so imperceptibly that no onlooker is aware that the fingers are active.

—Wynmalen, *Dressage*

This statement covers only part of excellence of riding, for the rapport between horse and rider, similar to that between ballroom dancers, is such that the entire horse, from heel calks to ear tips, is constantly responding; and much of the response, especially that of the rear quarters of a horse, results from what the rider does with his feet, legs, and other parts of his body.

For information on training of colts, teaching the gaits, correcting vices, jumping, and other specific matters of horsemanship see appropriate headings in this book.

Horsemanship Classes. *See also* HORSEMANSHIP

Many a youngster could be shielded from heartache if the nature and purpose of horsemanship classes were thoroughly explained to every competitor before he submitted his entry. In a horsemanship class, good hands class, or any other class in which the rider only is judged, the ability to elicit from a horse quietly, quickly, and exactly the entire range of his repertoire of performance and to maintain constant rapport with a horse (to say nothing of perfection of balance that cannot be upset by the caprice of any green animal) is not necessarily an advantage in winning a ribbon. Position of toes, feet, ankles, calves, thighs, placing of the buttocks, attitude of the torso, and position of arms and hands are of prime importance. Conventional use of the aids and knowledgeable procedure in the ring are equally important. In most classes in which the rider only is judged, a judge will attempt to take into consideration the difference in mounts (in regard to the difficulty any poorly trained ones may cause their riders). However, the rider on the perfectly schooled horse performing with a clocklike precision without any spontaneity certainly has an advantage in a horsemanship class over other contestants less fortunately mounted.

The American Horse Shows Association *Rule Book* includes as Rule XVII "Equitation Division." It states that this division is made up of three distinct sections (Hunter, Saddle, and Stock Seats). Under each section are various classes, limiting entries by age, experience, and type of performance. The *Rule Book* clearly explains in text and line drawings what is required of contestants in each class in which the rider is judged.

Horseman vs. Rider. *See* HORSEMANSHIP and HORSE, *Nature of*

Horseshoes

Horseshoes are a necessary evil. While it is imperative to watch a colt's feet and keep them level to prevent the legs from becoming crooked, no colt should be shod as long as his feet do not become overly sensitive because of wear on the terrain on which he is kept. Handmade shoes are too costly for the ordinary horse owner. Therefore, manufactured or "keg" shoes are worn by most horses. The ideal shoe is one made by the hand of an expert farrier. The thickness of the wall of the hoof varies greatly from horse to horse and since the nail holes are prepunched in the manufactured shoe, too much rasping is required when a manufactured shoe is put on an extremely thick-walled hoof. Or, to put the difficulty in another way, in order to have the nails placed properly in the wall in the hoof, the shoe cannot extend to the outside of the wall and give the horse the amount of bearing surface on the ground which he should have.

On the other hand, if the horse has an extremely thin wall, the nail holes force the farrier either to start the nails inside the white line of the hoof or to allow the shoe to extend out beyond the wall of the hoof, where it may be stepped on and pulled or strike the opposing leg.

For show horses and harness race horses worth thousands of dollars, competing for huge stakes, handmade shoes are imperative. Both the show horse and the harness race horse are performing learned gaits which they can execute only with the aid of expertly balanced and individually shaped shoes.

The running horse, who races under saddle, wears aluminum shoes. These are manufactured, but, because they must be so extremely light, the horse wears a set of them for a very short time, sometimes for the duration of only one race. Furthermore, the racer travels on a specially prepared track. Wearing manufactured shoes for such short intervals on such terrain seems to be relatively harmless. (*See* SHOEING.)

Horse-Show Classes. *See also under headings for specific types:* HARNESS CLASSES, BREEDING CLASSES, etc.

The number of kinds of horse-show classes to be seen in American horse shows runs into the hundreds. Historically, horse-show classes might be

Show classes for Arabians and some other breeds restrict length of feet. Method of measuring toe and heel: "The length of toe shall be determined by measuring the front of the hoof in the center from the skin line on the lower side of the coronary band to the ground. The height at heel shall be determined by measuring from the skin line on the lower side of the coronary band to the ground with the measuring device perpendicular to the ground. All measurement devices must be checked for accuracy."

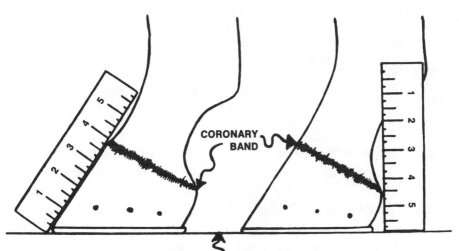

CORONARY BAND

SMOOTH FLAT SURFACE

divided into three general categories: those in which the horses are shown (1) in hand, (2) in harness, and (3) under saddle. The term *in hand* is still retained in Morgan classes. All of the classes in which the horse is shown in hand (led into the ring wearing only halter or bridle) are now called *breeding classes* in recognized shows and occasionally *halter classes* in small local shows.

There are 15 general divisions of classes specified by the American Horse Shows Association. Each division may have as many as three sections, exclusive of breeding classes, and each section may have a number of kinds of classes. A class may be exclusively for animals of one age, sex, or height, or for animals of a certain stage of maturity or experience, such as Maiden, Novice, or Amateur classes. Classes in which the rider alone is judged are divided along similar lines. Championship classes in each section and each division, very generally speaking, are for animals who have won first or second place in limited classes in their division.

Any horseman intending to compete in a horse show should apply for membership in the AHSA (*see* AMERICAN HORSE SHOWS ASSOCIATION). If he cannot afford or does not care to join, he should certainly examine the AHSA *Rule Book*. Privilege to study the *Rule Book* will be extended to any reliable, aspiring horseman by one of the officials or experienced exhibitors in the area in which the young horseman lives.

Horse-Show Judges

The American Horse Shows Association *Rule Book* states that "Recognized Judges shall be of four classes: Registered, Recorded, Special, and Guest." Only Recognized Judges in good standing may officiate at recognized shows in those divisions covered by the rules and specifications of the current *Rule Book*. The method by which Recorded Judges and Junior Guest Judges finally become Recognized Judges is a rather complicated procedure detailed clearly in the *Rule Book*.

Even though a small local show does not aspire to recognition by the American Horse Shows Association, it may well receive valuable assistance in selecting a judge by writing the AHSA for information (see address under its entry). There may be Recorded Judges or others who are quite competent to officiate at a small show. If someone is hoping to become a Recognized Judge, it is possible he will welcome the experience.

A good many years ago, before the AHSA was formed, either Bob Morland or Matt Cohen, two of the greatest showmen this country ever engendered, made a sage answer to a question about what might be done about inept or dishonest judging: "Go out and buy the best (blank blank) horse you can find and then let the judges worry."

Horse-Show Ribbons and Trophies

Ribbons and trophies at all recognized shows must be in accordance with the specifications of the current American Horse Shows Association *Rule*

Book. Any show, no matter how small, will do well to follow the *Rule Book* specification.

Horse Shows

In many parts of the United States horse shows have become so popular that there is rarely a weekend during the horse show season when at least two shows are not competing for attention in any given locality. Many of the smaller shows are independent affairs not associated with the American Horse Shows Association, the Pony Club, 4-H Clubs, or any other parent organization. They are undoubtedly useful in providing wholesome interests for the younger generation. If they are planned with wisdom and forethought and intelligently supervised, they are also entertainment for adults of the community.

Proponents of more serious and highly organized shows have defended horse shows on the ground that they are beneficial to breeders and increase the quality of animals. This argument is open to question and is countered by animal lovers who contend that there is not one type of domestic animal that has not been ruined by the show-ring. They cite the diminution of the teats of Jersey cattle and other conformational deterioration before the testing of production of milk cows superseded the show-ring as the center of competition for dairy breeds. They point to the hip displasia developed in German shepherd dogs and the shrinking of the "brain cage" of collies. Another favorite example is the American Saddle Horse, once noted for his beautiful head, good conformation, and endurance. Today, heads with eyes close to the ears and conformation marked by long legs and lack of heart girth are not infrequent in the breed.

Whether horse shows are good or bad, they are certainly much more prevalent today than ever before, and it is fortunate that the more important ones are organized under the rules of and classified by the American Horse Shows Association. Very recently, the Pony Club, started in England, has established branches in all parts of the United States and sponsors and regulates many of the smaller shows. Of only slightly less importance in the horse-show world is the 4-H Club, which now organizes and regulates horse shows.

Hunter

The most revered breed for use in the hunting field is the Thoroughbred. However, the Thoroughbred that is best in the hunting field may not be suitable for the racetrack, and many a winning race horse could never have been made into a very good hunter. In his "salad days" the writer felt that the only days not wasted were hunt days, and of all the good hunters he recalls, several came from a farm in Virginia on which more than one generation of a family by the name of Waller, if memory serves, bred Thoroughbreds exclusively for hunting. They were big-boned, tall animals of great heart girth and beautiful heads. Their level-headedness and great intelligence gave the lie to the snide remarks one sometimes hears about Thoroughbred temperaments.

Although level-headed Thoroughbreds can be found, the most usual temperament of the breed is not quite perfect for many riders to hounds, especially those who ride only to hunt. For this reason, the Thoroughbred crossed with other breeds, and sometimes purebred horses of breeds other than the Thoroughbred, are often used as hunters. In some parts of the Genesee Valley in New York State there are farms devoted to the production of hunters on which the best products carry one-fourth draft blood.

In the hunting field it is the horse, not his pedigree, who carries the hunter to hounds. Any level-headed big horse (16 hands or more) of good conformation with plenty of "heart" or impulsion can be made into at least a fair hunter.

Schooling of Hunters

There are almost as many ways of schooling a hunter as there are trainers; but no matter what method is used, the goal is a horse who will gallop and jump without excitement and one with perfect manners and a light, responsive mouth. Few amateurs ever produce a good hunter because they usually start putting him over jumps before he has learned to walk, trot, and gallop quietly and on a light rein. Or if they do not make this mistake, they put the horse over obstacles too many inches high and put him over them at a gallop before he has learned to walk quietly over low obstacles. It is regrettable, at least to the writer, that many, if not most, people who ride hunters ride only one end of a horse, the front end. Every inch of the perfect hunter can respond to the rider. Such a horse can sidepass, turn on the forehand or the quarters, or be moved forward or backward by his rider as readily as the rider can move when he is afoot (perhaps more readily, if he is as long in the tooth as the writer).

The first thing, then, to teach the hunter is to walk, trot, and gallop on a light rein. Though a hunter must be an animal always ready to move out freely, one of the first things he has to learn is to respond to restraint readily and without excitement. Before attempting to negotiate obstacles, he should be so trained that the entire horse responds to the rider. There is no one perfect method for every horse, but certainly teaching a horse to sidepass, to turn on the forehand, to turn on the hindquarters, and even to do rollbacks and inside rolls is helpful. (Each of the foregoing performances is treated in this book under its respective heading.)

When the horse has learned to respond in a relaxed manner at all speeds and to be so responsive that the rider can move any part of the horse's body as readily as he can his own, it is time for the trainer to think about putting the horse over obstacles. It might be well to add here that the writer is strongly of the opinion that much of any prospective hunter's training ought to be outside a ring or arena. He has never seen a horse trained exclusively to work in a ring or arena who would move out as freely as a hunter should.

There is no better way to start the young hunter over obstacles than by using a cavalletti (*see* CAVALLETTI). No definite rule will fit all horses, but surely a minimum of two weeks should be spent on the cavalletti before a single rail is elevated above the ground. When rails are raised, the raising should be extremely gradual. Vladimir S. Littauer, than whom there is no more reliable living authority on such matters, in his *Common Sense Horsemanship,* says that in the course of a month, height (of an obstacle) may be raised by three to six inches. If it is a matter of extending width, he recommends that it may be extended perhaps by one foot in the same amount of time.

When the horse has reached the point at which he will negotiate a three-foot jump in as relaxed a manner and as casually as he will step over the sill of his own stable door, it is time to begin to increase the variety of the obstacles he is put over. Each innovation should be a very gradual thing; any fright, tension, or excitement of the horse is an indication that the trainer has changed something too rapidly. However, ultimately the variety of shape, texture, and color of the obstacles to which the horse has become accustomed should indicate the unusual ingenuity and fertile imagination of the trainer.

If a hunter is to perform in horse shows, the radio is a great asset. Started with the volume very low, the horse can ultimately learn to endure calmly the most blatant and raucous of sounds that emanate from modern "musicians."

When young, the writer lived near a large state university and rode young prospective hunters on the campus (a stunt that would probably not be tolerated today) while cadets were drilling with a band blaring. That was an excellent way to prepare a young horse for horse-show activity. Of course, it would be easy to ruin any horse by using force to make him approach crowds or bands. Such an approach must be done little by little.

The making of a good hunter requires a great deal of time. This means that such a horse costs a lot of money, so it is important to start with an excellent animal of ample size.

Hunter Classes. *See* HORSE-SHOW CLASSES

Hunter Hack. *See* HACK, HUNTER HACK

Hunter Trials

As every good dealer knows, a certificate stating that a horse is a Qualified Hunter signed by the M.F.H. (Master of Fox Hounds) of a recognized hunt increases a horse's value considerably. Perhaps the most important aspect of the certificate is the proof that the animal has hunted regularly with a recognized pack; however, there are or at least have been masters who demanded that a horse must satisfactorily perform at hunter trials in order to qualify. The hunter trials, an annual event at some hunt clubs, simulate the obstacles encountered on the terrain over which the pack hunts. Also included may be obstacles to test the handiness of a hunter, such as an in-and-out jump, where two obstacles are close to each other and must be taken in sequence.

Hunting Calls

As hunts in America range from the extremely formal to those even more informal than the ones so charmingly pictured in Masefield's *Reynard the Fox*, the variation in hunting calls is extreme, to say the least. The huntsman may have a clarion voice to make himself heard by hounds and field, but he rarely enunciates in a fashion that allows his words to be distinguishable to the latter. It is the tone of his voice and what the modern grammarian would call juncture, stress, and pitch that communicate.

The huntsman's horn, capable of one note only, has a surprising repertoire. It makes up with tonal variation for lack of variation in pitch. The range of rhythm is also often surprising. Some huntsmen have developed their skill to the point of being able to double-tongue or, in rare instances, to triple-tongue on the horn.

When hounds are searching for Reynard in cover, the long notes of the horn tend to slur together. Double-tonguing comes into play when hounds are running. If the huntsman is not quite so gifted, he uses staccato single notes. Sometimes when hounds are drawing cover, the huntsman will give an occasional short single blast on his horn so that the hounds know that he is standing by. He is also usually using his voice to encourage them. Double- or triple-tonguing and an abundance of oral screams and yells indicate that the fox has been viewed and call the hounds to the huntsman so he can point them in the right direction. A sound somewhere between a rebel cry and a cowboy yell indicates that Reynard has "gone away," that is, has left cover and started to run. When the hounds are running properly, the huntsman is said to "blow them out"; he gives a series of long-short, long-short, or short-long, short-long notes or some similar rhythm. This is a very important call, for it brings the field in line behind the huntsman and hounds and prevents the possible heading of hounds by an ignorant or inexperienced huntsman. When hounds are casting themselves (looking for scent at random) the huntsman may decide they are working in vain, and if he has a pretty good idea of the general direction Reynard has taken, he may "lift" the hounds (call them to him and take them to where his hunch leads him). He lifts them with a whistle, a word, and perhaps a sharp note of the horn. If they pick up the scent, he cheers them on and blows some sharp notes to pull any possible stragglers onto the line. If the huntsman wants to move his hounds some little distance, he will collect them and head out on a hand gallop. Usually the hounds follow him readily, but the whip or whips are behind them, "just in case." As the huntsman moves along, he will double-tongue his horn occasionally, more to keep in touch with the field than to tell the hounds to keep following him.

At the end of the hunt, whether a kill or a "gone to ground," there is a chaos of sound including shrill notes on the horn. After the excitement dies down, the field is "blown home" with a series of long slurred notes.

Hunting Cap

In a formal hunt, local gentry who are not members of the hunt, the servants, and the master wear a special kind of velvet cap. The crown is lined with hard cork, the button is high, the visor is narrow. The cap is encircled by a grosgrained ribbon which ends with a bow at the back. The bow on the caps of the master and servants is turned down; others wear it turned up.

Hunting Country

Different types of country for hunting require different skills for both horse and rider. It is sometimes difficult for a horse or rider accustomed to one kind of country to negotiate a different kind of country. For example, the rocky fields and stone walls of New England might seem quite formidable to the huntsman from Ohio used to less rocky terrain and wire fences that can be jumped safely only over the "chicken coops" (paneling) provided by the hunt. Country that is heavily timbered is as easily negotiated as any other but does not seem so to one accustomed to the open rolling country seen in some parts of Pennsylvania and Maryland. Very recently, hunts have been organized in Arizona. Some parts of the state have country so rough that drag hunting is the only possibility. In drag hunting hounds follow a scent made by dragging a bag of anise or other scent producer over the terrain. However, the hunting country around Sonoita is open and relatively free of fences and may well be a place where the hunting pace will require the best of Thoroughbred blood.

Hunting Horn

The hunting horn of fox hunters is of metal and considerably shorter than the trumpet. It is capable of only one note (*see* HUNTING CALLS). It is carried either by the master or the huntsman, in the latter case on the front of his saddle or tucked in his vest.

Hunting Thong

The long, braided, leather lash terminating at one end in a loop attachable to the loop of a crop is called a *hunting thong*. Its use is said to be that of

Traditional Eastern North American hunt. Huntsman Gordon Errickee with pack at Potomac opening meet. V. C. Wilson, M.F.H., in far background to the right of huntsman.

rating (correcting) hounds. A professional rides with the lash hanging nonchalantly looped along his horse's shoulder, but the amateur must discreetly keep his coiled in his hand.

Huntsman

In some hunts the same person officiates as master and huntsman. Whether or not this is the case with any specific hunt, the huntsman is the most important of professionals. He is to hounds, whips, and field what the coach is to the personnel of a football game, so far as decisions on strategy are concerned (placing and performance of hounds, whips, and field). However, in the field, his attention must be focused entirely on his hounds. Like the coach, the huntsman is the target of all blame if his hounds consistently fail to find and kill, and if many foxes are accounted for during the season, all laudation is directed at the huntsman.

In the field the huntsman rides first, next to his hounds, cheering them on. In the field matters of discipline are attended to by the field master.

Fox hunting in the Southwest. Here are the Tritton Hounds of Cananea (a town on the International Border between Arizona and Sonora). Patrick Tritton, M.F.H., unconventionally wearing silk hat (see APPOINTMENTS), and William Clyde, Whip.

However, in any silly antics over jumps, riding too close to hounds, making a disturbance when hounds are being cast (put to work), or other transgression of important rules, the huntsman, through the master, will make the offenders regret the day of their birth. The writer still recalls the worst tongue-lashing he ever received in his long life. It was delivered by F. Everson Powell, Master of the Rocky Fork Hounds, because the writer, a member of the field, galloped across his own wheat field, and it was the ironclad rule that growing crops were not to be ridden on in the Rocky Fork hunting country.

Hurdles

The terms *hurdle* and *fence* are interchangeable in referring to obstacles used in jumping or hunter classes in horse shows, steeplechases, and races. The term *hurdles* is also used to denote the kind of portable panels used by sheepherders (*shepherds* is the word east of the Mississippi).

Iceland Pony

The Iceland Pony is usually gray, dun, brown, or black, very drafty in build, from 12 to 13 hands in height. His characteristic gait, called the *tølt*, is described and named in an amusing number of ways by observers who are not familiar with gaited horses. A backwoods Kentuckian would say that Iceland Ponies "saddled" (*see* FOX-TROTTER). Most characteristically, they can do a true rack identical with that of the Paso and the gaited horses of our own country, though they do not attain much speed. Their ancestors are said to have migrated from Norway in the ninth century. The only thing in their history that seems to account for their movement is the statement by one historian that they share with the Fiord Pony descent from animals brought back from Constantinople by Varangians in the eleventh century, which would suggest kinship with the jennets (*see* JENNET).

Inclination of the Body. *See* FORWARD SEAT

Inclines (maneuvering steep)

Thanks to Captain Caprilli and his discovery of the value of the forward seat, horses are saved much misery in negotiating steep descents today by their riders' use of the forward seat. In going up steep inclines, it is just as important to keep weight off the horse's loins as it is in descending, though sometimes more difficult if the horse has no mane to hold onto.

In making a steep descent, leaning back and placing weight over the horse's loins puts the weight of the rider so far behind the bearing of the hind feet that those hind feet will slide from under the horse and disaster will result.

Independence (of rider's seat as opposed to his hands)

As long as the rhythm of the rider's body (or any nonrhythmic movement of his body, for that matter) has an effect upon the movement or position of his hands, he is not competent to ride a fine horse and should confine himself to school hacks. Early bareback riding, especially if one's mount has a tough mouth, is likely to make a rider depend upon his reins for balance. To gain body balance that is independent of hands, it is good practice to ride one's horse in a ring without using the reins or to ride him outside the ring, led by a companion, with the reins tied up so that they will not drop under foot. Absolute independence of body and hand movement requires time and patience. It is one of the most important aspects of good riding.

Indiana Pants

Because of the area in which hobbles (hopples) first gained acceptance (*see* HARNESS RACING) they were sometimes called *Indiana pants*.

Indian Horses and Ponies. *See also* AMERICAN INDIAN HORSE REGISTRY, INC.

Indian horses and ponies range from starved and stunted, spraddle-footed, sickle-hocked, ugly-headed creatures to horses of excellent conformation, temperament, and "heart." On the Navajo Reservation it would be possible to find a carload of animals that would give stiff competition in any competitive ride and others that would do well in any one of a variety of performance classes in any horse show. In 1958 the writer had the good fortune to be the weekend guest of the Chief Justice of the Navajo Nation. While being shown a newly cut tunnel through rimrock, which shortened the horseback or pedestrian distance from the bottom of Canyon de Chelly to Window Rock by several miles, the writer spied far below him a moving speck that could be identified as a horseman on the floor of the canyon. The trail from that floor to the tunnel was at least two miles in length, and every foot of its tortuous curves was a grade of at least 6 percent. Four people watched that horseman make the ascent. When they could distinguish the gait of the animal, they saw that he was doing an extended trot. The pony never varied his long trot, and all members of the observing party flattened themselves against the rock as the little well-formed, lean, blue-roan cleared the tunnel on that long swinging gait, showing no sign of distress whatever. The rider he carried was a young Indian weighing at least 160 pounds, who looked neither to right nor left as he passed the observers, but there was on his stoic countenance just a hint of the pride he felt in his mount.

Indian Riders

The quality of horsemanship of the American Indians of frontier days varied greatly from tribe to tribe. They were almost universally devoid of any feeling toward their mounts, and many were extremely inept riders. However, the Nez Percé Indians were so highly skilled in breeding horses that they developed one of the most excellent breeds ever brought forth on this continent. As a result of their defeat at arms, the breed (the Appaloosa) was practically destroyed, and it so seriously deteriorated that at present, when breeders want to bring it back to excellence, outside blood has to be used.

The following story is illustrative of the kind of horsemanship soldiers in the Indian wars occasionally encountered. A troop of cavalry of the

Texas frontier, to amuse themselves during a lull in their official duties, wanted to have a horse race with the Comanches among whom they were temporarily quartered. They had difficulty arousing the Indians' interest, but a quarter-mile race was finally arranged. An Indian brave came to the meeting place on what seemed to the cavalrymen one of the funniest little off-colored horses they had ever seen. They brought out their third-best horse. The Indians bet buffalo skins and other possessions against flour, coffee, sugar, and bacon. The 170-pound Comanche carried a ridiculously heavy club which he swung about his head as he raced. The troopers roared with laughter, but their jaws soon dropped as the pony shot ahead of the cavalry horse and won. The soldiers then brought out their second-best horse and made more bets. The Comanche never changed horses or clubs. The outcome of the second race was the same. Finally, the troopers brought out their best mount, a Kentucky-bred racer. The Comanche threw away his club. At the start of the race he gave a war whoop. His pony jumped into the lead. As he drew near the finish line, with a comfortable distance between himself and the trooper, he reversed himself on his horse like a trick rider in a rodeo. Facing the losing racer, he beckoned to the soldier to catch up, but the soldier never did.

Indirect Lighting

Horses are naturally creatures of the open spaces. When a horse is kept in a box stall with a small window he will, like the prisoner in "Reading Gaol," stare with "wistful eyes at that little tent of blue which prisoners call sky." If there is but one small window in the stall, and if it is so placed that when the horse stares out at it he looks directly at the sun, the effect on his eyes will be the same as it would be on human eyes forced to stare at the sun. Horses hauled in horse trailers may have their eyes damaged when carried toward the sun for any great length of time unless the windows or windshields of the trailer are properly tinted.

Indirect Rein (Indirect Rein of Opposition). *See* REINS

Indoor Riding

In many parts of the country, for much of the year, riding must be done largely indoors. Some people consider this a poor substitute for riding outside. Perhaps they ride only to see the country; they forget that the intelligent horseman learns something every hour he spends in contact with his horse, whether he is on the horse in the open fields or merely beside the horse in a stall. A great deal of the schooling of the horse and of the education of the rider can be done more readily indoors than elsewhere. Indoor riding provides or may provide more concentration on these things than can be attained in the open. The indoor ring is an excellent place to teach the horse to sidepass, to turn on the forehand or turn the forehand around the croup, to back properly, to two-track (see each of these maneuvers under their respective headings), and to perform other useful maneuvers. The cavalletti (*see* CAVALLETTI) can be used indoors to start the young jumper or to improve the old one, or to increase the handiness or responsiveness of any horse. Proper use of the leads can best be taught and learned by the rider, in the beginning, indoors.

Indoor riding demands greater attention to etiquette, perhaps, even than outdoor riding. The indoor rider should remember that the person who is riding at a slow rate of speed should keep to the wall. No rider should ever pass another one between the one being passed and the wall. If one is schooling his horse on the leads, flying change of lead in particular, he should be sure to do it when the indoor ring is not full of riders, especially timid or beginning riders. Whatever is done in the ring should be done in a manner that does not excite or interfere with other riders.

A cavalletti or jumps may be set up equidistant from either side wall of the indoor arena and toward one end, but not close enough to the end to interfere with other riders passing around it. Any rider using the cavalletti or jumps should be very careful as he finishes putting his horse over the jump or through the cavalletti not to let him proceed into the path of riders coming around the end of the arena. Certainly, there is no better place to teach a horse manners than in an indoor ring. If the ring is being used by any number of riders, it is quite necessary for the rider who does anything except proceed slowly around the ring close to the wall to be able to ride both ends of his horse and to have that horse exercise good manners at all times.

Indoor Riding Rings

With the increase of population, even in such areas as the Southwest, California included, real-estate developments are ruining bridle paths and riding trails. It is becoming more and more necessary to have indoor riding rings. Of course, when the weather is good most of the year as it is in some parts of the West Coast, the ring may be outdoors. But when riding is confined to a ring in most areas in the United States, that ring had better be under roof.

In many parts of the country, communities are constructing cooperative riding arenas. It is imperative that when this project is undertaken, the arena be large enough to accommodate the community. The proper size for the professional or community riding hall is 150 by 300 feet. Overhead beams should be at least 14 feet high. Windows should be at least five feet above the floor. Some provision has to be made to keep the interested spectators out of the arena. A gallery may be built, or the kickboard may be a little more than ordinary height, which is 3½ feet, and a place made for the spectators to stand behind the kickboard.

Of course, there should be no sharp corners in the riding arena. This matter can be taken care of by rounding the corners of the kickboard. All lights should be high, so there is no danger of their being touched by horses or riders, even during jumping. The lights should be so constructed that they flood the arena and do not throw spots on the floor.

The best flooring is the flooring that has been conventional for many, many generations in this country: tan bark. However, it is frequently hard to come by. Whatever material is put on the floor, it must be of sufficient rigidity so that the horse's feet will not sink into it (if they do, all his movements will be restricted); and it must not be so hard that he will damage his feet. If sand or shavings or a combination of those is used, the material must be cleaned and replaced with some frequency. Hence there should be doors at least at one end of the arena that are large enough to admit trucks and tractors; that is, they should be 12 or, still better, 16 feet wide. All doors should open outward from the ring. Any door opening inward is likely to cause an accident because someone will open it just as a horse is coming around the ring past it. The main construction of the building will depend upon the money available and upon the amount and kind of material available. In some places airplane hangars have been taken over. Since they are made of steel, they are pretty hot in summer (in hot parts of the country) and very cold in winter. The amount of insulation that goes into the riding hall depends upon how much money can be spent. An ideal riding ring is to be seen at the Brusally Arabian Ranch in Scottsdale, Arizona. It is in a riding hall that is extremely well insulated and has complete air conditioning so that any desired temperature or humidity can be maintained, regardless of the temperature or humidity outside. The ceiling of the hall is very high—a great advantage in maintaining proper temperature and pleasant air.

In the large professional or community riding hall canvas or curtains may be used when classes of various types of horsemanship (for instance, jumping and gaited-horse work) are conducted at the same time. In smaller communities, where the kind of horsemanship engaged in is fairly uniform, much smaller indoor riding halls may serve very well. One of from 75 to 100 or 130 feet is probably fine. Such a riding hall is large enough for jumping, and it may be divided up for simultaneous use by people engaged in two or more kinds of horse activity if none requires a length of space greater than 50 feet.

Influenza

Equine influenza is caused by a virus infection. Its symptoms in the horse are quite similar to those of influenza in people. The temperature may reach 106° and may persist for from two to ten days. In early stages, the cough is usually dry, but mucous discharge soon appears and affects the cough. If complications do not occur, recovery usually is complete in from one to two weeks. Bronchitis and pneumonia are the complications most often found. The latter is the most common cause of death following influenza. Since influenza is a viral, not a bacterial, disease, antibacterial drugs do not affect it; but they are useful at proper stages of the disease in the prevention of complications. Intelligent horsemen seek competent veterinary diagnosis and treatment when their animals become ill.

In Hand

The phrase *in hand* has two distinctly different meanings. (1) A horse shown in a ring by a handler who is on foot and handling the horse by the use of a halter or bridle is said to be in hand. (2) Keeping a horse in hand is keeping him in at least a slight degree of collection (*see* COLLECTION).

The rider who keeps his horse in hand is exactly the opposite of the rider who may be called a passenger, a person who sits on a horse and is transported by it much as the animal would transport 150 or so pounds of freight.

Insanity in Horses

Insanity is less common in horses than it is in human beings. One reason is that the horse is not confused by language as we are; the level on which his nervous system operates does not extend to the understanding of abstraction that ours does. Furthermore, he does not have public schools, churches, and newspapers to add to his mental confusion. If a horse becomes insane, he can only be destroyed.

Inside Roll

The inside roll, a maneuver that is becoming a conventional part of Western competitions, includes the rollback (*see* ROLLBACK). The inside roll may be performed in the following manner:

First, take plenty of time to teach the horse and yourself the rollback. Perfect it so that you and your horse can perform it anywhere and any time. However, always remember that no one maneuver is to be repeated over and over again on any one ride in such prolonged and rapid sequence that the horse becomes "soured" on it. If he performs well a time or two, caress him for so doing, and do something else for a while, coming back to the maneuver a little later. Perfecting the rollback may take days, weeks, or months, depending upon the temperament of horse and rider and upon the circumstances under which the riding is being done. Generally speaking, the longer the time, the better.

When the rollback is perfected, take your horse into the chosen area or arena. Walk him until he is moving freely and calmly. Then start him around the ring turning to the left (counterclockwise) at a gallop. This will, of course, call for a left lead. When you are midway down one side of the arena, or at any place in a circular corral, turn your horse toward the center—that is, toward the left. Since he is already on the left lead, he does not change leads as he turns toward the center of the ring (or open area, if you are not in a ring or arena). When he has taken from five to ten strides toward the center, turn him again to the left so that he is heading straight back toward the arena fence you have just left (or edge of the area). As he comes to the fence, not slackening speed, turn him to the right, so he will change to the right lead.

What you have done is to reverse and then do a half rollback, the kind of rollback you did on your first attempt at that maneuver.

Gradually, you will get your horse to the point at which you can simply describe a short reverse circle followed quickly by a right-angle turn with change of lead. You must be able to do this going either way of the arena, starting with the appropriate lead for the direction taken (always lead with the inside foot). Some horses who are very proficient at the rollback will do the inside roll more easily if the turn toward the inside is almost a complete circle the first few times, followed by a rollback, which will of course head them in reverse direction proper for the new lead. After some practice, you can merely reverse your direction, turning toward the center of the ring, and as soon as your horse reaches the rail or fence (or outside of the area), he will take the proper lead for going around the ring in the new direction.

Intelligence of Horses

Most horses have little chance to display a very large portion of their intelligence. If we are to speak of the relative intelligence of horses and people, we might point to the fact that when we are dealing with a very "low" level of abstraction, the horse's nervous system is far superior to that of a man, as is the dog's. These so-called lower animals (the ones incapable of speech, wars, and production of slums) can hear sounds and see things that are entirely beyond our perceptions. An animal can be closed up tightly so that he cannot see out and then be shipped across the country. When he is released, if he is not interfered with by people (which, of course, is an impossibility today), he will return to his home no matter what part of the country that may be located in. This feat is far beyond the ability of any human being. In the days before the automobile, almost any horse owner (and that included anybody who could afford a means of transportation other than shoe leather) could tell of instances in which his life had been saved or at least in which he had been saved from serious accident because his horse's perception was better than his own, and the horse insisted on doing something or refraining from doing something contrary to the owner's demand (e.g., refusing to cross the unsafe bridge in floodtime though the horse had willingly crossed the bridge not many hours before).

Most horse responses which indicate intelligence escape notice by human beings. The dog goes more than halfway in his communication with people. If the owner does not notice some subtle movement by which the dog is communicating something, the dog will go so far as to jump up and put his paw on the owner (frequently to be rewarded by having his hind toes trod upon). But the horse, when his subtle movement of nostril, ear, neck, foot, or what not is not recognized and responded to by the person, will soon quit attempting to communicate with his owner. So most people underrate the intelligence of their horses.

If a horse is treated like a "thing" over a period of time, he becomes a "thing" and loses many of his abilities. In early Kentucky in the backwoods when the horse was such a vital part of life, the family horse was certainly treated as an important part of the ménage. His intelligence was remarked upon continually, sometimes in a rather derogatory fashion, for such horses frequently learned to untie all kinds of knots and open gates. There was one, the writer recalls, whose intelligence caused himself a severe case of colic and caused his owner loss of considerable property. That horse could open almost any gate. He finally learned that if he opened the gate and was followed by other animals, some human being immediately discovered his sin and returned the animals to their proper places and closed the gate, shutting it with wire or something else that presented a little more difficult puzzle to be solved. On one occasion, this horse opened the gate and then turned around and closed it so that other animals would not follow. He then proceeded to a field of corn that had not quite matured, gorged himself on it, and knocked down a good deal of it. His ensuing bellyache was a painful affair, and the ruination of the corn was costly to his owner.

Another family horse lost his eyesight. The owner of the horse decided not to use it anymore for normal purposes, and a 10- or 12-year-old girl in the household said that she would like to have it for her own. This wish was granted; the girl had, previous to his loss of sight, ridden the horse sometimes when he was not busy doing more practical things for the family. She continued to ride him after he lost his vision. Before long, she was riding this blind horse with other youngsters, and the horse performed in a manner that did not reveal his loss of sight at all. He was so responsive to the rider that he could gallop with the other riders through the woods over fallen logs, escaping trees. The writer of these lines was so skeptical when he heard the story that he traveled some distance to satisfy himself that the horse was capable of this feat. When he asked if he could mount the horse and ride it, the little girl was somewhat hesitant but finally agreed. Mounted by a stranger, the horse was reluctant to move forward, though he was a free goer under the girl. When urged to go forward, he broke out in a sweat, so great was his nervous tension, and the rider, of course, immediately dismounted and returned the horse to the child, who quickly calmed him.

Literature abounds in stories about the Arabs' war-horse. Arabian colts grew up in and out of the tents of the nomads, joining the children in their play and sharing with them the mare's milk. Certainly, the story of the phenomenal intelligence of these animals has a basis in fact, as any one of those not-too-frequent owners of Arabians who use them outside the show-ring can testify.

It is perhaps fortunate that most books about horses and horsemanship insist on the lack of intelligence of horses, because they may save the horse from considerable grief from people who expect things of him that he is not capable of. Much of the difficulty amateurs encounter with horses is the result of what might be called projection; that is, when a horse does any one certain thing, they assume that he does it for the same reason that they themselves would do it. This is very frequently not the case. Many times a horse does something because he is frightened, but the owner interprets his action as a result of anger, or of wanting to take advantage of the rider, because that is the reason the owner would perform in the given manner.

If amateurs can be made to believe in the lack of intelligence of the horse, they may go to greater lengths to make him understand what they want and proceed by more gradual steps. Certainly, all beginning horse-men should have impressed upon them the horse's entire lack of ability to use language as we use it—that is, to use a set of symbols in an infinite variety of combinations to "mean" an infinite variety of things. Horses, of course, may learn certain words as signals, but they are utterly incapable of reaching that level of abstraction which is necessary in our use of language and which is the one thing that is typical of all mankind. Anthro-pologists tell us that in the most primitive societies, where the vocabulary is extremely limited, there is always a grammar—a system of putting sounds together for a variety of meanings. This is beyond the intelligence of a horse. Fortunately so, for our use of language makes us, in Kipling's words, "all islands shouting lies to each other across a sea of misunder-standing."

Communication with a horse is almost entirely kinetic, that is, by movement, whether it is movement of the reins or the body. If one will watch horses working at liberty in a ring at a circus, he will notice that it is the movement of the trainer and his whip, if he uses one, rather than audible signals that does most of the communicating with the liberty troupe. It is highly probable that most of the noises the trainer makes are to impress the audience rather than to communicate with the horses. A remarkable example of the use of movement to communicate with an animal may be seen on the sheep ranges of Montana and Wyoming. The little border collies used by the sheepherders may move ("work") a band of sheep (a band is usually a thousand or more) on a ridge so far distant from the sheepherder that his voice is not audible. Yet as long as the border collies can see the waving of the sheepherder's arms, they will do with a band of sheep whatever it is he wants them to and do it precisely and immediately.

The horse uses movement to communicate with his rider just as a rider uses movement to communicate with his horse, and one is not a competent horseman until he is continually aware of his horse's "kinetic communication" while he is on his horse's back or in contact with him in his stall.

Interfere

If, when moving at any gait, a horse strikes a leg with the opposite foot, he is said to "interfere." Sometimes, faulty shoeing or faulty leveling of the feet is to blame. More frequently, it is a matter of faulty conformation, a congenital thing. If the horse is very young and the faulty conformation very slight, a good farrier may correct it. Veterinarians frown on one method of correcting the interference by horseshoeing that has been held in considerable favor in the past, that is, by changing the level of the foot. This, if done too drastically, may cause the horse to go lame because it injures the joint. Most veterinarians today prefer to have the toe of the foot squared so that the horse has to "break over" (turn the foot over) properly and in this fashion avoid hitting the other foot. Sometimes the inside of the striking foot is "boxed" or drawn in slightly. Whatever method is used should be under the direction of a competent veterinarian.

International Arabian Horse Association. *See also* ARABIAN HORSE CLUB OF AMERICA, INC., and ARABIAN HORSE

Address: 224 East Olive Avenue, Burbank, California 91503. The association is the breed promotion organization for Arabian horses. The literature about Arabs is prepared and mailed from its offices. The official yearbook, containing pictures of the champions and contestants from the shows across the country, is available at $10 per copy or may be procured by becoming a member. The association acquired the Half-Arab and Anglo-Arab Registries from the American Remount Association and has continued to maintain records and accept new registrations in keeping with the standards set by the latter in the past. Any wise owner of a foal sired by an Arabian will certainly make an effort to have him registered in the Half-Arab Registry because such registration increases the value of any animal.

Irish Hunter

The term *Irish Hunter* is a broad one. From the kind of Irish Hunters that have come to our shows, the standard here is pretty largely that of a horse of considerable size, tremendous bone, good heart girth, good shoulders, powerful quarters, excellent disposition, and some coarseness of head. In Ireland, the Irish Hunter may be a straight Thoroughbred. No country in the world has produced greater horses of the breed than has Ireland, and John Masefield, in a short essay, wrote perhaps the greatest description of a breed of horse, a tribute to the Irish Thoroughbred. Of course, in Ireland, as in this country, the Thoroughbred is a bit "hot," that is, too sensitive and too responsive, possessed of too much heart (impulsion), for many riders to hounds. So he is crossed with horses of colder blood to produce an animal who can take handling by inept horsemen. In the old days of resident magistrates who rode to hounds, the magistrate had to be mounted on something that would keep him at least reasonably well up in the field and still would not injure him. Perhaps this is one reason why the Irish Hunter was developed. In some parts of Ireland these horses are trained to go over an obstacle consisting of a bank and a ditch by pushing with the hind feet on top of the bank, much as a dog would push on the top of a fence when jumping over. The best Irish Hunter ever encountered by the writer, who had the good fortune to be asked to ride this horse, was one owned by Major Harry Brown of the Rocky Fork Hounds. The writer had read about the way Irish Hunters are trained to push at the top of a bank, but that did not come to his mind when he mounted this grand gelding, whose trot gave the sensation of being kicked down a flight of stairs—although his gallop was a joy. Hounds found (started a fox) in timber that was being logged off, and the first jump was over a felled tree. The trunk probably presented an obstacle that was close to four feet in height, and it was good and solid. The big bay gelding took it in stride, but as his hind feet were clearing it, they gave a tremendous push which whiplashed the neck of his rider violently! The rider heard the laughter of one of the whips, who had evidently anticipated what would happen and was observing it with some amusement. If one wishes to hunt and can procure an Irish Hunter trained in Ireland, he is bound to be mounted on a fearless animal who, if provided with a big bridoon and no other bit, can be ridden in any fashion, even by hanging onto the reins to maintain balance.

Irish Martingale. *See* MARTINGALE

Isabella

Isabella is the Spanish word for a horse the color of our Palominos (*see* PALOMINO). There are as many stories about the origin of this term as there are about the word *Palomino*, from religious to scatological; but none seems to be based on fact. The word is sometimes spelled *Ishbel* or *Isabel*.

Italian Influence. *See* FORWARD SEAT

Jaquima. *See* HACKAMORE

Jay

The jaybird and some of his kin are sometimes participants in a fox hunt, as John Masefield so beautifully points out in his *Reynard the Fox:**

> A blue, uneasy jay was clacking
> (A swearing screech like tearing sacking)
> From tree to tree, as in pursuit
> "That's it, there's a fox afoot."

* From *Poems* by John Masefield. © Harper & Brothers, 1913.

Jennet. *See also* HINNY

The two very different meanings of *jennet* are the cause of considerable confusion.

The result of breeding a stallion to a female ass is a hinny, sometimes called a jennet or genet. These last two terms were also used to designate a type of Spanish horse well thought of in the twelfth century, valued for his easy gaits. He was quite popular in England at the time when the saying was current that "a trotting horse is fit only for servants to ride or for packing." These easy-gaited animals were probably the ancestors of the Galloways and the Hobbies, highly prized for transportation in England just prior to the seventeenth century. It is also probable that the easy gaits of the Pasos of Peru and Colombia can be traced to the Spanish jennets. The Narragansett Pacers, so sought after by the planters of the West Indies that they entirely disappeared from this continent by Revolutionary times, carried a large proportion of the blood of the jennets. The Tom Hal and Cockspur families of the American Saddle Horse were uniformly easy gaited and undoubtedly could trace their lineage to the jennets if records had been kept. The Tennessee Walking Horse could trace his lineage through the same channels to account for his easy gait.

Jenny

Jenny is the term used for a female ass. It is not to be confused with *jennet,* the name for an easy-gaited Spanish horse of bygone days (*see* JENNET).

Jewelry (for riding)

Until recent years jewelry was considered in very bad taste as part of riding apparel. However, in horse shows today this rule is passé, especially in fine-harness classes.

The only place where the old attitude toward jewelry seems still to prevail is in the hunting field and in the show-ring classes for hunters and jumpers. In these situations the only jewelry which is in good taste is a plain gold bar or similar pin worn in the stock. It should be placed horizontally in the stock, for a perpendicularly placed pin can jab the neck or the chest of the rider in some situations.

Jigging

The term *jigging* signifies a slow trot that some horses will execute instead of a walk. There is perhaps no more annoying habit. Many horses cannot walk over 2 or 2½ miles an hour and if forced beyond this will trot. Some horses when they become warm or nervous will not walk at all and can trot almost standing still. When restrained, they will twist from side to side or otherwise attempt to resist the rider.

Jockey (noun)

A jockey is a professional who rides a race horse. In spite of the fact that the horse race has been described as "the chasing of half broken colts around the track by midget morons," the jockey is often a horseman of extreme skill "on equines that know not the meaning of indirect rein or other aids."

Jockey (verb)

The term *to jockey* means to maneuver for an advantageous position when lining up for a race or for competing in a group for any other purpose. It also sometimes means to trade sharply or dicker.

Jockey Club

The Jockey Club was started in 1893, organized along the lines of The Jockey Club of England, which was formed in 1750. The Jockey Club was created to develop the Thoroughbred race horse and establish racing on some sort of ordered basis. It created or re-created rules for racing and scheduled racing meets to avoid conflict. It gained some authority of law in 1895 by the Percy-Gray Racing Law, providing that any race meet had to be licensed and that the racing was subjected to conditions and race laws of The Jockey Club. While the club operates in New York and Delaware, it has helped in forming race associations all over the eastern United States, and its *Rules of Racing* are recognized on all tracks. This publication defines types of races, duties of race officials, weights, handicapping, conduct of jockeys, and insurance employers must carry. The Jockey Club is responsible for the registration of all American Thoroughbreds in its *American Stud Book*. No horse can be registered unless his sire and dam are registered in the *American Stud Book*. No horse may race on a recognized track unless he is so registered. The offices of The Jockey Club are at 300 Park Avenue, New York, New York 10022, and contain a library of some of the most famous Thoroughbred paintings.

Jockey Seat

Until Tod Sloan, a farm boy from Kokomo, Indiana, started to ride race horses and was sent to England, we had trouble winning on English tracks. However, Sloan invented the present *jockey seat* or "monkey seat" and by using that and the lighter shoes for which he is also given credit proceeded to give the English plenty of competition. The seat he invented is one with extremely short stirrups. It puts the rider's weight right over the horse's withers. When the horse runs, these extremely short stirrups place the rider's knees on the horse's shoulders just below the withers; he crouches over the horse and has all his weight over the horse's forehand.

Jog Trot

A jog trot is merely a very slow trot, not to be confused with jigging (*see* JIGGING). It is done in a relaxed manner and is one of the required gaits in some Western classes.

Joint Evil

This disease is also called by horsemen shigellosis, sleeper foals, dummy foals, wanderers, viscosum infection, joint ill, and pysopticemia. It is also called navel ill or navel disease. The symptoms may be confined to those that could indicate any one of several other kinds of infection. However, there is one symptom that occurs sometimes which is obvious to the horseman, and which some horsemen think always occurs: a swelling of the joints and increasing crookedness thereof. Until fairly recently it was generally thought that joint ill was the result of prenatal infection and that the infection occurred sometimes in the uterus. Modern veterinary findings indicate that such infection may occur in rare instances but that the disease is usually contracted after birth through the mouth or through lesions of various kinds, especially through the newly severed navel cord of the newborn foal. That is why veterinarians recommend that the navel cords on all foals be painted with iodine at the time of foaling. This is only one kind of prevention. There should be others, especially in areas in which the disease is endemic. If joint ill is known to occur in an area in which a foal is expected, the stall in which he is to be dropped should be disinfected, clean bedding should be used or even a foaling sheet, and a veterinarian should be consulted as to whether a preventive vaccine for the specific disease endemic in the area is available and advisable. The life of affected foals is usually very short. Although modern veterinary science has developed some remedies, successful in some instances, they are not as yet overly gratifying in their results.

Jumper

A jumper is a horse who can jump. In horse shows he is usually rated for his ability to clear obstacles, and the way he clears them does not count in most classes. Jumpers occur in all breeds and among horses of unknown breeding; they occur in horses of all sizes, although the big horse always has some advantage. Great Heart, who a number of years ago set a record of something over eight feet, was part draft animal. Many high jumpers have been part Hackney.

One of the most widely known and successful horses in America's Olympic competitions was a little horse named Olympic Don, a Saddlebred gelding scarcely 15 hands high. He was won by an army officer, stationed in Kansas, in a poker game. When the officer moved to Florida, he took the horse with him because officers were entitled to two mounts kept at government expense in those days. In Florida he had very little use for the horse, but the officer's children and others used to use him in amateur shrimp fishing.

The story goes that one day at an impromptu post horse show a relative of the officer was willing to participate in the show but had no horse. Olympic Don was offered her as a mount. One of the classes included a three-foot jump. The rider had never jumped, but she was willing to try. So far as anyone knew, Don had never been asked to jump. But these two, both new at jumping, negotiated the jump in such a fine manner that they won the class. From then on, Don jumped over everything, including six army cots piled one on top of the other with a recruit lying on the top one. At a subsequent Olympic contest in which a French horse with a great reputation was expected by everyone to be the winner, Olympic Don won.

It is said that none of the torturing devices frequently used to make horses jump high were ever used on Olympic Don. He was certainly an exception in his escape from such devices. Usually the high jumper is put over jumps to which a rapping bar has been attached. A rapping bar is a bar attached to heavily springed triggers which release the bar as the horse's leg clears the top of the jump. It is often provided with nails or short spikes and causes the horse's legs great pain. This makes him want to clear the jump as high as he can; since it also makes him terrified of jumping, he has to be made more afraid of not jumping than of jumping. In consequence, many jumpers are very roughly handled even in the show-ring, but clearing the jump is the object. Whether or not jumpers are subjected to more cruelty than are Tennessee Walking Horses or five-gaited horses is open to question, but it certainly is a matter that humane societies might well deal with.

Jumping (learning to jump)

The most sensible procedure in learning to jump is first to learn balance and to be aware of and constantly in movement with the horse's rhythm. This requires a great deal of time; sometimes it is helped by competent instruction. Before thinking about jumping, it is wise to learn the use of all the aids and of the direct and indirect rein, and how to move the horse as readily as one moves his own body. When one can do this, he is ready to start his horse over the cavalletti (*see* CAVALLETTI). His first jump may well be not over a foot high at the end of a cavalletti. The jump should be raised only after the rider has learned to negotiate perfectly this one-foot jump. Then, if the raising of the jump is done sufficiently gradually, the rider's hands and balance can develop easily and excellently.

However, this slow method is not for the riding school because riding masters are paid to teach people to jump, and the people who pay the bills are frequently the parents of children, and they want to see results and see them soon. In such situations the riding instructor will do well to have a jumping lane provided. The young rider then can be put on a steady horse; the reins of the horse can be tied up and a belt or other wide strap put around the horse's neck just ahead of his withers so that the young rider can hold on to that if need be. Starting thus with a one-foot-high jump, continual practice may result in balance good enough so that the young rider can negotiate the foot-high jump without hanging on to the belt around the horse's neck. The jump should not be raised even one inch until the rider can negotiate it with arms outstretched at either side and perfect balance maintained. The forward seat (q.v.) on a good forward-seat saddle is the proper one to use in such instances. Jumping should proceed very, very gradually as far as increasing height of the object is concerned. When the rider can negotiate three feet in perfect balance without putting weight on his horse's mouth, he can begin to think about jumping at hunting speed.

At this point it is important to be sure that the learner can go over a three-foot jump maintaining absolutely constant pressure on the reins— preferably light pressure, but the amount of the pressure will depend in considerable part on the mouth of his mount. The reason is that when the horse reaches the top of his jump and starts to descend, he thrusts his head forward, his nose out; at this time it is crucial that the hands go with the mouth and neither decrease nor increase the pressure that was exerted on the reins as the horse approached the jump. Many horses have been ruined by hands that did not go with the mouth as the horse started to descend. Such hands have the same effect on the mouth as if the horse were on level ground and the hands gave a tremendous jerk, enough to cause a convulsive straightening of the horse's hind legs and bring him quickly to a stop on level ground. When the horse is in midair, his hind legs are likely to do the same thing and knock off the top bar of the jump. Not only should the height of obstacles be increased very gradually, but the nature of obstacles should be changed gradually until the horse will jump over a collection of chains, automobile parts, etc., fastened to a pole at either end by men stout enough to jiggle the pole and make the collection of obstacles dance and make a noise. If transition to such a jump is too rapid, the horse will become excited. Then it will be obvious that progress has been too fast, and the learner should go back to the previous stage of his learning and continue from there. Of course, moving from the jumping lane for the beginner to jumps of the same height used in the lane but outside with wings to prevent the horse from jumping out is quite a transition. Sometimes it is best to have this transition occur by placing the jump just a few feet beyond the end of the jumping lane and then moving it farther and farther away from the jumping lane. Little by little, the learner can develop the skill to keep his horse in the jump by using his reins. Wings can be gradually lowered and shortened and finally dispensed with. When a horse will jump, let us say, a half-dozen army cots with a man lying on top of one of them as did Olympic Don (*see* JUMPER), he may be called a competent jumper.

Proceeding from single jumps to in-and-out jumps must be a very slow, step-by-step matter. The first in-and-out jump should be not more than one-fourth the height of the single jump a horse can negotiate easily. Making transitions slowly may tax the patience of teacher and learner, but it is the only way to produce a fearless rider; and by the same token, it is the only method that will result in the sort of fearless, quiet jumper that wins hunting classes. Of course, the horse who is being trained to win jumping classes can be trained in the same fashion. The temperament of the horse should be taken into consideration when he has become a competent jumper and it is time to carry him on to greater heights. One big help in increasing the height which a horse can and will jump is to be sure never to jump him until he is in the pink of condition and furthermore, never to jump him after he has become tired.

While it is true that some of the greatest international jumpers have carried the scars of the rapping bars, it is equally true that such horses as Great Heart have broken records without ever having been subjected to cruelty. If the trainer has the art of keeping the horse in such condition and in such surroundings that he wants to jump, the chances are pretty good that he will equal or exceed the performance of the horse who has been subjected to agonies.

Jumping Competitions

The kind of competitions that are useful in a riding school or small show are almost infinite in number and are limited only by the ingenuity of the person or persons in charge. Courses can be set up containing from eight to a dozen or more jumps, each of which may be of a different kind and of a different type of difficulty. Some jumps can present largely mental hazards (*see* MENTAL HAZARD JUMPING); others can be so constructed that they entail trappy jumping, that is, jumping that can be negotiated only by a horse that can jump when he is well in hand. The difficulty and nature of the jumps should be determined by the degree of excellence of the people competing.

The course can be marked by flags in such a manner that the rider will have to continue keeping a flag always on his right, or it can be marked by large numbers placed on each jump. But the course should be so arranged that the rider has to cross the ring several times. If the course is laid out for team jumping, a very useful kind of jumping in gymkhanas and in riding schools, jumps can be marked to indicate which ones the team should jump together and which the team should take in sequence. A useful kind of in-and-out jump in such a competition is one in which the rider has to turn at right angles to jump out. Many times a quadrillelike jumping event over low jumps two or three feet high is more interesting and sometimes more dangerous than a jump over an elaborate course consisting of high and more difficult jumps.

Jumping Faults (scoring of)

Scoring of jumping faults had best follow the rules of the American Horse Shows Association. These rules are very clear regarding knockdowns, disobediences, the falling of horse or rider, the scoring of pairs, teams, unicorns abreast or in tandem, the scoring of jumpers, the scoring of working hunters, etc. As the contents of the *Rule Book* of the AHSA change slightly from year to year, the current *Rule Book* should be consulted by any person or committee engaged in setting up rules for any specific show.

Justin Morgan

The only single horse who founded a breed all by himself was Justin Morgan. For many years he was considered to be an animal of unknown breeding. However, when the Morgan Horse Club was organized, considerable research was done and the members decided that he was sired by a horse called True Britain. He was also known as the "beautiful bay." He was sired, it is said, by Imported Messenger, a Thoroughbred. No claim is made as to the certainty of the breeding of Justin Morgan's dam, but because of what we know of Justin Morgan's appearance and the appearance of his progeny for several generations, he must have carried some of the stout, good-boned, good-footed blood of the horses the Dutch imported from their native land. Justin Morgan was foaled in 1793, the property of a teacher whose name was Justin Morgan. He called the little fellow Figure. In 1793 the only horses considered to be of great value were the Thoroughbreds; they had just come into popularity with the wealthy folk. (The Thoroughbred was scarcely known in this country until after the Revolutionary War.)

Nobody paid much attention to the teacher's colt. He grew up and learned to work in harness. His teacher-owner moved to Randolph, Vermont. Being frequently in need of money, like most men in his profession, the teacher rented his young horse for $15 to a Robert Evans, who had contracted a job of clearing 15 acres of land for a Mr. Fish. The trees growing on the land were large, but when felled and cut into logs, none was too large for the teacher's horse to drag to the nearby sawmill. At the end of one day's work on his contract, Evans, seated sidewise on his rented horse, was riding home, one hand on the hame, one heel dragging against a trace chain. As he passed the local tavern, he was hailed by a friend. He tied Figure to a hitch rail and went into the tavern to join his friends. They were all excited about a pulling match, a common sport in those days. There was a log, they told Evans, about 200 feet from the logway at the mill. The team (two horses) that had dragged it there had not been able to get it any farther.

Evans walked back to the mill and took a look at the log. When he returned, he said, "I'll wager a gallon of rum that my horse can pull that log in the logway in three pulls."

Cheering, the little crowd followed Evans and Figure to the mill. Taking a singletree from the doubletree abandoned by the team that could move the log no farther, Evans fastened it to the log chain and hooked Figure's traces to it. Then he stood back and surveyed the log.

"That's a mighty small log to move for a gallon of rum," he said. "Why don't two or three of you men jump on it?"

Three men piled onto the log; Evans gathered up the reins; the 950-pound, 14-hand horse gently began to mouth the bit. Evans spoke quietly to him. Figure settled into the collar and dug in with his feet. The great muscles of his loins and haunches bunched up and began to ripple. The chain ground tight on the log and the log began to move. At an ever-increasing speed it moved until it had covered half the distance to the logway and the three riders, spattered by dirt thrown up by Figure's digging hoofs, had tumbled off.

A quiet "Whoa" from Evans stopped the little horse for a breathing spell. In two more pulls, Figure landed the log in the logway.

From that day, the fame of the teacher's horse began to spread. Farmers around Randolph brought their mares to Figure to get colts that were strong. Parade marshals asked for him to lead parades on the Fourth of July and other days of celebration. With bands playing behind him, Figure stepped so proudly that everyone cheered him. Today our parade horses wear special heavy shoes held on with bands and have long toes so that they have to pick up their feet very high. Without special shoes or long toes, Figure's feet snapped back like steel springs. His full-crested neck was proudly arched. His big wide-apart eyes took in everything. From his delicately curved, alert ears, with their tips so close together, to his sensitive muzzle, his head was more beautiful than any ever before seen in Vermont.

"Sure, he's a pretty horse, and he can pull when he wears harness," said a jealous onlooker while Figure was prancing past him at the head of a Fourth of July parade.

"Yep, he may be a pretty prancer and a workhorse, but I have a horse that can outwalk him or outtrot him any day under saddle!"

So other contests were planned for Figure, and other wagers were won by his backers. In 1796 two horses, Sweepstakes and Silvertail, were brought all the way from New York to race him. They were the winners of many running races, which means races at the gallop. Figure beat both of them easily. His master must have felt sorry for the owner of Silvertail, because he offered him two chances to win back his money. He would put up the money as prize for a walking race or trotting race, he said, whichever Silvertail's owner wanted, but the offer was refused.

Today such a remarkable horse would bring a high price if sold. He would be kept in a fine stable with the best care; but in 1800 only Thoroughbreds were fashionable and merited such treatment. Figure was sold again and again for a modest price, and always to a man who needed a horse for work, though he might run him in a matched race now and then. Four times the little horse was taken as part payment of a debt.

His original name, Figure, was forgotten. It was not a very catchy name for a horse anyway. Perhaps Justin Morgan, the teacher, had chosen it because a schoolmaster was supposed to teach children to read, write, and figure. As word about this horse who could do so many things spread among men who used horses to earn a living, he became known as "that Morgan horse." Finally, he was referred to as Justin Morgan, the name we know him by today.

Though he changed hands many times, the stout little horse always worked for his owners. He continued to win fame by defeating all challengers in running, walking, trotting, and pulling contests until one evening, at the end of a hard day in work harness pulling a wagon, he was turned into a lot with other horses and was kicked. The night was cold, and snow started to fall. There was no shelter and no one to care for the wound in his side. Inflammation set in and he died. He was 32 years old.

Though the great Justin Morgan died in 1821, his fame continued to grow through his sons and daughters. One of the most unusual qualities of the "the big little horse" was his ability to pass on to his sons and daughters his strength, speed, and beauty. Two of the six most famous sons of Justin Morgan were known only by the names of the men who raised them—the Hawkins horse and the Fenton horse. They were foaled in 1806 and 1808 respectively. Two others of the famous six were known by the names of their sire and the names of the men who raised them. They were Sherman Morgan, foaled in 1808, and Woodbury Morgan, foaled in 1816. Another of the six, foaled in 1812, was called Bullrush Morgan. Perhaps he, like Moses in the Bible, was found in the bullrushes. Only one of the six had a name not connected with an owner or sire. He was called Revenue, foaled in 1815.

These six sons of Justin Morgan not only were famous in their own day but through their descendants are represented in the most fashionable breeds of American horses today—the American Saddle Horse, the Quarter Horse, the Standardbred, and the Tennessee Walking Horse. Of all important breeds today, only the Arabian and the Thoroughbred owe no debt for their success to Justin Morgan. (*See also* MORGAN HORSE.)

Kicking Strap

A kicking strap should be used on every animal the first time he is put in harness. Under the proper handling, the chances are pretty good that the strap will never be stretched, but many a young horse has been ruined by being hitched with harness not supplied with a kicking strap, and with his first kick breaking loose from the vehicle to which he was hitched. The kicking strap is made with heavy trace leather, very wide. Far enough from either end to permit the kicking strap to encircle the shaft, a buckle with keeper is attached to it. The strap passes over the horse's croup a few inches ahead of his tail, underneath the crupper. A narrow strap with buckle is attached to the kicking strap so that the crupper can pass under the narrow strap. It is a good idea to tie this securely to the crupper with a string so that the kicking strap will not slide back on the crupper and pinch the tail. Sometimes a kicking strap is provided with an extra narrow strap which attaches to it about midway on the hip and then attaches to the harness at the top of the croup. This tends to keep the kicking strap from sliding backward on the shaft. The kicking strap should be so adjusted that it does not exert any pull on the horse and does not interfere with his natural movement, but it should be short enough so that if he kicks, he cannot raise his croup high enough to enable him to do damage with his heels.

Lameness (in horses)

Most lameness, in spite of the diagnoses of wiseacres and would-be "hoss doctors," occurs in the feet. Years ago, a study of lameness of horses on racetracks published in *Blood Horse Magazine* found that some 75 to 80 percent of horses on our racetracks were unsound, and of that percentage the majority were unsound in the feet. This is a rather surprising assertion because any photo-finish picture of a race will show the tremendous strain put on the pasterns and other parts of the foreleg of a racer. Sometimes the pastern joint is in contact with the track and the knee is bent back.

Lamenesses are usually caused by either concussion or deficiency in diet. If we want to add a third, it could be congenital defect of conformation; however, such a defect simply makes the horse more susceptible to the effect of concussion. The effect of concussion is also heightened by hardness and dryness of the hoof. This in itself may be a sort of subsidiary cause of lameness because when the heel of the hoof contracts, the bars of the hoof, instead of sloping outward toward the ground, are straight up and down, and the frog is often narrowed to one-fourth or less of its normal width. Thus the sensitive inside structure of the hoof is pinched as the human foot would be pinched by a shoe too narrow.

Continued use of a horse with a contracted heel will cause bruises and inflammation. As a result, the periosteum, the covering of the bone, will become inflamed, a callosity will be formed on the bone, lesions of the joint will occur, and inflammation will lead to permanent disturbances of the circulatory system of the foot. The most usual lamenesses are joint lesions or calcium deposits on various parts of the joint. Deposits on the joints in the foot may be in the form of splints (*see* SPLINTS), sidebones (*see* SIDEBONES), or ringbones. The ringbone, to the layman's eye, resembles the sidebone, but the bulge of bone is not confined to the sides of the foot; it continues entirely around it just above the coronet.

On the hind leg, joint lameness arising from causes mentioned above occurs in the hock. Most common are two kinds of spavins and thoroughpins (*see* SPAVIN and THOROUGHPIN). There is another lameness, thought by many horsemen to be associated with a defect in conformation called "sickle hocks." These are hocks curved in such a way that the cannon bone, instead of dropping straight down from the hock, tends to slope forward so that the pastern is abnormally farther forward than the hock. (The writer has failed to observe any association between the sickle hocks and curbs that cause lameness.) The curb is an enlargement of the big tendon at the rear of the hock, and it occurs just below the hock.

There are, of course, other lamenesses too numerous to mention, but these are the chief offenders, except one, founder, which is in a class by itself and explained below. Lameness in a horse may be detected by a variation in the rhythm of his gait. The horse's natural nodding in his walk will be more pronounced; that is, the downward nodding will be more pronounced, as the foot impact following that of the lame foot occurs. When a horse trots, the same thing happens; the head nod is greater as the sound feet have contact with the ground than when the unsound foot strikes the ground.

The first thing to look for, the instant a horse shows any sign of lameness, is a nail in the foot. In the event one is discovered, it should be removed immediately, iodine poured into the wound, and a veterinarian called to give the wound further attention and to administer tetanus antitoxin to the horse. Occasionally a horse will get a stone lodged between the hoof and the frog, or, if the stone is of the proper size and shape, so lodged inside the shoe that it presses on the sole. It may cause rather intense lameness. Of course, the proper thing to do is to remove the stone. It is very handy to have a short screwdriver or a hoof-pick in one's pocket on such occasions. If a horse is valued at all by the owner, he will immediately call a veterinarian when the horse gives evidence of lameness. Farriers very frequently can diagnose lameness and prescribe proper cure, but it is much safer to depend upon the advice of a competent veterinarian.

Founder

There is one kind of lameness in horses that is prevalent and that is in a class by itself. It is ordinarily not caused by concussion, although it may be so caused; nor it is due to a nutritional deficiency of any kind. It is called laminitis or founder. To a good many horsemen, *founder* means simply that a horse has overeaten and then immediately been given water. This has produced a very painful swelling of the feet and eventually dropping of the sole (the sole loses its concavity). The horse is permanently lame. After such a founder, the hoof is characterized by a series of ridges. Founder is almost a mysterious ailment. Its causes are many, and some of them are not completely understood. It can be the result in some horses of a sudden, violent change of temperature on the feet. It can follow improper cooling out of a hot horse. Sometimes it is caused by a radical change in diet. In any case, the feet become fevered and swollen and the horse is lame, usually in both forefeet (the disease more frequently affects the front feet than the hind).

When a light case of founder is diagnosed immediately, it is possible that the fever in the feet can be reduced by letting a horse stand in water and giving him veterinary remedies. The horse can then become completely useful again. However, as a rule the horse is never as useful after he has had laminitis as he was before he was afflicted. Many, many cases of founder are the result of overfeeding on grain over a long period of time.

Laminitis (or founder). *See also* LAMENESS

Founder or laminitis is characterized by a separation of the lamina (the layers of the hoof), a dropping of the sole, and the formation of a series of horizontal ridges around the hoof. Its many causes are discussed under the heading LAMENESS. When a horse is badly foundered, his trouble can be diagnosed by any layman. His lower legs begin to swell, and it is difficult for him to walk. In days before competent veterinarians were available in many parts of the country, home remedies, in addition to getting his feet into water, included giving him a physic and heavy doses of saltpeter. Remedies of a more effective sort are now used by veterinarians, and any horse worth keeping merits the aid of a competent veterinarian when he is foundered.

Lampas

Lampas is a term indicating congestion of the mucous membrane which covers the hard palate (roof) of a horse's mouth and terminates in a ridge just behind the upper incisors. Not quite literate horsemen call it "lampers" and attribute it to *bad blood*, a term that is more amusing than meaningful. They insist that it is a disease, which it decidedly is not, and advocate scarifying the mucous membrane as a "cure." This ridge of mucous membrane behind the incisors, however, is normally filled with blood when a horse is eating and may project below the bearing surface of the teeth. It also may become filled with blood when the horse is cutting teeth or if barley beards or foxtails or some similar substance work in the mouth between the cheek and the gums or under the tongue and cause inflammation.

Ignorant horsemen have, for generations, resorted to a barbarous custom which is something like the following: "This horse has lampers. Put a twitch on 'im and gimme your knife and open his mouth and we'll cut 'em." Then the knife is used to scarify and cause bleeding of the ridge of the mucous membrane.

The horse is capable of resisting an enormous amount of bad treatment and usually survives this scarifying or cutting of his "lampers."

Of course, the proper thing to do if the mucous membrane is enlarged over a long period of time is to seek out the cause and remove it. Certainly, there is nothing to be gained by cauterizing or scarifying the mucous membrane, which is not diseased.

Landing

The term *landing* is used to indicate the terrain on the side of a jump opposite the takeoff. It is the ground the horse lands on after he has cleared a jump.

Lark (verb)

The term *to lark* denotes the iniquitous activity of taking jumps unnecessarily in the hunting field. This will bring down the wrath of the master or anyone else in the vicinity, although the members of the field have no authority to scold the person who is doing the larking. No jump should be taken in the hunting field unless hounds are running. By taking the jump hunters can follow a straighter course in pursuing the hounds than they can by going through a gap or around the end of a fence.

Latches (on doors)

Latches for stall doors, as well as latches for corral gates, should be so designed that they will not injure a horse if he should lunge or brush against them when passing in or out of the door or gate. They should also be so designed that the clever horse cannot readily open them. They should be heavy enough to keep the door from opening should a horse rub himself against them.

Lateral March. *See* TWO-TRACK

Laxatives

The sensible horseman keeps a close watch on his horse's droppings. If the manure is passed in tight, hard balls, the bran ration in feed should be increased. If the horse fails to drop manure for an abnormally long time, say, between feedings, a veterinarian should be summoned. The administration of home remedies to a horse without the advice of a veterinarian can be not only extremely costly but also extremely painful to the horse.

Where green forage is available, the horse who becomes slightly constipated can benefit from nibbling at fresh grass. However, a horse who has not had any grass for some time should be allowed only a small portion of it. Lawn-mower cuttings may be fed to a horse. If he is not used to them, just a small handful at a time should be given at first. Great care should be taken when feeding grass cuttings to see that they contain no oleander leaves (which are deadly poisonous even in extremely small amounts to horses) and to see that they are fresh. Grass cuttings heat very quickly when piled up and should not be fed to horses when they have started to heat because they begin to ferment right away.

Lead. *See* CHANGE OF LEAD

Leading (the horse)

All equines should learn how to be led from earliest foalhood. The horse should be led if the handler is on foot by the handler walking or running beside his shoulder. There is nothing more ridiculous than a person who leads a horse, especially into a show-ring, the way he would drag a pull toy on a string, with the animal following, frequently somewhat reluctantly, behind him. A horse used in situations in which he needs to be led by a person who is mounted on another horse should be trained to stay up beside the other horse. The handler may then grasp the reins of the unmounted horse above that horse's withers and handle him just as if he were mounted on him. This is not safe procedure at all unless the horse being led has been perfectly trained and stays up. If the led horse starts to lag back and the handler has to use the reins to pull him forward, he will be pulling the reins across the horse's neck; if he pulls hard enough, he may cause the horse to rear or even to fall. Unless the horse has been perfectly trained to lead properly in the manner just described, he can be safely led only by taking the reins over the head and using them as one would use a lead shank on a halter.

Leading the Balky Horse

If one is forced to lead a balky horse (that is, one who refuses to move forward at times), the remedy may be to turn the horse quickly to one side and then to the other and before he is entirely aware of what's happening start him out on a straight line, the one the handler wants him to take. If this does not work, circling the horse rapidly several times and then moving him out of the circle in the direction or path desired may do the trick. The worst thing that can be done in attempting to move a balky horse forward is to strike him with a whip or with the end of a halter shank. This will make the animal rear, tear loose, or do some other undesirable and violent thing; it will not make him move forward.

Leading by the Foretop

Many a willing and well-disposed horse has been spoiled by having some ignorant or overly optimistic handler attempt to lead him by the foretop. However, if the horse is extremely quiet and has great confidence in his handler, it is possible to lead him in the following manner: Grasp the foretop with the right hand and place the left hand on the horse's nose above the nostrils. Do not press on the nose unless such pressure is necessary to keep the horse from pulling forward too rapidly. To start the horse being led by the foretop, turn him slightly to one side and return him to the direction you desire him to follow.

Leading with a Short Rope or Strap

If the handler is confronted with a situation in which he has nothing more than his own belt or a short rope to lead a horse with, he may follow a procedure very similar to that described under *Leading by the Foretop* (above). The belt is a little better to use than the foretop. It should be placed around the horse's neck immediately behind the head. The left hand should be used as in leading a horse by the foretop.

Leading Through a Narrow Passage

When leading a horse through a narrow passage it is best to take the reins in both hands, face the horse, and walk backward. This method will keep the horse from rushing forward at too great a speed and will also enable the handler to direct its movements. Of course, if the horse is not entirely tractable, it is unwise to attempt to lead him through a narrow passage.

Leading a Horse over Rough Terrain

Only a horse capable of choosing his own footing safely should be led or taken over rough terrain. A horse who cannot pick his own footing should never be ridden outside a prepared bridle trail, ring, or arena. If the terrain to be traversed so frightens the rider that he does not want to stay on his horse's back, he may get off and lead the horse (though he is much safer on the horse's back than he is on foot) by giving him plenty of slack on the rein. The reins must be over the horse's head at this time. The thing the rider should be most careful of is that he does not drop the rein so that it falls under the horse's feet and jerks on his mouth when he steps on it. This accident may be disastrous, for it will upset the horse's balance. If the terrain is uphill or downhill, the rider should be careful to stay far enough ahead of the horse so that there is no danger of the horse's treading on the feet of his owner. Sometimes one side of the rein can be unattached at the bit so that the entire length of the rein can be used in this procedure. If the reins are open ended, they can be knotted so that the length of both reins can be used.

One very difficult problem may be encountered when leading the horse in the manner just described. That is the problem created by the very eager horse or the one who has not been ridden enough in rough terrain to travel steadily whether going uphill or down. On such a horse, leading on a slack rein may permit him to lunge up a bit of rough terrain or run down a rough slope. When he reaches the end of the lead rein, he is jerked up short and if the footing is not too good he may stumble or even fall. The only thing to do is to make the horse stand still until the rider progresses a few feet ahead of him, stands directly in the trail, and puts both arms straight out, moving them slightly so that the horse knows he cannot go farther than the few feet between him and his handler. Then he can be allowed to move forward. This maneuver, of course, can be done only a few feet at a time. The method has to be varied to fit the terrain encountered. Since rough country is of infinite variety, no directions can be given that will fit all regions, but the general principle of allowing a too eager horse to move forward only a few feet at a time is fundamental and imperative. The number of feet that may be included under the phrase *few feet* will depend upon the nature of the terrain. It is possible the horse may have to move as far forward as 10 or 12 feet without stopping because in that distance there may be no spot on which a horse can stand still. This kind of country calls for a little intelligence on the part of the rider. No rider should attempt to go into country of an extremely rough nature until he has developed considerable skill in handling a horse.

In the West there are group rides. One of those conducted in Maricopa County, Arizona, is a ride on which totally inexperienced riders go. Sometimes as many as one-third of the horses included in a ride of 150 people are rental horses. The writer never ceases to marvel at the wisdom and skill of these rental horses in carrying completely inexperienced horsemen over the roughest of mountain trails. As long as the horsemen stay in the saddle and do not interfere with the reins, these gallant creatures will get their riders to their destination in perfect safety.

Lead Rein

Use of the lead rein when one is teaching a young or inexperienced rider is sometimes advantageous when no ring is available. When such a method is used, the rein should remain slack at all times except in emergencies. Direction of a horse mounted by a beginner should come from his rider. The lead rein should be used only as an emergency device.

Leather (selection and care of)

For English equipment the horseman had best look only to leather imported from England, and of the finest quality. This may be more costly in the beginning, but it is the least costly eventually. Such leather should be oiled before being used. Pure neat's-foot oil is the one the writer prefers. However, there are many products on the market now which other horsemen find just as good or even better than neat's-foot oil. A new saddle oiled with neat's-foot oil is a source of considerable irritation for several rides after first oiling because the oil comes out on the clothing of the rider. The remedy is to use saddle soap rather than oil on the parts of the new saddle that come into contact with the rider's clothing. Many of the patent products now available for preserving leather do not have this objectionable feature of coming out on clothing and possibly are good for use on new saddles. If the rider expects to keep his equipment usable for as long as possible, he will clean it with saddle soap every time it is used on a sweaty horse or gets mud splashed on it. In soaping the leather, use plenty of lather and a minimum of water. Before applying the saddle soap to any leather surface, take off whatever mud and sweat you can with a soft cloth. All leather should be hung in a manner to keep its shape.

Western equipment is usually made of domestic leather. Like English leather, this should always be well oiled before using and soaped after use when sweat or other soil gathers on it. Whether the Western saddle (and other equipment) is used or not, it should be well oiled every six months at least. Care should be taken to see that the oil does not get on the wool lining of a Western saddle. All saddles and other leather goods should be so hung when not in use that they do not assume shape other than that which they have when on a horse.

Saddles, bridles, etc., are made of various grades of leather and various kinds. The only general direction to give the nonprofessional about choosing Western leather goods is that leather that is extremely stiff and hard to bend *may be* (not that it universally is) of inferior quality. It is possible to purchase good Western gear south of the border of the United States, but a good deal of leather in Mexico, especially that available in border towns, is of very poor quality, and the person choosing to buy leather goods there should have with him an experienced horseman. The best way to choose leather goods is to find a reliable saddler or saddlery store and depend on it for an honest statement on the quality of leather on any item to be chosen.

In choosing Western gear for use other than display and parades and show-ring classes, it is well to keep in mind that anything made of leather may be broken. A bridle rein, for instance, that is made of three plies of leather stitched together is much more difficult to repair than a bridle rein made of a single layer of unstitched leather. Round leather is especially hard to repair. The fancier or more ornate the bridle, as a general rule, the more difficult it is to repair. Sometimes a fancy or ornate bridle has its advantages because it may cover up a very ugly and coarse head. Aesthetically, without regard to show-ring requirements, it may be said that the finer a horse's head, the less it should be covered up with leather, and the split ear bridle of the West is certainly a most fortunate choice for the owner who has a horse with a fine head.

Leather (to reach for)

When the West was young, the rider who "reached for leather," that is, who took hold of the horn on his saddle, was the object of great derision. In rodeos today, a rule in saddle bronc events is that one must never touch the saddle with his hand. In fact, he must keep the right hand high in the air and the left hand on the braid of rope attached to a horse's halter. Among riders who use English equipment there has long been and still is some prejudice against grabbing for leather or reaching for leather (holding on to the saddle to help maintain balance). However, it is far preferable to hold on to the saddle than the reins for balance. If the inexperienced rider is forced to ride in the open without the aid of an instructor or friendly, experienced rider, it is much better for him to keep a hand close to the horn or pommel of the saddle or even to hold on to it than to run the risk of pulling the reins or tumbling off. No sensible, experienced rider whose opinion is worth any attention at all will even smile at the rider who does this. In fact, he may applaud his good sense in taking such precautions to avoid pulling on the reins.

Leathers (noun)

The term *leathers* is used at times to indicate the straps that attach the stirrups to the bars of an English saddle. It does not apply to Western saddles. Western stirrups are held on by wide straps provided with what are called fenders. These are pieces of leather that keep the legs of the rider from coming into immediate contact with the body of a horse.

Legs (of the horse)

Next to feet, the legs are the most important things to consider when selecting a mount. The old saying, "No foot, no horse," could well be modified, "No feet and legs, no horse." Probably cocktail party conversation among horsemen has done the horse as much harm as any other single thing. Certainly, it is in part responsible for the small feet of well-bred horses of some strains and the lack of bone in their legs. The writer has heard horsemen owning horses who cost thousands of dollars boast about the dainty feet or legs of their mounts, meaning small feet or small legs. The shock of a running horse on a single foreleg supporting his weight when running is tremendous. If that foot and that leg are not large enough, the horse will break down (suffer lameness) in his forelegs. Another old saying, "An ounce of blood is worth a pound of bone," means that evidence of fine ("hot") breeding in the leg of a horse is more valuable than size of bone.

The horse of Mediterranean origin (the "hot blood") has a flat leg between knee and pastern. That is, when the leg is viewed from the side, it is relatively wide from front to back. When viewed from front or rear, it is quite narrow. The leg from knee to pastern of the horse of origin other than Mediterranean has a rounder conformation. It is interesting to note that in the Percheron breed, one of the largest of the draft breeds, the foreleg is shaped like that of the hot blood (the horse of Mediterranean origin, including the Thoroughbred and Saddlebred, Standardbred, and other so-called light-legged horses). This conformation is attributed to the fact that the Crusaders brought back from the Orient horses of Mediterranean blood, and these were crossed onto the animals of France, etc.

A cross section of bone of a horse with some Mediterranean blood in his veins looks dense, while the cross section of bone of a horse of entirely other blood is porous or spongy. So the saying that an ounce of blood is worth a pound of bone has some basis in fact. However, to follow the saying to extremes is rather silly, for no matter how well shaped or dense a leg is, if that leg is too small, it will not hold up.

There is another dictum from the past: A horse must have a leg on each corner. This means that the forelegs should not be placed too far back of the shoulder. A leg placed too far back of the shoulder indicates that the arm of the horse is horizontal rather than approximately perpendicular and is also probably too long. The hind leg should be placed so that a plumb line dropped from the point of the horse's hip (the part of his body farthest to the rear) will touch the hind leg from the cap of the hock to the back of the pastern joint. The forelegs from elbow to knee and the hind legs from stifle to hock should be much longer than the leg from knee to pastern and hock to pastern. The pasterns should be neither short and stubby nor long and too sloping. If they are too short and stubby, the horse will give the rider a hard ride; if they are too long and sloping, they will be weak and break down. (*See* LAMENESS.) Both the forelegs and the hind legs should be straight when viewed from front or rear. That is, from the body of the horse to the shoe, the leg should not twist either inward or outward. The toes should point straight ahead. The hocks of the horse should be as far apart as and no farther than his pasterns. The same is true of the relation of knee and pastern. If a horse's toes point outward, he is said to be *base wide* and if they point inward (pigeon-toed) he is said to be *base narrow*. When the hocks are closer together than the pasterns, the horse is said to be cow-hocked. If he habitually stands with his hind pasterns farther forward than his hocks, he is said to be sickle-hocked. That is, the hind leg is shaped somewhat like a sickle.

Legs (of the rider)

The Creator must have had equitation in mind when he made the horse, for the animal has what we call a *saddle groove*. It is a part of his body just behind the shoulder and just in front of the spring of the ribs. The legs of the rider for most purposes (exclusive of those of the jockey or the parade or gaited show-horse rider) should be kept in this saddle groove. The inside of the calf of the leg and the inside of the knee should be used for gripping whenever gripping is necessary. Of course, the rider who grips his horse all the time will be miserable and will certainly present a ridiculous figure when he rides. But it is the *inside* of the calf of the leg and the *inside* of the knee that should be kept in contact with the horse in the saddle groove, not the back of the calf. The exact position of the legs of the rider differs with each seat, and there is a specific seat for each particular purpose of riding. For information as to the exact position of legs, the reader may look under the appropriate heading: FORWARD SEAT, BALANCED SEAT, SADDLE SEAT, JOCKEY SEAT, etc.

Leg Up

The phrase *leg up* means assistance given by a person to one who is mounting a horse. There are several methods of giving a leg up. Around racetracks, the helper puts his hands under the part of the rider's leg just in front of the rider's knee and helps lift him up. Another method, used in riding schools, is for the helper to bend his knee and place his hand palm upward on his leg just above the knee; then the horseman sets his ankle on the palm of the helper's hand. As the horseman starts to mount, the helper straightens his leg, thus raising the leg of the horseman. A still better way is for the assistant to bend his knee and place his own hand on his own leg as indicated; then the horseman puts the sole of his foot on the helper's hand, using it much as he would use a mounting block as he rises. If the rider attempts to spring onto his horse and push on the helper's hand before the helper has it on his own leg, an injury to the muscle of the helper may result, as an old injury to the writer attests (*see* MOUNT).

Leper

The word *leper* does not indicate a horse with a serious disease but is rather a term common in Ireland for an excellent jumper.

Leukoderma

Sometimes white patches (leukoderma) occur on the hairless parts of a horse's hide. These may be merely places where pigment is lacking and indicate no injury or disease.

Levrette

This French term, for which the American equivalent is *herring gutted*, means a horse whose belly is much smaller around toward the rear than elsewhere; the belly may be likened to that of a greyhound.

Liberty Horses

Liberty horses are those who perform in a ring without a rider on their backs. The most charming perform with absolutely nothing on them in the way of equipment—no saddle, no bridle, no surcingle.

Lice. *See* PARASITES

Lift (verb)

The term *lift* is used in the hunting field to indicate the performance of the huntsman when hounds are not able to pick up a scent in a given area. In such an event, he will call the hounds to him, summon the aid of the whips to keep them following him and not nosing for scent (*heads up* is the extremely proper term), and move them to a place he thinks is more likely to contain a fox.

Light Dressage

The term *light dressage* is a rather loose one and indicates the kind of dressage work that might be done by a dilettante, or in some instances it designates a person at the first level of dressage (*see* DRESSAGE).

Light Hands

Hands that are used on the reins only to signal and are used as economically as possible are called light hands. The well-trained horse under the expert rider is communicated with in such a subtle fashion that onlookers rarely see any movement of the hands. The rider with light hands seldom exerts any considerable amount of pressure on the reins. He is constantly in communication with his horse on the reins, which means that he is being communicated *to by* the horse as well as communicating to the horse. Such a rider always anticipates what the horse is going to do, and strangely enough, the horse usually anticipates (sometimes to too great an extent) what the rider is going to do and what the rider wants.

Lighting (in stable)

No stable ever seems to have enough light. However, it is important to see that light is properly placed (*see* INDIRECT LIGHTING).

Lightweight Hunters

The American Horse Shows Association *Rule Book* states that a "lightweight hunter is one that is up to [capable of] carrying 165 pounds."

Limit Class

According to the current *Rule Book* of the American Horse Shows Association, "*limit class* is open to horses which have not won six first ribbons in Regular Members Shows of this Association or the Canadian Horse Shows Association in the particular performance division in which they are shown. This rule does not apply to winning at Regular and local Member shows."

Line (hunting)

The *line* is the route or course pursued by a fox.

Liniment

The use of liniment on horses is as old as the art of riding a horse, perhaps older. It is sometimes harmful; that is, a liniment that causes blistering or scurfing of the skin may be unnecessary and may cause the horse to misbehave, and the rider may then do things which no sensible person should do. The extreme use of liniments to cause a horse pain is common among Walking Horse trainers as illustrated in pictures in "The Agony of the Walking Horse," *Life*, October 3, 1969. The use of mild liniments to relieve sprains is possibly beneficial in some cases. A liniment is simply an irritant that increases the circulation of an affected area. Where a liniment is beneficial, it is probably so largely because of the rubbing the person who is applying it does. To be sure that one is using a liniment helpfully, he should use it only on the advice of a veterinarian.

Linseed

Linseed is the common name for flaxseed. Linseed is part of the ration of most of the best patented horse feed mixtures. If one is feeding grain of one sort only, such as oats or corn, it is advantageous to give a handful of linseed meal to the horse two or three times a week. Linseed tends to have a laxative effect, but it is also a source of valuable vitamins and minerals.

The custom that was once more common than it is today of giving a gruel of flaxseed to pregnant mares has been known to cause trouble. During the spring of the year in which this book was being written, a neighbor of the writer's had a very fine Arabian mare. She gave the mare flaxseed which she cooked into a gruel about the consistency of oatmeal. When the mare foaled, she refused to let her foal nurse, and there was considerable to-do because a foal has to have the first of the mother's milk, the colostrum, if it is to survive or at least if it is to become healthy. Many things were done to get the foal to nurse, before the veterinarian finally discovered the trouble. The mare had been given too much milk-producing food, and her udder was so distended, swollen, and sore that she could not stand to have it touched. The mare was twitched while some of the milk was removed by hand, and at last the foal was allowed to nurse in a normal fashion.

The cooking of flaxseed destroys the enzymes it contains, but evidently, especially in the case just cited, it does not destroy the things that promote milk production. One of the best ways to feed linseed, and the way that has been used from time immemorial by people who wanted to promote good shiny coats on horses, is to buy flaxseed at the drugstore, put a handful of it in a teacup, cover it with water, and let it sit overnight. This concoction is poured over the morning feed. If it is given two or three times a week, it will certainly improve the coat of a horse unless he is badly afflicted with lice or some other ailment.

Lippizaner

The Lippizaner is the best-known breed of Austria and also a favorite of the small farmers of Yugoslavia. In both Austria and Yugoslavia the horse is used under saddle, in both light and heavy harness, and for farm work. He is basically warm-blooded (stemming from the Arabian and North African breeds) but carries enough cold blood (North European draft blood) to give him an amenable temperament and good bone and substance, though at the price of some coarseness of head in some individuals.

The breed originated in very early times in the Karst region of Yugoslavia near Trieste and is still used on farms there and in the northern and northwestern part of the country as it was originally. However the Lippizaner is best known today as the horse of the Spanish Riding School of Vienna (*see* SPANISH RIDING SCHOOL).

Lips (of the horse)

Horsemen prefer that the lips of the horse be firm but flexible. A pendulous, relaxed lower lip is thought by some to be a sign of great age in a horse. However, there are exceptions. One of the many symptoms of sleeping sickness (encephalomyelitis) is the dropping of the lower lip and the horse's inability to contract it. Unfortunately, the disease has usually progressed too far to remedy it by the time this symptom is obvious to the layman. Of course, every sensible horseman has his horse inoculated against the disease once a year. There are three known varieties on this continent and the horse should be inoculated against any variety in the locality.

Log (verb)

The term *log* means to educate a team roping horse by having him pull a log or other heavy object while he is being driven in longlines by a man on foot. It has been said with considerable basis in fact that the difference between an excellent, experienced team roper and an amateur is indicated

Logging the team roping horse.

by the amount of logging he gives his horse. The amateur has little patience for such education as a rule.

Longe or Lunge. *See also* COLTS

The use of the longe line, or lunge line, is a matter of much disagreement among horsemen. A top Western writer on horsemanship starts his discussion of it with an argument, "Longing, often miscalled lunging . . . ," while a more experienced horseman and unexcelled writer, much admired in the East for his works on English riding, Henry Wynmalen, uses the term *lunging*. The spelling l-u-n-g-e comes from a very long history that substantiates it.

One reason the practice of longeing is frowned upon in remote quarters in the West is that it is entirely of Continental origin, coming to America from the English, who got it from the French. Many an old waddy would turn red in the face if a friend found him dangling a colt on a 30-foot web line or cotton rope. Such a sight might elicit from the friend the comment, "I thought them critters was made to ride, not to play skip-rope with." It is very easy to ruin a colt by misuse of the longe line. A colt can cut all kinds of capers when loose in corral or paddock without injuring his feet or legs, but if his head is pulled by a longe line at the wrong time, his balance is destroyed and he may turn on his forequarters, injuring a foreleg or foot; or he may make an improper turn on his hindquarters and throw a curb (*see* CURB). However, the longe line can be used to considerable advantage in making the kind of horse now in demand. It is especially useful on the urban-raised colt who has no place to exercise naturally as range-raised colts do. Web longe lines are manufactured usually 30 feet long with a swivel and snap on one end. They are the ordinary tool used today.

A colt's education begins as soon as he is foaled, whether by human intention or not, though as old-timers firmly believed, no horse should be put to work before he is five. Any veterinarian will give good reason for this. However, the education starts with breathing, and a colt's attitude toward human beings depends upon his first encounter with them and upon his early experiences. Although many colts are crippled and made permanently useless by being put to strenuous exercise too young, a healthy one is never too young to be halter broken. The first touch of a human hand, if kindly, is the most helpful one.

It does not take many days to let the little fellow know what is wanted. His attention span is extremely short, and he should be handled with that fact in mind; but as soon as he can keep his mind for five or ten minutes on what is wanted, he can be taken into a corral, a round one if possible, and walked slowly, or "steady by jerks" if he insists, around it. As the colt

Working colt on longe line. 1–6. Starting colt and working to the left; 7, 8. stopping colt and coming to center; 9, 10. reversing direction; 11. working colt to the right; 12. stopping colt.

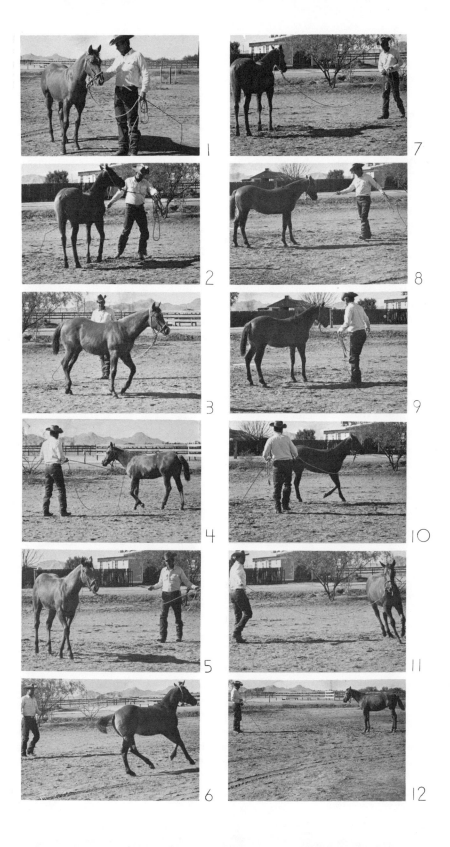

grows and his attention span becomes longer, the distance between him and his handler can be increased. Finally, without any use of whip, the colt will be working in a circle. I do not wish to imply that the use of a whip is bad. The longeing whip, properly used as a signal, is a very useful tool. However, when the little colt is started very gradually, the whip is frequently superfluous.

As soon as the colt learns to start around the circle at whatever signal the handler has decided upon—it may be a slapping of the hand on the thigh or a simple word spoken distinctly, but always the same—he can be taught to stop at the command "Whoa!" by a simple flip of the longe rope, which at all other times has been held slack but high enough to clear the ground and to be safe from a playful foot getting over it.

Colts vary, and a very light flip of the rope, which is always the first thing to try, may not stop the little fellow. Then a more definite flip should be given. As soon as the colt stops, the handler should walk up to him and let him know he has done well.

After learning to stop on command, the colt can be taught to come in to the center of the ring and then to reverse direction. Usually, with a colt at this stage, the handler can get an increase of speed to a trot just by taking a few running or shuffling steps in a small circle concentric to the larger one the colt is traversing. This should always be done with the giving of a definite signal, like the distinct speaking of the word "Trot!" or a slap of the hand on the handler's thigh. An increase of speed to the gallop can be obtained in a similar manner. As soon as the colt learns what is wanted, a definite signal can be used without the excitement employed at the first gallop.

If the colt is a particularly ambitious one, or is a well-bred, range-raised one, a bit on the fractious side, the method outlined may not be as suitable as it is for the more tractable or friendly colt. So here is an alternate method, differing only slightly, but importantly, from the foregoing one.

The colt is taught to lead, as usual. Then when he has learned to go around the circle at the end of a line of rope, he may be so ambitious that any flip of the rope, instead of stopping him, excites him to more speed. In such an eventuality he should be gradually brought into the center of the ring by shortening the line. This takes considerable judgment. If the colt is "high" and is playing violently, kicking up his heels and striking with his forefeet, he should not have his balance interfered with until he gets the tickle out of his feet. A hard pull on the rope when a colt is not balanced to respond to it may, as stated at the outset of this discussion, do permanent damage to him. He won't play forever. Let him work off some energy at the end of the line *without any pull*, so the corral fence will keep him from twisting his hindquarters away from you and going sideways around the ring. Then bring him up to you. Stop him. Stroke him quietly, and make him stand a few seconds. Then start him quietly in the other direction. Change the rope in your hands before you do so. If you are holding a whip, it, too, should be changed from right to left, assuming you have started originally to work him counterclockwise.

The novice will have all he can do, when he first uses the longe line, without adding a whip to the sum of things he has to attend to. However, the more experienced hand will find it useful as a signaling tool. *A wise horseman never uses a whip to inflict pain when he has a horse on the end of a longe line.* On those rare occasions when a welt-producing cut with the whip is needed, the horse should be well in hand (*see* IN HAND), not dangling on the end of a line. A skilled handler keeps the whip low. He brings it in toward the rear of the colt as a signal to start. Obviously, this may first be done by stirring up a little dust or even by touching the colt, if necessary. The same handler may use the whip as a stopping signal by bringing it toward the colt from the front. The whip can also be used to signal for reverse, for change of gait, or for change of speed. It should always be used in the same way for each signal. The particular movement of the whip used for each particular response can be left to the discretion of the handler. It may not be the same for any two colts. With one colt, the whip may have to be moved quickly and shaken a trifle, or raised from the ground slightly; with another, it may have to be moved very quietly and even in a different manner.

As the colt goes counterclockwise of the ring, the whip is carried in the right hand, the hand which also has the job of taking up slack or letting the line out as needed. The whip is carried back toward the heel of the thumb, leaving the fingers and thumb free to work the rope. When the colt reverses, going clockwise of the ring, the whip is carried in the left hand and the coil of rope, or folds of web line, are carried in the right hand, which now, of course, is also controlling the line to the colt.

Galloping or Cantering on the Longe

The longe line has two very valuable possibilities. One is that of educating the colt while he is still too young to be ridden (though the longe is not the only way to do this); the other is that of teaching the colt from babyhood to gallop straight. That is, gallop with the proper lead on a turn and without "cross-firing," as some old-timers called it, or "doing a disunited canter," as it is more fashionable to say today (*see* DISUNITED). If the colt is going counterclockwise he should, of course, be on the left lead. That is, he should strike the ground with his right hind foot alone, then with right fore and left hind feet at the same time (or so nearly the same time that only a camera can tell the difference), then with left fore alone. The left fore is the one that rises a little higher than any of the others. Variation from this sequence when the colt is galloping to the left calls for stopping him and starting over. If he persists in taking the wrong lead, he can be started a little more quickly and his head can be given a little sharp pull as he starts. This latter movement on the part of the trainer will tend to make the colt reach out with the proper foot. If it fails, the colt can be headed into a fence obliquely and made to begin his gallop as he begins to circle. This maneuver starts the colt when he is diagonal to his line of progress and also gets him to reach out with the proper foot.

The youngster should ordinarily be galloped equally on both leads, a few times around on one, then reversed and given a few turns on the other. If one is more difficult than another, it may be wise to give the difficult one a little more time. However, the easy one should not be neglected. He should learn to take the inside lead on either way of the circle.

It is now common to hear the term *canter* used to refer to a slowed-down gallop, though formerly the term was applied by professionals only to the extremely collected gait of gallop rhythm, done with balance well on the hocks. A canter of the latter type is not executed on a longe line. With the use of a bitting rig, something that appears to the spectator to be such a gait can be achieved; however, the rider who steps up on a horse so trained is soon disillusioned, usually with great discomfort. A stock saddle is an excellent substitute for the major portion of a bitting rig. The reins can be adjusted to the length desired and placed around the cantle, even held in place by the rear saddle strings. I do not like the results usually achieved by the use of a bitting rig on a Western horse, though there are exceptions, and I have seen coveted awards won by horses so trained. The Eastern horse who is to be hard against the bit at all times is not as likely to be harmed in training with a bitting rig. It will teach him to go with his chin in or "tucked," as some term it. Success has been achieved if a colt will do a slow lope on the longe line on either lead on command. Do not fuss with him about balance and collection on a line. Merely demand that he hold the proper lead. If he drops out of it as you slow him down, stop him and start him over again, whether he has dropped into a trot, gone into the other lead, or become "disunited."

A saddle, appropriate in weight and size for the animal, can be carried by the colt on a longe line. It should be first used without stirrups, or with stirrups tied down so they will not flop. It is even wise to tie down the skirts if a flat (English) saddle is used. As soon as the colt begins to learn what is wanted, the stirrups can be added, or untied. After a colt has learned to respond to signals for each gait he is capable of, and will stop, reverse, and stand on command, he can usually be mounted in the corral without any excitement and can soon be ridden outside with comfort.

Longline. *See also* COLTS

To longline a colt is to walk behind it and control it by a pair of lines long enough for the driver to stay out of the range of the hind hoofs.

Loop

In most rodeo roping events, two "loops" are permitted. Thus if the roper fails to catch the pursued animal with his first throw he is allowed a

Team-tying father and daughter, Sonny and Barrie Beach, both illustrate the need for the "second loop."

second chance. This is why most ropers carry a spare rope with them in such events. There is, of course, no time to spend coiling up the first rope so that it can be thrown a second time.

Loose-Rein Riding

Riding with a loose rein means distinctly different things to the Eastern rider and to the Western rider. To the former it means riding without communicating through the rein. Eastern riding masters advise their more advanced pupils to do this occasionally because it rests the horse. After all, keeping a horse in a high state of collection over a long period of time is rather tiring, and it is certainly necessary to rest a horse by throwing the reins on his neck and allowing him to walk at will for a while. However, this relaxation must be done in a place where there is no danger of the horse's shying or jumping suddenly or playing unexpectedly unless the rider is extremely experienced and has excellent balance.

To the Western rider, *loose rein* means simply that the reins are held with no tension. To the Western-trained horse, *any* movement on a rein communicates something. It might be said by Eastern riders that the

Western horse works behind the bit, for he is just as aware of movements on the loose rein (that is a rein with some slack in it) as the Eastern horse is aware of movement of the rein that continually has pressure on it. Some horse-show classes, notably hunter hack classes, and Western pleasure classes, require that the horse work on a loose rein. In this case it is not the loose rein obtained by throwing the reins on the neck of a horse. Rather, the reins are kept slightly slack, but communication with the horse is maintained.

It is just as impossible for the Eastern rider to imagine maintaining communication with a horse on a loose rein as it is impossible for a Western rider to understand how the school rider of Germany, let us say, can be any kind of horseman when he maintains a stout pull on the reins at all times. As Kipling put it, "East is East and West is West, and never the twain shall meet."

Lope

Lope is the term probably originating in the West to indicate a very slow gallop, sometimes called a "crowhop." In Western pleasure classes one does not see a canter (at least what used to be called a canter, that is, a gallop slowed down and highly collected so that the horse rocks on his hindquarters). The lope is as slow as any canter, but it is not done in a collected fashion.

Lunge Line. *See* LONGE

M

Maclay Cup

The Maclay Cup is offered annually at the National Horse Show in Madison Square Garden in New York City, held during November. It is competed for by youngsters who have won a Maclay Class in a registered show in the past 12 months. The riders are judged on their ability to take eight jumps (only the rider's ability is judged).

McClellan Saddle

The McClellan saddle was designed for the United States Cavalry by a Union officer whose name the saddle carries. Of all saddles ever designed, this one can probably be used without harm on a greater variety of horses than any other. It also can be ridden with comparative comfort by a greater variety of human anatomies. It is a very simple saddle consisting of a leather-covered tree. The leather covering fits the tree very tightly so that the space between the two bars of the tree that rest on either side of the horse's backbone is exposed. The stirrups are hung forward, which feature makes it superior at least in one respect to Western stock saddles. The seat is perfectly flat, but both cantle and pommel are raised slightly. The saddle is provided with rings, loops, etc., for carrying the full equipment of a cavalryman. Because the metal bars that hold the stirrup leathers do not open, the stirrup leathers will not come off the saddle if the stirrups are pulled rearward, as they will on English saddles. It is, therefore, not particularly safe to ride a McClellan saddle without hooded coverings to keep the foot from going entirely through the stirrup and dragging a fallen rider.

The McClellan saddle has two distinctive advantages aside from being usable on a great variety of horses and by many kinds of riders: (1) It is extremely cool and (2) it is extremely light, considering its strength. Its one disadvantage is that it requires a fairly thick saddle blanket, for there is no padding on the underside of a McClellan saddle. The cavalryman used a full-sized bed blanket as a saddle pad. He folded the blanket lengthwise and then made two more folds in it, thus achieving six thicknesses of woolen blanket to be placed under his saddle, with the final fold toward the front of his horse. In case of dire necessity, he could take the blanket from the horse at night and use it to cover himself.

Maiden Class

According to the American Horse Shows Association *Rule Book*, a Maiden class is "open to horses which have not won a first ribbon at a Regular Member Show of the Association or the Canadian Horse Shows Association in the particular performance division in which they are shown except for winning at Regular Member Local Shows."

Making a Cast

Making a cast is a hunting term to indicate that the huntsman is using his hounds to investigate a given locality in hopes of finding a fox or the scent of a fox (*see* LIFT). The huntsman may make a cast as the initial activity of the day or, if hounds have lost the line (lost the scent of the fox they were following), he may "lift" them and make a cast in a place he thinks the fox may have gone or one the fox may have crossed. Or if he feels the original fox is beyond reach, he may make a new cast in hope of discovering a new fox.

Mallenders

Mallenders is a name for the little callosities that grow on the inside of the horse's legs. Another term for them is *chestnuts*. There seems to be no total agreement as to the origin of chestnuts. However, some horsemen think they are vestigial remnants of toes of prehistoric horses.

Mambrino

Mambrino is the name of one of the most famous of early horses. He was the sire of a horse called Imported Messenger. Imported Messenger is considered the foundation sire in this country of trotting and pacing horses, and he is also one of the most potent of progenitors of the American Saddle Horse and the Tennessee Walking Horse. He was a foundation sire and head of a famous family of English coach horses. He is said to trace directly to the Darley Arabian. It was Rysdyk's Hambletonian (or as he was most often called, Hambletonian Ten), a grandson of Mambrino by Abdallah, who founded the family from which come all modern trotters and pacers. The family is called the Hambletonians. Until the Hambletonians took the center of the stage, the descendants of Justin Morgan were the leading breed of harness horses on the track.

Mambrinos

Mambrinos is a family name applied to the descendants of Hambletonian Ten. There is no explanation to why the term *Mambrinos* is used to indicate this family almost as frequently as is the term *Hambletonians*, for the entire family stems from Hambletonian Ten (*see* HAMBLETONIAN TEN).

Manege

The term *manege* denotes a riding hall, academy, or school devoted to educating riders and horses in the kind of equitation called dressage. Until recently this kind of activity was engaged in in this country only by one cavalry officer by the name of Tuttle. In very late years, thanks in no small measure to the Pony Club (*see* PONY OF THE AMERICAS CLUB), dressage has become extremely popular in this country. *Manege* is used almost interchangeably with *dressage*.

Manes

Styles of manes and tails of horses change sometimes from year to year, and the way the mane and tail are combed and trimmed or pulled usually indicates the purpose for which the horse is used and sometimes his breeding. Some horsemen seem to feel that hot-blooded horses (those tracing their ancestry to Barbs or Arabians) have finer textured manes and tails than do other horses. Horses with luxurious manes and tails are likely to have a considerable amount of cold blood in their veins (blood that does not stem from the horses of the Mediterranean area).

Caring for a horse's mane or tail is similar to caring for human hair, and the style in which it is kept depends upon the current fashion. Before entering a show-ring, a horseman should become familiar with the current styles for manes and tails for his particular kind of horse. For example, at the present time, three-gaited horses have their tails clipped several inches from the body; just a few years ago, any clipping of the tail was an indication of ignorance on the part of the owner. The tails of such horses were pulled very carefully and clippers were used surreptitiously only, mostly on the underparts of the tail where the clipping would not show. Quarter horses may have their manes clipped off entirely except for the foretop, and hair on the withers should be allowed to grow, at least during recent years. Five-gaited horses and fine-harness horses have long flowing manes and tails. Harness horses on the racetrack have their manes shortened somewhat by careful pulling and their foretops clipped off entirely. Styles of manes on hunters and jumpers change in given localities from time to time. At one time in one locality, for instance, it was the style to clip the manes of all hunters and jumpers. Later it became stylish in the same locality to pull the manes to an even length of three or four inches and then to do them up in little braids which were looped up and fastened on top of the mane at intervals so that the horse looked as if his crest had sprouted rosettes. Each breed and type of horse has its own style of "hairdo," and owners can only keep up to date by watching the horse magazines that are concerned with their own particular breed of horse.

Mange

The term *mange* is used by horsemen in general to cover what is a variety of ills to a veterinarian. There are many proprietary remedies for mange on the market. But before any such remedies are used, exact diagnosis is necessary. This can be made by an expert veterinarian. Some kinds of mange are extremely contagious. Any scaling, itching, or hairless spots on a horse merit an examination by a competent veterinarian.

Manners

Manners count heavily in the judging of horses in many kinds of horse-show classes. The horse with good manners is one who is immediately, willingly, and cheerfully obedient to every wish of his rider. He stands quietly and shows no tendency to interfere with other horses with whom he may be ridden. He responds so well to his rider that any signals given by use of aids, cues, etc., are scarcely observable by onlookers. A person who enjoys spontaneity in his mount may well spoil his chances for winning ribbons in many kinds of classes by allowing the horse to show his good spirits if he does it in a way that does not unseat the rider or interfere with his companions. Vitality of a mount, his observance of his surroundings (even in stopping to look at interesting sights), may be a source of great pleasure to some riders, but to indulge in this pleasure always lessens one's chances to win ribbons in the show-ring.

Manure (care of)

Daily cleaning of quarters is extremely necessary if horses are kept in a stall or small corral. Without regular cleaning, stalls or corrals tend to produce thrush in the feet of horses (*see* THRUSH). When manure is taken from the stall or corral, it should be piled where it will not be a nuisance. There are now preparations on the market that can be put over it to kill flies. However, the writer is rather timid about using any preparation of a toxic nature where animals may ingest it. Horses are prone to nibble at a manure pile. The spreading of lime over a manure pile is a big help in

Markings—face. 1. Star and snip   2. strip (or stripe)   3. blaze

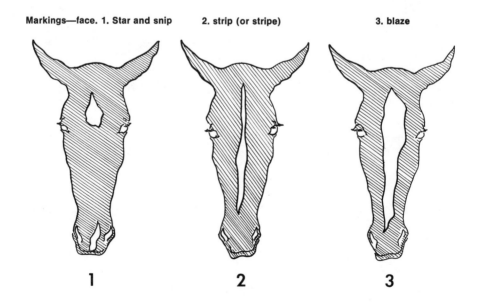

1   2   3

keeping down the flies. Of course, the biggest help is to have the manure pile removed regularly. In some parts of the country where the climate is extremely arid such as Arizona, some parts of California, New Mexico, and Nevada, dried manure is used in lieu of tanbark on small training rings and serves very well. When so used, the manure must be spread out so that it will dry quickly.

Mare

Mare is a term used to designate a female equine over the age of four. Prior to that, but after weaning time, she is known as a filly. Prior to her "fillyhood" she is known as a foal (the term *foal* includes youngsters of both sexes, though a male foal is usually referred to as a colt).

Mark a Fox (mark to ground)

The terms heading this entry mean to run a fox into his den, or, as hunting folk say, *to run him to ground.*

Markings

The breeds of horses that place great emphasis on distinctive colors or color patterns have definite nomenclature for the markings or color patterns. Each is discussed under its appropriate heading in this book. However, there are certain markings used by livestock inspectors, and by horse-show programs, that the horseman should learn to recognize and name.

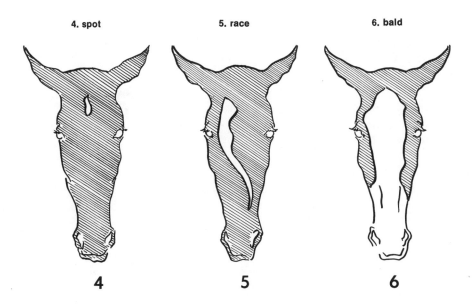

4. spot   5. race   6. bald

4   5   6

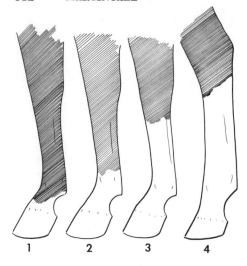

Markings—feet and legs. 1. Sock: white extends from hoof to pastern or fetlock; 2. boot: white extends from hoof into lower half of the cannon bone; 3. stocking: white extends from hoof above the middle of the cannon bone toward or up to the knees and hocks; 4. stocking (hind leg).

When a horse has a black mane and tail and sometimes a dark stripe down the center of his back, he is said to have black points. This is most distinctive of the bay horse. The markings of the head are known as follows: A white spot between the eyes or a little higher on the head is known as a *star;* a white spot between the nostrils or lower is known as a *snip.* White that extends from the nostrils to the eyes is known as a *strip* if it is narrow; if it is wider, it is called a *blaze;* if white covers the entire front of the face, the horse is said to have a bald face. White on the legs is indicated as follows: When it is just above the hoof, it is said to be a *white coronet;* if it extends approximately halfway from the hoof to the pastern, it is called a *white pastern;* the term *sock* designates white from hoof to midway between pastern and knee; the term *stocking* designates white from the hoof to the knee or hock.

Variations of the classification of markings occur in many places, notably in the records kept by livestock inspectors (many Western states require that any horse to be transported on highways carry papers of permission issued by a state livestock inspector). Then there are variations of the classification to be found in show-ring catalogues and in the breed registration requirements.

Martingale

Martingales are pretty generally of three types. The standing martingale is in essence a strap that goes from the girth or cinch to a noseband. It may run through a breastplate. The conventional hunting martingale has a breastplate of wide leather that encircles the horse's neck at his shoulders and is attached to the saddle just below the withers on either side. The so-called tie-downs of the polo field are of this variety. The tie-down of the

Western horse is simply a martingale, frequently of the simplest sort (just one strap that runs from cinch to noseband). On the Western horse the noseband is often made of rawhide, steel cable, or even metal of small diameter.

Another kind of martingale is the running martingale. This consists of a strap attached to girth or cinch which divides into a Y at the front of the horse's shoulders. Each arm of the Y terminates in a ring through which the snaffle reins are run. Curb reins should never be run through these rings, for with some horses the following accident may occur. A horse will simply bow his neck and bring his chin in until the bottom of the curb bit is against the martingale ring; then any pull the rider exerts on the reins is a pull on the martingale, not on the horse's bit; the horse can then perform as he will. He is forced to perform with his neck arched and his chin in as do some circus horses, but he can do so and he can attain almost top speed in spite of anything the rider may do on the reins.

The so-called Irish martingale consists of a strap a few inches long with a ring at either end; the reins are put through these rings. The purpose of the Irish martingale is simply to keep the reins from moving up over the horse's ears if he sticks his nose out and tosses his head. In many horse-show classes, the use of any kind of martingale is forbidden. It is best, therefore, to train a horse to work without a martingale if possible.

Some hunter classes permit martingales. A standing martingale is required on all polo ponies. On some horses whose mouths have been hurt so that they continually toss their heads or come up in front (rear), a

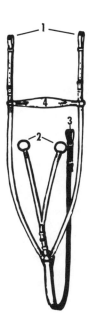

Running martingale (in hunting breast-plate). 1. These loops go through D's on either side of pommel of saddle; 2. reins go through these rings; 3. fastens to girth (or to ring on girth); 4. rests in front of withers.

Irish martingale.

German martingale—variation on draw rein.

martingale may be a must. Many horsemen look upon the use of a martingale as an indication of a spoiled horse or bad hands of a rider.

Care must be taken when a martingale is first put on a horse, especially a standing martingale. Occasionally, if a standing martingale is put on too short, a horse will fight it; he may even throw himself.

German Martingale

A piece of gear more suggestive of draw reins than martingales is called the *German martingale*. It has been found useful by many in starting colts in the snaffle bit, especially if they are naturally stargazers (*see* STAR-GAZER), and in correcting some faults of spoiled horses. It fastens to the center of the cinch, then runs through pulleys attached to bit rings and snaps into a D on the bridle rein. When properly adjusted, the draw rein operates only when a horse's head is too high.

Mashes

For centuries, horsemen in civilized countries and possibly in some not so civilized have been fond of cooking up what are called *mashes* for their horses. The beneficial effects of mashes have never been definitely established by veterinary science, but they certainly have some beneficial effects in some situations. The bran mash, made by half filling a 2- or 2½-gallon bucket with bran, pouring in enough hot water to make it the consistency of breakfast oatmeal, covering the bucket with a blanket, and allowing it to stand until it is cool, makes a very satisfactory bran mash. Many horsemen prefer feeding bran to a horse by giving bran mash once or twice a week than by giving dry bran in daily feed. The writer has found the latter method better. Mashes are also made in a similar fashion with linseed (flaxseed); a linseed mash is much richer than a bran mash and must be fed in tiny quantities only (see LINSEED).

In *Ride American,* the author has included pictures and an explanation of how a horse in his 30s in an almost fatal state of emaciation was brought to the pink of condition comparable to that of any show horse by the feeding of moistened feeds (moistened because the old fellow had few teeth left). The feeds so moistened were alfalfa and Bermuda pellets, red bran, and a little rolled barley. The last ingredient was varied in accordance with the variation in the condition of the old horse's manure. Bran was also varied in amount in accordance with the condition of the manure.

Feeding of any kind of moistened feed must be done with the exercise of a certain amount of intelligence. Vessels in which the feed is mixed and feed mangers must be kept scrupulously clean, for traces of moistened feed left in mangers or utensils draw flies, and any feed left over after a horse has finished eating will sour and be a source of indigestion or fatal colic to a horse. Alfalfa in any form, whether leaves or what not, must be moistened with great care; the best way is to dip the fingers in a bucket and shake them over the alfalfa. The alfalfa must be fed immediately after moistening, for if it stands any length of time before it is eaten, it will produce colic.

Mask

Mask is a hunting term meaning the head of a fox.

Massage

Massage certainly is as beneficial to a horse as it is to a human. However, the horse, because of his bulk, presents problems for many kinds of massage. The use of liniments, according to some veterinarians, is beneficial largely because of the massage that usually accompanies their application (see LINIMENT). Massage has been useful in some cases of colic (see COLIC).

Master of Fox Hounds Association of America

The Master of Fox Hounds Association of America, established in 1907, has as one of its most important functions the designation of "recognized" hunts. Such recognition is made use of in the rules of the American Horse Shows Association *Rule Book.* It is also involved in qualifying hunters (see HUNTER TRIALS). The address of the Master of Fox Hounds Association is 1044 Exchange Building, Boston, Massachusetts 02109.

Matinees

Some years after the Civil War, harness racing fell into considerable disrepute. To bring it back to favor in the eyes of respectable owners, in 1871 the Waverly Park Gentlemen's Pleasure Driving Association instituted the *Matinee*. This was a program of weekly races exclusively for members and guests of the club. The emphasis was on the winning of prizes and a very fancy trophy. These events became very popular. The term *matinee race* is still used today for certain kinds of amateur races held in the afternoon.

Maze Jumping

For maze jumping, a course is set out in a show-ring. It consists of all sorts of jumps, the variety being limited only by the ingenuity of the committee in charge of the show. The course the jumper must take through the jumps, laid out in various angles, is marked by a red flag on each jump, and the rider takes each jump with the flag on his right. Time is the chief element in maze jumping, and faults are not counted as they are in other jumping events (*see* FAULTS).

Meet

The term *meet* designates the gathering place of the participants in a hunt. The word suggests the most charming and perhaps the most completely explanatory writing ever done on a fox hunt, John Masefield's "Reynard the Fox." That long narrative poem opens with the line "The meet was at the Cock and Pie."

Megrims (or staggers)

Megrims and *staggers* are two old-time terms used to designate what happens when a horse faints. A horse faints from as many causes as does a human being, and the treatment is the same as the treatment for a human when he faints. The wise horseman will get a veterinarian, if possible.

Mental Hazard Jumping

In mental hazard jumping, the jumps are not necessarily of great height or width, but they are constructed of as many different kinds of things as the ingenuity of the designer can achieve. Each is made of something that normally frightens a horse, whether by its materials, the sound it makes, or its smell. Of course, such jumping is supposed to test the level-headedness and the manners of the horse.

Messenger

Messenger, or, as he was frequently called, Imported Messenger, was a not too handsome, flea-bitten gray Thoroughbred stallion imported from England in 1788. He had no very successful record on the English tracks before he was brought to this country. However, he is the progenitor of all the fastest trotters and pacers we have today and one of the progenitors of the American Saddle Horse, the Tennessee Walking Horse, and the Morgan. (*See* MAMBRINO, HAMBLETONIAN TEN, and MORGAN HORSE.)

M.F.H. (Master of Fox Hounds)

The Master of Fox Hounds is what might be termed the commander-in-chief of the hunt. His word is law. He may hunt his own pack or another. He may employ professional huntsmen or hunt his hounds himself. He is faced with a very severe problem, for he must satisfy people of rather opposing interests. The field, of course, is interested in the sport of the day, whereas in this country the terrain over which he hunts is almost always owned by farmers who are most concerned about keeping their crops from damage by a horse's hooves. (The writer, as stated elsewhere, had the most severe tongue-lashing he had ever experienced from a master who berated him for galloping over his own wheat field when hounds were running.)

Much hunting country today is obtained by an agreement with farmers in which the hunt agrees to pay for any damage done to crops, arranges for chicken coops (panels over wire fences), and frequently agrees to pay for any livestock or poultry killed by fox. This last provision is in the hope that the farmers will not find their own means of ridding the country of any fox that may be disturbing their property.

In addition to attempting to keep such divergent interests more or less peaceful and happy, it is the master's job to see that all goes well in the kennels and stable and to select places for casting the hounds, time of doing so, etc. Gentleman riders always tip their hats to the master, and no one in the field passes him except at his suggestion. At the end of the hunt, it is a great breach of etiquette to fail to thank the master for the fine day's sport.

Middleweight

A middleweight is a horse who is suitable for carrying a rider of up to 185 pounds. That is, he is a somewhat stouter horse than the lightweight hunter, who is supposed to be up to carrying a rider of 165 pounds. The heavyweight hunter is presumed to be up to carrying a rider up to 205 pounds. The implication seems to be that people over that weight do not ride to hounds, but the writer has seen at least two excellent riders to hounds who weighed considerably more. One of them habitually hunted a mule in stiff Virginia hunting country.

Missouri Fox Trotter. *See* FOX-TROTTER

Missouri Fox Trotter Horse Association

Address: Ava, Missouri 65608; Joe R. Hinds, president. (*See* FOX-TROTTER.)

Mixed Gaits

Many horses who have been trained to perform easy saddle gaits and have been ridden by ignorant horsemen tend to slide from one gait to another with no regard to the wishes of their riders. Such horses can be quite exasperating. One of their commonest faults is to slide into a pace because the pace seems to be easier for the gaited horse to do under an ignorant or difficult rider than any of the other gaits known to the Saddler. Another cause of pacing in a horse who has learned easy gaits is discomfort in the feet. The gaited horse who has been shown has feet so long that they are very likely to cripple him permanently. When the feet are thus crippled, the pace seems to cause much less discomfort than any other gait a horse can do (*see* GAITS).

Molars

The term *molars* designates the twelve large grinding teeth in the upper part of a horse's jaw, separated from the front teeth by a considerable space of gum. They do not always oppose each other directly. That is, the lower molars are somewhat inside the upper ones. The hard covering of the teeth therefore grows faster than the rest of the teeth and forms sharp edges which cut the cheek and sometimes the tongue. In this event, a veterinarian must be called in to remove the sharp edges. Development of the sharp cutting edges sometimes is the cause of a bad general condition of a horse, for he will not chew his feed properly.

Morgan Horse. *See also* JUSTIN MORGAN

Justin Morgan, the founder of the Morgan horse breed, had to earn his oats and hay by spending most of his life wearing a collar and harness with chain traces for pulling heavy loads. He was given no more care than any ordinary workhorse. The lives of his famous sons were different. Fast trotting horses were becoming fashionable. No longer was the imported Thoroughbred the only horse favored by the rich and stylish city folks. Then, too, the Revolutionary War had taught Americans the importance of good roads. And with roads came new wheeled vehicles. More and more, the rich rode on wheels, and trotting horses were much better than any others to pull them.

In 1825 a group of fashionable New Yorkers organized the New York Trotting Club. In 1826 they built a racetrack, called the Centreville Course, near an important road, the Jamaica Turnpike. Three years later, a group of fashionable Philadelphians organized a club to promote trotting races, which they called the Philadelphia Hunting Pack Association. Until this time all organized races had been run under saddle. But many trotting-horse owners wanted to race their horses in harness, hitched to carts. The Philadelphia club finally wrote into its rules that trotting matches in harness could be held if a majority of the club's members voted for them.

The growing popularity of trotting races gave Justin Morgan's sons and daughters and their offspring the chance they needed to become famous in the big cities of America. Sherman Morgan, one of his most famous six sons, sired a colt by a mare called Old Narragansett, a Narragansett Pacer (see NARRAGANSETT PACER). The colt was called Black Hawk. He was a champion trotter, but his greatest fame came from his son, Ethan Allen.

No horse could beat Ethan Allen at the trot under saddle. Then he was challenged to races in harness. No single horse could beat him. Finally, he was challenged to race in a team—two horses pulling a vehicle. No trotter could be found who was fast enough to keep up with him, so one of the fastest running horses of the day was hitched beside him. The matched race agreed upon was five one-mile heats. That is, the horses were to have five contests, each one mile in length, with sufficient time in between to rest and cool off. On the Fashion Course racetrack on Long Island on June 21, 1867, Ethan Allen not only won, with a mate galloping at his side, but won over the fastest horse of his day, Dexter, who was not hampered by a mate. More than that, Ethan Allen broke all trotting records of the day by trotting the three winning heats in 2 minutes, 15 seconds; 2 minutes, 16 seconds; and 2 minutes, 19 seconds.

In 1876 the best breeders organized into the National Association of Trotting Horse Breeders. This was the beginning of systematic horse breeding in America. The breeders adopted a "registry," the only means of keeping a breed pure. The association called its breed the Standardbred, because one of its rules stated that no horse should be registered unless he could trot a mile in 2 minutes and 30 seconds, which was called "the standard of speed." From this time on, speed and speed alone over a specially prepared one-mile track was the objective, and the Morgan horse was superseded *on the track* by the Hambletonian (see MAMBRINOS).

Early in this century, just before the automobile drove the horse from the city streets as a means of transportation, a club was formed to maintain a registry and promote the breeding of the Morgan horse. One extremely wealthy man was interested because this was such a useful horse with such a great variety of capabilities. His name was John Y.

Batelle of the Batelle Institute. As the automobile became more and more popular, the Morgan horse, whose forte was that of a using animal, became less and less popular. In fact, he finally came to be valuable only as a showpiece. However, John Batelle was determined that the breed of the Morgan horse should not become extinct. Through his efforts and finances, a breeding farm was established in Vermont to perpetuate the breed. The farm was finally given to the government because, after Batelle died, the Morgan Horse Club had difficulty staying alive financially. During the very rough years in the history of the Morgan Horse Club there were many changes in the methods of keeping track of the breeding of Morgan horses and of admitting horses to the registry. One man in charge of the breeding farm in Vermont decided that the best thing to do was to make the Morgan horse into a high-stepping harness horse. Consequently, the excellent bone and feet of the Morgan were somewhat neglected. He was taught to change his way of going entirely. The old Morgan could do his work with a minimum of effort, but the horses bred on the Morgan Horse Farm became high-stepping horses of the kind still seen in Morgan classes. There is some disagreement among Morgan people today whether their horse should be cultivated with extremely high action to be used in three-gaited classes (especially in three-gaited park classes) and in harness classes or should still be shown as a using animal, one who performs with ease to himself and his rider. There are today almost two types of Morgans.

In spite of the many changes in the objectives of Morgan breeders, certain distinctive characteristics of old Justin Morgan are still to be seen in the Morgan horse. A Morgan head can be recognized as far as it can be seen, and the general contour of the body is still distinctive. However, it is regrettable that the bone and the feet have changed considerably. The disposition of the Morgan seems to have maintained most of its original identity. He is a prompt, high-strung, willing horse, amenable to the wishes

of women and children when properly treated, but a horse who resents abuse and will fight until he kills himself if he is improperly handled.

Attesting to the fact that Morgan conformation has persisted down into modern times is the report of the postmortem examination of General Gates, the best-known sire of the Morgan Horse Farm in Vermont. He was found to have only five lumbar vertebrae (six is the usual number). The postmortems of other Morgans showed the same peculiarity (common only to the Arabians, the Barbs, and the Goas of India). Whatever the source of this characteristic, it is astounding that the prepotency of Justin Morgan was such that it was still found so many generations after his death. This skeletal peculiarity is one thing that gives the Morgan horse his short back and long croup, qualities that partially account for his great strength.

Morgan Horse Club, Inc.

Address: P.O. Box 2157, Bishop's Corner Branch, West Hartford, Connecticut 06117.

Morral

A morral is a feed bag made from a gunnysack (burlap bag). Two people can make a very good feed bag from a gunnysack in a very few minutes. In his left hand, one person grasps the seam at the open end of the bag. With his right hand he stretches the mouth (open end) of the bag open and holds it firmly. He keeps the bottom of the bag equally stretched and held firmly to the ground by standing on the bottom corners of the bag. He keeps the outstretched open end of the bag pulled firmly upward. The bag now forms a double thickness of burlap rectangular in shape.

With a sharp knife, the second person makes an incision about two inches from and parallel to the seam of the bag, starting at the top (open

Constructing a morral from a gunnysack (burlap bag).

end) of the rectangle of double burlap and continuing downward two-thirds of the way to the ground. The incision is made through both thicknesses of the burlap. He then makes a second cut parallel to the first, two inches from the side of the rectangle opposite the seam. This one also runs from the top downward two-thirds of the way to the ground.

The result should be a feed bag with two long strips, one formed by the seam and the other by a four-inch strip of burlap opposite the seam. These two strips (when the horse's nose is in the bag) are tied over the horse's head to keep the bag from falling off. The two broader pieces of burlap now dangling from the feed bag are each given a slight twist and tied together at the side of the bag after the bag with feed in it is put on the horse. They should be tied just tight enough to keep the horse from throwing feed out of the bag when he tosses his head, as almost every horse learns to do when he eats from a bag. (The tossing enables him to get the last grain from the bottom of the bag.)

Mount (verb)

There are many methods of mounting a horse, including jumping leapfrog over his tail. Fashions change in requirements in equitation classes in horse shows. (For a while it was imperative that the rider take both feet from the stirrups before dismounting and throw his body upward in the air, landing on both feet beside the horse. This was supposed to be the proper thing to do to avoid getting one's foot hung in the stirrup as he dismounted.) Anyone anticipating competing in equitation classes should determine the required method for mounting before he enters a show.

For most practical purposes, the following method for mounting will be satisfactory. It is advocated because it obviates the possibility of the horse's moving forward and freeing himself from the grip of the rider while the latter is mounting. It also puts the rider in position to fling himself on his horse if the animal moves while he is still in the process of mounting.

Stand on the left side of the horse's shoulder facing his croup; grasp the reins all together in the left hand, and in the same hand take hold of a good handful of mane just in front of the withers. If the horse has no mane, grasp the pommel of the saddle in the same hand that is holding the reins. The reins should be held just tight enough so that if the horse attempts to go forward the rider can restrain him, but they should not be tight enough to signal a horse to back up. It is very important for beginning riders to learn that this hold of the left hand should be relinquished for no purpose on earth between the time the horse is approached for mounting and the time the rider is in the saddle. If it is necessary to use a hand to help the left foot meet the stirrup, the right hand should be used. *On no account should the hold of the left hand be relinquished.*

After the hold of the left hand has been established, place the ball of the left foot in the stirrup, and grasp the cantle of the saddle with the right

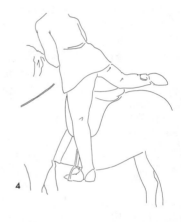

Mounting.
1. Take up reins in left hand. Take a good hold of mane—or pommel of saddle—with bridle hand (for equitation classes place bridle hand on withers).
2. Grasp stirrup leather with right hand and insert left foot in stirrup (help foot with right hand if necessary, but keep firm hold of mane and reins with left hand).
3. Straighten left leg before starting to swing right leg over horse.
4. Swing right leg clear of horse.
5. In mounting stock saddle use same procedure except that horn instead of mane may be held in same hand with reins. (In a Western equitation class take up reins in left hand and place hand on horse's neck in front of the withers with romal or end of reins on near side.)

hand. Then step up on the left stirrup just as if you were stepping up on a ledge. Do not turn your body until the left knee is straightened. When the left knee is straightened and you are standing up in the left stirrup, move the right hand from the cantle to the pommel of the saddle, lean over the pommel toward the far side of the horse, and swing your right leg around over the horse's croup, high enough to avoid touching the horse. Place yourself in the saddle, putting your right foot in the right stirrup.

When one is learning to mount, he puts considerable pull on the left side of the saddle; the horse must therefore be girthed or cinched very tightly or an assistant must be at hand to place his hand in the right stirrup and put enough weight in it to compensate for the weight of the rider in the left stirrup. After one becomes adept in mounting, he can place his right hand far enough toward the far side of the horse on the cantle to keep the saddle from turning. It is possible for an experienced rider to mount a horse of ordinary height with a saddle that has no girth and not move the saddle from the horse's back. In dismounting, the movements of mounting are performed in reverse order. The *Rule Book* of the American Horse Shows Association states, "To dismount, rider may either step down or slide down." This means that both feet may be taken out of the stirrups before the right leg passes over the croup. When this is done on a 16- or 17-hand horse, the rider will do well to keep his torso against his mount and slide gently to the ground after clearing the croup, in order to avoid landing with an ungraceful thump.

Mud

Mud is a source of concern to many horsemen in climates where it is the order of the day in spring and fall (and other times of the year "spasmodically"). Mud may cause a horse to develop what is called *scratches*, a dermatitis which occurs just above the hoof on the back of a horse's foot. If this condition is allowed to persist, it can become very serious. However, if it is detected immediately and the horse's foot is kept as dry as possible and zinc oxide ointment is applied to it regularly (of course, the affected area must be cleaned and dried daily before the ointment is applied), the ailment may be of no particular consequence.

Mud can be most beneficial to the feet of the horse who has been kept on hard, hot, dry terrain over a long period of time. However, the horse whose feet are alternately kept in mud and then in a dry, heated area for any length of time will deteriorate badly. This alternation between soaking and drying is as bad for a horse's foot as it would be for the handle of a hammer or ax.

Mud is difficult for a horse to travel in. Many a horse has had his limbs broken by being forced to travel in mud at too high a speed.

Mud Fever (scratches or cracked heels). *See* MUD

Music (of hounds)

Music is the term used to denote the cry of hounds when they are running in full pack. It is certainly music that is sweetest to the ears of all hunting enthusiasts.

Musical Chairs

Musical chairs is a game played in gymkhanas and some smaller local shows. It is exactly like the game of musical chairs that children play at birthday parties. When the music stops, each child must find a chair. The chairs, of course, have been lined up back to back with one less chair than children in the group that marches around them. When this game is played by mounted people, it is often lost by the rider who cannot dismount from the right side of his horse.

Musical Rides

Musical rides are those in which a group performs various maneuvers in a given routine to music. Some of the most fascinating of these rides are to be seen in the quadrille teams which appear in connection with some of the largest rodeos. One musical ride is performed by horses wearing no bridle or tack collar and ridden by girls.

Musical Stalls

Musical stalls is a game played like musical chairs but the rider, instead of dismounting and sitting on a chair, rides his horse into one of a series of portable stalls around which the horses are ridden until the music stops. The stalls can be made of eight- or ten-foot bars. Cavalletti can be made into good stalls. They can be put up above the ground at any desired height and placed so that the horses face each other or so that each must enter from a direction opposite to that from which his neighbor enters.

Mustang. *See also* NATIONAL MUSTANG ASSOCIATION

In Spanish, the word meaning a group of horse breeders is *mesta* and the suffix *-eño* means "belonging to." The horses which escaped from the mesta were therefore called "mesteños," which means those belonging to the mestas. The settlers who came after the Spanish Americanized *mesteño* to *mustang*. The Spanish horses were of true Andalusian breeding and so were the escapees of these herds, or the Mustangs. They gave rise to the legends of the beautiful and untiring Mustang stallions and their bands.

The term *Mustang* today refers to a horse who is the object of considerable controversy. The Bureau of Land Management until recently sought to have him eliminated and sanctioned that elimination regardless of the

cruelty and agony of the method used. There are, on the other hand, several organizations who are putting up an effective fight to preserve the Mustang. Another area of intense disagreement about the Mustang concerns his origin. One group of scholars claims that the Mustang is descended as much from horses who moved westward from the East Coast as he is from the Spanish stock that came up from south of the border. Some authorities claim that the Spanish blood brought in by De Soto was the source of the mysterious breed called the Chickasaws, sturdy little animals, and highly thought of at one time, about whose origin there is a great deal of dispute.

It is hard to establish the fact that any of De Soto's horses survived. Certainly, as soon as government troops and covered wagons started west, the horses of the West were infused with the blood of North European animals. But up until the beginning of the seventeenth century it is doubtful that any of such blood ran in the veins of the horses of our West.

The first horses trailed into the United States came in in 1598 when Juan de Oñate crossed the Rio Grande with 83 wagons and 7,000 horses, cattle, and sheep. Oñate prospered and proclaimed himself governor of the Spanish colony of New Mexico. He established the capital colony of Santa Fe. His horses were descended, of course, from the mounts of the conquistadores and were of Arabian and North African blood, blood that we now refer to as Andalusian, Barb, and so on. Oñate's spectacular success did not last long, for in two or three years the Pueblo Indians teamed up with the Navajos, the Apaches, and some of the Utes who came down from the north and wiped out the Spaniards. The latter abandoned Santa Fe and took with them what little livestock they could lay their hands on.

Certainly the blood of the Oñate horses is not exclusively that which courses in the veins of all the herds of wild horses still existing. Blood from the troopers' horses, horses from the covered wagons, and so on was mixed

(Far left) Mustangs running free and protected on National Mustang Association's ranch.

(Left) Captured on open range, this two-year-old Mustang will be released to run free on National Mustang Association's ranch.

(Right) Tom Holland, president of the National Mustang Association, feeds rescued Mustang colt.

These two orphaned Mustang colts are guaranteed a good home for life on the National Mustang Association's ranch.

Only two hours off the open range, this orphan Mustang colt has found a lifetime buddy.

into the blood of these wild animals. However, in certain areas those Spanish horses seemed to have remained apart from foreign intruders. There are places in the Bad Lands, certain places in Wyoming, where Mustangs of the purest Spanish blood are found. According to the January–February 1971 issue of *New Mexico*, the publication of the New Mexico Department of Development, there was one place where the foreign blood was deliberately kept out by human intervention. For several generations the Romero family protected the horses of Lucero Mesa. In 1957 the Lucero Mesa was taken under the care of the McKinley family, which is now extremely active in working to preserve the blood of the Mustangs.

While the Northwest affords no such large concentration of pure Spanish Mustang blood as that of Lucero Mesa, one of the most dedicated protectors of the breed is Robert Brislawn, Sr., of Oshoto, Wyoming. He put forty years of effort into hunting for specimens whose descent could be proved to include no infusion of foreign blood whatever. His son Bob Brislawn in 1925 located two mares, and two years later he trapped a stallion which he chose to use. as a foundation sire. Later, with two mares he obtained from New Mexico and another from Old Mexico, the Brislawn herd of Spanish pure-bloods was on its way to success. When asked about proof of purity of blood, the Brislawns state that the final proof is in the skeletal structure of the animals. Buckshot, the original foundation sire, had only five lumbar vertebrae instead of six. Other animals showed five lumbar vertebrae and one extra small sacral vertebra. The true Spanish Mustang has only 15½ pairs of ribs. Roundness and density of the cannon bone is another distinctive characteristic.

Height of the Mustang is from 13 to 14½ hands and weight is from 700 to 900 pounds. The Mustang is short-coupled; the distance from his poll to his withers equals that from his withers to his croup. His forequarters are powerful, and heart girth is extremely large, which feature of course would be necessary for him to endure the hardships he has lived through. His chest is not extremely wide, but his fork is a nice V. The Spanish Mustang Registry was organized by Robert Brislawn, Sr., in 1957 and is probably the most active registry for Mustangs existing today.

Another association for the registry of Mustangs, the American Mustang Registry, Inc., is located in Phoenix, Arizona (P.O. Box 9243, 85020). However, this registry is not as dedicated to nor insistent upon purity of descent as is the one set up by Brislawn.

The National Mustang Association, Newcastle, Utah 84756, is an ardent, hardworking group devoted to the protection and preservation of the Mustang, but it does not maintain a registry.

The American Horse Protection Association, 629 River Bend Road, Great Falls, Virginia 22066, has as one of its many laudable objectives the protection of the Mustang, and it has been the major factor in attracting public attention to and in getting legislative action for the protection of the Mustang.

Nail in the Foot. *See* LAMENESS and PUNCTURE WOUNDS

Narragansett Pacer

Narragansett Pacer is the name of a distinct breed of horse that flourished in the region of the Narragansett Bay in Colonial days. The horses were easy gaited and evidently of great beauty. They had a little more size than most of the early Colonial horses. Bays and chestnuts predominated as their colors. These horses were extremely popular with plantation owners in the West Indies. Ships carrying cargoes of rum from the West Indies would carry back Narragansett Pacers, and at one time buyers from the West Indies searched the counties for these horses. So great was the demand, not only in the West Indies but also in other parts of the New World where roads were difficult or impossible for wheeled vehicles to use, that the breed absolutely disappeared from the Narragansett country. Undoubtedly, the progeny was dispersed in diluted form to other parts of the then frontier, and some of this blood must flow in the veins of the Tennessee Walking Horse and the American Saddle Horse. (*See* GALLOWAY, HOBBIES, and JENNET.)

National Chickasaw Horse Association, Inc.

Secretary, Mrs. Duane Sunderman, Rural Route 2, Clarinda, Iowa 51632. Formed to conduct registration and promote breeding, showing, and racing of the Chickasaw horse, the association is now ten years old. In its promotional literature, it states that the Chickasaw is a breed originating during the time of De Soto (circa 1519). Some of the horses of De Soto, the association declares, stampeded and were later captured by the Chickasaw Indians. This assertion is contrary to the findings of Frank Dobie, but it probably gladdened the heart of Francis Haines. (Dobie and Haines are two of the most eminent scholars who disagree about the history of the Western horse.)

If the association's assertion has basis in fact, the Chickasaw horse carries a heavy percentage of blood of the Spanish jennets, Andalusians, and Arabians. The association describes the horse as being between 53 and 59 inches in height. It must be of solid color (no spots are allowed). It cannot have glass eyes. "No high tails are permitted." Whether this means no set tails or no tails carried naturally high is not quite clear. Chickasaws have long been prized as hardy, quick, intelligent horses.

Very early in the seventeenth century, plantation owners in Maryland and Virginia were complaining about bands of wild horses that were grazing on their grain fields. The plantation owners farther south were talking about the fine horses owned by the Indians of South Carolina and Georgia. Descendants of these horses are the ones that are known in their native territory as Chickasaw horses and have been so known for a long time.

All the old written accounts say that the Chickasaws were pretty horses suitable for both riding and heavy work in harness. The quality of prettiness does certainly suggest that they might have come from the best Spanish stock. Whatever their history, there is now a registry for them.

The Chickasaw Registry resembles somewhat the early Quarter Horse Registry; that is, horses are accepted by inspection, and they are registered under several classifications—tentative, permanent, etc. The promotional efforts of the association may well find the little Chickasaw horse a place in the show-ring and racetrack sun.

National Cutting Horse Association

Address: 4704 Benrook Highway, Fort Worth, Texas 76116.

While the literature of the National Cutting Horse Association is completely devoid of information concerning the date of the formation of the association, it is a relatively new organization, because formal cutting horse contests, whether in horse shows, rodeos, or other such places, have been occurring only within the last quarter of a century. Interest in cutting horse contests has grown at a surprising rate, and cutting contests are featured events today at the Houston Livestock Show, the Cow Palace in San Francisco, and the San Antonio Livestock Show. Three annual events featuring cutting horse competitions are the NCHA Cutting Horse Futurity, the NCHA World Championship Cutting Horse Finals, and the NCHA Team Cutting Horse Tournament.

The NCHA Cutting Horse Futurity is the only cutting horse event solely underwritten and managed by the National Cutting Horse Association. This event is now in its eighth year and is limited to three-year-old horses. Each contestant has paid a minimum entry fee of $300. The event has grown to be the largest cutting horse contest, in both numbers and monetary value, in the world. More than 550 horses were nominated to the 1969 NCHA Cutting Horse Futurity. The gross purse exceeded $100,000. It took place in Fort Worth, Texas, Will Rogers Coliseum, on December 9–14.

The NCHA World Championship Cutting Horse Finals have been held independently since 1962. This is the big purse show of the year for cutting horses. At its conclusion, the World Championship Cutting Horse of the Year as well as the Top Ten Cutting Horses of the Year are named. The finals have so far been held yearly in Las Vegas, Nevada, on the grounds of the Stardust Hotel in November.

The NCHA Team Cutting Horse Tournament was first held in 1965 and has become a popular part of the Annual Association Convention program.

National Mustang Association, Inc. *See also* MUSTANG

Address: Newcastle, Utah 84756.

The National Mustang Association is an organization of valiant souls doing effective work in preserving the Mustang. It does not maintain a registry. One of its most important projects in 1971 was purchase of a 44,000-acre ranch in Nevada to be a preserve for the Mustang. Among the members of the organization are many people who own Mustangs or who belong to the Spanish Mustang Registry, Inc. Anyone who is interested in membership in the National Association should write Mrs. Gerry M. Owen, secretary, National Headquarters, Newcastle, Utah 84756.

According to the association, one should not confuse the Mustang with the malformed "wild horse" frequently seen at auctions. Though many of them have some Mustang blood, such animals are of mixed breeds and lack the graceful proportions, intelligence, and willingness to learn of the Mustang.

Navel (treatment at birth)

Because of the prevalence of *joint ill* or *navel ill* (though the disease so named is contracted by means other than the infection of the navel), the navel of every newborn foal should be painted with iodine.

Navicular Disease

The navicular joint of a horse is in the hoof. It is so located that it is subjected to injury from concussion and also from pressure when a horse's hoof is contracted. If this joint or the navicular bone is bruised, a callosity will form on the covering of the bone, which causes pressure and pain. It is very rare for a horse who has been afflicted with navicular disease to be completely useful during the rest of his life; however, expert farriers have ways of shoeing a horse who has had the disease that enable him to travel with comparative comfort. Veterinarians can prescribe treatment that will alleviate the suffering. There is no way for the layman to diagnose navicular disease, but a veterinarian is able to make such diagnosis. In some cases the severing of the nerve in the foot will eliminate the pain, and for some purposes the horse can then be quite useful. Until fairly recently, any severing of the nerve to relieve pain in a horse's foot was accompanied with some danger to his rider, for it robbed the horse of all sensation in his foot. Surgical techniques in the field of veterinary medicine have now enabled the veterinary surgeon to sever only that part of the nervous system that makes the navicular area sensitive, and the horse still retains some of the feeling in the foot.

Near Side

If you are mounted, the *near side* of your horse is the side on your left. It is the side on which all fastening and unfastening of the gear is done. It is the side on which the horse is conventionally mounted. It is a mistake when educating a young horse to fail to get him accustomed to being handled on either side, to having his gear handled from the off side (the side opposite the near side), and to be mounted and dismounted from the off side. Some horses whose training has been neglected in this area are so "one-sided" that farriers have difficulty in picking up the feet on the off side.

Neck (noun)

Notions about how long a horse's neck should be, how it should be shaped, and how it should be carried, vary with the breeds and with the purposes for which the horses are used. The Saddlebred, for instance, should have considerable length of neck and flexibility; he should carry it fairly high and well flexed but not overly flexed at the poll. A hunter should have a neck of at least medium length. It should not be arched too much, and he should not carry it too high. The fashion now in Western horses is to have horses with a neck of medium or a little less than medium length with head carried low.

This fashion came in with the rise in popularity of the cutting horse, and it reached almost ridiculous proportions, so that a piece of iron pipe taped at one end for a handle was standard equipment in most Western training stables. It was used to beat a horse over the head or on the heavy muscle just behind the head every time he raised his head above the level of his withers. Fortunately, there seems to be some sign that this fad is passing. Even a cutting horse, when he is out of the cutting arena, carries a fair head. He does not go along the trail with his nose in the dust.

No matter what his breed or for what purpose a horse is used, his owner is likely to agree with other horsemen that the ewe neck is highly undesirable. The ewe-necked horse is one whose neck dips down immediately in front of his withers. He is sometimes said to have his neck put on upside down.

Neck (verb)

Before the West became overcivilized and when animals ran wild on many of the rougher parts of open ranges, the method used to "tame" young critters was to *neck* them to burros. A good stout burro was always chosen for this purpose. Around his neck was put a broad leather band or soft, heavy cotton rope. The unbroken wild colt to be necked was choked down with a lariat. Then either a rope was put around his neck, tied with a bowline knot so that it would not slip tight, or a halter was put on him and he was tied to the neck of the burro. He was tied close enough so that he could not whirl and kick and so that he could not get a straightaway pull from the burro. These two might be turned loose for some time; or, if the animals were roped some distance from the home ranch, they might be driven to the home ranch where the young creature was to be turned out. The procedure was a little rough on the burro sometimes, but it always taught the young animal to lead.

Neck Reining

Neck reining is the use of the pressure or touch of a rein on the side of a horse's crest as a signal for him to turn. In Western reining classes one sees horses who respond immediately to the slightest touch on the side of the neck. A good reining horse will spin on his haunches with a very slight pressure on his neck used as a signal. It is possible to teach a horse to respond in a passable fashion to the neck rein by using the direct rein or plow line in conjunction with the neck rein. If every time a horse is turned by the plow line the opposite line is put against his neck, the plow line (direct rein) use can be diminished as the use of the neck rein is increased, and gradually he will come to respond to the neck rein. This training can take place either in the ring or in the open. The writer has found that it can be done more readily (at least in the beginning) in the ring, but it can also be done on the trail. (*See also* REINS, *Use of.*)

In the West, neck-reining has always been the one way of turning a horse because the rider has to handle his reins with one hand only while he is roping or shooting or, possibly, drinking with the other hand. However, response to the neck rein is an asset for the horse no matter what his field of usefulness may be. Even the five-gaited horse can profit from knowing the neck rein. For instance, if the gaited horse at the rack hops up on one corner, as the saying goes (that is, he tends to hop up with one forefoot or the other or even with a hind foot), the fault can usually be corrected by using the neck rein to keep him slightly oblique to his line of progress.

In all dressage work (although authorities on dressage use the term *indirect rein* rather than *neck rein*) the neck rein plays an important part. In dressage, whether it be the Continental school or the English variety, there is a rule to the effect that no rein should cross the top of the horse's crest. This means that if the reins are held in one hand, that hand can move only very slightly from one side to the other. If the reins are held in two hands, the right hand must not cross the center of the neck toward the left side and the left hand must not cross the center of the neck toward the right side. Unless the horse is a beautifully trained reining horse, the neck rein must always be supplemented by the plow rein or direct rein or lateral pull.

In sharp contrast with the reining of a dressage horse is the reining of a Western horse in show-ring competition. In this case the reins must be held in one hand. The rules vary slightly from year to year about how they are to be held, but it is never permissible to separate the reins held in the one hand by more than two fingers. Usually the rule book says the reins are to be separated by not more than one finger. This stricture, of course, precludes the use of the lateral pull on the plow rein. The Western horse in reining competitions responds instantly to the slightest pressure of the rein on the side of the neck. In riding him, therefore, one never moves the bridle hand very far to either side. Thus one is following the rule that is applicable to all kinds of exhibition horsemanship: any signal or cue given the horse should be so slight that it is hardly noticeable by spectators.

Neckwear. *See* APPOINTMENTS

Nipping

Many a horse has been made head shy (developed a habit of jumping violently away from any movement of a person's hand toward the horse's head) by inept horsemen attempting to break him of the habit of nipping. Almost all very young animals have some tendency to use their mouths much as a baby uses its fingers—that is, to test anything that is new. Violent punishment of a horse for this is not necessary. The ounce of prevention should certainly be taken. That is to be sure one refrains from going up to the young animal and placing a hand on his face to pet him. This is simply a signal to the young animal that the person wants to play with him, and the only way he can respond is to use his lips. If one must pet or fondle a young animal, the petting or fondling should be done back of the animal's head, on his neck, shoulder, etc. A little observation of colts playing in the field will show that one of their favorite games is to come up and nip at each other's faces or necks or the back of each other's legs. If an animal has developed a habit of nipping, it is best to keep a halter on him so that whenever he is approached the handler may take a good firm hold on the halter. If the horse must be punished, he must be held by a halter and he should be punished by striking him with a whip or what not on the shoulder or rib cage, not on the head. He should be held firmly and not be allowed to jump away when he is chastised.

Noseband

The noseband of the bridle goes around a horse's nose a few inches above the place where the bit is attached. If the noseband is attached to the cheekpiece and is tight, it will interfere with the operation of a bit. It is much better to use a cavesson (a noseband with its own separate strap going over a horse's head to hold it in place). About the only good use of a noseband other than possible decoration (if the horse's head is so ugly that he needs decoration) is in conjunction with a standing martingale or tie-down. A standing martingale should never be attached to a bit. It should be attached to a ring in the noseband or cavesson, or to a bosal (*see* BOSAL and DROPPED NOSEBAND).

Novice Class

According to the current *Rule Book* of the American Horse Shows Association, "*A novice class* is open to horses which have not won three first ribbons at Regular Member Shows of the Association or the Canadian Horse Shows Association in the particular performance division in which they are shown except for winnings at 'regular member and local shows.'"

Numnahs

A *numnah* is an extremely useful piece of English equipment. A good English saddle is provided with padding on the side next to the horse. Such a saddle fits better and feels better to the rider because it puts him closer to his horse (no extra pad is used under the saddle). However, if the saddle is used without a pad, the sweat and heat of the horse will quickly harden the leather and make it crack unless it is cleaned and soaped after every use. A numnah is a piece of leather or rubber cut in the shape of an English saddle. It is usually provided with little straps that go around the front of the tree of the saddle and then back under the skirt, terminating in loops. The straps to which the girth is buckled are passed through those loops. The straps, of course, keep the numnah from sliding out from under the saddle. The numnah keeps the saddle padding free from sweat and yet does not separate the rider and saddle from the horse as would a thicker pad.

Nursing

In Illness or Labor

Nursing is just as important, as efficacious, and as necessary in the care of animals as in the care of human beings. In the natural environment of a horse, a mare foals without any human help. She also escapes some of the hazards to which a mare kept in a stable or corral is subjected, especially in the matter of infection and also in the matter of overfeeding and having so much milk that her udder is sore, making early nursing painful. In establishments where horses are of great value, foaling is attended not only by a "nurse" but also by a veterinarian.

One of the most remarkable instances of the efficacy of nursing is that of the saving of the great Arabian horse Raffles. This horse was a son and grandson of the great Skowronek. When he was well along in his 20s, he broke his hind leg between hock and stifle. Of course, the most merciful thing to do in such a case is to destroy the horse as painlessly as possible. The news of this accident somehow reached Mrs. Alice Paine in California. She was an admirer of Raffles, as were all Arabian breeders at that time. She immediately purchased the horse so that a young couple, employees on the Selby Farm in Portsmouth, Ohio, on which Raffles was located at the time, could nurse him (they had begged for such an opportunity). Not only did the leg heal, but the horse recovered complete use of it, as is attested by one picture which has been published more than once. It shows him playing, rearing with all his weight carried by the hind leg that had been broken. The veterinarian whose skill was in very large part responsible for the recovery of the horse gave a great deal of the credit to the 24-hour-a-day nursing by the faithful young couple who loved the horse so much. It may be worth noting here that Raffles was shipped to California and lived long enough to perpetuate (by being used in a program of very close breeding) one of the greatest Arabian families. Such perpetuation was undoubtedly a great contribution to the Arabian breed, for in its rapid rise to popularity, the practice of breeding winner to winner is diluting purity of strains.

Of Newborn Foal

A foal is able to stand on its feet very shortly after it comes into this world; and very shortly after that, it should be imbibing fresh mother's milk. This first milk of the mare contains colostrum, which is important in starting the proper functioning of the colt's alimentary canal. If the mare has been fed extremely rich feed, she may have developed so much milk that her udder is painful, and she will not permit the colt or anything else to touch it. In such an event, all that is necessary many times is a little hand milking, not enough to rob the colt of all the colostrum. However, this is not always the case. There are unfortunately instances in which the mare is so sensitive to pain that many expedients have to be resorted to to get her to allow the colt to nurse. Twitching is not always satisfactory because when a nose twitch is put on a mare she will hold up her milk. Sometimes a little milk can be hand milked and warm compresses can be put on her udder. Water tends to dry out the skin and so is undesirable. Lotions or salves may help soften it, but care has to be taken that they don't get on the nipple and make a taste that the colt will not stand for. Sometimes the mare can be hand milked and the milk collected in a nursing bottle. Then the baby can be induced to suck the bottle. There are also instances in which the difficulty is with the foal. Once in a while the foal seems a bit on the stupid side and will put his nose on anything except the mare's teat. A helper may then take the little fellow in hand, place a leg behind his buttocks, with one hand direct his nose to the proper spot, and with the other milk a few drops of milk onto his nose or into his mouth. This may start proceedings in the proper direction. Whenever any difficulty is experienced during the foaling, a veterinarian should be summoned immediately.

Oats

For centuries oats has been the preferred grain for horse feed in England and America. In his famous dictionary, Doctor Samuel Johnson defined oats as a cereal grain used for horse feed in England but (because of his antipathy for Scots) a part of the staple diet of Scotsmen.

One of the merits of oats is the bulk provided by the hulls. Horses can be foundered by overfeeding on oats, but because of the bulk, foundering on oats is less common than foundering on other grains. Because some of the grains of whole oats pass through a horse without being digested, some horsemen prefer to feed this grain after it is processed by crimping, crushing, or steamrolling. Heat above certain temperatures destroys the enzyme content of food. The damage done to oats by steamrolling is open to investigation, though steamrolling probably makes it more easily digested. Crushing or crimping involves no heat and probably makes the grain more readily digestible. However, the amount of oats fed whole that passes through a healthy horse with good teeth is negligible.

There is great difference in the quality of oats. The best in this country comes from the Northwest. A measured bushel of good Northwestern oats will greatly outweigh the legal standard for a bushel of oats. Each grain of such oats contains a far greater proportion of available nutrients than does a grain of oats raised elsewhere, and horses show a decided preference for oats of excellent quality.

Offset

In many Western reining classes the execution of an "offset" is required. This is a quarter-pivot on the hindquarters (*see* PIVOT). It must be done with the horse giving the appearance of doing it comfortably, that is, without tossing his head, opening his mouth, or switching his tail (though attention to the last-named fault seems on the wane!).

Off Side. *See* NEAR SIDE

Open Jumper

An open jumper is a horse who has won $2,000 or more in jumping classes in Regular Member Shows affiliated with the American Horse Shows Association or the Canadian Horse Shows Association in the two years preceding the date of a show in which his owner wishes to enter him.

Open Jumper Classes

Open jumper classes are those in which open jumpers compete (*see* OPEN JUMPER).

Ophthalmia (periodic)

Periodic ophthalmia (known to the layman as moon blindness) is the most common cause of defective vision in horses. It occurs in horses of all ages and breeds and in both sexes. It is known to the veterinarian as a recurrent iridocyclitis that produces alterations in the eyes as a result of reactions to the acute inflammatory process. Much research has been done on this disease, but no treatment has been discovered that is effective in preventing its recurrence. The symptoms may include some that occur in many other diseases of the eye. However, an experienced horseman can usually detect moon blindness, at least the second or third time it occurs, by a faint, rather lacy curtain over the iris of the horse's eye.

The only advice that can be given in regard to this disease is *Caveat emptor* ("Let the buyer beware"). When one is purchasing a horse, the only guarantee he can have that the horse is not afflicted with moon blindness is either a written statement of soundness signed by a reliable and financially responsible seller or an examination of the animal by a veterinarian.

Opposition (reins of). *See also* REINS

Sometimes, as an aid in performing some movement with the horse's hindquarters, a rider may use the neck rein (*see* NECK REIN), also called the "indirect" rein, in opposition to the plow rein, also called the "direct" rein. For example, if the rider wants to keep the forehand stationary and move the hindquarters to the left, he may (in addition to the leg aid) use direct pull on the right rein and at the same time use the same rein as a neck rein against the horse's neck (indirect rein) to prevent it from turning the forehand to the right in response to the direct pull on that rein. It would, of course, be just as logical to say that he is using the direct rein in opposition to the indirect rein.

Whatever it is called, such use of reins (combination of neck rein and plow rein) is a subtle and very necessary part of all horsemanship beyond the level of the Sunday rider. It reaches its most highly developed use in the dressage work becoming so popular today.

Orejano

An orejano is a wild critter (*see* CRITTER).

Ornaments (bridle)

If an owner has a horse with a very beautiful head, he will want the head as free from covering as possible. In the West, owners of taste whose horses have beautiful heads use split ear bridles. These are bridles with a single strap that goes over the head and splits for a space of several inches to allow the right ear to protrude through the slit. This prevents the bridle from falling too far backward on the neck and from slipping off the front of the head. Of course, if the horse has a head that is not extremely attractive, he may appropriately wear a bridle that covers up a portion of it. In modern horse-show classes, the five- and three-gaited horses and Tennessee Walking Horses frequently have heads on which the eyes are set high and the nose is long. Such horses wear broad, highly colored browbands and broad, highly colored nosebands. These bands cut the extreme length of ugly noses and are conventionally used now in all such classes. It is perhaps unfortunate that in some Arabian classes, even not costume classes, the Arabians with their exquisite heads wear bridles that interfere with the fine and delicate lines of the head. Of course, in costume classes and parade classes, the greater the ornamentation of the gear, bridles, saddles, etc., the better.

Orphans. *See* WEANING

Outlaw

An outlaw is a horse who has been thoroughly and completely spoiled. In Oscar Wilde's words, he has "learned what evil things the heart of man can dream and, dreaming, do." Such a horse, of course, is unsafe for anyone to handle.

Overcheck

An overcheck is a piece of harness attaching to either side of the bit. Straps from the sides of the bit join each other just above the horse's nose. From there the overcheck is a single strap up the bridge of the nose, between the eyes, and split so that it runs over the crownpiece through two loops an inch or more apart on top of the bridle. Thence the overcheck runs to a hook on the ring on the top of a surcingle or on the "saddle" of a driving harness (see illustration of harness race horse under HARNESS RACING).

Overfeeding

A horse cannot be injuriously overfed on hay unless the hay is one of the legumes or is made of one of the grains and cut after the grain is matured. A horse must become accustomed to legume hay or extremely rich grain hay very gradually. With the exception of those two kinds of hay, overfeeding will result in nothing more serious than an attack on the owner's pocketbook, for the horse will waste under his feet what hay he does not eat.

On the other hand, overfeeding with grain usually has serious consequences. They may be immediate; or, especially if it is slight overfeeding, they may be cumulative, and seen only after it has been carried on for some time. Overfeeding of the latter variety will eventually result in laminitis (founder) just as frequently as will extreme overfeeding, which may cause acute laminitis immediately (*see* LAMINITIS).

While it is rather difficult to put too much weight on a horse who is used regularly (the writer always strives to keep as much weight as possible on a horse he is using regularly), the horse who is not used and carries an excess of fat will certainly not live as long as one who is not fat. Furthermore, if a horse has been overfed until he is too fat, he will be so soft when used that he will be short of wind, and his sweating will be profuse. In the wintertime it is almost impossible to cool out and dry out such a horse properly.

Overrun (to overrun the scent)

Foxes are clever animals; they have to be to survive through centuries of pursuit. Sometimes, when being pursued, they make a very sharp turn. If the turn is made to enable them to cross a stream, or even to hop on stones over a stream or to leap on top of a rail fence and run along it for a ways, the hounds may not make the quick turn but continue running in the direction they were going. In such an instance, the hounds are said to overrun the scent.

Own (to own the scent)

The voice of a hound is meaningful to a huntsman or to any other person knowledgeable about foxhounds. The noise a hound makes is never spoken of as baying or barking by hunting people. They say the "hound speaks," and when the hound speaks in a certain way, as he is looking for scent, the huntsman knows that he is expressing success in his search. The hound is then said to own the scent or to honor the scent.

Oxbow Stirrup

An oxbow stirrup is made of a piece of wood bent into a U shape and held together at the top of the U by a metal bolt long enough to accommodate the stirrup leather.

Oxer

An oxer is a special kind of obstacle, either natural or simulated, in the show-ring. A natural oxer is a hedge bordering a ditch which is also protected by a guardrail. If it has a guardrail on both sides, it is called a double oxer. While oxers and double oxers do not naturally exist in hunting countries in the United States, with the increase of the sport in the West, it is possible that in some irrigated areas an oxer may actually be encountered in the hunting field in America.

Pace

1. The word *pace* is loosely used as synonymous with *rate of speed*. In some classes in the show-ring designed for hunters, horses are required to perform at a "hunting pace." This means that they are to take their jumps, execute the turns at the end of the ring, etc., at a rate of speed that might be comparable to average speed in the hunting field.

2. The word *pace* is used to designate one of the gaits of the horse. Almost without exception, it is an uncomfortable gait to ride unless it is done very slowly or at extreme racing speed. The exception is the "stepping pace" done naturally by some horses. It is almost impossible to discern or describe what these horses do that makes their pace rideable with comfort, because the relationship of foot impacts with the ground is exactly the same as for other pacers whose ride is so distressing. The difference is in the flexibility of their bodies and their body movements. Such pacers are extremely rare. The writer has seen only three in a long lifetime.

When a horse paces, the two feet on the same side have impact with the ground simultaneously or so nearly simultaneously that any difference escapes detection by eye or ear. On the racetrack, this gait is slightly faster than the trot but not quite as fast as the gallop (the gallop is done under saddle, not in harness as the pace is done). In pacing races, all horses wear hobbles (*see* HOBBLES).

Pacers

Pacers is the term designating horses used on a racetrack in harness in an attempt to win races at a pace. They are, today, all descendants of a horse called Hambletonian Ten or Rysdyk's Hambletonian. Hambletonian Ten was a son of Abdallah, who traces to Imported Messenger on both sides of his pedigree (*see* HAMBLETONIAN TEN).

Paddling

A horse is said to *paddle* when he throws each forefoot outward at each forward step, a fault in any horse except a Paso (*see* DISHING).

Paddock

The word *paddock* is an Eastern or English term for the Western corral (small enclosure). No horseman ever has enough paddocks or corrals, but it seems that every horseman has to learn this the hard way by having some emergency need for one. He may, for instance, have a horse suffering from an affliction which the veterinarian says may be remedied by allowing the horse to exercise in a small corral or paddock, or an animal may have contracted feet and need to be turned into a small enclosure which can be dampened with a hose if the weather is too dry. The needs for small corrals or paddocks are often extreme and too numerous to mention.

Paint. *See* AMERICAN PAINT HORSE ASSOCIATION

Pair Classes

Horse shows have pair classes for many kinds of horses—three-gaited horses, hunters, jumpers, even parade horses. In the late 1930s in the Intermountain Northwest, the writer encountered five-gaited pair classes, though he has not found them elsewhere. In all pair classes, manners are the most important requirement because horses perform together at all times.

Palomillo

Palomillo is a term sometimes used to denote an equine lighter in color than a Palomino (from cream to off-white). A few Palomillos were registered by Dick Halliday, the pioneer champion of the Palomino, but they are not acceptable today as Palominos (*see* PALOMINO).

Palomino

In almost any discussion of the Palomino a heated question arises: "Is the Palomino a breed?" It is a nonsense question. If the term *breed* means a group of animals of relatively uniform characteristics, sufficiently pre-potent to transmit those characteristics to their offspring, the answer to the question is "No," for a Palomino bred to a Palomino usually results in get that is not Palomino color. If, on the other hand, by *breed* we are referring to a group of animals possessing common characteristics, and all of them are recorded in a register kept by an organization devoted to the promotion and improvement of that group of animals, the answer is a very strong "Yes." Either use of the term *breed* is legitimate.

The outstanding common characteristic of the Palomino is his color (the term *palomino* is frequently used to denote a color, whether it be that of a Shetland pony or 2,000-pound draft horse). According to breeders of Palomino horses, the ideal body color is that of a newly minted gold coin. The mane and tail should be white or ivory. White markings on leg or face are permissible if the face white is limited to a strip, star, or snip (*see* MARKINGS) and the leg white does not extend above the knee or hock.

There are two breed associations devoted to the Palomino, recognized by the National Stallion Enrollment Board. They are the Palomino Horse Breeders of America, P.O. Box 249, Mineral Wells, Texas 76067, and the Palomino Horse Association, Inc., P.O. Box 446, Chatsworth, California 91311. There is also a National Palomino Breeders' Association, Inc., Mrs. Lewis Howard, Secretary-Treasurer, East Dixie Street, London, Kentucky

40741. Requirements of skin color, eye color, and the amount of deviation from the ideal body color to be permitted have never been permanently fixed. There is disagreement among the associations on requirements. However, each association has to permit registration of animals having one parent who is not a Palomino. This practice will continue unless breeders are able, some day, to produce Palominos who will get Palomino color when bred to Palominos.

Origin

Though it would probably be impossible to find an Arabian horse today of palomino color, most students agree that our Palominos can trace their color to Barb and/or Arab ancestors. The color occurs now and then in most breeds of equines, from Belgians to Shetland ponies, but the ancestors of most registered Palominos today were probably of Spanish origin.

Chief Quanah Parker of the Comanches was proud of the Palominos he bred in the 1800s. Old Fred, a Palomino and progenitor of many modern Quarter Horses of note, was foaled in 1890 in Missouri, when Ben Swaggart of Lexington, Oregon, was also breeding Palominos (which he called Cremolines). The Waggoner Ranch of Texas (which also bred Suffolk Punch horses, animals of uniformly sorrel color, ideal for crossing with Palominos to get Palomino offspring) and other isolated breeders produced Palominos half a century or more ago. However, the color was generally not in favor and was considered suitable only for circuses (though some early Missouri Saddlebred breeders stoutly championed it for their breed) until the late 1920s.

One man may be given much of the credit for bringing respectability to the palomino color, a man unique in the history of horsemen. Coming apparently from nowhere, about 1925, he preached the gospel of the superiority of the Palomino through magazine articles and by word of mouth to all horsemen, singly or in groups, who would listen. He set up the first registry (which admitted some animals that would not be accepted by any registry today) and fired the enthusiasm of several affluent breeders. Dick Halliday he called himself. His devotion to the Palomino was so complete that he scarcely bothered about his own welfare and died possessed of very little of this world's goods in Florence, Arizona, in the late 1940s. Local authorities' efforts to locate relatives and origin of Dick Halliday were fruitless with the exception of the word-of-mouth information friends had received from him that he was born in Australia.

Much that Halliday wrote and said about the Palomino is difficult to substantiate—stories of the golden horses of the Dons and of the desert of Arabia. However, his evangelism bore fruit (or it was very timely). Today, as the result of judicious infusion of blood from appropriate breeds, Palominos are distinguishing themselves in all equine fields from parade and three- and five-gaited show horses to stock horses (some are doubly registered in Quarter Horse registry and Palomino, or in Saddle Horse and Palomino registries). There is a separate registry for Palomino Saddlebreds, but all other breeds seem content to leave the matter of color in the hands of the Palomino registries.

Panel (noun)

The word *panel* is sometimes used to designate any solid, upright obstacle encountered in a hunting field. However, it most strictly means the "chicken coops" that are put over wire fences in hunting country at appropriate intervals so that these fences may be jumped with safety. A "chicken coop" is simply two platforms leaned and fastened together at the top which are high enough so that they cover the top of the wire fence.

Panel (verb)

When stone or wire fences are common in hunt country, panels may be constructed at appropriate intervals so that horses may jump the fences with comparative safety. On a stone wall, a piece of timber or rail is placed on top of the stone so that any leg that is dragged over the jump will not be injured as badly as it might be if dragged over stone. Wire fences are paneled with "chicken coops" (two platforms leaned against each other at the top, high enough to cover the top wire of the fence).

Paneling in stone-wall country serves a very important secondary purpose—that of keeping a hunt in the good graces of landowners. A farmer who finds stones being knocked from the tops of his fences during a hunt is quite likely to become sufficiently irate to forbid use of his land by the hunt.

Paper Chase (hare and hounds)

In the horseback game of hare and hounds, often called a paper chase, a part of the group called the "hares" carry a bag of popcorn, rolled oats, or other material that will be visible and will be consumed if left on the ground so that it will not add to pollution. The hares lay a trail with this material, dropping some of it every 20 or 30 feet. They may make false cross trails or they may cross streams or think of other ways to mislead the "hounds." However, they must mark well all legitimate forks or turns. The first "hound" to sight the "hares" is the winner in this game. Variations can be played; in one of them, the trail is marked by bits of red tape tied to branches. The trail leads to a place where a good meal is enjoyed, and the winner, of course, gets his meal "for free."

Parade Horse. *See* FAULTS

Parasites

Internal Parasites

Internal parasites are one of the curses of modern horse care. Undoubtedly, internal parasites have plagued horses for many years; but certainly, with the increasing density of the horse population that we have had recently, they have increased. The history of parasite control on any organized basis dates from about 1925. During the 1930s, in an effort to control internal parasites, many fields containing virgin bluegrass sod were turned over. However, plowing up of virgin sod was not the answer because new horses turned out to pasture bring in the eggs of parasites, and the only method of keeping internal parasites under control is to pursue a successful program of parasite management on each horse. This can best be done under veterinarian supervision or advice.

Usually, if a horse has not been subjected to systematic parasite control, the first worming should be done by way of a stomach tube applied by a veterinarian. Thereafter, it is possible to use appropriate proprietary vermifuges on the market that can be administered through the feed. Each of these vermifuges covers a different spectrum of internal parasites, and it is wise to consult a veterinarian as to which is best for any particular horse. It is especially wise to consult a veterinarian as to which one is appropriate to give a pregnant mare or a mare nursing a foal.

External Parasites

External parasites are not a problem among well-cared-for horses. The external parasites that do occur among horses in this country are lice and ticks, which are easily controlled by the use of any of the proprietary remedies sold for the purpose of controlling external parasites. In each one the active ingredient is rotenone. The horse infested with lice or ticks will be in poor condition. Lice rarely attack a horse in good condition, and ticks don't seem to multiply on horses in good condition.

The most bothersome problem that ticks can create is an infestation in the ears. If a powder containing rotenone does not rid the ears of ticks, a veterinarian should be called. There are two reasons: (1) The old-time remedy of pouring in the ear a preparation that will kill the ticks (a combination of chloroform and sweet oil is lethal to ticks in the ear) usually results in making a head-shy horse. Veterinarians today have a less painful way of eradicating ear ticks than the old painful remedies. (2) Ticks located deep in a horse's ear are invisible to the eye, but you can be sure that a horse is bothered by ticks if he continually shakes his head and wants to rub his ear. If the ear is badly infested, he will be very touchy about the ear and will not want it handled at all. The danger of doing the ear serious damage, because of the horse's violent movement when the ear is touched, is considerable if a nonprofessional attempts to cure the trouble himself.

It should not be necessary to state that the horse who has become emaciated because of an infestation of external parasites (and probably concomitant causes) should be carefully brought back to a normal condition before he is put to any kind of work. His feed should be increased gradually, and he should be examined for infestation of internal parasites and dental ills.

Until recently the so-called screwworm, which is the larva of a fly, was of great importance in the Southwest, but it is now under control. Nevertheless, the horseman should watch any scratch or wound closely; if larvae appear, the authorities should be notified, for only by constant watch on screwworm infestations can the livestock sanitary boards of the Southwestern states keep the screwworm under control.

The owners of a stallion should watch the end of the urethra for possible infestation of larvae of any variety. If the stallion is washed well after each service, there is little danger. However, if the larvae do attack the urethra of a stallion and are not checked quickly, very serious trouble can ensue. The larvae, of course, must be removed immediately and the urethra kept clean. A veterinarian should be called if the stallion's urethra is attacked by larvae.

Park Hack

The term *park hack,* a rather unusual one, is sometimes applied to a horse who is suitable for general riding on prepared trails in parks or in similar situations. Classes for park hacks are about as uncommon as classes for five-gaited pairs, but when they do occur, the horses are expected to have attractive action, good manners, and a generally showy appearance.

Park hack classes are not to be confused with park horse classes, which are becoming quite popular with Arabian exhibitors (*see* PARK HORSE CLASSES).

In the American Horse Shows Association *Rule Book* there is a provision for a Three-Gaited Park Saddle Horse class, in which the horse is to be shown at a walk, trot, and canter. The class is "to be judged on performance, quality and manners."

Park Horse Classes

Park horse classes are becoming popular with Arabian fanciers. According to the American Horse Shows Association *Rule Book,* Arabian park horses are "to be shown at an elastic and animated walk, an animated, natural trot and a canter. To be judged on performance, presence, quality, manners, all around brilliance and conformation."

Trainers of Arabians destined for competition in park horse classes usually have their horses wear chains on their hind feet while they are in their stalls in hope that they will develop the habit of picking their feet up quickly and high behind. Front action striven for is fairly high at the trot but most remarkably characterized by a pointing and dwelling of each forefoot an instant before it strikes the ground. Since the *Rule Book* limits the length of toes of Arabians to a maximum of 4½ inches and the weight of shoes to 12 ounces, and forbids the use in the show-ring of any artificial appliances to produce special action, Arabian park horse action is not as artificially high as that of horses in Three-Gaited Park Saddle Horse classes.

Park Riders

Park riders is a derogatory term used in a few parts of the United States to designate riders whose only purpose in riding may be for what Veblen called "conspicuous consumption." They seem to be riding only to be seen, ride only in parks, and can stay mounted on only the gentlest of horses.

Parrot-mouthed

The term *parrot-mouthed* describes a horse's mouth in which the upper jaw extends beyond the lower one, and the upper incisors extend below the lower ones. Some foals are born with such an extreme parrot mouth that they cannot nurse and have to be destroyed. Those with milder cases of parrot mouth seem to survive without too much difficulty; unfortunately, horses cannot wear bands on their teeth as can the human young.

Pas de Côté

Pas de côté is a French term for side step or sidepass (*see* SIDEPASS).

Paso Fino. *See also* AMERICAN ASSOCIATION OF OWNERS AND BREEDERS OF PERUVIAN PASO HORSES, AMERICAN PASO FINO PLEASURE HORSE ASSOCIATION, INC., CRIOLLO, and JENNET

Paso Fino is the name given to a type of horse found with very slight variations in this hemisphere from Colombia to Peru. The preferred conformation of the Paso is described in the pamphlet entitled *Paso Fino Horse* (published by the American Paso Fino Pleasure Horse Association, Inc.) as follows:

GENERAL IMPRESSION. A light horse of great natural grace and style with definite, but controlled, spirit. No extreme muscling.

HEAD. The ears are short, often curved inward at tip. Eyes widely spaced and large—should have a soft expression and not show white at edges. The profile is straight or slightly convex just above nostrils—not between the eyes. This feature comes from the Andalusian blood. A concave or dish face is not typical and an extremely Roman nose is not desirable. The lips should be firm and well formed, and the nostrils should be large and dilatable.

NECK. Medium in length, set at an angle permitting rather high carriage, but

Sentencia, Peruvian Paso by imported sire and out of an imported dam. As three-year-old was first in Gaits for Mares class at All Paso Show in California. As four-year-old, in 1968, was crowned Champion of Champions Mare at All Paso Show. Note gait of foal is easy saddle gait, identical with that of mare. Imported and owned by Mr. and Mrs. F. V. Bud Brown, Scottsdale, Arizona.

neck is carried in an arch. Throat latch should be well defined, but not too narrow. A slightly swan neck is not uncommon.

FOREHAND. Shoulders are sloping with great depth through the heart. Moderate width through the chest. Withers defined, but not pronounced.

BACK. May vary from very short to quite long and still be typical. This conformation feature is greatly influenced by the bloodline and breeders must use great care to select stock that will produce balanced looking foals. Extremely long backs should be penalized in halter classes as this is definitely a structural weakness.

CROUP. Sloping, but rump should be well rounded. Tail is set low, but carried gaily when horse is in action. Extremely low set tails are undesirable.

LEGS. Straight, rather delicate in appearance, but have strong tendons well separated from the bone. Some have a tendency to show sickle hocks; this must be penalized in halter classes. Hoofs are small and do not show much heel.

MANE AND TAIL. As long and as full as possible. Forelock also left long.

SIZE. 13 to 15.2 hands with 13.3 to 14.2 being the most typical. Weight from 700 to 1100 lbs. Full size may not be attained until the fifth year. Paso Finos mature slowly and live a long time. It is not considered too unusual for them to live to be over thirty.

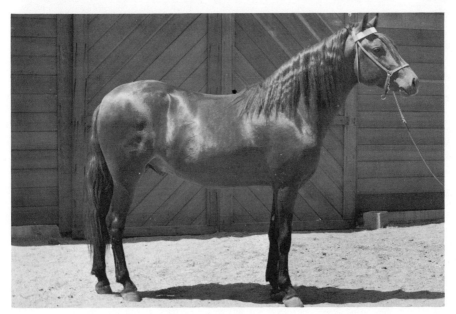

Dulce Sueño, Peruvian Paso stallion, photographed at 2 years and 9 months of age; sire and dam were champions in shows in Peru. This stallion is now the Junior Sire at the B-Bar-B Ranches.

COLOR. Every color can be found, but blacks, bays, chestnuts, and palominos are most common. White markings are common.

From personal observation it is added here that in hand the Paso Finos are gentle and amiable from foaling time on. Under saddle, handled by human beings of good will, they are invariably kindly but always possessed of ample impulsion, "heart."

In recent years some Paso Finos have been imported into the United States. A perusal of the publications of the American Paso Fino Pleasure Horse Association, Inc. (incorporated in 1964) suggests that certain characteristics of the breed are eliminated by selective breeding (characteristics such as paddling, long backs, and low-set tails, the first of which is considered as asset in Peruvian show-rings, and the last two, not overly common in the breed). The little horse from south of the border may supply us with all the desirable features of our gaited horse breeds without the attendant cruelties and artificialities which are turning many horsemen away from our gaited horses. The Paso Fino traces his ancestry in part to the twenty stallions and five brood mares Christopher Columbus gathered in the Spanish provinces of Cordella and Andalusia and brought to the New World on his second voyage. In this little band undoubtedly flowed a strong infusion of the blood of the Spanish jennets (or genets) who were long famed for numerous qualities, mainly their comfortable saddle gait and the ability to pass this gait on to their offspring (*see* GALLOWAY, HOB-

Lucerito, Senior Peruvian Paso Sire at B-Bar-B Ranches, winner at Peruvian shows before importation, Grand Champion of the Show at All Paso Show, Los Angeles, California, November 1966.

BIES, JENNET). The gait of the Paso Fino was the one most highly prized in England for all outdoor riding until the latter part of the seventeenth century. It was called a "pace" until the early part of this century, when a distinction was made between the lateral gait in which the two feet on each side hit the ground simultaneously and the easy saddle gait in which each hoofbeat follows its predecessor by exactly the same time interval.

For the lateral gait the term *pace* was kept. The new term, in this country, was *rack* (*single-foot* enjoyed popularity in some areas for a few years). The rack is in rhythm and relation of hoofbeats exactly midway between a pace and a trot. However, to the eye it resembles the pace. So today some writers describe the *paso* (which is identical with the rack) as a broken pace. *Running walk* was used until very recently to designate a gait done with the same rhythm and relation of hoof impact as the rack, but without leaping and therefore at a much slower rate. The running walk as described by Burt Hunter, who might be called the "Father of the Tennessee Walking Horse," was a gait "done at six to eight miles an hour with economy of effort to horse and rider." Today, it is done at from 15 to 20 miles an hour, a rack done by a horse so sore in front that he has to hump his back and scoot his hind legs under him.

The Paso Fino does his four-beat gait naturally. In the Peruvian Paso Fino the ability to trot is so rare that a member of the breed who can trot is considered a freak. The Peruvian Paso does not gallop. For extreme speed he may execute a fast pace. In Colombia, the trot is permissible as well as the gallop or canter, and many of these horses are naturally double-gaited. The Colombians more nearly subscribe to our standards of conformation than do the Peruvians. However, Peruvian Pasos may readily be found that satisfy the eye of a gringo horseman. All the Pasos have uniformly excel-

Passage. One of the movements of the Lippizaner horses of the Spanish Riding School of Vienna—the origin of dressage.

lent feet and sturdy legs; unsoundness is a rarity. Their weight-carrying ability is astounding; many a 14-hand animal displays no difficulty in carrying a load of well over 200 pounds over any sort of terrain. They readily learn to execute all the movements of a reining horse or stock horse; they make excellent rope horses. This is not surprising, for they are the horses used for working cattle in their native lands. They become foolproof mounts for babes and grandparents with a remarkably small amount of training in the hands of an intelligent horseman.

Passage

The term *passage* is a source of some confusion. By a few devotees of dressage (sometimes called high school) it means the movement called elsewhere "sidepass," (*see* SIDEPASS). However, the word *dressage* is French, and the French designation of *passage* is, in the late Henry Wynmalen's words, "nothing but a very elevated trot, wherein the horse appears to 'dance' from one diagonal to the other." In the ideal passage, the horse swings forward from one pair of diagonal legs to the other, suspending each pair in the air higher and for a longer period than for a trot. This ideal passage gives the impression of floating above the ground free from weight.

Passage des Singles

Passage des singles is a French term designating the bottom of a horse's belly under which a girth or front cinch passes. If the ribs spring too close to the horse's elbows or if the arm is too horizontal, the girth or cinch may be forced against the elbow so tightly that it develops sores.

Passenger

When someone refers to a rider as a "passenger," he is indicating that the rider has no rapport with the horse—that he lacks communication with him and is simply so much freight being transported by an animal.

Passing Other Horses

Serious accidents have occurred because of the ignorance or viciousness of a horseman when passing other horses on bridle path or trail. Whenever a rider is overtaking another rider or other riders, he should slow his mount and come up rather gradually. If the horse or horses being overtaken display excitement, he should certainly stop his mount and remain standing until the excited horse gets far enough ahead to regain composure. If he cannot find a way to get out of the trail or path and pass the overtaken horse at sufficient distance to avoid exciting him, he had better wait until that animal has returned to the stable or turned off the path. If the person overtaken is able to control his mount, he will, if courteous, pull off on a side trail as soon as possible so that the overtaker may pass. However, this may not be possible for an inept horseman, so it is the obligation of, and the way of self-preservation for, a more experienced rider to allow plenty of leeway if the overtaken rider is mounted upon an excitable horse.

When attempting to pass another horse on trail or bridle path, one is always wise to watch his ears to see whether they are laid back (a signal that the horse will kick). Courtesy demands that the rider of a horse given to kicking should turn him around to face the overtaker. However, wisdom demands that anyone passing another horse had better rely on his own observation and skill rather than the possibility of courtesy in an overtaken rider. There is a timeworn jingle: "Here lies the body of poor Willie Gray; he died maintaining his right of way. He was right—dead right—as he sped along, but he's just as dead as if he'd been wrong."

Pastern

The pastern is the part of a horse's leg between the hoof and the next joint above the hoof. The pastern should be a little straighter than a 45-degree angle when a horse is standing still and at rest. It should be neither too long nor too short. If it is too short and too straight up and down, the horse will give a rough ride. Also, the concussion on his feet will be extremely great. If the pastern is too long and too sloping, it is likely to break down. Observation of almost any picture of race horses, especially a photo finish, will reveal that the pastern of the foot carrying the horse's weight is horizontal or even slopes downward from the hoof until it touches the ground. Looking at a few such pictures relieves one's mind of all wonder that most race horses are unsound by the time their skeletal structure has reached maturity.

Pastures. *See also* HORSE, *Handling of, in Pasture*

Many a horse has come to grief because his owner has an idea that any large area in which some grass is growing is a good place for a horse to be for a while. The horse may meet disaster because the fences are such that he is torn up by barbed wire, or the particular kind of grass growing in the pasture may be unfit for equine consumption. The best pastures are those that are well fertilized and rotated so that the grass is eaten fairly short periodically and then allowed to grow several inches before horses are turned into it. Grass is richest in vitamins, minerals, and available nutrient content when it is only a few inches high and before it has developed a head, that is, before any blossom has formed on it.

The fences of a pasture are extremely important. It is possible to make a pasture safe for a horse even though it is enclosed by barbed wire by using an electrified wire (*see* FENCING) a few feet inside the barbed wire. While overworked and underfed horses can be run together in an enclosure without great danger, any horse who has been properly fed and not overused should never be put in a pasture with other horses who are shod. He should also never be turned into a pasture in which there are more horses than that pasture will easily support. If a horse has been confined for a considerable period of time and his owner wishes to turn him out to pasture, it is wise to mount the animal and ride him around the perimeter of the pasture a few times before turning him loose.

The author well recalls one grand mare, a big hunter who had been in a box stall and not used for several months because of her owner's illness. Finally, it was decided to turn her out in a pasture of about 20 acres. The pasture was enclosed by a good number nine woven wire fence topped by barbed wire, as is very necessary to keep horses from riding a woven wire fence down. The mare was turned loose at a gate to go as she would. She became so hysterical at being free that she started to run and never checked until she ran full speed into the wire fence at the opposite side of the pasture. The veterinary bill which this episode caused was considerable.

Pecking

The term *pecking* is used to denote the act of touching the top of a jump with the forefeet.

Pelham. *See also* BITS

A Pelham is an English curb bit (straight sidepieces with loops for a lip strap) provided with four rings for reins. One pair of rings is at the ends of the mouthpiece, so reins attached thereto operate as snaffle reins; reins attached to the other pair, at the bottom of the shank, are used as curb reins.

Percheron. *See also* PERCHERON HORSE ASSOCIATION OF AMERICA

Information circulated by the Percheron Horse Association of America states that the Percheron horse originated in the ancient province of Le Perche in Northern France. There is, however, evidence that a Percheron type was in existence as long ago as the Ice Age, but the true development of the breed, of course, belongs to the time of its usefulness to man.

It is believed that some of the sires playing a part in the early refinement of the breed were Arabian; for by the time of the Crusades the Percheron was already outstanding not only for his substance and soundness but also for his characteristic beauty and style. Historical records of medieval "chargers" undoubtedly refer to Percherons.

Topper's Hope II, 250012, a Grand Champion Percheron mare.

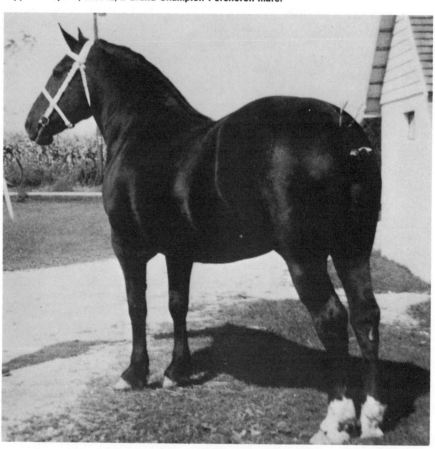

In the seventeenth and eighteenth centuries, horses produced in the Perche district attained widespread notoriety and were in demand for many uses. The Percheron of that time was not as large as he is today. He showed less scale and a lighter weight, was more active, and ranged in size from 15 to 16 hands. He was a superior general-purpose horse of drafty conformation, used as a saddler, a hunter, and a carriage horse. Some of the sires were English horses of the Thoroughbred type, and some were listed in the government stud book as Turkish horses.

In the nineteenth century, the French government established an official stud at Le Pin for the development of army mounts and for the encouragement of the breeding industry. The horses were selected with great care, and an invaluable contribution was made to the development of the breed under this supervision maintained for so long a period. In 1823 or 1824 a horse called Jean-le-Blanc was foaled. He was destined to become the most famous Percheron sire, for all of today's Percherons trace their bloodlines back to this great stud in one way or another.

The first Percherons shipped to America arrived in 1839. They were sent by Edward Harris of Morristown, New Jersey, who was then traveling in France. Other pioneers were importing Percherons by 1850, and in 1870 the Percheron trade had gained the status of an established business.

The first American stud book was published in 1876 under the name of the *Norman Stud Book*, but shortly thereafter the title was amended to *Percheron*. The Percheron Society of America, now called the Percheron Horse Association of America, was established in 1905. After the appearance of the American stud book, the French breeders published a register of French horses (1885).

The 1880s were years of remarkable expansion for the Percheron business. Breeders paid as high as $2,000 for a single Percheron, and it was not unusual to hear of an outstanding animal going for $5,000.

Depression struck the country in the '90s, and the resulting curtailment of importations caused farmers to rely more than ever before upon American breeders for stock. In addition, many large breeding herds had to be dispersed, and the top-quality horses thus became evenly distributed throughout the country. By 1900 business was again expanding. Reportedly, 1,634 breeders were producing Percherons in America in 1900 and 5,338 by 1910. Registrations of Percherons increased from 1,490 registered between 1890 and 1900 to 31,900 recorded during the next 10 years.

This period inaugurated the era of the nearly perfect draft horse, with many remarkable individuals coming into existence. The cumulative effect of careful breeding programs, pursued for many generations, produced Calypso, once chosen as the all-time ideal Percheron stallion; Carnot, sold at one time for the record high of $40,000; Dragon, Laet, Lagos, Hesitation, Don Degas, and many other sires of wide distribution.

In 1936 the breeders of this country held a conference to study the changing commercial need for drafters and to draw up some principles to govern the future breeding program. The ideal Percheron, according to 100 prominent breeders consulted, is a medium-sized heavy bone, up-headed horse. Sires weigh from 1,800 to 2,000 pounds and mares from 1,500 to 1,600. Males stand 16 to 17 hands high and mares are 15 to 16 hands. Colors are predominantly gray or black, with a few sorrels, bays, etc.

Percherons are noted for extra-heavy muscling in the lower thighs and for an aspect of unusual ruggedness and power. Also characteristic of the Percheron is the clean action and the quality conformation of the feet and legs. An ideal horse should have a fairly long croup with a big, round hip. He should be close coupled and wide and deep through the chest, with plenty of back rib. The muscles of the arms, forearms, croup, and gaskins are especially emphasized in a good drafter, and ease and balance of gait are essential. He is also expected to be of marked tractability and intelligence, and an easy keeper. The Percheron head and neck are typical of the most attractive draft-horse character. The ideal Percheron has a full and prominent eye, a broad and full forehead, straight face, strong jaw, and ears refined and attractively set, and carried with animation suggesting the Arabian. Sires should have a ruggedness about the head; the mares show more feminine refinement.

Percheron Horse Association of America

Address: Belmont, Ohio 43718. *See* PERCHERON.

Periople. *See also* HOOF

Periople is a hard, thin varnish covering the hoof. It is secreted by a band of papillae located at the top of the coronet (*see* CORONET). The periople aids in preserving the natural moisture of the hoof. It is impossible to shoe a horse without some rasping of the periople below the point at which each nail protrudes from the wall and is cut off and clinched. However, farriers almost invariably rasp more than is absolutely necessary. This, they say, is done to give the kind of smooth-looking job their customers demand.

In horse-and-buggy days, when wise horsemen insisted more on preservation of the periople than do those of the present era, there was an old saying addressed to farriers: "The hoof below the clinches is yours for rasping; the rest of the hoof is the horse's and not to be touched by your rasp."

Pet Colts. *See* SHOWING and TRAINING

Phaeton

The term *phaeton* was used in the horse-and-buggy days to designate a rather wide variety of vehicles, but each was the epitome of comfort and quiet luxury. In the city a rather light variety of phaeton was used for comfortable transportation, and it was usually pulled by one horse. It had a top which could be put up and let down much like the top of a convertible. The phaeton used in heavy-harness classes was at least twice the weight of the phaeton found on the city streets in most places. It was pulled either by a heavy-carriage-type horse or by a heavy-harness pair.

Piaffe

Piaffe is a dressage term for trotting in place. This artificial maneuver is performed with very high action. *See* SPANISH RIDING SCHOOL.

Pick-me-up

Before the days of modern veterinary science, a horse that was near exhaustion from overwork would be "drenched" with a mixture consisting of whiskey and milk or water. After such drenching, he was blanketed and rubbed down quickly and allowed to rest until the effects of the "booze" wore off. Modern veterinarians warn against drenching (*see* DRENCHING).

The writer recalls more than one occasion on which his father, a physician, was forced to drive until his horse approached the state of

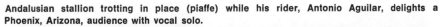

Andalusian stallion trotting in place (piaffe) while his rider, Antonio Aguilar, delights a Phoenix, Arizona, audience with vocal solo.

exhaustion. On such occasions the doctor would stop the horse, open his medicine case, and extract a bottle of tincture of nux vomica, which is a derivative of strychnine. He would shake the bottle, pull out the cork, then pull out the horse's tongue and touch the cork to the tongue as far back as he could. These few drops of nux vomica always revived the weary animal so that the doctor could get home.

Another physician, using starved native ponies for hunting in the Sierra Madres of Mexico, said he could revive an exhausted pony by feeding a bit of panocha (crude native brown sugar), which he always carried in his pocket for emergencies.

Pigeon Toes

A horse with pigeon toes is said to be "base narrow." He almost invariably paddles (*see* PADDLING). This fault can be lessened somewhat by corrective shoeing, but too drastic efforts to correct it may result in lameness because of injury to joints above the hoof. Such drastic remedies usually entail changing the level of the foot by rasping the inside wall until it is shorter than the outside.

Piggin' String

A piggin' string is a braided rope tucked under a rodeo contestant's belt or held in his teeth. It is used to tie a bovine's feet together after it is roped.

Pin Firing. *See* FIRING

Pink Coat or Hunting Pinks

Contrary to popular opinion, the term *pink* used in referring to the red coats customarily worn by male members of a hunt is not derived from the color of the coats but rather from the name of a very famous London tailor who spelled his name either Pink or Pinke.

Pinto. *See* AMERICAN PAINT HORSE ASSOCIATION

Pirouette

The pirouette is a pivot on the hindquarter; that is, the hind feet move very little, while the forehand turns around: 180 degrees in the half pirouette, 270 degrees in the three-quarter, or 360 degrees in the full pirouette.

Pivot

The completely responsive horse, when ridden by an intelligent rider, moves with his rider much as a ballroom dancer moves with his or her partner. When such rapport exists, the horse can pivot either on the forehand or the hindquarters. A pivot on the hindquarters is called a pirouette. In a pirouette, leg aid and reins are used to move the forequarters. When a horse pivots on the forehand, the reins are used to hold the forehand and the legs are used to push the hindquarters around. If rapport is complete, the use of aids is extremely slight.

Plantation Walker

The term *plantation walker* is now obsolete. In its place we use the term *Tennessee Walking Horse* (*see* TENNESSEE WALKING HORSE).

Plate

The term *plate* refers to a very plain shoe devoid of calks (*see also* PLATES). It is also used to designate a race that is run for one prize, as distinguished from a race run for stakes (in which money is divided into several prizes).

Plater

A *plater* is a derogatory term for a horse who is not good enough to race for stakes and is only raced for plates.

Plates (racing)

Racing plates are extremely light aluminum shoes having tiny steel calks used for running races. Such shoes do not last any length of time. Sometimes they do not last for more than a single race.

Pleasure Horse

In horse shows there are classes for English pleasure horses and for Western pleasure horses. There is a feeling on the part of many horsemen, with some basis in fact, that a so-called pleasure horse is one not good enough to compete in horse shows in classes other than pleasure horse classes. However, if we think of the dictionary sense of the word *pleasure,* we are talking of a very different kind of animal. A horse capable of giving the utmost pleasure to his rider is one who has never been subjected to abuse and so is of good disposition. He enjoys being out of his stall and being ridden on a trail or bridle path. He is as responsive to his rider as a partner is to a leader in ballroom dancing. He could certainly perform any but the spectacular and above ground movements of dressage if his rider were inclined to follow such a routine. A genuine pleasure horse has at least one of the easy gaits in addition to his ability to do a good four-mile-an-hour flat-footed walk without any objection, a trot, and an easy, collected rocking canter. The extra gait may be a running walk, a fox-trot, or a slow rack. If he can give his rider the exhilaration of a fast rack or smart

Probably the most celebrated organized use of pleasure horses in the West—the Twain Harte Ride, conducted annually in the High Sierras.

trot, so much the better. But the horse must have no tendency to change gaits except as he and his rider together wish to change them. This pleasure horse must be able to clear, cheerfully and easily, any three-foot obstacle. The rider of a genuine pleasure horse can move his horse in any direction as easily as he can move his own body, or even more easily. He can lift his horse's forehand and execute a half-turn on the haunches. He can move the horse backward, either in a straight line or in any desired direction or series of directions more easily than he can move himself when he is afoot.

Every movement of the kind of pleasure horse being discussed here is graceful. It is a movement that has, in a golfer's terms, "follow-through." Such a horse does not have the excessive artificial, mechanical high action seen in the three- and five-gaited and Tennessee Walking Horse classes, nor does he have the daisy-clipping stride seen in other kinds of classes (forward and backward movement of feet very close to the ground at all times). He is free of the short choppy gait exemplified by some reining and roping horses. On the pleasure horse here considered the rider can carry a child if he wishes, or any kind of utensil or equipment, without frightening the horse because the horse has never learned to fear his rider. On such a horse it is possible to swing a rope or polo mallet without causing any fear. Of course, the first time a mallet or rope is swung on him, he may want to stop and take a look at the queer thing; and the rider will, of course, allow him to do so before he proceeds any farther.

The horseman who has $75,000 to $100,000 to spend may find little difficulty in obtaining a horse who will win almost any kind of horse-show class for which he has been trained. However, regardless of how much money the horseman is able to spend, he will have a hard time locating a pleasure horse of the kind just described, and he is fortunate indeed if during a long lifetime he owns one or two such animals.

They are confined to no specific breed. One of the best today is owned by a Phoenix businessman, a cowboy, a polo enthusiast, whose pleasure horse is excellent at the game. That horse is thought to be of Standardbred and possibly of Cleveland Bay origin. Another pleasure horse recalled by the writer was an Arabian of classic type; still another, a Morgan-Saddlebred cross. The writer's own pleasure horse is an Amerian Saddle Horse differing greatly from the type of the breed seen in the show-rings today.

Pointing

When a horse habitually stands with one foot forward and heel raised slightly, he is sometimes said to be pointing. This is an indication of lameness of one kind or another.

A more common use of the term *pointing* is to indicate a kind of trot that is frowned upon by devotees of all breeds other than the Arabian. It is a trot in which the horse points the front foot far forward at each stride in the trot before bringing it to the ground. The Arabian horse owners say that the horse "dwells."

Point-to-Point

Originally, a point-to-point race was one in which riders could choose their own route in going from one point—say, a church steeple—to another. In more recent times, point-to-point races have been held by hunt clubs and other organizations, and the courses have been laid out and marked by flags.

Policed (to be)

The term *policed* is synonymous with the term *come a cropper*. Both terms mean to fall off a horse. It is the mark of the tyro, of the uninitiated, to talk about being thrown. The more experienced person is aware that most of the time when the rider is unseated (unless he is a contestant in a rodeo) his fall is caused by his own ineptitude and not by viciousness on the part of the horse. One is reminded of an incident during the life of the late John F. Kennedy. The newspapers published a little item stating that Mrs. Kennedy was thrown from her horse. She (being an excellent horsewoman) indignantly made some of them retract the statement and say that "she fell off her horse."

Police Horse

For some inexplicable reason, the police horse has survived the cavalry horse as a public servant. There are still, in some large municipalities, stables of police horses. Horses used for this purpose may be of any breed; however, they are usually of some size (around 1,200 pounds seeming to be preferred) and about 16 hands or more in height. They must be level-headed and possessed of good bone and feet. A police horse undergoes considerable training. The ideal police horse is one who responds in much the same manner as the horse described in this book as the pleasure horse, distinguished from the pleasure horse in the show-ring.

Poll Evil

Poll evil is an infection of the occipital bursa or cushioning sac on the spinal column just behind the poll. Until recently it was thought that the initial cause of poll evil was always a blow of some kind. This belief certainly has some basis in fact because all horses used in coal mines had poll evil from running against the top of the tunnel. Today, however, veterinary science tells us that trauma is not necessary, and some types of infection can cause this disease without the aid of a trauma.

The lay horseman can diagnose poll evil after it has progressed slightly. It is characterized by a swelling of the top of a horse's head just behind the highest point. This becomes extremely sensitive and sore, swells still more, and is soft to the touch. It is hardly safe for any but an experienced horseman to attempt to touch it because the excruciating pain will cause an immediate, violent reaction on the part of the horse.

Any sign of poll evil should be a signal to summon a veterinarian, who is the only person able to treat it successfully. Many, many supposed cures or remedies have been tried through generations of horsemen. None will do much more than add to the agony of the horse. Yet, it is possible for a modern veterinarian to effect a complete cure.

Polo

The name of the game called polo is some indication of the excellence or at least of the acrobatic skill of the horsemen of Tibet (*see* HORSEMANSHIP), for it comes from the Tibetan language—*pulu,* meaning "ball." The exact age of the game has never been determined; certainly it goes back many centuries before Christ. The earliest written record of it is dated about 600 B.C.

The game was used by the British military in India to while away the long hours spent in that rather disagreeable climate. Introduced into the

United States about 1876, it was played at that time on ponies, the best of which came from Texas. The rules of the game have changed, and it is now a spectator sport of great speed and violence. Height limits of ponies have been removed, and the horses played in all the important games are almost entirely Thoroughbred.

The tremendous change in styles in polo, including styles in equipment, is illustrated by an experience of the writer. When he was in graduate school at Ohio State University, he practiced occasionally with the then budding polo team, which was under the guidance of a wise captain of artillery by the name of Hill. One day, out to practice came one player whose horse was wearing a standing martingale.

The captain demanded, "What in blazes do you call that thing?" pointing to the martingale.

"A martingale, sir," was the apologetic reply.

The captain snapped, "Take it off and lead your pony back to the stables. If your hand is not good enough to keep that animal's head out of your face, you are not fit to ride him."

Today no pony is allowed on a field without a tie-down. There are two reasons: the change of the breed of horse used, and the change of the speed and rules of the game. It is far more important for a polo player to be a good man at teamwork and mallet work than an excellent, all-around horseman in modern polo.

Variations of the game are popular in some areas of the country. Indoor polo is played with a softer ball and on a much smaller field than a regular polo field. In some riding academies and riding clubs broom polo affords a great deal of fun. This is played with brooms instead of mallets, and the ball is fairly large and soft.

Polo Ponies. *See also* POLO

Polo ponies today are really not ponies. They are Thoroughbred horses. Their training is the training given a good reining horse. However, they are asked for speed far greater than that of any reining horse, and there is a great variety of devices used to induce these Thoroughbreds (bred for centuries to run, not to stop) to stop quickly enough to be useful as polo ponies. Some of these devices are excruciatingly painful. For many years, ponies coming from Argentina were considered the best in this hemisphere. They received training exactly like the best of animals used for stock work.

Ponies

The term *ponies* covers a multitude of types of animals. Any animal under 14 hands in height is usually considered a pony. The use of small ponies, such as Shetlands, for children is frowned upon by many horsemen

David Namesnik illustrates the excellence of the Shetland pony as a pleasure mount with CoCo, his Shetland gelding.

because such ponies are very frequently unamenable. They are so small that they are not usually trained by a full-sized horseman. However, it is possible to train the smallest of Shetland ponies by using them in harness; then when the saddle is put on him, the trainer can teach the animal a great deal by walking beside him and handling the reins above the saddle as if he were mounted.

Many Shetland ponies make perfect mounts for any person small enough for them to carry. Their ability to carry weight in proportion to their size is far greater than the full-grown horse's. The natural disposition of Shetlands, contrary to popular belief, is excellent. Their reputation for meanness comes from the fact that many of them are not trained by competent adult trainers.

Pony of the Americas

The Pony of the Americas (POA) is a developing breed being established by the Pony of the Americas Club, Inc., which was incorporated in 1954

Connemara pony herd, one of the many types of ponies popular in America. Mavis Connemara Farm—Rochester, Ill.

for "the purpose of developing a distinct using type pony for the child who has outgrown a Shetland and is not ready for a horse."

To be eligible for registration as a POA a pony must be 46 inches and not over 54 inches high at maturity. In color he must have white or partially white sclera and some mottled skin. Striped hooves (as in the

Model POA (Pony of the Americas).

1. **Stadium jumping, national rally, the United States Pony Club National Competition.**
2. **Stadium jumping, the United States Pony Club National Competition.**
3. **Cross-country, the United States Pony Club National Competition.**
4. **"Water" splash on cross-country, the United States Pony Club National Competition.**

Appaloosa) are desirable but not mandatory. Six color patterns are permissible: (1) snowflake type—white spots over solid-colored body; (2) frost type—white hair intermingled in coat, often forming blanket as pony matures; (3) blanket type—dark body with light blanket over croup; (4) leopard type—diamond, square, or teardrop spots over entire white body; (5) white body—white with black spots over croup, loin, and back; (6) marbleized roan—roan body with varnish marks on head, elbows, stifles.

Pony of the Americas Club, Inc.

Address: P. O. Box 1447, 1452 North Federal, Mason City, Iowa 50401.

Port

A port is the upward curve in the center of the mouthpiece of a curb, Pelham, or Weymouth bit (*see* BITS).

Posing

The term *posing* was long the only correct one to indicate what the three- or five-gaited horse does when he is lined up in the show-ring. Until very recently, such a horse stood with his forelegs perpendicular to the ground and his hind legs pushing forward slightly. As horse shows became more popular and, in the words of one old horseman, "anyone who could afford a derby hat, a blue coat, and a long shanked curb called himself a horse trainer," the stance taken in the lineup changed. Today, one can see horses in three- and five-gaited classes standing with their feet stretched apart as in a position taken by a horse when urinating or by one whose feet are so sore that he cannot stand in a normal position. Today, *posing* is often called *parking* or *stretching*.

Post Entries

Post entries are entries made after the advertised closing date for entries in a show. The acceptance of post entries is discouraged by the American Horse Shows Association, but its *Rule Book* makes provision for them for such shows as insist on accepting them (sometimes with penalties).

Posting

Posting is a rhythmic movement of a competent rider on a horse at a good open trot. In posting, the rider rises very slightly from the saddle and returns to it in rhythm with the two-four time of the footsteps of his trotting horse. The height to which one rises from the saddle depends on the speed of the horse and the nature of the trot. Posting was for many years the butt of jokes in the West, but today many judges in Western pleasure classes require the rider to post the trot.

When one has learned to post well, it is as easy to post the trot as to keep oneself rocking in a rocking chair. One way to learn to post is as follows:

The first thing to do is to have your horse stand perfectly still while you learn the movement. If your horse is a bit fussy, have a friend stand at his head while you devote all your attention to your own movements, with your horse stationary. Be sure your stirrups are adjusted with the leathers just long enough to reach your ankle joints when you sit with feet out of the stirrups and legs extended toward the ground as far as possible. It does not matter greatly whether you use a flat or stock saddle for learning to post. The stock saddle is a little easier for most beginning riders because the stirrups are hung farther back than are the stirrups on a flat saddle (*see* SADDLES). It is thus easier to rise in the stirrups. The beginner may find it a bit harder to sit far enough forward in some flat saddles to get the weight of the body directly over the stirrups. Sit with the balls of your feet in the stirrups and the weight of your body carried by the bony structure, not the fleshy part of the buttocks. This will necessitate leaning forward, with the shoulders a few inches farther forward than the hips. You should sit far enough forward in the saddle so that the weight of your body is directly over your stirrups, with stirrup leathers vertical.

Now, using your knee joints as a pivot, rock forward so that the entire weight of your body is carried by your stirrups. As you do this, your hip joints should not straighten. Your knees are the pivotal joints. The hip joints do not function. In other words, the angle formed by the upper leg and the lower part of your body does not change. It is only the angle at the knee joint that changes. Note that we are now considering the most elementary kind of posting; later on, you may learn useful variations if you learn this part of posting well.

With your horse standing still, practice this rocking from seat to stirrups until you can do it in time to counting or to a whistled tune in two-four time. It will take much more effort than will posting a real trot after you have learned to do it, because at the trot the horse's rhythmic movement provides the momentum for your rise at every other hoofbeat. When you are able to rock forward and back in a regular rhythm, you are ready to try posting a real trot.

For the first few trials at posting, it is helpful to have a friend ride with you and lead your mount while you are making your first attempts to rise to his trot. This measure obviously guards against your jerking on the reins because of the unsteadiness of your body in the beginning. However, assistance is not indispensable. Try the very slow trot at first. It takes much more effort on your part to post a very slow trot than to post a moderately fast one, but try the slow one until you can post without having the movements of your body translated into unsteadiness on the reins. As soon as you can rise up and down on the slow trot and at the same time keep your hand perfectly still on the reins, you can urge your horse to go a little faster at the trot. You must, of course, at all times keep your reins short enough so that if he becomes disturbed by the movements of your hands or body you can slow him down and quiet his fears. Do not try posting very long at a time at first. Gradually lengthen the time from day to day.

If you are riding a stock saddle, it is no disgrace to keep your left hand on the saddle horn for the first few days of posting. Continuing to do so will of course spoil your balance and make you a lopsided poster; but for the first few times, a hand on the horn may enable you to keep your other hand, your bridle hand, steady on the reins while you are learning to rise in your stirrups. The rhythm of your rising and sitting should be exactly in time with the two-beat rhythm of your horse's trot. If you are at all out of time, you will probably get a double bounce when you sit and have to use unnecessary effort to rise. If you can keep in time with two-four music on the dance floor, you can quickly learn to keep in time with the trot of your horse. The height of your rise will depend on the length of stride of your horse and on the amount of spring in his movement. If you are in perfect time with your horse, you should rise only as high as the stride of the horse sends you. Also, you should note that you cannot be in time with your horse if there is a moment of pause either at the height of your rise or at the moment you are seated. Your movement is like that of the rocking chair or the swinging hammock, continual movement.

On a horse with a short stride and little spring, the posting rider hardly leaves the saddle. On the long-gaited trotter with lots of spring and high action, the rider will rise very high, and will do so without effort. When properly done, posting makes riding any trot easy and requires little effort. A good rider on an alert and healthy horse can ride a trot many miles without fatigue and without tiring his mount if he changes diagonals occasionally (*see* DIAGONALS).

Potatoes (in feeding)

Potatoes, like carrots, are useful supplements in feeding. Such supplements sometimes make a great change for the better in horses. When potatoes are fed, they should be cut up in small pieces and sprinkled over the feed. It is a little more difficult to get some horses to eat potatoes than to eat carrots. Rare indeed is the horse who will not eat carrots the first time he encounters them. Not more than a few handfuls should be given at first.

Potato Race

In a potato race, potatoes are laid out in rows several feet apart—far enough apart to allow a horse to travel and turn around. A pail is set at the end of each row and each contestant is armed with a pointed stick. He starts down his row jabbing potatoes and carrying them to the pail. The rider who fills his pail first is the winner. The rules may state that the rider can spear only one potato at a time or he may be allowed two or three.

Poultices

Poultices are sometimes beneficial to a horse. They are useful for about the same variety of ailments on the horse as on human beings. One thing that is sometimes eased by a poultice on a horse is fever in the hoof (not encountered in human beings). A poultice for this should be cool, and it can be of bran or anything else that will hold moisture. Boots are made especially for such purposes but they are expensive and their life is not usually long. A poultice for the hoofs can be made with a burlap sack or two or more burlap sacks put inside each other, or with an inner tube.

Prepotency

Prepotency is the ability to pass characteristics on to get. The best-known example of a prepotent sire is Justin Morgan. Not only did his immediate get uniformly possess his characteristics, but so did his descendants for many generations.

The breeding of Justin Morgan is too controversial to shed much light on the source of prepotency in the sire. However, we do have a record of the establishment of what is considered by many horsemen to be the greatest family of Quarter Horses ever developed. It was almost entirely a result of creating prepotency and was developed on the King Ranch of Texas under the careful eye of Dr. J. K. Northway.

According to Jack Widmer in his *The American Quarter Horse,* a stallion named Solis was mated to 50 of his half sisters. Then he was bred to his own daughters out of his half sisters. Widmer tells us that this was the first time desirable traits of an exceptional sire did not begin to disappear with the second generation. Prepotency was established; and contrary to most old wives' tales, absolutely no undesirables resulted from this concentration of blood.

When Dr. Northway was taken to task for what had hitherto been considered dangerous inbreeding, he replied, according to Widmer, "We call it concentration of desirable blood. When you do it, I call it in-breeding; when I do it, I prefer to call it line breeding."

Certainly this kind of creation of prepotency is no plaything for the dilettante. In the hands of lesser men than Dr. Northway, such close breeding is usually disastrous. However, Colonel Hughes, one of the most astute and influential of the horsemen who brought the American Saddle Horse to its place in the sun, said, "Of all great horses whose breeding is known, there is not one who is not somehow or other intensely in-bred."

Prepotency, the ability of an animal to pass on its qualities, *may* occur in animals that are not inbred, but there is no reliable record of such a phenomenon.

Pressure Bandage. *See also* BANDAGES

According to the veterinarian attending the highest-priced Arabian alive, as well as other leading veterinarians, more harm is done by the use of bandages in the hands of untrained caretakers than can be remedied by a great deal of professional treatment. The vascular system of a horse's leg, to say nothing of the complex functioning of the fluid that lubricates tendons, joints, etc., is too complex to be tampered with, though the horse is such a marvelously durable creature that he has survived centuries of crippling by grooms and "practical hoss doctors."

Any pressure bandage should be applied only with the advice of a competent veterinarian. Such a bandage is usually applied over copious amounts of sheet cotton and wrapped spirally with even pressure so that fluids will be forced neither up nor downward.

Fortunately the pressure bandage that was once the sole remedy for bowed tendons (effective only if applied immediately, continuously, and professionally) is now superseded by a semirigid type of cast which works wonders on most cases if attended to promptly.

Pricked Sole. *See* PUNCTURE WOUNDS

Privet Hedges

Privet hedges have several advantages as jumps. They can be trimmed to any height or assortment of heights, and they are safe. However, some horses, if jumped too often and continuously, become careless about clearing a privet hedge. A remedy in this event is to place a heavy rail at or near the top of the hedge.

Privet must be protected from animals and people until it has attained substantial growth, for it succumbs to maltreatment easily when immature; but a good stocky well-trimmed privet hedge will stand considerable wear and tear.

Profile

In examining a horse for purchase or in judging conformation for any other purpose, one should pay critical attention to his profile. No two breeds have identical profiles, and what is considered a virtue in one breed may be a fault in another. Nevertheless, there is general agreement on most important matters of the profile (*see* CONFORMATION).

Protests

At a recognized show, any exhibitor, agent, or parent of a junior exhibitor may file a protest against the violation of any horse-show rule. The protest should be made to a show committee. It must be in writing, signed by the protester, addressed to the secretary of the show at which the violation occurred, accompanied by a deposit of $25, and received by a member of the show committee within 48 hours of the alleged violation.

Proud Flesh

Proud flesh is rapidly growing tissue that often forms in wounds and prevents healthy, more slowly growing tissue from healing. The healthy tissue grows from the edges of the wound and is a bright pink color. Proud flesh may develop over the entire surface of the wound and build up so rapidly that it makes a bump which protrudes out of the wound above the level of surrounding normal skin. Any blanket prescription for treating all wounds is misleading and harmful. But very generally speaking, *minor* wounds should be treated immediately with one of the caustic powders especially prepared for this purpose or swabbed with one of the blue or violet liquid swabs available from any veterinarian. Certainly every stable should always be supplied with such first-aid material. The swabs and powders mentioned above prevent the swelling of tissue and subsequent opening of the wound. Daily treatment until the wound heals is, of course, necessary, both to keep the wound clean and to promote healing.

While salves, especially those with appropriate vitamin content, will promote healing, they also seem to promote growth of proud flesh. Lightly touching the center of the growing patch of proud flesh with a stick of silver nitrate will control it. However, care must be taken to avoid touching the healthy, growing tissue at the edges of the wound. Burning this growing healthy tissue with silver nitrate or other caustic will cause scar tissue to form.

Przhevalski Horse

The western part of the Gobi Desert is considered the evolutionary cradle of the horse (and other mammals). Today the last remnants of the oldest type of wild horse are still running on the slopes of the Tachin Schara Nuru Mountains on the edge of the Gobi. Discovered by Colonel N. M. Przhevalski in 1881, these little equines stand 12.1 to 14 hands. Their colors are of a dunnish persuasion running to lighter hues around the edges. They have dorsal stripes and often stripes on neck, withers, and legs. The supposition is that about 40 of them still exist in Mongolia. Hunting them is forbidden by both the Mongolian and Chinese governments.

Puffs

Horses used continuously on hard roads (and some others) usually develop what are called *wind puffs, wind galls,* or *road puffs.* These are small swellings at and just above the pastern joint, occasionally running several inches up the leg. When the horse works, there must be fluid inside the tendon sheaths for lubrication. Excessive work calls for excessive lubricant. That is what makes at least one kind of puff. Such a puff is usually harmless unless the owner starts to bandage the leg for aesthetic improvement.

It must be added here that there are other kinds of swellings in the region of the pastern that may be indications of serious trouble, and they are not easily distinguished from harmless wind puffs by the amateur. It is best for all but experienced horsemen to have any swelling about the legs examined by a veterinarian. Horses that are overridden on hard roads will go lame; and the owner or his advisers may think the lameness results from the wind puffs when in reality the trouble is probably in the foot.

Pulling. *See* VICES

Pulse

The easiest place for the layman to feel a horse's pulse is where a large artery passes under the jaw a little nearer the place where the throatlatch goes than the place where the chin chain is worn. The pulse can best be felt if the ball of the third finger is placed lightly on the artery where it crosses the inner edge of the jawbone.

A normal pulse rate is from 36 to 40 beats per minute.

The wise horseman will practice taking the horse's pulse until he can do so readily.

Puncture Wounds

Any puncture wound is a serious matter for an equine. The pathogenic organisms that are the chief factor in tetanus (lockjaw) live in a horse's intestines and in horse manure, so they are usually present on the skin or sole of a horse. If a horse has not been inoculated against tetanus, his chances for surviving a bad puncture wound are not enviable. Such a wound may be cleansed just as it would be on a person. A veterinarian should be summoned immediately to give appropriate inoculation (a "booster" shot is indicated if the animal has previously had regular inoculations).

When the wound is a nail in the foot, the veterinarian may find it necessary to resort to some paring of the hoof. If fortunate, he may be able to get to the bottom of the wound with a probe and cleanse and disinfect it without radical surgery. He may then instruct the attendant in the use of penicillin applied by means of a fine-nozzled tube daily.

The writer recalls one instance of great good fortune many years ago when, in the desert country of Arizona (the most unlikely spot on earth for a nail), his mount went suddenly lame after passing through an old, much-patched but long-abandoned gate. A nail had punctured the gelding's sole. One member of the party had a small first-aid kit containing a bottle of iodine (in those days iodine had not been supplanted as a first-aid necessity). The nail was removed. The hoof had been traveling in what must have been sterile sand and gravel. It was clean. Iodine was poured into the wound, and the party proceeded on its way. That gelding, innocent of inoculation, never took a lame step the rest of his life. The writer is sure that that incident used up all the luck he has coming to him this side of the Great Divide, and he is therefore extremely careful about having every equine in his life regularly inoculated against tetanus.

Purchasing the Horse. *See* BUYING A HORSE

Purgatives. *See* LAXATIVES

Push Polo

Push polo is played with an inflated ball at least three feet in diameter. The ball is pushed toward and through the goalposts of an opposing team by players riding against the ball. Riders do not use their hands on the ball but may use other parts of the body. Smart ponies soon learn to push the ball with their noses at times.

Quality

Quality is a rather indefinite term referring to the refinement of a horse. For example, the Arabian usually has a head that exemplifies quality (as distinguished from the head of the ordinary plug horse or even the "ant-eater" type of head often seen today on American Saddle Horses). Both Arabians and Thoroughbreds exemplify quality of bone (leg), though the bone may not have size (substance) enough to satisfy some horsemen.

There is an old saying: "An ounce of blood [quality possessed by blooded horses] is worth a pound of bone [size or substance]." Certainly a combination of quality and substance is the ideal. However, many show programs state for specific classes whether emphasis is to be placed on quality or substance.

Quarantine

On any breeding establishment it is wise to have a stall or stalls where newly purchased animals can be quarantined from other stock for a few days if their place of origin is not well known to be free from influenza or other contagious diseases.

Horses returning from a show should be kept from home stock until the danger of bringing home shipping fever, influenza, or other disease germs (always prevalent at shows and sale barns) is well over.

Quarter (of the hoof)

The term *quarter* may refer to the side of a horse's hoof just in front of the heel.

Quarter Boots

Quarter boots are of two general varieties (though of a multitude of distinct kinds or brands). One is the bell boot, shaped like a bell, fitting rather snugly around the pastern just above the hoof and extending to the ground. The other is the hinged quarter boot, which fastens with a narrow strap tightly around the coronet and (below the hinge) with two straps around the hoof.

Both varieties serve to keep the quarters of a forefoot from being struck by a hind foot.

Quarter Clips

Quarter clips are triangular bits of iron drawn up from the outer edge of a horseshoe and pressed in against the wall of the hoof after the shoe is nailed on the hoof. In some parts of the country, clips at the toe (toe clips) are commonly used. For some special uses, pathological and otherwise, clips are used at the quarters (quarter clips). Quarter clips should be employed with caution, preferably under veterinary supervision. If they are placed too far to the rear, they prevent normal expansion of the hoof and may lead to contracted quarters, which will cause lameness.

Quarter Cracks. *See also* HOOF

A perpendicular crack in the quarter, starting at the shoe and extending upward, is called a quarter crack. A good farrier can prevent a quarter crack from increasing and causing lameness if he attends to it promptly. (*See* SAND CRACK.)

Quarter Cuts

A quarter cut occurs when a horse cuts the quarter of a forefoot with a hind foot. It usually happens only at high speed or at a learned gait. (When a horse trots or paces faster than 10 or 12 miles an hour, he is doing a learned—not "natural"—gait. For most gaited horses, the rack is a learned gait.) Quarter cuts can be prevented by the wearing of quarter boots (and sometimes a little corrective shoeing and/or better handling of the reins).

Quarter Horse

(From quarter-mile race horse, also called short horse because of use in "short" races.)

There was no registry for any breed originating in the West until the establishment of the American Quarter Horse Registry in 1940. However, the endeavor to get horses more suitable for work and play than those roped out of wild bands (or bought from the Indians) started over a century ago. Good blood from Kentucky and other Eastern areas was imported, often at considerable expense. These early importations were generally known in the West by the names of their most illustrious progenitors. Thus, there were many Steeldusts and many Copperbottoms, to say nothing of the Morgans. In the Northwest there were several Kentucky Whips, indicating blood from one of the early families to which the American Saddle Horse owes a debt.

In addition to the blood of known origin, some stallions of unknown breeding produced get that attained fame in the West: Sykes Rondo, Old Billy, Shilo, Traveler, and, perhaps most illustrious of all, Peter McCue.

Speed was always sought by horsemen and any horse who could win races was valued far above any work animal. Backwoods farmers of the East, though far from the sophisticated tracks of the more populous areas, began horse racing almost before they had land cleared for farming. The races were of necessity short, for long courses were not available. These

The ideal American Quarter Horse. This oil painting hangs in the headquarters of the American Quarter Horse Association.

short races or "quarter races" (approximately a quarter of a mile) were in a very early day dominated by one horse and his descendants. He was a son of Janus, who was a grandson of the Godolphin Barb. This little horse, because of his unusual coloring (probably indicative of his Barb blood), was called Bloody Buttocks. Because of the speed of his descendants some of his blood traveled west.

When in 1940 at Fort Worth, Texas, the American Quarter Horse Association was born and set up (*see* AMERICAN QUARTER HORSE ASSOCIATION), no foundation bloodlines were designated as prerequisites for registration. Three types of Quarter Horses were designated as acceptable for registration upon inspection: (1) the stocky "bulldog," (2) the more racy "greyhound" type, and (3) the medium type. These three were obtainable by use of the strains of horses already highly valued in the West, mentioned above.

A remarkable example of the way in which breeders established the Quarter Horse type is the breeding done on the great King Ranch of Texas, where one of the most highly respected and uniform families of Quarter Horses was created. Old Sorrel, a grandson of Peter McCue, was considered the best stallion on the King Ranch. His son, Solis, was bred to his own half sisters and then to the daughters resulting from those matings (*see* PREPOTENCY).

As the Quarter Horse breed developed, rules for registration changed. When it became well established, the book was closed; that is, only foals from registered sires and dams could be registered.

In conformation, the ideal Quarter Horse has a fairly short head which is not large in proportion to the size of his body. The eyes are wide apart and set about midway between poll and nose. The muzzle is firm and the jaw strong, with powerful cheeks for chewing roughage. The neck is flexible at the poll. The ideal Quarter Horse's neck is not as long as that of some other breeds. It has to be flexible and set on sloping, powerful shoulders.

The ideal has long, powerful arms, short cannon bones, strong pasterns neither too long nor too sloping. His stifles should be large and his gaskins well muscled.

One outstanding characteristic of the Quarter Horse is a tremendous heart girth. This means great depth of body. Width is not a defect as long as the inside of the juncture of front legs with body is a Gothic arch. There should not be any flat expanse of chest between the front legs.

The back should be strong, loins powerful, and hips long, powerful, and well muscled. In general appearance this ideal is a compact, powerful animal, well muscled but also flexible and quick.

In addition to the American Quarter Horse Association (P.O. Box 200, Amarillo, Texas 79105), rival Quarter Horse associations have organized and set up registries. They are as follows:

Model Quarter Horse Association
   Mrs. Lavonne Foster
   P. O. Box 396
   Lincoln, California 95648

National Quarter Horse Registry, Inc.
   Cecilia Connell, Secretary
   Raywood, Texas 77582

Original Half Quarter Horse Registry
   I. M. Hunt, Secretary
   Hubbard, Oregon 97032

Standard Quarter Horse Association
   4390 Fenton Street
   Denver, Colorado 80212

Quartering

The practice of quartering illustrates how much more importance is placed upon tradition and authoritative prescription in many areas of the horse world than upon common sense and logic. It is conceivable that in some climatic situations quartering might be of value, but they certainly are not common today in modern stables.

Quartering is simply the process of grooming a part of a horse while the rest of him remains blanketed. After head and neck are groomed, the blanket is folded back uncovering the forequarters for grooming. Then the forequarters are covered and the hindquarters are uncovered and groomed. This procedure is a sort of ritual around some race stables before a race. It was originally done with incantation to promote speed for the race, but the words have been lost.

Quarters (of the horse)

The term *quarters* refers to the hindquarters of the horse. It rather loosely designates the part of the animal behind his rib cage.

Quittor

A quittor is a sinus connecting the coronet with a suppurating lateral cartilage. It was common when draft horses, wearing shoes with large calks, were worked in teams (pairs). Turned and backed by careless and ignorant teamsters, the horses would of course be forced to step on each other's feet occasionally, and a quittor often resulted. It is conceivable that horses hauled in trailers by ignorant or careless owners can be so tossed about on a turn that they will tread on their own feet, but according to veterinarians such accidents are extremely rare and quittor is, fortunately, almost unknown today.

R

Race Horse

The term *race horse* conventionally denotes a horse used solely in organized racing. Therefore, his advent in the English-speaking world resulted from the occurrence of the first organized racing, during the reign of Charles II. After the death of Cromwell, Charles returned to England from France, bringing with him his good friend William Cavendish, Duke of Newcastle, and a taste for excellence in many things, including horses. Until this time, the most highly prized horses of nobility and royalty ranged in type from the Great Horse of England (*see* GREAT HORSE) to the Spanish horse (*see* ANDALUSIAN) depicted by Velásquez and other artists, a horse with a breast like a pouter pigeon and a general conformation suggesting an enlarged Shetland (*see* SHETLAND PONY). Outside the elaborate establishments of the manege (*see* MANEGE) supported by the nobility, England had been developing, more or less by chance and convenience, a type of horse that was to be a cornerstone of the Thoroughbred (*see* THOROUGHBRED), even though the later proponents of the breed were to claim as its foundation three Oriental horses. Of these English horses, at the time of the Restoration, Newcastle wrote, "Certainly the best English horses make perfect horses for hunting or riding and to hawk, and some are as beautiful horses as can be anywhere, for they are bred out of all the horses of all the nations."

As the breeding of this light-legged horse began to gain favor, supporters of the Great Horse (*see* GREAT HORSE) petitioned the king to prevent the type of horse "fit for the defense of the country" from dying out. However, the Duke of Montrose (possessing firsthand knowledge of the horsemanship of Italy and France) had shown the efficacy of light cavalry by conquering all of Scotland with it for his king, and the argument of the Great Horse fans was out of date.

Charles II set up the best breeding establishment that the island had ever beheld. Some authorities claim that he sent abroad for his mares, which were to go down in history as the famous Royal Mares. But one of the most reliable books, *Royal Studs,* maintains otherwise. Then, as now, the label *imported* impressed the fashionable set; and owners of progeny of the Royal Mares probably did all they could to establish foreign ancestry of their stock. Some of those mares undoubtedly were imports, but others (possibly the best) were of English stock.

The first volume of the *Stud Book,* the oldest record we have of pedigrees of English race horses, was not published until 1808. It includes the pedigree of a horse called Counselor, bred by a Mr. Edgerton in 1694. The *Stud Book* gives his pedigree as tracing to imported Oriental stock on both sides within three or four generations. However, the Duke of Newcastle in his *A New Method* includes this horse among a list of horses of the manege, none of which were the light-legged, hot-blooded Oriental type, and I would trust the word of the Duke in preference to that of a compiler of records in the employ of his betters. Such discrepancies support the supposition that fashion rather than fact credits Oriental blood with so much influence in the development of the English race horse.

Whatever the breeding of the Royal Mares may have been, from the time they were ensconced in the king's stables, the term *Thoroughbred* was used by careful horsemen only to designate animals descended from them and the stallions in the royal stables. These "Thoroughbreds" soon demonstrated their superiority as race horses on the racecourse established by Newcastle. Hopefully, English nobility imported Oriental stock to beat native racers, but in vain. However, it was soon learned that crossing the fastest of the Oriental imports on native mares produced racers of great speed. Consequently, today credit is given to four Oriental stallions for the racing supremacy of the Thoroughbred. They were all brought into England in the first half of the eighteenth century. Within a few years after their being established as sires in England, only horses who descended from them through their fathers or the male members of their father's family (that is, whose grandfathers were sons of one or more of the four foundation stallions) could be called Thoroughbreds. Even today, every Thoroughbred in England and America traces his ancestry through his male ancestors to those four stallions. They were the Byerly Turk, the Darley Arabian, the Godolphin Barb, and the Alcock Arabian. Only Thoroughbreds could be raced on recognized tracks.

Until 1825 the only horses considered race horses by the general public, and especially by the gentry able to pay substantial prices for horses, were Thoroughbreds. Justin Morgan (*see* MORGAN HORSE), later to become one of the most famous of American horses, spent most of his life looking through a collar (at hard labor), passing from owner to owner at very modest prices, often in payment of a debt. True, he won matched races at walk, trot, and run, and he won pulling contests, but he was not regarded as a race horse. This attitude was soon to change. American cities were growing. Roads were being built between them. *Porter's Spirit of the Times* (December 20, 1856) tells of an actor, Thomas Cooper, "a tragedian" of the day, buying a horse who had won a $1,000 wager by trotting a mile in three minutes—a feat then thought to be impossible—and using the horse harnessed to a light rig as transportation between New York and Philadelphia, "thereby enabling him to perform his engagements in either city on alternate nights." It was the building of roads, many of them made of planks, and the manufacture of lighter-wheeled vehicles that made such transportation possible and, in turn, gave rise to a new kind of race horse, the trotter, later known as the harness race horse.

The National Association of Trotting Horse Breeders called its breed the Standardbred (*see* HARNESS RACING) because one of its rules in 1876 was that no horse should be registered unless he could trot a mile in 2 minutes,

30 seconds, which was called the standard of speed. So a new kind of race horse, the Standardbred, a trotter, became a part of American life.

Until almost the middle of the next century, the Thoroughbred and the Standardbred were the only "real" race horses, the only ones allowed to race on organized tracks. While early American aristocrats were importing and racing the first Thoroughbreds on organized tracks, backwoods farmers were betting on matched races, necessarily short because they had no long tracks to run them on. Most tracks were approximately one-fourth of a mile long, so they came to be called quarter races, or sometimes short races. The horses used were known as Quarter Horses or Short Horses. In fact, they were not recognized by the gentry at all except on those occasions when some farmer could scrape up enough money to bring a mare to the court of a Thoroughbred stallion.

The gentry raced their horses over considerable distances. If a Thoroughbred could not win races at least four miles long or produce get that could make four-mile race horses, he was peddled to a backwoodsman, if one could be found gullible enough to buy him. Janus, grandson of the Godolphin Barb, was just such a horse. He was a stocky little sorrel with one white hind foot, a stripe on his face, and speckles on his rump (many of his modern descendents are perfect Appaloosas) (see APPALOOSA). One of the most famous of his progeny was called Bloody Buttocks, an indication that Janus transmitted his color.

Janus did win a few four-mile races, but only a few; his sons did not seem to be able to stay a course four miles long. So Janus was sold to a Carolina farmer. He was resold many times (like Justin Morgan), but for 19 years he was used to produce short horses. His get were such consistent winners of matched short races that the aristocrats of Virginia became interested in him. A Mr. John Goode of Mecklenburg, Virginia, offered a handsome sum for the old horse to be delivered to his stable. The game little horse was started on the journey one cold winter day. He got as far as the stable of Colonel Haynes in Warren County, North Carolina, where he died.

This horse, once cast out by the gentlemen of Virginia, is now considered the father of a new breed of race horse, or, perhaps more exactly, a new breed of horse now running on organized tracks. The American Quarter Horse (see QUARTER HORSE) Registry was created May 15, 1940. In a very few years Quarter Horse tracks were established in the Southwest and a few years later Quarter Horse racing was permitted on many of the recognized tracks throughout the country. Thus a third kind of race horse became part of American life.

Lately, Appaloosas have been permitted to run on some organized tracks. Still more recently, Arabians (see ARABIAN HORSE) have been permitted on some tracks. Whether we call Appaloosas and Arabians "race horses" is probably now a matter of personal preference.

Racing. *See also* HARNESS RACING

Horse racing is one of the oldest activities of man. Since the dawn of written history evidence has existed that racing attracts all classes of humans, but its most avid fans come from the dregs of society and from the most privileged classes. Its opponents have usually arisen from the middle classes. Today, revenue from racing (via taxes on pari-mutuel wagering) gives substantial support in some areas to schools and other public institutions supposed to be of benefit to mankind.

While races for Arabians, Quarter Horses, and Appaloosas are permitted on some tracks today, Thoroughbred racing alone is a multibillion-dollar industry in America today. Harness racing, trotting and pacing, is not far behind in financial importance. Quarter Horse racing, though not yet comparable in magnitude to Thoroughbred racing or harness racing, is running a good third in national popularity.

In the latter part of the nineteenth century, much confusion existed in the racing world because control was in the hands of several racing associations. They set up dates for race meets, rules of tracks, etc. To bring order out of chaos, the Jockey Club was organized in 1893. It was patterned on the Jockey Club of England, founded at Newmarket in 1750. While the Jockey Club originally included under its authority all activities on and off racetracks, its powers have grown until today it also controls registration of Thoroughbreds as well as a breeding bureau foundation. In fact, practically everything pertaining to the sport is controlled by the Jockey Club, unless we except pari-mutuel wagering, in which the United States government has some say.

Rack

Until the National Saddle Horse Breeders' Association (founded 1891) changed its name to American Saddle Horse Breeders' Association (1899) and agreed upon terminology for the gaits of the Saddle Horse (and many other things), terminology for the movements of the gaited horse was confused and varied from place to place. Colonel Theodore A. Dodge, writing in the 1870s in the excellent book on horsemanship *Patroclus and Penelope* uses the term *rack* to designate what the ASHBA agrees to call *running walk*.

What is now, because of the decision of the ASHBA, a *rack* was formerly called a single-foot. The same gait done today by the Paso Fino (*see* PASO FINO) is called the paso. The only difference between the old *single-foot* and what is now called *paso* by owners of Peruvian mounts is one of speed and action.

The rack may be considered to be midway between the trot (in which the two diagonal feet strike the ground simultaneously or so nearly so that

Sequence of hoof impacts on the ground in the rack. There is an interval following each impact when no foot is on the ground. 1. Left hind foot; 2. left front foot; 3. right hind foot; 4. right front foot.

the eye and ear can perceive only one beat for each pair of feet) and the pace (in which the two feet on the same side strike the ground simultaneously).

The rack has the same sequence of hoof impacts on the ground as the walk (left hind, left fore, right hind, right fore), but the horse leaps, so there is an interval following each impact when no foot is in contact with the ground. This interval must be of exactly the same length after each impact. The rhythm must be true four-four time. Any tendency toward syncopation is unpardonable. If anyone wonders why, he need only sit on a horse whose rack is not true. (The true rack is delightfully smooth; the untrue, unbearably rough.) (*See also* SINGLE-FOOT.)

Range Horse

Range horse is a very loose term usually indicating a horse of nondescript breeding raised and used on a cattle ranch in the West. It is a little broader than *cow horse*, for it may include unbroken stock.

Rapping Pole

The rapping pole is one of the many corrective devices common in stables that train for horse shows. It is a pole, sometimes provided with spikes, which is held either by hands or by triggers at the top of a jump. If, as is usually the case, the hind feet are the ones the trainer wishes to elevate, the pole is quickly raised either by hand or by release of the triggers just after the forefeet have cleared the jump.

The French seem to be more adept at the use of this particular method

of torture than other people. A friend of the writer raised and trained a very fine mount who had been completely cured of a bowed tendon, but some white hairs on the leg resulted from the semirigid cast used in the cure. Whenever the owner was questioned about the white hairs, he would reply with grim humor, "Yes, he's from France, you know; trained to jump high."

There are reliable horsemen who maintain that rapping poles, if light and skillfully handled, can be humanely and profitably used in training high jumpers. However, they certainly have no place in the training of a hunter, in whom manners are important. No horse on whom a rapping bar has been used will take an obstacle calmly, cheerfully, and comfortably, as a good hunter should.

Rarey, John S.

At the end of the nineteenth century, just before the automobile super-seded the horse as a most important part of human life, many great horse trainers performed publicly in this country and abroad. None was more successful and probably none possessed greater ability than John S. Rarey, a native of Groveport, Ohio, and an alumnus of Ohio Wesleyan University. He performed in 1858 at Buckingham Palace before more crowned heads than had ever before been assembled under one roof. As a consequence, he was asked by the heads of state of various countries, including Germany, Austria, and Russia, to present his art in their homelands.

Rarey's method was not as spectacular as that of some of the other horse trainers of his time. He was a very kind and quiet man. One of the most dramatic things recorded about him in this country is his leading a Fourth of July parade in Chillicothe, Ohio, mounted on a Thoroughbred horse named Cruiser who had been a notorious man-killer in England and subsequently tamed by Rarey and given Rarey as a present by the nobility who had owned the animal. Accompanying Rarey on either side in the parade was a child riding on a Shetland pony. The original records that we have of this man's performances suggest the ironic line from Byron's *Don Juan,* "He was the mildest manner'd man that ever scuttled ship or slit a throat."

Rarey Strap

For the modern horseman, perhaps not so gifted as Rarey, the most useful piece of equipment designed by Rarey (*see* RAREY, JOHN S.) is the "Rarey strap." It is similar to the strap sometimes used instead of a breeding hobble for mares. It is a wide strap from 36 to 40 inches long with a buckle at one end. Immediately behind the buckle on each side of the strap are loops for keepers. The strap is used to keep one foreleg off the ground for as long as the horseman desires it to be so kept.

To apply the Rarey strap on the left foreleg, let us say, the strap is first attached to the pastern, the flesh side of the strap next to the horse's leg. The buckle is on the outside with the tongue pointing to the rear. The strap is run through the keeper on the flesh side of the strap and pulled up snug so that the keeper and buckle are very close to the horse's pastern. Then the foot is lifted and the strap passed around the horse's forearm and buckled up tightly. When the strap is properly applied, the horse cannot

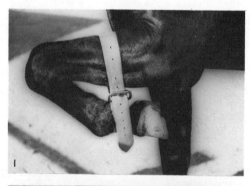

1. Rarey strap used to keep horse's foreleg off ground. 2. End of strap lifted to show how strap fastens around horse's pastern.

put his foot down. He will sometimes make considerable effort to do so. The trainer should be calm. The horse should be in a box stall or other place where he cannot hurt himself as he hops about trying to get his foot to the ground. When the horse finds that it is impossible for him to get his foot down, he will usually stand very quietly and the horseman can approach him and pet him. From that point on, the procedure should depend upon the aim of the horseman, the temperament of the horse, and other factors. Rarey sometimes used the strap to tire the horse sufficiently so that he could cause him to lie down on a deep straw bed. The strap may be used just to calm a horse so that he cannot be hurt. It should not be used by an excitable horseman or by an impatient one. The horse should simply find out that he cannot get his foot down. It usually is good to have a halter shank on the horse, although it is not advisable to restrain him with the halter until he finds he is unable to put his foot to the ground. Then he can be led about the stall hopping on three feet if he needs further discipline. But this maneuver should be done very quietly and calmly.

Rate (the horse)

1. To rate a horse is to have him go at a designated or controlled rate of speed.

2. In calf roping, the term is used to designate putting the rider in a position for roping and maintaining that position until the calf is roped, no matter how the calf dodges or changes speed.

Rate (hounds)

When a master or huntsman punishes his hounds either by voice or whip (thong), he is said to "rate" them.

Rations. *See* FEED

Rearing. *See* VICES

Reata

A reata is a lasso made of rawhide. Reatas were favorites in Mexico for some time and are still used by Mexican cowboys. They are usually much longer than other types of lassos, sometimes as long as 80 or 85 feet. The slang term for reata is "gut line," an expression used in some Western songs and stories.

Recovery (after stumbling)

There are two strongly opposed views as to what to do with the reins when a horse stumbles. The United States Cavalry, when it used horses, had a rigid rule that the reins should remain loose after a horse stumbles, to give the horse a chance to use his head for balancing in gaining his feet. On the other hand, some riders stoutly maintain that the horse who is not collected immediately after he stumbles will continue to go down until he is on both knees or completely prone. Probably the truth of the matter is that no one method is best for all horses. The writer has known horses who had to be collected after stumbling to prevent them from falling down; he has also known horses who recovered better when left completely alone. The best thing to do with a horse who stumbles habitually is to pension him or sell him. It is true that bad shoeing may cause any horse to stumble. So if one is not acquainted with his horse and finds that the animal stumbles, it may be wise to look into the matter of his shoeing before deciding to dispose of him. *See* STUMBLING.

Refusals

Horses refuse jumps for many reasons, of course. But perhaps the most common one is that they have been jumped by people whose hands don't go with their horses' mouths so that when the horse reaches the top of the jump and thrusts his head forward in preparation for landing, he receives a blow on the bars of his mouth. This causes the hind feet to drop just as a jerk on the mouth will cause the hind legs to stiffen when the horse is on the ground. A few experiences of this kind will make any horse refuse.

Another common cause of refusal is asking a horse to take a jump for which he has not been properly trained or experienced. Then there's the opposite cause. It affects the horse that has been jumped so much that he's gone sour; he's just fed up with the whole business. One of the best remedies for any horse who refuses is to use the cavalletti (*see* CAVALLETTI).

If a horse has been in the hands of a person who trains high jumpers by using a rapping bar, he will usually refuse when he is ridden by an ordinary rider who does not put the fear of God into him when he brings him into a jump. If a horse refuses in the show-ring—that is, a horse who is presumably ready to show and normally does not refuse—he should be taken back and jumped the second time with a shorter takeoff, and strong impulsion should be given him. If a horse refuses in the hunting field when he is jumping a panel or any other obstacle which horses are taking in turn, he should be immediately taken out of line and kept from the jump until the field has passed over. Undoubtedly he will be quite willing to take it then, for no horse likes to be left behind.

Registration of Horses

The number of registers for horses kept by appropriate associations listed in this book is over two score. It is possible today to register many animals not from registered stock on both sides of their pedigree. Half-Arabs, of course, can be registered; and there is a registry for easy-gaited riding horses, upon inspection. The owner of a horse who thinks his animal might be registered will do well to write the association that keeps the registry. It will give him information as to the requirements. Addresses of such associations are given in this volume.

It is desirable to have a horse included, if possible, in almost any kind of register, even though some registers do not command quite the respect of the old and long-established registries. If a horse is registered, there is no doubt about his age, for one thing. Also, registration is a strong selling point for any horse. The mere fact that a horse is registered indicates that somebody thought enough of him to write a few letters and go to the trouble of having him registered.

Reining Back. *See* BACKING

Reins

The kinds of reins used in riding horses are almost infinite. The conventional reins used with flat saddles are of as wide a variety as reins used in conjunction with Western gear. The conventional reins of the full bridle, called also *double bridle* or Weymouth bridle, are of English leather. The snaffle rein is always a trifle wider than the curb rein. The snaffle is fastened together at its ends with a buckle so that it can be run through the rings of a running martingale; the curb reins are stitched because no horseman in his right mind runs the curb reins through a running martingale (*see* MARTINGALE). Reins used in the hunting field may be the conventional reins of the double bridle or the reins used on racing horses, that is, reins which are made of broad leather, split and braided where the hands take hold. Of course, if a single snaffle is used on a hunter or jumper, a single wide rein may be in order. Usually, such reins are fastened together at the end with buckles. The reins of an English bridle are fastened to the bits with buckles or they are stitched (stitching is more frequently used on hunting bridles than on others). The reins may also be fastened to the bit by what are called French hooks, a kind of metal hook in front of and behind which the billets pass through loops or keepers.

Western reins may be of leather, braided rawhide, braided mohair, braided cotton, or even some synthetic material. For several years when the cutting horse began to appear in horse shows, the rein used on him was a very large one made of braided cotton. The purpose was to enable the judges and the audience to see that the reins were slack and the horse was working cattle "on his own." Western reins are frequently open at the ends and longer than English reins. The custom of using such reins originated in parts of the West where horses were trained to be "ground tied," that is, to stand as if tied when reins were dropped to the ground. Few horses today are ground tied, but the open-ended long reins are still preferred by some Western riders. Then there is the short roping rein. It is continuous from one side of the bit to the other and fairly short so that when the calf roper leaps from his saddle and the reins fall on the horse's neck, they are not long enough to get entangled with the horse's legs or the gear of the saddle.

Western reins are fastened to bits in a variety of ways. Sometimes they are buckled; frequently the long open-ended reins are fastened by running them through a loop of leather fixed to the bit end of a rein. Or they are fastened to the bit by running a leather thong through holes in the end of the reins and tying it securely. Once in a while a rein is fastened to a bit by merely passing it through a slit in the bit end of the rein. All these Western methods, other than the conventional buckle, have a history that dates back to the days before a horseman could go to a harness store or hardware store to get supplies.

Use of Reins

The ignorant or inexperienced rider uses reins usually for just two purposes: When he wants a horse to stop, he yanks or pulls on the reins; when he wants to go forward, he uses the ends of the reins to whip the horse's shoulders with, or if they are longer, to whip the hindquarters with. The reins in the hands of a skillful rider might be likened to violin strings, for he "plays" upon them with "infinite variety." Of course, the reins are never used without the accompanying use of the other aids (legs, body, and sometimes voice). Even the most skillful rider might on rare occasions use the reins to exert an extreme pressure on a horse's mouth for a moment or two (never for more than a moment or two). But the reins are usually employed only for subtle variations of pressure and direction which are, in the show-ring, too slight to be observed by spectators and, much of the time, even by judges. No piano note extends over a great length of time though any note may be repeated sometimes in rapid succession. Similarly, pressure on the reins should be of short duration, though as a signal it may be repeated quickly and as many times as necessary. In the matter of direction, there are two general methods of using the reins. They are called by some riders plow rein (because this is the kind of pull used to direct a plow horse) and neck rein. By other horsemen, they are called direct rein (plow rein) and indirect rein (neck rein). If the neck rein or indirect rein is used to keep the horse from turning to the right, let us say, while at the same time pressure is being exerted on the right rein to get a horse to move his quarters to the left, that neck rein is called, for this maneuver, the rein of opposition. That is, it opposes the command to turn to the right which seems to be given by the backward pull on the right rein.

The horse who has been trained to respond well (quickly and subtly) to the neck rein is always ridden with a very light or slack rein. Any tightening or backward pull on a rein will tend to move the horse's hindquarters away from the side on which that tightening or pull is exerted. A horse who is excellently reined, as the saying goes in the West, meaning he is trained to respond perfectly to the neck rein, will sidepass (move sideways in a straight line), move the croup (hindquarters) around the forehand (with the forefeet remaining approximately in the same spot as the hindquarters circle around them), or turn or spin on the hindquarters by appropriate combined use of direct and indirect rein, supplemented by subtle leg aid— usually merely moving the leg an inch or two backward from its normal position in the saddle. It is by properly shifting the relative use of direct and indirect rein ever so slightly when a horse is backing that he can be kept in a straight line or turned in his backward progress. (*See* PIVOT and PIROUETTE.)

Until a rider has learned to use both direct and indirect reins, he will not be a completely satisfactory or entirely safe riding companion for others or entirely safe himself in all situations. Once he has learned to use indirect and direct reins in their proper relationship, at the proper times in connection with the proper aids, he moves his horse's feet and other parts of his horse as readily as he does his own feet and body. Needless to say, he has much greater enjoyment in riding than do people who are not as skillful.

Position of Holding—English and Eastern

When one is using a full bridle (English), the reins may be held as follows: With the back of the hand facing the horse's ears, the curb reins

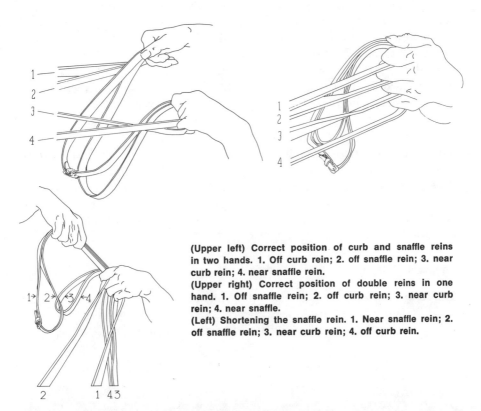

(Upper left) Correct position of curb and snaffle reins in two hands. 1. Off curb rein; 2. off snaffle rein; 3. near curb rein; 4. near snaffle rein.
(Upper right) Correct position of double reins in one hand. 1. Off snaffle rein; 2. off curb rein; 3. near curb rein; 4. near snaffle.
(Left) Shortening the snaffle rein. 1. Near snaffle rein; 2. off snaffle rein; 3. near curb rein; 4. off curb rein.

come into the hand on either side of the ring finger, and the bight (end) of those reins passes out of the hand between the thumb and index finger. The near snaffle rein comes into the hand just outside the little finger and the bight passes across the palm and out between the thumb and forefinger. The off snaffle rein comes into the hand between index finger and middle finger, the bight passing out between thumb and forefinger.

If the reins are held in two hands (in English full bridle) the near curb and snaffle are held in the left hand just as they are when holding all four reins. The off reins are held as follows: The back of the right hand faces the horse's ears. The curb rein comes into the hand between the little finger and third finger and the bight passes out between finger and thumb. The snaffle rein comes into the hand just outside the little finger and the bight passes out between finger and thumb. The bight of the reins should fall on the off side of the horse just as it does when the reins are held in one hand.

Position of Holding—Western

In Western classes two different ways of holding the reins are permissible. It may be stated at the outset, however, that with either method the bight of the reins should fall on the off side of the horse. If the rider is using a romal or is using the reins with split ends (ends that are not fastened together) and holding those ends in his right hand, the reins may be held as follows: With the back of the left hand or knuckles toward the horse's ears, both reins come into the hand outside the little finger. The bight of the reins passes across the palm and out between finger and thumb, falling across the thumb and down on the off side of the horse. The alternative to holding the reins thus is to use reins with split ends and not hold the bight in the right hand. In this case the bight falls on the near side of the horse. With this alternative method the left hand is held with knuckles or back of hand toward the horse's ear, the reins come into the hand between thumb and forefinger, and the bight crosses the palm and passes out of the hand where it is held by the little finger. With this method of holding the reins— that is, the reins with split ends not held in the right hand—it is permissible to have the reins come into the hand on either side of the index finger instead of having both of them come in between index finger and thumb. When a romal is used, or when the bight of the reins with split ends is held in the right hand, romal or bight should be held at least 16 inches from the bridle hand and the hand holding the romal or bight should be kept free of the saddle.

Remount

The term *remount* was used when the United States Army had horses in its cavalry. The term indicated a cavalry horse. Obviously, when a horse was shot out from under a soldier, he had to have a remount.

Remuda

A remuda is a herd or band of horses used by a working cow outfit in the Southwest. The remuda includes the animals assigned to each cowhand at work on the job as well as the animals belonging to or assigned to the foreman, cook, etc.

The term comes from a Spanish word *remudar*. In the Northwest the term for such a band of horses is *cavvy,* from the Spanish word for horse, *caballo;* since the Spanish *b* is pronounced somewhat like the English *v*, the word *caballo* finally became cavvy.

Renting a Horse

The best way to make the owner of a string of rental horses suspicious of your ability to take care of a horse you rent is to tell him that you are an experienced horseman and want a spirited horse. Chances are good, unless his business is pretty slow, that he will tell you his horses are all taken. It is wise to tell the owner honestly how much experience you've had with horses and let him judge what kind of horse to give you. Many people who try to rent horses have no notion at all about how they should be cared for. Most owners of rental stables can tell stories by the hour of how they have had horses ruined. Often the careless rider will ride a horse onto a pavement at a trot or gallop and have the horse slip and fall. Such a rider is always quick to try to sue the rental stables for his damages, but it is very hard to get money out of him to pay for a horse who had to be killed because of a broken leg or sent to the chow works because his knees were so badly injured that he was unfit for further service.

Again, there are the almost endless stories of rental horses ridden until sweaty and then tied while their owners went in for a sandwich. Any horse who is hot and made to stand still is likely to suffer what is called laminitis or founder (*see* LAMINITIS). If you anticipate the need to tie a horse up, it is well to ask the owner whether the horse will stand tied, because many rental horses, improperly tied by ignorant renters, will tear loose and break bridle and halter.

One wise old owner of a rental string says you can always tell how much a person has ridden by the rate at which he wants to ride. If he has ridden very little and is afraid of falling off, he will walk almost all the time. If he has ridden just enough so that he can stay on top of a horse by clutching the saddle, he insists on galloping to show that he can ride. He will gallop his horse until the poor animal drops unless a more experienced horseman cautions him. Then, of course, there is the person who really enjoys the feel of a good horse under him; he will walk most of the time because he enjoys the movement. He is well aware that a horse has many ways of walking and will respond to proper handling on a walk just as he will on various other gaits.

The average rental horse, of course, is not particularly responsive. The responsive horse in a rental string either loses his responsiveness or does not survive because no two riders "talk" to a horse on the reins the same way. Most people who rent horses don't "talk" to a horse on the reins at all. They merely use the end of the reins if they want him to stop. It is the sturdy wise horse who survives this kind of treatment and adjusts to it so that he becomes useful in a rental string. If it is possible to try a horse out in the corral or stable yard before renting him, the renter may avoid taking a horse who throws his head annoyingly or continually tugs on the reins or has to be constantly prodded to keep moving. However, most owners of rental strings will tell the rider about the characteristics of the horse if he takes the trouble to ask.

Resting the Horse

In competitive rides or endurance rides some rest is afforded the horse by change of gait, that is, a change from walk to trot or trot to walk. The wise rider uses only those two gaits in competitive riding. In addition to the slight rest afforded by change of gait, a horse on an endurance ride should be rested by having his rider dismount and lead him at least five minutes out of every hour. At the noon stop the horse can be rubbed down, watered, and fed whatever the occasion allows.

On a hunt, whether a fox hunt in the East or a lion hunt in the West, after the horse has strenuously exerted himself and there is a check, he should be rested by having his rider dismount. There is an old saying, "Never sit a standing horse." This is good advice because, first of all, a rider who has ridden for some time or at some speed and stands for a while is likely to relax and slouch in the saddle, causing the horse discomfort in his back. Secondly, if the rider dismounts, he can lift the saddle slightly so that air can get under it. Whenever possible, as at a noon stop, the saddle should be removed and the horse rubbed down. A proper rubdown is as restful to a horse as it is to a human being.

Rewards

A bit of carrot or lump of sugar as a reward, if used judiciously, is helpful in teaching certain acts such as posing (see POSING). However, judgment must be exercised or the horse will want to stop and reach around for a reward every time he thinks he has done something that merits one.

The horse whose rare relationship with a human being includes being responded to as well as responding can be rewarded by a pat on the neck or even an approving tone of voice. However, most professionally trained or conventionally trained horses have early in their careers abandoned all attempt at communicating with human beings. The horse, unlike the dog, will not go more than halfway to communicate to a man. If a human does not respond to a dog who wants to get a response, the dog not only will wag his tail but may jump up on the human and get his hind toes tramped. The horse's communication to a person is a very subtle matter, a slight movement of the head, the ear, nostril, eye, or what not. Of course, the hungry horse will nicker for food or paw at his manger. Whether this action should be included under the general heading of communication is open to debate. But the horse whose subtle signals have been ignored by human beings will cease to attempt such communication, and a pat on the neck or a word of approval will mean nothing to him. Something more substantial in the form of a bit of carrot or sugar must be given him.

Ribs of a Horse

The ribs of a horse should be "well sprung." The first and second ribs should not bulge out at the side suddenly, but the middle ribs should bulge out enough to give plenty of room for the lungs. A horse whose ribs do not curve out sufficiently for lung room is said to be "slab sided."

Ride in the Huntsman's Pocket

Occasionally a newcomer to the hunt field, in order to be sure of not getting lost, will attempt to follow very closely after the huntsman. This "riding in the huntsman's pocket" is, of course, an annoyance to the huntsman. The newcomer had better follow one of the older experienced riders in the field.

Ride Straight

The person who rides as the crow flies on a fox hunt, that is, who takes his fences as they come rather than pursuing a zigzag course in order to jump fences where they are most easily negotiated, is said to ride straight.

Ridgeling. *See* CRYPTORCHID and RISLING

Riding

A member of one of the first families of Virginia, an excellent horseman and for many years the occupant of a departmental chair at Ohio State University, once remarked to the writer:

"Louis, you can always tell how much a person has ridden by the rate at which he rides. If he is mortally afraid of falling off, he walks all the time. Just as soon as he has ridden enough to be over his first fear of falling, he gallops all the time to prove to everybody that he is a 'horseman'; but old-timers like you and me [the writer was not over 12 or 14 years of age at the time] walk most of the time enjoying communication with the horse and the infinite variety of which it is capable."

In this art of riding, as distinguished from merely being a passenger on a horse's back, it may be said that complete harmony of horse and rider is the goal. When that is reached, the horse will flex with a smile and champ the bit while the rider holds the reins lightly in sensitive fingers.

Belle Beach, on occasion, to make a point, rode with silk sewing thread for reins. Major Tuttle, for many years the only exponent of dressage in this country, for purposes of exhibition would ride with threads for reins.

There is a story of a great showman of the early part of this century which is still told in Missouri and Kentucky. The showman was Tom Bass. He won many of the most coveted prizes in his day for five-gaited horses as well as for fine-harness and three-gaited horses. It seems that on one occasion he reached over and removed the bridle from the head of a very famous mare and displayed in the ring for all to see, a wonderful performance in all five gaits.

There are few Belle Beaches, Major Tuttles, and Tom Basses; but the ability to communicate with a horse and to perform *with* a horse as readily as one performs with his own body is the ultimate goal in riding for every horseman, no matter what kind of riding he does. Any argument about which is the "best" kind of riding is rather senseless, for nobody lives long enough to become perfect in any one type of horsemanship, and each type can be an avenue leading toward the goal mentioned above. At the time when Spanish horsemanship was considered the finest in the world, Spanish horsemen rode *à la brida* and also *à la gineta*. The former was with the very long stirrup, the "forked-radish" seat of the Crusaders; the latter was with the very short stirrup and the crouching seat of the Moors. The highest compliment that could be paid a Spanish horseman of that era was to say that he could "ride in both saddles." (Few modern horsemen can "ride in two saddles.")

The Restoration saw the advent of great riding halls in England and a style of riding brought from France by Charles II. It was performed on horses capable of only three gaits—walk, trot, and gallop—quite a contrast to the easy gaits of the Hobbies, Galloways, and other easy-gaited types hitherto most highly prized as mounts. Though capable of none of the easy gaits, the riding hall horses performed varied movements both on the ground and aboveground. This particular kind of aristocratic riding reached its height in the rococo period during the eighteenth century, in the Spanish Riding School of Vienna (*see* SPANISH RIDING SCHOOL), and it was the parent of what came to be known as the only educated form of riding. It is, perhaps, about all we have left alive today of the activity of the rococo period. The Spanish Riding School is still operating in Vienna and employs a form of dressage. *Dressage* is the word for training in the kind of performance horses were asked to do in the days of the great riding halls. It is enjoying what may even be called a rebirth in the United States, encouraged, if not sponsored, by the Pony Clubs of America.

The oldest kind of riding, the riding of the easy-gaited horse, may be seen in our horse shows, though the sort of riding done there is certainly different from what the eleventh- or twelfth-century Londoner did to get from one place in town to another. And it may be seen being performed by owners of the Paso Fino horses, fox-trotters, and other easy-gaited horses. Still another kind of riding, almost as old as the riding hall variety, is that done by the hunter and jumper devotee and the fox hunter.

Scorned in polite equestrian circles in the more populous areas of America until after the first quarter of this century, but older by far, at least in its original form, than any other done in America, is the kind of riding brought to Spain by the Moors, who occupied Spain for over five centuries. The Spanish brought it to this hemisphere at the beginning of the sixteenth century. Horsemanship of the conquistadores, so well portrayed in Tom Lea's *The Hands of Cantu*, has been modified to be used by hands less subtle than those of the horsemen of Baja California (who introduced it to what is now the United States). The bosal of the conquistadores has changed in construction and in the placing of its authority (*see* BOSAL). The spade bit is (fortunately for horses ridden by modern hands) replaced by the snaffle. However, today's Western riding is closer to the original Iberian variety than is any other kind of riding done in America.

Originally the ultimate in Western riding was done on a horse who had spent plenty of time in training—at least one year on the bosal during which he carried an unused spade bit in his mouth while he learned the meaning of reins by means of the bosal only. Subsequently and gradually the bit reins came into use, and the bosal reins were discarded. This method achieved an extremely light mouth, so light that to an Easterner the horse appeared as though ridden with an entirely slack rein or ridden "behind the bit." Modern Western riding is done on horses not as quickly and subtly responsive as the horses of old Baja California days, but the best of them will shift balance completely at the slightest lift of the reins, and the lightest laying of a rein against the neck will precipitate a spin. Direct rein (*see* REINS) is never used on such a horse, and a turn is executed by a subtle sideways move of a rein.

Riding Etiquette. *See* COURTESY

Rigging

The word *rigging* applies to the manner in which cinches are put on a saddle (*see* CENTER FIRE RIG and SADDLES).

Ringbone. *See* LAMENESS

Ringer

A ringer is a horse who has been entered in a race in some false manner—sometimes under another horse's name. Such false entry may be made in order to get better odds in wagering.

Riot, Riotous

When hounds start to pursue game other than the game which is the object of the hunt, they are said to *riot*. In some areas domestic cats cause young hounds to riot more than any other game. In the West, where the term is scarcely known although the act is just as bothersome as it is elsewhere, deer frequently cause young hounds to riot when they are supposed to be after lion or bear.

Risling, Ridgeling

The words *risling* and *ridgeling* are obsolete terms for *monorchid* or *cryptorchid* (*see* CRYPTORCHID). Both the cryptorchid and the monorchid are likely to be extremely irritable and they are difficult to control around mares. Although surgery can now be successful, it is not advisable to resort to surgery until after the animal is two years old because sometimes the testicles do not descend until as late as the second year.

Among the illiterate or semiliterate the word *ridgeling* is often corrupted into *original*, though this corruption has not yet been recorded, even as slang, in a dictionary.

Road Hack

In former years, many horse shows included a class labeled Road Hack. The American Horse Shows Association *Rule Book* includes no such class, but one that is very close to the old Road Hack class is entitled Bridle Path Hacks.

The *Rule Book* specifies: "Bridle Path Hacks (hunter type) to be shown at a walk, trot, canter, and hand gallop. To back easily and stand quietly while rider dismounts and mounts. Emphasis shall be placed on actual suitability to purpose."

In the old Road Hack classes, more emphasis was placed on the horse's ability to cover ground over a long period of time. This meant that he should have a good long trot and that his hand gallop should be one which he could maintain for a considerable time. Programs frequently specified that the horse had to be ridden on a slack rein.

Roadster

According to the American Horse Shows Association *Rule Book,*

The Roadster should be a standard or nonstandard bred horse, of attractive appearance, balanced in conformation and with manners that make a safe risk in the ring.

Horses shall be serviceably sound and shown without artificial appliances (e.g., wired ears) except quarter boots and inconspicuously applied tail switch or brace.

There are two types of Roadsters for show—those suitable for bike and those suitable for road wagon. Occasionally, there are horses suitable for both purposes. Usually the Road Wagon Roadster will have more scale and height than the Bike Roadster.

Roan. *See* COLOR OF THE HORSE

The gray roan and gray are sometimes a little difficult to distinguish between. However, most gray horses are foaled some color other than gray—frequently black. Arabians destined to become gray (and later white) may be foaled almost any color.

Rodeo

The word *rodeo* comes from the Spanish verb *rodear,* which means "to surround." In the early days of cattle ranching in the Southwest, *rodeo* was used to designate what might now be called a roundup. This was a gathering of cattle from over a vast area for any one or all of several purposes. One of these might be to select certain animals for shipment or for putting in fattening corrals. The most usual purpose was to sort out animals as to ownership. The Mexican roundup of this sort was called rodéo. In a rodéo there was plenty of horseplay, and informal contests of various kinds took place.

The modern rodeo is a far cry from that early activity. There is no rounding up of range animals in today's rodeo, although it includes the use of a great number of cattle and horses. The competitions have become formalized. The bucking horses are encouraged to buck (*see* SEAT, BUCKING, BUCKING STRAP, BULLDOGGING, ROPING, etc.). They are not simply horses brought in off the range to be broken. Some kinds of competition that were very popular in the old days are now banned. The most striking of these is the technique of "steer busting," in which a rider roped a steer by horns or neck, flipped his rope around the rump of the animal, spurred his horse rapidly past and away from the steer, and jerked it in a somersault to the ground. This stunt, of course, not infrequently broke the neck of the steer. Practically every event in today's rodeo differs in some way from the competition of the days of the big roundups. Rodeos are highly organized. Contestants have an organization, Rodeo Cowboys Association in Denver, and rodeo is extremely big business in this country.

There is considerable controversy as to whether the rodeo is cruel to animals and should be barred. Some people claim that the rodeo animal is used for only a few minutes and compared to some show horses, notably the Walking Horse and the Saddler, is treated exceptionally well. This controversy has resulted in the past in the closing, for a period of years, of some of the biggest rodeos of the East. At the present time, rodeos are again big business in the metropolitan centers of the East. Professionals in the rodeo field pronounce the word ro'deo (accent on the first syllable).

Eastern visitors in the West usually give the word the old Mexican pronunciation with the accent on the second syllable, rō-day′-o.

Rollback (For English variation, *see* HALF-TURN.)

The invasion of the show-ring by Western horses is relatively recent, having occurred within the memory of most living horsemen. It added a new vocabulary to horsedom and a host of new movements and types of performance to show-ring competition. Neither the movements nor the nomenclature associated with them has quite jelled into standard or permanent form. A quarter-turn on the haunches was for several years called an *offset*, a term not so popular today. What used to be called *cross-firing* a few years ago is now referred to by an old English term, *disunited canter*.

The term *rollback* was made popular by Monte Foreman in his clinics, which have found favor across the country, often conducted under the auspices of universities and horsemen's organizations. The word refers to a reversal and change of lead (*see* CHANGE OF LEAD) at the gallop. While not at present included in the requirements of the AHSA (*see* AMERICAN HORSE SHOWS ASSOCIATION) for Western classes, the movement is becoming more popular in nonrecognized shows and may well be included in official requirements of the future. It is a relatively easy movement to teach a horse. A stout arena is the ideal place to do a rollback.

Teaching the Rollback

To start teaching the rollback, one should have the horse galloping fast enough so that he has no tendency to drop out of the gallop into a trot, but no faster than necessary to be sure to keep him in the gait. If an arena is used, gallop around the arena keeping close to the rail (a horse should *always* lead with the shoulder which is nearer the inside of the ring). About midway of the arena, turn the horse toward the inside and ride straight across the arena toward the opposite side. Do not allow the horse to slacken speed as he nears the opposite fence. As he reaches the fence, turn him toward the side away from the leading shoulder. This of course means a right-angle turn and will head him around the arena in the direction opposite to that in which he had been galloping before being turned across the arena.

Make the turn quickly just *as* the horse gets to the fence, but do not do it with a jerk. To avoid disturbing the horse's natural balance, use both plow rein and neck rein in turning him. Neck rein alone tends to divert the horse's head from his line of progression and to pull his nose in the direction opposite the one toward which he is turning. Use enough plow rein pull to point his nose in the direction you want him to turn. If the horse has been trained in an Eastern hunter-jumper stable or show-horse establishment, he probably will not know the neck rein. In such event, of course, use the plow rein (lateral pull) alone for turning, but steady him slightly with the outside rein. If he tends to slow down out of a gallop, either you have used too much pull on the outside rein or the horse must be urged on a bit by squeezing with your legs, or by a touch with the whip just as you ask for the turn.

Keep well forward in your saddle to help your horse get his hind legs under his weight for change of lead. *Do not lean way out to the side in the direction of the turn*, but lean enough to keep your body in line with the thrust of the horse's hind legs as he makes the turn. Lean slightly forward and allow the horse to increase speed as he comes into the new lead, for he may be disunited for two or three strides, and a little burst of speed should help get "both ends" galloping on the new lead.

Some horses (with some riders) can do a complete rollback on the first try. That is, instead of turning merely at right angles as they reach the rail, they can do a reverse and gallop back across the arena following the tracks they have just made. This is not a usual occurrence, for a horse will tend to slow down and drop into a trot as he is pulled around away from the rail to complete the reverse turn. The complete reverse gives more assurance that the horse will change lead satisfactorily, if he does not lose speed as he turns. So if the horse is extremely handy and amenable, you may be able to make the whole rollback the first try and be fairly certain of changing leads admirably. However, do not try to *force* the horse into a complete reverse turn the first time. Just ride him at the fence, turn him at right angles in the direction away from the old lead, and let him gallop on down the arena close to the fence. If you try too much force in an effort to get a complete reversal, you may have to call for the farrier to replace a shoe, or, worse, pick yourself up out of the dust of the arena while watching your horse scramble to his feet.

The operation just described may disturb the sensibilities of any old horseman of the West who is forced to listen to such a description. Much of the new method brought into respectability by the advent of Western classes in horse shows is contrary to old traditions—especially the story-book version of old traditions—of the West. Posting, for instance, has been the butt of many mossy Western jokes. Use of the plow rein on anything but a very green colt is also something new to many horsemen of the wide-open spaces. However, nobody attends a Monte Foreman clinic or seminar without acknowledging the value of the method, and most modern Western training stables give evidence of its worth.

This initial training (as well as practice at complete rollback) is a valuable part of the kind of skill required of both man and mount in the horsemanship now popular in the West and very prominent in the East. Handiness, the ability to start, stop, turn, change leads, etc., is one trait most in demand, and the rollback is an important aid in developing it. It is also very useful in what older horsemen call "suppling." The horse who has been "suppled" will "give" to the bit and bend his neck at a touch of the rein, with or without use of the leg aid. He will turn easily and promptly.

By gradually asking the horse to turn farther and farther from the fence and by increasing gradually the degree of turn—first a right-angle turn and gallop away from the fence, then more than a right-angle turn and gallop away from the fence—one can bring the horse to the point of doing the complete rollback. At signal (sharp turn in either direction) he will totally reverse his direction and change leads without dropping out of his gallop. When proficient, he will execute the turn mainly on one hind foot. He will perform this rollback at any place, in the arena or out of it, on demand.

The lack of an arena for teaching the rollback is not a great obstacle. Though a good arena is the ideal place, any relatively smooth area with firm but not hard footing will do if it is adjacent to a wall or fence of any material that is not dangerous wire. The horse can learn to gallop in an oval or circle in the area. When he has become accustomed to using the area for such galloping, he can be turned directly toward the wall or fence from a point at right angles to it. Then he can be turned as he reaches it, just as he would be at the fence or rail of an arena. The lack of an arena merely requires that a little time be spent in getting the horse in the habit of working within a given area. This must, of course, be done before starting to teach the rollback.

Roller

A roller is a surcingle used to hold a blanket in place.

Rolling Up

The phrase *rolling up* is of European origin and is used in the East to designate the practice of making a horse turn rapidly in a short circle for a short time when he refuses to leave the stable or perform some other desired act.

This same technique of making a horse turn in a small circle, frequently as rapidly as possible, is used in the West and is called "circling." A similar maneuver, called *bending,* is helpful when a horse does something objectionable when he is going at speed. Of course, a horse traveling at some speed cannot be turned in a very small circle without the danger of throwing him. (That particular technique is sometimes used in throwing a horse in the making of a motion picture, especially if the Humane Society is on hand and prevents the use of the running W or other more violent means of throwing a horse.) The phrase *bending the horse* simply means that if the horse is doing something at some speed that the rider objects to, he simply takes hold of the rein as close to the bit on one side as he can and starts pulling the horse's head around to make him turn. As stated above, this must be done with caution to prevent accident.

Romal

A romal is a length of braided rawhide terminating in a single or double tapered strap. The overall length of a romal is usually between three and four feet. It is attached to the posterior extremity of closed, braided rawhide reins. In some Western classes in the show-ring, the method of holding the romal is prescribed. The *Rule Book* of the American Horse Shows Association states that the romal is held 18 inches from the bridle hand.

Roman Nose

A Roman nose might be considered the opposite of the dish-faced profile of some of the families of classic Arabians. It is a nose that bulges out below the eyes. If the nose is long and the bulge is quite pronounced, the Roman nose is regarded as a defect and by some horsemen is believed to indicate draft blood or cold blood, that is, blood of the coarse horses of North European origin. However, a little study of breeds will dispel this notion, for there are certain North African (Barb) strains in which the Roman nose is quite common, and some families of the Criollo of South America, which is undoubtedly descended from horses of the Mediterranean area, almost always have the Roman nose, as sometimes does the Lippizaner of Austria.

Rope Burns

A rope burn on a horse can become a very serious matter. Treatment is the same as for any other burn on a horse or on a man. The difficulty in treating most rope burns and effecting a cure arises from the fact that they frequently occur at the back of the pastern just above the hoof, where the skin is in motion a great deal of the time. Veterinarians now have semirigid casts that immobilize the joints. In the case of a severe rope burn on the back of the pastern, such a cast may be useful.

Rope burns have many causes, but one that is too frequent, because it is so easily avoided, comes of tying a horse with too long a shank or picketing a horse who is not used to being picketed. The latter procedure will always result in a rope burn or some other more serious injury; when the horse reaches the end of his rope and starts to turn, he will always get the rope caught just above the heel of a hind foot. At this point he will panic and kick with his hind foot, making the rope saw back and forth on it. A severe rope burn should be brought to the attention of a veterinarian, and his advice should be followed in treating.

Roping

Roping, as now done in rodeos and other special contests, is of two varieties. (For what is usually an illegal exception, *see* STEER BUSTING.) One is called calf roping and the other is called steer roping or team tying.

The horse trained for the former type of roping comes to a sliding stop the moment his rider lays an arm on the horse's neck in preparation for leaving his saddle and running to the roped calf to hog-tie its legs. The horse will keep the rope on the calf taut until its legs are hog-tied.

The steer-roping horse has to do one of two things. He has to perform either for the head roper or for the heeler. As soon as the former has roped the head of the steer, the horse immediately turns with his tail toward the steer and makes the rope taut. The horse keeps tension on the rope while the heeler ropes the heels of the steer. Then both horses pull in opposite directions, stretching the steer out so that it can easily be rolled over on its side. The head roper dismounts as soon as the heeler has roped the heels of the steer, and it is the head roper who ties the legs of the animal so that it cannot get up.

Obviously, the two kinds of roping entail two different kinds of training for horses. The calf-roping horse has to be trained to come to a sliding stop immediately and keep the rope taut while he is facing the calf. He must continue facing the calf until his rider returns to him and mounts. The

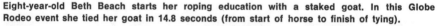

Eight-year-old Beth Beach starts her roping education with a staked goat. In this Globe Rodeo event she tied her goat in 14.8 seconds (from start of horse to finish of tying).

Roping. Sonny Beach, header, and his son Bret, heeler. Top, steer's head is roped; above, heeler catches by one foot.

steer-roping horse, the one used in team tying, has to learn to turn around and pull on the rope much as a plow horse pulls on a plow. His training entails what is called "logging"—that is, driving the horse with long lines while he pulls a log or some other object on the ground. This process teaches him not only to pull but also to stand still and to keep tension on the rope to whatever he is dragging.

There are rare horses who are good at both kinds of roping. However, many an excellent calf-roping horse has been ruined in an attempt to teach him to be both a calf-roping horse and a team-tying horse. Proper training of a rope horse requires as much skill and as much time as proper training of any other kind of horse. And a good rope horse will command as high a price as a good five-gaited horse or a good hunter. (*See also* SCORE.)

Rosettes

Rosettes on a riding bridle are usually a nuisance. Some riding bridles are so made that the throatlatch is a separate and single strap running through the looped ends of the browband behind the crownpiece or headpiece, which also runs through the loop ends of the browband. On such bridles, rosettes are needed to keep the throatlatch and headpiece in their proper positions where they pass through the ends of the browband. Unless the throatlatch is buckled after it is taken off the horse, the tab end of the throatlatch will inevitably slip up through the end of the browband and allow the rosette to fall off. Almost inevitably, the rosette will be lost in bedding on the ground. There may be places where one can buy a rosette to replace the missing one—that is, a rosette that matches the remaining one on the bridle—but the writer has never found such a place. About the only thing to do when a rosette is lost is to beg a piece of the heavy linen harness maker's thread from a harness maker and tie that around the browband where the rosette once performed its function.

Roundup. *See* RODEO

Rubber Numnahs. *See* NUMNAHS

Rubber Pads

Rubber pads go between the horseshoe and the horse's hoof. They were invented for use on delivery horses working on city streets and are still universally used on police horses. One type of rubber pad is thick where it covers the quarters of the foot. With this type, the shoe is cut off behind the last nail, and the pad alone protects the back part of the hoof.

Other types of rubber pads are used with an entire shoe. The pad is thick enough over the frog and bars of the foot so that when the horse is standing the pad carries as much weight as the shoe. This kind of pad is helpful in maintaining frog pressure, when it is desirable to keep a fairly long foot

Rubber pad used inside shoe to give frog pressure and decrease concussion. Shoe is placed against surface of pad shown in picture.

on a horse (not the length, however, of the Walking Horse or gaited show horse—no shoe on earth can keep such feet healthy).

The rubber pad is always useful in maintaining frog pressure, which is extremely necessary for proper circulation in the foot. The frog has been called "the horse's second heart."

A word of caution is appropriate in a discussion of rubber pads. The horse used on turf, or on terrain other than paved roads or very hard ground, is usually better off without pads of any kind. When one starts to use rubber pads, the chances are great that the use will have to be continued. Just as a boy's foot becomes tender in wintertime when he wears shoes so that next spring going barefoot is painful, so the horse's foot becomes tender with the use of pads. It is possible, in most instances, to accustom a horse to going without pads if the process is a gradual one and done with great care. However, without such care, the foot may be bruised and permanent damage may be caused. As every competent farrier knows, rubber pads must never be put on a horse unless tar and oakum are placed between the pad and the sole of the horse's foot. Oakum should be pushed well down into the crevices between the frog and the bars of the foot. Some farriers have a hoof dressing they prefer to pine tar. This undoubtedly is satisfactory. The tar and oakum prevent gravel and mud from working up under the rubber pad. They also keep the frog soft. Without them there is nothing to soften the frog, for it can't reach the moisture on the ground.

If one is considering buying a horse who is shod with rubber pads, the prospective buyer should be sure to have a veterinarian make a thorough examination of the horse's feet. Rubber pads are sometimes used in pathological shoeing, and the horse may be shod with rubber pads to correct navicular disease or some other trouble in the foot.

Rubbing Down

Properly rubbing down a horse is as vigorous exercise as a human being can indulge in. It is not a gentle wiping. A Turkish towel will suffice for the purpose, but the best rub rags are linen (the kind once used for bags of salt imported from Ireland) or raw silk. Whatever the kind of rag, it should be washed frequently. The rag is grasped by its middle so that the ends will flap about and add to the cooling if a horse is being rubbed after a workout.

One of the best methods is to start at the horse's hocks and work the skin over completely from hocks upward and forward to the head of the horse. The rubbing should be a back-and-forth motion with plenty of pressure and the ends of the rag flapping. Special care should be used to see that the loins and shoulders of a horse are properly rubbed. If the rubdown follows a hard workout, the horse should be moved while being rubbed until he cools slightly. The cooler (*see* COOLERS), which is a large blanket covering a horse from ears to hocks and hanging almost to the ground from front to rear, should not be removed immediately; the first rubbing must be done under the cooler. This, of course, will prevent the flapping of the ends of the rub rag described above. It should always be borne in mind that any sudden change in temperature is likely to cause laminitis (*see* LAMINITIS). Such a change certainly is created by allowing a sweating horse to stand still in a hot, dry climate, especially if there is any wind blowing. When a horse's temperature has returned nearly to normal, he can be crosstied so that the person giving the rubdown can work to best advantage.

Rub Rag. *See* RUBBING DOWN

Rug

Rug is a British term applied to any heavy wool blanket worn by a horse.

Runaway

Most runaways, or boltings, are caused by the rider. A very usual runaway follows this pattern:

An inexperienced rider takes a horse out of the riding ring before he (the rider) is sufficiently educated for outside riding. The horse makes a sudden move. The rider's fear causes him automatically to grip the horse with his heels, and the horse's response is to move forward. This adds to the rider's fright. He crouches forward on the horse and raises his hands because his reins are so long that he has no other place to pull. This, of course, is the signal for the horse to break into a gallop. The rider screams, thus encouraging the speed of the horse. The rider finally grasps the horse around the neck and throws the reins to the wind.

The foregoing may be an exaggeration. However, such things do occur, and they are the cause of most so-called runaways. Some horses, of course, have been so misused that they have learned to run away or bolt at the first chance they get. They are not fit mounts for anybody except the person who enjoys "challenges" of the kind such horses afford.

Another common cause of runaways is the idiot who rushes up behind another rider on a bridle path or a trail. In the event one's horse is made to run away from the cause just mentioned, the way to stop him is to reach forward on one side and take hold of the rein as close as possible to the bit so as to pull the horse's head to the side (*see* ROLLING UP). This must be done with caution, for if the horse's head is taken away from him too quickly and violently while he is running, he may fall. However, turning the horse who has started to run in panic is the best way to stop him, and the circle he describes can be made shorter and shorter as he begins to slow down. The one thing to remember is that a steady pull on a horse running in panic will not cause him to slow down. A seesaw movement on the reins or the holding of one rein steady and the pulling of the other one in rhythm to the horse's gallop is sometimes useful.

An experienced rider can usually stop a horse by collecting him. To collect the horse running in panic, no impulsion need be given, but the forehand of the horse can be raised by rhythmic lifting of his head. The rhythm should be merely an exaggeration of the natural rhythm of his head as he runs. If a horse can be sufficiently lifted in front, he will slow down; a horse cannot run at top speed unless he can throw his center of balance forward and his nose out.

A gag rein may be helpful in curing a horse of the habit of running away (*see* GAG REIN).

Running Walk. *See* GAITS

Rushing

A horse who rushes his jumps may have been trained in too big a hurry, that is, he was perhaps forced to take obstacles that were too high for the amount of training he had. Or he may have been ridden by a rider with bad hands, who pulled him at the top of a jump causing pain on his mouth. In other words, the horse who rushes is one who is fairly convinced that jumping is associated with pain, and he jumps because the fear of refusing is greater than the pain he associates with jumping.

The foregoing is an oversimplification of a very complex problem. The solution, if such there be, is to give the horse plenty of slow, quiet work, using him over low obstacles occasionally, with plenty of work on the cavalletti. A high-class funeral of an employee (or even of an owner) may help solve the problem.

Saddlebags

Until very recent years, no one thought of making a saddlebag of anything but leather. Today, some saddlebags of canvas are offered in saddlery stores. The saddlebag is about the only piece of modern equipment that is an exact replica of the army issue of mounted cavalry days. The type of saddlebag here referred to is the one seen frequently in television and motion pictures of cowboys and Indians. It consists of a pair of large pouches held together with a strip of leather. Leather and bags fit around the cantle of the saddle and extend downward almost as far as the bottom of the skirt of an English saddle. These saddlebags were originally designed to fit on a McClellan saddle, which is provided with a hook located just behind the center of the cantle. The hook fits through a hole in the leather of the saddlebag, and the leather is reinforced at this point. There are rings on the bag lower down, which were provided to fasten to the rigging of the McClellan saddle. However, it takes some ingenuity to attach these rings to saddles other than the McClellan. They can be attached either to the cinch ring of a Western saddle or to the girth of an English saddle by long heavy shoestrings. It is necessary to attach these rings to the saddle; otherwise the bags will flop in an annoying fashion whenever a horse moves faster than a walk.

While the old cavalry-type saddlebags described above are probably the most useful ones for carrying any amount of luggage, other types of saddlebags are certainly preferable if one is "traveling light," for two rea-

(Left) Near (left) half of saddlebag originally designed for U.S. Cavalry. It became the most popular of all saddlebags. With minor alterations, it is still manufactured and sold in all major saddleries. (Right) Sandwich case.

sons: first, because the old saddlebags cover a great deal of the horse and therefore add to his heat; second, because they are so large that it is almost impossible to keep them from flopping to a certain extent even when they are tied in all the places that they are designed to be tied. If one is using a flat saddle, it is possible to purchase at any good saddlery a piece of very useful equipment (designed for the hunting field) called a sandwich case. This case is meant to hold a little box that will carry sandwiches and a flask for a beverage. The sandwich case attaches to the two D's on the off side of the flat or English saddle. It is so cleverly made that it does not flop and fits very closely to the saddle. Of course, these cases can also be tied to a Western saddle; if one wants to carry only a light lunch and a beverage, they are preferable, even on a Western saddle, to any other kind of saddlebag.

Saddle Classes

Saddle classes are offered in horse shows for every breed except the Hackney. Most of them require the horse to perform at only three gaits. There are classes for five-gaited horses, and there are also classes for Walking Horses who perform in three gaits; but they are not the traditional walk, trot, and canter, which the term *three-gaited* ordinarily designates. The three gaits of the Walking Horse are supposed to be the flat-footed walk, the running walk, and the canter. The requirements for horses in classes under saddle are slightly different for each breed. However, most of them are explained under the following headings in this book: FIVE-GAITED HORSE, THREE-GAITED HORSE, PLEASURE HORSE, PARK HACK, PARK HORSE CLASSES, and AMERICAN SADDLE HORSE.

Saddle Horse

The term *Saddle Horse* usually indicates an American Saddle Horse (*see* AMERICAN SADDLE HORSE).

Saddler

The term *Saddler* is used to denote an American Saddle Horse (*see* AMERICAN SADDLE HORSE).

Saddles

One kind of saddle in its most primitive form was made by an Indian who borrowed an ax from a white man encountered on the trail. With the ax the native American cut down a cottonwood tree. Next, he selected and cut from the felled tree two forks, symmetrical and of similar size and shape. Then he split two slabs from the trunk of the tree, each a couple of inches wider than the palm of his hand and about three times that long. Out of consideration for his horse's comfort he rounded off the edges of one side of each slab; then, for his own comfort, he treated the other side in similar fashion. With a ramrod heated in a fire, he made two holes in each end of each slab. Then he made two holes in each leg of the forks he had cut. Taking some rawhide thongs he had put to soak when he started to make his saddle, he laced the forks onto the slabs so that each slab would rest on the side of a horse's rib cage just below the spine and the forks at either end would arch high enough over the backbone to avoid pressing upon it. He tied the rawhide as tightly as possible and set the finished product close to the fire so the rawhide would dry and shrink still tighter.

Indians had many ways of attaching stirrups, but our Indian simply tied a loop of rawhide around each bar so that each loop hung down far enough to serve as a stirrup on each side. A strip of hide tied around the horse's barrel and the saddle served as girth.

Another type of saddle was also once made by an Indian, probably a Central American Indian. He cut two squares of hide about as long as his arm. He laid one square on top of the other and with maguey fiber stitched them together with two seams two or three inches apart right down the center of the squares. Then he stitched around the edges of the squares, leaving an unstitched opening on each side so he could stuff dried grass between the hides. When he had stuffed the grass in, with a little more of it fore and aft than in the center on each side, he stitched the opening shut. The seams down the center lay on either side of his horse's backbone. The saddle was held in place by a strip of hide which encompassed horse and saddle. Stirrups were a long loop of maguey rope thrown over the saddle and hanging down on either side far enough to serve as a stirrup.

Every saddle used today is of one of the two types made by the hypothetical Indians just described, or it is a combination of the two (English saddles have wooden trees *and* pads). The cottonwood slabs used by our first Indian are a little more cleverly whittled today and covered with fabric, leather, or heavy rawhide ("bullhide"). We call them the "bars" of the saddle. This word causes some confusion, for on English or flat saddles our stirrups are attached to these bars by little metal devices which also go by the name of "bars," "safety stirrup leather bars," or "safety bars."

The part of the saddle that holds the bars (slabs) together in front is still called a "fork" if the saddle is a Western one. However, the rear fork of the Indian's saddle has evolved into a "cantle," which not only holds the bars together but adds to the comfort of the rider when he wearily slouches in his saddle.

Modern Saddles

Saddles in use in this country in the 1970s may be generally classified as flat saddles and stock saddles. If one prefers the classification English and Western, it may suffice. However, there are so-called English saddles that are of distinctly American design and American manufacture, such as the very good Whitman saddle. Then there is the English-type saddle used by the New York City police force, an excellent saddle for general purpose. It is of American design and American manufacture, though it makes use of the open safety bars for which we have English saddlemakers to thank, and the stirrups are set forward as they are in English saddles. The profile of the New York City police saddle resembles that of a deep-seated hunting saddle from England. Viewed from the top, the layman may confuse the New York policeman's saddle with the old McClellan saddle of cavalry days; in both, the seat is open between the bars of the tree.

Just as there are English-type saddles of American design and manufacture, so there are stock saddles designed and manufactured as far east as St. Louis, Missouri, and Louisville, Kentucky (both extremely "Eastern" places in the mind of a Western cowhand).

The Kentucky springseat saddle can be classified only as a flat saddle. It would be difficult for one to associate it with things English. The springseat was the saddle designed for what was once called the Plantation Horse and is now called the Tennessee Walking Horse. It has a quilted, padded seat. Frequently, it has a tree of heavy stiff rawhide rather than the usual rigid tree of beech or other wood. It is a comfortable saddle for an easy-gaited horse. The stirrups are set well forward. The seat is fairly short, so the rider is in no danger of sitting back on his horse's loins. There is one great drawback to the saddle. It is a very dangerous saddle for use on any but the quietest of horses on terrain which affords no possibility of stumbling or falling. The stirrups are held on by closed stirrup leather bars. Thus if the rider and horse part company and the rider's foot hangs in the stirrup, there is no way for the stirrup to come loose from the saddle where it is held by the bar to the tree. Of course, stock saddles or Western saddles do not have open bars, either. The stirrups are permanently attached to the tree. However, on the Western saddle the stirrup is usually of such a design that there is little danger of a foot's catching in it. The heavy fenders also are useful in preventing the stirrup from flopping up and capturing the foot of a fallen rider.

The choice of a saddle should depend upon the kind of riding one intends to do and also upon the kind of riding done by one's friends and associates. There is a common mistaken notion that one should choose the kind of saddle one's horse has been used to; that is, if one purchases a horse who has been ridden under a Western saddle, one should buy a Western saddle for him. This is slightly amusing.

The only possible difficulty one might find in changing the kind of a saddle on a horse would be in changing from a stock saddle or English saddle, which has no saddle strings or straps flapping from it, to a stock or Western saddle supplied with long saddle strings and latigo straps and with a hind cinch. If a horse is used to an English saddle and one wishes to ride him with a stock or Western saddle rigged with a hind cinch, it is best to shorten the spacer strap, the little strap under the center of a horse's belly, which connects the front and hind cinches. The spacer strap should be short enough to keep the hind cinch within an inch or two of the front cinch under the center of the horse's belly for the first few rides or until the horse is perfectly at home with his new saddle.

The hind cinch should not be pulled tight. At no time does an experienced Western rider pull a hind cinch tight. It is there, primarily, to keep the saddle from tipping up on its nose when a large bovine is roped. In addition to keeping the hind cinch fairly loose for the first few rides, one may tie the saddle strings up so they will not flap. They may be let down gradually after the first few rides. This is the only sort of problem ever encountered in changing from flat saddle to stock saddle or from stock saddle to flat saddle.

Choice of a Saddle

If one has learned to ride or started to learn to ride (it is doubtful that the process of learning to ride is ever completed by anyone) on a flat saddle, he will undoubtedly find a stock saddle very uncomfortable. The stirrups on a flat saddle are hung farther forward than the center of the seat, while the stirrups of the stock or Western saddle are hung directly from the center of the seat, unless one has ordered a special design or buys a specially designed saddle like the Monte Foreman saddle.

If, on the other hand, one has started riding on a Western saddle, he may feel a little insecure in changing to a flat saddle. The feeling of insecurity will not last long, and soon the flat saddle will seem at least as comfortable as the stock saddle, if not more so. This fact has been attested by many a cowboy who has taken up polo.

If one decides to use an English design, he has a choice of a forward-seat saddle or the older, more conventional type which includes the deep-seated saddle used by some people who are devotees of fox hunting and by some polo enthusiasts—also by some dressage riders. It sometimes comes as a surprise to Western riders to learn that the deep-seated English saddle has a seat that is identical with Western or stock saddles used a quarter of a century ago. The deep-seated English saddle (and also the New York policeman's saddle) has a seat that is four inches lower at its lowest point than the top of the cantle and pommel. This four-inch rise, as it is called, is about the same as that used in the saddles seen in roping contests and rodeos 35 years ao. Of course, the saddles used for roping today have a much smaller rise than that. Some of the "low-down" ropers have less than a two-inch cantle. This enables the calf roper to dismount a little faster than he could if his cantle were higher. The only way one can make sure what kind of flat saddle is best for him, if it is a flat saddle he chooses to ride, is to spend some hours on two or three different kinds.

The choice between the forward seat and the conventional seat of the flat saddle is not so difficult to make. If one is to spend any time in the hunting field or in jumping, the forward-seat saddle is best. If one's riding does not include much jumping, he will be wise to choose the saddle of the more conventional type. The so-called park seat or Somerset seat is excellent for general riding, as is the seat of the Whitman saddle, an American manufacture.

Among forward-seat saddles there is as great a variety as among the saddles of the old conventional English type, and one should spend some time in each of several of these varieties before he makes a final purchase.

A first saddle can well be a used saddle. One will not have as much money invested as if he bought a new saddle. So if he finds he has made a mistake, he can rectify it without extreme expense. Furthermore, most horseman's furnishings stores are willing to allow one to take a used saddle home and try it before purchase. Obviously a storekeeper cannot allow a new saddle to be so tried, for one or two trials will make it unpresentable as new merchandise. When trying out any saddle, one should put a sheet under it to keep it clean; also, riding for a few minutes with a sheet between a flat saddle and the horse will reveal any pressure spots that might hurt the horse. If there are any such places, the sweat will begin to appear very quickly on the sheet.

In choosing any new saddle, one should make sure that the bars of the saddle press equally from front to rear. Neither end of the bars of the saddle should poke into the horse's back. On cheap saddles of English persuasion, sometimes the back end of the bars will poke into a horse's loins. There should be plenty of room between the center of the saddle (from front to rear) and the backbone of the horse when the weight of the rider is on the saddle. As far as comfort of the horse is concerned, one of the best English saddles is the extended-bar saddle, sometimes called an officer's saddle or semimilitary saddle. In such saddles the bars extend a few inches behind the cantle, preventing the rider from sitting back over his horse's loins. However, in cheap versions of this saddle the back end of the bars may poke into a horse's back. Be sure this doesn't happen.

Any English saddle should be provided with two or three billets on each side to which a girth or girths can be buckled. A folded leather girth is satisfactory if it is kept clean and pliable. It will make sores on any horse if it is allowed to collect dirt and to become hard and cracked.

The most satisfactory girth for general use is a mohair girth to which the galvanized or stainless steel buckles are attached without leather. Such a girth can be put in the washing machine. In showing horses under flat saddles, white webbed girths are in order. The flat saddle used in the show-ring in classes other than the hunter and jumper classes (in which, of course, the forward-seat saddle is used) is called a cutback. It gets its name from the fact that the pommel is cut back, usually about four inches, so that the withers of the horse are not touched by the saddle, even though this particular kind of saddle lies closer to the horse's back at all points

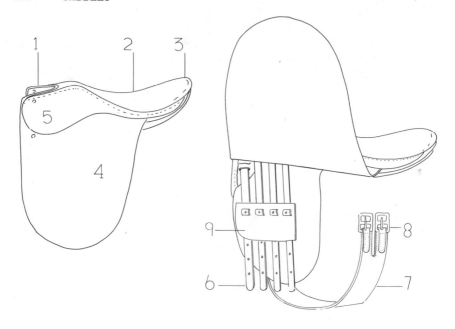

(Above) Flat saddle, English or Eastern. 1. Pommel; 2. seat; 3. cantle; 4. saddle skirt; 5. stirrup bar flap; 6. billets; 7. girth; 8. girth buckles; 9. buckle guard. (Right) 10. Safety stirrup bar; 11. stirrup strap; 12. stirrup; 13. detail of open safety bar; 14. stirrup tread.

than any other kind used. The billets for the girths of this show saddle are attached far forward on the saddle so that the saddle can be made to stay far back on the horse.

The purpose of this saddle is to show off the good front of the horse. Since the saddle is close to the back, the horse's neck seems to extend all the way to the back end of the withers. The saddle gives a much longer and bolder appearance to a horse's neck than would a saddle with a pommel that perched up over a horse's withers. Such a saddle sitting back over the loins of the horse, as it does in the show-ring, would not be suitable for general riding. However, a show saddle can be used for general riding in case of necessity if a breast strap is used to keep the saddle far enough forward. But since the billets are placed far forward on the saddle, it is wise, if such a saddle must serve for general riding, to attach the girths to the billets farthest to the rear. Thus the girths can be kept from chafing a horse just behind his elbows. These extremely flat, cutback show saddles are always supplied with four or more billets, so it is possible to take an ordinary four-buckle girth—that is, a girth with two buckles on each side—and place it on the last two billets of the saddle to avoid making the horse sore behind the elbows.

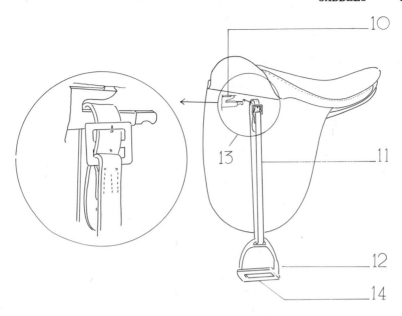

Western Saddles—Rigging

Early Western saddles were secured on the horse's back by two stout straps. One went over the front of the tree, terminating at each end in a big ring at the bottom of either side of the front of the tree. The other strap went over the rear of the tree just behind the cantle. It, too, terminated in big rings on either side at the bottom of the tree. These rings were just below the cantle. The four rings—two on either end of the front strap and two on either end of the rear strap—were called "rigging rings."

On double-rigged or full-rigged (both terms were used for the same rigging) saddles, the front cinch was attached to the forward rings by latigo straps, and the hind cinch was attached to the rear rings (the cinches were held the correct distance apart under the horse's belly by a spacer strap).

In those areas of the West where a single cinch was preferred, the straps over the front and rear of the tree terminated in one large ring on either side, both front and rear straps being attached to the same ring. When the rear strap was considerably longer than the front strap, allowing the ring on each side to be well forward, the saddle was said to have a three-quarter rig. If the front and rear straps were of approximately equal length, allowing the ring on each side to be below midpoint of the tree, the saddle was said to be a center-fire.

On steep-shouldered horses who have arms (the arm is the bone between the most forward point of the shoulder and the elbow—the joint just in front of the cinch) that are almost parallel with the ground (good ones

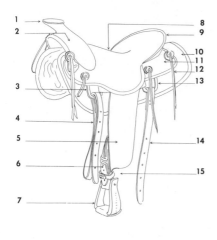
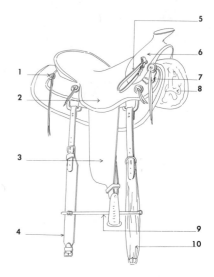

(Left) Western stock saddle, near side. 1. Horn; 2. fork; 3. front rigging ring; 4. latigo; 5. fenders or tapaderos (these are made in one piece with stirrup leathers); 6. stirrup leather; 7. stirrup; 8. seat; 9. cantle; 10. skirt; 11. upper flank skirt; 12. strings; 13. hind cinch ring; 14. hind cinch; 15. stirrup leather buckle strap.
(Right) Western stock saddle, off side. 1. Leather buttons or metal conchas; 2. seat jockey; 3. fenders or tapaderos; 4. hind cinch; 5. rope strap; 6. swell fork or front; 7. latigo carrier; 8. sheepskin lining; 9. cinch spacer; 10. front cinch.

are more nearly perpendicular), a full-rigged saddle is very likely to chafe the horse right behind the elbow. The chafing can easily cause an injury that is hard to cure.

For inexperienced horsemen the double-rigged saddle may be dangerous. First of all, the hind cinch, which is actually a two-inch strap, must always be loose enough to allow the whole hand to be inserted between it and the horse's belly. The green horseman may pull it too tight so that it interferes with the horse's breathing; or he has it so loose that the horse gets a hind foot through it or brush gets under it. The writer has seen at least one serious accident resulting from an inexperienced horseman's using a full rig with the spacer strap so long that the hind cinch got back into the horse's flank. A frequent accident is the tearing up of a saddle and ruining of a horse by undoing the front cinch first on a double-rigged saddle—that is, undoing the front cinch before the hind one is unfastened. If the horse happens to move or shake himself when only a hind cinch is fastened, the saddle will move, tighten up that hind cinch, and make the horse panic. Of course, a similar accident will happen if the hind cinch is buckled before the front cinch is fastened while one is putting the saddle on.

The advantages of the full rig, amounting to absolute necessity in some kinds of work, are several. The double-rigged saddle will stay in place without having the cinches pulled uncomfortably tight. Most ropers con-

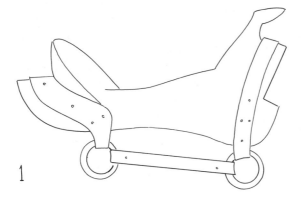

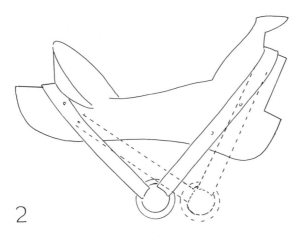

Double-rigged tree. 1. Stock saddle tree with full rigging; 2. stock saddle tree with center-fire rigging (three-quarter rigging shown in dotted line).

sider the full rig essential, because when an animal is roped and the rider steps off his horse, the hind cinch prevents the saddle from tipping up on its front end. Steer ropers use a full-rigged saddle and add a breast strap to it. The center-fire saddle will slip backward on most horses in going up a steep hill unless a breast strap is used. A horse accustomed to a single cinch is likely to be frightened and become hysterical when a double cinch is put on him unless for the first few times the hind cinch is held within an inch or two of the front cinch under his belly by a spacer strap, and is very loose. Of course there is no problem in changing from a double to a single cinch.

Seat

The type of seat a saddle should have is a matter of even more controversy than the rigging. Early Western saddles had nothing between the tree and the man in the saddle except one layer of rawhide (with which the tree was covered) and a layer of saddle leather. More than 90 percent of the Western saddles used by experienced riders today have built-up seats, and many of them have quilted seats with foam rubber padding. The built-up seats slope from the front of the seat toward the base of the cantle. Monte Foreman, whose riding clinics are known from coast to coast, denounces built-up seats because they prevent the rider from getting his weight forward. He also objects to the way stirrups are hung on most Western saddles and insists on having stirrups hung farther forward because it is difficult for a rider to get forward for rapid work if his stirrups are hung in the middle of the saddle, as is customary. Foreman has designed and marketed a saddle that bears his name and incorporates the features he advocates.

On the other hand, many expert Western horsemen insist that because the cantle of the Western saddle is ahead of the rear of the tree there is no danger that, in ordinary riding, the horseman will get too far back in his saddle. For fast work they claim the built-up seat assists, giving the thighs a chance to carry the weight comfortably forward. I have heard little support for the hanging of the stirrups from the center of the saddle other than that it is the easiest and stoutest way to hang them.

Comfort vs. Misery

In all the controversy about the seats, rigging, hanging of stirrups, etc., it is odd that one hears little argument about the relative comforts of different types of Western saddles. There seems to be scant consideration given to the comfort of the beginning rider and the experienced rider who has ridden only English saddles. For such a horseman, the saddle with stirrups hung in the old-fashioned way, directly under the rider's crotch, is sheer torture for a ride of any length. A saddle without a built-up seat adds to the misery. Saddles with such stirrups and seats have convinced many riders that it is impossible to ride a Western saddle with comfort.

Another cause of misery for the beginner or the person who has started riding a Western saddle later in life is the saddle that is wide through the front part of the seat. Width at this point is also an impediment to getting forward on a horse when necessary. Only an expert saddlemaker can tell how narrow a saddle can be behind the fork and still be strong enough to stand roping; for comfort's sake, it should be as narrow as possible without sacrifice of needed strength. There are at least two saddlemakers who make stout saddles, with built-up padded seats comfortably narrow in front, and with forward-hung stirrups if the buyer asks for them.

The most recent innovation in seats finding some favor among veteran horsemen in the West is the padded, quilted, seat. Some horsemen object to them because they know that the closer the horseman is to the horse the better. However, on the long, slow ride, the quilted, padded seat is a comfort; and the writer knows cutting horse riders who swear by such seats because they lessen the shock of the sudden stops in the arena. Perhaps a half-inch of foam rubber and a thin layer of leather do not separate horse and rider sufficiently to interfere with good riding.

Novel Saddles and Economy Saddles

Ever since Juan de Oñate established the first cattle ranch in the West in 1610, ranchers have been looking for stronger and lighter saddles. Saddlemakers for two centuries have striven to combine lightness with strength. Within the past decade or two, the bullhide-covered, hardwood tree, the unchallenged standard of strength for many years, has been challenged. Aluminum, fiberglass, and some other materials have been used and put on the market with startling claims for strength and lightness. It is too soon to say that they offer a real challenge, for ranchers are not eager to give them a trial. However, the makers of one aluminum tree claim they are willing to stand behind their saddle in any comparison with the standard tree. They also claim that their tree fits the back better than the wooden tree and that it will not warp.

The fiberglass saddles the writer has seen are certainly lightweight. They seem to have a comfortable seat, but they are provided with "widow-maker" stirrups—small wooden stirrups—and are without fenders. The writer would certainly not want his foot to be caught in one of those stirrups if he tumbled off the horse or the horse fell. This danger can be avoided if hoods (or tapaderos) are put on the stirrups. Because fiberglass saddles are light enough for a child to lift onto a horse's back and because they are low priced (less than one-third the price of a conventional Western saddle), they are finding favor as children's saddles.

If the writer were looking for a low-priced light saddle for a beginner, a saddle not necessarily as stout as a roper's saddle, he would consult the proprietor of a good riding stable or guest ranch. Such men always have on hand many light, comfortable saddles. Some of them occasionally use Mexican saddles, but most use saddles manufactured especially for their purposes by reputable American saddleries. There are good saddles made in Mexico, but only the practiced eye can distinguish between the good ones and those that "have teeth" (which will injure a horse's back) and are otherwise undesirable. Sometimes an obliging guest ranch operator who buys his saddles in wholesale lots will let a friend or guest have one at cost. Even if the saddle has had a season or two of use, it is a much better and safer buy than a novice would be likely to get if he shopped around for a cheap saddle at bargain counters.

Stirrups

From the simple iron ring seen in Montana to the oxbow of the Southwest, the variety of stirrup styles in stock saddles is almost infinite. Without entering into controversy on which stirrup is the best, we may make a few generalizations. A stirrup should be large enough, especially from top to bottom, to permit a boot to leave it easily in case of accident. It should be heavy enough to hang down as the boot leaves it. It should not be made of aluminum or other material that will bend and trap the boot if a horse falls on it.

Tapaderos—leather coverings or hoods—serve at least two purposes. They are a necessary protection when riding in heavy brush, and they are a safeguard against a boot's hanging in a stirrup when an accident occurs.

New Inventions

The new role of the horse as plaything and backyard pet has led to an urban horse population explosion, particularly in the Southwest, where riding is a year-round activity. The majority of users of horses in this new role are youngsters. (An aside worth making here is that a record kept one year by the Western Saddle Club of Phoenix, Arizona, showed that more than 80 percent of youngsters participating in its activities were on the honor role in school every month of the year; wise parents are encouraging the horse population explosion.) This juvenile influence is felt in the saddle business and has affected styles in saddles.

Many youngsters do not have the money to buy saddles of the kind the ropers use. Most of them have no need for such saddles. In considerable numbers they have turned to the use of pads, some with stirrups and some without. The pad is a great improvement over bareback riding, for the horse's sake as well as for the sake of the launderers of jeans. A horse continually ridden bareback by a youngster will develop bumps on the spine where the pinbones of the rider habitually press. These little bumps enlarge when a saddle is added to the gear.

Pads

Useful as the pad may be, it is attended by some danger, especially when stirrups are added to it. There is nothing to keep the pad from slipping sideways, and it certainly will slip when the horse turns sharply unless the rider is very skillful. Stirrups provided on pads are the small, light, wooden variety. There are no fenders to keep them from flipping up and catching the foot if the rider slides off on a turn. The remedy for the danger of a slipping pad is to put a breastplate on the horse and attach the pad to it. A cheap and even better safeguard that can be made with a couple of straps and rivets is a Y-shaped strap, the base of the Y can be attached to the bottom of the cinch, and the ends of the arms of the Y can be fastened securely to either side of the pad at the front, a few inches below the horse's backbone. The remedy for the danger of the stirrups is to cut hoods out of old boot tops and fasten a hood (tapadero) on each stirrup to prevent the foot from going through the stirrup farther than the ball. Heavier and larger stirrups than the ones supplied by the manufacturer are also a help.

Saddle Seat

The term *saddle seat* as used in the American Horse Shows Association *Rule Book* applies to a seat identical with that described in this book as the balanced seat, with the exception that the hands are used in a specified fashion as follows: "Both hands shall be used and all reins must be picked up at one time. Bight of rein should be on the off side."

The *Rule Book* gives considerable leeway to the position of the hands. The diagram given for the saddle seat indicates hands held so that there is a straight line from the elbow of the rider to the bit of the horse. The arm from shoulder to elbow drops slightly forward and the knuckles of the hand are almost perpendicular to the ground.

The saddle seat designated by the *Rule Book* is not to be confused with the seat used by the most expert professional riders of three-gaited and five-gaited show horses. The seat of these professionals has one, and only one, purpose: to show off to best advantage the front of their horses. To accomplish this, the saddle is set farther back than it is for any other purpose. The rider's legs are as nearly straight up and down as possible. This position keeps the knees back so they do not obscure the shoulder of the horse. Keeping the legs straight, of course, means that the stirrup leathers are extremely long, and any posting done cannot be high. Some trainers believe that the pounding of a rider's weight on a horse's loins increases his action. Such riders, though they are sufficiently expert to sit a trot properly, bump slightly at each stride of the horse.

Saddling the Horse. *See also* COLTS, *Mounting the Colt*

When saddling a horse with a flat or English saddle, one should be sure the stirrups are run up on the leather and the girth is laid up across the seat of the saddle (not buckled to billets on the off side). Usually the pad for such a saddle is the shape of the saddle and is attached to it by having the billets run through the little straps on either side of the pad. If this is the sort of pad used, the pad may well be put on with the saddle. However, even with this pad, it is not amiss to put the pad on the horse before the saddle is applied.

The pad or blanket under the saddle should be placed several inches farther forward than is normal. Then it can be slid back and will smooth all the hair. The saddle should then be placed on the pad; if the pad has narrow straps through which the billets should go, the billets should be placed through the loops at the ends of these straps. The saddle is put on the horse from the near side, and the horse is always approached quietly. The saddle should be placed on the back so that the front of it almost touches the shoulder blades but not quite. The fault of most beginners is to put the saddle too far to the rear. In this event, the saddle and blanket should not be slid forward on the horse's back, for the hair will be ruffled and irritation possibly caused. The process should be started anew if a mistake has been made.

After the saddle has been put on, the horseman should go around to the off side, attach the girth to the billets after the billets have been placed through the strap to hold the pad in place (if there is such a strap), and pull the right stirrup down on the leathers. He should then return to the near side of the horse and take the girth up moderately. Then he should pull the irons down on the stirrup leather. After leading the horse a few steps, he may tighten the girth a little more.

The girth should ride at least three or four fingers behind the horse's elbow. Put on too close to the elbow and too tight, the girth is very likely to cause a sore. The girth should be tight enough to keep the saddle from turning when one mounts (of course, an inept rider can turn a saddle no matter how tightly it is girthed) but not so tight that one cannot get two or three fingers between the girth and the horse's ribs. Placing two or three fingers between the girth just below the saddle pad and running those fingers down to the bottom of the girth is good insurance that the horse's skin has not been wrinkled when the girth was pulled up.

Putting a Western or stock saddle on a horse is a procedure similar to that of putting on a flat or English saddle. Of course, the stirrups cannot be run up on the leathers, but the off stirrup, as well as the cinch or cinches, can be put over the back of the saddle before the saddle is placed on the horse's back. The placing of the saddle blanket under a Western saddle is very important. If the saddle does not have excellent lining, several saddle blankets are advisable. The saddle blankets should be put on so that the front of them is well forward on the horse's withers. When the horse is finally saddled, more blanket should show in front of the saddle than behind it. If more of the blanket is behind the saddle, the rider will soon lose his blanket. The Western saddle should be placed on the horse's back (from the near side) carefully and quietly, not swung onto it so that stirrups and cinches bang the off foreleg or the belly. If the saddle is full-rigged (provided with both front and rear cinches), one should be sure that the spacer strap (a narrow strap that rides at the bottom of the cinches and keeps them a proper distance apart) is buckled and in good repair. The front cinch should be fastened first, then the hind cinch. This is just as important as the reverse order when unsaddling (that is, hind cinch to be unfastened before the front cinch).

For discussion of cinches, spacer straps, and other matters pertaining to the Western saddle, *see* SADDLES.

While the correct side from which to saddle (and bridle) a horse is the near side, *every horse should be accustomed to having a saddle put on him from the off side,* just as he should be accustomed to being mounted from either side. A horse not so trained may become so "one-sided" that he will even be nervous and possibly make trouble when the farrier works on the animal's off side.

Safety. *See* ACCIDENTS and COURTESY

Saliva Test

A saliva test is done on a race horse to determine whether or not he has been given a sedative or a stimulant prior to a race. Such "doping" is, of course, forbidden by law.

Salt

Horses, like other animals, should have free access to salt at all times. There is on the market a little device that holds a small block of salt and can be nailed on the wall. With such a device, a horse can lick the salt block from the bottom. It has been the writer's experience that this is not satisfactory because, first, it is not natural for a horse to lick upward to get his supply of salt, and second, the blocks that fit into these contrivances are so hard that a horse does not get sufficient salt by licking them. The ordinary salt blocks that are used by stockmen weigh about 60 pounds and can be placed in paddock, corral, or stall for a horse to lick at will. These are fairly satisfactory. Adding loose salt to the feed is rather a nuisance, and one cannot always gauge the amount of salt necessary. Furthermore, most of the commercial horse feeds contain salt so that any salt added to them will probably overdo the salt intake of a horse. Mineralized salt blocks are useful. Some of them are good because they are not quite as hard as the plain salt block.

A horse who has been deprived of salt for a long time should not be given free access to loose salt, for he may get too much and suffer a malady called "blind staggers," similar to fainting spells or extreme vertigo in human beings.

Obviously, a horse at hard work during warm weather will need more salt than other horses. For him, a little box containing loose salt located near his grain manger will be very helpful, for he will not get enough salt by licking a hard, compressed block.

Sand Crack

Sand crack is a term for a perpendicular crack in the quarter (of the hoof) which starts at the coronet and runs downward. A sand crack is usually the result of an injury to the coronet. It may or may not be infected. If the injury to the coronet was severe, the danger of a permanently deformed hoof is great. A small sand crack may yield to the treatment of a competent farrier. However, if the horse has any value and the injury to the coronet was severe, a veterinarian should be called.

Sandshifter

Sandshifter is an old-fashioned slang term for a pacer, that is, a harness race horse.

Sandwich Case. *See* SADDLEBAGS

Saumur

Saumur is a cavalry school that is to France what Fort Riley (cavalry school) once was to this country. When horses were used by our cavalry, gifted officers were now and then sent to Saumur to study.

Scalds

Burns or "galls" caused by friction of saddle or other gear can become chronic and serious. Sometimes the saddle gall, if the offending saddle can be replaced by one that fits the horse better, can be cured without giving the horse complete rest. The favorite remedy for many, many years was a proprietary salve called Bickmore's Gall Cure. This medicine was put on the market years ago as a healing ointment for collar sores on workhorses, and it carried the slogan, "Work the horse," explaining that the medicine worked best if the horse continued in his ordinary work while the ointment was applied. Of course, all such scalds or burns must be kept clean and a fresh application of the ointment made each day.

Schooling

The word *schooling* is used more frequently by trainers of jumpers than by other horsemen. By it they mean putting a horse over jumps to improve his education. However, the term can also be legitimately used by other horsemen for the process of putting a horse through any movement one is trying to teach him. The oldest horseman's term of this variety is *dress*. In very old books on riding, the word *dress* is used to mean "train" or "school." That is where we get the word *dressage,* which originally meant training. Today we sometimes forget that what we ask the dressage horse to do is merely what we had him do in order to train him to be handy and responsive. So dressage work is actually training or schooling (*see* DRESSAGE).

Score

1. In team roping, the score is the distance from the barrier in front of the horse to the line the steer must cross before the barrier is released. In calf roping, the score *may* be the same as in team roping; however, in some rodeos the horse's barrier is released the instant the calf is released. In such events *score* means getting to the calf, putting the roper in proper position for the throw.

2. In harness racing, the word *score* refers to the process of warming up a trotter or pacer for a race. This is done by trotting or pacing him a short

distance on the track, in a clockwise direction (the harness race is run in a counterclockwise direction). A harness horse may be scored many times before his race, and the driver may let the horse work a little faster at each succeeding score.

Scoring. *See* SCORE (2)

Scotch

The word *scotch* indicates a fault in performance of a rope horse caused by cruel, unnecessary use of reins in stopping the horse. As a result of this, the rope horse anticipates the pain and stops before he is signaled to do so.

Scouring

The word *scouring* means diarrhea. Its causes are almost infinite, but it is always a sign that some condition of the horse needs immediate attention. Very frequently, scouring is caused by a change in feed, especially a change from old hay to newly cured hay. The feeding of hay that is newly cured and improperly cured can cause diarrhea, and the horse owner is fortunate if that is the only ill result of feeding such hay. Some horses scour when excited, and no remedy is needed but the removal of the cause of excitement. The feeding of bran (*see* FEED) is good insurance against scouring, contrary to the opinion of many horsemen. Bran, fed dry every day, in amounts not to exceed one two-pound coffee-canful twice a day with other feed is not extremely laxative, and it does have a soothing effect on the alimentary canal. A horse that is scouring violently should be kept on dry hay until the advice of a veterinarian can be obtained. Of course, the animal should have access to water at all times, and he should be kept quiet until professional attention is given to him.

Scratch (to start from)

The term *to start from scratch* means to race without handicaps. This phrase goes back to Colonial history, when a race was started from a line scratched on the dirt with a stick.

Scratch (verb)

To scratch a horse in a race is to withdraw him from a race for which he has been entered.

Scratches

The word *scratches* refers to a condition of the back part of a horse's pastern just above the heel. It more frequently occurs on the forefeet than on the hind ones. It is somewhat similar to chapped hands or chapped skin on a human being, but much more severe and, as far as we can tell, more painful. The condition called "scratches" occurs most frequently during a time of year when roads or trails are muddy. The horse develops scabs and sores on the back part of his pastern just above the heel, and they become so painful that he will limp. The first thing to do is clean the affected part very carefully and gently. Compresses of warm water to which a little Epsom salts has been added will usually soften up the encrusted dirt. After the scratches have been cleaned thoroughly, they should be dried and a salve such as zinc oxide ointment applied. This treatment, with the possible exception of the application of wet compresses, which may not be necessary more than once, should be given every day. A horse with a bad case of scratches should not be worked and should be kept as quiet as possible in a clean, dry stall until the affected part heals. Use will prevent healing and increase the cracks in the skin so that the condition may become chronic and very severe.

Screw

Screw is an old slang term for a very cheap hack horse in a rental string.

John Galsworthy (an excellent horseman as well as novelist and dramatist) in the *Forsyte Saga* has George Forsyte refer to his three race horses as "screws" when on his deathbed he is dictating his will to his less jaunty and more legally "correct" cousin, Soames.

"Make me a codicil. . . . My three screws to young Val Dartie, because he's the only Forsyte that knows a horse from a donkey. . . . What have you said?"
Soames read: "I hereby leave my three race-horses to my kinsman, Valerius Dartie, of Wansdon, Sussex, because he has special knowledge of horses."

Scurry

Scurry is a kind of jumping contest seen rarely today. It was a contest of time. Each horse's performance was timed, and a fault was discounted as a second or a specified number of seconds.

Seat. *See also* BALANCED SEAT, BASIC SEAT, FORWARD SEAT, SADDLE SEAT, CHARRO, *and* RIDING

Much to-do is made about the distinction between Western and Eastern or English seat, but it is a distinction without a difference. Competent Western riders, when working, ride the balanced seat, with weight well forward most of the time. On the long trail, they sit at ease in the basic seat. On parade, they ride the charro seat, which is practically identical with the seat used in the show-ring by professional riders of gaited horses. This last-named seat is part of the *à la brida* riding of the ancient Moors (*see* À LA BRIDA).

The rodeo bronc rider's seat is the extreme example of the balanced seat. His weight is always over the center of the balance of his mount, and his torso is perfectly aligned with the line of thrust. The instant either condition alters in the slightest degree, horse and rider cease to be moving in unison, and the contestant ends his ride, usually by a sky dive followed by a rapid descent. (As long as the bronc rider's torso is over the center of balance and his body is aligned with the line of thrust, he can move his legs forward and back to spur in front of and behind the cinch, as the rules require.)

All the above-mentioned seats are common to both Eastern and Western riding. The extreme forward seat and the "monkey seat" of the jockey are impractical if not impossible on a Western saddle.

Second Horseman

The term *second horseman* designates a groom who, in the middle of the day, brings a fresh horse for his master to ride on the continuation of a hunt.

Secretary

The hunt secretary is a very important member of the hunt. It is his function to keep all books and be useful in many other ways.

Seedy Toe

The term *seedy toe* applies to a separation of the laminae of the hoof. The layers of the hoof separate, and a rather mealy substance forms between them. This condition usually occurs in one area of the hoof. If the area is not too large, the hoof can be pared so that it does not press on the shoe, and the horse can be shod with a leather pad under which his hoof is packed with tar and oakum. There are various kinds and many causes of separation of the layers of the foot. These separations are most common in the dry, arid regions of the Southwest. When the condition is severe and covers much of the foot, the only way to save the horse is to employ the services of a competent veterinarian. Sometimes even the best veterinarian cannot make the horse entirely serviceable after he has had trouble with separation of the layers of the hoof.

Selecting a Horse. *See* BUYING A HORSE

Serape

The modern serape serves no practical purpose. It is worn as a symbol of its historical importance to horsemen of the part of this continent first invaded by mounted Europeans.

In the days of the great haciendas of Mexico and California, when wheeled vehicles were a rarity, the serape, or *manca,* as it was then also called, was as universally worn as the sombrero. It was 2½ meters long and 1½ meters wide, made of heavy, tightly woven wool with rounded edges and a hole with collar of velvet or corduroy in the center. Such a garment protected man and part of his mount from rain and dust storms.

With the advent of roads and wheeled vehicles, riding became a matter of elegance rather than practical necessity, and the serape evolved into a finely woven circular cape. The collar was narrow, often of fine, soft leather and fastened with a silver ornament. This serape, also called a *ruana,* was superseded by a more elaborate rectangular serape with gold or silver fringes that brushed the stirrups when worn extended. It was ordinarily neatly rolled and tied behind the saddle with fringes all on the near side so that the off spur would not become entangled during dismounting. These serapes were often of the same colors as the saddle blanket and were highly decorative. They were the peak of the evolution of the serape. Today, though beautifully woven and gaily colored, the serape is small, a mere token of convention, worn neatly rolled in a compact bundle behind the charro's saddle. To display such a serape unfolded or "extended" is a great breach of etiquette.

Serpentine

The serpentine is an exercise used in some riding halls. In the serpentine the rider goes from one end of the hall to the other making half-turn after half-turn. When this is done at a canter or gallop, a horse should change leads at each turn. It can be performed at any gait. If it is performed so that the half-turns are of uniform size, it may be an interesting exercise and beneficial practice for a learning rider. In the beginning, standards can be set alternately so that the rider is forced to make a complete half-turn as he negotiates the posts. An accomplished rider who can easily execute flying change of lead and the rollback (*see* FLYING CHANGE and ROLLBACK) can make a very pretty exercise of the serpentine, and he can add to its charm by performing a rollback at either end of the hall.

Servants

In hunting parlance, the whips and the professional huntsman are sometimes alluded to as the "hunt servants."

Set Tail

The uninformed sometimes speak of the "broken tail" of gaited horses. Even some horsemen who should know better refer to setting the tail as "breaking the tail." Of course, there is no breaking of the tail in this hideous operation. It is a process of cutting the two large muscles that are used to pull the tail downward. They are cut very close to the horse's body.

Then the tail is held upward (usually by ropes that go through pulleys and are attached to weights) until the wound has healed and the muscles have lengthened. Then the tail is put into a contraption made of iron covered with wool. This is attached to a surcingle by a back strap, side straps, and straps between the horse's legs and to the belly of the surcingle. In this affair the tail assumes the waterfall form seen on five-gaited and three-gaited show horses. The waterfall in recent years has been forced to run uphill; that is, the tail, instead of being held up from the body, is actually held forward for a few inches and then bent sharply downward.

Of course, with the modern methods of anesthesia, the operation itself can be performed with little pain to the horse, but no one in his right mind can maintain that forcing the tail into the position it finally assumes in the show-ring can be done without discomfort. With use of modern antibiotics, much of the disfigurement that formerly resulted from infections and crude surgery in cutting the tail is overcome. However, the operation frequently so affects the circulation of the tail that it is difficult to grow hair on it. For this reason wigs are frequently used on gaited horses and on Walking Horses.

Sew a Button

In the game of "sew a button," contestants line up, race to a distant line where assistants are waiting to sew a button on the sleeve of each contestant, then return to the starting line. Of course, the first contestant to return with a button sewed on his sleeve is the winner.

Shadbelly

The shadbelly is a very dressy kind of hunting coat having some similarity to a cutaway. Usually it is worn with a top hat.

Shetland Pony. *See also* AMERICAN SHETLAND PONY CLUB

The Shetland pony is a native of the Shetland Islands, of which there are about 120. They lie about 200 miles north of Scotland and within 350 miles of the Arctic Circle. Five or six of them are habitable the year round. There is not sufficient documentary proof to establish facts about the origin of the ponies. However, the late Henry S. Vaughan, an eminent authority on breeds of livestock, asserts the probability that the Shetland represents a distinct species of the equine race which has always been small. He also speculates that the "privations endured by the breed have kept it quite small and have also impressed upon it the good constitution, strength and hardiness which are characteristic."

Since December 1, 1927, no Shetlands over 42 inches tall have been eligible to registry in the American Shetland Stud Book. In England, the

natural type of the breed has been favored. It has a rather drafty conformation and action that is not high. Americans prefer another kind of
Shetland and by selection have achieved it. It resembles a heavy-harness
type of horse or the Hackney pony type with extreme action and style. The
American ponies also show much more refinement of head than do
Shetland ponies elsewhere. The natural disposition of the Shetland is
uniformly docile and pleasant. The notion among laymen that Shetlands
are stubborn and tricky has probably arisen from the fact that many Shetlands are not trained by adult trainers. Of course, any animal improperly
educated will show all kinds of disagreeable characteristics. Under proper
guidance, however, an intelligent child can train the Shetland pony to be
an ideal mount.

Shire

The most direct modern descendant of the Great Horse is the Shire horse
(*see* AMERICAN SHIRE HORSE ASSOCIATION). The Flemish Great Horse is
generally considered the foundation of most modern draft breeds and is
assumed to be the source of the size of the horses used by the Crusaders
and other men who fought in armor on horseback. However, at least one
reliable researcher insists that the Great Horse existed in England during
the time of the Roman invasion (*see* GREAT HORSE).

The Shire resembles the Clydesdale somewhat (see CLYDESDALE), but
the Shire maintains slightly bigger size than the Clydesdale and is coarser
in head and bone. He has more feather (hair on the legs) and less
muscling and crest of neck. The Shire's action is not as high or springy as
that of the Clydesdale. However, when the draft horse was in his heyday in
this country, Shires demonstrated a superior ability to increase draft qualities in the horses of any farming community in the United States. The
great size and substance, the rugged build, power, strong back and coup-
lings, good middle, superior coat, good topline, excellent position of legs,
and straight, powerful action (though not high and showy) found favor
among draft horse breeders in this country.

There is an old British saying, "Plenty of bone and lots of feather; top
may come, but bottom never." Certainly, the Shire horse had plenty of bone
(though some American breeders thought it a little coarse and the pasterns
a little short and steep), and the beautiful feather on the Shire horse was
not equaled by that of any other breed. His topline was also unexcelled by
any other breed.

Shoe Boil

A shoe boil, also called a capped elbow, appears at first as a rather soft and
sometimes pendulous swelling at the horse's elbow. It is caused by a bruise
from the inside heel of the forefoot when the horse lies down in a stall that

has insufficient bedding or a very rough floor. Usually the shoe boil becomes hard and extremely sore. A veterinarian should be summoned if the horse has any value at all. One treatment consists of waiting until the boil comes to a head and then opening it (after proper sterilization of the knife and the area to be opened). The tender part should not be squeezed or irritated, and it has to be irrigated daily with a rubber ear syringe or similar device with an antiseptic solution. The opening should not be allowed to close until all drainage has stopped. Improper treatment or failure to prevent further bruising may result in a permanent and incurable malady.

One method for preventing further bruising is the use of a shoe boil boot or, as it is called in England, a sausage boot. This is simply a roll of heavy padding covered with leather and buckled around the horse's pastern. If the horseman is clever with his hands, he may be able to make a similar kind of boot from a portion of a small inner tube filled with sand. Another way to prevent bruising, popular in England, is to use a "straw bandage." This is simply the bandaging of enough straw around the cannon bone so that the heel of the shoe cannot press against the horse's elbow.

Shoe Boil Boot. *See* SHOE BOIL

Shoeing

For several decades after the automobile replaced the horse on city streets it was difficult to find a farrier (a horseshoer) of any competence. However, in recent years farrier schools have sprung up, especially in the Southwest, which are doing excellent jobs in training horseshoers. These young shoers help relieve the load of the few competent, experienced older shoers so that today it is possible for the owner of a good horse to locate a good farrier with mobile equipment who will come to his stable and do good work.

There are a few matters that every owner should have in mind when he is having a horse shod. First, a farrier must be able to keep the horse's foot level. That is, the foot must be level when viewed from front or rear. Second, the angle of the foot when viewed from the side should be the same as the angle of the pastern. The horse who is shod with an extremely long toe and low heel puts undue strain on the tendons of the leg. If his heels are too high, he will not put pressure on his frog, which is often called a horse's second heart because frog pressure, as a horse puts weight on a foot, aids in the circulation of blood in the foot. No good farrier will pare away the frog of a horse's foot or the bar of the foot (see illustration).

Shoes on a horse—shoes of any kind—are a necessary evil. The horse who is used very little and only on soft ground can usually go barefoot. It is wise to let a young animal go without shoes as long as possible—that is,

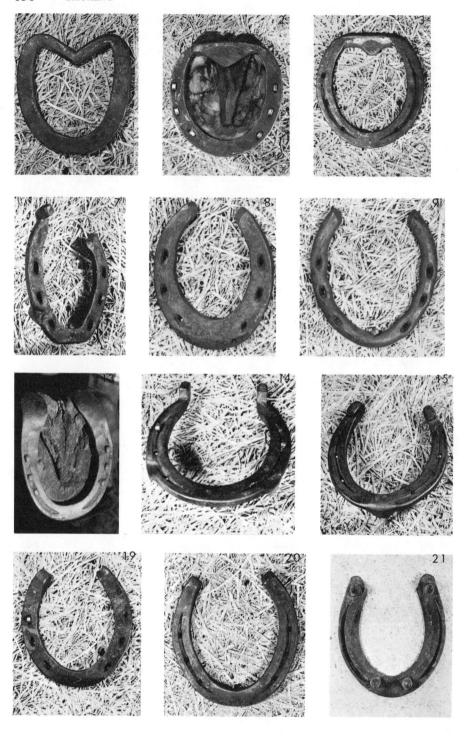

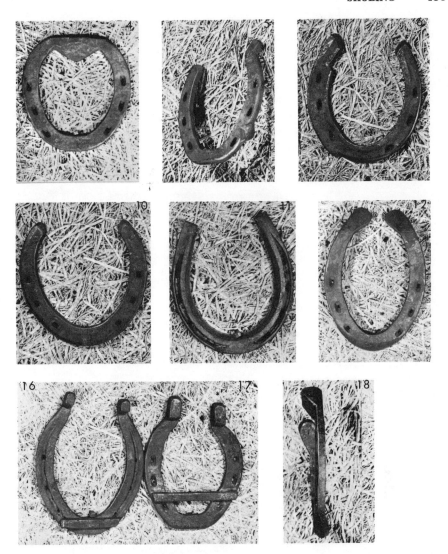

Shoes. 1, 2. Bar shoes applied to increase frog pressure; 3, 4. bar shoes for use on quarter cracks or for other pathological purposes; 5. square toe and outside trailer behind to correct lateral twist of hind action; 6. front lateral extension to correct interfering; 7. squared toe, outside trailer with heel calk to correct twisting action ("lateral twist") of hind foot; 8. 18-ounce toe weight with rolled toe to increase front action; 9. half-round 6-ounce trotting horse front shoe for speed; 10. hand-made (turned) light plate for saddlers; 11. machine-made light plate for saddlers; 12. front shoe with spoon heels to prevent over-reaching; 13. hind shoe with spoon heels used on reining horses in horse shows to facilitate execution of long sliding stop (also used on some very rocky ranges to protect heels when working cattle); 14. heel calks and quarter clips (calks give traction); 15. toe clips and blocked heels (latter for elevation of action and for traction); 16. toe grab—traction for draft horse; 17. hind shoe Memphis bar and blocked heels to elevate hind action or induce lateral gait; 18. side view of 19; 19, 20. front shoes with swelled heels and rocker toe—pathological (ringbone, laminitis, navicular disease, strained ligaments, etc.); 21. shoe with replaceable screw-in calks, still in use in wintertime on work stock in the Northwest and sold in general stores in farming and ranching areas.

until he is put to sufficient use to make his feet tender. This does not mean that no attention should be given to his feet, for the colt's feet from the time he is foaled should be watched carefully to see that both the level and the angle are proper. (Often, especially if a youngster is running on rocky ground, one side of the hoof will break off and the level of the hoof will be so destroyed that a farrier must be called to level the foot, or even to put a very light plate on the foot until it grows sufficiently to be properly leveled.) A foal's feet should be handled from the time he is dropped, so that when it comes time to have a farrier attend to them the farrier can give all his attention to his job without having to take time to be a horse-breaker.

If the owner of a horse happens to be so situated that he cannot locate a good farrier, he will do well to have his horse shod, at least for the first time he is using a new farrier, under the supervision of a veterinarian. All good colleges of veterinary medicine today give excellent instruction in the anatomy and care of the feet and the legs, and any modern veterinarian can supervise and instruct a farrier.

Shoes

The variety of horseshoes in use today is almost infinite. It ranges from the racing plate (see PLATES) to the heavy "Scotch bottom" shoe used in shows on draft horses weighing a ton or more. (The Scotch bottom shoe is so beveled on the outside that the angle of the hoof is continued downward from hoof to ground.)

For most ordinary purposes, a steel plate is used. A plate is a shoe without calks (or calkings) but thick enough to withstand ordinary wear for at least a month to six weeks. In some instances, to make the plates wear longer on a horse who is used excessively, a farrier will fuse a spot of borium (a metal that is extremely hard and long wearing) on the toe of each shoe and sometimes on the heel of each shoe. Such spotting of borium may be done on shoes for horses who are to be ridden in a parade, for the borium helps prevent slipping on the pavement. The best shoe for this, however, is the rubber pad.

Some rubber pads are a little thicker than a shoe and entirely cover the back part of a horse's foot, the shoe being cut off behind the last nails to accommodate the rubber pad. Rubber pads are also used to increase frog pressure on horses suffering from contracted heels.

For wintertime when horses are ridden on icy roads, sharp calks are put on shoes. There used to be shoes manufactured that were provided with threaded holes at toes and heels into which sharp calks could be screwed. These calks could be replaced when they became worn. Ordinarily, it is inadvisable to use calks on a horse for any purpose other than to prevent slipping.

In the show-ring a variety of shoes promotes the kind of action desired for each specific kind of class. The horses in whom high action is desired are usually shod with very heavy shoes and long feet. These shoes are frequently, especially in front, held on by steel bands brazed to each side of the shoe and passed over the hoof. Where the bands pass over the hoof, turnbuckles are provided to keep the bands tight.

Shoeing of harness race horses is an art in itself, for the shoer in collaboration with the driver enables the horse to obtain more speed than Mother Nature originally endowed him with.

The variety of shoes used for pathological purposes is great. Any pathological shoeing should be done by a well-trained farrier under the supervision of a veterinarian. A word of caution is in order in any discussion of shoes or shoeing. It is implicit in an old saying, "The amateur often expects the farrier to do what should be done from the top of the saddle." This means that much of the improvement in action or correction of action is the province of the trainer and cannot be done by the farrier alone.

Shoulder

The shoulder of a horse is a very important point in judging conformation. What is usually referred to when the shoulder is spoken of as being sloping or being too heavy (too loaded) is the part of the horse from the foremost section of the body just below the neck to the withers. This should be as sloping as possible. A steep shoulder means more jar to the rider and more jar on the horse's feet. In a jumper it means more probability of a fall. A shoulder that is too meaty is said to be too heavily loaded. The shoulder should be lean and sinewy in appearance. When the shoulder is properly sloping, the withers come well into the back, and a surcingle on the horse, because the withers are well back, will come under the horse's belly several inches behind his elbow. On the steep-shouldered horse the surcingle will come close to the elbows. For the hunting field and many other areas the horse should not be too thick through the shoulders, but he should be deep from top to bottom; that is, the distance from withers to the bottom of his rib cage should be relatively great. It is this measurement that gives the large "heart girth" that is so desirable in any horse.

Shoulder-in

Shoulder-in is a very special one of the general class of movements loosely called two-tracking (see TWO-TRACK). The shoulder-in movement can be done on any reasonably flat area, but if done in an arena or school, the hind feet of the horse make a track close to and parallel with the wall or rail, and the forefeet make a track one foot (or slightly more) farther away from the rail or wall. As he makes these two tracks, the horse bends his spine from poll to tail in an arc directed away from the rail or wall. The proper degree of the arc is that of a circle with a radius equal to the length of the horse (usually slightly under 10 feet).

Showing

Many if not most urban and suburban youngsters owning horses are passionately concerned with showing them. Such youngsters cannot seem to imagine why anyone owning a good horse would have any object in mind other than showing that horse.

Under proper guidance a young horseman (more often, young horsewoman) can survive this phase of growth with relatively little trauma. If he can direct his energies toward small local shows, confining his competition to classes limited to animals similar to his own in natural endowments and training, he and his family may enjoy a few years of participation in showing. However, failure to realize that many show classes are competitions between animals costing thousands of dollars, and on whom more thousands have been spent in professional training, may result in heartbreaking competition by young amateurs and bitter regret for money "thrown away" by indulgent parents.

"Horse-show fever is a disease for which there is no cure," said a wise old horseman. Enjoyment of showing horses and enjoyment of riding (*see* RIDING and PLEASURE HORSE) for its own sake, the pleasure of moving with a versatile and powerful animal as dancing or skating partners move together, are not mutually exclusive. Yet when a professional retires from the show-horse world or turns from it to another vocation, he may talk fondly of bygone equestrian experiences, but he does not ride. He may have wedded his employer's daughter and become owner of a fine stable, but he hires another to do the riding.

The point is that showing horses and enjoying them, apart from the glory they bring us as owners, are two different things. A question is often raised whether genuine affection for a horse would preclude the possibility of making him suffer to bring satisfaction to his owner. (*See* RAPPING POLE, SET TAIL, and TENNESSEE WALKING HORSE.)

Shows. *See* HORSE SHOWS and SHOWING

Shying. *See* VICES

Sidebones

A sidebone is an ossified (turned to bone) lateral cartilage on the side of a horse's foot just above the coronet. Veterinary authorities, though they point to concussion and bad shoeing as possible contributing causes, name heredity as the most important cause of sidebones. They strongly advise against breeding animals afflicted with sidebones.

To diagnose a sidebone in any but advanced stages is not easy for the layman. He must familiarize himself with the feel of a normal lateral cartilage and compare the suspected one with normal ones on the same animal. Whether the sidebone has reached the stage of causing lameness or not, a horse must be pronounced unsound by a veterinarian who examines him and definitely establishes the existence of sidebones. While the layman, with his respect for gadgets beyond his understanding, assumes the x-ray to be the sure means of diagnosis, the diagnosis of sidebones is not so simple, according to veterinary authority, though the x-ray is a valuable adjunct in a difficult diagnosis.

Although there is no cure for sidebones, in some cases the horse may be enabled to do light work without pain if proper pathological shoeing is done. We repeat, this is not always the case.

Side Gallop

What is called a side gallop is a gallop done on two tracks (*see* TWO-TRACK). It differs from the lateral pass and other two-track movements in that the outside forefoot does not pass in front of the inside foot. The horse must be leading with the inside forefoot. Obviously the outside forefoot cannot cross over in front of the leading foot.

The side gallop is sometimes used to slow down a jumper when he attempts to rush a jump. It is also occasionally employed to cure the tendency to "bolt" or run away. However, great caution is called for because it is essential for any horse to gallop straight and to hold a lead as long as the rider desires. Use of the side gallop, especially on a horse who is not responsive to the leg aid, is quite likely to result in the habit of twisting from side to side and changing lead with every twist. The horse who will not hold a lead is even more objectionable than the one who will not change leads properly.

Sidepass. *See also* PAS DE CÔTÉ

The maneuver here called the *sidepass* has gone by other names, notably *side step*—used to include more movements than the sidepass. In no other part of the new method made popular by inclusion of Western classes in horse shows (starting about 1925–1930) is its borrowing from dressage as obvious as in insistence on the "sidepass." Here we see the meeting of East and West, as we do less spectacularly in the use of the plow rein and the insistence upon correct change of leads, things unheard of in the West until the second quarter of this century.

The sidepass is certainly the minimum of dressage essentials that any well-trained Western horse should know. The horse who can perform it is responsive to leg aids and has at least a fair mouth. The rider who can perform it must know more than how to yell "giddyap" and flail with his heels.

Here is the way I have found best to teach the sidepass.

Teaching the Sidepass

Contrary to the practice of some proponents of the new method, start work dismounted. The horse may be ignorant of the meaning of pressure against his side by heel or spur, or he may have associated a certain very definite response to it quite different from the response needed in the sidepass. Therefore, have him face a wall or fence, close enough to it so he cannot move forward. Standing at his left shoulder, hold both reins in your left hand a few inches from the bit. Place your right hand on the horse's side behind the cinch (front cinch if the saddle is full-rigged) just below the saddle. Push with your right hand until the horse moves sideways a few steps; at the same time use your left hand on the reins close to the bit to keep him at right angles to the wall or fence. Do not ask for more than a step or two the first try. Repeat the process a few times while standing at the horse's left shoulder. Then go to his other side, reverse hands, and move him in the opposite direction. Do this several times a day for a few days. Gradually, just the tip of your finger or thumb will be sufficient to get the horse to sidepass.

If you are a perfectionist, you may (by forcing the horse slightly forward) get him to cross over behind exactly as he does in front. That is, if his forefoot near you crosses in front of the one on the opposite side, the hind foot on your side should also cross in front of the other hind foot. However, the more casual rider will merely teach the horse to move away from the pressure of finger or thumb and move sideways without changing his angle to the fence or wall.

Gradually, you can move the pressure of thumb or finger to the spot on the horse's side where your heel will touch him when you are mounted. The finger or thumb tip can be replaced by a dull spur held in your hand (a substitution that may have to be made very early if the horse is sluggish).

As soon as the horse learns to respond to finger or spur pressure on his side by moving as you want him to, mount him and ride to the place at fence or wall where you have taught him. Place him at right angles to the fence exactly as you did the first time you tried to push him sideways. With your left hand use the rein lightly to neck-rein the horse to the right. In your right hand hold the rein out at least a foot to the right of the horse and at the level of your knee. Use a very light plow-rein pull on it so that the neck rein will not pull his nose to the left. At the same time you use the reins, or a split second before you put pressure on them, use your left heel or blunt spur just as you had been using your finger or spur when dismounted. As soon as the horse responds by taking a step or two to the right, dismount and caress him to let him know he has done well.

Difficulty at this point may come from one or more of several causes, but the most usual one is either use of the wrong bit or a nervous, hasty rider. Be sure that your horse is calm and that you are calm in the saddle before you ask for the first mounted sidepass. If the horse violently tosses his head even though your hands are steady and your right hand stays well down, the bit may be the trouble. If you are using a curb or Pelham (*see* BITS), try a snaffle or put the reins in the top rings if your Pelham has four rings. If you are already using such a rig, try using two sets of reins, one through the martingale (*see* MARTINGALE) and one free, using some pressure on each set of reins—just enough on the one through the martingale to give a downward pull when the horse tosses his head up. Sometimes two sets of reins on a four-ring Pelham will work if the reins attached to the bottom rings are just tight enough to give pressure only when the horse tosses his head. Use your wrists, not your whole lower arm, to manipulate the reins. Keep wrists bent so that knuckles are toward the horse. Your hands, generally speaking, should follow the horse's mouth, not jerk it.

As is obvious, your heel keeps the horse's hindquarters moving to the side and your hand moves his forequarters. It is up to you to see that he maintains a right angle with the fence as he sidepasses. You will learn to anticipate the horse so that your hands increase or decrease pressure of the right kind *as* it is needed, not after it is needed. Likewise, your leg aid (heel pressure at first) will become skillful. Gradually, the mere increase of the pressure of the calf of your leg will move the horse's hindquarters. This is the chief value of the sidepass.

When you have perfected the sidepass, two-tracking (moving the horse at walk or trot on a line diagonal to the direction the horse is facing), offsetting (making a quarter-turn with the forequarters with practically no movement of the hindquarters), complete turn on the forequarters, complete turn on the hindquarters, and other stunts can be readily learned. Furthermore, you and your horse will be moving together so that you can move a part of your horse as readily and "unconsciously" as you move your own feet in a dance movement that you do well. In fact, a good horseman and his mount move together much as do a couple of excellent ballroom dancers.

Side Step. *See* SIDEPASS

Side-wheeler

Side-wheeler is a slang term for pacer.

Signals

Usually the word *signal* is used synonymously with *aid*. However, it may also indicate such communicative movements (cues) of the rider as the firm touch on the middle of the top of the crest which is the conventional signal for a trot on a gaited horse. Such a movement can hardly be considered one of the aids (*see* AIDS).

Silks

Silks are the gaily colored blouses worn by jockeys and drivers of harness race horses. They indicate the stables to which the horses belong, each stable having its own distinctive colors.

Single-foot

Single-foot is an obsolete term for *rack*.

Because of the extremely long feet of contemporary gaited show horses (7 to 7½ inches) and the artificial action they induce, some horsemen maintain that the single-foot is a gait much slower and lower in action than the rack (*see* RACK).

Sire

Sire is used instead of *father* in speaking of a horse's parentage. Sires worth speaking of all have one quality in common—prepotency (*see* PREPOTENCY).

Sit-fast

Sit-fast is a layman's term for an injury to the horse's back caused by an ill-fitting saddle and allowed to become a chronic sore. Surgery and subsequent rest may restore the animal to near-normal condition if the surgery does not result in thick scar tissue.

Size (of horses)

Because the show-ring sets the standard for price outside the racetrack, a big horse will bring a higher price than a small one of equal quality.

Though a 13-hand Welsh pony, Little Squire, and a 15-hand American Saddle Horse, Olympic Don (to name but two great stars), are among the most famous jumpers America has produced, size is a very important factor in the price of hunters, and especially hunter prospects.

This emphasis on size not infrequently results in unsuitable mounting of children and small riders. The child or very short rider on the very large mount cannot use leg or heel aids in any manner that is meaningful to the horse. Furthermore, the long stride of a large mount is, to say the least, not comfortable for a child or short person.

Skewbald

In America the terms *paint* and *pinto* (the second, a Spanish word for the first) are used to designate the colored horses called *skewbald* or *piebald* by the British. A Paint or Pinto may be any combination of colors, but a skewbald is a horse of white and any other color except black; a piebald is a horse whose colors are black and white (*see* COLOR PATTERNS).

Skinner

1. In horse traders' parlance, a "skinner" is an animal worth only what he will bring for conversion into dog food. Obviously, the term comes from the days when such an animal was valuable only for what his hide would bring.

2. In the days of freight wagons pulled by multiple hitches of mules or horses, the driver was called a "skinner."

Sleeping Sickness

"Sleeping sickness," equine encephalomyelitis, until 1971 occurred in only two varieties in the United States: "Eastern" and "Western." Since the late 1940s effective preventive vaccination for each kind has been available. All knowledgeable horsemen have had their animals properly vaccinated with the appropriate vaccine against the disease annually, and it has ceased to be the scourge it was for a few years.

In 1969 a new form of the disease, Venezuelan encephalomyelitis, started moving northward. In 1970 it killed over 6,000 horses in Mexico. By April of 1971 it had traveled to within 250 miles of Texas. It is over 80 percent fatal. Immunization is now available, and every horse in the Southwest should be immunized. With the modern mobility of show and race animals, the chances are considerable that the disease will soon spread to other parts of the country unless a nationwide program of immunization is instituted.

Sliding Stop. *See also* STOPPING

One of the hallmarks of the Western horse, whether he is displayed in New York or New Mexico, is the sliding stop. There is probably no other movement required of him in which he gets more needless abuse, and in which the rider displays more ignorance. Most roping pictures show a horse tossing his head because of pain or straining against a tie-down. The picture of Monte Foreman in this book shows a perfect sliding stop. The horse's mouth is relaxed; his head shows no reaction to pain; *and how he is stopping!*

The perfect sliding stop, Monte Foreman up. Note position of horse's head and his closed, relaxed mouth indicating light hand on rein. Note also the absence of tie-down, the position of rider, and his use of leg aid.

The horse who is brought to a sliding stop properly will stop a split second faster than the one who is yanked to a standstill. He will jerk a calf down just as hard, and his rider will be better able to dismount for calf tying than if the horse has been yanked.

To teach the sliding stop, never stop a horse twice in the same spot. The stopping should be at the signal of the rider, not because a certain place has been reached. This admonition, of course, is contrary to the teaching of other maneuvers; for with the sidepass, the rollback, and the inside roll, the beginning horse is helped by being asked for the maneuver at the same spot for the first few days. It helps him realize what is wanted. However, the sliding stop must be performed from a full gallop; if the horse antici- pates it, he will shorten stride or slow down.

Teaching the Sliding Stop

Start teaching the stop by riding the horse around the arena or the chosen open area at a full gallop but not at extreme speed. To execute the stop, squeeze with both your legs enough to draw his hindquarters up under him. At the same time slightly increase your rein pressure *as* his head comes up in the normal head movement in the gallop. The next time his head comes up normally, increase the pull on the reins; at the next stride, rein pressure should be increased sufficiently to stop the movement of the hind legs, as they are stopped in the picture of Monte Foreman's horse doing the sliding stop. It takes considerable practice to give these three pulls properly, each one progressively stronger, each one strongest as the horse is at the top of his stride in front, and the three given in even, rhythmic progression. If the stop has been made perfectly, you can dismount, go back and look at your horse's tracks, and see three tracks that look like number 11s each evenly spaced, the second a few feet longer than the first and the third just slightly longer.

Start with only enough speed to have a full gallop (not collected canter, no slide in early stage of teaching). As your hand gets better, increase speed of gallop and quickness of stop. Keep your hand low enough and your pulls light enough to avoid making the horse throw his head up violently. However, you do raise the forequarters as you push the hindquarters up under you with the squeeze of your legs. Also, you must get forward in the saddle and lean forward. Obviously, as the horse gets his hindquarters under him for the sliding stop, he seems to squat, so that his back is at almost a 45-degree angle with the ground. If you sit at right angles to his back, you are actually getting your weight *behind* the ground support of his hind feet! More than one professional roper buys boots (to protect the fetlocks behind), makes the horseshoer put trailers on the hind shoes, and indulges in profanity, when all the time the cause of the trouble is on top of the saddle. This troubled roper leans back when he stops and gets his weight all behind his horse. No wonder the horse takes the hide off his hind pasterns. (Let me hasten to add that there are a few exceptional horses with a tremendous stop, flexible pasterns, and other peculiarities that make boots and special shoeing necessary.) Keep forward in the saddle and over the horse's balance, not behind the center of gravity.

The perfect sliding stop is one performed with an ordinary curb. (In the picture, Monte Foreman is using a Monte Foreman Pelham that measures six inches from mouthpiece to the center of the bottom ring for the rein.) It is sometimes performed with tie-down (standing martingale). Most professional Western horsemen use spurs because a light signal with a spur is more definite than a squeeze with a leg or a rub with a heel, either of which may often be given accidentally. However, many horses with a perfect sliding stop are not touched with the spur, the rider merely giving a good squeeze with his legs or a turn inward of the heel as he signals for the stop. Voice signal is sometimes used—sharp, distinct "Whoa!"—as the other signals are given, though many horsemen disapprove of the voice signal, feeling that a bystander or competitor may yell "Whoa!" at an inopportune time and the horse respond.

With some naturally high-headed horses, the good sliding stop cannot be achieved with a simple curb. A standing martingale may be necessary, adjusted so that it operates only when the horse gets his head too high for proper balance at the stop. However, use a martingale only when needed, never to make up for lack of skill of the rider. Never use a martingale when all that is needed to prevent head tossing is elimination of the pinching of the corner of a horse's mouth caused by a too-long curb strap or chain. The Monte Foreman Pelham, and some others, are specially designed to prevent this pinching. With ordinary curbs a close watch must be kept, especially if a strap rather than a chain is used, to be sure the strap has not stretched just enough to make it pinch the corners of the mouth when pulled for a stop.

Remember, if the horse does not stop the way you want him to, look for the trouble on *your* end of the reins.

Slip Fillets

Before the advent of the American Horse Shows Association, slip fillets were sometimes used in jumping classes. These were strips of wood laid on the top rail of a jump so that they would fall and indicate a touch when one was made.

Slip fillets are now forbidden by the *Rule Book* of the AHSA. Modern scoring of touches is more complex than mere observation of slip fillets. For example, a touch with any part of the horse behind the stifle counts as half a fault; a touch with any other part of the horse counts as one fault; touch of the wing with any part of the rider or equipment counts as one fault; etc.

Slipper

The term *slipper* may designate a light shoe that is put on for temporary protection of a hoof. Before the use of the extremely long feet seen in contemporary shows, a horse who was shown with a shoe weighing four pounds or more, for example, would have the heavy shoes carefully removed after a show and replaced by a "slipper," using the same nail holes. The "slipper" would be worn during transportation to the next show.

Snaffle

The word *snaffle* has for many years been used to denote a bit made of a jointed mouthpiece and jointed sidepieces. The latter usually have rings or rings with bars to prevent the rings from pulling into the side of the horse's mouth. If the bars extended upward and downward from the ends of the mouthpiece, the snaffle was called "full cheek." For use in driving a horse in harness, the upward extension of the full-cheek sidepiece interfered with the overcheck when the latter was fastened directly to the main driving bit (not attached to an extra bit sometimes used for the overcheck). To obviate this problem, the upper half of the bar at each end of the mouthpiece was omitted. Such a snaffle was said to be of the "half-cheek" variety.

Bridoon is another name for a snaffle bit (*see* BRIDOON). The conventional English "full bridle" or "double bridle" is sometimes referred to as a "bit and bridoon" bridle. Obviously, the word *bit* here means *curb*.

In very recent years, at least one authority in the field (Monte Foreman) uses the term *snaffle* to mean any bit that does not have leverage action. He even refers to the top rein on a four-ring Pelham bit as the "snaffle rein." (*See* PELHAM.)

Very generally speaking, the snaffle bit tends to put the horse's center of balance forward, while the curb (Weymouth, Pelham, and the almost endless variety of Western curb bits) tends to bring the chin in, hocks forward under the horse, and, as a result, center of balance farther back on the horse. When used without a running martingale (*see* MARTINGALE), the snaffle presses against the corners of the mouth when reins are pulled, not on the bars of the mouth as do other bits. For this reason it is generally believed that an inept or heavy-handed rider is less likely to ruin a good horse's mouth if he uses a snaffle bit rather than a rigid bit.

Some excellent riders in the hunting field use a snaffle with two pairs of reins, one going through the rings of a running martingale, the other running free. This arrangement gives a range of control or communication similar to that of a full bridle (curb and snaffle). The martingale will keep the pressure of the snaffle down on the bars of the mouth, and the pair of reins running free gives the usual effect of the snaffle.

Unless he is in the hands of an exceptionally fine horseman, the young horse will consider his introduction to the bit a challenge, an invitation to resist. It takes some time to get him to realize that pressure on the reins is communication, not an act of war. For this early part of a horse's education, most horsemen find the snaffle the most useful bit. (*See also* GAG REIN and DRAW REIN.)

Snubbing Horse

A snubbing horse is one from whom an unbroken or green animal is led. One method of breaking horses to saddle used to be to "snub" the unbroken animal to the saddle horn of a "snubbing horse." (To "snub" is to secure by taking two or three wraps of a lead rope or lariat around a saddle horn, tree, or post.) Horses could become very clever assistants when used for some time as snubbing horses. They would anticipate the movements of the unbroken animal, staying the proper distance from him and nipping him on nose or neck when he tried to lunge around in front of the snubbing horse.

Soring

Soring is the use of caustic liquid called "scooter juice," chains, or shackles to make a Walking Horse's fore ankles sore. This process, combined with feet seven or more inches long and some drastic training, creates the movement of the show-ring Walker.

On February 13, 1972, the Arizona *Republic* ran an Associated Press story as follows:

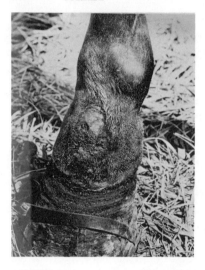

An example of soring—the foreleg of prize-winning Tennessee Walking Horse Papa Charcoal. This deliberate injury of leg to produce show performance was featured on NBC program *Chronolog* in January 1972.

The Agriculture Department has announced the adoption of regulations providing fines up to $2,000 and six months imprisonment for anyone engaged in the practice of horse soring to produce special gaits in the show ring.

Officials said the regulations, which implement a 1970 law banning the practice, will go into effect upon official publication scheduled for February 15.

If horse-show judges and officials had adhered strictly to the policy and rules of the American Horse Shows Association, such regulations and laws would not have been called for. The AHSA has never knowingly tolerated the exhibition of a sored animal in a recognized show; and in the AHSA *Rule Book*, Rule XXXIII, specific instructions are given for examination of Tennessee Walking Horses for soring. Any evidence of soring calls for immediate dismissal of the horse from the ring and the rest of the show and subsequent penalties for the owner.

Sorrel

Until about the time the automobile began to replace the horse and buggy on city streets, the word *sorrel* was the designation for a vast range of color in horses. Any horse of a reddish, "goldish," or chocolate color, unless he had a black mane and tail, was called sorrel. If he was of a chocolate hue, he was called chestnut or chestnut sorrel. The ones of chocolate persuasion were most highly esteemed. Considerable heat was generated by owners of dark sorrel horses when show officials refused to list them as chestnut. The line of distinction between chestnut sorrels and other sorrels became such a bone of contention that the term *sorrel* was dropped from show-ring vocabulary; all horses once called sorrel, as well as those originally entitled to the cherished "chestnut," were listed as chestnut, which is where the matter stands today. (*See* COLOR OF THE HORSE.)

Soundness

A sound horse is one who shows no "evidence of lameness, broken wind or impairment of vision," if we may borrow apt phrasing from the *Rule Book* of the American Horse Shows Association.

There are many kinds of unsoundness that are periodic, especially in their early stages (e.g., periodic ophthalmia or "moon blindness" and some joint lesions), so it is most important to have a veterinarian examine any horse before he is purchased by a nonprofessional horseman.

Spade

A spade bit is one patterned after the Moorish bits brought to this continent by the conquistadores. Its authority derives from the spade or spoon which rises from the center of the mouthpiece as does the port of an English curb or Weymouth (*see* BITS). The spoon exerts pressure on the roof of the mouth. There are braces running from each sidepiece to the bottom of the spoon. These braces keep the mouthpiece a little lower than the corners of the mouth, where an ordinary curb usually rides, and thus puts pressure on a more sensitive part of the bars of the mouth than does the simple curb.

Only in the hands of one whose life has been devoted exclusively to the art is the use of a spade bit excusable. In such hands (as so well portrayed by Tom Lea in *The Hands of Cantu*) it can achieve a perfection of unity of horse and rider seldom attained otherwise.

Spanish Horse. *See* ANDALUSIAN and JENNET

Spanish Mustang Registry, Inc. *See also* MUSTANG

Address: P. O. Box 26, Thompson Falls, Montana 59873.

Spanish Riding School. *See also* RIDING

In the latter part of the sixteenth century the Spanish Riding School of Vienna was organized to teach to aristocracy, nobility and royalty "riding in its highest form" (which had reached its peak of development and popularity in Spain). The most obvious aspect of this form of riding was the execution of five movements—the piaffe, the passage, the capriole, the levade, and the courbette. Piaffe and passage are explained under their own headings; the capriole is a leap straight up with body level, forelegs bent, and hind legs kicking straight out behind; the courbette is a leap straight up from a rearing position; the levade is collection (*see* COLLECTION) so extreme that all the weight is carried by the hind legs, and the forefeet rise a foot or so off the ground—the horse seems to squat.

Much of the training of the horses was done with the horse tied between

Movements of the Lippizaner horses of the Spanish Riding School—the origin of dressage. 1. Levade; 2. capriole.

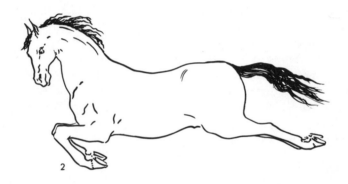

two pillars while being lashed with a whip some 20 feet in length, wielded by two hands. Other parts of the training were done by the use of long ropes held by a goodly number of assistants while another horseman plied the long whip.

It is interesting to note that the Duke of Newcastle, close friend and equerry to Charles II of England, was the author of reforms in this "highest form" of riding in England. He (1) reduced the number of pillars to one, and greatly restricted the use of that; (2) whereas the Austrians tied the horse's head (by a cavesson) securely to the saddle, Newcastle put the reins in the rider's hands and instituted the draw rein (*see* DRAW REIN).

In 1735 the Riding Hall, constructed for classical riding, was completed. This rococo structure is still the home of the school today. Though the school was named Spanish because it originally used only Spanish horses

The courbette, one of the airs above ground of the Spanish Riding School, performed by Antonio Aguilar, Master Horseman of the Americas, on one of his Lippizaner stallions.

(at the time of its origin deemed the best ones for the purpose), it now uses only Lippizaner stallions, white in color (all dark when foaled but turned white when mature).

One who completes a course of training (a matter of 10 to 15 years) at the Spanish Riding School may be called a Bereiter. The course is rigorous for either a human or an equine trainee, and the percentage of casualties and/or dropouts is high.

Spanish Walk and Trot

The Spanish walk and trot are not included in any of the recognized national or international dressage competitions. They are, however, the movements of the high school horse that make the greatest impression on nonprofessional audiences. Whether they are, as some contend, sheer circus stunts or, as others maintain, a useful part of dressage (or high school training), any attempt to teach them must be made with caution and knowledge, for it can easily result in ruining a good horse, to say nothing of failure to achieve the end desired. The best explanation of the method of teaching and riding the Spanish walk and trot is contained in a book entitled *Equitation* by the late Henry Wynmalen.

In the Spanish walk, the horse lifts each forefoot in turn as high as his shoulder, or higher. Each foot must return to the ground without any bending of the knee. The cadence of the gait is the four-beat rhythm of the flat-footed walk. It must be absolutely regular and the horse must progress a uniform distance at each step.

The Spanish trot has similar requirements, though lifting of the hind feet is more pronounced (but of necessity not so great as front action).

Spavin

In lay parlance, there are two kinds of spavins: the bog spavin (*see* BOG SPAVIN), which is a vascular disorder of the hock joint, and the bone spavin or "jack," which is a calcium deposit or growth on one of the bones of the hock joint making movement painful. Though some bone spavins are not detectable by the layman, most of the bony enlargements can be seen or felt toward the inside forward and lower part of the hock joint. In some cases firing (*see* FIRING) will enable the horse to go sound. Veterinary advice is necessary in any case of spavin. Home cures almost invariably raise false hopes and end by making a bad matter worse.

Speak (hounds)

When a hound becomes vocal while following a scent, he is said to "speak" or "cry."

Speed

The "natural" speed of a horse at the walk is about three miles an hour. A stopwatch will dispel the delusion of many horsemen who boast of having a four-mile-an-hour walking horse. There are, of course, exceptional horses who can do a flat-footed walk at five miles an hour, but they are extremely rare. The true running walk, according to the late Burt Hunter, one of the most influential early proponents of the Tennessee Walking Horse, "is a gait done with a minimum of effort to both horse and rider at a speed of six to eight miles an hour." (The crippled show specimens of the breed today do something at about 18 miles an hour.) A horse will trot "naturally" up to 8 or 10 miles an hour and then break into a gallop. Harness race horses are taught to trot a mile in considerably less than two minutes. Pacers can go a little faster. The running horse can do a mile in about a minute and a half.

Of the easy saddle gaits, the rack (formerly called single-foot) is the fastest (*see* GAITS). Top show horses can rack at considerably more than 20 miles an hour for a short spurt in the ring. The Paso Fino can do the same gait at a little less speed but if pushed can go into a straight pace and increase his speed considerably. The Missouri Fox Trotter can do his famed gait easily at eight or ten miles an hour.

Speedy Cuts

When a horse strikes the inside of a knee or hock with the hoof on the opposite side, he is said to suffer a "speed cut" or "speedy cut." Such an injury occurs only in horses used at high speed in some competitive work or in those with extremely high action, usually artificially induced. Frequently speedy cutting indicates that an animal is being forced to perform beyond what he has been properly prepared to do, or that he is weak (from improper feeding, recent worming, or what not). In some instances a good farrier can correct the trouble by a very slight change in the level of the foot or weight of the shoe.

Of course, any wound resulting from speed cutting must be healed before the animal is again asked to perform, regardless of what the farrier can do.

Splints

The splint bones of a horse are tiny skeletal vestiges that lie beside the cannon bone from knee and hock downward but do not extend to the pastern joint. They seem peculiarly susceptible to injury. Any injury to them, like injury to any other bone, results in the formation of a callus or enlargement over the place of injury. Such an enlargement on a splint bone is called, very simply, a "splint."

There are many theories about the causes of splints, ranging all the way from malnutrition to concussion on hard roads. Whatever the cause, the splint will usually do no harm unless the owner becomes enthusiastic about home remedies, or unless it is the result of the horse's interfering (striking the leg with the opposing hoof) and the cause is not removed. However, some splints, especially in horses under six years of age, form near enough to the joint to make movement painful. In such cases a veterinarian may prescribe blistering (which will at least have the benefi-

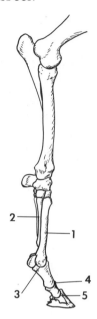
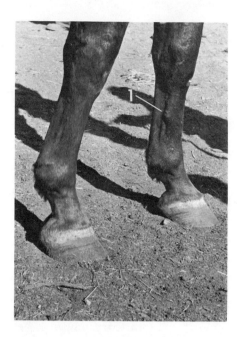

(Left) Front leg, inside. 1. Cannon bone; 2. internal small metacarpal bone (splint bone); 3. fetlock joint; 4. pastern joint; 5. coffin joint. (Right) Front leg. 1. Indicates splint.

cial result of resting the horse) or pin firing (*see* FIRING). If a veterinarian determines that the splint has been caused by improper leveling of the foot by the farrier, removal of the cause will be easy. (*See also* LAMENESS.)

Spoon. *See also* SPADE

The spoon of a spade bit may vary from a fraction of an inch to two or more inches in length. Some spoons have small rollers at their upper edge. Just below the base of the spoon there is a slot in which a cricket rides loosely (*see* CRICKET).

Sprains

Equine sprains, if responsive to treatment, will yield to the kind of treatment useful in human sprains. Immediate treatment should be the application of cold water or ice packs. After the first day, heat is better than cold. Most permanent lameness resulting from sprains is caused by the failure of the owner to give the horse the weeks of rest needed to mend the torn tissues of the sprain.

If the "sprain" is what is called a "bowed tendon," which is a tearing of the lateral ligaments between knee and pastern, prompt attention by a veterinarian can usually effect a complete cure of what used to be considered an injury from which a horse never completely recovers. Modern veterinarians have a type of cast (made of fiber, not plaster) which holds the big ligaments in place until the lateral ones heal and are ready to take over their job again.

The layman can usually determine that the lateral ligaments are torn by observing the extreme lameness of the horse and the tendency of the big upright ligament behind the cannon bone to bow outward slightly. However, if the horse has a severe sprain, the wise horseman lets a veterinarian do the diagnosing. The old method of treating bowed tendons and other sprains by tight bandaging over plenty of cotton sometimes effected a partial "cure," but the effect on the vascular system of the leg by nonprofessional bandaging and the inability of any bandage to hold upright ligaments in proper place for the healing of lateral ligaments always resulted in a "cured" leg that would go lame again under severe strain of hard work.

Spurs

As has been said by many excellent horsemen, putting spurs on the heels of an unskilled rider is like giving a monkey a razor to play with. On the other hand, spurs properly used increase the rapport between man and mount. The heel is too large and its touch too indefinite for some of the most subtle communication between rider and mount. The expert horseman rarely if ever causes pain with spurs. When punishment is necessary, he uses a cutting whip. Spurs, contrary to popular opinion, are not used (by accomplished horsemen) to excite a horse to greater speed. They are an adjunct, a very useful adjunct, to the leg aids (*see* AIDS).

The only place where the experienced horseman uses a spur to inflict pain is in the rodeo. Even there, the infliction of pain is a side effect, for the reason for use of spurs in bronc riding events is to gain points of record in the judges' box. The flank cinch and whatever was done to the horse as he left the chute (procedure varies with each individual) will make him buck as spectacularly as his natural endowments permit.

Bronc riders' spurs have fairly short shanks and small rowels. The latter are so shaped that they will readily scratch hair (to gain points) but rarely break the hide. Rodeo bronc riders usually buckle their spurs on the outside. Traditionally, Western spurs were buckled on the inside, for at least two reasons. First, buckles will catch on brush and drag a spur into a horse. Second, the outside buttons of Western spurs were often highly decorated, never the inside ones; and the spur strap would hide at least part of the button if spurs were buckled on the outside.

It is anybody's guess whether the cause of rodeo contestants' breaking with convention in the matter of spur buckling is their exposure to English riders (who always buckle spurs on the outside) or to keep the inside of the boot as smooth as possible to facilitate swinging the foot to scratch both in front of and behind the cinch (which must be done to gain points). The latter seems more plausible.

The length of shank desirable on a spur, English or Western, may well be governed by the relative size of horse and rider. A short-legged man on a big-barreled horse had better have short shanks or he may be touching the horse's hip, not its side, when he uses his spur. The long-legged man on the small horse may have to use fairly long shanks to avoid standing tiptoe in his stirrup every time he wishes to touch his mount with a spur. Of course, the English rider may obviate the last-mentioned difficulty by adjusting his spur strap to keep his spur high on the boot; but the Westerner must wear his spurs where they hang.

No rowels are permitted on polo spurs. The rider who is not extremely adept at using spurs should use spurs without rowels, if he wears English spurs. If he is a Westerner, he may use a large rowel (if he can find one in this modern age) with many dull points.

No horseman should wear spurs until there is absolutely no chance that he will touch the horse with them unintentionally and until he is adept at using leg aids (*see* AIDS).

Square Trot

A square trot is one in which the hoofbeats have the one-two rhythm of two-four time in music. This means that the diagonal pairs of feet are working together. If the rhythm is a bit on the syncopated side, the gait is verging toward the fox-trot, in which the forefoot of each diagonal pair strikes the ground a little before the hind foot strikes. Any soreness of the horse's feet or legs may cause this "syncopation" of the trot. Among gaited-horse fanciers, a square trot is demanded to be sure that the horse executes each gait on command and does not mix them (slide from one into the other at will).

Stables

While most of the atrocities committed on horses arise from the human desire to "keep up with Joneses" (or, better, surpass them), horses are free of this human ailment and can be comfortable in the most modest of stables. In fact, the horse there may be happier than his brother kept in an elaborate establishment, for he may receive more individual attention and response from his owner.

Whether a horse is housed in a backyard stall or an elaborate stable, certain principles must be adhered to if owners are to avoid difficulties. From a nationwide view, the simplest and, in urban areas, the most common stable is the converted garage (the modern car can stand in the carport or at the curb, but Rosinante must have his stall). So let us start this discussion of stables with suggestions about conversion of the garage to a more worthy use.

To convert a garage into a one-horse stable, one four-by-four upright and a few two-by-sixes to fence off one end of the garage for tack are all the lumber that is needed. Box stalls should be not less than 10 by 10 feet and larger if possible; 16 by 16 is ideal. Three cautions are *imperative* when converting a garage:

1. If grain cannot be kept behind a closed door in a service room on the back porch of the residence and must be kept in the garage, make a strong box for grain, with a lid that a horse cannot open. The ways by which a horse can get into a tack room seem to be many and mysterious. Personal knowledge of tragedies to much-loved mounts of amateurs makes the writer very insistent upon this point.

2. Remove all exposed electrical wiring from the horse stall. Just one example of a freakish accident may serve as warning. The late Dr. Richard Sigler of Bozeman, Montana, and Mesa, Arizona, had a beautiful and playful animal electrocuted accidentally by a light socket that hung very high, suspended from the ceiling of the stall. It is not certain whether the horse reared and touched the socket with a wet muzzle or whether a damp ear found the live point of contact. Exposed wires can be shorted by teeth or striking hooves. Strange to most novices is the fact that a very small amount of current can be fatal to a horse. (The current from all properly underwritten electric fence units is of sufficiently low voltage to be perfectly safe.)

3. Any small door through which the horse is to pass must be provided with a catch to hold it open. If a door swings shut on a horse as he is entering, he will usually be startled and lunge forward. His hip may be broken or "knocked down" from such an occurrence.

With these cautions observed, any bright teen-age youngster can convert a garage into a good home for a Saddle Horse.

Size of Stall and Paddock

If room permits, a box stall of 16 by 16 feet is a comfortable size, though a horse can live well in a 12 by 12 or even 10 by 10 area. If eight feet is the only convenient width in a given stable, lengthen the stall by a few feet, opening up a wall and extending the stall into the yard with a four- or five-foot fence if necessary.

Where space is available, a paddock will eliminate most of the work of grooming and stall cleaning. Even a paddock 1,250 to 1,500 square feet will help a great deal. It should be needless to say that a small paddock should not be enclosed by barbed wire. Also, some wooden fences invite destruction by chewing. (*See* FENCING.)

Three major factors must be considered when deciding about the general type of construction for a stable: (1) climate, (2) the kind of use the horse is to have, and (3) the amount of money the owner wishes to spend.

Where winters are extreme, there is a temptation to want to make stables airtight. This leads to no harm if care is taken to air the stable out well daily and to be sure the horse has some chance to be outdoors some time during every day the weather permits. However, more horses are made ill by heavy blankets and tight stables than are harmed by braving the elements in an open feed lot well supplied with good roughage and fresh water at all times. Whether storage space is to be provided for a quantity of hay in climates where hay spoils is an individual matter. Over a period of years, money can be saved by building a hay storage space and buying hay in quantity in proper season. But if reliable feed stores are available, good baled hay can be bought in small quantities as needed and a few bales stored outside under canvas when necessary. Better still is the use of pelleted hay that is now available in stout paper bags at all feed stores. It is always higher in price than hay in other form, but because of absence of waste and the better digestibility, it is more economical than other forms of hay unless the difference is extreme—say, more than 20 percent.

Hay is sometimes pelleted with a certain amount of grain and sold as a "complete ration," of course at a slightly higher price than other pellets. The objections to this are two. First, the horse used very lightly is better off with no grain except a two-pound coffee-canful of bran twice a day (no wise horseman omits regular feeding of "red" bran). Second, bran may be absent from the pellet or included in insufficient quantity.

If pelleted hay is the only roughage given, the horse will always ravenously chew wood. If he cannot get to any wood (mangers and stalls all metal), he will undoubtedly experience as much uneasiness as the wood chewer. A very small addition, say about one-third normal ration, of timothy, Bermuda, redtop, or other nonleguminous hay to the horse's daily ration will usually stop the craving for more bulk. The writer uses threshed Bermuda when he can get some of good dust-free quality because, though it adds little food value, it is quite low in cost and suffers little from exposure to weather.

To be healthy, a horse needs fresh air as much as a human being does. In hot climates, such as the Southwest, shelter from the sun is about all the stable that is needed for comfort.

In Tempe, Arizona, the writer built a stable that proved very satisfactory. A ramada or shed roofed with aluminum was constructed 60 feet long and 20 feet deep. The roof was 9 feet high at one side and 8 at the other. Chain link fence 6 feet high separated the first 40 feet of the ramada into stalls 10 feet wide, making box stalls 10 by 20. The next 10-foot length was left open to be used for hay storage or as a breezeway where shoeing, grooming, or saddling could take place when the sun was hot. The final 10-foot length was enclosed with stucco walls, floored with cement, and provided with a door at either end; this was the tack room and grain storage room. The end stall had an electric wire around it at the height of the point of the hips of the stallion occupying it. This wire served as tailboard and also deterred the occupant from crowding the stall to get at the horse in the adjoining compartment.

This sort of stable is suggested as the simplest to construct. It is not satisfactory if a short coat is desired on the occupants.

Floors (*See Model Small Stable at end of this article on stables*)

Almost any material will serve for the floor of a stall if the bedding is heavy enough and is cleaned well daily. The busy city dweller, however, can rarely be meticulous about his barn work; he must have a floor that will not be full of great holes in a few weeks. Nevertheless, the nearer the floor comes to duplicating the conditions of natural sod, the better off will be the condition of the horse's legs and feet.

In pre-automobile days, heavy plank flooring was perhaps the most common material in city barns. Concrete with a not-too-smooth surface and brick were also very common. These latter two materials are certainly not recommended; especially are they to be avoided if the horse stands in the stall most of the time. Two-by-sixes or two-by-tens on edge, spaced a half-inch or less apart to allow for drainage, make a satisfactory floor. Perhaps the best wooden floor this writer has ever seen was in the Woodside establishment at Columbus, Ohio, home of the great Laet, champion of all Percherons. Smooth cedar posts some 18 inches long were placed on end as tightly together as possible. Then sand was pounded in to fill all cracks and crevices. That floor had great wearing quality. Horses did not slip on it, and it was easy to keep clean.

Local supply will dictate the kind of material for most inexpensive floors. In some localities there is a kind of clay that makes excellent floors. Near the writer's home in Scottsdale, Arizona, a material called "decomposed granite" makes good floors, easy to clean, wearproof, nonslippery, and springy enough to be kind to feet. Around Butte, Montana, there is a fine black cinder that is good for flooring, though most cinders are bad for that purpose. Some places have a variety of limestone that makes a good floor when finely crushed.

Whatever the material, the floor should be perfectly flat and should slope very slightly away from the manger. If the floor is of clay, crushed stone (fine enough to avoid lodging of small stones in feet), or similar material, it should be properly sprinkled, packed, and dried before it is used. Parts of the floor that will get the most stamping and tramping, such as the area in front of the manger and just inside the door, should be tamped extra well.

Tailboards

Tailboards are advantageous not only for horses who have to wear their tails in sets but also for horses who have a tendency to rub tails. The perfect height for a tailboard is the height of the point of the hip (the point that sticks farthest out behind) of the horse who is to occupy the stall. Twelve inches is narrow enough for the board. It should be at least a two-inch plank and should be very securely bracketed to the walls of the stall and the door. Useful as tailboards are, they are certainly not a *must* in a pleasure horse barn. It is here recommended that the beginning horseman, unless he intends to start right off with showing a horse with a set tail, avoid the use of tailboards until apparent need arises.

Electrified Wire

To stop manger and corral chewing, and also to substitute for tailboards, the writer has used electric wire. It may be installed on insulators, according to directions that come with the unit that may be purchased at most large hardware stores. It may be placed on the corral fences where chewing occurs and on the edge of mangers opposite the side from which the horse eats. Wire must never be put where a horse has to reach over it to eat or drink. To substitute for tailboards, put the wire on insulators at tailboard height all around the stall.

If a horse must be kept behind barbed wire or woven wire (through which many horses delight in sticking a foot), an electric wire is imperative. It should be located at least three feet inside the barbed or woven wire fence. It should be the height of the point of the shoulder of the horse or not higher than where the bottom of his neck comes out of his body.

Homemade fence units are to be avoided. A horse can stand very little current. He is so susceptible that the current of many good fence units is not readily felt by a man if he is wearing leather or composition soles. Good electric fence units, operating on a six-volt battery, are properly underwritten and guaranteed. Current from such units is perfectly safe for any equine. The only source of danger that the writer has observed from the use of an electric fence arose from the carelessness of the owner. If the fence is "shorted" by a stray piece of baling wire and the owner is counting on the electric fence to protect his horse, he may come to grief. An electric fence that is "shorted out" will not stop a horse.

Mangers

There are as many notions about mangers as there are about horses. The most usual type of hay manger is of wood. A two-by-four or two-by-six frame is used with boards at least a full inch thick. Where elm is available, it is the best wood. The part of the manger nearest the horse when he is feeding should be a few inches higher than the point of his shoulder. From front to back, the manger should be large enough for the horse to get his head into easily. The front wall of the hay manger is usually slanted inward at the bottom, presumably on the theory that the horse can readily get at the feed in the bottom if the corner next to him is square. The bottom of the hay manger should be flat and smooth so that it can be easily cleaned from time to time. Some people prefer a removable bottom. The hay manger should be three or more feet wide. The bottom should be just above or on the floor of the stall.

Other types of mangers for hay are too numerous to list here. The corner rack type is preferred by those who think that the dust and chaff will sift out if hay is fed in a high rack or those who feel that such a manger will tend to make a horse hold his head high. The writer is not of either of these schools.

The most common grain manger is built in the upper half or third of one end of the hay manger. It should be about one-third as deep as the hay manger or a little more. If it is too shallow, the horse may throw his grain out.

Many horsemen prefer to feed salt loose in a little box much narrower and shallower than the grain manger. The salt box should be just wide enough for comfortable licking and about one-third the depth of the grain manger. The writer uses commercial mineralized salt blocks (the kind less hard than ordinary salt blocks, which are a bit too hard for some horses to lick readily enough to get sufficient salt in their diet).

The beginning horseman who wishes to keep his horse comfortable as economically as possible may dispense with all carpenter work on mangers. At almost any city dump or junkyard he can procure two 50-gallon metal drums. No matter if they leak, just so long as they are not so badly rusted that rough edges which will injure the horse may be exposed.

If the tops are not already removed, they can be cut out with a cold chisel and the rough edges smoothed with a file; or the local welder can cut them with a torch, after he has filled them with water to be sure no gasoline or other combustible fumes are in them.

Each drum should be a little more than half filled with dirt after it has been placed in the stall where grain can easily be fed from one and hay from the other. On top of the dirt, smooth out by hand about two inches of cement (a sack of dry, ready-mixed cement can be gotten at any lumber yard and at most hardware stores), leaving the edges a trifle higher than the center. When the cement has hardened for 24 hours, the mangers are ready for use.

Another 50-gallon drum can be cleaned out and kept full of clean water, or a five-gallon bucket can be securely fastened in one corner of the stall at manger height and kept full of clean water.

If the writer had to choose between keeping a horse on short rations but with clean water available at all times and keeping a horse on full rations but with water only a couple of times daily, he would without hesitation choose the short-rations-constant-water alternative.

Model Small Stable

One of the most useful and well-planned stables serving a private family living in a suburban area is to be found at the home of Joseph and Marylou Namesnik of Scottsdale, Arizona. The Namesniks own a few of the finest Arabians in the Scottsdale area.

The Namesnik stable is an incorporation of some of the most desirable features of the stables of the late Mrs. Anne McCormick in one of modest size. Flanking both sides of a 12-foot center aisle are rows of stalls. Each

A

B

An ideal small stable, owned by Mr. and Mrs. Joseph Namesnik. A. The interior of the finished stable. B. Front exterior. Louver and roof are lower than specified by the architect's plan. This deviation affords conformity with adjacent buildings but decreases the natural circulation of air. 1. Interior elevation (the dry wells are actually eight feet deep, backfilled with various courses of rock, instead of the five feet indicated in the architect's drawing); 2. front exterior elevation; 3. side exterior elevation (showing double gates to each stall); 4. floor plan (p. 464).

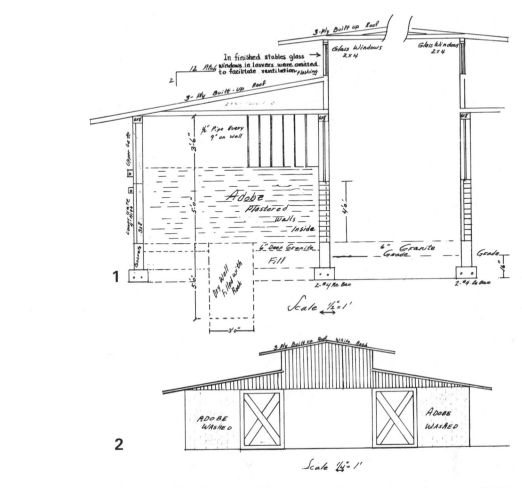

1 Scale ½"=1'

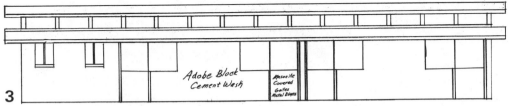

2 Scale ¼"=1'

3

stall is 12 feet square. One stall on each side is finished and enclosed, one to serve as feed and tack room, the other as trophy room and office. Each stall opens onto a corral 20 feet long and as wide as the stall or as two stalls at the ends of the rows.

In the center of each horse stall an eight-foot hole, three feet in diameter, was bored and filled with river rock to within four or five inches of the top. It was filled the rest of the way to the top with decomposed granite. The granite was also used for the floor, which slopes gently upward from the center of the stall. The subsoil in the area is sufficiently porous to make unnecessary any drainage from the bottoms of the eight-foot holes in the

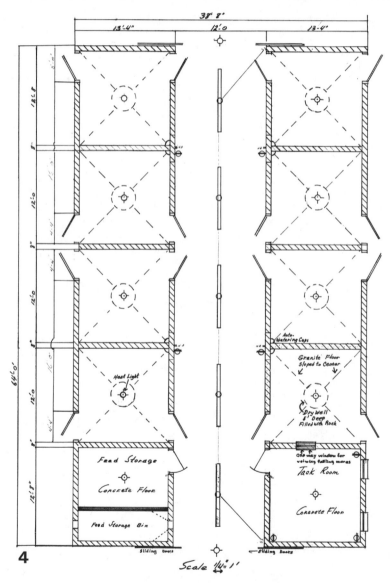

4

Scale ¼"=1'

centers of the stalls. In less fortunate locations, a system of drainpipes leading from the rock-filled holes in the stalls to a central sump or cesspool is necessary.

The Namesnik stable exemplifies all aspects of construction, ventilation, lighting, safety, and convenience discussed in this book, with the exception of tailboards. As the Namesnik "remuda" consists of Arabians, Joseph, Jr.'s, Quarter Horse, and young David's beautiful little Shetland, tail rubbing is no problem. (If tails are washed regularly and not set or kept in sets, horses seldom rub their tails unless infested with pinworms. Shetland show ponies sometimes have set tails, but David Namesnik would most furiously defend his pony against the knife if anyone dared suggest setting its tail.)

Staggers. *See also* BLIND STAGGERS

When a horse has the staggers (faints), he should, of course, be allowed to rest, even if he does not go down. Cool compresses on the head may comfort him. A veterinarian should be summoned immediately (and probably an officer of the law for the owner). (*See* MEGRIMS.)

Stake Classes

Stake classes are those in which the prizes are substantial amounts of prize money, such as the Ten Thousand Dollar Five-Gaited Stake held annually at Louisville, Kentucky. The money is usually divided into more than the conventional four prizes and may be offered in several divisions, as the one mentioned above.

Stake Horse

A stake horse is one considered good enough to compete in stake classes.

Staking Out Horses

The owner who ties a horse to a stake driven into the ground, unless he knows the horse has been properly trained and he does the tying properly, should be reported to the Humane Society.

A horse tied at ground level, unless he has been carefully trained, will immediately become hysterical and get his feet entangled in the rope. If the rope is long enough, his first move will be a quick turn wrapping the rope around the hind pastern, which he will then proceed to saw back and forth on the rope.

When the writer lived in the Arizona desert, he learned the convenience of teaching a horse to "ground tie," or be stake tied. During those years he taught this trick to every horse he owned. Returning to Kentucky one summer, he took with him a favorite stallion, which he stake tied on the spacious lawn of the house he lived in. When a group of friends rode up to invite him to join them en route to refreshment at a neighboring farm, the stallion behaved as would any hot-blooded "entire" (the English word for stallion) and threw the visitors into a panic. However, the instant he reached the end of his 30-foot rope, he stopped without stretching it and danced back and forth across it carefully. This was probably the first, last, and only time a well-bred stallion was ever staked out in Kentucky, but it demonstrated how an intelligent horse can learn to handle himself on a rope.

To start a horse on a ground tie, the first 10 or 12 feet of the rope (which must be of cotton) can be run through a large-diameter garden hose, or it can be secured to a sapling with half hitches close enough to keep hooves from getting between sapling and rope. The rope must be tied to a swivel at the top of the stake (such special stakes were common a generation or so ago in rural villages where every home that could afford it kept a cow), or the horse must be watched constantly so he can be un-wound when he winds himself around stake, tree, or whatever holds him. A little watching and help when he needs it for the first day or two, and the horse will have learned a useful trick.

The Oriental custom of teaching from tiny colthood the ability to be tied by a foreleg is probably the ideal method of stake tying, but Americans so far have not taken the gentle care and forethought to handle their animals in this manner.

Any ground tying should be done with a soft cotton rope from 20 to 40 feet long and should be so accomplished that the horse will not wind the rope up and shorten it.

Stallion

In America we commonly think of stallions as hard to handle, excitable, and usually dangerous. In many other countries, castration is not common, and nobody makes any fuss about stallions.

Xenophon used only stallions in his cavalry, as have other generals of other lands. A stallion is, generally speaking, whatever he is made to be. If he is kept for breeding and ridden very little if at all, he is certainly likely to be unsafe for any but the most expert horseman, especially in the spring of the year. However, a stallion who has plenty of work to do and learns something about discipline can be handled as casually as any other equine, though if he is used for breeding he may need a little extra discipline in spring.

Stalls. *See also* STABLES

The conventional size of a box stall (one in which the horse runs loose) is 12 by 12. The tie stall or "straight stall" is customarily 5 by 10.

Standardbred

The Standardbred (so called because the first requirement for registration was the ability to achieve a certain standard of speed) is the horse used for harness racing (*see* HARNESS RACING). Horsemen in general would profit from a wider appreciation of this horse. He has qualities of conformation and temperament that all breeds desire and he has not been spoiled by selection and breeding to meet show-ring demands for freak action or details of conformation. His bone and feet are usually superior to those of the Thoroughbred, the other racing breed. (*See* HAMBLETONIAN TEN.)

Standing Martingale. *See* MARTINGALE

Star

A star is a white mark on a horse's forehead.

Stargazer

A horse who habitually holds his head high and nose out is called a star-gazer. Such a horse, though he rarely refuses to take a jump, is not a safe jumper. For any other work he is usually equally unsuited, for it is difficult to get him to flex or balance properly.

Starting the Horse

Just as a horse reveals his quality, or lack of it, in the manner in which he starts from a standstill, the rider reveals much about the quality of his horsemanship by the manner in which he starts his horse.

On the reasonably well-trained horse, the good rider will always stand for a moment or so before he asks his horse to move out. He may adjust stirrup leathers or get the feel of his reins, taking them in two hands if he is of the "hunting, jumping" or "saddle seat" (though not professional) persuasion or taking them up lightly in his left hand if a Westerner. When ready to start, the rider will collect his horse and almost at the same time give a trifle more impulsion than restraint (*see* COLLECTION). The amount of impulsion must be determined by the horse's temperament and amount of training. The amount of restraint is also so dependent. The sluggish horse may require a smart touch of a cutting whip. The well-bred, well-trained one will need but a slight lift of the reins and the merest backward move of the legs for collection, the leg movement supplying the added appropriate impulsion.

The horse who is sluggish or a bit difficult to start, perhaps because he is not acquainted with his present rider and does not understand what is wanted, may be turned one step to the side as he is given impulsion. He can, of course, be immediately turned back into the desired direction as soon as he starts.

Steeldust

Before any organization for registration and promotion of any breed of Western horse existed (the American Quarter Horse Association was formed in 1940), a highly esteemed and distinctive type of horse was to be found on some of the better cattle ranches throughout the Southwest. This type was called the Steeldust and was supposed to come from a very prepotent sire of that name.

Since Western horses have become respectable, and recognized classes of various kinds for them are included in recognized horse shows, effort has been expended to identify the original Steeldust. Because of the custom of naming colts after illustrious sires, it is doubtful that any of the "original" Steeldusts "discovered" is the extremely prepotent progenitor of that strain of horses, which antedated the Quarter Horse as the most highly prized Western horse in the Southwest. However, the Steeldust blood has contributed to the Quarter Horse through several families.

Steeplechasing and Hurdle Racing

Though there is no official record of steeplechasing until the time of our Civil War, the sport is very old, perhaps the oldest form of racing with any semblance of organization. The courses were originally laid out by sighting on church steeples; hence the name.

Hurdle races are usually run over dirt tracks. The first one of which there is record in this country was run in Washington, D.C., in 1834, with "every gent riding his own horse," according to rule.

Steeplechases and hurdle races are not restricted to Thoroughbred horses, as are the races on our highly organized tracks featuring pari-mutuel wagering. Steeplechasing calls for the most rugged of hunters. In 1928, of the 42 horses starting in the Grand National (reputed to be the most demanding of all steeplechases), only one finished. In 1946, in the Grand National, in which one horse was killed and another critically injured, of the 34 entries, 6 finished. That steeplechase was won by a level-headed "lady's hunter" named Lovely Cottage. She was Irish bred, as winners of the Grand National frequently are.

The Maryland Hunt Cup is the most notable American steeplechase. It was founded in 1894 by five gentlemen who were in some disagreement over the relative merits of hunters in their country.

Steer Busting

In recognized rodeos and shows today, with the exception of those in three states, steer "busting," tripping, or flipping is not permitted. However, where it is practiced today, it is done a little differently from the old-time method common when wild cattle ran on unfenced range.

In those days, according to one old-timer, the cowboy, with his rope tied hard and fast, would overtake a renegade, rope it by the horns or neck, toss the slack over the hips so that it pulled across the hind legs just above the hocks, turn about 45 degrees to the left, and increase his speed. When the horse hit the end of the rope, if cinches and rope held, the steer would flip high in the air in a backward somersault and land hard enough on his back to knock himself into docility for a moment, usually long enough for the cowboy to get to him and hog-tie him before the animal came to his senses.

Most steer jerking today is done, not with the rope tied hard and fast, but with it dallied around the horn. When the steer is roped, the slack is flipped to come across his hind legs, the rope is dallied, and the horse is turned at a sharp right angle away from the steer. This maneuver does not cause the high backward somersault of the old method, and it requires weight and size in the rope horse rather than extreme speed.

In the early days, especially in the Southwest, horses used on the range were small. I have seen a little 850-pound cow pony make a 1,000-pound steer take off skyward in a somersault that broke his neck on landing. Today we rather frown on breaking steers' necks, especially in public; so we use the big horses and roll the steers over on their sides. (See illustrations on pages 470–471.)

Stern

A foxhound does not have a tail; it has a *stern*.

Stiff-necked Fox

A "stiff-necked" fox is one that runs in a straight line. In hunting country comprising some woodland, meadow, and stream, with a few rail fences, a smart fox sometimes takes advantage of natural objects in a manner that is quite confusing, especially to young hounds. The so-called stiff-necked fox, on the other hand, runs in a beeline. He may even eschew the usual circularity of course (large for red fox, smaller for gray) and take a straight line out of the country.

Stifle

The word *stifle* is used to denote the joint immediately behind the flank and sometimes to include the muscles behind that joint.

Stifled

When a horse dislocates (throws out of joint) the stifle joint, he is said to be "stifled." If the dislocation is more than momentary (as it sometimes is), a veterinarian will be needed to normalize the joint. In many cases the

1

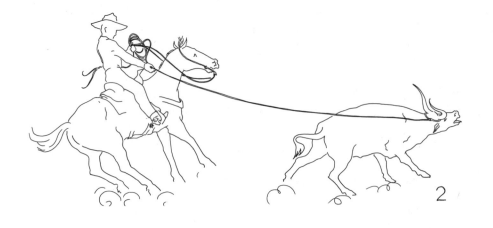

2

3

Steer busting. 1. Steer buster casting loop; 2. taking up slack; 3. flipping rope to right side of steer and starting to turn horse to left; 4. increasing speed and busting steer (rider then shifts weight to left stirrup preparatory to dismounting, causing horse to stop).

stifle will almost immediately dislocate again, and pathological shoeing will be necessary on both hind feet until the joint is completely normal again.

Stimulants

A horse will respond to alcoholic beverages given as stimulants in the event of chill or collapse about the way a human being will. However, the administration of any liquid to an ailing equine by a nonprofessional is extremely risky and may result in death from foreign-body pneumonia, as discussed in this book under DRENCHING.

An amusing incident of use of stimulant by a professional occurred in Montana. The late Richard Sigler, a surgeon of well-deserved fame throughout the intermountain Northwest, was a close friend of the writer. Between us, however, was a spirited rivalry over a stallion owned by Dr. Sigler, a son of Chester Dare, and a grandson of that stallion owned by Charles LaDue of Sheridan, Montana, and William Belknap of Goshen, Kentucky. The latter horse was being shown during summer vacation by the writer.

The old horse was the finer of the two animals but was a bit sluggish and unwilling to show the speed at the rack of which he was capable. So, piloted by Mrs. Sigler, the old horse had been consistently second at the little intermountain shows, placing under his grandson.

At Missoula, Montana, Dr. Sigler had a plan to change this routine. He appeared at the stables a short while before the five-gaited stake class was called. He walked to his box and sat down with a canary-swallowing feline smile on his face, evidently expecting some surprise. It was, however, the doctor himself who was surprised.

The old son of Chester Dare (to whom, it was later revealed, the doctor had administered a fifth of good bourbon) came rolling into the ring on a very high-stepping slow gait whoofing at every tiny piece of paper he saw and otherwise giving a fair imitation of a human being with a silly jag on. The old horse placed out of the ribbons in that class, but everyone agreed he gave all appearance of having "one hell of a good time," as his owner put it.

The moral of this tale, if any, is this: The effect of stimulants on equines is not entirely predictable.

Stirrup Leathers

English stirrup leathers are not provided with fenders to keep the sweat of the horse off the legs of the rider as are the stirrup straps of Western saddles (on which the fender may be part of the stirrup leather). However, for the horseman who finds much of his fun on horseback to be what Anglophiles call "hacking," the leathers can be run through slots at top and bottom of properly shaped pieces of saddle leather, with considerable contribution to his comfort.

The stirrup leathers should be of the best English leather for safety's sake. Good English leathers are numbered. The numbers are on the flesh side of the leather, for the bearing of saddle bars and stirrups should be on the grain side of the leather. On all good leathers, the buckles are sewed on so the flesh side of the leathers will be out.

On Western saddles the stirrup straps should be equally good in quality and about twice the width of English ones. This width, plus the weight of the fenders, keeps the stirrups down when a rider leaves his horse unintentionally and helps prevent hanging a boot in a stirrup. The safest and oldest way of fastening Western stirrup straps is with thongs, well laced. However, since any change of length of leathers is a major undertaking if they are laced, many Westerners use one of the several patent fastenings now on the market. These do well enough if they are properly applied, but if holes for them are bored with a pocketknife (instead of being made with a leather punch) or allowed to become worn, they are unsafe.

Stirrups

Metal stirrups are conventional on English saddles, but children and beginners sometimes find wooden stirrups easier to hold. If wooden ones are used, they should be provided with leather hoods and with straps attached to toe of hood and stirrup (so toes cannot be poked through space between hood and stirrup and be lodged there). This arrangement is necessary because the wooden stirrup is light and may fly upward and catch a foot if the rider falls. Any wooden stirrup must be much wider than the boot and higher from tread to top than are metal stirrups.

Good Western saddles are equipped with stirrups of wood or other material that cannot be crushed into a trap for the boot if a horse falls on it. Oxbow stirrups of narrow width of tread or rounded tread are comfortable only for those who ride with their insteps on the stirrups and wear boots with strong steel arches. The same thing may be said of the stirrups which are merely circles of steel, used in some parts of the Northwest. For brush country, tapaderos are a necessity.

Cheap "Western" saddles are often equipped with small wooden stirrups. They are very dangerous. The addition of tapaderos is of some help.

Stock

When a horse's legs swell as he stands in the stable, he is said to "stock" or "stock up." This may be a sign of infection. If so, it is frequently accompanied by a swelling of the lymphatic glands under the belly. Circulatory sluggishness accompanying age in geldings and stallions is sometimes the cause. More frequently, the cause in geldings and stallions is an accumulation of smegma in the horse's penis. At times the accumulation builds to such a size in the head of the penis that it makes urination difficult, painful, or even impossible. A stallion or gelding should therefore be examined periodically and, if necessary, cleaned by a veterinarian or a careful, hygienic, and experienced horseman.

Stock Horse. *See also* COW PONY

A stock horse is one who is useful in work with livestock. The American Horse Shows Association *Rule Book* in its "Stock Horse Section" carefully explains the details of performance of the stock horse in each of the many classes it specifies for him. He may perform in the ring either with or without cattle. The general characteristics of a good working stock horse, according to the *Rule Book,* are as follows:

1. Good manners.
2. Horse should be shifty, smooth and have his feet under him at all times. When stopping, hind feet should be well under him.

Typical stock horse—Western horse for ranch use—ridden by actual working cowboy in working gear. Note tapaderos, indicating work in brushy country.

3. Horse should have a soft mouth and should respond to a light rein, especially when stopping.

4. Head should be maintained in its natural position.

5. Horse should be able to work at reasonable speed and still be under control of its rider.

Stockings

When white on a horse's leg extends above the pastern joint, it is called a stocking. (If below that, a "sock.")

Stock Saddles. *See* SADDLES

Stomach

A horse's stomach is very small in comparison with his size. The most economical and effective way of feeding, therefore, is in small quantities and very frequently. Also because of this small stomach, feeding a thirsty horse and then allowing him to drink is a waste of feed and a possible cause of illness.

In his natural state, a horse may graze 22 out of the 24 hours, especially if "the picking is slim." The writer has achieved remarkable results in getting a thin horse into show shape by feeding five times a day at regular intervals. It must be emphasized that cramming a manger full of hay so that the horse has chewed-over hay in front of him most of the time will yield bad results.

Stone in the Foot

If a horse goes suddenly lame, the first cause to suspect is a nail or stone (*see* PUNCTURE WOUNDS). If a stone is found to be the cause, it will probably be lodged between shoe and frog or bar. If it is very firmly lodged, some force may be required to dislodge it. Another rock may be used to drive it or, if there is an English saddle at hand, a stirrup can be quickly pulled from the saddle bars by a backward pull on the leather. A metal English stirrup has hammered out many a rock from a hoof.

The rock should be driven out toward the toe rather than toward the heel. Any use of screwdriver or other such instrument should be made with the instrument pointed forward (toward toe, not heel), because it is easy to damage the structure of the hoof by driving or forcing such a tool toward the heel.

Stopping. *See also* SLIDING STOP

The rider gives about as much evidence of his horsemanship when he stops a horse as he does when he starts (*see* STARTING THE HORSE). And the quality of training given and the breeding of the horse are equally disclosed. No good horseman yanks a horse to a stiff-legged stop with his head tossed high and mouth yawing open. The genuine horseman demands no more speed of response in stopping than the horse by training and natural endowment is capable of giving without strain. Even the well-trained horse can be ruined through being stopped by inept riders. Around almost any rodeo and most horse shows can be seen good animals in Western gear who have cocked hind ankles attesting to riders with poor hands and the habit of leaning back when asking a horse for a quick stop (*see* SLIDING STOP).

In no use of a horse under English saddle (except in polo) is the quick stop any considerable asset. The ability to stop smoothly in response to a light hand and to stop squarely, with head in natural position, jaw relaxed, and feet under the body, is a mark of a good horse well trained and well ridden. For extremely quick stopping, no time is lost by warning the horse a stride or two in advance of the stop (as explained under SLIDING STOP), and keeping the rider's weight forward over the horse's center of balance is

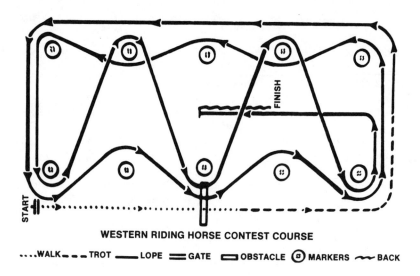

WESTERN RIDING HORSE CONTEST COURSE

....WALK --- TROT ——LOPE ≡≡GATE ▭OBSTACLE ⊙MARKERS ～BACK

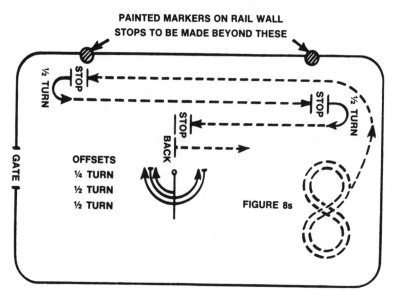

PAINTED MARKERS ON RAIL WALL
STOPS TO BE MADE BEYOND THESE

½ TURN   STOP

GATE

STOP
BACK

OFFSETS
¼ TURN
½ TURN
½ TURN

STOP   ½ TURN

FIGURE 8s

not only helpful but imperative for best results and preservation of soundness of the horse.

Strangles (Distemper)

Strangles, or distemper, is a highly contagious disease. Two varieties of *Streptococcus* are the cause. The mucous membranes of the nasal passages and larynx are affected, and in some cases only a tracheotomy by an expert veterinary surgeon can prevent suffocation. Veterinarians use, among

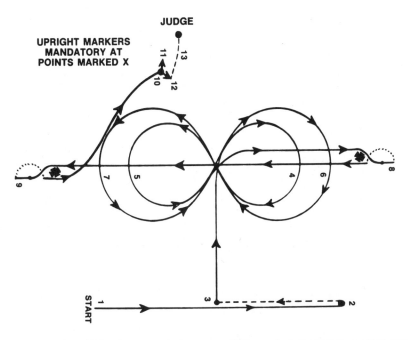

JUDGE

UPRIGHT MARKERS
MANDATORY AT
POINTS MARKED X

11 13
12
10

9 7 5 4 6 8

START 1 3 2

(Upper left) Western riding horse contest course. "This contest is neither a stunt nor a race. It is a competition in the performance and characteristics of a good sensible, well-mannered, free and easy moving ranch horse. A judge may require an exhibitor to repeat or reverse any part of the routine. Any Western equipment of the exhibitor's choice may be used, but the kind of equipment necessary for control and the severity of such may be considered by the judge in making awards. Extra credit will not be given for fancy or expensive equipment or dress."

(Above) An approved American Quarter Horse Association reining pattern. "1 and 2. Run at full speed at least 20 feet from any fence or wall; 2. stop and back; 3. settle horse for 10 seconds; 4 & 5. ride small figure 8 at slow canter; 6 & 7. ride large figure 8 fast; 8. left roll back over hocks; 9. right roll back over hocks; 10. stop; 11. pivot left; 12. pivot right; 13. walk to judge and stop for inspection until dismissed. (Other reining patterns from which the judges may choose are available from the American Horse Shows Association.)"

(Left) Pattern for Stock Horse Class (when not worked on cattle). "Suggested procedure is for horses to enter ring at walk, taking jog-trot and a slow lope upon request. They then shall line up or retire from ring at walk, taking jog-trot and a slow lope at judge's direction. Horses then shall be worked individually. Rider shall start his workout with a figure eight, executed at a lope two or three times and of sufficient size to avoid short, choppy turns. Failure of horse to change both front and hind leads shall be faulted. The smoother and more even the gait, the more credit to the horse. Entry shall then go to the end of arena, turn and run full length of arena to a straight sliding stop, turn away from the rail and run to the other end of the arena and make a straight sliding stop. After allowing the horse to gather itself, back the horse in exactly the opposite direction in a straight line for 10–15 feet. Horse shall then be brought up to the judge, stopped and, with weight on the hind quarters and with legs in one position, make a quarter turn to the right, half turn to the left, and a half turn to the right. After all entries have been shown, indicated horses may be worked on a rope sack (optional)—sack is to be roped, horse run from side to side, turning squarely back as end of rope is reached with not to exceed 25 feet of rope out, to show horse can work accurately and fast after an animal has been roped, and is not rope shy. (If rope or sack is to be used, prize list must so state.)"

other things, antibiotics in therapy. Abscesses may appear, even a week or so after apparent cure. They should be treated with warm compresses and, when ready for rupture, may be opened by a veterinarian. In some cases the entire lymph system of the horse is involved and internal abscesses may occur.

During an epidemic of distemper, the wise horseman avoids causing fatigue in his animals, keeps them away from public watering and feeding places, uses red wheat bran regularly in feeding, and avails himself of any grazing of clean fresh grass that may be unexposed to other horses. The use of bacterin injections (as preventive) during an epidemic may possibly add to susceptibility under certain conditions, according to most recent veterinary scientific authority; so the wise horseman follows the guidance of his veterinarian in this matter.

If by taking his horses to a show or meet of other kind a horseman learns he has exposed his animals to distemper, he should immediately inform his veterinarian and take such preventive steps as are advised.

Strapper

Strapper is British slang for what we would call a stable hand, one who curries horses. *Strapping* is British slang for currying or grooming.

Straw

Wheat straw is better than that of other kinds for bedding, though little different from rye straw. With barley straw, there is some danger of getting barley beards embedded between the cheeks and the gums if horses tend to eat it. Straw is more economical than peat moss for bedding, though not as absorbent. Bermuda straw, threshed Bermuda, is not very good bedding, being neither highly absorbent nor resilient. However, if one is feeding rich, pelleted hay, Bermuda straw, if free from dust, is a good addition to the ration. It contains a small amount of nutrient and supplies bulk enough to stop most horses from the wood chewing they indulge in when fed only pelleted hay.

Stretching

Before the advent of the automobile, carriage horses were often taught to stretch (as do male horses during urination and street-sore horses whenever they are at rest). This pose tended to ensure that the horse or horses stood still while milady and her escort entered the carriage. When the American Saddle Horse finally assumed the exclusive role of showpiece, he was taught invariably to pose with forelegs perpendicular and hind legs pushing slightly forward. This pose gave the level topline of croup so highly prized by Saddlebred and Arabian show people and also tended to make the shoulder appear more sloping.

While top professional trainers for many years were careful to teach their Saddle Horses to pose as described above and not to overpose or "stretch," amateurs almost invariably overposed or "stretched" their horses in a cantileverlike fashion as if they were diabetic or sore in the forefeet. For some strange reason the amateur fashion of posing (now even called "stretching") won out in popularity in the show-ring and is seen more frequently today than the original "pose" of the gaited horse.

Striking

Striking is another word for *interfering* (*see* INTERFERE and SPEEDY CUTS).

Stringhalt

In the peculiar and unfortunate malady called stringhalt the point of the hock jerks violently upward whenever the hind leg is moved, and the foot returns to the ground with a forceful thud. Sometimes one and sometimes both hind legs are affected. Very rarely is a foreleg so afflicted. Surgical optimism has, according to leading veterinary authorities, so far led to no successes. The supposition of such authorities is that the source of the trouble is not, as has often previously been thought, in the leg but in the spinal cord. No remedy has yet been found.

Stud

The word *stud* is used (1) for a collection of animals kept for breeding purposes, (2) for the place in which they are kept, and (3) for a stallion. Among the fastidious, the term *stallion* (*entire* in England) is preferred.

Stud Book

A stud book is a record kept by an association or other authority for the purpose of registering animals who qualify as purebred members of the breed for which the association or authority exists.

Stud Fees

A stud fee is the charge for the service of a stallion in breeding a mare. Such fees are usually paid in advance (*before leaping* was the phrase used on some handbills and posters advertising stallions in horse-and-buggy days). Some stallion owners guarantee a live foal ("that will stand and suck," state some advertisements).

Fees range from $50 or less for common stallions in some rural areas to a considerable part of a million dollars for some Thoroughbred race horses. The Arabian stallion Naborr, standing in his twenties in Arizona, commands a $10,000 fee.

Stumbling

Under a rider with meaningless hands (making no use of reins as communication) who burdens a saddle like a sack of potatoes, even a good horse may become so bored that he will stumble, especially on relatively smooth ground which makes no demand on his attention. A very bad shoeing job may cause stumbling, as will emaciation from starvation or illness. If none of the foregoing causes is present and a horse stumbles with any frequency, he is unsafe for use and should be sold to a human being deserving such an affliction.

When considering purchase, one should keep in mind that if a horse has any scar on his knee stumbling may be suspected, though bad handling over an obstacle or any one of the causes mentioned above could be responsible for the accident that made the scar.

Unsoundness such as sidebones or ringbones (*see* SIDEBONES and LAMENESS) is not an uncommon cause of stumbling.

Substance

The term *substance* is the horseman's word for apparent hardiness, ruggedness, and stamina in a horse. The animal who elicits the term is usually one with plenty of bone (*see* BONE) for his size, well muscled and short coupled. Substance and quality or refinement are not necessarily mutually exclusive qualities, but a horseman looking for one of these qualities may tolerate considerable lack of the other. The old arguments over which quality is more worthy probably engendered the saying "An ounce of blood is worth a pound of bone" (*blood* signifies the refinement stemming from a preponderance of Thoroughbred or Oriental blood).

Sudadero

Sudadero is the Mexican cowboy's term for the leather lining of a saddle skirt. The word also means a *handkerchief* or *sweat cloth*. It has been incorrectly applied to the fender of a saddle by at least one Eastern writer. The Spanish for the fender is *tapadero,* a term also applied to a part of a jaquima (*see* HACKAMORE).

Suffolk or Suffolk Punch

The Suffolk, originally called Suffolk Punch, is the oldest of the draft horse breeds. It shares with the Percheron the distinction of being one of the two draft breeds having "clean" legs, i.e., legs free of long hair. The horses are uniform in color, a chestnut ranging from a light sorrel to dark true chestnut, which fact gives some support to the claim that they carry the blood of horses brought to England by early Norse invaders. If so, infusion of considerable Flemish or Dutch blood must have been used to give the horse its size—a range from 1,600 to 1,800 pounds, only slightly smaller than the other draft breeds.

This very docile, prompt, and willing horse has been bred in Suffolk County, which borders on the North Sea, since about 1500. All registered animals trace their male bloodline to one sire, a horse owned by and carrying the name of one Mr. Crisp. That sire was foaled in 1768.

Though not common in the United States, the Suffolks in use here have won for the breed a reputation of being the most useful, hardy, and long-lived of farm horses. One of the largest dairy ranches in Arizona uses only Suffolk horses for power and stoutly maintains that they are much more economical and dependable than tractors. Each year the farm brings one or more teams for exhibition to the Arizona State Fair, where they attract much favorable attention.

The registry for the breed is kept by the American Suffolk Association with headquarters in Spencer, Indiana 47460.

Sugar

Many horsemen condemn the feeding of sugar and suggest carrots or bits of apple for reward, if such is given. It is doubtful that the amount of sugar fed in proportion to the body weight of a horse has an adverse effect on his health comparable to that of the ordinary use of sugar by people; but, say the antisugar horsemen, once a horse acquires the taste for sugar (never natural for a horse) he becomes "nippy" and disagreeable to handle.

The writer's experience has not borne out this notion. It is true that some horses become almost "hooked" on sugar, being quite frantic about it when they suspect its presence on the person of a handler. But a little common sense will enable a horseman to maintain discipline.

One horseman found it lucky that a valuable stallion was "hooked" on sugar and even associated the word with the object of his desire. The stallion was being hauled in a trailer when, by misfortune during an unloading for a rest stop, he got loose in a cholla-infested part of an Arizona desert where unbranded horses were considered fair game by both Indian and Mexican residents. A horse unacquainted with cholla usually becomes hysterical and runs at top speed until exhausted when he picks up the huge cholla burs with their fishhooklike spines. Before the stallion ranged far enough to get into the cholla, the owner walked casually toward him with outstretched palm and called, "Sugar, Dare." The horse had learned to associate the word with the sweet. He came briskly forward and got his reward (and a line placed quietly under his throttle and over his neck).

Suitable to Become

A class labeled "Suitable to Become" is frequently seen in shows in hunting country. It is for colts and fillies. Obviously, they are judged on their apparent suitability to become hunters.

Sulky. *See also* HARNESS RACING

A sulky is the vehicle used in harness racing. In pre-pneumatic-tire days it was a high-wheeled, cumbersome thing. Today's sulky, with its ball-bearing, pneumatic-tired wheels, is very light and puts the reinsman close to his horse, whose tail is usually braided and trails an extension which can be placed on the seat of the sulky to keep the tail from switching the face of the horseman. The shafts of the modern sulky are shaped to facilitate easy turning for the horse, and the vehicle is so light that very light-weight and (to a layman's eye) very scanty harness is needed.

Sunfishing

Sunfishing is a type of movement peculiar to some bucking horses. It resembles the movement of a flopping fish, for the horse twists his body crescentwise alternately from side to side, tipping his belly upward on first one side, then another.

Suppling the Horse

There are various exercises recommended for suppling the horse. Any of them consistently used by a horseman with good hands will increase suppleness (the ability to shift center of balance easily with appropriate change of flexion and collection in response to a light hand on the reins). However, the horseman with good hands and the ability to be communicated with as well as to communicate to the horse will more profitably spend his time teaching the horse to understand and respond to requests for flexing, collecting, extending at each gait (except canter, of course, for the canter by definition is a collected, slowed-down gallop), and backing properly. These performances are all treated under their respective headings in this book.

Surcingle

A surcingle is a band of leather or webbing passing around a horse's body just behind his withers.

Sureness of Foot

The terrain on which a horse is raised and the manner in which he is confined while growing up usually have a good deal to do with his sure-

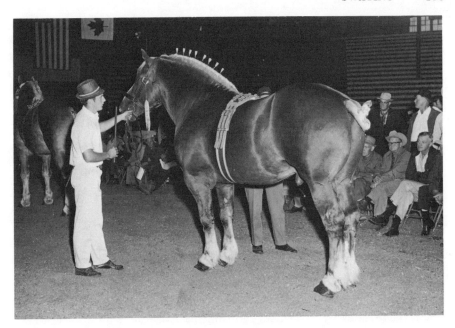

Jan Rubis, a Grand Champion Belgian stallion owned by Jacob W. Ruby, Brookfield, Massachusetts. The belt around the stallion's girth is a surcingle which came from Scotland. It is used strictly for show purposes.

footedness. Knowing this, the late Honorable William B. Belknap, when planning to develop a summer home in a mountainous part of Montana, sent a small band of breeding stock to a Montana friend to raise on mountain range some well-bred horses on shares, so that when the Belknap ranch was ready for occupancy the owner would have some surefooted mounts of the quality he was accustomed to in Kentucky. Surprisingly enough, one three-year-old stallion sent out proved to be one of the best and fastest working mounts in that mountain area. He, alone, when a four-year-old, captured (with a competent young rider on his back) the remnant of a bunch of wild horses that had been eluding authorities and local ranchers for two or three years. This young stallion had been raised in smooth grass pastures in Kentucky.

The above incident illustrates the fact that, while terrain and early handling usually have much to do with sureness of foot, the quality is sometimes congenital and more closely related to breeding than to environment.

Swaying

Any deviation from usual stride or movement in a horse is meaningful to a wise horseman. Quick detection, for instance, of slowing of hindquarter movement or of difficulty in normal collection (*see* COLLECTION) may enable an owner to save a horse from severe effects of azoturia (*see* AZ-OTURIA). Swaying, particularly of the hindquarters, may indicate internal ailment or soreness of loin muscles. It may be a prelude to very serious disorder if proper immediate steps are not taken. The first sign of encephalomyelitis (sleeping sickness) detectable by an expert but not medically trained horseman is a lessening of response of the well-trained horse to the reins. Keen observation will save a horse owner much grief.

Sweating

Perspiration varies among horses as it does among people. Furthermore, the amount one individual sweats is affected by his physical condition and his physical fitness for the work being done. A horse should be gradually worked up to the point of fitness for difficult work just as the human athlete is conditioned for his maximum effort.

When the horse has been properly fitted for maximum output of energy and "gives his all" in any kind of performance, he must not be allowed to stand still while sweating (*see* COOLERS AND COOLING). Under extremely cold and windy conditions, the sweating of the horse may not be evident. The writer witnessed two riders returning to camp in a group ride in the San Gabriel Mountains a few winters ago. The last couple of miles were in deep river sand. The two riders pushed their horses ahead of the group and arrived in camp far ahead of the others. By the time the body of riders arrived, frantic efforts were being made to locate a veterinarian. The riders said their horses were not sweating when they arrived in camp, and they gave them what water they wanted. One of those two animals died and the other was in serious condition. They had undoubtedly perspired while traveling too fast in the difficult footing, but the cold wind prevented the sweat from being obvious to the two "horsemen" who had overridden and watered them.

Sudden breaking out in sweat, either over the entire body or on portions of it, such as the hindquarters, may be a sign of sudden illness or "tying up" (*see* AZOTURIA). Cessation of sweating while a horse is continuing hard or fast work is also a sign of trouble and probable need for a veterinarian.

Sweat Scraper

A sweat scraper is a slightly curved piece of wood or metal (usually aluminum today) about 15 inches long and 1¼ inches wide. It is somewhat spoon-shaped, rounded on one end and provided with a hole for hanging in the other. Deft, forceful, long strokes *with the hair* enable a good groom to remove most of the sweat (or water from a bath) and greatly facilitate the cooling-out process. Similar but not so effective results can be obtained by using any dull-edged object, such as a piece of shingle.

Swollen Legs

Swollen legs can be indicative of any one or more of a host of ills and should be heeded as a grave warning by the horse owner (*see* STOCK).

Any use of bandaging, which is often prescribed as a cure for swollen legs by self-styled "horse doctors," may increase the real trouble (*see* BANDAGES).

Syringes

Unsterile syringes or syringes of any sort used without veterinary supervision or advice have caused horses much misery and horse owners many more dollars than would have been spent to obtain proper veterinary aid.

Tack

1. *Tack* denotes anything a horse wears. The term also includes all the small tools and accessories used in connection with the horse, especially at horse shows.

2. To *tack up* a horse means to saddle and bridle him (*see* APPOINTMENTS).

Tacking Race

A tacking race is fun as a gymkhana event and useful as an incentive in riding schools. Horses are led by halter to the starting line. Tack awaits at a distant line to be properly applied before each contestant returns to the starting line. Any rider returning with improperly tacked-up horse must return to the tack line and place the billet through the keeper or do whatever else is necessary before he returns to the finish line (originally the starting line).

Beginners may be confined to a walk in a tacking race.

Tack Room

Running water and proper racks to facilitate cleaning of tack are very necessary adjuncts for even a modest tack room. Proper shelf room for cleaning materials and cupboard or shelf room for first-aid materials, grooming tools, and spare stirrup leathers, saddle pads, and other accessories are essential. While the modest horseman may admire and enjoy the elaborate tack rooms equipped with bar and trophy case in many show stables, if he keeps his own clean and convenient, it needs no apologies and may prove more useful than some of the more elaborate ones.

Tail

The particular style of tail favored by the proponents of any breed of horse changes as frequently as does the style of human hair arrangement. If interested in competition, the horseman should watch the magazine featuring his kind of equine for pictures of the tails of current stars.

The harness race horse is probably the most fortunate of all breeds as far as his tail is concerned, for his proponents are content to let it grow to normal length and do not whittle on it with knives or put it in sets as do the gaited-horse fanciers (*see* SET TAIL) or pull or shorten it as do owners of other breeds.

Western horsemen, fearful of having their mounts identified with broomtails (wild horses, which frequently have long and full tails) pull their horses' tails to about hock length. Some ropers claim this keeps the tail off the rope.

To date, the rattail of the Appaloosa is maintained as a distinctive feature of the breed, but with the present fashion of crossing outside blood into the breed, this style may shift.

Hackney ponies are the only popular show animals wearing docked tails. This fashion stems from the old idea (upheld by one of America's greatest authorities and most competent horsewomen, Belle Beach) that it was not safe for a woman to drive a horse whose tail was not docked (some horses would panic when they clamped their tail on the reins).

Thoroughbred people and their kinfolk, the hunter and jumper proponents, maintain that their breed has fine, thin manes and tails, so if nature does not support their contention, the comb will do very well.

For those who like to let their horses have long tails, problems arise, especially in hot dry climates. Unless tails are washed very frequently and the skin treated with just the right amount of oil, frantic itching will cause the horse to rub its tail (*see Tailboards* under STABLES). Infestation of pinworms will have a similar effect.

Many horses destroy tail hair while being hauled in a trailer. Unless the trailer is perfectly fitted to the horse, it is best to wrap his tail when he is being hauled. Wrapping may destroy some Derby bandages, but it may save tails. (Modern self-securing bandages now used on polo pony tails are very useful in trailers.)

Takeoff

The takeoff is the point at which a horse leaves the ground for a jump. Argument abounds over whether the horse should take off at a signal from his rider or should be allowed to do what comes naturally. During the years when the Italian cavalry was at the height of its fame and Caprilli was introducing forward-seat riding to the world, the Italians insisted that the horse must be signaled for the takeoff. They would ride a horse into a jump frequently and not take it, returning to a starting point. This, however, was a "to jump or not to jump" signal rather than the signal of the rider who feels he can direct the exactly proper spot for the takeoff. Some horses, of course, especially those who rush their jumps, tend to take off too close or too far from the obstacle. This result of bad or cruel handling can be overcome better by use of the cavalletti (*see* CAVALLETTI) than by an attempt to signal the already confused and fearful horse from on top. The horse who jumps in a pleasant, unafraid manner will do better if allowed to do his own taking off. It is true that an expert rider on a beautifully trained mount is much like the leading partner in ballroom dancing and is in constant subtle communication with his horse. He and the horse together determine the takeoff.

Tallyho

1. *Tallyho* is the shout of the one who first views (sees) the fox in a hunt. Propriety demands that he keep his horse's head pointing in the

direction he assumes the fox to be taking and points with hat in hand in the same direction while he gives the good cheer, "Tallyho."

2. The name *Tallyho* was given to a four-horse pleasure coach imported to this country from England about a century ago. Since then, all similar coaches have been called tallyhos.

Tandem

The custom of driving two horses in harness in single file is said to have arisen to enable a gentleman to take his hunter some distance to a meet without tiring it. The hunter was, of course, the lead horse and not required to pull the load. Early vehicles used for a tandem hitch were designed with a large box or crate under the seat for carrying hounds, so the driver's seat was quite high.

As the use of a tandem hitch became stylish, tandem classes were included in horse shows, and the appointments became quite conventionalized. The American Horse Shows Association *Rule Book* states:

Tandem Hackney or Harness Ponies shall be shown to a suitable two- or four-wheeled vehicle, with side checks. To be shown at a smart trot and to be judged on performance, quality, uniformity, and manners. The wheel pony should be of proper size for the shafts and possess substance and power for the work in hand, with some action. The lead pony to be slightly smaller and notable for brilliance of action and beauty. A smart leader is essential for a good tandem.

There are also tandem classes for hunters under saddle. In such classes the pair of hunters works single file, and failure to keep proper "hunting distance" apart is counted as a fault.

Tapadero

Tapaderos (usually shortened to taps in the West) are leather hoods for stirrups, very necessary for work in brush country. They are also highly decorated and used on parade saddles. When so used, they are often extended far below the stirrups.

In early days of showing Western reining horses, tacks on the sides of taps next to the horse were used to increase speed of turns, offsets (*see* OFFSET), etc., so the contemporary *Rule Book* of the American Horse Shows Association forbids the use of tapaderos in performance classes. However, they are seen in parade classes with elaborate decoration.

Tattersall's

Tattersall's in London is the best-known sale barn in the English-speaking world. The name of this great sale stable is given to the strikingly colored vests worn occasionally in the hunting field and elsewhere.

Team Roping—Team Tying. *See* ROPING

Teaser

A stallion or cryptorchid (*see* CRYPTORCHID) kept in a breeding establishment solely for the purpose of determining the readiness of mares to accept a stallion is called a teaser.

Teeth

The adult equine has 10 incisor teeth and 12 molars in each jaw. A male (and rarely a female) has two "bridle teeth" or "tushes" immediately behind the six front teeth and just ahead of the toothless space of the lower jaw (the bar) on which the bit rests.

A horse with a lower jaw a great deal narrower than the upper may develop a sharp outer edge on his upper molars. This will cut his cheeks, and he will not chew his food properly. In such event, his teeth will have to be ground down (*floated* is the horseman's term) by a veterinarian, whose services are also needed if the horse develops "wolf teeth," tiny teeth that grow in front of the molars and sometimes interfere with proper mastication or use of the bit. If the horse loses a molar and the opposing tooth grows and interferes with proper occlusion or bruises the gum, a veterinarian must remove it.

If a horse on adequate feed, a ration that has formerly kept him in good flesh, loses weight (without increase of work or change of rider or driver), the first cause to suspect is internal parasites. If laboratory check of the droppings proves negative, suspect one or more of the dental ills mentioned above.

Determining Age

An experienced horseman without training in the science of veterinary medicine can tell a good deal about a horse's age if he is aware of the following facts:

Until a horse is nine years old, his lower front teeth reveal his age. Unless he is unusually precocious, the foal's two front baby teeth appear at ten days. At four months he has four of them; and at a year, six. The three-year-old has replaced the two front baby teeth with permanent teeth. At four years, four have been so replaced, and some evidence of bridle teeth may exist. At five years, all front baby teeth have been replaced, and the bridle teeth (of the male) are fully developed. At this age there is a depression in the center of the grinding surface of each front tooth, called a cup. At six years of age the bearing surface of the two center teeth has been worn smooth; the cups have disappeared. At seven, only the two outer cups remain; and at eight, the horse is said to be "smooth mouthed"—his cups have all gone.

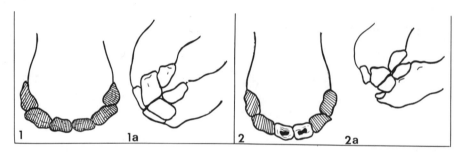

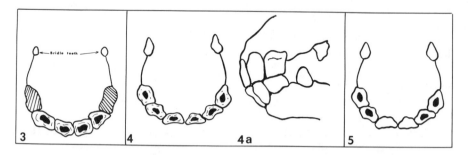

Determining age by teeth. 1. One year old: All temporary teeth visible; surfaces of centrals show wear. 1a. One year old: Upper and lower corner incisors do not contact. 2. Two and one-half years old: Permanent central incisors are in; chewing surface of intermediates (still baby teeth) is worn and the temporary corners show definite wear. 2a. Two and one-half years old: Permanent central incisors are not in contact and have gum on much of their surface. 3. Four years old: Permanent intermediate incisors are in; bridle teeth (also called tushes or tusks) have appeared. 4. Five years old: All permanent teeth are in; chewing surface of centrals and intermediates shows wear but still has visible cups encircled with enamel. 4a. Five years old: Incisors meet; permanent corners are beginning to show wear. 5. Six years old: Cups in central incisors are worn smooth. 6. Seven years old: Intermediate incisors are worn smooth. 7. Eight years old: All cups are gone. 8, 8a. Ten years old: 8a. Beginning at about nine years a brownish colored groove (Galvayne's groove) appears on the upper corner incisor. By the age of 10 it has extended gradually downward from the gum line to about one-third of the length of the tooth. 9. Fifteen years old: The Galvayne's groove extends halfway down the upper corner incisor. Teeth are becoming longer and more oblique. The chewing surface of the lower centrals and intermediates appears triangular in shape. 10. Twenty years old: The Galvayne's groove extends entire length of the upper corner incisor. After 20 years the mark begins to disappear, starting at the top. The slant of teeth is quite oblique. The teeth have spaces between them. The chewing surface of lower incisors is triangular, and sometimes the lowers are worn almost to the gum line.

From this time on, any layman's guess as to the age of a horse must be based upon the slope of the teeth (front teeth slant forward with age) and upon the "Galvayne mark" or "Galvayne's groove." Not until Sidney Galvayne, a renowned horse trainer who appeared before Queen Victoria in 1887, noted the correlation between this mark and a horse's age had anyone been observant or intelligent enough to use this means of calculating

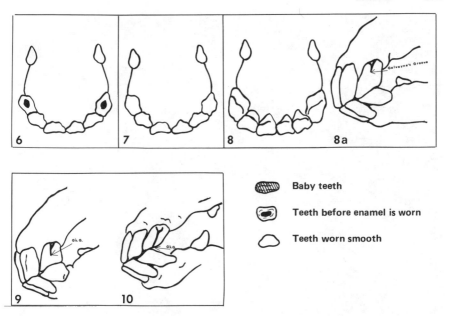

Baby teeth

Teeth before enamel is worn

Teeth worn smooth

the age of a horse. This dark mark runs downward from the gum in the middle of the outside of the upper corner incisors, starting when the animal is 10 and reaching the bottom of the tooth when he is 20. The mark then gradually disappears, beginning at the top, and is gone at age 30.

In addition to the dental indications of age, which are easily recognizable by any good horseman, there are some indications recognizable by a veterinarian. For example, the newborn foal has three cheek teeth, which are temporary, to be replaced by permanent ones later. A yearling has four cheek teeth. A two-year-old has five cheek teeth, and at four to five years, there are six cheek teeth.

Among the other dental details scrutinized by a veterinarian in exact determination of a horse's age is the state of the bearing surface of the teeth. During the horse's years up to seven, this bearing surface or bearing table is oval. At nine years, the surfaces of the central teeth are triangular. At 10 years, the laterals (those next to the center teeth) become triangular. At 11, the corner teeth have triangular surfaces. After the horse is 13, the surfaces become rounded and have a central pulp mark. In extremely old horses the tables again become oval, but whereas the oval shape in younger horses was from side to side, the length of the oval in very old horses is from front to back.

Another dental detail which, considered in addition to the other indications, helps the veterinarian to an exact determination of age is the incisor "hook." This "hook" or projection develops at the posterior edge of the upper corner incisor (front), first appearing at the seventh year. It gradu-

The running walk of the Tennessee Walking Horse is shown here by West Coast Champion Mare "Lady About Town Again," ridden by 14-year-old Heidi Harris, holder of the West Coast Championship for Show Riders 17 and Under.

ally wears away, and by the time the horse is nine years old the surface of the tooth is level. At 11 years it reappears and at 13 it becomes quite noticeable. It usually remains for the rest of the horse's life.

Temperature

The normal temperature of a horse is 100.5° F. It is taken rectally.

Tennessee Walking Horse

Of all the many breeds of horses man has developed through the ages, America has developed two that are the epitome of excellence as riding horses, the two that give the most elegant and delightful ride. They are the Tennessee Walking Horse and the American Saddle Horse. Unfortunately, if one were to attempt to point out the modern breed that is subjected to the greatest suffering by man, he would be hard put to it to decide between the two breeds just mentioned. (See *Life*, October 3, 1969, and the series of articles by Alice Higgins entitled "The Torture Must End" published in *Sports Illustrated* early in 1960.)

Painting of Allen F-1, foundation sire of Tennessee Walking Horses.

Aware of the difficulty of finding fine, easy-gaited horses who could be ridden with pleasure outside the show-ring, some astute horsemen of Tennessee conceived the idea of forming an organization to promote the market value of horses of their area. In the backcountry of Tennessee there were good easy-gaited horses of unspoiled disposition. They were perhaps not as speedy or as handsome as American Saddle Horses but they were beautiful nonetheless, and their easy gaits made them a delight to ride. So on April 27, 1935, horsemen met in Lewisburg, Tennessee, to discuss methods of organization and promotion. The type of horse they were discussing at that meeting had previously been called a Plantation Horse or the Plantation Walker because his sale had been largely to plantation overseers in the cotton belt states. However, they decided upon the name Tennessee Walking Horse and shortly thereafter formed themselves into an association called the Tennessee Walking Horse Breeders' Association of America. It was an appropriate name because their horse could do a running walk (*see* GAITS and AMERICAN SADDLE HORSE) a little differently from the way it was done by any other horse. He could do it at from six to eight miles an hour and with a loose flowing motion that was more delightful to ride than was the running walk of any other horse. Burt Hunter, who was elected as the paid secretary of the organization, described the running walk (in an issue of the *National Horseman* published shortly after the formation of the association) as a gait done from six to eight miles an hour with an economy of effort to both horse and rider. What Hunter was talking about was not a "leaped" gait, that is, the horse did not spring through the air after each hoof impact. In the true running walk, one foot is in contact with the ground at all times. It is a four-beat gait with the same interval following each hoof impact. Their horse, the gentlemen meeting in Lewisburg declared, should also do a flat-footed walk, and his running walk could be squeezed by the feet of his rider into a slow, rocking, easy canter on either lead. On that day they also made up a list of the finest horses in Tennessee, to be named foundation sires in the registry. At the head of the list was a horse called Allen. They wrote him down finally as Allen F-1 because he was Foundation Horse Number One.

Allen was a beautiful stallion, 15 hands high. He had a long graceful neck, a short back, and long powerful hips on which the tail was set high and carried proudly. One of his great-grandfathers was a grandson of Justin Morgan. Another was descended from famous winners of trotting races on the tracks of America. The easy movement of the Walker was also inherited from other great-grandparents who were members of the old families of easy-gaited Saddlers, the Tom Hals, Cockspurs, and others. Many of the first Walking Horses registered by the American Walking Horse Breeders' Association were "double registered." That is, they were registered both in the Walking Horse Registry and in the American Saddle Horse Registry. In those early days, the Walking Horse Association, through the watchdog eyes of its secretary, Burt Hunter, saw to it that no Walking Horse was shown with excessively long feet or weighted shoes and that he performed the gaits as they were designated originally by the association.

In a very few years Tennessee Walking Horses became popular as fine pleasure horses. Because of their fame, horse shows from New York to California began to include classes for them. But the secretary saw to it that the gaits done were those originally described in the *Rule Book*. Not until after the death of Burt Hunter did the Walker join the Saddlebred as a high-priced show-ring attraction. Today the Walker performs a gait called a running walk but he does it at more than twice the speed of the running walk designated by the association when it was first formed. His feet are now so long and his shoes so weighted that they can be kept on only by steel bands over the hooves in addition to nails. The gait he does is a four-beat gait, perhaps closer to the rack of the Saddlebred than to any other gait, but the trainers "sore" him in front by the use of blistering liniments, chains, etc., so that he does this gait as any horse would when lame in both front feet, by scooting his hind feet up under him to take the weight off his forehand.

In spite of what is done to the Walking Horse by his trainers (the blame for such cruelties should rest on owners, not on the trainers, for the latter are merely trying to make a living and satisfy their employers), he will give an elegant and delightful ride to any owner who can get him before he has been sored by trainers.

The Walking Horse, because of high prices paid for show specimens, has increased in size since the formation of the association. Most Walkers now to be seen in horse-show classes are 16 hands high or higher. Some of them tend to be a little coarse in conformation, but refinement is still plentiful in the breed, and it is possible to find excellent mounts on any of the Walking Horse breeding farms. Certainly, no horse has a more kindly or amenable disposition; for proof one can cite the "discomforts" with which the Walking Horse puts up without becoming vicious or difficult to handle.

H. Tom Fulton, secretary of the Tennessee Walking Horse Breeders' Association of America, gives the following very interesting information about the breed:

The Tennessee Walking Horse is a light horse breed founded in the Middle Basin of Tennessee, but predominantly in five or six counties of Middle Tennessee where native blue grass abounds and the soil is rich in limestone and phosphate. This, with an abundance of pure limestone water, had much to do toward building the breed as a hardy, healthy horse with great stamina. This breed of horse is a composition of the Standard-bred, the Thoroughbred, the Morgan and the American Saddle-Bred stock. Foundation animals of these breeds were brought to Tennessee from the Carolinas, Virginia and other states by the pioneers who settled this territory. North Carolina is especially known for its fine breed of Narragansett and Canadian Pacers along with some Thoroughbreds. This particular section of Tennessee previously mentioned was populated mostly by pioneers from North Carolina. An early history of Tennessee refers to these horses being ridden back and forth between the two states as early as 1790. There are statements in documents of the great General Andrew Jackson in reference to the horse named Free and Easy being sent to Warren County, North Carolina, for breeding purposes. As was his name, so were his gaits. Also, he refers to the great horse Copperbottom, a Canadian and Thoroughbred brought from Kentucky as a colt, being brought back from North Carolina at the age of twenty to spend the remainder of his life in Tennessee. He was a great sire of saddle horses, being the founder of the great Copperbottom strain, and many of our good horses of today trace back to him. One of his sons, Morrells Copperbottom, established the great Slasher family, most notable of which is Mountain Slasher F-59. Another great horse about this same time was McMeens Traveler, by Stump the Dealer, and he by the great Timoleon. It is said that Traveler never sired a sorry horse and his colts were in great demand and brought fancy prices. There were 47 horses sired by him in General Forrest's Cavalry and not a one of them was lost during the Civil War. The records show that one of his sons, a twelve year old grey gelding, brought a thousand dollars in gold during those hard times. I shall not dwell longer on the older horses, but will say that the blood of the pacing horse from the strain of the Hals, Brooks, Snow Heels, Joe Bowers and Grey John, not to miss Pat Malone, the great pacer, left their mark in the future generations of their wake. The family of Stonewalls who came from the great Cockspur and Denmark breed that you find in gaited stock also contributed their outstanding characteristics to our horses of today. These different breeds were well established in Tennessee more than 175 years ago, and our breed has continued to advance from the utility and work horses used by our forefathers, to the World's Greatest Pleasure Horse, and finally on to our present day leaders in the horse show field.

Mr. Fulton also gives the following interesting information about Allen F-1, who was the foundation sire of the breed:

Allen F-1 was by Allandorf by Onward, by George Wilkes F-54, by Hambletonian (10). His dam was Maggie Marshall, by Bradford's Telegraph, by Black Hawk (5), by Sherman Morgan. Allen F-1 was a black horse with a blaze, off hind coronet, near hind sock; foaled in 1886; was bred by E. D. Herr of Lexington, Kentucky. He was a double-gaited horse (trotter and pacer) with a record of 2:25 speed which was excessive for that era. The sire Allandorf was the acme of fashionable harness breeding of his day. His dam was of the best Narragansett pacing blood in existence. He had been bred with the hopes of being a great trotter, but he wanted to pace and, therefore, was not raced. He was later sold in Kentucky and eventually wound up in Tennessee where he was ignored for many years until the late J. R. Brantley of Manchester, Tennessee, obtained him and started breeding the good native mares to him. If he had done nothing more than sire Roan Allen F-38, Merry Legs F-4 and Hunter's Allen F-10, I would say he had done his part in establishing the Tennessee Walking Horse Breed.

Tennessee Walking Horse Breeders' and Exhibitors' Association

Secretary: Tom Fulton, P.O. Box 286, Lewisburg, Tennessee 37091. (*See* TENNESSEE WALKING HORSE.)

Tetanus

Tetanus or lockjaw is attributed to a pathogenic organism that abounds in horse manure. Any puncture wound is likely to infect a horse with the disease, but wounds about the lower extremities are more dangerous than others. Administration by a veterinarian of tetanus toxoid in proper dosage is an established preventive. Foals at birth and animals suffering puncture wounds will increase their chances of survival if immediately given serum.

Theodore

Theodore is a gringo corruption of the word *fiador,* which is the name of a rope throatlatch attached to a bosal at the heel knot (*see* BOSAL and HACKA-MORE).

Thoroughbred. *See also* ENGLAND

Of all breeds of horse in America, the Thoroughbred is the most highly prized. Individual animals have sold for millions of dollars. Small fortunes are often spent on the training of one animal, an animal whose winnings stagger the imagination. His reason for being is performance on the race-track, though he can be found at work on ranches, in the hunting field, and elsewhere. When the United States Cavalry used horses, he was used to improve native stock for remount purposes (*see* REMOUNT).

Because of the selection for a short dash (a mile or so) of speed over a specially prepared track, carrying a very light rider, the modern Thorough-bred has lost some of his original typical qualities, especially those appeal-ing to man's aesthetic sense, such as the finely chiseled, diamond-shaped head and the beautiful flexible neck.

Perhaps the most representative gallery of pictures of outstanding Thoroughbreds of this century in America is the collection of photographs of all the winners of the Kentucky Derby. It hung for years in the dining room of the Pendennis Club of Louisville, Kentucky, with the new winner being added each May. The most striking aspect of that awe-inspiring collection was the great variety of conformation it displayed. It dispelled any notion that the speed of a horse can be predicted by observing his conformation. There were long backs and short backs; steep croups and relatively level ones; long legs and short legs—as well as tall horses and one or two not very tall. The qualities common to all were few indeed. They might be summed up as follows:

Long, sloping shoulders, a body not thick but extremely deep from top to bottom of the rib cage; short cannon and long forearm; arm nearer the perpendicular than horizontal. It might be added that none of those winners have the appearance of lacking amplitude of hindquarters, what-ever shape the hindquarters might have. The majority of them, as far as one can tell from the poses in the pictures, seem to be slightly higher in the croup than at the withers.

Origin

Though the oldest pedigrees go back to a white stallion owned by Oliver Cromwell, most students of Thoroughbred bloodlines claim as the male source of the breed three stallions and a possible fourth. The three are the Godolphin Barb (appearing in England in 1730), the Byerly Turk (im-ported circa 1689), and the Darley Arabian (imported 1706). The possible fourth is the Alcock Arabian. All present-day Thoroughbreds trace to one or more of these sires.

On the distaff side, the foundation of the breed is older. About 1670, Charles II gave his good friend and Master of Horse, the Duke of New-castle, the responsibility of selecting brood mares for the Royal Stud at Hampton Court. The progeny of those mares proved that Newcastle did an excellent job. There is no doubt that mares imported from the Orient comprised part of that band, but some of our most reliable scholars insist that most of the mares were of native English strain (which no Oriental horse had ever been able to equal in the contests of speed, begun in

England in the last half of the twelfth century). Others insist that all the mares were Arabian and Barb imports. Whatever the source, the collection was called the Royal Mares and it is the maternal foundation of the Thoroughbred breed.

Before the Godolphin Barb died on Christmas day in 1753, organized racing began in England, and in 1750 according to the Honorable Francis Lawley, a careful authority, the British Jockey Club was formed. This organization, of course, records the breeding of every registered Thoroughbred, in addition to its other manifold duties.

While the Thoroughbred was not generally known in this country until after the Revolution, earlier in the century wealthy gentlemen of the Carolinas, Maryland, and Virginia were importing some of the best blood of England, such as Othello, who has been called the Godolphin Barb of Maryland. He was foaled in 1743 in England, a grandson of one of the Royal Mares. He stood at James River, Virginia, in 1761.

A Virginia gentleman, Colonel Benjamin Tasker, Jr., imported Selima, a daughter of the Godolphin Barb foaled in 1746. This mare was unbeaten on the turf and became equally famous as a brood mare. Practically every race horse of distinction in this country can trace his pedigree to her.

In 1798, when he was 21 years old, Diomed, said to be "the most impressive stallion ever upon American shores," was imported to Virginia, where he founded one of our greatest Thoroughbred families. His son Sir Archy, foaled in 1805, was the first great American Thoroughbred. This 16-hand four-mile bay racer lived to be 32. He was the great-grandsire of Lexington, perhaps the foremost of American Thoroughbred sires. He was a bay, 15.3 hands high, and set a record of 7:19¾ for four miles, carrying 103 lbs. His greatness as a sire was not confined to his own breed; his influence on the Standardbred and American Saddle Horse is acknowledged by devotees of those breeds.

For some 75 years, Thoroughbred races were four miles long. Gradually tracks were improved and races shortened to a mile or a mile and a half. This change caused more value to be placed on horses capable of a tremendous burst of speed for the shorter distance than on those capable of sustaining the four-mile speed. Sire lines that were most successful in producing get to conform to new standards of speed emerged.

One of the most outstanding lines descended from a horse called Domino, principally through Peter Pan and Ultimus. (Ultimus was sired by Commando, son of Domino; Ultimus's dam was a daughter of Domino. Peter Pan was also a son of Commando.) Domino carried an intensification of Lexington blood. Among the most notable Thoroughbreds ever produced was High Time (foaled in 1915); his sire was a double grandson of Domino and his dam was a daughter of Domino.

Another emergent sire line was that of Ben Brush, transmitted through his sons Broomstick and Sweep. A third great modern sire line stems from Spendthrift, principally through his son Hastings, grandsire of Man o'

War, who, according to *The Blood-Horse* (Nov. 8, 1969) "towers above all the great horses which have thundered over the American turf."

A fourth important sire line that emerged with the advent of shorter races is that of Hanover, who sired Sir Barton, the first Triple Crown winner (*see* TRIPLE CROWN).

Barring of American Thoroughbreds from English Stud Book

Many American-bred Thoroughbreds are barred from registration in the English stud book because of a "flaw" in their pedigree in Colonial days when the breed was about as nebulous in England as in the United States. Some of the early dams in this country were not from stock registered in the English stud book. However, American-bred Thoroughbreds carrying lines of breeding blacklisted by the English stud book have won the Derby and other great English races. Gallant Fox, one of the greatest money winners of all time, is ineligible in the English stud book because of a

Doc Pardee, the "dean" of Arizona Thoroughbred breeders, up on Man o' War. Thanks are due to the late Colonel Sam Riddle, owner of Man o' War, for permitting this picture (the only one mounted by anyone other than his regular jockeys) to be taken of two of the greatest turf personalities of our time.

(Upper left) Man o' War at three, Clarence Kummer up.
(Above) Stakes winner of 1970, Mrs. E. D. Jacobs's Personality, champion at three.
(Left) Sir Barton, the first Triple Crown winner, as depicted in a painting by F. B. Voss which hangs in the National Museum of Racing.

Commando line in his pedigree. The blood of Lexington and Hanover is also on the English blacklist.

Size Increase

The size of Thoroughbreds has increased in this century. Man o' War stood at 16.3 and after his retirement weighed well over 1,300 pounds. Whether or not this increase in size is in part accountable for increase in speed, it is a boon to breeders of hunters, for, all other things being equal, the bigger the hunter, the higher the price he will command.

Thoroughpin

A thoroughpin results from strain on the flexor tendons as they pass around the hock. To the layman a thoroughpin appears as a puff on either side of the hind leg just above the hock. The puffiness is usually greater on one side of the leg than on the other. Immediately following the strain, the horse may be lame. If he is rested, the lameness may disappear, though the unsightly puffiness will remain. Most attempts at removing the puffs result in making a bad matter worse.

Three-gaited Horse

The three-gaited horse walks, trots, and canters.

In today's show-rings, a three-gaited horse displays extremely high action both in front and behind at the trot. This gait is done at moderate speed. The canter is done on both leads in a very collected and animated fashion. The walk is often a very slow, broken trot. (*See* GAITS.)

Throat

The throat or throttle of the horse is the object of much attention in conformation classes (halter classes). Many if not most show horses, therefore, wear fleece-lined leather-covered "sweaters" around their throttles. These devices are presumed to reduce the size of the throttle and make it look "fine." What their effect is on the horse's susceptibility to respiratory ailments deserves study. Arabian breeders strive to accentuate the "mitbah," an Arabian word denoting "the direct way in which the neck leaves the head for a slight distance before curving."

While the show-ring demands a fine throttle, a roomy throat and wide jowls, once the boast of Asil Arabians, are far superior functionally to the small throat and narrow heads of many modern ribbon winners.

Throatlatch

The throatlatch is the narrow strap that runs under the throttle in all English and some Western bridles. One mark of the inexperienced horseman is his habit of buckling the throatlatch snug and neat. If the throatlatch is snug on the horse at rest, when he flexes his neck properly for collection, the strap will restrict his respiration. If a throatlatch is properly buckled, three or four fingers can easily be inserted under it when the horse is at rest.

Throttle

Throttle is another term for throat (*see* THROAT).

Thrush

Thrush is a rather loose term laymen use for fungus infections of the hoof. In the parts of this country that are not extremely dry and hot, it usually occurs where the frog and bars of the foot join. In its early stages, it does not cause lameness but can be detected by its very offensive odor. If not treated, it can become a serious incurable disease. Keeping the hoof clean by daily attention and regular application of Coppertox (a proprietary preparation) or medication of identical formula under any other patented name will cure the disease if attended to early.

In some parts of this country fungus diseases of the hoof are exasperatingly prevalent. They may attack almost any part of the hoof. Some of them cause a separation of the layers of the hoof wall. In very early stages, the treatment described above may help. Keeping stalls and corrals clean and the use of the hoof dressing detailed in this book under HOOF will help prevent fungus infection of the feet in localities where it is most prevalent.

Tie-down

Tie-down is a Western term for the standing martingale (*see* MARTINGALE).

Tie Rope

The best tie rope is a halter shank (*see* HALTER SHANK). No horse except a dull and sluggish one or one who has been specially trained for such treatment should ever be tied by a rope around his neck. A horse with any life will pull back until he chokes to death or breaks his neck if the rope slips around while he has his head to the ground and comes on top of his poll (between his ears). A rope tied around the neck with a knot that will not slip and allow the rope to tighten can be run through the halter ring or through a bit ring (of a snaffle only), or a bridle noseband can be used without the danger of the above accident.

Toe. *See* FEET (*of horse*) and FEET (*position of rider's feet*)

Tonics

Old wives' tales still persist in abundance around stables, in spite of the progress in the science of veterinary medicine in recent years. Tonics "for the blood" (such as ferrous sulfate) and "for the kidneys" (such as saltpeter) are often recommended. Probably a little ferrous sulfate will do no harm—though the balance of ferrous sulfate and copper sulfate would be a more reasonable thing to consider. Saltpeter in small doses is probably also innocuous. However, if the horse is sluggish or off his feed, it would be wise to consult a veterinarian to find out whether the condition may be due to internal parasites, bad teeth, or some other trouble. If the animal is male and has urinary trouble, he probably has an accumulation of smegma in the head of his penis and needs cleaning (*see* BEAN). Feeding a horse a "tonic" selected because of nonprofessional advice or advertising can be much more costly in the long run than the employment of a veterinarian.

One of the oldest tonics used to put bloom on show horses is Fowler's Solution of Arsenic. If the horse is healthy, a tablespoonful of the solution given daily for 10 days, then omitted for 10 days, then fed again for 10 days will stimulate bloom and spirit. However, arsenic is cumulative and if fed continuously, or intermittently over a long period, will produce an effect exactly opposite to that desired. Horses like the taste of the solution, so it can be fed with the grain. Like many other poisons, it has been known to produce sterility.

A much wiser way of producing bloom (*see* BLOOM) is proper feeding and care. In areas where some basic nutrients are known to be deficient, such as those lacking iodine or phosphorus, supplements should be added to the ration. Horses who do not have access to green growing forage can be improved by the feeding of supplements containing proper amounts of vitamins. Wheat-germ oil has benefited many horses. Though it is known chiefly as an aid to fertility, it has other beneficial effects, probably rivaling Fowler's Solution as a bloom producer.

Topline

Topline refers to the top of a horse's profile. The preference in the topline varies somewhat with breed preference. However, most breed preference is for a short back and a level croup (from highest point of hips to root of tail). Horsemen who are more concerned with power and performance than with aesthetics prefer a croup that is long and sloping or rounded. Practically all horsemen prefer shortness in the back (from withers to croup) and length of croup.

Touch-and-Out

Touch-and-out classes used to be quite popular. As the name implies, horses would continue jumping, the jumps sometimes being raised with each completion by all contestants, until all but one had touched a jump and been dismissed. The remaining horse was of course the winner. In judging such classes, slip fillets were used. They are now forbidden by the American Horse Shows Association, which has set up some rather complicated definitions of faults (*see* SLIP FILLETS and FAULTS, *In Hunter Classes*).

Today we have fault-and-out and knock-down-and-out classes rather than touch-and-out.

Trailers

Any horseman who shows or who participates in group riding is almost obliged to own a trailer. For the sake of conspicuous consumption, the sky is the limit in interior finish and exterior decor. However, sturdy, safe trailers are on the market for little over $1,000.

In selecting a trailer, the inexperienced will do well to have a knowledgeable mechanic with him. Sturdy axles (four wheels are mandatory), frame, and floor are of primary importance. Many a fine horse has met a horrible fate by having a foot go through a trailer floor. A standard brand of electric brake that operates either from the brake pedal of the car and optionally from hand lever or from pressure at the hitch is satisfactory; the writer prefers the former type. The hitch must be extra strong and of such design that it will not jar loose. The lighting system must conform to highway department requirements, and all wires must be protected from mud and dust where they pass under the floor (if they do so pass). Most commercial trailers have adequate mangers, but some do not have dividers in them, and horses will quarrel over feed and sometimes make trouble. Padding must be provided for knees and chests, and a chain or crossbar can keep horses from "sitting on their tails" on the endgate. Commercial trailers are universally long enough and wide enough, but for owners of breeds taller than Quarter Horses, many trailers are too low. Six and a half feet is low enough for any horse of the larger breeds. When hauled in a low trailer, the horse is uncomfortable and, what is worse, he will invariably strike the top of his head as he steps out of the trailer.

There is no conclusive answer as to whether the ramp-type endgate or the step-up type is better. The writer prefers the ramp and a partition consisting of a steel pole from which drops a rubber matting to absorb any possible kick. The pole can be swung to the side for leading the first horse.

Some horsemen like an escape door at the front of each horse. The writer does not. It adds weight and certainly does not add strength. A large, strong ring should be sturdily anchored in front of each horse. Though no horse should feel the restraint of a tie rope while he is being hauled (any such restraint will make him fight a trailer), it may be necessary at some time to tie a long cotton rope in one of those rings, bring it back alongside a horse who is refusing to lead, then up across his hind legs above the hocks, and from there to the hands of a stout assistant who can pull and take up slack until the goal is reached. Sometimes the first reaction of a horse to this method is a strong kick. If the assistant is deft enough to pick up the slack, that first kick will usually land the recalcitrant animal right where he is wanted—inside the trailer.

WARNING: *Never* pull forward on halter or lead rope while asking a horse to enter a trailer. A knowing hand kept on the halter *to guide* the horse will help while hands behind him or a rope pushes him forward. Picking up a foot and placing it on ramp or floor sometimes helps.

Heavy fiber or rubber matting saves floor and feet.

Training. *See also* COLTS, REINS, ROLLBACK, INSIDE ROLL, BACKING, HUNTER (*Schooling of Hunters*), CAVALLETTI, JUMPING, LONGLINE, ROPING, SLIDING STOP, and other headings pertaining to specific kinds of performance

There are many kinds of training for each kind of performance. No one of them can be called *best*. The choice of training should depend upon the kind of relationship the owner wants to maintain with his horse. If the horse is to be a thing with which to win prizes or a tool with which to play polo, rope calves, or the like, it is wise never to make a pet of the animal. The best show is put up by an animal who performs with a certain amount of fear and confusion. The dressage mount must be drilled like a soldier and respond like a machine.

When a trainer of reining and roping horses was asked how his horse knew he had done well if the trainer never petted him after a good performance, the reply was, "When I stop beatin' on him he knows he's OK."

While there is a touch of Western humor in that reply, it reveals the kind of relationship desired in a horse, that is, to be an important tool in fast and possibly dangerous work. The pet colt is anathema to most professional trainers. Before any training can begin, such a colt has to be taught to relate to human beings in a brand-new way.

Pet colt is a broad phrase. It covers the animal who has been so handled that he will nip, kick, fight any kind of restraint, and be generally obnoxious. It also includes the young animal who has become fond enough of human companionship to habitually come toward his owner when he or she enters the corral, paddock, or stall and enjoys being cross-tied and groomed and handled in other appropriate ways. Such a colt learns early that a halter on his head is the signal for cessation of play and a sign of working with his handler. He has been handled by an owner smart enough to communicate with the animal. Training has progressed by such gradual stages that the colt has experienced neither fright nor confusion. On the rare occasions when the animal has been punished, the punishment was perfectly timed (occurred *as* the infraction was committed) and was severe enough to be more than a mere irritation. An animal trained in the manner just outlined can become the kind of pleasure horse described at length under PLEASURE HORSE, though he will probably not make a very good showing in a pleasure horse class at a horse show, for animals trained in more conventional ways will put up a flashier appearance in the ring.

A note of exception is in order here, fortunately. At the present time (early 1970s) hunter class awards seem to be going to the animals who come into the ring quietly in hand (*see* IN HAND) and take obstacles cheerfully and calmly. Such equines can well be the products of training without fear.

One sure cause of failure in any attempt to make a fearless, calm horse, whether hunter, ideal pleasure horse, or what not, often escapes notice. That cause is ignorant or careless and ill-bred stable help being allowed contact with young horses. For example, a horseman was doing well with a two-year-old filly. She had been longed, longlined, and ridden enough to begin to understand what a bit is for. She was fearless, fond of learning, and curious. She lived in a box stall adjoining a small paddock or corral. The owner, to save time for his growing legal practice, began to allow the neighbor boy to clean the filly's corral. The lad had apparently been getting along well with the attorney's older horses when he cleaned their corrals.

As the owner learned later from an observant neighbor, the boy entered the filly's corral with barrow and tools while the young equine was munching hay. At the sound of the intrusion she trotted out to see what was up. Curious about the novelty of someone other than her owner pushing a barrow into her quarters, she approached the barrow with outstretched nose. The boy, possibly thinking she meant harm, waved a scoopshovel violently at her and yelled. She whirled and kicked like a bronc wearing a bucking cinch, though her heels were many feet from the boy. This initial meeting of boy and filly set a precedent. Soon a routine was established. The boy would enter the corral. Immediately the filly would rush out of her stall or toward him from another part of the corral. The boy would throw up a shovel and yell. The mare would then whirl and kick. Before long it was considered unsafe for anyone to move about in the filly's quarters without first haltering her.

The instance just cited was a mild example of the effect of stable help on horses. Many a biter, kicker, or stall crowder has been created by such help. Experiences in stall or paddock affect a young horse's entire response to people. From the moment he is foaled, the equine destined to become an ideal mount of any sort should come into contact only with people who are as nearly well bred as the equine as possible and who will accord him as much respect as they hope to cultivate in him for his human friends.

Trandem

Some years ago there was a vogue among sporting folk for driving three horses single file. Such a hitch was called a *trandem*. It is perhaps regrettable that the vogue was short-lived, for driving trandem is certainly an act of skill and a demonstration of well-trained horses.

Transportation

The most comfortable way to transport a horse is by riverboat. It has one drawback: Some docks, usually the busiest ones, are of steel or other material on which a horse cannot stand unless he is specially shod with rubber. The cheapest overland horse transportation is the van. One or more horse van lines can be contacted at any major racetrack and at most of the more important shows. The biggest drawback of this means of transportation is that owners of one or two horses must suit their time to the schedule of the van. Sometimes there is considerable delay before a van has a load going in the desired direction. By far the most popular means of transportation is the two-horse trailer (*see* TRAILERS).

Shipment by railroad entails the building of a stall or stalls in a boxcar unless one is shipping a carload. There is an old federal ruling which obliges the railroad to give half rate to purebred breeding stock shipped from the East to the West, but it almost requires the employment of legal aid to get compliance from some rail lines.

Traveller or Traveler

The name *Traveller* is associated with several famous horses and many not quite famous (because of the custom of giving colts the name of an illustrious sire). The earliest record of a famous Traveller is of a Thoroughbred by that name bred just before our Revolution, owned by a Mr. Morton of Colonial Maryland. A son of Morton's Traveller, called Tasker's Traveler, was bred by Colonel Benjamin Tasker, Jr., whose estate was known as Belaire. It was located in Prince Georges County, Maryland. There is no way of tracing the descendants of this famous horse down to the time of our Civil War; however, it is probable that the blood of Tasker's Traveler ("a fine, strong bay horse, upwards of 16 hands") flowed in the veins of General Robert E. Lee's favorite mount, also called Traveler. Judging from pictures and such meager descriptions as are extant, Lee's Traveler too was a "fine, strong horse," though gray and not over 16 hands. Lee commented upon the excellent walk of his animal and his endurance.

In any list of famous Quarter Horse sires, the name Traveler is included, though blood connection between any Quarter Horse and the Travelers mentioned above would be difficult to prove. Nevertheless, there is a strong probability that the bloodline continued with the name.

Treasure Hunts

Treasure hunts as well as paper chases (*see* PAPER CHASE) are very helpful in stimulating interest in riding clubs, schools, and breed associations. It is difficult to understand why they are practically unknown among horsemen in the West. The treasure hunt is a game played on horseback just as it is on foot except for the fact that clues are scattered over a much wider territory.

Tree

The tree is the wooden foundation of a saddle. It is conventionally made of hard wood (preferably beech). Western saddle trees are covered with heavy rawhide, usually referred to as bullhide, before the exterior leather, horn, and undercovering (almost invariably sheepskin) are added (*see* SADDLES).

English saddle trees are much lighter than Western ones and are necessarily strengthened by steel strips especially across the front and rear of the tree. On excellent (and expensive) ones, such as the Smith-Worthingtons (made in the United States), the steel is of the highest quality and so placed that it does not create pressure on the backbone. In the so-called cutback saddle the pommel is open over the withers so that the saddle will not detract from the appearance of a long neck in the show-ring. This type of saddle requires very strong irons in front. American ingenuity has excelled in combining strength with lightness and desired appearance in the cutback show saddle, which is an English saddle.

Trials. *See* HUNTER TRIALS

Triple Bar Jumps

The triple bar jump is the simplest form of what the *Rule Book* of the American Horse Shows Association classifies as a *spread jump,* "an obstacle or combination of obstacles taken at one jump" (in the triple bar, three bars). The bars must, according to the *Rule Book,* have a minimum height of three feet, and the difference in height of the bars must be at least nine inches. In the case of a tie, bars are usually either raised or spread or both until one animal commits a fault.

Triple Crown

The horse who wins the three best-known races in this country is known as the "winner of the Triple Crown." These races are the Kentucky Derby, which is run on the first Saturday in May; the Preakness, two weeks later; and the Belmont, three weeks after the Preakness.

Trip Rope

1. A trip rope may be a rope attached to the latch on a gate of a chute, trap, or pen for the purpose of remote control.

2. A trip rope may be a rope attached to the fore pastern of a horse. From the pastern, it passes through a ring at the center of girth, cinch, or bellyband and thence to the hands of the driver of a vehicle (if the animal is being broken to harness) or to the hands of a trainer or an assistant (if the animal is destined for use under saddle). Such a device is used to break an animal of kicking, stampeding, or some other vice. Some trainers use a trip rope on every animal during the first few lessons in harness.

Trotters. *See* HARNESS RACING

Tucked Up

A horse whose abdomen, especially in the region of the flanks, is extremely deficient in circumference (giving him a greyhound appearance) is said to be "tucked up" or "herring gutted." If this is a congenital characteristic, not a result of starvation or extreme thirst, it is a major fault.

Turf

Turf is a rather slangy word for *racetrack.*

Turkish (Turkoman, Tukmon)

The Turkish horse is one of the several breeds of North African horses often loosely referred to as Barb. The Byerly Turk is one of the three best-known and highly respected sources· of Thoroughbred blood (*see* THOROUGHBRED).

Turk's-Head Knot

A Turk's-head knot is a complicated but very neat knot customarily used on all rope ends in the West to prevent raveling and/or to prevent a rope from passing through a narrow opening. The greenhorn or newcomer uses Scotch tape to hold the end of a rope together; the knowledgeable Westerner uses a Turk's head.

Turning

Turning a horse at any considerable speed without properly collecting him is quite often the cause of a bowed tendon (*see* BOWED TENDON). The person who "rides only one end" of his mount is not a horseman. A horse and rider turn as do partners on the ballroom floor—harmoniously in unison of entire bodies (*see* COLLECTION, PIVOT, ROLLBACK).

Turning Out to Grass

Vacationers and devotees of the hunting field turn horses out to grass seasonally. This practice may benefit the horse or may do him serious damage. If the pasture is good, the fences are safe, and the pasture is not overcrowded or infested by one or more shod animals or animals who fight, shoes may be removed and hooves properly prepared for going barefoot, and the horse can be safely and carefully introduced to his new quarters. A horse who has been confined and highly fed may put on a burst of speed when first turned out. This burst may carry him crashing into a fence or a fight.

When the horse is returned home after a season on grass, he must be gradually accustomed to work, after his feet have been properly attended to by a farrier. If flies have been bad or the pasture deteriorated during the season, the horse may be in very poor condition. His droppings should be examined for worms (*see* PARASITES), and he should gradually be put on full feed and kept there until he returns to normal.

Tushes

The "bridle teeth" which appear in male horses (*see* TEETH) during their fifth year are often called *tushes* or *tusks*.

Twitch

A twitch is a loop of rope or chain fastened to the end of a handle. The horse who has been spoiled for standing while being shod, as well as horses in some other situations in which force is the only recourse for obtaining immobilization, can best be handled by use of a halter chain (at end of a shank—*see* HALTER SHANK) or by use of a twitch. The latter is ordinarily preferable because the former requires more skill and frequently results in some sloughing of tissue.

The loop is placed over the end of the horse's upper lip. Then the handle is twisted until the loop holds the lip firmly. The user of the twitch must stand at the horse's shoulder, for some horses strike quickly and violently when being twitched. Most horses will remain motionless when the twitch is properly in place. A few will stand but gradually lower the head and finally "explode" (strike and fight hysterically). An experienced horseman, by shaking the twitch slightly at just the right instants, can usually avoid catastrophe.

The process described above may shock the inexperienced, but it is a much more humane method of handling a spoiled horse during shoeing than the beating and kicking often resorted to.

No horseman has the right to ask a first-class farrier to be a horse-breaker. To do so adds to the expense of all who own well-mannered animals and are careful about educating their colts for shoeing. Often a brief application of a twitch at the right time will save a colt from being spoiled. The considerate owner of young animals has his twitch ready in case need arises during shoeing time.

Two-Track

Two-track is a nonprofessional term loosely applied to a general class of dressage movements in which a horse progresses in such a manner that his hind feet and forefeet make two parallel tracks, usually about one foot apart. This maneuver is done in some movements by following the outer edge of an arena and in others by cutting diagonally across the arena. Some movements, e.g., shoulder-in (*see* SHOULDER-IN), must be done with extreme collection (*see* COLLECTION) and curving of the spine. The simplest one, the lateral march, is performed with very slight collection or none at all. In this movement the horse's body is kept diagonal to his line of progress, and each outside foot crosses in front of its partner as the horse progresses. The movement is usually done in a diagonal across arena or hall.

Tying the Horse

Every horseman knows that no sensible horseman ties a horse by the bridle reins, but practically every horseman sometime in his life has a horse he ties by the reins, as every harness repairman knows. It is well to remember that if a horse is tied by one bridle rein only, there will probably be a rein left to ride home with after the one rein is broken—provided the other rein has been tied up to the saddle so it does not get under the horse's feet.

For proper methods of tying a horse *see* COLTS, HALTER SHANK, and TIE ROPE.

An additional caution may be timely: Never tie a horse so that the rope will slip down on the post and exert a downward pull on the horse (and don't tie him so long that his forefeet will get over the rope).

Uniforms. *See* APPOINTMENTS

United States Trotting Association. *See* HARNESS RACING

Urticaria (Nettle Rash)

An affliction similar to hives in human beings occurs in some horses, usually the young, when brought off pasture and range. The bumps or "hives" may or may not come to a head and scab. Time and plenty of bran in the ration will usually cure the ailment if it is nothing more serious than this rather mystifying trouble, urticaria.

The writer has encountered urticaria many times and has found no appreciable help in veterinary advice and none in external applications. However, he always calls a veterinarian when a case occurs, just to be sure the animal is afflicted with no serious disorder.

Vaquero. *See also* BUCKAROO

Vaquero, the Spanish word for cowboy, occurs in colloquial use in the Southwest.

Varmint

The term *varmint* is used for *fox* by some hunting folk.

Ventilation

Ample cross ventilation is as necessary in a stable as in a house. Horses kept in a poorly ventilated stable in summer will lose weight and become weak. Eventually they will succumb to some respiratory ailment.

If built in proper relation to prevailing winds, stables with large double doors at either end of the runway will provide enough ventilation for a row of standing, or "tie," stalls. Box stalls should be provided with half doors or outside windows for additional ventilation.

No horse should be allowed to stand in a direct draft, so stall doors and windows must be made so they can be closed when wind causes draft directly on the horse. In hot parts of this country, stables must be constructed so that upper walls can all be opened, and roofs must be high enough to avoid radiating their heat on animals.

Veterinarians

No area of science has made greater progress in the last half-century than veterinary medicine. Though there is a great need for more colleges, as there is in the field of medicine for human beings, 18 colleges of veterinary medicine and surgery span the country. To name only three, Cornell, in New York; Fort Collins, in Colorado; and the University of California school at Davis compare with top medical schools in discriminating selection of students, scientific quality of curricula, and rigorous training, time, and money required for graduation.

Unfortunately for horse owners, the easiest and quickest road to affluence for a graduate is small-animal practice (though all good veterinarians are overworked and none acquire riches of great magnitude). However, in practically all areas in which any considerable number of valuable horses are owned, veterinarians will be found whose love for horses and cattle is greater than the attraction of small-animal practice. Every purchaser of a horse should locate a licensed veterinarian in his area and find out how he can be reached in emergency. In the area in which the writer lives, for example, some veterinarians have their pickups (which are well equipped with necessities for treatment of most emergencies) provided with "walkie-talkie" radios and can be contacted through a phone call to a central answering service. In some areas the veterinarian has a radio-operated buzzer which signals him to call his office or home.

The wise horseman becomes acquainted with his veterinarian *before* emergencies arise.

Vices. *See also* BARN RAT, BALKING, BOLTING, BUCKING, and CHARGING

Getting Behind the Bit

The peculiar, and often dangerous, vice called *getting behind the bit* is not as common as the vice of pulling on the bit, often called *getting ahead of the bit*. It is caused by a heavy hand, by pain from a chin chain or strap that pinches, by a crudely made bit having sharp points or corners that hurt, or by constant overcollection to get high action or appearance of animation. When a horse has suffered from any one of these causes sufficiently, he will bow his neck quickly to remove all hold on the bit. He will even tuck his chin back against his neck or chest. If the rider immediately takes up the slack, the horse will attempt to rear. If thwarted in this attempt by a clout over the head or a drastic lowering of the hands, he will fly back, often running backward at considerable speed for several rods.

The cure, of course, is to remove the cause. The first thing to do is to throw away the bit and ride the horse with a hackamore (*see* HACKAMORE) or bosal. No bit should be put in his mouth until all fear of his rider's hands is dispelled. Then a bit should be hung in his mouth but no reins attached, and he should be ridden on the bosal or hackamore with a bit hanging useless for several days. When the bit is equipped with reins, the reins should be used very lightly and only as a supplement to the bosal. The variety of bit used is not as important as the quality of the hands on the other end of the reins. However, a snaffle (*see* BITS) with a big mouthpiece and the reins run through a running martingale (*see* MARTINGALE) is about as nearly foolproof as a bit can be. If a curb (*see* CURB BIT) is used, the shorter the shank and the bigger the mouthpiece, the less damage it can do. Of course, the chin chain or strap must be properly adjusted.

If the horse still flies back at any touch on the rein after several weeks of unfailing care in the use of the method described, a competent professional should be employed. He may decide that with expert timing a cut with the whip as the horse tenses to fly backward may be indicated. If the professional is really competent, this may help. However, most use of the whip or spur on the horse who is getting behind the bit is like pouring kerosene on a blaze.

Uncompromising kindness and patience are the best remedy for most horsemen to use in curing this vice.

Shying

Shying is frequently caused by the inept or sadistic trainer who forces the colt under whip and spur to go up close to objects that terrify him. It may also be caused by the timid rider who begins to tighten up on the reins and use leg grip whenever he approaches anything he thinks his horse may be afraid of.

Horses, like people, are afraid of what they cannot understand and of the unfamiliar. Any force to make them come close to the feared object increases the terror and makes them fear the one who uses the force. When the horse encounters a fearful object, he should be allowed to go out of the trail and around it, but not in panic. How far he should go from it is a matter to be determined for each situation. Certainly, he should be firmly held to some discipline, but forcing him up to the object just for the sake of discipline is making a bad matter worse. He should be kept going and not allowed to turn around and head toward home. If the horse is very young and a little on the green side, he will want to stop a moment and stare. This is allowable if he is not permitted to jump to the side or turn. It is also understandable, for a horse normally has binocular vision, and a monocular focus for staring takes a conscious effort on his part, as conscious an effort as it does for you to hold your breath. He has to stand still and concentrate (*see* EYES).

The old offender who is constantly and unexpectedly jumping sideways at real or imaginary objects just enough to unbalance his rider is a different problem. He has been spoiled by experts. A skillful rider with expert timing, a deft heel for the spur, and a quick, light hand can catch the horse *every* time he shies and catch him *as he shies*, with heel to drive him on and with rein to keep him in the straight and narrow path. Regular riding by such a rider for thirty days will usually have a salutary effect on the confirmed shyer. If that will not cure him, he is not worth working with further.

The Puller or Cold-Jawed Horse

It is the pulling rider, not the pulling horse, who makes the cold jaw. When a horse becomes hard-mouthed and habitually pulls on the bit, most riders start looking for more severe bits. This is an unfortunate response, for under the sustained torture of a severe bit, the nerves become insensitive and the trouble is increased.

On television I once watched Pablo Casals giving a lesson. The pupil played a passage. The master stopped her and said, "No, crescendo, crescendo, diminuendo, diminuendo! Not all on one level!" So it is with the reins. It is the dead-level pull with no crescendo or diminuendo that makes the cold jaw. A good hand cannot be described. It is learned largely by trial and error and by a sort of sixth sense, an ultrasensitive response to the horse. It also requires as keen a sense of timing as does the dance or the drama. The best way to prevent a bad mouth on a horse is to develop a good pair of hands on the rider.

If the puller with the bad mouth can be cured, the first thing to do is change riders or change bits. If he has been ridden on a curb, change to a snaffle with a draw rein or a gag rein. If he has been ridden with a snaffle, change to a short-shanked, rubber-mouthed curb or a leather-mouthed bar bit (*see* BITS) with reins through running martingales (*see* MARTINGALE).

The horse should be worked alone for a while and set down hard and quickly each time he takes a hard hold of the bit. This procedure is done by holding one rein very firmly and steadily and with the other giving a hard, quick pull that swings the horse's head to the side. It is similar to the quick snatch on the reins often used to throw a running horse for the movies. Considerable skill is required to snatch a horse back properly, so professional help should be employed for the job if at all possible. However, it should be *skilled* professional help, not just a would-be bronc buster.

For the puller who has been ridden with a bit, sometimes a change to a hackamore bit (*see* HACKAMORE BIT) is helpful. But here again the trouble is merely aggravated if the rider has dead hands on the reins. Any sort of hackamore or hackamore bit calls for a deft, quick hand, not unlike that needed in trout fishing. With the hackamore rein, the letting go is just as important and requires just as much skill as the pull. There are good books in print on the use of the hackamore. They are advertised in *Horse Lover's Magazine* and in *Western Horseman*. Before attempting the first use of the hackamore or hackamore bit, one of such books or my *Out of the West* should be studied carefully. The biggest harm done with hackamores and hackamore bits by the ignorant is done by improper adjustment. The nose-piece should come just where the bone and cartilage join on the nose, never down on the soft part of the nose where the wind will be cut off. There is a widespread notion among amateurs and new arrivals in the West that the hackamore, bosal, or hackamore bit is used to cut off a horse's wind. It may be so used, but if it is, unless the horse is utterly foolproof, trouble will result. The hackamore and similar devices work by pressure on the nose and, even more, by pressure on the jaw. It is largely the jaw pressure that does the work in many instances, but the pressure is always momentary only.

Halter Pulling

A horse is sometimes tied too low, too short, or so long that he gets a foot over the tie rope, or he may be tied to a pole or tree at proper height but so loosely that the rope slides down on the tree or pole. He is sometimes tied with a halter or rope too flimsy, or is tied too close to something terrifying, like a steam exhaust or automatic pump, so that he flies back and breaks the halter or rope. If a horse is tied and breaks loose, he is a potential halter puller. The number of times required to make him a confirmed halter puller depends upon the intensity of his fright when he pulls loose and upon the temperament of the horse. One bad experience may make a halter puller that is hard to break.

There are many time-honored gimmicks to break halter pullers. Each old-timer thinks his is the best. All of them are successful in the majority of cases if used by an experienced hand. The most common gimmick is the use of a rope, which must be of cotton and five-eighths of an inch or larger. The rope is doubled and the middle is placed under the horse's tail or under his belly where a flank cinch goes (the kind used in rodeos to make horses buck). Each end of the rope is passed through a large ring just in front of the croup (*see* CROUP). Then the ends are passed through the halter ring and tied to a very stout tree, tall post, or solid ring in the side of the barn. When the horse flies back and gets the pull under his tail or belly, he will lunge violently up and forward, so he must not be tied to an ordinary post or rail on which he could easily injure himself. A variant of this gimmick is to tie a cotton rope around a front pastern (*see* PASTERN). The rope is then passed through the halter ring and finally tied to a tree or ring in the side of the barn.

There is some danger of injury to the horse in each of these gimmicks, but I have seen them used many times, sometimes with the horse being flogged over the head with a sack or blanket to make him fly back. I have never seen an injury result, with the exception of a slight rope burn under the tail, which was easily cured by application of Corona Wool Fat, a useful patented product, or thuja and zinc oxide ointment (an excellent remedy).

Laurence Richardson, an old friend and one of the best horsemen of my acquaintance, has a gimmick I have never seen anyone else use. He has better success with it than I've seen from any other. The horse stays broken; you can tie him with a shoestring and he leads up promptly when led from another horse or on foot. Richardson uses the same system to break a horse who rebels at going into a trailer.

His gimmick is simple. He replaces the crownpiece of a stout halter with a piece of number 9 smooth fence wire. I would not have the temerity to employ such a contraption myself, but I have seen him use it many times, once on a spoiled mare we bought in partnership, and he has never had an injury result from it.

I have used the rope under the tail and the rope around the belly and was always successful with both. I quit use of the tail method because I disliked having to cure rope burns.

One grandson of Bourbon King I bought in Kentucky as a five-year-old was a bad halter puller. But in his early show training I knew he had suffered so much that I did not have the heart to subject him to any more misery in which he could see no sense. I started tying him with a three-quarter-inch cotton neck rope, tied with a bowline knot, passed through the halter ring and tied to a stout limb of a tree at the height he normally carried his head. I made sure the limb was strong enough to hold the entire weight and pull of the horse but had just a little give, so when he went back on it he would not hit a solid pull.

For months I tied the horse no other way. When I finally tied him to a ring bolted solidly to the heavy timber of the stable, he went back on the rope a time or two, but did not become hysterical as had been his habit before I started to work with him. Eventually I could tie him anywhere.

The method I have just described obviously takes more time and requires much more sustained care and attention than the use of the tail or belly rope, all of which illustrates an important point: Any gimmick, from long line or bitting rig to tail rope for a halter puller, is a shortcut substitute for time and the patient skill of a competent horseman. Sometimes the result of use of the gimmick is as good for the end in view as the longer method, though usually not as safe for the horse.

Kicking

The timid horse is most likely to become a kicker. The mule is a much more timid animal than the horse and is subjected to even worse abuse than horses, outside show stables. He is quite usually a kicker.

The way to prevent the vice of kicking is to be ever watchful that you do not frighten a horse by stepping up behind him suddenly when he does not know you are around. Always speak to him before you approach from the rear. Never, never approach him with arms extended and torso leaning forward. You would not slip up on a friend from the rear and poke a hand out at him to see if he would kick. To keep a horse from becoming a kicker in company, be always watchful for the idiot or ignorant one who rides up on the heels of other horses.

There is no one method that will help cure all kickers. A trace chain from a work harness (or chain of similar weight or length) buckled around the hind pastern with a soft, heavy strap, such as a strap off a pair of hobbles, will help in some cases. The chain or chains, if one is used on each hind leg, can be left on while the horse is in a stall or corral. If there is a competent reinsman still alive in the neighborhood, he can drive the horse in a breaking cart with stout hickory thills. With a deft snatch of the rein and flick of the whip as the horse starts to kick, the reinsman can throw him, and an assistant who rides on the step of the breaking cart can get to the horse's head and hold him down for a few minutes of thoughtful repentance.

This method was standard practice in horse-and-buggy days and was usually effective, though some horses had to be thrown several times. Throwing should always be done on sod, sand, or some other soft surface free from stones, though in the horse-and-buggy era it was often done on a gravel road with considerable loss of hide and sometimes broken knees. The method of throwing in harness is the same as that sometimes used in Hollywood by stunt riders.

The horse who kicks at other horses in company is especially dangerous and should never be taken on a trail ride. In the hunting field, such a horse should wear a red ribbon on his tail, and the rider must be constantly vigilant to keep out of the vicinity of other horses, especially while hounds are drawing cover or the field is waiting for anything else.

I do not like the job, but I have broken horses from kicking in company by the following method: The kicker, ridden with a full bridle, was tempted to kick by a skilled mounted assistant, the assistant being careful to ride just close enough to tempt a kick but not close enough for his horse to receive it. The instant the kicker's heels left the ground, I would collect him and use a whalebone or rawhide whip around his belly. The more definite the mark made, the better. Even a little blood was not bad. However, one cut with the whip and one only was the ironclad rule. More horses have been ruined by repeated cuts than have ever been helped by any kind of use of the whip. Continuous pain never makes the horse do what is wanted; it usually aggravates a bad action. The puller on the reins is usually made worse by the rider's use of a severe bit and constant pull.

The more a balking horse is clubbed, the stiller he stands. It is the sharp, well-timed cut with the whip, touch with the spur, or pull on the bit that gets results, when results can be obtained by a whip, spur, or bit.

When riding a colt or horse of unknown disposition, the rule is always to keep the animal well collected and his head up as other riders approach. A horse cannot do much damage with his heels while he is extremely collected and has his head well up. Of course, a skilled and careful rider can ride any horse and keep him from kicking in company. The spoiled confirmed kicker, however, will watch his chance and may catch even the best of riders off guard, so don't ride a kicker in company.

Biting

Many good colts raised in backyards are spoiled and made into biters. I do not subscribe to the notion that pet colts necessarily make mean horses. It all depends on what kind of pets they are. A colt can be taught to lead a few days after he is foaled—just as soon as his legs quit wobbling. He can be taught to cooperate with and not to fear human beings, but at the same time he must be taught to mind. Never caress a colt by putting a hand out toward the front of his head or stroke the front of his face or nose. A colt's automatic reaction to such gestures is to nip. Watch colts at play; they illustrate what I am talking about—a reach for the head and a nip in return.

It should be unnecessary to say that the person who allows a small colt to be teased and made to nip should never be permitted to own an animal of any kind.

There is a wide assortment of "cures" for biting. An old favorite was a small paddle stuck full of nails and hidden in a sock or glove which the horse was encouraged to bite. Variations of this are easy to imagine. A farrier uses a sharp-pointed punch or divider. A cowboy uses a hot-shot electric prod. The expert horseman, if the horse is young, frequently puts his faith in time, removes the cause (ignorant handling), and waits for the youngster to grow out of the nippy stage. If no time is available, the expert will use a whip. If the colt tends to nip when groomed or when held, the horseman will keep a firm hold on halter or bit and put one welt on shoulder or ribs each time the horse nips, restraining him from lunging forward by the hold on bit or halter. Rarely is it possible to punish the horse about the head without making him head-shy. Any horseman is ashamed to have a horse in his stable who jerks up his head whenever a hand is moved in front of it. The horse who gives evidence of fear of being struck about the head is a disgrace to his owner.

Very rarely is a horse a biter in company, but such a horse should wear a muzzle.

Rearing and Whirling

Almost any young horse may overcollect and get his forefeet off the ground once in a while. This action will only become the habit of rearing if he is mishandled.

When a horse comes up off the ground with his forefeet, the rider should release pressure on the reins at once and lean forward over the horse's neck, being careful to put his head down *beside* the horse's neck, not on top of it where he may well have his nose broken. The instant the horse is on all fours again, the rider must push him forward by whatever impulsion is required, using only enough restraint to keep contact on the reins. The idea is to prevent the horse from coming up a second time.

The rearing horse is usually the product of the heavy-handed rider. Almost any horse can be made to rear if he is kicked or whipped and jerked at the same time. The extremely sensitive horse with plenty of heart will rear if given almost any signal of impulsion (a light squeeze with the legs, a slight backward movement of the heels, or a clicking noise made by the rider's tongue) and is restrained by the bit from going forward. If he is made to rear this way a few times, rearing will become a habit. The first thing to do for a cure is to remove the rider by any legal means. Then a martingale can be used and the horse ridden by a more experienced rider. If a standing martingale (*see* MARTINGALE) is used, it should be attached to a noseband or bosal, never to a bit. It should be just long enough to allow the horse to carry his head comfortably in his normal or natural way, but short enough to prevent his putting his head up to rear.

If a running martingale (*see* MARTINGALE) is used, only snaffle reins should go through the martingale ring. It should be so adjusted that there is no downward pull on the reins unless the horse puts his head higher than he usually carries it.

Some horses become so confirmed in this habit that they can rear in spite of martingales. They often combine rearing with whirling, refusing to leave the stable or a group of riders in the field. Such a horse is called stablebound or herdbound (*see* BARN RAT).

Gimmicks for curing such cases range all the way from a paper sack, filled with water and broken over the horse's head as he rears, to a hot shot applied by an assistant as the horse whirls. If the rearing horse is pulled on over backward and the rider steps off and holds the horse prostrate for a few minutes, the animal loses its enthusiasm for two-legged walking. Once will usually break the horse of the vice, but if not, he should be pulled over and held down each time he comes up. Three times is the limit I have ever known a horse to rear when so handled. This trick is, of course, useful only to skilled riders and should be done on sod or other soft footing. It is dangerous and should never be attempted by any but expert riders of long experience and by them only after all other methods of cure have failed.

Cribbing and Wind Sucking

In some parts of America *cribbing* is used to designate the chewing of wood, corral fences, mangers, and stalls.

The term *cribbing* in other parts of the country means only the act of hooking the upper teeth over a post, stump, or other solid object, pulling back, and swallowing air.

The mere chewing of wood often leads to the more harmful vice just described, also called *wind sucking* or *stump sucking*. Theories about causes and cures of cribbing and stump sucking are numerous. Certainly the horse suffering from a nutritional deficiency is more prone to eat wood than is a healthy horse. However, I am not the only horseman who has tried all the vitamin and mineral supplements known and found nothing that will stop wood chewing. In a few cases a bale of straw (opened and wire removed, of course) kept available to the horse helped some, but it was not a complete cure. Some horses chew wood all their lives, regardless of condition. Others chew only at times. Some never touch the stuff.

There is no sure prevention of this vice except to keep the horse where there is no exposed wood. A creosote-base white paint helps. Painting all exposed wood with creosote is as near an effective prevention, or cure, as I have found where it is impossible to keep wood away from the horse, or the horse away from wood, but this method is not very sightly. Stripping boards with metal is sometimes effective but dangerous, especially in the arid parts of the country, because the roofing nails tend to drop out or are easily pulled out when the wood shrinks from the heat of the sun. As every old horseman knows, roofing nails are the worst kind of hardware for getting in a horse's foot.

In my own corrals I use an electric wire to keep horses from wood. Once in a while a smart animal will find a place I have not protected. Then I put in some insulators and string more wire. Any electric fence unit adequately underwritten is probably safe, but I use only the battery-operated variety, powered by a six-volt hot-shot battery.

Fortunately, few horses become wind suckers or stump suckers. This vice is even more baffling in regard to cause and cure than wood chewing. It occurs more frequently among horses who are constantly confined in small quarters than among others. It is very rare, so rare that I have never seen it, among horses who work regularly. The only "cure," which is merely a deterrent, is a fairly wide leather strap buckled tightly around the throttle (*see* THROTTLE). The best such strap is made with an extra bit of leather that serves as a pad under the throttle. These so-called cribbing straps can be bought at most saddlery stores. The strap is tight enough to prevent distention of throttle muscles, but not so tight as to interfere with eating. Some wind suckers do not take in enough air to damage their general health. With such mild offenders nothing need be done except remove from their corrals all objects that will tempt them to hook their teeth on something solid, pull back, and swallow air. Other horses seem almost frantic to suck in air and will use almost any solid object to crib on. They lose weight and vigor. A strap should be used on them.

Weaving

Weaving is a vice seen usually in young horses in poor condition kept in tie stalls or very small box stalls, though a horse of any age or condition may be a weaver. The weaver will stand in relatively the same spot for hours but will continuously shift weight from one front foot to the other as do some carnivores in cages in the zoo. Both the prevention and the cure are to keep animals where they have ample room for exercise and are free from fear and tension. One competent horseman recommends putting the horse in a stall where he can look out of a window at traffic.

Stall Pawing and Kicking

The horse who pawed or kicked in the stall used to be very common in horse-and-buggy days in city stables where horses had to stand in tie stalls, sometimes for weeks in winter, without being out. I suspect, therefore, that the cause is largely confinement. If so, prevention is simply a matter of giving the horse room to exercise. A cure is a leg chain such as I have described for kicking. A more humane and possibly more effective cure is advocated by another horseman. It is a rubber ball attached to a rubber band which, in turn, is fastened to the horse's leg by a strap. Whenever the horse strikes or kicks, the ball bounces on his leg. Though I have never seen this device tried, it should be effective, for it is the timing of punishment, not the severity, that makes it effective.

Villain

The word *villain* is used for *fox*, probably a carry-over from the day when foxes were actually a menace to small stock and poultry.

Vixen

A vixen is a female fox (a less harmful creature than the one for whom the term is used figuratively), and destroying her is legal in most places.

Voice

In the hunting field, though the words of the huntsman as he encourages or "rates" his hounds are rarely distinguishable, by the tone of his voice, the rhythm and inflection of his utterances, and his use of the horn, he clearly communicates to experienced members of the field what the hounds are doing. In a similar fashion, though a horse's brain is not constructed to comprehend words as symbols used in meaningful combinations, a mount accustomed to the human voice is as vitally affected by it as is any human being, and he is probably aware of more subtleties than is his master.

One warning in the use of the voice can never be too often repeated: *Don't cluck* to your mount, especially when in company. First of all, such practice labels one as rude or ignorant; secondly, it may startle a companion's horse and cause an accident.

Quiet, calm, continuous use of the voice has taken many a young and inexperienced horse through many a bad spot.

A kind and careful stroke usually better conveys approval than does a pat. Unless the horse is well aware of the peculiarities of humans, a pat may startle rather than reassure.

Waler

In Australia, the states of New South Wales, Queensland, and Victoria comprise an area so favorable to the breeding of horses that we might call it the "blue grass" of Australia (comparing it to that small part of Kentucky surrounding Lexington which has become so famous for breeding fine horses). The best horses developed in that region are called *Walers* (though they are as common to Queensland and Victoria as to New South Wales).

The original horses of Australia were brought by explorers in the sixteenth century. Like our own Southwestern ones, they were of Barb and Arabian blood—directly or indirectly. Later importations of different breeds were made, of course, including the Thoroughbred. By careful selective breeding, the Waler became an animal sought after as a cavalry and artillery mount. In 1940 a Waler made the world's record jump of eight feet and four inches.

Walk. *See also* GAITS

Careful usage reserves the word *walk* for a gait done without any leaping between hoof impacts on the ground. In other words, the horse has a foot in contact with the ground at all times while at the walk. To distinguish this gait from the running walk and the prancy "half trot" done in the show-ring by many horses when asked to walk, a genuine walk is called a flat-footed walk.

For all except the gaited show horse (and some not gaited), the walk is the most important and most used gait a horse has—and usually the one most neglected by trainers. The neglect is understandable because most owners want something showier for their money. However, if the owners were going to ride their horses after training, they might well insist that the animals be taught to do at least a four-mile-an-hour extended walk and a collected walk at a not much slower rate. The writer has seen a few horses who could walk five miles in an hour, and he has owned two such gifted animals. Most claims to a five-mile-an-hour walk will dissolve with an application of the stopwatch.

A wise old horseman once said, "A horse that can walk properly can do anything else well." That statement may stretch truth a trifle, but it is certainly food for thought. The horse who walks perfectly does have a good mouth, is responsive to the aids, and is in harmony with his rider.

Walking Horse. *See* TENNESSEE WALKING HORSE and TENNESSEE WALKING HORSE BREEDERS' AND EXHIBITORS' ASSOCIATION

Walking Race

A walking race, one in which any horse breaking out of a walk between start and finish lines is disqualified, is usually considered a beginners' event. It might well be a contest between experts, for few horsemen are skilled at teaching a horse to walk properly and almost as few can keep him at the peak of performance at the walk even if he has been well trained.

Walk-Trot Horse

A three-gaited horse is often referred to as a walk-trot horse. His three gaits are, theoretically, the walk, trot, and canter.

Wall (of hoof)

The wall is the horny covering of a horse's hoof from the ground to the coronet. It is laminated (consists of layers), and under some adverse conditions the layers tend to separate. Then the hoof is said to be "shelly." Such a hoof will not hold a shoe properly, and the condition is often difficult to cure (*see* HOOF).

Walls (fences)

In some country, stone walls are used as fences on farms. If the footing on either side of a wall is free of booby traps, such as overgrown holes or boulders, the wall makes a good jump. However, a wise horseman always inspects the footing on both sides of a wall before he attempts to take it. Placing a rail on top of a wall one is in the habit of jumping may save skinned pasterns and also prevent lowering the wall by knocking off the top stones. The rider who disturbs a fence not only makes himself unwelcome in the country but often closes the country to all riders.

Waltzing

The circus stunt of waltzing is merely the alternation of pivot on quarters and pivot on forehand. Any horse perfectly trained to respond to the aids can perform it (*see* PIVOT).

Warbles

Warbles are lumps under the hide caused by maggots which hatch there after the sting of the warble fly. If a lump is located where no pressure of saddle or harness is exerted on it, it will come to a head, and the maggot will emerge. The wound can be kept clean until it heals, which will take little time. If a saddle is used over a warble, a serious and permanent sore may result. If world-shaking events depend upon immediate use of the horse, a competent veterinarian should be called to excise the larvae.

'Ware Wire!

Any participant in a hunt calls " 'Ware wire!" or " 'Ware hole!" or " 'Ware quicksand!" whenever he encounters unexpected dangers so that following riders will take warning. Whenever a rider hears the cry " 'Ware hounds!" he had better look sharp and have his mount instantly well in hand, for that cry may be a reprimand for his riding too close upon hounds, a very serious offense. Of course, that same cry may mean that hounds have suddenly encountered difficulty in following the line and are momentarily casting for scent in brush where they may not readily be seen.

Warts

Warts sometimes grow to considerable size. Unless they are under the saddle, where they will necessitate veterinary attention, the owner may experiment with tying a silk thread around the base of the wart or touch it with silver nitrate. Such remedies sometimes are efficacious. However, the writer recalls one horse afflicted with warts, an excellent animal, whose owner allowed it to go for some time without veterinary attention while the son of the household experimented with home remedies. When a veterinarian was called, he found the growths to be malignant, and the animal could not be saved. Whether earlier attention could have prevented the tragedy is a moot question.

Water Fountains

All feed and saddlery stores have for sale or available on order drinking fountains for horses. They are simple to operate. The horse quickly learns to press the paddle in the bowl, thereby opening a valve. These devices are excellent for providing constant, clean water; the bowl is easily removed and cleaned. However, in climates where the temperature drops very far below freezing, special valves must be used on the fountains and all pipes leading to them must be well insulated. Equal insulation of pipes is necessary in extremely hot climates. Water standing in uninsulated pipes or hoses in Arizona in summer, for instance, is often scalding hot when it is released.

Watering

Clean water should be available to the horse at all times. It is less harmful to him to cheat him on feed than to fail to give him constant access to water. In a horse, the stomach is a much smaller part of the digestive tract than in most other animals. It was developed for the nibbling of forage intermittently throughout the 24-hour day, and drinking water frequently (and in small quantities) when possible. A horse who is watered only once or twice daily may wash undigested grain into his intestines and cause colic, or he may wash all digestive fluids out just before mealtime.

It should not be necessary to warn that giving an overheated horse water will probably cause founder. A few sips every few minutes until he has his fill is the method to use in watering a hot horse. (Of course, during this time he will be walked and rubbed with a good linen or terry-cloth rag.)

While the kind master shades the water tub when the thermometer climbs far above 100 degrees and removes the ice when water freezes, a horse can tolerate warm water in summer and cold water in winter if it is constantly available so he can take it a little at a time.

Watering Out

Around some racetracks the process of giving a hot horse a few sips of water every few minutes until he has his fill is called watering out.

Weaning

Milk from a mare on excellent pasture or otherwise properly fed is the best food for helping a foal grow into a fine horse. If the mare is not pregnant and the owner has no urgent need for her at hard work, the colt will do best if allowed to nurse as long as his dam will put up with him. She may do so for a year, but she will eventually wean him unless the pair is confined in small quarters where the offspring has unfair advantage.

It is customary on breeding farms to wean foals at five or six months. Weaning can be done without damage to the foal if he has been taught to eat grain early (starting when a few days old) and is accustomed to a daily ration of all the grain he wants. (Whole oats is the most foolproof feed for colts, especially if they have access to grain in a "creep," which is so constructed that the little fellows can enter it but the mares cannot.) The weanlings should have all the good, green, leafy legume hay they want and good pasture if possible. Patented feed supplements for foals are used by many good horsemen, but because they are high in protein, it is possible for them to become the source of food poisoning. One brand of such feed reportedly caused fatalities in Arizona in 1971. If for the sake of the dam's health or for any other reason a foal has to be weaned early, such supplemental feed must be given, but the wise horseman will consult his veterinarian about the safety of the particular feed he uses. Unfortunately, baby equines cannot digest cow's milk, which curds in a solid mass. Mare's milk curds in a form that somewhat resembles snow. Goat's milk can be digested by foals. More than one orphan foal has nursed a goat with excellent results (sometimes the goat takes a little persuasion). It is possible to use cow's milk if rolled oats (in the form people eat for breakfast) is added to it to make it into a gruel.

Whenever the foal is weaned, he should be confined in a clean, safe box stall, corral, or paddock preferably far enough from his dam so the two animals cannot hear each other. If the foal is extremely high-strung, it is best to confine him in a fairly small area so he will not run in panic and injure himself. Weaning two foals together or confining the weanling with a gentle old animal a few days is often helpful. The weanling and his dam should not be turned together until the mare has completely dried up and is in no danger of allowing the foal to attempt to nurse. This may well be a matter of several weeks. Mares usually dry up best if the udder is not touched; however, poultices of strong tea sometimes relieve the discomfort of a heavy milker. The mare should be taken off grain until she dries up. Her hay ration should not be increased to compensate for the withholding of grain, for eating hay prompts drinking of water. It is not wise to restrict the water, for an impaction could result. If the mare has been used to daily ration of bran in her grain, it is best to continue the bran, especially if the mare has some years to her credit.

Welsh Pony

The Welsh Pony Society of America, 202 North Church Street, West Chester, Pennsylvania 19380 (Mrs. Louise E. Geheret, secretary-treasurer), maintains the registry for Welsh ponies in this country. There is no more versatile breed of pony. In conformation and temperament it uniformly exhibits features most highly prized among fanciers of fine breeds of full-sized horses.

The breed is very old. Its proponents say that it has been cultivated in Wales since Saxon times. In the early nineteenth century, Thoroughbred blood was introduced, and the influence of the fine, old-time Thoroughbred is evident in the refinement of head and quality of coat of many Welsh ponies. Little Squire, a Welsh pony of scarcely more than 13 hands in height, was for years the open jumping champion of the United States. Thousands of Americans have seen motion pictures of this valiant little fellow taking five- and six-foot jumps (some of which he could not see over) in his competitions in Madison Square Garden in open jumping classes. As one horseman remarked, "Rarely has so much horse been wrapped up in such a small hide!"

Among important shows featuring Welsh pony competitions are the following: (1) All-Pony Show in Lebanon, Indiana, held in June; (2) All-State 4-H Pony Show, Pontiac, Illinois, also held in June; (3) Heart of Illinois Fair Pony Show, Peoria, Illinois, held in July; (4) Illinois State Fair, Springfield, Illinois, held in August; (5) Stephenson County Fair, Freeport, Illinois, held in August; and (6) National Dairy Cattle Congress, Waterloo, Iowa, held in September.

Western Chunk

Until the last few decades, Western horses were shipped by carloads to Midwestern and Eastern sale barns for auctions. Many of them were classified as "Western chunks." Such animals were the result of using draft stallions on range mares. They were rather heavyset animals of good-sized bone and feet. They were especially adapted to light farm work, and some went south to cotton plantations. In fact, they were sometimes called "Southern chunks."

Western Horse. *See* QUARTER HORSE, MUSTANG, and WILD HORSES

Western Saddles (stock saddles). *See* SADDLES

Western Seat. *See* SEAT

Weymouth (Bit, Bridle)

A Weymouth bit is the conventional English curb bit. It has straight shanks, or sidepieces, provided with lip-strap loops and it usually has a moderate port.

A Weymouth bridle is the conventional English full bridle or double bridle (consisting of curb and snaffle). (*See* BRIDLES.)

Whang Leather   ·

Whang leather is very soft, tough leather usually used in strips for tying other pieces of leather together.

Whips

A properly timed, severe cut with a whip has improved many a horse, but misuse of the whip has spoiled many more. In the hands of an expert, a whip may be used either as punishment when a horse misbehaves from a cause other than ignorance, misunderstanding, or fear; or it may be used as a signal, as in work on the longe (or lunge) line. Usually a good trainer prefers to have his finished horse work without whip under saddle, though there are numerous exceptions arising from the congenital temperament of individual horses or from peculiar previous training.

The rider who pecks at his mount intermittently with a light whip is an irritation to the animal and to human companions. However, the child on a sluggish mount should have a whip and be taught to use it rather than make a nuisance of himself by lagging behind when in company. Of course, the sluggish horse is never ideal for a child or anyone else; but the responsive, prompt, and safe horse is so hard to find that necessity sometimes dictates the sluggish mount for a child.

Whip Breaking

As stated above, there are those rare times when a severe cut with a whip, even severe enough to draw blood, may be necessary. Prolonged lashings

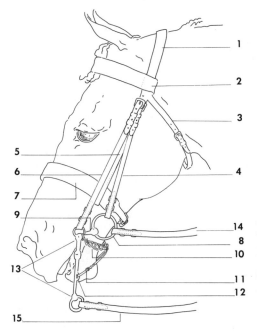

Bit of bridoon or full bridle with cavesson. 1. Crown; 2. browband; 3. throatlatch; 4. snaffle cheekpiece; 5. cavesson headstall; 6. curb cheekpiece; 7. cavesson; 8. snaffle ring (bridoon); 9. snaffle mouthpiece; 10. curb chain; 11. lip strap; 12. lip-strap loop; 13. curb shank; 14. snaffle rein; 15. curb rein.

serve no purpose other than to expose the ill nature and ignorance of the handler. The nearest thing to an exception to this rule is the "whip breaking" sometimes used to teach a horse to come to the trainer's hand when he snaps his finger. It is accomplished thus: The horse is whipped each time he turns his rump toward the trainer, and the whip is applied repeatedly until the horse turns to face his tormentor. When this course is embarked upon, the trainer must not relent for one instant until he gets the desired result, even if he miscalculates and stops a flying hoof with some part of his own anatomy.

Such a method is not justified except with a horse who has been so badly spoiled that a more reasonable method of correction would consume more time than the animal is worth. Even then, the result will rarely if ever be the kind of response one desires in a personal mount.

Whippers-in (Whips)

The whippers-in (frequently referred to simply as whips) are, unless officially appointed Honorary Whips, hunt servants who act as assistants to the huntsman. Because the latter maintains the friendliest possible relations with the hounds so that they look to him for comfort and protection, he never rates (punishes) them. All punishment of hounds is administered by the whips, hence their title.

Whirling. *See* VICES

Wild Horses. *See also* MUSTANG

The ancestry and nature of present-day wild horses is discussed at some length under MUSTANG in this book. The spectacle of wounded and dying horses dragged into trucks (or left to slow death on the desert) and hauled to pet-food canneries after an airplane horse hunt is not as common today as a few years ago because most Western states have laws against hunting horses from the air. The American Horse Protection Association, 629 River Bend Road, Great Falls, Virginia, is doing courageous work on this problem, though it is far from solution.

Until 1968 the Bureau of Land Management was relentless in its policy of eradicating the wild horses. However, thanks to the efforts of people like Bob Brislawn of Wyoming (*see* MUSTANG) and especially to the seemingly untiring and fearless efforts of Mrs. Velma B. Johnson, better known as "Wild Horse Annie," a 33,000-acre area on the border between Montana and Wyoming was, in 1968, dedicated as federal range for the protection of wild horses. It is known as Prior Mountain Wild Horse Range and in 1971 was the home of something less than 200 head of wild horses. Under the direction of the Bureau of Land Management, study of the habits, needs, and nature of these wild horses is being conducted. Methods of study are humane and scientific. They include the use of tranquilizing shots administered by well-trained, careful men on foot and of observation and photography from the air. One interesting note: The herd may be located by men in a pickup truck and approached to within a reasonable distance; however, workers must get out of the pickup while it is moving, for the instant a vehicle stops, the herd is terrified and takes off in flight. If men stalk the herd quietly and use their tranquilizing pellets, they can mark (lip tattoo is usually employed) or treat an animal.

Wind

When horsemen speak of a horse's wind, they have reference to the health of his respiratory apparatus. Great demands are made on this part of a horse's anatomy. Soundness (*see* SOUNDNESS), which means normal healthy condition, of this part of the horse is just as important, as far as his value is concerned, as is soundness of feet and legs.

Unsoundness of wind can usually be detected by listening to his breathing immediately after he has been moved at his top speed for a minute or so. One ailment, heaves, treated under its own heading in this book, is discernible by the eye. It causes a secondary movement of the flank after each exhalation.

Unsoundness of wind exists in many forms, some caused by prolonged illness, some by misuse, some by inherited conformational defect (*see* THROAT). A very few kinds of wind trouble yield to surgical treatment. A veterinarian examining a horse for soundness will of course include an examination of his wind.

Windows

Windows in a stall should be located high enough to prevent drafts from blowing directly on the horse. They should also be located so that the horse is not staring directly out at the sun a major portion of the day (*see* VENTILATION).

Windpipe. *See* THROAT

Wind Puffs, Wind Galls. *See* PUFFS

Wind Sucking. *See also* CRIBBING and VICES

Wind sucking or cribbing is a serious vice and should not be confused with chewing wood of stalls or fences, though the latter habit may lead to cribbing.

Winkers, Blinkers, or Blinders

A horse's eyes are so placed that he has practically a 360-degree range of vision (*see* EYES). Some horsemen for certain purposes want this range restricted. Some tribes of the Near East use blinders or blinkers on horses they ride. One wonders whether the purpose is to keep the horse from becoming terrified by the flowing robes of the riders. Many draft horses on farms used to wear blinders to prevent their seeing the high loads of loose hay or machinery behind them. In many driving classes in horse shows, horses are required to use blind bridles.

A horse who has always been driven with a blind bridle is very likely to panic the first time he is driven with an open bridle and sees the wheels of the vehicle following him. A carefully educated young animal can be introduced to work in harness without the use of blinders by proper preparatory work in longlines (*see* LONGLINE); then, if necessary because of his timid nature, he can be worked between a pair of saplings carried at one end by an assistant and gradually introduced to a cart. So handled, the horse never needs restriction of vision, though if he has to wear a blind bridle for a show-ring competition he can do so.

Winkers are sometimes worn with hoods on the racetrack. Some runners are distracted by competitors or shadows, or for some other reason (real or imagined by trainers) they do better with restricted vision.

Wire Cutters

At least one of the whips carries a pair of wire cutters on a fox hunt. In riding in any area where there is the lightest chance of encountering wire fences that have been allowed to go down or fences that have been destroyed to make way for real-estate development or what not, wire cutters are a very necessary part of a horseman's equipment. However, a rider carrying wire cutters while riding on a Western range is suspect and certainly extremely unwelcome unless he is an employee of the owner of stock running on that range.

Wisping

To remove dried or half-dried mud and sweat from a horse, nothing is better than a wisp of good hay or straw twisted and doubled in a careful and energetic hand. Using a wisp of hay or straw in this manner is sometimes called wisping.

Wolf Teeth

Occasionally very small teeth develop just in front of a horse's molars. They have no function and sometimes hurt the tongue when a bit is used. A veterinarian easily removes them.

There is an old idea that wolf teeth have a bad effect on the horse's eyes. The writer has been unable to find scientific verification of this.

Worms. *See* PARASITES

Wrestling

Wrestling on horseback is used sometimes to add variety and zest to riding-school activity and sometimes as a gymkhana event. The horses must be steady, and they should be equipped with nothing more than halters to which bridle reins are attached. Bridles or even bosals may be so jerked that a horse's mouth or jaw may be injured. Of course, a loose bosal with fiador, as used in the Northwest, may be satisfactory if the bosal is not heavy. Wrestling should not begin until horses are standing side by side, each facing in an opposite direction. The first rider to touch ground is the loser.

Xenophon

Xenophon, who is known to all students as one of the participants in Plato's *Dialogues,* is the author of the oldest book on horsemanship that has been preserved intact until today. Its title is translated as *The Art of Horsemanship.* A complete translation by M. H. Morgan can be purchased from J. A. Allen and Co., 1, Lower Grosvenor Place, London, S.W. 1, England.

Much that Xenophon says about mouths, hands, and related matters is as true today as it was 24 centuries ago. He advises, for example, that a groom lead the young horse through the marketplace to dispel his fear of strange sights, smells, and sounds.

Xerapa

Xerapa is a gringo misspelling of *serape,* a brilliantly colored, finely woven, fringed blanket conventionally folded and carried at the rear of a charro saddle. The serape is never used as a saddle blanket. (*See* SERAPE.)

Yearling

Unregistered equines are considered yearlings for the first 12 months of their lives. Since the age of registered animals is reckoned from the first day of each year, a registered animal is a yearling only until he survives his first New Year's Day.

Young Entry

Young hounds getting their first hunting experience, which they normally do during cubbing season, and children getting their first experience on a hunt, are known as "young entry."

For Further Reading

American Horse Shows Association, Inc., New York, *1973 Rule Book*.

American Veterinary Publications, Inc., The Work of Sixty-eight Authors, *Equine Medicine & Surgery*, Wheaton, Illinois, 1963.

J. K. Anderson, *Ancient Greek Horsemanship*, University of California Press, Berkeley, 1961.

Lady Apsley, *Bridleways Through History*, The Mayflower Press, Plymouth, England, 1936.

J. Frank Dobie, *The Mustangs*, Bantam Books, New York, 1958.

R. B. Cunningham Graham, *The Horses of the Conquest*, University of Oklahoma Press, Norman, 1930.

Noel Jackson, *Effective Horsemanship*, Van Nostrand Reinhold, New York, 1967.

Tom Lea, *The Hands of Cantu*, Little, Brown & Company, Boston, 1964.

Vladimir S. Littauer, *Common Sense Horsemanship*, Van Nostrand Reinhold, New York, 1951.

Vladimir S. Littauer, *Horseman's Progress*, Van Nostrand Reinhold, New York, 1962.

Frank B. Morrison, *Feeds & Feeding* (Abridged), Morrison Publications Co., Ithaca, New York, 1963.

Louis Taylor, *The Story of America's Horses*, World Publishing Company, New York, 1968.

Louis Taylor, *Ride Western*, Harper & Row, New York, 1968.

Fay E. Ward, *The Cowboy at Work*, Hastings House, New York, 1958.

Jack Widmer, *The American Quarter Horse*, Charles Scribner's Sons, New York, 1959.

Charles O. Williamson, *Breaking and Training the Stock Horse*, The Caxton Printers, Caldwell, Idaho, 1971.

Henry Wynmalen, M.F.H., *Dressage*, A. S. Barnes & Co., Cranbury, New Jersey, 1952.

Henry Wynmalen, *Equitation*, Charles Scribner's Sons, New York, 1938.

Xenophon, *The Art of Horsemanship*, translated by M. H. Morgan, J. A. Allen & Co., 1962.

Index

Accidents, 1
Action, 1–5
Age, 5–6; birthday, 56, 536; in buy-
ing horses, 86–87; teeth and, 6,
489–492
Aged, 6–7
Agoraphobia, 7
Aguilar, Antonio, 43, 357, 451
Aids, 7–8, 251; signals, 441–442
Albino, 8, 9, 116–117; American
Albino Association, Inc., 8, 10
Alcock Arabian, 31, 161, 381, 497
Alfalfa, 207, 241–242, 315
Ali Pasha Sherif, 38
Allen F-1, 493, 494, 496
Alter, *see* Castrate
Amateur, 10
Amble, 10, 160, 199; broken, 79
American Albino Association, Inc.,
8, 10
American Andalusian Horse Associa-
tion, 10–11
American Association of Owners and
Breeders of Peruvian Paso Horses,
11
American Buckskin Registry Associa-
tion, 11–12
American Hackney Horse Society, 12,
218
American Horse Protection Associa-
tion, Inc., 12, 328, 532
American Horse Shows Association,
10, 12–13, 256–257
American Indian Horse Registry,
Inc., 13
American Mustang Registry, Inc., 13,
328
American Paint Horse Association,
13–16
American Paso Fino Pleasure Horse
Association, Inc., 16–17, 347, 349
American Quarter Horse Association,
17, 378, 468, 477
American Saddlebred Pleasure Horse
Association, 19
American Saddle Horse, 17–19, 75,
194; action, 1–3; American Saddle
Horse Breeders' Association, 17,
19; ancestry, 18, 194, 201, 284,
317, 329, 377; Chief family, 102–
104; cruelty to, 12, 85, 152; fine-
harness class, 185; gaits, 19, 198–
200; head, 239; height, 243; hoof,
249; horse shows and deterioration
of, 257; posing, 478–479
American Saddle Horse Breeders'
Association, 17, 19, 383; gaits
approved by, 198–200
American Shetland Pony Club, 19
American Shire Horse Association, 20
American Stud Book, 276–277
American Suffolk Horse Association,
20, 481
Anatomy of horse, 130
Andalusian, 20, 157, 160, 380;
American Andalusian Horse Asso-
ciation, 10–11; Spanish horses in
America, 326, 329
Anthrax, 20
Antitoxin, 20–21
Appaloosa, 21–22, 116, 265; harness
classes, 232; racing, 382, 383; tail,
486–487
Appaloosa Horse Club, Inc., 21–23
Appetite, 23–24
Apples, 24–25
Appointments, 25–30
Appuyer, 30
Arabian horse, 30–38, 75, 204, 272;
action, 2–4; bloodlines, 31–33;
bridles, 339; driving, 153; in
endurance rides, 158–159; gaits,
36, 37; Half-Arab and Anglo-Arab
Registries, 218; harness classes, 3,
232; head, 33–34, 238–239; International Arabian Horse Association, 273; mustang descended
from, 326; Palominos descended
from, 343; park horse classes, 346–
347; Percheron related to, 354,
356; pointing, 361; racing, 382,
383; Raffles family, 336; specifications, 33–36; throat (throttle), 502
Arabian Horse Club of America, Inc.,
39
Argentine horses (criollos), 138–139,
403
Arms (of horse), 39

Illustration Credits

Credits are listed by page number. All other illustrations not otherwise credited are by Rosemary Davison Taylor.

377   Photo courtesy American Quarter Horse Association
404   Photo by Louise L. Serpa
405   Photo by Louise L. Serpa
410, Right   Courtesy Miller Harness Company
434–435   All shoes handmade by Monk Maxwell, farrier (photos by Rosemary Taylor)
444   Photo courtesy Monte Foreman
448   Photo by Jack Corn, *Nashville Tennessean*
476–477   Courtesy *1970 Rule Book*, American Horse Shows Association
483   Picture by Cline, courtesy Jacob W. Ruby
493   Photo courtesy Tennessee Walking Horse Breeders' Association
499   Photo courtesy Doc Pardee
500-501   Photos courtesy of *Blood-Horse*, 17 36 Alexandria Drive, Lexington, Ky. 40504

73 74 75 76 77 10 9 8 7 6 5 4 3 2 1